The Healthcare Value Chain

"Criticisms of the healthcare system come from many directions. One frequent target concerns the roles played by Group Purchasing Organizations (GPOs) and Pharmacy Benefit Managers (PBMs). Hemingway wrote that the one quality needed, above all, to be a good writer was having "a built-in, shock-proof, crap detector." Professor Burns has taken Hemingway's sage advice by chronicling the evolution of these organizations and faithfully identifying the value provided by these much-misunderstood entities. Readers will understand what it takes, in an era of supplier consolidation and innovation, to be a valued agent for organizations that are so dependent on others to bring care to our population."

—Eugene Schneller, Ph.D., *Department of Supply Chain Management, Arizona State University*

"Professor Burns dives deeply into the two most opaque parts of the healthcare ecosystem - GPOs and PBMs. It is the most detailed and comprehensive assessment available of these two often misunderstood sectors. Anyone truly interested in understanding, as opposed to blindly criticizing, these key participants would benefit from a careful read of this important volume."

—Bradley Fluegel, *Former Chief Commercial Officer and Strategy Officer, Walgreens, Former Chief Strategy Officer, Anthem, Former Head of National Accounts, Aetna*

"In his introduction, Professor Burns alerts us to the "Dark Territory of GPOs and PBMs". He then proceeds to illuminate the darkness thoroughly and emphatically with humor, analogy, and extensive research. In so doing, he firmly establishes the historical roles played by GPOs and PBMs in the healthcare ecosystem. If "Past is Prologue" then Professor Burns' exhaustive chronicle of GPOs and PBMs sets the stage for a more nuanced, less biased interpretation of their role. This volume is an intense, but absorbing read. A "Dark Territory" no longer. You would be hard pressed to find a better researched view. Every healthcare executive, employer and policy maker should take advantage of these insights."

—Mike Taylor, *Principal, MT Healthcare Consulting, Former Senior VP Delivery System Transformation—Aon plc*

"Professor Burns, one of the nation's leading healthcare management scholars, provides an objective assessment of healthcare middlemen. Burns convincingly argues from research evidence and decades of experience that if you are looking for organizations to blame for the nation's health cost crisis, you had better look elsewhere. This is a must read for those who want to learn more about the complexities of our healthcare supply chain."

—David Dranove, Ph.D., *Walter McNerney Distinguished Professor, Professor of Management & Strategy, Kellogg School of Management, Northwestern University*

Lawton Robert Burns

The Healthcare Value Chain

Demystifying the Role of GPOs
and PBMs

Lawton Robert Burns
Department of Health Care Management
The Wharton School
University of Pennsylvania
Philadelphia, PA, USA

ISBN 978-3-031-10741-2   ISBN 978-3-031-10739-9   (eBook)
https://doi.org/10.1007/978-3-031-10739-9

This Palgrave Macmillan imprint is published by the registered company Springer Nature Switzerland AG
The registered company address is: Gewerbestrasse 11, 6330 Cham, Switzerland

Preface and Acknowledgments

This volume has been in the making for the past twenty-five years. In the late 1990s, with the financial assistance of a grant from the National Science Foundation and its sponsored Center for Health Management Research, I undertook a multi-year field study of the institutional supply chain in healthcare. That study investigated (1) the *manufacturers* of pharmaceutical, medical supply, and medical device products; (2) the *distributors* of those products; and (3) the organized *purchasers* of those products. The purchasers included the group purchasing organizations (GPOs) and integrated delivery networks (IDNs). That investigation resulted in a book published in 2002, *The Health Care Value Chain.*

While I have remained active in studying these organizations and their contractual relationships, I have broadened my scope to examine the retail supply chain in healthcare that is concerned with prescription drugs. That inquiry brought me into greater contact with drug wholesalers, pharmacy benefit managers (PBMs), and pharmacies. I confess that it has taken me longer to understand (to the extent that I do) the retail channel than the institutional channel, perhaps because I have studied physicians and hospitals (the two end customers of the institutional channel) for so long.

I have long been struck by the parallels (and contrasts) between the institutional and retail channels, and in particular, the similar roles played by two intermediaries in these chains: the GPOs and the PBMs. As best I can tell, none of my colleagues has bothered to analyze this topic. I have seen only a few cursory depictions of these parallels from industry publications—and I do not feel they are either accurate or thorough. My purpose is to establish an academic foundation for this topic, drawing on an extensive archival record that places these two intermediaries in historical context.

I am standing on the shoulders of many researchers and analysts who have gone before me and/or are still going. I have persuaded some of them to assist (and correct) me here as co-authors of several chapters. In particular, I wish to acknowledge David Cassak and Roger Longman—both long-time analysts and journalists covering these intermediaries. David has lectured in my Wharton classroom on many occasions; Roger has similarly lectured in my colleague Patricia Danzon's class. Much of my historical understanding of GPOs and PBMs stems from their decades-long investigations. I also wish to thank Adam Fein, Ph.D., who received his Ph.D. from Wharton in the late 1990s. His publications educated me about (a) mergers of pharmaceutical wholesalers and how they extracted scale economies from such combinations, and (b) the workings of wholesalers, PBMs, and pharmacies. I have been using those lessons in class for more than twenty years. Adam has also been most gracious in letting me utilize some of his slides as figures here. I also thank Allison Briggs, my doctoral student, who has helped me to analyze survey data on the GPOs and their performance over the past few years. Special thanks go to Tina Horowitz, who has been the most phenomenal administrative assistant I have ever had the pleasure of working with. Like many of my prior books, Tina edited this entire volume and helped with many of the source documents and figures. Finally, I thank my wife and son who, as with my last book on the healthcare ecosystem, tolerated me and my long hours of writing this volume from home.

Bryn Mawr, PA, USA   Lawton Robert Burns

Contents

List of Figures

List of Tables

Part I

Introduction

Part I

Introduction

1

Caution: Entering Dark Territory

Dark Territory

My son analyzes industries and companies for a hedge fund. The first industry he covered was the railroads. According to that authoritative research source, Wikipedia, "Dark territory is a term used in the North American railroad industry to describe a section of running track not controlled by signals." There are several elements here. First, there is no central control or centralized administration. Second, there are safety concerns due to the absence of direct or indirect train detection. Third, there is a lower ability to detect misalignment in track switches, broken rails, or runaway rail cars. Fourth, and most importantly, it is dark. Of course, I should have known all of this. It played a central role in Steven Seagal's 1995 action movie thriller, "Under Siege 2: Dark Territory."

Welcome to Healthcare's Dark Territory

Healthcare has its own version of dark territory. It comprises many intermediaries—i.e., firms that connect other firms (buyers and sellers)—who are widely mistrusted and disliked. Why? They are seemingly out of control, with little federal regulation of their activities; their actions purportedly threaten patient safety; they amplify (rather than correct) distortions in the market; they allegedly make big profits but don't make anything; and, of course, they are widely viewed as shady characters that evade transparency and sunlight.

© The Author(s), under exclusive license to Springer
Nature Switzerland AG 2022
L. R. Burns, *The Healthcare Value Chain*,
https://doi.org/10.1007/978-3-031-10739-9_1

In the 1990s, the firms with the "dark territory" bullseye on their back were the health maintenance organizations (HMOs), a subset of managed care organizations (MCOs). The HMOs helped to (briefly) contain the escalation in national health expenditures in the middle of the decade, largely by working with employers to channel employees into narrow-network plans that often required prior authorization by a gatekeeping physician to see a specialist and a second opinion before getting surgery, and pressured hospitals to discharge patients more quickly (e.g., "drive-by deliveries"). The public's dislike of these tactics led to the "managed care backlash" of the late 1990s, a loss of market share, and replacement by a less restrictive form of MCO known as preferred provider organizations (PPOs). In 2008, candidate Barack Obama targeted another subset of MCOs, the Medicare Advantage (MA) plans (HMOs for Medicare enrollees), complaining about the high rates of reimbursement they were paid by the federal government.[1]

MCOs are not alone. Other healthcare firms that have been frequently targeted for criticism are the pharmaceutical manufacturers ("Big Pharma") for the high prices attached to their new drugs. For 2021, population surveys rank pharmaceutical companies lowest in public trust (56%) among five types of healthcare firms, not far behind the MCOs (59%).[2]

These criticisms pale, however, compared to the invective leveled at two other intermediaries: the group purchasing organizations (GPOs) and pharmacy benefit managers (PBMs). They have perhaps been the two biggest scapegoats in healthcare for at least two decades. The following accusations typically accompany articles in the popular press about one or both of them[3]:

- monopoly power
- collusion with manufacturers
- market foreclosure of smaller, innovative startups due to exclusive contracts
- anticompetitive market structure
- distortions to supply and demand
- conflicts of interest
- stifling innovation and keep lifesaving technologies off the market
- harms to patient care
- deadly medical supply cartel that is killing healthcare workers
- excessive fees and outsized profits
- kickbacks
- secret rebates
- pernicious pay-to-play system
- cater to the sellers rather than the buyers
- lack of transparency and disclosure

- artificially higher product prices
- bamboozle hospital chief financial officers and purchasing managers
- influence what drugs a physician prescribes
- take decision-making out of the hands of physicians
- product shortages
- impeded patient access to medications
- higher patient co-pays for medications

Most recently, a Professor of Surgery at Johns Hopkins Medicine weighed in on the issue, publishing a short, two-page "viewpoint" (letter, not research) in the *Journal of the American Medical Association* and then a new book.[4] He restates many of the same accusations above.

This is a pretty long list of serious charges. Some readers may now be thinking, "what a bunch of #@&$!#@." No wonder healthcare is "broken." How come I did not know about this scandal? Why hasn't someone done anything about these problems? Has anyone gone to jail for all this wrong-doing? Or, as TV attorney Saul Goodman (from *Breaking Bad*) would say, "Who did this to me? And more importantly, who can I sue?" The journalistic assault on these intermediaries has continued for at least two decades.

The problem with these accusations is that they are very difficult to evaluate. The authors of the articles and reports on these intermediaries note the lack of evidence; others note the lack of understanding about what these organizations actually do. For example:

- "As for independent assessment of GPOs' effect on costs, they are hard to come by."[5]
- "...little empirical evidence exists to definitively assess the impact of the GPO safe harbor."[6]
- "How [PBMs] operate has remained mostly hidden."[7]
- "Debates about PBMs can be confusing in large part because their role is generally not well understood..."[8]
- "The evidence is scant that abolishing PBMs would reduce the amount that our country spends on drugs..."[9]

Instead, the stories are almost entirely based on opinions, case vignettes, and testimony of disgruntled parties in Senate Hearings. The lack of understanding is perhaps why GPOs and PBMs are not included in surveys of public trust.

Dark Territory for Academics, Too

Researchers who seek to objectively evaluate these intermediaries are often tarred with the same brush. In February 2002, I published my first book, *The Health Care Value Chain*.[10] The volume represented the culmination of a 3.5-year, field investigation of how the supply chain in healthcare operated—the first analysis of its kind. The study was underwritten by the Center for Health Management Research (CHMR), an industry/university consortium funded by the National Science Foundation (NSF). The industry members of the consortium, large integrated delivery networks (IDNs), wanted to understand the workings of their upstream trading partners: product manufacturers, product wholesalers, and group purchasing organizations (GPOs). The book's findings and conclusions were based on industry reports and executive interviews at a sizeable sample of firms drawn from each category of the IDNs' trading partners. These partners handled medical-surgical supplies, medical devices, and pharmaceuticals.

The book's sales were modest. However, the timing of its publication was impeccable, given that it was coincident with two external events. First, beginning in March (and extending through December) of 2002, the *New York Times* published a series of exposé articles on the practices of the GPOs. The articles aired complaints by small suppliers that (1) GPOs were plagued by conflicts of interest, (2) the GPOs allegedly erected barriers to new suppliers getting access to hospital markets, and (3) the clinicians and patients faced barriers getting access to the new technologies offered by these suppliers. Second, these articles sparked a series of Hearings conducted by the Senate Judiciary Committee's Subcommittee on Antitrust. These Hearings began in April 2002 and ran through 2006, covering many of the same issues reported by the *Times*.

I was approached that Spring by the lead counsel for the Senate Subcommittee to see if I could testify at the Hearings. The attorney then asked me what I thought about the GPOs. I relayed the contents of Chapter 4 of that book, which could be succinctly summarized as follows: "The GPOs may not be as good as they think they are, but they are certainly not as bad as others say they are." It was a balanced, academic response to the *New York Times* stories I had been reading. I was promptly dis-invited and dropped from consideration as a witness. It was my first hint that I had stumbled into a minefield filled with partisan politics; to use the vernacular, "the fix was in." Academic objectivity had little role to play in the Senate Hearings. To some, this may sound like sour grapes at being excluded. It may actually have been a blessing in disguise. As I and some of my colleagues have learned experientially, academics get vilified for any whiff of support their research offers the GPOs.

In 2008, I published the results of a national survey of hospital Vice-Presidents of Materials Management regarding their views of the GPOs.[11] Like the 2002 book, this study was funded by the CHMR and NSF. This was the first empirical article on GPO performance published in a peer-reviewed journal; it reiterated the theme of GPOs being not so good and not so bad. The Government Accountability Office actually cited the study as the only peer-reviewed evidence on the GPOs' impact on pricing.[12]

As my colleague, Mark Pauly, likes to say, "no good deed goes unpunished." At that time, a journalist and staunch GPO critic wrote a lengthy, 7-page, single-spaced letter to the Chairman of the Board of Overseers of the Wharton School—also copying the President of the University of Pennsylvania, the Deputy Provost, and the Wharton School Dean (among others)—accusing me of serving as "a friend, advocate and apologist for the GPO industry" and that I had committed "a serious breach of academic integrity." Moreover, the critic asserted that the NSF's funding of my research constituted "an egregious misuse of taxpayer dollars," and that my "so-called research" could embarrass both Wharton and Penn. These allegations rested on the assumption that, since I frequently spoke about the findings in my book and subsequent survey at conferences sponsored by the GPOs as well as product manufacturers and IDNs (the GPOs' trading partners), I must be "on the take" and have serious financial conflicts of interest. It never occurred to the critic that academics (generally) and business school professors (specifically) endeavor to disseminate our research findings to outsiders in the industry. The Administration of the Wharton School investigated all of this, quickly exonerated me, and informed the critic that if they did not like my findings, they should write a letter to the Editor of the journal that published them.

What happened to me was not an isolated event. My colleague at Arizona State University, Gene Schneller, wrote the second academic volume on the healthcare supply chain, funded by the same NSF research center and issued by the same publishing house.[13] Gene subsequently issued some GPO-funded studies on their contribution to lowering hospital costs. He has suffered the same (and perhaps more) calumny from the same critic. So has a former commissioner of the Federal Trade Commission.

Why relay this chronicle? It serves as an advisory to the reader that the topic of this new volume is "hot" and fraught with controversy. You will not make any friends writing anything objective or quasi-positive about GPOs. I have learned that my research (on GPOs and other topics) sometimes pisses people off. That is not usually the case with academic journal articles or books which are too obtuse to cause offense. I sometimes think that if my work is not pissing people off, it must not be very good. You can let me know. But, hopefully I have gotten your attention and you will read on.

Time for Some Critical Thinking

The question begs itself: do the GPOs and PBMs deserve their role as everyone's favorite scapegoat? How does one go about answering this question? (And, did I and my colleague deserve so much crap for studying them?) This is not an easy assignment, since (as noted above) there is not a lot of empirical or academic evidence on their market conduct and performance, and certainly no experimental data to satisfy the hard-core scientist. Like the MCOs, the GPOs and PBMs are "middlemen" who act as "agents" on behalf of other organizations ("principals") and thus are somewhat shielded from public scrutiny. The problem is somewhat akin to judging the managers who act as agents on behalf of firms and their shareholders (the principals).

I attempt to train my students in the art of "critical thinking." This can be defined as a mode of disciplined but open-minded thought that carefully weighs arguments and claims, gathers evidence to support or rebut them, considers alternative explanations, and maintains an attitude of "reflective skepticism." The motto over the entrance to the Royal Society in London (circa 1660) is *nullius in verba*, i.e., "take nobody's word for it." In short, I train my students to ask, "is what I just read really true?" Such deliberative thinking is in short supply. According to the famous Irish playwright, George Bernard Shaw, "two percent of the people think, three percent think they think, and ninety-five percent of the people would rather die than think."

Given the lack of hard data and real experiments, the Royal Society may not be convinced (either way) by anything that anyone says, including me. I do think academics can do a better job of marshaling the available evidence to construct a plausible theory and argument, however. That evidence consists of (1) an accurate historical chronicle of how the GPOs and PBMs developed, (2) an analysis of the "agency role" they play in the broader healthcare industry, and (3) an assessment of their performance using available information, including what their customers (the "principals" in the principal-agent relationship) say about them.

What this volume undertakes is the following four-fold task:

- Describe the agency roles of middlemen in U.S. healthcare and the industry context in which they operate
- Describe the roles GPOs/PBMs play in the broader healthcare industry
- Chronicle the historical development of GPOs/PBMs and functions they have assumed
- Analyze the host of performance issues surrounding the GPOs/PBMs

Sources of Evidence

Of course, following the Royal Society and George Bernard Shaw, you should not take my word for it any more than you should accept all of the accusations found in the non-academic literature. So, where do I draw my insights? What is my competitive advantage in assembling this volume?

First, I have been studying the GPOs for over two decades and the PBMs for one decade—all as part of studying the U.S. healthcare ecosystem and the various intermediaries that operate in healthcare. I continue to teach the introductory course on this ecosystem to MBAs and have continued to do so for roughly 35 years at three different business schools (as well as two more in India and China). Because my students are interested in business and the product manufacturing sectors of healthcare (e.g., pharmaceuticals, medical devices), I have had to master the business and revenue models of not only the hospital buyers and product suppliers but also the intermediaries that connect them.

Second, I have received a LOT of help along the way. MBA programs typically invite outside speakers from the industry to educate our students. I have been fortunate to have had a long-running interaction with executives from the manufacturers of healthcare products who explain how their sectors work. Their presentations often include analyses of their trading partners, including the MCOs, GPOs, PBMs, and wholesalers. In addition to the manufacturers, I have also invited in top consultants who cover the intermediaries. I have learned about the inner workings of the intermediaries for over two decades from (a) consultants such as Chris McFadden (Goldman Sachs), Adam Fein (Pembroke Consulting), and Karl Kellner (formerly at Booz, now at McKinsey) and (b) journalists such as David Cassak and Roger Longman (Co-founders of Windhover Information, which published *In Vivo*). Several of these individuals have graciously joined me in co-authoring certain chapters in this volume.

Third, I have the honor of co-directing one of the most innovative undergraduate training programs in the world hosted at the University of Pennsylvania: The Roy & Diana Vagelos Program in Life Sciences and Management (LSM for short). LSM may be the only dual degree program where students are admitted into the program as entering freshmen, jointly pursue dual degrees in Biology (College of Arts & Sciences) and Business (the Wharton School), and combine both skill-sets in a year-long practicum to advise life science startups on the two key issues they all face: validating their scientific contribution and then helping them commercialize it. I am now in my tenth year with LSM. The program has taught me considerably about life science companies (e.g., pharma, biotech, medical devices, information technology), their scientific platforms, and their business/revenue models.

Fourth, some of the major industry/academic consortia (e.g., CHMR) and professional associations—such as the American Hospital Association (AHA) and its Association for Health Care Resource and Materials Management (AHRMM)—have taken a personal interest in my work and funded my research. These organizations represent the hospitals, hospital systems, and IDNs in the industry. Because they serve as the principals who contract with the GPO agents, I have been granted generous access to the hospital membership of the GPOs as well as to GPO executives. During the course of this research, I have also come to know a considerable number of Vice-Presidents for Materials Management (VPMMs). A panel of VPMMs served as the advisory committee for the research contained in the 2002 book. They used their role as "buyer" to persuade their upstream "suppliers" (e.g., manufacturers, wholesalers, GPOs) to grant me interviews with them. The VPMMs have also proved invaluable in helping me construct the historical chronicle of the GPOs' development contained in Chapter 4.

Fifth, I have conducted and published a considerable amount of peer-reviewed research, much of it empirical and statistical, since the late 1970s. This research has spanned the entire U.S. healthcare ecosystem. These endeavors have broadened my purview of the industry and sharpened my analytic skills. I have also had a chance to work with several top healthcare economists. Such collaborations have enabled me to consider topics from multiple perspectives and disciplines.

Sixth, my research track record and broad areas of expertise have attracted the attention of attorneys, who engage me as a fact witness or expert witness in many cases. As the saying goes, "I have no dog in those fights." I am not working to advance the interests of one side over another. Rather, I participate in these cases to learn more about the industry. Such participation exposes me to information that researchers (let alone the public) never get access to. This includes the contractual relationships struck between the various parties in the healthcare supply chain (principals and agents) as well as strategy and board deliberations that explicate how the industry actually operates. Normally, I work alongside my economist colleagues who perform the statistical modeling while I offer "the color commentary." We all agree that this experience serves to test and (hopefully validate) our academic hypotheses on how the ecosystem functions.

Seventh and last, based on my academic research, I have observed a lot of promising innovations and innovative organizations on both the technology as well as managerial side. To my chagrin, most of these innovations have either failed or seriously under-performed. I have also taught many courses in Wharton's Management Department (where I am jointly appointed) and covered scores of Harvard Business School cases on strategy and strategic implementation. These experiences have helped me to develop a keen "BS Detector."[14] Scholars have linked BS detection to "critical thinking."[15] I have endeavored to practice both skills, in class as well as in my writing. Hopefully, this volume is BS-free.

Overview of Volume

This volume is divided into four parts. *Part I* encompasses this Chapter and Chapter 2, which constitute the "Introduction." Chapter 2 portrays the challenge of capturing the material contained in the second and third parts. This challenge can be summarized as one of manifold complexity: multiple chains of activity (vertical chain, value chain, supply chain), multiple channels of product flow (retail channel, institutional channel), multiple types of customers (consumers/end customers, physicians, firms in the supply chain), and multiple ways to conceptualize and measure "value." Welcome to the jungle.

Part II, encompassing Chapters 3–8, focuses on GPOs. Chapter 3 characterizes the complex landscape of GPOs as they operate today. Chapters 4 and 5 chronicle the historical development of GPOs, broken up into two periods (capturing events in the 20th and 21st Centuries, respectively). Chapter 5 examines all of the contentious issues and the criticisms leveled at the GPOs that give them the "dark territory" treatment. Chapter 6 then carefully reviews the research evidence on GPO performance to ascertain whether the criticisms have validity. Chapter 7 makes an evidence-based argument for how GPOs can be viewed more favorably and why GPOs may serve pro-competitive ends. Chapter 8, finally, considers whether GPOs are differentiated firms or commodities—e.g., are they as good as they think they are.

Part III, encompassing Chapters 9–13, focuses on PBMs. Chapter 9 characterizes the complex landscape of the PBMs, paralleling Chapter 3. Chapter 10 chronicles the historical development of the PBMs in the twentieth century; Chapters 11 and 12 analyze PBM development in the new millennium according to their tailwinds and headwinds, respectively. In this manner, Chapters 10–12 on the PBMs parallel Chapters 4 and 5 on the GPOs. Chapter 13 "looks under the hood" of the PBMs and their contractual negotiations upstream (with pharmaceutical manufacturers) and downstream (with health plans and employers). The chapter examines PBM contract terms to begin to evaluate the criticisms levied at the PBMs and demystify their operations. In contrast to Part II, there is no evidence base on the PBMs as there is for GPOs, and thus no parallel to Chapter 6. The PBM chapters do evaluate the available data and evidence to draw similar conclusions, however.

Part IV, finally, brings the volume to a conclusion. Chapter 14 summarizes the overall lessons of the volume and the similarities and differences between GPOs and PBMs. It includes a detailed side-by-side comparison of the GPOs and PBMs to document their common roles as intermediaries in the healthcare value chain.

As a guide to the reader going forward, I present two charts here that introduce the complex ecosystem in which GPOs and PBMs reside. The first chart (Fig. 1.1) borrows from my friend Adam Fein's depiction of the many intermediaries involved in the distribution and reimbursement of inpatient and outpatient drugs in the U.S. I have modified his slide to be even more exhaustive (and exhausting). Figure 1.2 simplifies Adam's chart to highlight how many intermediaries are engaged in aggregated purchasing:

- Group purchasing organizations (GPOs)
- Pharmacy services administrative organizations (PSAOs)
- Pharmacy benefit managers (PBMs)
- Third-party payers/health plans
- Employer purchasing coalitions

For the reader who wants more and cannot wait, Chapter 14 includes a third chart (Fig. 14.1) that highlights some of the similarities and differences between GPOs and PBMs. The remainder of this volume explicates these comparisons.

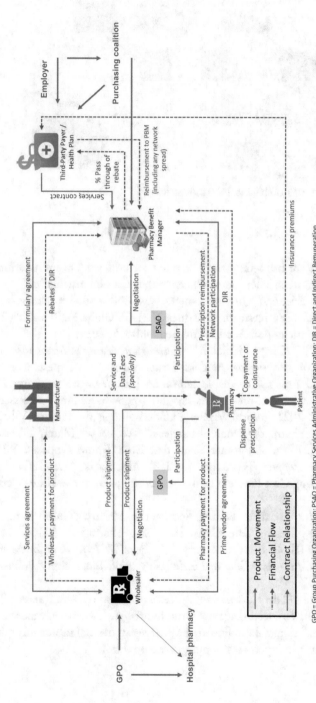

GPO = Group Purchasing Organization; PSAO = Pharmacy Services Administrative Organization; DIR = Direct and Indirect Remuneration
Source: Drug Channels Institute. Chart illustrates flows for Patient-Administered, Outpatient Drugs. Please note that this chart is illustrative. It is not intended to be a complete representation of every type of product movement, financial flow, or contractual relationship in the marketplace.

Fig. 1.1 U.S. Distribution & reimbursement system for inpatient and outpatient drugs

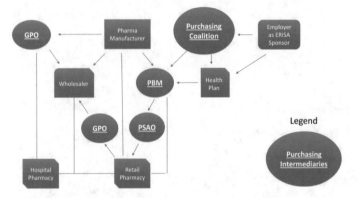

Fig. 1.2 Multiplicity of purchasing intermediaries

Notes

1. Other healthcare firms frequently targeted for criticism are the pharmaceutical manufacturers. They are producers rather than intermediaries.
2. 21st Annual Edelman Trust Barometer. Available online at: https://www.edelman.com/sites/g/files/aatuss191/files/2021-05/Global%20Health%20Sector%20Barometer.pdf. Accessed on September 5, 2021.
3. Mariah Blake. "Dirty Medicine," *Washington Monthly Magazine* (July–August, 2010). Physicians Against Drug Shortages. "Expert Commentary on GPO Abuses." Available online at: https://www.physiciansagainstdrugshortages.com/what-the-experts-say-about-gpo-abuses.html. Accessed on September 5, 2021. Jessica Wapner. "Understanding the Hidden Villain of Big Pharma: Pharmacy Benefit Managers," *Newsweek* (March 17, 2017). David Dayen. "The Corporate Scam that Even Trump Opposes: PBMs," *The American Prospect* (February 14, 2018). Alex Kacik. "Are GPOs, PBMs Part of the Drug Cost Problem or the Solution?" *Modern Healthcare* (January 19, 2019).
4. William Bruhn, Elizabeth Fracica, and Martin Makary. "Group Purchasing Organizations, Health Care Costs, and Drug Shortages," *JAMA* 320(18) (2018): 1859–1860. Martin Makary. *The Price We Pay: What Broke American Health Care—And How to Fix It* (New York: Bloomsbury Publishing, 2021).
5. Mariah Blake. "Dirty Medicine," *Washington Monthly Magazine* (July–August, 2010). Physicians Against Drug Shortages. "Expert Commentary on GPO Abuses." Available online at: https://www.physiciansagainstdrugshortages.com/what-the-experts-say-about-gpo-abuses.html.

6. American Medical Association. *Group Purchasing Organizations and Pharmacy Benefit Manager Safe Harbor*. Report 8 of the Council on Medical Service (A-19). Available online at: https://www.ama-assn.org/system/files/2019-07/a19-cms-report-8.pdf. Accessed on September 6, 2021.

7. Jessica Wapner. "Understanding the Hidden Villain of Big Pharma: Pharmacy Benefit Managers," *Newsweek* (March 17, 2017).

8. Ike Brannon. "Abolishing Drug Rebates May Push Consumer Drug Costs Higher," *Forbes* (September 26, 2018).

9. Ike Brannon. "Abolishing Drug Rebates May Push Consumer Drug Costs Higher," *Forbes* (September 26, 2018).

10. Lawton R. Burns and Wharton School Colleagues. *The Health Care Value Chain*. (San Francisco, CA: Jossey-Bass, 2002).

11. Lawton R. Burns and J. Andrew Lee. "Hospital Purchasing Alliances: Utilization, Services, and Performance," *Health Care Management Review* 33(3) (2008): 203–215.

12. Government Accountability Office. Letter to Senator Charles Grassley. "Group Purchasing Organizations: Research on Their Pricing Impact on Health Care Providers," (January 29, 2010). Available online at: https://www.gao.gov/assets/gao-10-323r.pdf. Accessed on September 6, 2021.

13. Eugene Schneller and Larry Smeltzer. *Strategic Management of the Health Care Supply Chain*. (San Francisco: Jossey-Bass, 2006).

14. Lawton R. Burns and Mark V. Pauly. "Detecting BS in Health Care." Philadelphia, PA: Leonard David Institute of Health Economics (November 2018). Available online at: https://ldi.upenn.edu/wp-content/uploads/archive/pdf/LDI%20Detecting%20BS%20in%20Healthcare_7.pdf. Accessed on September 6, 2021. Lawton R. Burns and Mark V. Pauly. "Detecting BS in Health Care 2.0." Philadelphia, PA: Leonard David Institute of Health Economics (February 6, 2019). Available online at: https://ldi.upenn.edu/our-work/research-updates/detecting-bs-in-health-care-2-0/. Accessed on September 6, 2021.

15. John Petrocelli. *The Life-Changing Science of Detecting Bullshit* (New York: St. Martin's Press, 2021).

2

The Challenge of Complexity: Chains, Channels, Customers (and Value Too)

The Challenge: Too Much Stuff?

In 1997, blues artist Delbert McClinton (along with John Prine and Lyle Lovett) released a song called, "Too Much Stuff."[1] The tune opens with some catchy "boogie-woogie" piano and then chronicles the junk that piles up around people—including the fat around their waist. It is an apt description of the challenge facing researchers, analysts, and students who want to understand U.S. healthcare. There is literally too much healthcare stuff that has been piling up for over a century. This confounds most people's understanding. Without such an understanding, it is really hard to grasp (let alone evaluate) the role of specific players in U.S. healthcare such as GPOs and PBMs—the task laid out in the prior chapter.

I have been teaching the introductory course on U.S. healthcare for roughly 35 years and annually face the challenge of how to cover an expanding array of topics and issues in a finite academic term. I have recently written an article with two colleagues on the trials and tribulations we instructors deal with in trying to capture and convey the material.[2] I have also just published a textbook that attempts to tame the beast and reduce it to written form.[3]

U.S. healthcare is not a "system." That is one reason why it is so hard to capture and comprehend. In a system, the players act in concert in orderly, coordinated ways toward a common purpose. By contrast, U.S. healthcare is an "ecosystem," a community of living organisms that merely interact with one another in a specific environment. Yes, the actors are interdependent,

© The Author(s), under exclusive license to Springer
Nature Switzerland AG 2022
L. R. Burns, *The Healthcare Value Chain*,
https://doi.org/10.1007/978-3-031-10739-9_2

but they do not work together. Their purposes are frequently orthogonal to or, worse yet, at odds with one another. Thus, these actors can be direct competitors or can transact as buyers and sellers seeking competitive advantage by undermining one another at the bargaining table (akin to the card game, "screw your neighbor"). It is not collaboration; it is what the Dutch might call *klobberation* or what the Germans might call *partner-shaft*. It is perhaps the opposite of what the Quaker minister Edward Hicks portrayed in his 1830 painting, *The Peaceable Kingdom*: e.g., "The wolf also shall dwell with the lamb, and the leopard shall lie down with the kid; and the calf and the young lion and the fatling together; and a little child shall lead them." Look for William Penn in the painting background. Instead of a peaceable kingdom, we have an unforgiving, dog-eat-dog, eat-or-be-eaten jungle. The Hippocratic oath, "do no harm," no longer applies once you leave the doctor's examining room. In such an environment it is difficult to assess the contribution of any particular player, given all the other players they are contending with.

To make matters more complex, the number of organisms populating the healthcare ecosystem has proliferated over time. The ecosystem sports a seemingly endless cast of characters that have taken the stage. We started with some apothecaries, physicians and quasi-physicians (bone setters, herbalists), and quasi-hospitals (almshouses) in the eighteenth century. In the mid-late nineteenth century, we added on more professionally trained physicians and nurses, hospitals, pharmacies, pharmaceutical companies, and pharmaceutical wholesalers. In the twentieth century, we then added a succession of other players: (in roughly chronological order) private insurers, nursing homes, employers offering health insurance benefits, GPOs, hospital outpatient departments, public insurers (Medicare and Medicaid), long-term care hospitals, emergency rooms, PBMs, hospices, medical device firms, ambulatory surgery centers, biotechnology firms, managed care organizations, home healthcare agencies, information technology firms, integrated delivery networks or IDNs, and retail clinics.

This proliferation in healthcare occupations and organizations has been going on perhaps for a century.[4] Much of this proliferation has taken the form of differentiation (i.e., increased division of labor) and specialization in both healthcare delivery and healthcare supply. On the delivery side, Milton Roemer documented that the ratio of non-physician healthcare professionals (e.g., nurses, dentists, technologists) to physicians rose from 0.58:1 (1900) to 3.35:1 (1950) and then to 12:1 (1973).[5] More recently, David Lawrence, former CEO of Kaiser Foundation Health Plan and Hospitals, noted that the number of categories of healthcare professionals mushroomed from 10–12 in the 1950s to more than 220 by the early 2000s. Similarly, the number of specialties in medicine grew from 6–8 following World War II to more than 100.[6] On the supply side, while wholesalers and GPOs have existed for a long time, a host of other intermediaries have taken the stage more recently, including insurers (now managed care organizations, or MCOs) and their agents, the PBMs. With the exception of the manufacturers of drugs and medical-surgical supplies, many of the technology firms occupying the medical device, biotechnology, and information technology spaces are relative newcomers.

Such proliferation has been interpreted in a variety of ways.[7] First, some view the growing sprawl as evidence of "Taylorism" in healthcare: an increasing specialization and division of labor that leaves medical professionals in ever narrow, bureaucratically confined roles. Second, some view this as a major contributor to the growing "fragmentation" of healthcare, where no one professional or organization takes account of the "whole person" in the delivery of healthcare. Third, some view this as contests—"turf battles"— among competing firms for control over healthcare tasks that used to be dominated by others. Fourth, some see this proliferation as a multiplication and lengthening of the routes needed to get product supplies to end customers. None of these interpretations sounds good. They may all be accurate.

For purposes of simplicity, I have elected to capture this growing complexity in terms of several "chains," "channels," "customers," and types of "value." The different chains are basically variations on a common theme; the different channels and customers are much more distinct. Some observers have sought to capture and assess the relative contribution of GPOs and PBMs in these chains and channels; more commonly, they offer recommendations for how they might improve their contribution (whatever it is). These recommendations often invoke the word, "value." As we discuss below, value is the *Zeitgeist* of the new millennium (i.e., spirit of the times). Value is always hard to define, let alone measure; several of my colleagues and I believe that a lot of "crapola" has entered the scene here. This is the context for analyzing the roles played by GPOs and PBMs.

Multiple *Chains*

Researchers usually refer to one of the three chains: the vertical chain, the value chain, and the supply chain. While they overlap considerably, they can nevertheless be distinguished—and then we can stop worrying about this.

The Vertical Chain

The production of any product or service usually entails a lengthy, vertical chain of activities. That chain spans the acquisition of raw materials and other inputs (e.g., labor), the production process utilized to turn those inputs into some tangible product or service, and then the sale and distribution of that output to customers. This is more generally known as an input-throughput-output model. Few firms do everything, however. Firms have vertical boundaries that demarcate what they do and what they do not do. Some activities are conducted inside the firm, while other activities are left to outside market firms to perform. The firm's choice as to one or the other is known as "make versus buy" (make in-house versus buy from outside). The former is known as "insourcing"; the latter is known as "outsourcing." Firms that outsource utilize a host of "trading partners" in the market for both acquisition of raw materials (upstream) and distribution of their output (downstream). Figure 2.1 depicts U.S. healthcare as a vertical chain of buyers and suppliers (in a sideways view). Any box to your right is a potential upstream supplier; any box to your left is a potential downstream buyer.

The Value Chain

Michael Porter, an economist at the Harvard Business School, popularized the term *value chain* among academic circles to encompass the entire vertical chain from the input of raw materials to the output of final product consumed by the end user.[8] This chain is called a value chain because each link in the chain adds some value to the original inputs. So, for example, raw lumber is of little value to most consumers but increases in value as furniture makers turn that raw material into wooden cabinets or bookshelves.[9] So, a value chain is a vertical chain with each firm's value-added contribution computed along the way.

There are really two value chains here. The first concerns the stream of productive activities *within* a given firm that allow it to manufacture a product or render a service (see Fig. 2.2). Thus, a firm acquires inputs (for

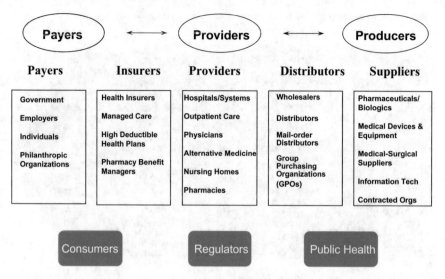

Fig. 2.1 The health care value chain (*Source* Lawton R. Burns, *The Health Care Value Chain [2002]*)

example, raw materials, labor, capital, and so on), integrates and processes them in a throughput stage, and then produces its outputs. The value-creating activities inside the firm include five primary activities (inbound logistics, production operations, outbound logistics, marketing, sales and service) and four support activities (back-office functions including finance/accounting, human resources, procurement, and technology). The second value chain includes the stream of activities *across* firms, where the outputs of one set of firms become the inputs for another set of firms. Thus, a firm has input suppliers, industry competitors, distributors, and end customers (similar to Fig. 2.1). An analysis of the value created within a given firm helps to identify its contribution to the value created along the interfirm chain.

The concepts of vertical chain and value chain are similar. Porter's value chain has received more attention in industry, while academic researchers talk about the vertical chain. According to economists, "the vertical chain is a series of activities that must be performed to produce a good or service, whereas the value chain is a series of activities that add value...In general, any activity on the value chain must lay on the vertical chain. At the same time, any activity on the vertical chain should be on the value chain. If not, then by definition it adds no value and should not be included in the vertical chain."[10]

This last sentence sets the stage for this volume. Many analysts of U.S. healthcare argue that there are a small number of intermediaries who offer questionable value and, thus, whose role in the vertical chain should be

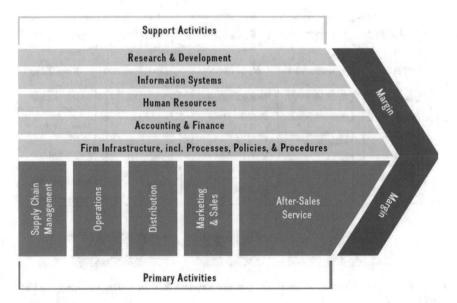

Fig. 2.2 The "internal" value chain

sharply circumscribed if not proscribed. In other words, these intermediaries ought to be "dis-intermediated." GPOs and PBMs have frequently served as the scapegoat for what ails the healthcare ecosystem and thus the target of such pronouncements. The problem is that the value offered by these intermediaries is difficult to quantify in a way that satisfies critics.

The Supply Chain

Vertical chains involve three types of flows: products, money, and information. In industry, product movement along the vertical chain is often referred to as the *supply chain*. A supply chain is a virtual (as opposed to vertically owned) network that facilitates the movement of a product from its earliest point of production, through packaging and distribution, and ultimately to the point of consumption. The supply chain is thus the path traveled by the product; each stop along that path defines a link in the supply chain. By contrast, problems with the other two flows (money and information) are often the source of criticism regarding product intermediaries. Product flows become problematic when there are allegations of shortages or inventory stockpiling.

Supply chains became part of mainstream discourse during the COVID-19 pandemic due to shortages of personal protective equipment (PPE) and worries about sourcing active pharmaceutical ingredients (APIs) used to manufacture generic drugs. Such supply chains are global. Researchers are now investigating whether such supply chains can be reconfigured into global value chains.[11] My horizon in this book is more circumscribed, with a focus on the domestic supply chain that links up U.S. manufacturers with their downstream customers.

Supply chain networks may operate to both (1) "push" manufactured products through the chain using sales forces and promotional campaigns and (2) "pull" products through the chain to continually replenish retailers' inventories and meet customer demand. In the former model, manufacturers promote and sell as many products as they can to customers. In the latter model, customers demand products from the preceding link in the chain; those vendors then become responsible for managing the customer's inventories.

What explains the existence of supply chains? There are at least two explanations, derived from organizational and industrial organization theory. First, supply chains exist because there is little vertical integration of manufacturers into the distribution and delivery of their products to the end customer. Vertical integration is low because manufacturers believe that the costs of transacting with the marketplace for distribution and delivery are much less than the costs of attempting to take distribution in-house and coordinate all of these exchanges using managerial hierarchies. That is, manufacturers believe that it is cheaper for them to "buy" distribution services from product wholesalers in the marketplace rather than "make" distribution services in-house. Consequently, manufacturers have elected not to enter the distribution business but rather let specialist firms produce these services for them.

Second, because manufacturers have left the provision of distribution services to others, they are now interdependent with external firms over whom they exercise no hierarchical or managerial control. Consequently, they need to develop contractual or strategic alliance relationships with these specialist firms in order to get their products to the end customer. Supply chains thus exist to coordinate and manage the exchanges of freestanding firms that are interdependent.

Multiple *Channels*

To make matters even more complicated, one can study vertical chains, value chains, and supply chains in terms of two channels: the retail channel and the institutional channel. The two channels share some of the same players; they also have some unique players. The two channels also share some of the same operating principles and dynamics, while differing on others. Finally, they differ partly in terms of the types of products they convey.

As an illustration, healthcare products such as ethical (branded) pharmaceuticals are dispensed in several different settings: community pharmacies, mail-order pharmacies, specialty pharmacies, hospitals, physician clinics, and nursing homes. The former three are known as the "retail" channel, while the latter three are known as the "institutional" (or non-retail) channel. Because the supply chain and competitive dynamics at different levels of the distribution chain differ based on the channel, it is useful to discuss the retail and institutional channels separately.

The Retail Channel

The retail channel is so named because, by and large, purchases are made at retail locations. The channel includes independent pharmacies, chain-based pharmacies (CVS, Walgreens, Rite Aid), supermarkets with drug stores (Kroger, Publix), and mass merchandisers with pharmacies (Walmart, Costco). The retail channel also includes mail-order pharmacies (as opposed to brick-and-mortar retail pharmacies) which fill prescriptions from a central location and deliver to the customer's home, as well as specialty pharmacies which focus heavily on high-cost medications for complex diseases and offer additional services for patients with complex conditions (e.g., education, therapy management).

The ultimate buyer in the retail channel is the patient, who finances the drug's purchase either through third-party insurance or on an out-of-pocket basis. Third-party coverage includes: employer-based health insurance (EBHI), Medicare, Medicaid, individually purchased private coverage, and the military. Many insurance plan sponsors (e.g., employers, private health insurers) outsource the management of their prescription drug benefits to PBMs. PBMs pool the purchasing volume of health plans and their enrollees and then enter market share-based contracts with pharmaceutical manufacturers for discounts off the manufacturer's list price. PBMs charge the manufacturers a contract administrative fee (CAF) as well as negotiate rebates (discounted prices) based on formulary placement and purchase volumes that can be documented. The majority of these fees and rebates are shared with plan sponsors.

In the U.S. retail channel, pharmaceutical manufacturers sell their products to wholesalers who hold the inventory and distribute as needed to downstream outlets in the retail channel. Wholesalers sell pharmaceutical drug products to retail pharmacies at a price including a markup, although some pharmacies buy directly from manufacturers.

The Institutional Channel

The institutional (non-retail) channel of the pharmaceutical sector consists primarily of hospitals, physician offices and clinics (that may or may not be run by hospitals), and nursing homes. As in the retail channel, the non-retail supply chain begins with pharmaceutical manufacturers. They sell their drug products to drug wholesalers at wholesale acquisition cost (WAC), which serves as the baseline price against which negotiations with wholesalers proceed (see Chapter 9 for details on drug pricing). Discounts and rebates may subsequently be applied to WAC, based on market share, purchase volume, and prompt payment. Hospitals then buy the drugs from wholesalers. Researchers estimate that as much as 90% of drug purchases in the institutional sector go through pharmaceutical wholesalers, with only 2% of sales going direct.[12]

Due to the large number of drugs required by patients and the number of manufacturers that make them, the vast majority of hospitals do not negotiate directly with wholesalers or manufacturers on the price for individual drugs. Rather, they purchase their drugs at prices negotiated by their GPO(s). For nearly half of all hospitals, GPOs negotiate pricing for 75% of the products sold by manufacturers to the hospital market.[13] The GPO functions in the non-retail channel much like the PBM functions in the retail channel: it pools the purchasing volumes and negotiates discounts for drug purchases for member hospitals for a contract administrative fee. The majority of these fees are, in turn, shared with GPO members, thus reducing unit prices. Hospitals use GPOs to bargain collectively with manufacturers in the hope of obtaining better pricing on pharmaceutical drug products compared to what they could obtain if they negotiated individually. GPOs that succeed in obtaining lower drug pricing have to document "control," i.e., the ability to deliver on market share and hospital compliance with GPO contracts. In contrast to the PBMs in the retail channel, GPOs in the institutional channel handle other products besides drugs, including medical-surgical supplies, medical devices, and capital equipment.

Multiple *Customers*

The existence of two channels indicates there are two very different types of customers. The first is the end customers—the retail consumers of products made by manufacturers, a.k.a., the patients treated by providers in the vertical channel. The second is the various institutions and firms arrayed along the vertical chain that buy from and sell to one another. This distinction is huge. The former channel is comprised of individuals who are entirely fragmented and disaggregated. They thus lack the market power to influence everyone else. They also lack information and the ability to gather and interpret it. This fosters great asymmetries in the vertical chain. The latter channel is composed of large firms (of varying sizes) that are all engaged in efforts to get bigger in order to exercise more pricing leverage in the vertical chain. Whether such leverage is designed to benefit them, their customers downstream, or their end customers (the patients) is ripe for inquiry.

Multiple Takes on *Value*

Intermediaries in the Chain

This volume addresses the general, core issue of "what role do intermediaries play?" and "what value do they generate?" One legal scholar writes (in typical academic jargon) that intermediaries "function as platforms in two-sided markets."[14] Translated into English, this means they mediate business-to-business (B2B) and/or business-to-consumer (B2C) transactions. What is the advantage (value) of the platform model? Here is the theory, according to one legal scholar[15]:

> In other two-sided market scenarios, buyers and sellers theoretically are able to transact with each other, but their transaction costs are too high to make it happen. A seller, for example, may be willing to sell its product for, say, $100 to an individual buyer. The buyer, however, would not buy the product because $100 is too expensive. He would only be willing to pay, say, $70 for the product—a price the seller would gladly accept as well if she had at least 1,000 buyers rather than just a few. In the 1,000-buyers scenario, the seller might even be happy to sell the product to each buyer for $60. There may be 1,000 or more potential buyers for the product, but they are dispersed and consolidating them would be too expensive.
>
> A cost-efficient platform, however, may still effectuate the product's sales. To be cost-efficient, a platform needs to make a profit by collecting a fee from both buyers and sellers. For example, it may charge a $10 access fee to each buyer in exchange for its undertaking to the buyer to sell her the product for $60. To be able to deliver the product for that price, the platform needs to secure the appropriate contract with the seller. Making and executing such contracts is much cheaper than making and executing a collective agreement that embodies 1,000 buyers' undertaking to buy 1,000 products for $60,000.

The platform, therefore, generates scale economies that benefit both the seller and the buyers of the product.

By using its expertise in the market for this and similar products, the platform also generates information. It reliably informs buyers about the products' availability, variety, and prices. It reliably informs sellers about the buyers' demand for the products. When a product's potential buyers and sellers do not have this information, they often decide not to transact. These failed transactions could have been mutually beneficial to buyers and sellers.

For the right price ("the access fee"), the platform can remove the coordination and asymmetric-information obstacles for such buyers and sellers. The fee is a fraction of the buyers' and the sellers' combined saving in transaction costs. In essence, the platform pockets the agreed-upon part of its end-users' saved expenditures on acquisition of information and coordination.

This is not necessarily a good thing when the intermediary is an MCO. As the legal scholar writes, "This [platform] function currently has negative implications for the quality of medical care"—for example, when the MCO focus to (a) compete on price and minimum loss ratio and/or (b) acquire other plans to boost its enrollment may lessen emphasis on building high-quality provider networks. When it comes to the GPOs and PBMs, much of the criticism of their platform role centers on the profits they make, the access fees they charge, and the information they do or don't share.[16] These issues are considered in the remainder of this volume. Other researchers suggest that intermediaries such as GPOs and PBMs nevertheless have a unique opportunity to promote health and generate value.[17] But, defining what that value is in terms of the three chains gets murky.

Value-Added Benefits

Each activity in the firm's <u>internal value chain</u> can potentially add benefit that customers get from the firm's product/service, and each can add to the cost that the firm incurs in producing and selling the product/service. It is quite difficult to isolate the incremental benefits and costs of each activity and, thus, to estimate the value of that activity. This, in turn, makes it difficult to estimate the value created by the firm and where that value creation resides. When different stages in the production process lend themselves to analysis as semi-finished or finished goods, then market prices for these goods can serve as estimates. This method is known as "value-added analysis." If that is not possible, then the value-added of the firm's internal value chain is more crudely estimated by the market value of its goods and services minus the cost of goods and services used in their production—in other words, the markup in the prices it charges its customers relative to the prices it paid for the inputs it used. This is known as "industry value added," or IVA. According to the Bureau of Economic Analysis,[18]

> The value added of an industry, also referred to as gross domestic product (GDP) by-industry, is the contribution of a private industry or government sector to overall GDP. The components of value added consist of compensation of employees, taxes on production and imports less subsidies, and gross operating surplus. Value added equals the difference between an industry's gross output (consisting of sales or receipts and other operating income, commodity taxes, and inventory change) and the cost of its intermediate inputs (including energy, raw materials, semi-finished goods, and services that are purchased from all sources).

What about the external value chain in which the firm resides? That type of value can perhaps be assessed by achievement of the external chain's objectives. Across firms engaged in trading relationships, a value chain is concerned with several theorized objectives:

- Optimize the overall activities of firms working together to create bundles of goods and services,
- Manage and coordinate the whole chain from raw material suppliers to end customers, rather than focus on maximizing the interests of one player,
- Develop highly competitive chains and positive outcomes for all firms involved, and
- Establish a portfolio approach to working with suppliers and customers; that is, decide which players to work with most closely and establish the processes and information technology (IT) infrastructure to support the relationships.

Thus, value chains are supposed to be collaborative partnerships between adjacent players engaged in economic exchange. Such collaborative activity includes coordinated planning of production and distribution to meet the customer's needs on a just-in-time basis that reduces inventory levels and delays in product availability. It is also designed to create a lowest total cost solution for the end customer and the manufacturer. Lowest total cost is achieved using demand planning, which relies on information gathered from the customer that "pulls products." Demand planning works backward from the customer toward the manufacturers and their suppliers and original equipment manufacturers (OEMs). This is all in contrast to traditional supply chain management, which starts with the manufacturer that "pushes product" (for example, using marketing and advertising campaigns) and works forward toward the customer. Here the manufacturer's aim is not to achieve lowest total cost but to increase product sales, greatest product differentiation, and lowest delivered cost. A later section below examines how feasible the accomplishment (let alone measurement) of all this is.

What is Value?

While many often use the phrase "value-added," embedded here is the word "value." It does not help that "value" is a murky term. Many of my Wharton colleagues are economists who, to paraphrase Oscar Wilde, understand the price of everything and the value of nothing.[19] For them, the value that someone places on a product reflects the intensity of gratification it provides. That gratification is known in economic circles as "utility" (or "utils"). Because measuring utility is not easy, many punt by studying the money price that people will pay. The problem is that different people are willing to pay different amounts, which may not really reflect differential value. Adam Smith tried to explain that value has two meanings—"value in use" (the utility of an object) and "value in exchange" (what that object can be exchanged for)—which can be quite different in magnitude. The latter meaning of value is based on what you can sell it for and others' are willing to pay (WTP) for it. Some of us non-economists do not find this approach particularly insightful for studying intermediaries.

Recently, spurred by the work of Michael Porter and Elizabeth Teisberg, value has taken on a definite meaning in healthcare as the quotient of quality divided by cost.[20] Indeed, "value" is the *Zeitgeist* of healthcare. We are confronted by the following panoply of terms:

- Value-based care (VBC)
- Low-value care
- Volume to value
- Value-based purchasing (VBP)
- Value-based insurance design (VBID)
- Value maximizing
- Innovating for value

Most people cannot distinguish (let alone define) these terms. "Value" as defined by Porter and Teisburg is incredibly murky: it is anything that increases the numerator and/or reduces the denominator in the quotient above. So, what is the problem? It turns out that quality and cost (the numerator and denominator) have a pretty complex relationship.[21] At the population level, there are conflicting findings. Dartmouth Atlas researchers reported a negative relationship in the Medicare population; others reported a positive relationship across both Medicare and commercial populations; still, others found no relationship. A meta-analysis suggests the overall correlation is nearly zero.[22]

Why might this be the case? One possibility is that the two aims (high quality, low cost) are orthogonal. This explains the zero correlation. A second possibility is that the data are generated by firms that differ in managerial efficiency so that, although cost and quality trade off in every firm, those firms that choose to produce at high quality are the more efficient, lower cost firms. A third likely explanation is that cost and quality have a more complex relationship that sums to zero—perhaps an inverted U-shaped curve (see Fig. 2.3). This curve reflects three types of process measures of quality—underuse, misuse, and overuse. The upward slope suggests cost and quality are positively correlated for a range of services that are under-used, such as vaccinations, taking prescribed medications (e.g., statins or beta-blockers for heart disease), guideline-based care, and both preventive and primary care. The downward slope suggests cost and quality are negatively correlated for a different range of services, such as antibiotics for simple infections, whose overuse can be harmful. The flat part in the middle suggests cost and quality are not related for another set of services, such as imaging for low back pain.[23]

One effort to apply the Porter and Teisberg framework suggests that PBMs be measured along three dimensions that might impact the quotient.[24] These three dimensions include:

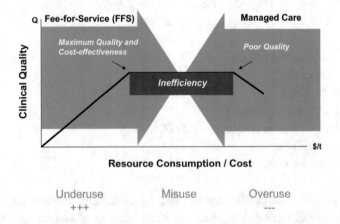

Fig. 2.3 U-shaped relationship of cost and quality (*Source* Brad Fluegel)

1. Use of cost-effective medications, measured by the generic prescribing rate or formulary compliance
2. Timely initiation of appropriate medication therapy for chronic conditions
3. Adherence to that therapy

The authors lay out multiple strategies that PBMs can implement to "improve value along the 3 dimensions of value promotion." One problem with this approach is that these three dimensions are not under complete or direct control of PBMs. Another problem is that variations in patient populations call for different targets for medication use and adherence. Thus, the value generated by PBMs needs to be patient-specific and risk-adjusted.

So, where does this leave us? Efforts to define and quantify the value of any given activity within a firm, as well as the value of the firm in the broader value chain, may yield little fruit. The situation may be even more complex. According to some academics, "In services, metrics are less precise and, consequently, the service value chain can be more complex. In fact, the value chain is comprised of several possible value chains, thereby forming a network of relationships, rather than the sequence customarily associated with the value chain."[25]

Two Other Value Frameworks

The Iron Triangle

One approach to gauge the value of intermediaries such as GPOs and PBMs is their ability to tackle "the iron triangle" and/or "the triple aim." The iron triangle, developed by William Kissick, encompasses the three goals of healthcare pursued by every country for decades: increase access, improve quality, and contain rising costs.[26,27] The logic of this triangle is that there are inevitable societal tradeoffs in pursuing any of the goals (vertices) in the triangle. Oftentimes these tradeoffs are illustrated using the tension between promoting access to care for everyone (e.g., by expanding insurance coverage) versus containing healthcare costs or using price as a tool to ration healthcare services. If the triangle is an equilateral triangle, and thus each angle is 60 degrees, policy initiatives that expand one angle beyond 60 degrees force one or both of the other two angles to contract below 60 degrees. Thus, efforts to promote access to care (e.g., via insurance coverage) will lead to higher demand for care, rising utilization, and higher costs. Similarly, efforts to promote quality by virtue of enabling access to modern technologies (drugs, medical devices, and equipment) will also likely raise costs.

Determining the right thrust and mix among the three angles constitutes the balancing act in resource allocation faced by most firms and countries. This explains why the impact of intermediaries such as MCOs (noted above) on quality may be negative: if the goal is to balance the three goals of health-care, and if the emphasis is placed on cost containment, then either quality or access or both may be sacrificed.

Trying to measure the "value" of an intermediary across three goals that can be negatively correlated may likely yield mixed messages about anyone's contribution. This volume suggests that GPOs and PBMs attempt a delicate balancing act among these three goals; such balancing acts involve tradeoffs, i.e., giving up something on one goal to get something more on another goal. Such tradeoffs make value assessments difficult. It does not help that remarkably few people can define what these three goals are. One reason is that they are all multi-dimensional.[28]

Visibility of the Iron Triangle

The iron triangle became visible in the private sector during the latter half of the twentieth century. The development of new medical technology placed pressures on insurers to provide coverage that allowed the public to access the new discoveries. Expanded access to high-tech care and increased utiliza-tion of that care rapidly drove health care spending higher, which increased the demand for insurance to cover the rising costs. As a result of this health-care quadrilemma,[29] rising access to sophisticated technology and its quality benefits were accompanied by rising costs (see Chapter 10). To deal with this quadrilemma, public and private sector insurers initiated technology assessment programs that analyzed its quality benefits starting in the 1970s. Providers also became interested in technology assessment programs since they had the *de facto* responsibility of rationing technology at the point of care. Provider technology assessment programs focused on both cost and quality of new innovation. Providers outsourced a portion of their technology assessment activities to group purchasing organizations (GPOs).

Management of the iron triangle grew even more pronounced with the advent of MCOs in the 1980s and 1990s. MCOs actively sought to reduce patient access to hospital services (i.e., reduced hospitalization rates and lengths of stay) in order to reduce healthcare costs. MCOs used strategies such as utilization review, prior authorizations, and second opinion surgeries to effect this balancing act.

The iron triangle became visible in the public sector following the passage of Medicare and Medicaid in 1965. The two entitlement programs expanded access to health insurance for the elderly and the poor, respectively, but also accelerated the rate of increase in healthcare spending. Various organizations subsequently developed in the U.S. healthcare industry to manage the trade-offs and balancing act between cost, quality, and access. MCOs, PBMs, and state Medicaid programs, for example, developed formularies that restricted patient access to specific pharmaceuticals made by manufacturers who agreed to price discounts (tradeoff access versus cost). These organizations also developed tiered networks that allowed patients access to specified pharmaceuticals at different price tiers based on their discounted price and efficacy (e.g., lower cost generic versus higher cost branded drug). State Medicaid programs also developed restricted networks of providers (selective contracting with hospitals) that patients could access in exchange for hospitals' agreeing to accept lower reimbursements to be part of the network and gain access to those patients.

Like the MCOs, PBMs, and state Medicaid programs mentioned above, GPOs also make tradeoffs between cost and access. GPOs typically develop contracts with subsets of suppliers across product categories and promise them increased market share in exchange for discounted pricing. In this manner, they reduce hospitals' access to the total market to secure lower prices or lower increases in product prices. GPOs also seek to assess the technological benefits of new and existing technologies they purchase from product manufacturers in order to balance cost and quality. GPOs have historically pursued technology assessment using (a) sponsored meetings attended by vendors and hospital members, (b) in-house committees of clinicians drawn from their member hospitals, and (c) external technology assessment firms such as ECRI. Product reviews conducted by committees of clinicians typically evaluate technologies based on their ratios of perceived clinical benefits divided by costs (i.e., how researchers define "value").

The Triple Aim

In 2008, the healthcare industry welcomed a "new triangle on the block" to improve the U.S. system: "the triple aim." Coined by Dr. Donald Berwick and colleagues in an article in *Health Affairs*, the triple aim recast the goals of the iron triangle discussed above as "care, health, and cost": patient experience of care, population health, and per capita cost.[30] Unlike Kissick's iron triangle, Berwick's triple aim downplayed (but still acknowledged) tradeoffs among the three goals. Borrowing from organization theorists, the solution was no longer "satisficing" but now "optimizing" on all three dimensions.[31] While there might be some tensions, the three goals could be harmonized and jointly pursued in the presence of (1) an "integrator"—whether an IDN like Kaiser, or policy actors with political will who could alter provider incentives and structures, (2) "disruptive innovation," (3) efficiency improvements, and (4) a population focus that included social services and preventive health. Thus, rather than tradeoffs, the triple aim holds out the promise of achieving all three goals simultaneously.

As with the iron triangle, most people cannot define the three dimensions of the triple aim either. What is worse, they conflate the triple aim with the iron triangle. It is not clear whether the new triangle on the block will help in any assessment of the contributions of intermediaries, since GPOs and PBMs are not involved in direct patient care and may not have much to contribute to a person's health status. Still, researchers have made several attempts at applying the triple aim's goals to the assessment of these intermediaries.[32]

Value Chains and Value Chain Alliances

There is a further problem with the value/value chain approach. Value chains are also supposed to develop as strategies of competitive advantage in which one set of trading partners (input supplier–product manufacturer–distributor) seeks to create more value (for example, higher quality and/or lower cost products and services) than a rival set of trading partners. Research on value chain alliances in the auto industry suggests some of the essential ingredients for success.

One key ingredient is dedicated asset investments in one's supply chain partners in order to increase productivity. These can include dedicated managers and account representatives who accumulate substantial understanding and know-how through longstanding relationships with trading partners. Another type of asset investment is the development of capital investments tailored and customized to a specific trading partner.

A second key ingredient is the effective management of knowledge and knowledge flows among trading partners. This requires sharing of information (both explicit and tacit knowledge) rather than secrecy. This is accomplished through supplier associations, learning teams, on-site consultation, joint-study groups, problem-solving teams, and interfirm employee transfers. In this manner, suppliers provide input to product development and process improvement initiatives.

A third key ingredient is trust among trading partners. The presence of trust lowers the necessity for contract enforcement and surveillance, which reduces transaction costs. Specific means to foster trust include selection of suppliers based on their capabilities and track record for performance (rather than competitive bidding) and previous contracting relationships, establishment of long-term contracts, stability of employment of managers involved in contracting, extensive two-way communication, financial investments in one another, and evaluation of the relationship on a broader scale than just unit price of inputs.

Research on the auto industry suggests that the presence of these three ingredients allows the formation of extended enterprises that span manufacturers and their suppliers. Such enterprises achieve competitive advantage over other manufacturers (that lack such alliances) in terms of the speed of product development, product development costs, transaction costs in procurement, product costs, quality, market share, and profitability.

Do Value Chains Exist in the U.S. Healthcare Ecosystem?

In 2002, I argued that this view represents more aspiration than reality in U.S. healthcare.[33] This is still largely true today. One basic reason (noted above) is that we do not really know what value is, let alone how to measure it. Within healthcare, information on the quality and cost added at each link in the vertical chain is severely lacking. We also suffer from a lack of transparency regarding the quality and cost of products produced and services rendered. There is still a great reluctance to share information within any given stage of the vertical chain (e.g., with competitors) as well as across stages (e.g., between payers and providers). As a consequence, multiple links in the vertical chain may (and do) perform duplicative functions that may not add value. Another, perhaps more fundamental reason is that real collaboration among firms located at different points along the value chain is in short supply.

There are, however, some interesting exceptions to this state of affairs. As noted above, as part of the value movement, players along the vertical chain have developed value-based partnerships. For decades, product manufacturers have endeavored to engage both payers and providers in risk-based contracts whereby they earn favorable reimbursement contingent on the outcomes observed among patients using their products. Payers and providers have also entered value-based contracts using centers of excellence, high-performing networks, tiered networks, and reference-based pricing. The evidence base that might support the success of these partnerships is weak, however (see Chapter 13).

Product wholesalers have developed another set of collaborative, value chain alliances with the manufacturers of specific pharmaceuticals and physician GPOs. At the same time, insurers, PBMs, specialty pharmacies, and providers have developed some novel, vertically integrated relationships (see Chapter 11). Such value chain alliances represent efforts to coalesce players across the vertical chain to work together—and perhaps increase integration, coordination, and cooperation.

Centrifugal Versus Centripetal Forces

On the one hand, these collaborative value chain alliances appear to represent a centripetal force to unite a fragmented ecosystem. Adam Fein from the Drug Channels Institute presents a more nuanced picture[34]:

> I believe that these insurer / PBM / specialty pharmacy / provider organizations are poised to restructure U.S. drug channels by exerting greater control over patient access, sites of care/dispensing, and pricing. If they can effectively coordinate their sprawling business operations, they will pose a substantial threat of disruption to the existing commercial strategies of pharma companies. Will they succeed by better managing care and costs, or merely by extracting higher profits from our convoluted system?

On the other hand, by virtue of forming such alliances, players across the vertical chain are diversifying into one another's space to occupy and control as much of the distribution channel as possible. Figure 2.4 shows the overlapping functions (rows) performed by different distributors and pharmacy chains (columns). This could suggest greater duplication and, thus, the existence of centrifugal forces at work. More to the point, this could mark the formation of "competing value chains" or "extended enterprises" which researchers have been discussing for decades as the new basis of competition in healthcare.[35]

In addition to the rise of duplication, there is also growing proliferation of players performing many of the same functions. These players are differentiated by the place they occupy in the vertical and supply chains.

	MCKESSON	AmerisourceBergen	CVSHealth	EXPRESS SCRIPTS	Walgreens Boots Alliance
Wholesale Distribution	✓	✓	✓*	✓	✓**
Pharmacy Benefit Management			✓	✓	
Dispensing to Patients	✓	✓	✓	✓	✓
Healthcare Provider Services	✓		✓		✓
Group Purchasing Organization (GPO)	✓	✓		✓	✓
Paid services for Manufacturers	✓	✓	✓	✓	✓

Fig. 2.4 Duplication among organized channel companies (*Note* *Self-distribution only; **Non-U.S. only. *Source* Pembroke Consulting Research)

Agency Theory: A Way Out of the Wilderness?

Clearly, there is "too much stuff" to determine the value contribution of intermediaries such as GPOs and PBMs. So, how should they be evaluated? Agency theory offers one solution (and a way out of the wilderness). Agency theory concerns itself with the congruence between the interests of the principal and the agent. Principals delegate work to agents and anticipate that the agents will act in the principals' best interest. In the corporate management literature, this is often studied as the convergence or divergence of incentives between the firm's owners (e.g., the principals, such as shareholders) and the firm's managers (their agents). Perhaps the central tenet of agency theory is that there is a "potential for mischief" when such interests diverge. In such circumstances, the managers may be able to exact "higher rents" than the owners would otherwise accord them.[36] The key research question then becomes, is there a disjunction in interests between the principals (owners) and agents (managers) of the firm? It is not just about incentives and interests, however. The issue also concerns information asymmetries between the two parties. Conflicts between the two parties can arise because (a) their relationships are governed by work contracts, (b) contracts cannot anticipate all contingencies or cover all details, (c) monitoring the work of agents is difficult and costly, and (d) efforts by principals to exercise their property rights may be difficult.[37]

Three approaches discussed in the literature include independence, equity, and the market for corporate control. Independence relies on governing boards to oversee the actions of their agent managers. Equity relies on giving managers an ownership stake to align their interests with the stockholders. The market approach relies on external market players to discipline managers who leverage their agency position to advantage themselves (which can lead to a degradation and an under-valuation of the firm's assets in the market and thereby invite acquisition). Agency theory is thus a subset of the broader academic inquiry into corporate social responsibility, stewardship, and shareholder value maximization. Unfortunately, there is very little evidence of systematic relationships between these three approaches and the firm's financial performance. Perhaps, to paraphrase Winston Churchill, agency is the worst theory of corporate governance, except all those other forms that have been tried over time.[38]

The U.S. healthcare ecosystem includes several well-known principal-agent relationships: physicians act as agents for patients in their demand for medical care, while MCOs act as agents for employers whose employees need medical services provided by physicians.[39] Agency theory has been applied to GPOs several times, but not always in depth. Some reports apply broadly to procurement[40]; others apply more specifically to GPOs.[41] One key question, not answered in the reports, is whether the GPOs are motivated to act in their own interests as opposed to the interests of their owners (customers). Self-interests include the generation of administrative and other fees, and thus the potential conflict of interest to negotiate higher prices that generate more fees. According to one report, experts conflict on the issue. Some believe that market competition among the GPOs mitigates this principal-agent problem.[42] Others argue that agents may indeed engage in self-interested behavior (often due to a lack of effort), but that such behavior may not be deceitful or willingly misrepresented to the principal. Another key issue is the presence of asymmetric information that may not be shared with the principal. Most authors acknowledge that the agent's privileged position in the supply chain affords them differential knowledge and leads to uncertainty on the part of the principal of the agent's actions. Regardless of their opinion, everyone agrees that empirical data to resolve or address these questions are limited.

Agency theory has also been applied to the analysis of PBMs. Academics broadly characterize PBMs as actors in a healthcare landscape who manage the tradeoff between access/quality (access to innovative medicines) and cost by virtue of their role as the managers of pharmacy benefits acting on behalf of health plans and other payers (e.g., state Medicaid plans).[43]

According to researchers, PBMs play a central role in drug markets as market intermediaries who have to offer value to both upstream branded drug manufacturers and downstream health plans. They have been subjected to intense scrutiny from policymakers. Little attention has been devoted to the economic functioning of these organizations, partly due to the opaque contracts governing their relationships with payers on one side and drug makers on the other. Not surprisingly, the researchers conclude that PBM intermediaries improve market efficiency but the gains do not accrue to consumers or drug manufacturers.

Conclusion

Parts II and III of this volume conduct a "deep dive" into the realms of the GPOs and PBMs, respectively. Each Part seeks to first explain how these realms operate and then to evaluate the value they provide to other stakeholders in the ecosystem—whether in terms of the goals in the iron triangle or the goals in the triple aim. To the degree that data are available, they also assess how satisfied the principals (customers) are with the agents (intermediaries) that serve them and how aligned they think their goals are.

Notes

1. Available online at: https://www.youtube.com/watch?v=U3PLjbuTI48. Accessed on September 3, 2021.
2. Lawton R. Burns, Howard Forman, and Carolyn Watts. "Teaching the Introductory Course on the U.S. Healthcare System: Issues, Challenges, and Lessons," *Journal of Health Administration Education* (forthcoming 2022).
3. Lawton Robert Burns. *The U.S. Healthcare Ecosystem: Payers, Providers, and Producers* (New York: McGraw-Hill, 2021).
4. See R.A. Davis. "Fresh Thoughts on a Growing Problem: How We Could Arrest Proliferation of Allied Health Professions," *C.M.A. Journal* 105 (July 24, 1971): 193–194, 213.
5. Milton Roemer. *Ambulatory Health Services in America.* (Rockville, MD: Aspen Systems, 1981).
6. David Lawrence. "Bridging the Quality Chasm," in Proctor P. Reid, W. Dale Compton, Jerome H. Grossman, and Gary Fanjiang, (Eds), *Building a Better Delivery System: A New Engineering/Health Care Partnership* (Washington, D.C.: National Academies Press, 2005): 99–101.
7. See for example: Darius Rastegar. "Health Care Becomes an Industry," *Annals of Family Medicine* 2(1) (2004): 79–83. Linda Aiken and Karen Lasater.

"Commentary on 'The Changing Medical Division of Labor,'" *Journal of Ambulatory Care Management* 40(3) (2017): 176–178.

8. Michael E. Porter. *Competitive Advantage: Creating and Sustaining Superior Performance.* (New York: Free Press, 1985, 1999).

9. David Besanko, David Dranove, and Mark Shanley. *The Economics of Strategy* (New York: John Wiley & Sons, 1996): p. 72.

10. David Besanko, David Dranove, and Mark Shanley. *The Economics of Strategy* (New York: John Wiley & Sons, 1996): p. 72.

11. Wendy Phillips, Jens Roehrich, Dharm Kapletia et al. "Global Value Chain Reconfiguration and COVID-19: Investigating the Case for More Resilient Redistributed Models of Production," *California Management Review* 64(2) (2022): 71–96.

12. Lawton R. Burns. *The Health Care Value Chain* (San Francisco, CA: Jossey-Bass, 2002).

13. Lawton R. Burns and Allison Briggs. "Hospital Purchasing Alliances: Ten Years After," *Health Care Management Review* 45(3) (July/September 2020): 186–195.

14. Alex Stein. "Healthcare Intermediaries," *Regulation* (Winter 2006–2007): 20–25.

15. Alex Stein. "Healthcare Intermediaries," *Regulation* (Winter 2006–2007): 21.

16. Marty Makary. *The Price We Pay: What Broke American Health Care – And How to Fix It* (New York: Bloomsbury Publishing, 2021): Chapters 14 and 15.

17. William Shrank, Michael Porter, Sachin Jain et al. "A Blueprint for Pharmacy Benefit Managers to Increase Value," *American Journal of Managed Care* 15(2) (2009): 87–93.

18. Available at: https://www.bea.gov/help/faq/184. Accessed on September 2, 2021.

19. Uwe Reinhardt. "On the Much Used (and Abused) Word 'Value' in Healthcare," *Journal of Health Administration Education* 28(4) (Fall 2011).

20. Michael Porter and Elizabeth Teisberg. *Redefining Health Care: Creating Value-Based Competition on Results* (Boston: Harvard Business School Press, 2006).

21. Lawton R. Burns and Mark V. Pauly. "Transformation of the Health Care Industry: Curb Your Enthusiasm?" *Milbank Quarterly* 96(1) (2018): 57–109.

22. Lawton R. Burns and Mark V. Pauly. "Transformation of the Health Care Industry: Curb Your Enthusiasm?" *Milbank Quarterly* 96(1) (2018): 57–109.

23. Lawton R. Burns and Mark V. Pauly. "Transformation of the Health Care Industry: Curb Your Enthusiasm?" *Milbank Quarterly* 96(1) (2018): 57–109.

24. William Shrank, Michael Porter, Sachin Jain et al. "A Blueprint for Pharmacy Benefit Managers to Increase Value," *American Journal of Managed Care* 15(2) (2009): 87–93.

25. Dennis Pitta and Michael Laric. "Value Chains in Health Care," *Journal of Consumer Marketing* 21(7) (2004): 451–464.

26. William Kissick. *Medicine's Dilemmas: Infinite Needs Versus Finite Resources* (New Haven, CT: Yale University Press, 1994).
27. John Hoadley. "Health Care in the United States: Access, Costs, and Quality," *PS (Political Science)* 20(2) (1987): 197–201.
28. Lawton Robert Burns. *The U.S. Healthcare Ecosystem: Payers, Providers, Producers* (New York: McGraw-Hill, 2021).
29. Burton Weisbrod. "The Healthcare Quadrilemma: An Essay on Technological Change, Insurance, Quality of Care, and Cost Containment," *Journal of Economic Literature* 29(2) (1991): 523–552.
30. Donald Berwick, Thomas Nolan, and John Whittington. "The Triple Aim: Care, Health, and Cost," *Health Affairs* 27(3) (2008): 759–769.
31. James March and Herbert Simon. *Organizations* (New York: John Wiley & Sons, 1958).
32. Association for Healthcare Resources and Materials Management. *CQO & The Triple Aim: Supply Chain's Strategic Connection* (Chicago, IL: AHRMM, 2016). Available online at: https://www.ahrmm.org/resource-repository-ahrmm/cqo-the-triple-aim-supply-chains-strategic-connection-1. Accessed on September 8, 2021. Karthik Ganesh. "Why Benefits Managers Need to Explore 'Value'," *BenefitsPRO* (November 3, 2020). Available online at: https://www.benefitspro.com/2020/11/03/why-benefits-managers-need-to-explore-value/. Accessed on September 8, 2021. Decision Resources Group. "Beyond the PBM: A New Order for Healthcare Delivery," *Pharma-Times*. Available online at: http://www.pharmatimes.com/__data/assets/pdf_file/0016/1235221/Beyond_the_PBM_-_a_new_order_for_healthcare_delivery_-_DRG.pdf. Accessed on September 8, 2021. Pharmaceutical Care Management Association. *PBMs Provide Clinical Value to Patients, Doctors and Other Healthcare Providers* (PCMA: 2017). Available online at: https://www.pcmanet.org/wp-content/uploads/2017/04/PBMs-Provide-Clinical-Value-to-Patients-Doctors-and-Other-Healthcare-Providers_whitepaper_final.pdf. Accessed on September 8, 2021.
33. Lawton R. Burns. *The Health Care Value Chain* (San Francisco, CA: Jossey-Bass, 2002).
34. Adam J. Fein. *The 2020 Economic Report on U.S. Pharmacies and Pharmacy Benefit Managers* (Drug Channels Institute, 2020).
35. Lawton R. Burns. *The Health Care Value Chain* (San Francisco, CA: Jossey-Bass, 2002): 10–11. David Dranove and Lawton R. Burns. *Big Med: Megaproviders and the High Cost of Health Care in America* (Chicago, IL: University of Chicago Press, 2021): 232–234.
36. Dan Dalton, Michael Hitt, S. Trevis Certo et al. "The Fundamental Agency Problem and Its Mitigation: Independence, Equity, and the Market for Corporate Control," *Academy of Management Annals* 1(1) (2007):1–64.
37. Kathleen Eisenhardt. "Agency Theory: An Assessment and Review," *Academy of Management Review* 14(1) (1989): 57–74.

38. Dan Dalton, Michael Hitt, S. Trevis Certo et al. "The Fundamental Agency Problem and Its Mitigation: Independence, Equity, and the Market for Corporate Control," *Academy of Management Annals* (1) (2007):1–64.

39. Thomas G. McGuire. "Physician Agency," in A. J. Culyer and J. P. Newhouse (Eds.), *Handbook of Health Economics*, volume 1. (Elsevier, 2000): Chapter 9, pp. 461–536. Mark V. Pauly. "Insurance Reimbursement," in A. J. Culyer and J. P. Newhouse (Eds.), *Handbook of Health Economics*, volume 1, (Elsevier, 2000): Chapter 10, pp. 537–560.

40. Wendy Tate, Lisa Ellram, Lydia Bals et al. "An Agency Theory Perspective on the Purchase of Marketing Services," *Industrial Marketing Management* 39(5) (2009): 806–819. Cliff McCue and Eric Prier. "Using Agency Theory to Model Cooperative Purchasing," *Journal of Public Procurement* 8(1) (2008): 1–35. Joe Sanderson, Chris Lonsdale, Russell Mannion et al. "Towards a Framework for Enhancing Procurement and Supply Chain Management Practice in the NHS: Lessons for Managers and Clinicians from a Synthesis of the Theoretical and Empirical Literature," *Health Services and Delivery Research* 3(18) (2015).

41. Government Accountability Office. *Group Purchasing Organizations: Funding Structure Has Potential Implications for Medicare Costs.* GAO-15–13. (Washington, D.C.: 2014). Carl Johnson and Curtis Rooney. "GPOs and the Health Care Supply Chain: Market-Based Solutions and Real-World Recommendations to Reduce Pricing Secrecy and Benefit Health Care Providers," *Journal of Contemporary Health Law & Policy* 29(1) (2012): 72–88.

42. Government Accountability Office. *Group Purchasing Organizations: Funding Structure Has Potential Implications for Medicare Costs.* GAO-15–13. (Washington, D.C.: 2014).

43. Rena Conti, Brigham Frandsen, Michael Powell et al. "Common Agent or Double Agent? Pharmacy Benefit Managers in the Prescription Drug Market." NBER Working Paper No. 28866 (Cambridge, MA: NBER, May 2021).

Part II

Group Purchasing Organizations (GPOs)

3

Group Purchasing Organizations (GPOs): An Overview

Introduction

Group purchasing organizations (GPOs) have been long-term players in the healthcare ecosystem for over a century, but have gained some unwelcome notoriety in the last two decades. During the early 2000s, they were the subject of (in turn): several exposé articles in *The New York Times*, four Antitrust Subcommittee hearings sponsored by the U.S. Senate Judiciary Committee, and several reports by the Government Accountability Office (GAO). They were named or unnamed co-conspirators in several lawsuits brought by small product manufacturers alleging restraint of trade and anticompetitive practices. They quickly became the most controversial, scrutinized, and (at times) vilified players—following the HMOs of the 1990s—until being recently supplanted by the PBMs (see Chapter 12).

What brought all of this on? Like the PBMs, the GPOs have consolidated into a small number of very large organizations that pose a considerable countervailing force to large product manufacturers. Their growing scale thus makes them more visible. At the same time, the GPO and PBM sectors are also somewhat invisible. Few academic texts cover these sectors; there are no prior histories written about these sectors; there is little empirical research on these sectors; and there are no industry-wide databases that researchers can access. Like the PBMs in the *retail supply chain* covered later in this volume, the GPOs are *middlemen* in the *institutional supply chain* (see Chapter 2)—two topics themselves that are not well understood. Supply chain management, in general, is not a topic that either the public or the

© The Author(s), under exclusive license to Springer
Nature Switzerland AG 2022
L. R. Burns, *The Healthcare Value Chain*,
https://doi.org/10.1007/978-3-031-10739-9_3

research community is familiar with (at least until COVID-19). Finally, like just about everybody else in the healthcare ecosystem, their contracts with upstream manufacturers (suppliers) and downstream hospitals (buyers) are not made public. As one critic put it, "GPOs are like PBMs in how they operate in a fog of transactions, making value difficult for any buyer to ascertain."[1]

To be fair, there are some differences between the two sectors.[2] The GPOs are not all publicly traded and thus do not all disclose information to shareholders. The PBMs, on the other hand, are now all publicly traded companies. However, they have recently vertically integrated with insurers and taken on a conglomerate form, making it challenging to decipher the information they do disclose. Unlike the PBMs, GPOs are very transparent to the point they report every administrative fee collected on every contract as part of the "safe harbor" (discussed below). A GPO sector initiative has also produced a lengthy annual report on themselves for the past sixteen years; the report includes some statistics as well as a Public Accountability Questionnaire.

Nevertheless, there are few champions or advocates for these firms. The GPOs made only a lukewarm effort to defend themselves early in the new millennium, presumably because of the adage "don't poke the bear" (e.g., the U.S. Senate); they have done a better job since then.[3] By contrast, their critics have been consistently outspoken. One has recently lambasted the GPOs for "not selling anything," charging "pay-to-play" fees, and engaging in other "perverse financial incentives" just for writing contracts and connecting product manufacturers with hospital buyers.[4] So, critics naturally ask, what value do they provide?

This chapter describes GPOs in terms of the functions they perform and the services they provide. It also distinguishes different types of GPOs based on who they serve and at what geographic level, the demography and market structure of GPOs, their revenue models, their contract portfolios, their downstream relationships with hospitals, their upstream relationships with manufacturers, and their efforts in product standardization. Finally, it provides a window into the contracts that GPOs negotiate with product manufacturers.

The next two chapters build upon this one. Chapter 4 provides an extensive chronicle of the history of GPOs, their parallel growth with hospital systems and integrated delivery networks (IDNs), and some of the differences between them. Chapter 5 addresses topics regarding alleged issues of antitrust, restraint of trade, and GPO performance.

GPO Functions and Services

Contracting

As its name implies, a GPO is an organization that *contracts for* the purchase of products and services that its hospital members can access. The GPO sources these products and services but does not actually purchase (most of) them[5]; instead, it negotiates contracts that its members can voluntarily use (or not use). Hospital members do the actual product purchasing.

When hospitals use these contracts, the GPO aggregates the purchasing of those products and services across as wide a membership base as possible in order to secure a lower unit price. While GPOs do more than just contracting, the core promise of collective purchasing bestows bargaining clout on the GPOs and enables them to extract lower unit prices with product/service vendors. This is a classic price-volume tradeoff strategy utilized in business. It exemplifies "pooling alliances" which bring together organizations that pool their resources (in this case, their purchasing dollars) to exert leverage over suppliers to obtain lower unit prices and thereby reduce hospital costs.[6]

Joint purchasing of supplies and services offers GPO members one specific avenue for achieving scale economies—economies which are difficult for individual hospitals to generate in their normal operations due to the fact they are small and labor-intensive firms. Such economies can generate savings that can support hospital improvements in their technology, the labor force, and provision of quality patient care. Hospitals have found these scale economies elusive using other strategic avenues, such as joining multi-hospital systems.[7] Some estimate that the GPOs' contracting function saves providers more than $2 billion annually in administrative costs.[8]

The advantages can flow both ways. By virtue of having a large membership base, GPO contracts hold out the promise of large-scale (volume) buying to suppliers. For example, suppliers who gain a sole-source contract with a GPO typically gain a larger sales base than at GPOs who offer them a dual-source contract. As another example, large diversified suppliers might be able to strike a handful of contracts that cover the vast majority of hospitals with a small set of price points with simplified rebate mechanisms. Suppliers also recognize that such contracts can lower their search costs for customers, the transaction costs of negotiations (i.e., negotiate multiple contract terms for multiple products across multiple suppliers and product categories) for them and their customers, their SG&A (sales, general, and administrative) expenses, and their manufacturing costs.

Products and Services

The *products* covered by GPO contracts can include medical-surgical supplies (e.g., drapes, gowns, sutures, etc.), pharmaceuticals used in inpatient and outpatient settings, laboratory items (e.g., reagents), diagnostic imaging and other capital equipment, dietary and nutritional products, and office supplies. The *services* covered by GPO contracts can include facilities and maintenance, insurance, laundry, utilities, clinical engineering, and product shredding (among others).

A GPO's contract moves a product from non-contracted to contracted status. This means there is an established, negotiated price for that product that is likely to be lower than what an individual hospital could have negotiated on its own in a vacuum (i.e., a world without GPOs). But, in a world with GPOs, some hospitals can utilize the GPO's contract as a price ceiling and try to further negotiate below it. Moreover, as Vice-Presidents of Materials Management (VPMMs) report, suppliers who are not on the GPO's contract always try to come into the hospital and beat the incumbent's pricing ("it happens every day"). Thus, best pricing is fluid. Nevertheless, GPO contracts may rest on three-to-five-year agreements, thus affording some price protection to GPO members. Such price protection has clear benefits in an inflationary environment.[9]

The contract thus represents "the minimum" the supplier can do for the hospital. Neither the contract, nor its price, nor the contract terms are binding on the hospital members; they become binding only when the hospital elects to activate a GPO contract. Hospitals can (and do) buy off-contract and at terms they negotiate on their own. Conversely, suppliers can do business with hospitals in most GPOs, regardless of whether they have a contract with that GPO.

This also means that GPO contracts are not "the key" to product sales. Hospitals and their clinicians derive value from product quality, clinical features, ergonomics, etc., as well as good pricing. In evaluating supplier bids, GPOs may construct their own value equation of non-financial considerations divided by financial considerations (pricing).

GPOs offer other benefits to their hospital members beyond lower product prices. These include reductions in price variations across suppliers, an array of cost reduction tools (in materials management, contract management, and operations consulting), lower head counts needed for materials management, improvements in product standardization or reductions in product utilization, training support on new products, improvements in clinical operations (benchmarking with peer institutions, clinical resource management, decision support tools, disease management, business process design), comparative data with peers on supply chain expenditures, networking/participation in "affinity groups" with peers in other hospitals, technology management programs (technology assessment and life cycle management), collaboration with the Food and Drug Administration (FDA) and other federal departments and agencies to address challenges in the supply chain, programs to address systemic problems such as drug shortages, local market trends and research, equipment (maintenance, repair and disposal), insurance services, human resources management, education, and marketing.

Of course, not every GPO offers all of these services. An earlier analysis conducted by the GAO reported the varying levels of service provision across six GPOs (see Fig. 3.1).[10] Other research conducted in 2010 indicates that some services are more important than others in the hospital's selection of a GPO and that these services are used or not used by hospitals to varying degrees (see Fig. 3.2).

Services the six largest group purchasing organizations (GPO) reported providing in 2008

Service	GPO					
	A	B	C	D	E	F
Custom contracting	✓	✓	✓	✓	✓	✓
Clinical evaluation and standardization	✓	✓	✓	✓	✓	✓
Technology assessments	✓	✓	✓	✓	✓	✓
Supply-chain analysis	✓	✓	✓	✓	✓	
Electronic commerce	✓	✓	✓	✓	✓	
Materials management consulting	✓	✓	✓	✓	✓	
Benchmarking data	✓	✓	✓	✓	✓	
Continuing medical education	✓	✓		✓	✓	✓
Market research	✓	✓	✓	✓		
Materials management outsourcing	✓	✓			✓	
Patient safety services	✓	✓	✓			
Marketing products or services	✓	✓		✓		
Insurance services	✓	✓				
Revenue management	✓	✓				
Warehousing	✓					
Equipment repair	✓					
Other			✓		✓	✓

Fig. 3.1 GPO services across GPOs (*Source* Government Accountability Office. *Group Purchasing Organizations: Services Provided to Customers and Initiatives Regarding Their Business Practices.* [Washington, DC: GAO, 2010]. GAO-10–738. Page 9, Table 2)

Attributes	Important	Not important	Don't use
Assistance with standardization	82%	11%	8%
Benchmarking– clinical improvement	68%	11%	21%
Benchmarking– supply chain	86%	5%	9%
Capital and asset management tools	54%	22%	24%
Consulting – clinical service line	41%	24%	35%
Consulting – pharmacy	46%	21%	33%
Consulting – physician preference items	53%	16%	31%
Consulting – revenue cycle /RAC review	39%	23%	37%
Consulting – supply chain	61%	16%	23%
Contracts – fair price with value added	90%	6%	5%
Contracts – negotiate lowest price	93%	4%	3%
Contracts for alternate sites	51%	19%	30%
Custom contracts	72%	15%	14%
Customer service/rapid response	86%	6%	7%
Data management (standardization, synchronization)	71%	12%	17%
Education	68%	19%	13%
E-sourcing, Web-enabled tools	72%	14%	14%
Group buys (e.g., capital equipment)	73%	18%	9%
Information materials (RFID)	73%	18%	9%
Item master mgmnt/cleansing	57%	21%	22%
Manage vendor contract compliance	48%	23%	29%
Outsourcing in-hospital supply chain Services management to GPO	88%	5%	7%
Peer networking	23%	29%	48%
Product research/product evaluation	74%	15%	12%
Safety/quality initiatives	81%	10%	9%
Technology assessment	77%	11%	12%
Value analysis assessment	61%	17%	23%

Fig. 3.2 Importance of services in GPO selection (*Source* 2010 Hospital GPO Use Survey. *Hospitals & Health Networks.* Survey sponsored by MMHC/AHRMM)

As part of contracting, GPOs screen the suppliers to contract with, manage the contracts, update contract price changes, and work with contracted suppliers to disseminate product information. This is no mean feat, given the wide array of product suppliers, line items, supply categories, total expenditures, and GPO members involved. For example:

Premier has a national portfolio of 3,100 product contracts with 1,350 different suppliers. These agreements, covering hundreds of thousands of line items in multiple product categories, totaled over $69 Billion in 2020 purchases from over 4,100 hospital members and 200,000 other organizations. Executives report that the non-acute care segment accounts for a growing share of the GPO business (now 35–40%), due to historically lower penetration and the shift of care from acute to non-acute settings.[11]

Vizient has a national portfolio of 2,100 contracts with 900 unique suppliers. These agreements, covering more than 725,000 line items on contract, totaled over $112 Billion in 2020 purchases in both the acute care ($66 Billion) and non-acute care ($46 Billion) space.[12]

HealthTrust Purchasing Group has a national portfolio of roughly 1,700 contracts with over 800 unique suppliers. Total spend under contract purchases in 2020 was roughly $45 Billion from approximately 1,600 hospitals in the U.S. and the United Kingdom, as well as 60,000 non-acute care locations (ambulatory surgery centers, physician practices, long-term care sites, etc.).

There is thus an array of contracts and prices paid by hospitals for any given product from any given supplier, both within and across GPOs.

Of course, the GPO statistics reported above are subject to considerable "noise," as the GPOs will tell you. For example, the total dollar volume of purchasing covers acute and non-acute; the former is easier to track because the national GPOs commonly track the hospital's "primary national GPO." However, even that can lend itself to duplicate reporting: if a hospital buys from the contract portfolio of a competitor, some GPOs count that hospital's entire supply spend under their aggregate spending. Moreover, the acute care spend covers not only owned facilities under its member systems but also those hospitals that are leased and managed by those systems. Furthermore, acute care spend can include alternate sites such as physician practices, skilled nursing facilities, or other post-acute care (PAC) settings if they are managed centrally by the hospital system. In those instances, the non-acute sites can access acute care pricing by virtue of their hospital system affiliation.

Nevertheless, some GPOs "keep score" based on these purchasing volume and hospital member metrics. One national trade journal, *Modern Healthcare*, used to publish such statistics that provided an initial set of GPO comparisons. Certain GPOs stopped participating in the surveys because they felt the metrics were not based on standardized reporting and thus were inappropriate. Those GPOs think the better metric for comparison is supply chain cost per adjusted hospital discharge, if such comparative data were widely available. GPOs can gain a glimpse of this only locally and sporadically whenever a hospital seeks competitive pricing bids from alternate GPOs on a mock product portfolio (what GPOs label a "shoot out").

GPO product portfolios are not static; new products can be added for a number of reasons. Moreover, hospital members can provide feedback to their GPOs on the latter's contracts; the GPO's field force can detect items that members want and that are not on contract; and new suppliers can approach the GPO to try to strike a contract. GPOs may also rely on external technology assessment firms to identify new products on the horizon and which ones appear technologically promising. In the past, these external firms included ECRI, SG2, Hayes, and the Health Technology Center.

GPOs can also offer services to product manufacturers beyond contracting efficiencies. GPO contracts are referred to as "licenses to sell" or "hunting licenses" in the industry. Sales representatives ("reps") are very expensive assets for suppliers. Many vendors view GPO contracts as drivers of greater market share, greater contract compliance, business stabilization, and strengtheners of demand for products with lower market shares—all of which can reduce the number of sales reps needed. Having contracts with stipulated prices frees up the manufacturer's sales reps to promote the product, educate hospital staff about its clinical benefits, and demonstrate its use. This enables reps to maximize their face time with clinicians to "inservice" the product and help clinicians determine the best mix of products.

For smaller and lower volume manufacturers that face difficulty in getting access to national GPO accounts, some GPOs offer a private label program. Smaller suppliers that might have difficulty gaining market access can sell their products using the GPO's label. These suppliers gain incremental sales in exchange for granting hospitals lower product prices. GPOs have also developed programs that facilitate suppliers that come from under-represented populations—and under-represented in the healthcare supply chain—to gain greater market traction. Such populations can include busi-nesses owned by people of color, members of the LGBTQ community, women, the disabled, veterans, and small sized enterprise owners. Such initiatives are profiled in HGPII's Fourteenth Annual Report to the Public.[13]

Classifying the Types of GPOs

GPOs can be classified along many dimensions, including ownership, geographic focus, and type of customer(s) served. These classifications are delineated below.

GPO Ownership

In prior decades, there were several large, national, nonfederal GPOs with a variety of owners (see Chapter 4). Today, there are three large national GPOs, all sponsored by hospitals.[14] One large GPO (Premier) used to be owned by its hospital shareholders but then offered shares to the public via an initial public offering (IPO) in 2013. It is now publicly traded and -owned, and reports its operating results to shareholders. Another large GPO (Vizient) is not publicly owned but refers to itself as a member-owned and member-driven health care services company ("participant member ownership struc-ture," according to Moody's Investors Service). Most GPOs have historically fallen into this category, being member-owned by the providers they serve and often functioning as shared services organizations (see Chapter 4). A third large GPO (HealthTrust Purchasing Group) is a subsidiary of another publicly owned company (HCA) that reports only consolidated results that do not break out the GPO activity.

GPOs can have other sponsors, including physicians, insurers, and distributors—and sometimes combinations of these as the GPOs change hands. For example, one physician-sponsored GPO, International Nephrology Network (INN), originated as a physician practice management company (PPMC) back in the 1990s. INN's founder started a specialty pharmacy to supply injected drugs to patients at home, and then sold this company to PhyMatrix, one of the early PPMCs, which had acquired oncology practices and included the group purchasing of drugs for its physician members as part of its business and revenue model.[15] The goal was to achieve scale economies through group purchasing of expensive pharmaceuticals for oncologists and to provide expertise in the management of physician practices. PhyMatrix eventually divested its assets and sold the specialty pharmacy back to the founder, who then sold it to Express Scripts (a PBM). In the late 1990s, the founder set up International Oncology Network (ION) as the authorized agent negotiating pharmaceutical purchasing contracts for office-based oncologists. With the acquisition of ION by AmerisourceBergen Corporation (ABC), a pharmaceutical wholesaler, the founder sought to replicate the ION model in other physician specialties (rheumatology, dermatology, urology, gastroenterology, and nephrology) under the umbrella, International Physician Network, or IPN. The founder sought to roll up many such specialties into one network to achieve a significant volume of physician members and product purchases. The founder then sold IPN to ABC as well.

GPO Geographic Focus

Historically, GPOs operated at a local or regional level, often initiated by state hospital associations or alliances between associations in neighboring states. During the 1970s and 1980s, several GPOs consolidated operations across state and regional lines to develop a handful of national GPOs (see Chapter 4). The latter has garnered most of the attention. Their numbers have fallen over time due to consolidation—from eight national GPOs in the early 2000s to just three national GPOs today. Their major attribute and competitive advantage is scale—i.e., the sheer number of hospitals and their purchasing volumes they bring to the bargaining table. They also exhibit healthy cash flows which can be used to (1) develop value-adding services for hospital members and (2) rebate savings back to the members as additional revenues or reductions to their supply expenses.

The growing scale of the national GPOs creates issues of "one size fits all." Aggregated purchasing clout at the national level can come at the expense of contract customization for some members at the local level and reduced ability to standardize purchases across a large number of hospitals. There is some sentiment that the national GPOs cannot do all of the following functions well, although the GPOs beg to differ (see endnotes to the bullet points below):

- Provide hands-on service in smaller and rural hospitals
- Provide face-to-face relationships with hospital members[16]
- Influence members' use of negotiated contracts
- Address idiosyncratic needs of hospital members
- Negotiate local contracts for hospital members with local vendors of supplies and services—appropriate for supplies such as medical gas, perishable food, medical waste removal, and equipment maintenance
- Offer scale economies to local vendors
- Assist local hospitals with shared services (order processing, distribution, warehousing, invoice processing)[17]
- Assist hospitals with shared information technology platforms to help them do the above and enable them to act as a single (virtual) organization.[18]

Many regional and local GPOs continue to operate and, indeed, have proliferated over the past three decades to perform the above functions. Evidence suggests that purchasing activity has become less concentrated at the national level and more dispersed to regional and local levels. The regional GPOs continue to be formed by providers and hospital associations in neighboring states. A 2010 survey reported that 83% of hospitals belonged to at least one national GPO, with an average of 1.45 memberships; 51% belonged to a regional GPO (typically only one), and only 2% of hospitals reported no GPO memberships.[19] A more recent 2021 survey likewise indicates that 53% of hospitals are associated with regional purchasing coalitions.[20]

There are reportedly hundreds of regional GPOs. Regional GPOs can operate under many labels, such as regional aggregation groups, purchasing coalitions, purchasing alliances, and custom supply chain networks.[21] What they share in common is pooling of non-related hospitals, hospital systems, and IDNs in the same geographic market. They may even belong to the same national GPO but work together locally to try to optimize their GPO contract portfolios. They also offer services beyond product purchasing in areas such as data sharing and utilization, networking and best practices, and trend identification to enhance performance.

Regional GPOs thus serve to complement the national GPOs and supplement their efforts, offering the advantage of local customization, agility, and nimbleness by virtue of working with a smaller number of hospitals in a defined geographic area. The smaller membership and geographic proximity of these regional groups are believed to confer upon them closer interaction and greater alignment of purchasing preferences and goals. They may also serve to support smaller, regional product suppliers who can face difficulties getting GPO contracts at the national level. Hospitals can thus earn savings at both national and regional levels. National GPOs have come to recognize the important role played by the regional GPOs, often partnering with them to support their efforts.

Which GPO level is more important? Survey data from FTI Consulting indicates that hospital members report their national GPO is more effective than local GPO alliances in providing financial value.[22] This mirrors 2014 survey data showing that VPMMs rank the role and impact of the national alliances higher than regional/local alliances.[23] Nevertheless, the two can play complementary roles. Research suggests that, at least for the purchase of medical and surgical devices, the hybrid national-regional GPO model delivers the lowest costs to hospital members, outperforming the national GPO and hospital self-contracting efforts.[24]

GPO Customers Served

GPOs can and do offer joint purchasing programs to lots of stakeholders. These can include general medical-surgical hospitals, specialty (e.g., children's) hospitals, independent physicians, physician group practices, nursing homes, community health centers, community blood centers, independent and chain pharmacies, specialty and infusion pharmacies, respiratory providers, ambulatory surgery centers, laboratories, imaging centers, PAC providers such as skilled nursing facilities and assisted living centers, state and local governments, school districts, the Veterans Health Administration, and the Department of Defense. National GPOs may serve several of these constituencies; by contrast, smaller and regional GPOs likely concentrate their purchasing business to serve a handful of stakeholders. Some of their business lies outside of healthcare in food service, grocery stores, manufacturing, legal, education, and government. National data published by IBISWorld suggests that healthcare is the major market and accounts for roughly 60% of all GPO revenues (see Fig. 3.3).[25]

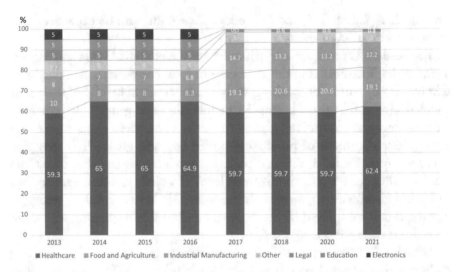

Fig. 3.3 Major markets for the GPOs (*Source* Jack Curran. *Group Purchasing Organizations.* Industry Report OD5963. [IBISWorld, August 2021])

GPO Market Structure: Numbers, Consolidation, and Concentration

GPO Numbers

For a long time, researchers, trade associations (e.g., the Health Industry Group Purchasing Association), and other observers commonly asserted there are 600 GPOs. To be honest, I do not think anyone really knows. GPOs can be sponsored by a wide range of parties serving different customer segments for different sets of products at varying geographic levels—all of which make it difficult to precisely ascertain their numbers. A slightly more conservative estimate advanced by IBISWorld suggests there are 583 GPOs, a number trending upwards since 2013 (see Fig. 3.4).[26]

The actual number of GPOs is somewhat irrelevant, for several reasons. First, the GPO market is quite consolidated, with a small number of big players and a large number of small, niche players. Second, it is nevertheless a competitive market with a lot of new entrants that can span the value chain. GPO startups do not require a lot of capital and do not have to undergo any registration process. Nevertheless, they do require a significant amount of infrastructure to ensure compliance with federal rules regarding safe harbors. Third, a lot of non-traditional GPOs can perform GPO-like functions; these include consulting firms (that maintain product pricing files

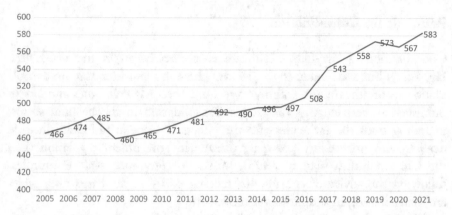

Fig. 3.4 Number of GPO enterprises (*Source* Jack Curran. *Group Purchasing Organizations*. Industry Report OD5963. [IBISWorld, August 2021, and earlier years])

for their clients that can be utilized in subsequent engagements) and wholesalers. Fourth, in recent years, the largest PBMs have developed their own GPOs (see Chapter 11).

GPO Consolidation

Historical Combinations

The GPO expansion (largely at the regional/local level) has occurred at the same time that the sector has undergone considerable consolidation (at the national level). In recent years, the GPO sector has witnessed several important mergers and acquisitions (M&As) involving the top national GPOs:

- 2007 pooling of Consorta members as an equity owner of HealthTrust
- 2008 acquisition of Broadlane by TowerBrook Partners
- 2010 acquisition of Broadlane by MedAssets
- 2015 merger of University HealthSystem Consortium (UHC) and its GPO Novation with VHA to form Vizient
- 2016 acquisition of MedAssets by Vizient
- 2019 acquisition of ROi by HealthTrust
- 2020 acquisition of Acurity and Nexera by Premier
- 2021 acquisition of Intalere by Vizient.

Rationale for Consolidation

Consolidation of the U.S. healthcare ecosystem began in the 1960s (see Fig. 14.1), but accelerated in the 1990s. There is a vast literature on consolidation in healthcare, too lengthy to recount here. My colleagues and I have published several lengthy analyses of consolidation in the hospital sector, including both the rationales and the effects.[27] General rationales include dealing with uncertainty posed by threatened government regulation (i.e., the Clinton health plan of 1993), pursuit of presumed scale economies, following the advice of consultants, seeking parity at the bargaining table, and participating in a bandwagon movement.

GPOs took part in the consolidation movement themselves as their upstream and downstream trading partners consolidated. One might argue that such upstream and downstream consolidation poses a threat to GPOs and their bargaining power vis-à-vis their trading partners. There is little written about GPO combinations, however, although two recent mergers provide a window in the espoused benefits.

In 2010, MedAssets (then the third largest GPO) acquired Broadlane for roughly $835 million. The strategic rationale for the deal was multi-fold:

- Create the market leader in the combined space of revenue cycle management (RCM) and cost management. The RCM solution would include both clinical and administrative solutions, drawing upon MedAssets' technologies.
- Access Broadlane's high rate of compliance (92%+) in its committed purchasing program
- Possibly gain/retain three key Broadlane hospital customers (Kaiser, Ascension, and Tenet) which would increase participation in the committed purchasing program.
- Increase savings (11–25%) across several product categories
- Provide a platform (e.g., customer base) for developing broader solutions that address quality management, cost management, alternative payment models, and analytics
- Sell a broader package of solutions to a combined membership with little overlap.
- Offer greater sales opportunities across the two businesses by virtue of (a) cross-selling existing services and solutions to each other GPO's members and (b) up-selling new products/services/solutions to existing members
- Enhance revenues, earnings per share growth, profitability, and cash flow.

In late 2015, Vizient offered $400 million in debt, largely to purchase the entity holding MedAssets' two businesses—MedAssets Clinical Spend and Resource Management and Sg2—from Magnitude Parent Holdings, a subsidiary of Pamplona Capital Management. The deal closed in January 2016. MedAssets' two businesses consisted of (1) group purchasing, strategic sourcing, and outsourcing and (2) advisory and consulting services, along with analytics and intelligence platforms. According to the offering, the combination would bestow several benefits:

- Manage a larger book of business ($90 billion of annual hospital member spending) that potentially offers greater market leverage over suppliers to reduce unit prices
- Reduce corporate overhead in back-office staff and services across the combined GPOs to yield cost savings
- Optimize GPO contracts across the two memberships to yield cost and revenue synergies
- Provide members with data-based insights into their cost and quality performance
- Offer an expanded range of advisory services
- Expand the GPO's footprint across both acute care and non-acute care providers that create cross-selling and up-selling opportunities for members that operate both lines of business.

Consolidation Impacts

According to economists, such consolidation can potentially impact market competition and public welfare.[28] One issue is monopsony power, which involves asymmetric power of GPO buyers over product suppliers. This is a potential issue since the very existence of the GPO relies on aggregated purchasing volume to compel price discounts; if GPO buyers restrict purchases or drive deep discounts, manufacturers may restrict output. A second issue is market foreclosure. GPO contracts may limit the suppliers available to their members (e.g., using sole-source contracts, volume-based or committed contracts) and thereby potentially exclude other, smaller, clinically superior, and/or efficient competitors. This may also stifle product innovation by smaller firms. A third issue is the use of contract administration fees (CAFs, covered below) that are earned as a percentage of members' product purchases using the contracts. Such fees, critics allege, potentially give GPOs the incentive to contract for higher-priced supplies that earn them higher CAFs but also entail higher supply costs to their hospital members.

These potential impacts are analyzed and assessed in greater detail in Chapter 5. Here we offer some brief comments. The first threat may not be realized since the hospitals that own the GPOs do not want restrictions on product supply; and, yet, history suggests this threat can become real if the discounted prices are so low that manufacturers reduce production (a possible cause, but not a primary cause of periodic generic drug shortages in the new millennium). The second threat hinges on the capabilities of these smaller vendors to make clinically superior products in sufficient quantities and then successfully market and distribute them to hospitals around the country—thereby solving the "twin pillars of product innovation."[29] Such capabilities may not be present in smaller firms, thereby limiting their own success. This threat is further mitigated by the fact that GPOs contract for products that their members historically utilize. The third threat may be counterproductive: contracts with higher product prices will lead to lower product purchases and thus lower CAFs earned by the GPO. In fact, according to hospital supply chain managers, suppliers raise prices to GPOs (and their members) "because they can," not because the GPOs incentivize them to do so.

GPO combinations may have other downstream impacts. Mergers leave fewer GPOs operating at the national level and, thus, fewer alternatives for vendors to contract with, fewer contracts offered, and fewer vendors with contracts. These can all serve to heighten vendor competition for GPO contracts.

Origin of Contract Administration Fees (CAFs)

The contract administration fee (CAF) business model is used in other industries, such as financial services, agriculture, real estate services, and online marketplaces; it is also employed by the federal government. Given the size (and notoriety) of CAFs in healthcare, it is important to sketch their origin and their protection under what has become known as a "safe harbor."

The safe harbor came about in a circuitous fashion.[30] The 1965 Amendments to the 1935 Social Security Act enacted the Medicare and Medicaid programs. The 1972 Amendments to the Social Security Act included a provision that criminalized solicitation and/or receipt of payments for referrals under these Federal healthcare programs. This provision became known as the "Anti-Kickback Statute" (AKS). The breadth of this statutory language required Congress to subsequently clarify what practices were included or exempt in the 1977 Medicare and Medicaid Anti-Fraud and Abuse Amendments Act. One exemption included price reductions negotiated by GPOs on behalf of their provider members, on the condition that they were properly disclosed by the former and reflected in the cost statements of the latter.

Product suppliers, who were asked by the GPOs to pay these discounts, countered that the GPOs were violating the AKS. The Office of the Inspector General (OIG) inside the Department of Health and Human Services (DHHS) requested that the Department of Justice (DOJ) issue a "blanket declination" that exempted GPOs from prosecution, arguing: "the use of volume purchasing through group purchasing agents clearly reduces the costs of purchases by hospitals." The DOJ stated that Congress needed to statutorily specify this exemption, which it did in the 1986 Omnibus Budget Reconciliation Act. The Medicare and Medicaid Patient and Program Protection Act of 1987 (P.L. 100–93) added new provisions to the Social Security Act and its Sect. 1128(b) Anti-Kickback Statute ("AKS"), and extended DHHS' authority to establish "safe harbors" under the AKS. The final regulation implementing this provision was released in July 1991.

Under the safe harbor, the GPO must have a written agreement with each individual or entity (e.g., hospital member) for which items or services are furnished. The agreement provides for either of the following: (a) the agreement states that participating suppliers from which the individual or entity will purchase goods or services will pay a fee to the GPO of 3% or less of the purchase price of the goods or services provided by that supplier, or (b) in the event the fee paid to the GPO is not fixed at 3% or less of the purchase price of the goods or services, the agreement specifies the amount (or if not known, the maximum amount) the GPO will be paid by each supplier (where such amount may be a fixed sum or a fixed percentage of the value of purchases made from the supplier by the members of the group under the contract between the supplier and the GPO). Where the entity which receives the goods or service from the supplier is a healthcare provider of services, the GPO must disclose in writing to the entity at least annually, and to the Secretary upon request, the amount received from each supplier with respect to purchases made by or on behalf of the entity.

GPO Concentration

Consolidation should lead to higher concentration of the GPO market: i.e., a smaller number of GPOs with larger market shares. National data are often used to construct concentration measures such as the Herfindahl–Hirschman Index (HHI), relied on by economists and government regulatory agencies to assess the market competition. The HHI is formally defined as the sum of the squared market shares of all competitors in the same market. HHIs below 2,000 reflect an unconcentrated (i.e., competitive) market; HHIs between 2,000 and 6,000 reflect a more concentrated (i.e., oligopolistic) market; HHIs above 6,000 reflect a monopolistic market.

The degree of GPO concentration is difficult to gauge. Measures of concentration are usually based on agreed-upon definitions of the geographic market and the product market. As noted above, GPOs vary in terms of their geographic scope of aggregated spending—such as national, regional, and local. At the same time, GPOs also vary in terms of the product markets for which they mediate spending: medical-surgical supplies, capital equipment, medical devices, pharmaceuticals, and purchased services (among others). For example, Vizient mediates $50 billion in pharmacy spend and has 20% share of the non-acute space.[31] Finally, GPOs vary in terms of their customer segments. Some estimates of consolidation focus exclusively on the acute hospital market where GPOs first originated; others include other customer segments such as ambulatory surgery centers, physician offices, and post-acute care.

Estimates of GPO market penetration rarely take these different dimensions into account and, thus, likely vary in terms of different types of spend they capture. There are some data on the product dimension, but much less on the geographic and customer dimensions. We will thus never have good estimates of GPO concentration until we resolve the multi-dimensional issue of GPO purchasing.

The "Local" Issue

One must keep in mind the adage that "all healthcare is local" and, thus, what happens at the national level may not be reflected at the local level. For example, national-level data indicate that the acute care hospital market is quite fragmented, with any hospital system having only single-digit market share; conversely, health plans appear to have consolidated considerably, with a smaller number of insurers controlling a much bigger share of the national market.[32] This would give the impression that health plans have much greater bargaining power than hospitals, and that health plan consolidation is a much more important issue than hospital consolidation. However, such national measures of concentration are not replicated at the local level in metropolitan markets. Locally, hospitals are more concentrated than health plans and have used their relative market power to extract higher payment rates from commercial insurers,[33] a development that has received increasing recognition.[34] For purposes of competitive analysis and antitrust enforcement dealing with hospitals and health plans, concentration ratios such as the HHI have thus been computed at the level of the metropolitan statistical area (MSA); the impacts of mergers of hospitals or health plans have also been examined at the MSA level in terms of their impact on the local HHI.

The "all healthcare is local" adage may be increasingly relevant to the analysis of GPOs. There are no corresponding HHI measures of GPOs at the national or local level, for several reasons. First, while national GPOs strike national contracts with suppliers, regional and local GPOs often negotiate additional discounts using the national GPO contract as a price ceiling.

The ability to do so depends on the number of hospitals belonging to these regional/local groups and their volume and level of committed purchasing—both of which vary geographically. Second, the regional and local GPOs contract for items that must be sourced locally such as dietary items and purchased services (e.g., utilities)—areas in which the national GPOs are less adept. Such contracts are struck between local GPOs and local suppliers, transactions which are not measured by national GPO activity. Third, as noted above, hospital systems and IDNs have increased both their size and market power at local and (increasingly) regional levels, allowing them to act as their own GPOs. Their local consolidation may pose a countervailing force to national GPO consolidation. Fourth, suppliers are motivated to increase their share in local as well as national markets and have regional/local sales organizations to assist with this end. They are thus interested in striking contracts with regional/local GPOs and hospital systems to drive that share.

National GPO Market Shares

Revenues. Researchers have sought to assess GPO concentration at the national level in terms of the national purchasing volumes. According to IBISWorld (see Fig. 3.5), two GPOs dominate the sector in terms of total revenue: Vizient (32.2% share) and Premier (24.2%).[35] Overall, depending on the analyst, the top four or six GPOs control nearly 90% of the market. Other analysts suggest that the top three national GPOs handle $220 Billion in spending; of this, Vizient controls 50%, Premier controls 30%, and HealthTrust controls 20%.[36] This level of spending may leave considerable "head room" for other GPOs to capture share in relatively under-penetrated areas such as physician preference items (PPIs) and capital equipment. Indeed, between 2004 and 2014, the percentage of hospital supply spending routed through the hospital's primary national GPO fell from 71 to 62%. As noted above/below, an increasing share of supply spending now flows through regional or local GPOs or is managed directly by the hospital in the form of self-contracting.

Additional survey data support a narrative of declining market concentration. According to a recent study, the percentage of hospitals serving as shareholders in the national alliances fell during the 2004–2014 period from 43 to 38%; similarly, the percentage of hospitals relying on only one national GPO fell from 59% in 2004 to 53% in 2014.[37] Why do hospitals belong to more than one national GPO? One answer is to cherry-pick contracts: one GPO may contract with a specific supplier but the other GPO does

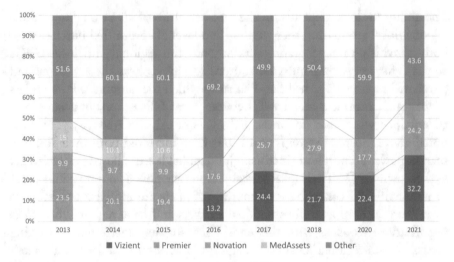

Fig. 3.5 GPO market share of major players (*Source* Jack Curran. *Group Purchasing Organizations.* Industry Report OD5963. (IBISWorld, August 2021, and earlier years)

not. Another possible explanation is that one GPO is used for medical-surgical items, while another GPO is used for pharmacy items. This can result from siloed contracting inside the hospital—whereby materials management contracts for med-surg items, while the pharmacy contracts for drugs.

Number of Members. Researchers have also attempted to measure GPO concentration in terms of the number of hospitals identifying a particular national GPO as their primary GPO. An earlier analysis of the GPO industry reported that, as of 1999, two-thirds of hospitals belonged to the top two GPOs. That figure does not appear to have increased since then and may actually have decreased slightly. One research group analyzed the database of the members of the American Hospital Association (AHA), which lists the GPO affiliation of each hospital.[38] Those 2014 data suggest that three GPOs commandeered the largest shares: Vizient (29.9%), Premier (17.7%), and HealthTrust (14.2%).[39] Another national survey of hospital VPMMs reported the following distribution: Vizient (43%), Premier (24%), and HealthTrust (15%).[40] Finally, another analysis of AHA data suggests the following market shares based on hospital membership[41]: Vizient (30%), Premier (14%), HealthTrust (12%), and Intalere (13%), which was just acquired by Vizient. Overall, market shares based on revenues and primary hospitals appear somewhat comparable.

GPOs compete vigorously for hospital membership. Membership is voluntary[42]: hospitals are free to sign up with any GPO, to sign up with multiple GPOs, and to negotiate purchasing agreements outside of GPO agreements.

GPOs keep track of "incumbent retention" and "competitive wins." The former are hospitals that renew their membership; the latter are hospitals that switch from another GPO. Wins and losses are tallied in terms of both hospital numbers and purchasing volume across all national GPOs. GPOs also keep track of top hospital customers who are up for membership renewal in a given year. Over a several-year period, according to data maintained by one national GPO, the ratio of competitive wins to incumbent retentions exhibited a 44–56% split, suggesting that turnover can be a frequent phenomenon. Such turnover occurs when (a) one hospital system merges with another system that belongs to a different GPO and/or (b) when the hospital/system changes its CEO. When GPO contracts are up for renewal, it is not uncommon for hospitals to solicit bids from three or more GPOs, and perhaps engage a consultant to help them. Some hospitals may do this to motivate the incumbent GPO into offering them more incentives to stay. In addition to staying or leaving their primary GPO, hospitals also have the option of switching some volume to a second national GPO. Finally, hospitals are periodically approached by other GPOs, and will often take a look at what they have to offer. As one purchasing manager described it, "the threat of switching is always out there."

Limits to GPO Concentration

There are two limits to GPO size and, thus, GPO concentration. First, large GPOs historically included only one major hospital or IDN in a local market to render a competitive advantage in terms of purchasing economies. GPOs thus did not roll up multiple, local competing hospitals. Second, at a national level, GPOs are subject to federal antitrust guidelines that create safe harbors for joint purchasing arrangements—specifically, the requirement that joint purchases account for less than 35% of the total sales of the purchased product/service in the relevant market.[43] In this manner, total GPO purchases cannot be so high as to drive down the product/service price below competitive levels. The relevant hospital product market here is national or regional in scope. Since the two major GPOs include close to two-thirds of hospitals and beds, they are already reaching this ceiling.

As a historical note, the Federal Trade Commission (FTC) scrutinized the 2010 acquisition of Broadlane by MedAssets. Although the FTC declined to confirm whether it had reviewed any potential GPO mergers, it did receive advance notice of the merger and took action to terminate the statutory premerger waiting period that allowed the transaction to occur. This may have reflected the fact that, at that time, the two largest GPOs (Nova-tion and Premier) enjoyed nearly 60% share of national purchasing volume, with MedAssets being a distant third. Moreover, the proposed merger would increase the countervailing power of the number three player (MedAssets + Broadlane), neither of whose constituent members competed against one another but rather competed against the two large incumbents. The proposed merger would thus increase the competitive rivalry and instability of GPOs in a "triadic marketplace." This invoked an old expression, "the rule of three"[44]: as long as there are three significant competitors, the antitrust agencies may be less concerned about mergers.[45]

Revenues and Revenue Models

Economic profiles of businesses usually include a description of their busi-ness and revenue models. Any given company can have multiple business and revenue models at the same time. A business model describes how the company generates value for its customers. The earlier section on "GPO Functions and Services" offers one depiction of the GPO business model. A revenue model describes how the company generates revenue or income across each of its customer segments. GPO revenue models are challenging to capture. Public information is not available for one of the three national GPOs; public data on the other two national GPOs come from different sources, making it difficult to draw head-to-head comparisons. GPO compar-isons are further hampered by differences in their contracting philosophies, services, capabilities, and organizational structures.

IBISWorld data suggest that overall GPO revenues totaled $5 billion in 2021 with an average profit margin of 6.1%. This marks a roughly 20% increase in revenues ($4.176 billion) since 2013 (see Fig. 3.6). Such growth in revenue may suggest continued use of and satisfaction with the GPOs' contracts.

GPO revenues come from different sources, which vary in importance over time. The revenues at one national GPO exhibited the following distribution: purchasing/strategic sourcing (49%), supply chain management/outsourcing assistance (24%), capital equipment solutions (9%), workforce management, oftentimes done for non-GPO members (6%), PPI consulting (7%), and operational efficiencies (4%).[46]

Historical data reveal that CAF fees used to account for 70–85% of GPO revenues in the early 2000s; the remainder was generated primarily by membership fees (5–15%), with little income from online or performance

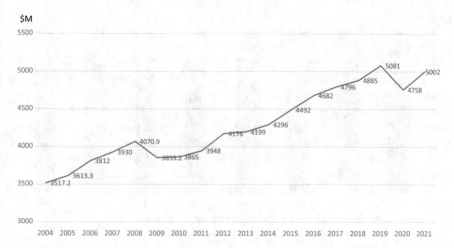

Fig. 3.6 GPO revenues ($ millions) (*Source* Jack Curran. *Group Purchasing Organizations*. Industry Report OD5963. [IBISWorld, August 2021, and earlier years])

services (less than 5%). Data collected from the five largest national GPOs by the Government Accountability Office (GAO) in 2013–2014 suggest a higher percentage of revenues from CAFs (mean of 91.8%, ranging from 83 to 98%) and a lower percentage from membership fees (mean of 3.3%, ranging from 0.2 to 12%). Altogether, the five GPOs reported collecting a total of $2.3 billion in administrative and licensing fees from vendors in 2012. This represented a 20% increase in the total amount of fees collected from vendors in 2008 when adjusted for inflation.[47]

While GPO revenues still tend to be heavily weighted toward procurement and supply chain functions, their share seems to be falling. Since 2013, contract administration fees (CAFs) have declined slightly over time in importance, accounting for as low as 67–70% of GPO revenues, according to IBISWorld data. GPO membership fees have fallen as a percentage of the total from 14 to 3%. Offsetting this decline has been a rise in the percentage of revenues derived from benchmarking and e-procurement services, each rising from 4 to 12% between 2013 and 2021 (see Fig. 3.7). GPOs report that gross administration fees remain core to their revenue stream but do not go as far as they used to. Less of these fees are used to fund ongoing operations (being returned to members as "sharebacks") but instead are deployed to expand into adjacent markets such as ensuring access to generic drugs (e.g., Premier's Provide Gx).

It is important to point out the variability in CAFs, which partly obscures their analysis and explains their continued notoriety.

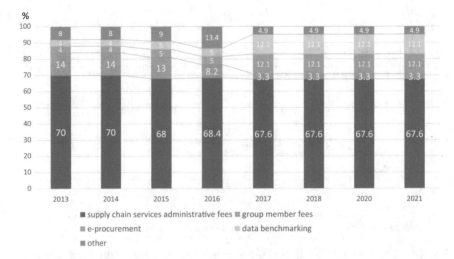

Fig. 3.7 Products and services (*Source* Jack Curran. *Group Purchasing Organizations.* Industry Report OD5963. [IBISWorld, August 2021, and earlier years])

- First, CAFs vary by GPO. Historically, the for-profit GPOs charged higher CAFs (closer to 3% as a percentage of sales) than the nonprofit GPOs (between 2 and 3%). According to some reports, the weighted average CAF in 2012 was 1.7%.[48]
- Second, CAFs vary across product categories (e.g., medical devices, pharmaceuticals, diagnostics) as well as across specific products within a given product category, making it impossible to infer the total amount and structure of any GPO's CAFs. In one GPO, CAFs ranged from 3.0% for purchased services, 2.4% for medical-surgical items, to 1.3% for pharmaceuticals. Medical-surgical accounts for the lion's share of purchasing volume (69%), followed by pharmaceuticals (30%) and purchased services (1%). CAF data from the five largest national GPOs suggest that fees for branded drugs were generally lower (ranging from 0.9 to 2.1%) than for generic drugs (ranging from 1.3 to 3.6%). Four of the 5 GPOs reported that, of the total amount of supplier fees they received in 2012, on average, 25% derived from commodities, 15% devices, 12% branded drugs, 8% generic drugs, and 41% other products and services (e.g., capital equipment, food service).
- Third, GPOs vary in how they allocate purchases across different product categories, often categorizing products in different baskets.
- Fourth, CAFs vary based on the prices that hospitals pay for products. There is considerable variation in the prices that hospitals pay.

- Fifth, CAFs vary by product vendor. Large, diversified suppliers (e.g., Johnson & Johnson, Medtronic, Abbott, etc.) each account for a sizeable share of any GPO's spending and thus the CAF fees it generates; by contrast, the operating companies within these diversified suppliers account for smaller shares of GPO fees.

Premier's Revenue Model[49]

Premier, Inc. (PINC) is a for-profit corporation that converted from hospital shareholder ownership to public ownership by completing an initial public offering (IPO) in 2013. As of June 2020, it was partly owned (41%) by 155 health systems and other organizations, with the remaining 59% owned by public investors.

National GPOs like Premier are large organizations. Premier reported fiscal year (FY) 2020 revenues of $1.3 Billion, up from $634 Million (FY 2013). This represents a compound average growth rate (CAGR) of 11%. Its earnings before interest, taxes, depreciation, and amortization (EBITDA) grew at a 9% CAGR from $313 Million (2013) to $564 Million (2020). Of the roughly $1.3 Billion in revenues, slightly more than half ($683 Million) derive from supply chain services. The vast majority of these services (98%) are "net administrative services." As noted above, suppliers pay administrative fees in the range of 1–3% of the total dollar purchase volume of goods and services sold to GPO members under the contracts Premier negotiates. "Net administrative services" are CAFs less the portion distributed to members in the form of "sharebacks." Net service fees have increased roughly 50% since 2013 ($414 Million). The remaining revenues derive from contract manufactured product sales ($270 Million) and performance services ($347 million), described in greater detail below.

Premier also offers an e-commerce platform called STOCKD. Initially focused on its non-hospital ("alternate site") customers, the program provides a public marketplace where providers can purchase from Premier's GPO suppliers utilizing a user-friendly, e-commerce platform as a more efficient ordering solution. STOCKD's growth has recently been driven by its ability to fulfill the needs of alternate site providers for personal protective equipment (PPE).

Sale of Contract Manufactured Products

Premier's subsidiary, S2S Global, assists members to access more diverse products at competitive prices and gain some degree of transparency into manufacturing costs. S2S Global facilitates customization of product specifications and direct sale to GPO members (as well as other customers or distributors) using contract manufactured products, as well as obviating unnecessary or unwanted product features and specifications that could add to product cost. Premier markets its direct sourcing activities to members primarily under the PREMIERPRO brand. Such programs used to be known as "private label," whereby the GPO approaches a supplier and asks to have its name stamped on their product; they are now referred to as "direct manufactured products." Such programs help to drive top-line revenue but do not add much profitability. According to Premier executives, the goal is to work with its clinical committees to "de-feature" products and standardize them (rather than paying for product differentiation features claimed by suppliers).

Performance Services

The Performance Services segment seeks to deliver value through a comprehensive, technology-enabled platform that offers critical supply chain services, clinical analytics, financial and cost analytics, operational/enterprise analytics, value-based care software as a service ("SaaS"), consulting services, performance improvement collaborative programs, insurance management services, direct to employer business, and an electronic invoicing and payables platform.

In 2021, Premier rebranded this business into three sub-brands, partly to incorporate artificial intelligence (AI) into its suite of solutions. The three sub-brands serve different markets at present. The first, PINC AI, seeks to use analytics and consulting services to help hospitals optimize cost and clinical quality performance in three areas: clinical intelligence, margin improvement, and value-based care. Clinical intelligence focuses on benchmarking data, ongoing clinical surveillance (prevent infections and hospital-acquired conditions), clinical decision support, patient safety, and standardization. Margin improvement draws on peer hospital data regarding savings benchmarks, enterprise resource planning solutions, consulting services for workforce management and clinical improvement, and liability and benefits insurance services. Value-based care draws again on benchmarked data for population health improvements, managing investments in medical groups via strategies for revenue enhancement, cost reduction, and implementing evidence-based practices.

The second and third sub-brands are Contigo Health and Remitra. Contigo Health delivers comprehensive services for optimizing employee health benefits, including: (1) a network of centers of excellence, built upon partnerships with top clinicians, to provide care through access to the highest-quality outcomes for a bundled cost and (2) a program to empower self-funded employers with a flexible approach to employee benefits to help improve access to quality care, achieve cost savings, and improve member satisfaction. Contigo is now selling third-party administrator (TPA) services into health systems' health plans (particularly their self-insured populations). Remitra is an electronic invoicing and payables platform designed to stream-line financial processes, reduce errors and fraud, and unlock cost and labor efficiencies.

Vizient's Revenue Model[50]

Vizient, in contrast to Premier, is a fully member-owned (not publicly owned) GPO. Vizient resulted from the 2015 acquisition of the University HealthSystem Consortium (UHC) by VHA (formerly known as Voluntary Hospitals of America). The two jointly owned a large GPO called Novation. Briefly, in 2015, it had 97 stockholders, including 96 legacy shareholders of VHA owning roughly 80% in equal shares, and one stockholder repre-senting the legacy UHC entity with 20% ownership. The UHC shares were then distributed to its participating members. Vizient had estimated revenues exceeding $700 million. There is much less public information available on Vizient's operations, compared to Premier. However, the $400 million debt offering in 2016 that was used to finance the acquisition of MedAssets provides some useful (albeit slightly dated) information on Vizient.[51] After summarizing this information, more recent data on Vizient's performance is presented from Moody's Investors Service, which rates the company's debt.

During the 12-month-period ending September 2015, Vizient's GPO members purchased $61 billion in supplies and services from roughly 750 suppliers using 2,200 supply contracts. Vizient members included 2,000 acute care providers (e.g., hospitals), 167,000 non-acute providers, and 96,000 non-healthcare providers. By virtue of its UHC component, Vizient served 117+ academic medical centers and 337+ of their affiliated hospitals. Such large institutions account for much heavier spending than commu-nity hospitals. With the MedAssets acquisition that closed in January 2016,

Vizient had a potential increase in annual member spend of $30 billion (2014 data), yielding a combined total of $90 billion in GPO-mediated spending.

Like Premier, Vizient offers its members analytics and intelligence platforms dealing with (a) clinical resource use and patient outcomes, (b) operational performance measures and benchmarked data from peer hospitals, and (c) supply chain informatics encompassing (among other insights) price benchmarks, supply utilization, and data management. Vizient's capabilities here rest on GPO member submissions of "clinical claims, lab, supply, pharmacy, cost accounting and their operational data (including labor productivity, cost center performance)" which facilitate cost and quality benchmarking with other members. These data, drawn from more than 960 facilities, reside in Vizient's Clinical Data Base (CDB) that covers both inpatient and outpatient settings.[52] Vizient also uses the data to help members examine their cost and quality profiles at the procedure and physician levels to identify sources of variation and opportunities for standardization (discussed below).

To do all of this, Vizient draws on more than 340 staff to perform consulting services that help members with performance improvement initiatives in areas such as supply and service cost management, clinical process improvement, operations and workforce optimization, physician alignment and governance, pharmacy optimization, service line strategy, and growth. Vizient also draws upon Sg2 for market analytics to help members forecast utilization, consumer movements in local markets, and referral patterns that inform physician alignment and ambulatory care strategies. Finally, like Premier, Vizient connects members in collaboratives for purposes of sharing insights among hospital executives, knowledge-sharing in other peer-to-peer networks, and shared investments in supply chain ventures.

Vizient's revenues fall into three categories: (1) membership fees and fixed core charges to hospitals that allow them to participate in national and regional GPO contract networks; (2) variable core charges based on a member's actual purchases under the supply agreements; and (3) custom revenue from consulting services and analytics subscriptions. As of September 2015, roughly 68% of Vizient's annual revenue originated from the first two categories (CAFs and membership fees). Tracking these fees is not a straightforward task for several reasons.

- First, Vizient's offering indicates that it distributed 65–100% of the CAFs it collects to members.[53]

- Second, other data in the offering reveal that $111 Million (25%) of the $440 Million in revenue Vizient generated in 2014 came from "net administrative fees" after fee distributions to shareholders, while $329 Million (75%) came from service fees.
- Third, market analysts opine that the level of CAFs returned to the member hospital ("sharebacks") varies based on the hospital's size and negotiations with the GPO. Such sharebacks serve as a rough proxy for pricing.
- Fourth, it may be the case that the fees returned to hospital members have risen over time, particularly as GPOs compete for membership.
- Fifth, market analysts suggest that the sharebacks contribute relatively small value for the hospital compared to the per-unit price savings (attributable to GPO contracts) and utilization savings (attributable to GPO consulting services). This view is also expressed by senior GPO executives. As one shared with me:

> With all of the precision of a dull pencil and a cocktail napkin, supplies typically account for 15% to 20% of a hospital's costs. If the hospital has a 5% operating margin, 20% of costs equate to about 19% of revenue. If a GPO saved 20% of that 19%, the benefit would be about 3.8% of revenue. For a hospital having a 5% margin, 3.8% amounts to roughly 75% of their operating margin. In that respect, one might argue that hospitals would struggle to do much of anything without the savings generated by the GPO. Perhaps worth a note is the fact that price concessions are only a portion of the savings that GPOs generate. Significant benefit results from increased utilization efficiency and standardization across product lines. Those savings account for a substantial portion of a typical hospital's net margin.

Vizient's GPO business incurred few capital expenditures (4% of total net revenue 2013–2015) and had only modest working capital requirements. This enabled Vizient to grow its revenue and operating margins over time. Total revenues rose from $390 Million in 2013 to $440 Million in 2014; EBITDA also rose from $69 Million to nearly $88 Million, with an EBITDA margin of roughly 18–20% (2013–2014). According to the offering, the pro forma adjusted EBITDA following the MedAssets acquisition was estimated to reach $376 Million.

More recent data provided by Moody's shows that Vizient's revenues have grown from $1.1 Billion in 2016 to $1.2 Billion in 2017 to nearly $1.3 Billion by 2020 and then $1.5 Billion by 2021 (December figures). By end of 2019 (compared to 2015), its customer base had grown to 3,100 acute care providers (up from 2,000) and 230,000 non-acute care providers (up from

167,000). Its contracting base had grown to $112 Billion in 2020 (compared to $90 Billion following the MedAssets acquisition); its number of unique suppliers had grown to 900 (compared to 750 in 2015). Margins (defined by EBITA, without factoring in depreciation) have consistently hovered around 31–32%.

The most noticeable change has been the shift in Vizient's revenue mix. In 2015, Vizient earned 68% of net revenues from its GPO business (which covers contract administrative fees, GPO services, and membership fees) with the rest coming from its professional services (advisory/consulting and analytics) business. By 2021, net revenues were more evenly split between the two businesses: 58% vs. 42%. The transition reflects the company's intentional "pivot" from being a GPO to being "a healthcare performance improvement company" to help its hospital members manage the total cost of care.[54] The transition was also based on the reality of (1) lower revenue growth in the GPO business (flat to low single digits) compared to higher growth in the advisory and analytics business and (2) continued pressure on hospital margins and pressures to embrace value-based care. However, the latter business reportedly has lower margins.

Vizient's goal is to create a "clinically integrated supply chain" that draws on the company's data assets—$140 Billion in supply spend data, 62 million patient records, 29 million inpatient encounters, and 411 million outpatient encounters—and the company's personnel assets (e.g., reportedly the 3rd largest consulting firm, now with 550 experts). This strategy faces severe headwinds on at least three fronts: clinical integration, supply chain management, and physician engagement. None of these is a strong capability in its hospital members.[55]

In addition, Vizient partnered with the Mayo Clinic in 2019 to establish a provider-sponsored PBM ("Alluma") to serve self-insured employers such as health systems that are operating owned/affiliated pharmacies. Private equity-backed startups are now partnering with other health systems to develop their own PBMs, independent of the GPOs (see Chapter 11).

HealthTrust Purchasing Group's Model

The third largest GPO is HealthTrust Purchasing Group (HPG), whose members include the hospitals owned and operated by HCA Healthcare (formerly Hospital Corporation of America), Tenet, Consorta, and hospital members of ROi (former GPO for the Mercy system acquired in 2019). This encompasses roughly 1,600 hospitals, 60,000 alternate sites, and $45 Billion in supply spending. Five of the nation's seven largest IDNs belong to HPG.

HealthTrust is the only national committed-model GPO. It is led by a Supply Chain Board that sets strategy and member-led Advisory Boards that govern all contract awards. It maintains a broad portfolio featuring flexibility and choice for PPIs and can execute custom contracts in the areas of cardiovascular, spine hardware and osteobiologics, and orthopedics.

HealthTrust delivers value by assisting members in evaluating clinical and operational data, benchmarking performance across multiple entities, and tracking success in achieving financial targets, compliance, clinical/process outcomes, physician engagement, and patient satisfaction. The focus is on improving the overall performance of service lines by managing spend and eliminating unwarranted variation. Its Medical Device Management specialty concentrates on the utilization of high-value implants and the reduction of unnecessary waste. Its Clinical Services group is focused on care processes and protocols to reduce complications, readmissions, and value-based purchasing penalties by leveraging clinical evidence and physician alignment strategies to standardize care for like patients.

According to HealthTrust, it is differentiated from other GPOs by virtue of its deep operator expertise in *running* the supply chain for some of the largest healthcare systems in the country. "HealthTrust executes collaborative methods of working with members, innovative control systems, and shared service solutions that have been tested and proven at the leading health systems to ensure immediate and sustainable value and the best patient outcomes. Every engagement that we provide has known references and benchmarks, and every recommendation is supported by proven real-world implementation, results, and performance metrics. Our committed model— with unmatched aligned scale—yields the industry's best pricing, minimal clinical disruption, and maximum Day 1 value."

GPO Contract Portfolios

Overview of Portfolios

GPOs contract for a large number of products across a wide range of product areas using an array of purchasing options. Collectively, this comprises the GPO's "contract portfolio." There are at least three major options that hospitals can choose from in buying from the contracts their GPO negotiates. GPOs can offer their hospital members a choice between (a) sole-source versus dual-source versus multi-source contracts; (b) pre-commitment versus no commitment contracts; and (c) bundled versus unbundled contracts.

The GPO's contract portfolio allows it to address the different needs of different members and accommodate the manifold factors that influence these needs, including hospital size, service mix, and the degree of integration between hospitals in a health system. The contract portfolio also reflects existing member preferences for specific vendors in a given product category, as well as variation in member preference for lower cost products (via sole-source) versus greater product variety and access (via multi-source). The portfolio thus builds considerable flexibility to allow an individual member to make the tradeoffs it wants in a given product category—e.g., between lower price from a supplier tied to purchase commitment level versus greater choice among suppliers with fewer restrictions on amounts that have to be purchased.

These contracts also include an array of pricing tiers. It is important to note that hospitals request the pricing tiers (not the suppliers or the GPOs) and often tell their GPOs when they want more tiers. More tiers allow for more flexibility and customized tradeoffs. At one national GPO, 56% of contracts had only one pricing tier; 7% had pricing tiers tied to volume purchased; and another 27% had tiers tied to standardization (i.e., committed purchasing) opportunities. For one product category in the urological space, the tiers took the following form, with better pricing at higher tiers tied to purchasing commitment levels:

- Tier 1 = Access tier, no percentage commitment required
- Tier 2 = Commit to purchasing 50–84% from a specific supplier
- Tier 3 = Commit to purchasing 85%+
- Tier 4 = IDN that commits to purchasing 85%.

There is a distribution of hospitals within a given GPO that fall across these four tiers. Hospitals select the specific tier and, thus, the price/volume tradeoff they prefer. In the case of this national GPO, nearly all hospitals and hospital purchases fell under Tier 3, with small but equal shares in the other three tiers. Hospitals are not discouraged from buying under Tier 1 because they may buy only a few items in low volume or they may not be able to shape their clinicians' preferences regarding standardizing on one vendor. Hospitals can be in Tier 4 but purchase off-contract for the remaining 15% of items using individual contracts or local agreements.

Sometimes a GPO's contract with a specific supplier is structured around the rebates rather than the price tiers. For example, tiers can consist of higher per-unit rebates based on the market share that the supplier achieves across different product lines purchased by the hospital. In this case, Tier 1 consists of one rebate level for 50%+ share, Tier 2 consists of a higher rebate level for 70%+ share, and Tier 3 consists of an even higher rebate level for 90%+ share. Alternatively, the rebate levels can be pegged to (a) the number of product units purchased rather than the percentage share or (b) both the number of units purchased and market share targets. Rebates reflect net price while price tier discounts reflect invoice price. Some suppliers may prefer rebates as a mechanism to obscure their average selling prices (ASPs) from third-party firms conducting price benchmarking and yet still meet customer pricing demands and sales thresholds.

GPOs generate the majority of their purchasing revenues from a relatively small number of contracts in their portfolio. In one GPO with 1,500+ contracts, two-thirds of purchases (and CAFs) derived from less than 15% of those contracts. Only one-quarter of such contracts offer possibilities for standardization and, thus, the use of single- or dual-source contracts. The array of contracts across all product areas at one GPO exhibited the following distribution: 69% medical-surgical, 16% capital equipment, 14% pharmaceutical, and 1% purchased services (total of 1,600). The distribution of purchase volume across these categories was: 62%, 27%, 10%, and <1%.

Contract Portfolio Variations and Strategic Considerations

GPOs frequently ask for a sole-source or dual-source contract bid—usually based on the requests of their hospital members (who wish to reduce stocking levels on inventory shelves). Hospitals and their GPOs may prefer one supplier and sole-source contract which yield lower prices and higher CAFs; suppliers can only achieve and keep these if they have products that are clinically superior. Suppliers can have larger share at one national GPO and much smaller share at another—reflecting each supplier's competition to be on contract. The choice of sole- versus multi-source contracts involves trade-offs for the GPO: more work to service and standardize purchasing but higher CAFs *versus* less work for the GPO but lower CAFs. As more suppliers are added to the GPO's contract, the portfolio gets diluted across more suppliers which provides less value to the hospital buyer, its GPO, and the supplier.

Sole-Source Contracts

The GPO can strike *sole-source contracts* with just one supplier in a given product category. Such contracts are designed to route as much buyer volume to that one supplier in exchange for large price discounts. Such contracts can yield other efficiencies for the hospital buyers. HealthTrust pioneered the shift from dual-source to sole-source contracts during the 1990s in an effort to standardize products, reduce multiple sets of sales representatives in their operating rooms, and multiple sets of products on their inventory shelves (see Chapter 4). Suppliers who win sole-source contracts also benefit. While they yield bigger price discounts up front, they often conduct product selling efforts to increase product uptake, yielding bigger market share and overall revenues on the back end.

These contracts can usually only be done when the GPO's hospital members already prefer the same supplier for the bulk of their purchases, but split lesser volumes with its rivals. That supplier is incentivized to lower its price to gain an opportunity to further increase its market share at the expense of the competitors with smaller market shares. The contracts can yield higher savings or other forms of added value for members (e.g., differentiated clinical quality based on evidence-based research). The more exclusive relationship also allows the GPO to contract for products that meet its members' specifications. Sole-source contracts may be more common for commodity items and generic drugs. They may also be struck for proprietary ("branded") products and technologies for which there are no effective competitors.

Such contracts reportedly represent less than ten percent of contracted products in GPO portfolios. They are struck based on the oversight and approval of the GPO's hospital members and their expert committees (covered below). It should be noted that sole-source contracts are not a guarantee of sales. There are historical examples of suppliers with such contracts being outsold 2:1 or even 3:1 by preferred manufacturers not on contract.

Dual-Source and Multi-Source Contracts

Dual-source contracts are struck with two suppliers who split the members' purchasing volume. GPOs utilize such contracts when there are two dominant manufacturers that hospitals (and their clinicians) utilize heavily and prefer. GPOs may be more likely to use sole-sourcing with product distributors (e.g., with Owens & Minor, Fisher) than with product manufacturers.

Multi-source contracts are struck with 3 or more suppliers in a given product category. Such contracts make sense when hospital members express variable preferences across manufacturers for a given product they all make; these variable preferences need to be accommodated in the GPO's contract. Multi-source contracts can offer pricing tiers based on the amount of purchasing volume and/or commitment to a specific percentage of that purchasing volume. In committed multi-source contracts, the GPO provides the particular supplier with a list of members that have pre-committed to a specified amount or percentage, and then the supplier directly handles the tracking and monitoring of fulfillment of such purchasing volume.

Within hospital-owned GPOs, the selection among the use of sole-, dual-, and multi-source contracts is driven by the type of product and hospital/clinician decisions regarding what is the best value and quality. At some GPOs, the usage mix among these three contracts is 10–20%, 15–20%, and 60–70%. Utilization of any particular sole-, dual-, and multi-source contract is driven by the individual hospital member, perhaps with assistance from the GPO's field force. No specific fulfillment requirements are needed in these contracts to obtain certain pricing levels. Each hospital and supplier come to an agreement on the appropriate pricing tier based on expected purchasing volume, with tracking and ongoing validation of such purchasing volume provided by the supplier. Thus, each hospital member, along with its clinicians, engages in its own customized tradeoff between unit price and supply quantity (volume). Chief Medical Officers (CMOs) are, reportedly, often "not on board" with sole-source contracts. Oftentimes they have to deal with vocal medical staff who dislike these contracts and their restrictions on product choice.

Pre-commitment Versus No Commitment Contracts

In the last two decades, GPOs and their product suppliers have migrated to tiered pricing which ties economic savings (and thus value) to the amount purchased. Higher tiers (i.e., lower prices) are linked to either higher purchase volumes or higher levels of commitment participation (in the form of percentage buys) in the GPO's contract for a given item or set of items. Hospitals reportedly earn better pricing by using higher volumes, price tiers, or both. According to some GPOs, participation in pre-commitment (compliance) programs can yield product savings of 6–8%, and perhaps 20% better pricing. Commitment can also lead to higher volume for the supplier, which can translate into lower manufacturing and selling costs, both of which yield savings that can be shared back with the hospital buyer.

Pre-commitment Contract Terms and Mechanisms

Pre-commitment contracts require that a certain amount of hospital members commit in advance to a specified amount or percentage of purchasing volume before entering into a contract with a particular supplier. Pre-commitment contracts are reserved for product categories with a minimum threshold level of GPO-wide spending (e.g., greater than $10–15 million). Such contracts are also struck where there are two viable suppliers competing in the market who have equivalent products/services. Such contracts require a heavy lift from GPO staff to gain hospital participation and commitment, and thus are limited in number (e.g., 10–15) in any given year. GPOs usually seek hospital compliance levels in excess of 85–90% of purchases in those product categories, using contracts typically struck for 3-year terms. Such duration is needed to consider the products under contract, conduct evaluations of their performance, and do conversions of non-users to these products. Another reason for the contract length is that hospitals do not want to repeat this time-consuming process every year. The hospital members pull the trigger on the specific suppliers chosen, usually in the form of value analysis committees (VACs) which the GPO facilitates but does not participate in.

Hospitals are not required to buy anything under pre-commitment contracts and are not precluded from buying those products from other suppliers. Hospitals can buy products off-contract from other manufacturers and yet still remain on the preferred contract tier. Most nonprofit GPOs do not force their members to utilize contracts, and most hospitals do not feel obligated to use them if they can secure lower pricing on their own. Indeed, their local representatives may assist the hospital with off-contract purchasing. Nevertheless, starting in the early 2000s, some hospital systems and IDNs increased scrutiny of new technology and made it more difficult for clinicians to buy off-contract, e.g., requiring them to first route their requests through new technology committees and VACs.

Only one GPO, HealthTrust, relies on its hospital members to utilize its negotiated contracts the majority of the time (e.g., 80%). It has higher compliance by virtue of the fact that (a) its members can only belong to one national GPO, and (b) the GPO monitors their membership and their purchasing. By contrast, the other major GPOs have established programs of committed purchasing that their member hospitals can opt into or out of. The pre-commitment program at Premier is profiled below.

All sides of the transaction benefit from such contracts. GPOs can earn higher CAFs from greater product sales of GPO-mediated contract purchases. Hospitals can earn not only lower product prices paid up front but also increased revenues on the back end (sharebacks) in the form of a percentage of the CAFs collected. According to several VPMMs, these fees are not a huge financial incentive but rather a vehicle to reduce supply expenses; other VPMMs at smaller hospitals counter, saying the sharebacks are often a significant boost to their margins. Manufacturers can earn increased product sales, greater penetration of the local hospital market, and potentially greater production efficiencies derived from guaranteed purchase levels of their products. The gains for incumbent manufacturers can be substantial (e.g., 10% more market share); the gains for non-incumbent (new) manufacturers can be whopping (e.g., as much as 60%).

Premier's Pre-commitment Program

Premier members can participate in its ASCEND and SURPASS "performance groups." The ASCEND group aggregates purchasing data for members and enables them to benefit from committed group purchases. Members receive group purchasing programs, tiers, and prices specifically negotiated for them, along with knowledge-sharing with other member participants. According to Premier, by June 2021, the approximately 1,100 hospitals participating in the ASCEND group identified approximately $696.4 million in additional savings beyond their U.S. hospital peers not participating in the ASCEND Performance Group since its inception in 2009.

The SURPASS Performance Group seeks to build upon ASCEND by driving greater savings for members willing to make a higher level of commitment. This higher level is achieved by coordinating purchasing decisions among member hospitals in a system, reviewing product utilization, and achieving product standardization across their facilities. SURPASS brings together clinically led cohorts to make evidence-based decisions about physician and clinician preference items with the goal of materially reducing the total cost of care. As of June 2021, a core group of 19 members reportedly identified roughly $186.2 million in additional savings via their efforts in more than 150 product categories.

Issues with Pre-commitment Programs

Pre-commitment programs are not without their issues, however. Use of a high-compliance model can generate friction with some hospital members (and their clinicians and CMOs) who believe the savings do not warrant the effort. This can lead to lower levels of GPO satisfaction. Such dissatisfaction can lead to a variety of outcomes such as turnover (switching GPOs) or cherry-picking contracts from other national GPOs; more likely, hospitals demand better terms from their national GPO at membership renewal time (e.g., higher sharebacks, provision of free services). It is important to note that commitment programs are struck between the GPO and the supplier; the actual compliance with such programs is driven by the myriad of decision-makers at the local hospital level.

The effectiveness of commitment programs is debatable. One issue is accurate measurement of hospital purchases—a process that entails a lot of effort. Suppliers measure compliance either via purchasing records, deviations in sales numbers at an account, or compliance reports run at the hospital level by their sales reps, who estimate sales based on storeroom checks or bedsize calculations. Suppliers are contractually required to provide statistics to GPOs on their hospital members' behavior which may or may not coincide with data kept by the GPOs. These data may cover the hospital system or IDN, rather than specific hospitals. A given hospital may belong to more than one GPO, making it difficult for the supplier to know which GPO contract the hospital utilized. The GPO sends these data on to the hospital, and the hospital may report discrepancies back to the GPO to make sure their contracted purchases are accurately recorded. Of course, hospitals do not always collect such information. GPO reps may do a manual reconciliation by reviewing the hospital's purchasing orders from that supplier. The CAFs are generated off of these purchasing data.

Another issue with the effectiveness of compliance programs is that hospitals do not generally buy products based on the CAFs that are earned. Few hospital executives know what the CAFs are and what their facility actually earned, since the CAF revenue becomes known only later on (e.g., in the form of semi-annual payments from GPO); clinicians clearly do not know or care about these payments. Moreover, the CAFs are aggregate figures and not pegged to specific product items, making it virtually impossible to connect aggregate GPO payments with disaggregated purchase decisions by individual physicians.

Even if hospitals are found not to be compliant, the GPO may not take any action. This is because the GPO may not want to discipline the hospital or drop it from its membership; the GPO may also still earn a CAF if the other supplier used by the hospital is on contract. Instead of disciplining hospitals, the GPO may instead prefer to let them know "how much money they are leaving on the table" by not adhering to the contract.

Bundled Versus Unbundled Contracts

In some cases, the GPO may contract with one supplier whose aggregate pricing terms for an array of products are better than for individual products. These "product bundles" may cover up to 6–12 different categories of products. Bundled contracts represent "standardization on one supplier," or one-stop-shopping convenience. Hospitals may prefer full-line suppliers with one-stop-shop that minimizes having to pick products from multiple suppliers. Hospitals may also reap financial incentives if they use products in each of these areas. There are several conditions that make bundling feasible:

- The presence of large, diversified suppliers like Johnson & Johnson, Abbott, Medtronic, Boston Scientific, etc., who offer both breadth and depth in their product lines (see Chapter 14)
- High acceptance by clinicians for the products made by these suppliers
- Historical and functional relationship among the products in the bundle (e.g., sutures and endomechanical devices)
- Product bundles purchased by one department or clinical area in the hospital (e.g., imaging/radiology)
- Real risk of suppliers losing contracts, as evidenced by contract turnover.

There are, nevertheless, stumbling blocks to product bundling. Hospitals have fragmented decision-making and lots of "ports of call," making a coordinated sale difficult. Moreover, different specialists prefer different suppliers. Research on hospital contracting with imaging manufacturers shows that it is easier to standardize within one clinical department than across clinical departments, let alone across hospitals within a system.[56] Within academic medical centers, academic departments and clinical areas represent "Balkan States" and medieval fiefdoms. They may each have their own historical relationships with specific manufacturers and display considerable heterogeneity in their approach to (a) best-of-breed versus (b) one preferred supplier.

Demystifying GPO-Mediated Contracts Between Suppliers and Buyers (Hospitals)

As noted earlier in this volume, the healthcare ecosystem operates based on a myriad of buyer-seller relationships up and down the value chain. One cannot really understand these relationships without understanding the contracts struck between the two parties. Unfortunately, such contracts constitute trade secrets and are rarely, if ever, disclosed. This is not necessarily undesirable, however. As discussed later on, such secrecy can be pro-competitive in two respects: opaque contract pricing induces suppliers to discount their products (since competitors are unaware) and precludes supplier price collusion. Nevertheless, such lack of disclosure contributes to the perceived secrecy and opacity of middlemen like GPOs and PBMs and public suspicions about their motives.

Demystifying this is no easy task. There are thousands of hospitals, hundreds of hospital systems, hundreds of GPOs, and thousands of product suppliers engaged in such contracting—covering (likely) hundreds of thousands of products. I do not claim to have reviewed a large number of contracts or even a representative sample of such contracts. I have read many, however, and seek to distill some of their constituent elements below. Chapter 13 offers a similar analysis of PBM contracts.

First, these contracts can be lengthy. This is not because of contractual details and clauses that require considerable attorney oversight. It is because they usually itemize two relevant laundry lists: the "eligible participants" and the products. The former lists the facilities (e.g., hospitals) that are authorized to purchase under the contract; the latter lists the products that are covered under the contract. The former are subsets of the GPO members, usually belonging to the same hospital system or IDN, each hospital having its own unique supplier number. The latter includes each product covered, including:

- Product category
- Part/item number
- Product description
- Unit of measure (UOM)
- Product quantity per UOM
- Access price (e.g., less than 50% committed purchases)
- Tiered contract price(s) (e.g., greater than 50% committed purchases).

Another, short section of the contract covers "pricing discount opportunities" and provides definitions of the following contract features:

- Vendor status—stipulation of whether the contract is sole-source or dual-source
- Net purchases—total invoiced purchases during a compliance period, net of all returns, exchanges, credits, and rebates
- Net unit purchases
- Applicable products

- Compliance period—often the supplier's fiscal quarter—for measuring the buyer's commitment
- Compliance form—completed by the buyer at the end of each compliance period—that quantifies the dollar value of the buyer's net invoice purchases from the contracted supplier and other suppliers. Under a sole-source contract, commitment is measured as net invoice purchases from the contracted supplier divided by total purchases from all suppliers. Under a dual-source contract, commitment is measured as net invoice purchases from the contracted supplier and the next most widely used vendor, divided by total purchases.
- Compliance processing—whereby the customer agrees to report the cost of any product purchased and/or all discounts and rebates earned under the agreement to federal and state payers to satisfy the discount safe harbor to the Anti-Kickback Statute
- Tier performance targets
- Tier pricing levels—which are usually extended to hospital members after they select the tier they want and complete a "tier designation form" (TDF).

Another short section of the contract covers any applicable "rebate program" or "market share rebate program," and provides definitions of the following terms:

- Applicable products
- Invoiced purchases of applicable products, net of all returns, exchanges, credits, and rebates
- Net unit purchases of applicable products
- Rebate period—usually the supplier's fiscal quarter
- Rebated products
- Rebate opportunity and requirements—usually tied to a "rebate target" (number of units purchased)—that stipulates the dollar value of the rebate per-unit for specific products
- Rebate payment period
- Compliance processing—customer required reporting of discounts.

Finally, the contract includes the general "terms and conditions of sale," which encompasses the term of the agreement (e.g., 2-year, 3-year), restrictions on product resale by the customer, customer payment terms, product delivery, return policy, confidentiality of contract pricing and other terms, and treatment of discounts. Contracts may also include clauses regarding termination with or without cause, introduction of new products into the category of committed products as well as pricing for such products, and perhaps stipulation that the GPO has not provided legal advice to either the supplier or the buyer in the negotiation of contract terms and conditions.

GPOs and Downstream Buyers: Hospital Systems and IDNs

Who's Who

It is important, but difficult, to disentangle GPOs from their major constituents (e.g., hospital systems and integrated delivery networks, or IDNs). The GPOs facilitate product contracting; the hospitals and IDNs do the actual purchasing. The former offers consulting services on how to improve clinical care; the latter renders the actual care. The former are product intermediaries; the latter are service providers. Chapter 4 chronicles the intertwined, historical development of both; more detailed histories of the systems and IDNs have already been published.[57]

While hospital systems and IDNs are often used interchangeably, they should be distinguished. They are "integrated" along two different dimensions. First, they can be *horizontally* integrated systems of formerly independent hospitals that now operate as part of a chain. Second, they can be *vertically* integrated as a continuum of care (or value chain) that includes physicians, one or more hospitals, and perhaps PAC providers. The former are hospital systems; the latter are IDNs. Needless to say, hospital systems can vertically integrate to become IDNs, just as IDNs can horizontally integrate to become hospital systems.

Several realities blur the two lines between GPOs and these integrated providers. First, some for-profit GPOs (HealthTrust) are subsidiaries of for-profit hospital systems (HCA). Second, some nonprofit GPOs like Vizient can be owned by their shareholders (e.g., member hospitals, hospital systems, and IDNs). Third, some former GPOs like AmeriNet are really strategic alliances among large IDNs such as Intermountain Healthcare. Fourth, a growing number of systems and IDNs have expanded their membership to the point where they can and now do act as their own GPOs. Since the late 1960s, there have been four waves of horizontal integration of hospitals[58]; since the early 1990s, there have been two waves of vertical integration of hospitals with other providers.[59] Trend data presented by one of my colleagues shows that, between 1998 and 2012, there was a 15.6% drop in independent hospitals and a 5% rise in hospital systems with 2–5 hospitals, a 10.6% rise in systems with 6–20 hospitals, and a 17.9% rise in systems with 21+ hospitals.[60]

Competitive Issues

The larger size of hospital buyers (both system and IDN members) poses both (1) a management challenge for GPOs, since the members can have ill-defined governance structures that hamper decision-making and cooperation with GPOs, and (2) a competitive threat in the form of a product substitute and source of uncertainty. As systems and IDNs grow in size (number of hospital members, physician groups, nursing homes, and other alternate sites), they develop the potential for aggregated purchasing clout in the local (or even regional) market and, thus, the ability to negotiate product discounts on their own. This can take the form of either self-contracting and/or developing their own GPO affiliate model.

The larger size of systems (based on horizontal integration), combined with their growing employment of physicians and ownership of PAC sites (based on vertical integration), means that systems have the potential opportunity to explore product buying across a wider array of categories (and even be candidates for product bundling). This may be of interest to product suppliers. The horizontally and vertically integrated providers can offer an incentive for suppliers to (1) develop full product lines that follow the patient across different treatment settings, (2) develop disease management systems of care, and (3) bundle together products with services in clinical pathway programs or clinical trials.

In addition, most of these systems and IDNs operate in local or regional markets, presenting an interesting buying opportunity. They may exhibit more similar patterns of resource utilization and share enough overlap in their physician membership to standardize their purchasing around a smaller number of products and stock-keeping units (SKUs). As a result, they may develop purchasing programs with higher levels of compliance than those achieved by the national GPOs with their more diverse membership. The system's hospitals may also be numerous enough and in close enough geographic proximity to share a common warehouse and operate as their own distributor as well as GPO. Indeed, the local nature of systems and IDNs may coincide with the local nature of product distribution.

While they do not collectively account for the same purchasing volume as large GPOs, systems and IDNs offer a product supplier an alternative set of advantages including greater contract compliance, greater standardization on that supplier's products (over a rival's products), and increased market share penetration in that local area. This situation can quickly give rise to some short-term, win-win scenarios for both sides: the supplier offers the system/IDN a lower price than that negotiated by their GPO in exchange for increased product sales.

Finally, the growing number and size of systems/IDNs may be particularly important to those (often smaller) product suppliers that encounter difficulty in obtaining long-term contracts with the large, national GPOs. Partly due to the need to broadly appeal to its hospital members, large GPOs have shown a tendency to contract with large incumbent manufacturers with leading market share. Vendors that fail to win one GPO's business must compete vigorously for the others and/or compete for the system/IDN's purchases. Larger vendors are reluctant to grant big price concessions to gain market share, since it may hurt total profits. Smaller vendors with lower market shares are able to cede greater price discounts to win the system/IDN's business, thereby increasing local market share for their products without hurting total profits. Alternatively, smaller or regional suppliers may have a lower cost structure or be willing to work at lower margins in order to get the system/IDN's business.

In sum, systems and IDNs may thus have both the opportunity and incentive to act as their own GPOs. While larger GPO alliance membership may increase purchasing volume and the potential for lower contract prices, it also makes it harder to tailor its services to meet the needs of its hospital members. Over time, the national GPOs have beefed up their regional and local affiliates to improve their responsiveness to the local needs of their members.

The threat posed by hospital systems and IDNs may, nevertheless, be subject to constraints imposed by the adage that all healthcare is local. Research by my colleague shows that providers' efforts to increase bargaining ability by increasing organizational scale are largely thwarted by an increase in asymmetric preferences (rooted in the diversity of physicians and the hospitals they work in) that limits efforts to standardize and centralize purchasing.[61] Thus, the adage applies to supply chain operations in the following sense: larger, centralized hospital systems may be unable to manage the preferences of disaggregated physicians who are dispersed across the operating units in a multi-unit chain.

Upside to Hospital Consolidation and Regionalization of GPOs

Hospital consolidation presents another opportunity to GPOs. GPO executives admit their hospital customers are increasingly fewer in number, larger in size, and more sophisticated in handling their supply chain functions. VPMMs are gradually being replaced by "chief supply chain officers" and "chief resource officers" who have responsibilities beyond supplies that encompass all non-labor expenses (i.e., anything a hospital buys that is not an employee). Such hospitals are hiring world-class supply executives, often-times trying to emulate the performance of large logistic-based enterprises like Walmart. These executives are devoting less of their attention to extracting small reductions in the price points achieved by their GPOs and more energy to reductions in clinical utilization. They draw on the data and analytics offered by the GPOs to drive down costs of PPI utilization, often in tandem with their value analysis committees and programs in physician engagement. A further step is to drive toward higher quality of care in addition to lower total cost.

GPOs view the growth of regional and local GPO affiliates in much the same way. The affiliates supplement the work of the national GPOs and leverage the hospital's role as (often) the largest employer in the local community. As the central employer, the hospital and regional affiliates can support local service providers and supplier diversity. Sometimes the national GPO co-invests in the local affiliates and provides the technology and back-office support functions (e.g., Premier's "OnHand" joint venture with Texas Health Resources).

The GPO's Value Proposition for Systems/IDNs

There are several ways to assess the value that hospitals, hospital systems, and IDNs derive from their GPO membership. One simple way is the prevalence of hospital use of GPOs. Another major way is the hospital's utilization of the GPO for supply purchasing. This is an important metric since many hospitals report that (a) medical-surgical supplies consume anywhere from 10 to 30% of their operating expenses (with an average of 15–24%), and (b) total supply chain costs account for 30–40% of expenses. These are the costs that GPOs seek to target and reduce for their members. Hospitals report routing the majority of these expenses through GPOs, albeit using a mix of national, regional, and local players. National survey data from 2014 reveal that 62% of supply spending went through the hospital's primary national GPO (55%) and its regional/local affiliates (7%); another 5% and 3% went through unaffiliated regional and local groups, respectively. The share accounted for by the primary GPO seems to have fallen slightly since an earlier 2004 survey.[62] Over this ten-year interval (2004–2014), the national GPO mediated a sharply increased share of hospital purchases of some items (commodity items, purchased services), a modest increase in other items (e.g., PPIs, capital equipment), and a falling share of other item purchases (e.g., pharmaceuticals). Other surveys similarly suggest that the majority of hospitals route 60% or more of their medical-surgical supplies through GPO contracts.[63]

Another way to assess GPO value is the hospital's tenure with (and turnover from) its primary GPO. One set of survey data indicates that the average tenure is nearly 11 years, suggesting relatively infrequent turnover.[64] Another, earlier survey reported that 33% of hospitals had never changed their GPO, 21% had belonged to their current GPO for 10+ years, and another 19% had belonged for 6–9 years.[65] By contrast, data presented above suggests that GPO turnover may be more frequent.

GPO turnover often occurs when one hospital or IDN is acquired by another, and the target's purchasing migrates over to the acquirer's GPO. Turnover can also occur when the hospital feels that it can improve pricing and total savings, finds a GPO whose culture and business practices are better aligned with it, or the hospital hires a new CEO. Such GPO loyalty is not across the board, however. As noted above, hospitals have routed a falling percentage of their GPO-mediated purchases of products through the national GPOs and re-routed them to regional and local players. At the same time, academic research suggests that hospitals are more likely to add a GPO affiliation in a given year (14.5%) than to drop an affiliation (8%). Whether affiliations are added or dropped seems to be partially driven by how many affiliations the hospital currently has: those with fewer affiliations add and those with many affiliations drop.[66]

One can also measure hospital tenure with (loyalty to) specific GPO contracts. Hospitals often belong to multiple national GPOs to cherry-pick the contracts that they want to use. Market analysts suggest that, on an annual basis, contracts are "sticky" with retention rates of 99%.[67] While hospitals frequently go to market to test the economics of their current relationships, the cost of conversion to another supplier can be quite high due to the need to persuade clinicians to change their product/supplier preferences.

Another way is to ask hospitals what they value in a GPO and whether or not they get it. Survey data reveal that low product prices and contracting convenience are, at once, the most valued GPO services and the most satis-fying GPO services. Other, similarly rewarding services are e-Commerce solutions (e.g., Web-enabled contract catalogue), product cross-referencing, and sharing experiences and networking with peers. The hospitals' ratings of importance and satisfaction with other GPO services are more variable, and tend to be middle-of-the road.[68]

Proprietary survey data can also profile the performance of all national GPOs across an array of performance criteria: savings, contract portfolio, service, and non-source offerings. In the past, GPOs rarely ranked the highest across all four criteria, but could rank highest on one or two. These data showed, however, that ranking was not necessarily dependent on hospital usage of that GPO.[69] The first two criteria tend to be the most important in hospitals' eyes.

A final way to assess GPO value is how much money they save for their hospital members. This is a most controversial topic, since estimates are drawn from a range of sources including hospital self-reports, hospital use of secondary product markets, and aggregate analyses. Some common metrics include supply expense as a percentage of net patient revenue, supply expense as a percentage of total operating costs, and supply expense standardized by case-mix index (CMI) or CMI-adjusted discharge; alternatively, the GPO and hospital member can develop customized (and validated) savings goals. The reader should know that this is a polarizing question. The topic is taken up in Chapter 5.

Suffice it to say that the ability of national GPOs to deliver lower prices and savings to members may diminish as hospitals, hospital systems, and IDNs continue to consolidate. Larger systems/IDNs are reportedly applying greater pressure on product suppliers for price discounts, using the national GPO contracts as price ceilings, benchmarks, and leverage in negotiations.[70] This is important since the top 125 IDNs represent roughly 2,200 (or 43%) of U.S. hospitals and 54% of total spend on acute care. Not only are they a presence numerically, but they may also have a competitive advantage over the national GPOs in driving supplier rationalization, product standardiza-tion, and committed purchasing among their owned members. A 2016–17 LEK survey of 125 hospital executives reported high and growing levels of receptivity to bypass GPOs in a range of medical technology areas.[71]

My colleague published some interesting findings on hospital purchases of medical devices.[72] His work shows that product savings accrue to bargaining transactions where hospitals are large buyers and have historically paid rela-tively higher prices. At the same time, his work suggests that the savings are limited by transaction costs, the stickiness in the transactions (e.g., multi-year contracts), and the age of the technology. For example, savings accrue to older technologies such as bare metal stents, rather than the more recent (and more expensive) drug-eluting stents; moreover, the price discounts are small (low-mid single digits). We may need to curb our enthusiasm about GPO- and self-contracting. Research suggests that hospital negotiations with buyers (insurers) should not be treated the same way as hospital/GPO negotiations with suppliers (medtech). The latter involves lots of smaller firms and lots of end-users whose buy-in is needed.

GPOs and Upstream Suppliers

GPO critics oftentimes mention the possibility of collusion between GPOs and upstream suppliers. Such collusion rests on the undocumented belief that GPOs allow suppliers to inflate their prices to generate higher CAFs—even if such inflated prices hurt the supply budgets of the GPOs' member hospitals.

One flaw in the collusion argument is the fact that large suppliers themselves recognize what they call "a lack of alignment around contracting philosophies" with GPOs.[73] This mis-alignment has several dimensions:

- Suppliers seek annual price increases while GPOs seek price-protected agreements
- Suppliers seek extended contract terms while GPOs often prefer 12–36 month terms
- Suppliers prefer letters of commitment while GPOs may seek to avoid them
- Suppliers seek tiered or "value-based" CAFs while GPOs seek flat CAFs and CAFs based on access pricing and member sales
- Suppliers seek contract extensions while GPOs pursue a request for proposals (RFPs) for expiring contracts
- Suppliers prefer facility-based pricing while the GPO's owners (e.g., hospital systems and IDNs) prefer system-wide pricing that includes affiliates
- Suppliers prefer a strategic approach to pricing for clinically preferred products and PPIs based on value (quality divided by cost, or total cost) while GPOs and their members prefer (a) best price extended by vendors to other GPOs, (b) cost alone, or (c) multiple pricing levels to meet member needs
- Suppliers prefer only limited contracting for new technology while GPOs want greater access to new technology and special pricing contracts

- Suppliers want preferred positions on the GPO contract while GPOs may prefer to use dual- or multi-source awards.

It is also important to note how suppliers view their sales profile. They oftentimes segment their sales as follows: GPO-contracted sales, other contracted sales (e.g., hospital system or IDN), non-contracted sales, and Government. While GPO-contracted sales may be the largest category, the number two category can be non-contracted sales. Suppliers prefer not to contract with GPOs if they can be avoided; suppliers with new, proprietary technology not offered by any other manufacturer do not need to contract with GPOs (and don't).[74]

One issue facing GPOs today is the ongoing consolidation of suppliers (e.g., Becton Dickinson's 2015 acquisition of Care Fusion and subsequent 2017 acquisition of Bard). Other volumes depict the ongoing consolidation among pharmaceutical and medical technology manufacturers.[75] Consolidation means fewer suppliers that products can be sourced from, which reduces gains from competitive bidding for contracts. It also leaves GPOs and their members more vulnerable to product stock-outs at contracted suppliers, with fewer alternative sources to consult. Finally, it diminishes the bargaining leverage that GPOs have with suppliers. According to some national GPOs, large diversified suppliers dwarf the size of any hospital, hospital system, or even GPO.

GPOs will tell you that suppliers contract by "class of trade," yielding greater discounts to organized hospital systems while making higher margins in more fragmented settings such as PAC sites which often lack sophisticated materials management. As demonstrated in a recent volume on the hospital market, consolidation results in higher prices charged to customers, which may thwart the GPO's *raison d'etre*.[76]

Product Standardization

What Is Standardization

Standardization is a commonly used strategy in healthcare. For example, hospitals seek to reduce time and monetary waste in their clinical processes, oftentimes employing methods drawn from industry like the Toyota Production System (TPS). Hospitals and payers also seek to reduce variations in physician practice patterns that may contribute to either lower quality and/or higher cost healthcare (i.e., "low-value care").

In the healthcare supply chain, standardization is defined as the process of gaining efficiencies and lower product cost by reducing the number of products/services used that serve the same function. Standardization can yield important benefits in the following areas:

- reduced administrative costs by virtue of lower product ordering cost, lower cost of product processing and checking, improved tracking of information dealing with price/vendor/usage, decreased accounting cost, fewer purchase orders (POs), and thus fewer discrepancies in invoice payments and problem resolution
- reduced logistics and inventory costs such as one purchasing order, one slot on the product shelf, reduced space requirements, lower carrying cost, improved productivity in such areas as receiving/storeroom/inventory, higher inventory turns, reduced supplier costs, and enhanced distribution and logistics support from vendors
- higher clout and reduced cost of shipping out-of-date items back to the vendor (since they all go out-of-date at the same time)
- higher quality (particularly for PPIs) in the form of higher accuracy and quality of documentation, and improved item inspection and handling
- fewer chances for clinical errors among nurses, particularly as they float across floors or hospitals within a system/IDN
- faster turnaround in procedure rooms due to more standardized procedure kits for different clinicians
- higher end-user (patient) benefits including higher quality, safety, and consistency in product use, lower cost of educating and training staff, and fewer stock-outs.

Avenues to Standardization

Single-source contracts and committed-buying programs—discussed above—both rely on one key capability: the cooperation of hospital members and (most importantly) the clinicians within them to agree on a particular supplier and its product. This is known in the industry as "clinical standardization." Standardization can be pursued in hospital/GPO partnerships with suppliers. Typical partnerships revolve around specific cost containment, utilization reduction, and standardization initiatives. GPOs publicize these initiatives to attract new members and improve efficiencies among their current membership. For example, one GPO used to publish guidebooks on standardization and utilization each year. These volumes included case studies, written by the hospital members and product manufacturers, describing hospital efforts to (1) minimize the number of products performing the same function, or product standardization, and (2) ensure that the products selected are the most cost-effective.

In a typical case of standardization, representatives from the product supplier come into the hospital to (1) audit clinical departments' product needs and use, including practice variations; (2) develop quality specifications and/or best practices for products and packaging systems; (3) recommend and implement changes that match the appropriate product or package for the appropriate application, patient, or procedure; and (4) thus reduce waste and cost. Often, these programs consist of product and therapeutic conversions—that is, switch from one SKU or drug to another—and improved processes for utilizing them. Programmatic success is gauged by expense reductions in the specific clinical area, inventory and SKU reductions, and improved human resource utilization. Such efforts may now be conducted by consultants inside the national GPOs. Conversions are time-consuming and expensive processes—involving lots of clinician input, trading out inventory, and training costs.

Factors that Foster Success with Standardization

Some GPO-sponsored research suggests that VPMMs view product standardization as one of their most cost-effective strategies, although certainly not as important as lower prices.[77] Older case studies of standardization programs now under way suggest savings in the range of 1–2% of medical supply costs.[78]

As part of these efforts, the GPOs may commit specialized staff (for example, consultants and/or nurse clinicians) to work with supplier reps and hospital members to examine the custom packs or contrast media packages that hospitals are utilizing and often wasting (for example, by throwing away certain items in the pack). The GPOs then work with the suppliers to pare down the custom packs and remove SKUs in order to reduce product cost and increase hospitals' efficient use of the supplies purchased. Such partnerships are encouraged and developed as part of the bidding process.

Some GPO executives assert that managed care has abetted their efforts here. Managed care exerts pressure on physicians not only in their practices but also on the hospitals where they admit patients. As hospitals seek to constrain physician choice and discretion, physicians respond by asking for greater involvement in the decision-making processes that limit their choice.

Conversely, in markets where managed care pressure is weak, physician resistance is strongest.

This model requires that the GPO and its members know the physician practice behavior and supply utilization patterns in their hospitals. Armed with such information, the GPO can then proceed with a version of procedure case management that links outcomes to practice styles and resource use, and then shares this information with clinicians across hospitals. Physicians may not be fully convinced to change products based on practice variation data, however. Hospital executives claim the model works well when individual clinicians across system hospitals conduct extensive clinical trials involving competing products to gauge their effectiveness and afterward agree to use a particular supplier's product. In such cases, suppliers lack direct access to any decision-making body to influence physician decision-making. Moreover, individual physicians now collectively persuade suppliers of their willingness to shift their business elsewhere. The model also works well when GPOs can demonstrate willingness to shift contracts in other product areas from a larger supplier to a smaller supplier that threatens the incumbent. The resulting benefit for the GPO is, at a minimum, physician buy-in on the basis of quality, increased physician compliance in using the products contracted for, and perhaps higher quality at a lower cost.[79]

One determinant of success in driving standardization is whether or not substitute products are available for physicians to utilize. This may be impacted by supplier consolidation. Success in driving standardization is also a function of the clinical nature of the disease and available therapies. GPO executives state they achieve high rates of standardization on products where they are not dealing with the cutting edge of medicine, which often requires everything to be available. Sometimes standardization is influenced by the physician specialty involved. GPO executives report that some specialists (e.g., interventional cardiologists) may not be that cooperative. Finally, success may depend on selection effects. For example, investor-owned systems actively select the hospitals they wish to acquire and decide which procedures they wish to do within them. In this manner, they may concentrate on general community medicine where a high rate of standardization can be achieved.

Headwinds to Standardization

Standardization of PPIs

There are particular challenges in trying to standardize PPIs among physicians. First, physician product preferences likely reflect higher quality and ergonomic convenience, but not necessarily lower cost. Second, suppliers may factor physician preferences for higher quality into the prices they charge for their products. Third, wide-ranging physician preferences may require multi-source contracting that limits any group leverage over specific suppliers. Fourth, these preferences may change quickly, especially in innovative, high-tech product areas where new product iterations occur frequently. Such changes may prevent effective programs in product standardization. Fifth, physicians are subjected to enormous marketing messages from suppliers that compete with local hospital efforts to change their behavior. Sixth, there is past physician resentment at not being involved in decision-making, and current sentiment that physicians lack a financial incentive to get involved and/or are just not interested. This is especially true for office-based physicians aligned with IDN members. In their practices, supplies are only a tiny percentage of practice expenses compared to labor; moreover, office staff (for example, head nurse or nurse manager) rather than physicians order the supplies and may allow medical sales representatives to come in, inspect the inventory, the examination rooms, and restock the shelves.

One key issue for GPOs is obtaining clinician buy-in and committed buying for their programs in clinical standardization. Such programs focus on clinical preference items in key areas (e.g., cardiovascular, orthopedic, and ophthalmic) rather than commodity supply items. For example, the purchase of cardiovascular products accounts for much of the spending at the top GPOs. Many of these purchase decisions are physician-driven, based on direct detailing and marketing by product manufacturers. GPOs seek greater influence in these decisions in order to bring those products under GPO contracts and reduce their hospitals' expenditures in these high-cost areas. There is another reason for the salience of this area for GPOs. Besides relying on GPOs, the manufacturers of these products invest significant SGA (selling, general, and administrative) effort in their own sales force to gain access to IDNs, pull through their products, and determine compliance. They thus feel they have to invest in and support GPO contracts substantially.

In some preference areas, the GPO tries to winnow down the number of suppliers from double digits to single digits. In areas such as orthopedics, there are four major hip and knee implant manufacturers: Stryker, Zimmer Biomet, DePuy, and Smith & Nephew. In other areas such as cardiac pacemakers, there have been three major manufacturers: Medtronic, Boston Scientific, and St. Jude. Physicians develop preferences for one manufacturer over another based on their prior medical training or preference for particular product features. GPOs identify the major players based on their national market share and product pipeline and then try to get the physicians from member hospitals to agree on using some subset of them. If physicians cannot agree but insist on having all major manufacturers on the contract, the GPO cannot drive any economic value itself, but instead must rely on market forces to drive down prices. If physicians can at least agree to go with just two suppliers (dual-source the agreement), then incremental business and shares directed to those two can be exchanged for lower prices.

In orthopedics, hospitals can try to make their orthopedic surgeons convert from one vendor to another, but that strategy is difficult since surgeons trained on these suppliers' products are quite "sticky" in their vendor preference, and are also trained on the suppliers' instrumentation used alongside the implant, and can take their patients to other hospitals where they have privileges. In such cases, hospitals employ other strategies and negotiating tools that accommodate their surgeons' particular preferences but still yield lower prices and contracting terms. These can include:[80]

- Requests for Proposals (RFPs) or Invitations to Bid (ITBs)—which invoke competitive bidding for a committed portion or share of the purchases made by the GPO's members, often for a multi-year period. Sometimes, the bidding can take the form of "winner-take-all" (or at least a substantial share) which increases supplier rivalry for the contract and, thus, pricing concessions.
- Vendor certification (or pre-qualification) prior to soliciting bids to avoid unqualified suppliers from bidding (and then claiming they were unfairly treated in the bidding process). Hospitals can consider multiple factors here, including sales force size and geographic availability, production size, product distribution capability, product reputation and knowledge among clinicians, education and training, hospital demand for that supplier's products, and breadth of the supplier's product line.
- Value Analysis Teams (VATs) or Committees (VACs) composed of clinicians from across the hospital to facilitate standardization processes and decision-making. Like Pharmacy & Therapeutics (P&T) committees, VATs are designed as a disciplined process for assessing various products and determining the "value added" by certain product features to patients' outcomes and safety, weighed against relative costs. These assessments of comparability are then used when making contracting and other strategic decisions regarding product equivalencies.
- Physician involvement in decision-making—to give clinicians a sense of ownership of the process of PPI standardization. This may include developing a "partnership mentality."

- Price/payment caps which generate savings over current pricing and allow any supplier to participate as long as their product price falls below the ceiling. The payment-cap model does not explicitly restrict particular products or suppliers but instead standardizes costs by restricting the price paid for products in a particular category. The main assumption underlying this approach is that the suppliers of similar products will compete to offer an equivalent product within a price ceiling established for that product's specification. A variation of the payment-cap model is the *reverse auction*, in which prequalified vendors are offered a short time to bid on a carefully defined product, with committed volumes going to multiple low bidders.
- Device formularies restrict the number of choices of suppliers from which PPIs are purchased or of the range of products that are bought for a given procedure. In practice, restrictions on product choice also mean restrictions on supplier. The formulary model resembles the standardization strategy used for pharmaceuticals within hospitals and is consistent with the supply source reduction efforts used by other industries. The assumptions underlying this approach are that (1) a hospital's commitment to use a particular supplier will result in lower prices from that vendor; (2) the chosen suppliers will have a sufficient range of products to meet the physicians' demands for their various patients' needs; (3) the wide range of products currently available on the market is unnecessary because there are genuine product equivalencies; and (4) patient safety is enhanced when the operating team uses familiar products with which they have experience, even when individual members may rotate from one team to another.
- Trim the list of contracted vendors to allow the major vendors to still participate but allocate them some additional share from any excluded vendor in exchange for a lower product price.

Commodity Items that Mimic PPIs

For non-PPIs and products for which there are no demonstrable quality differences, additional savings can be generated through supply chain rationalization and complexity reduction—i.e., reduce the number of suppliers and SKUs used inside the hospital. This requires the hospital to standardize on as few suppliers/products as possible consistent with the provision of high-quality healthcare. Standardization can be pursued using some of the same techniques outlined above for PPIs, including RFPs, winner-take-all bidding, and long-term contracts (which amplify the ramifications to the vendor of winning/losing contract bids).

It should be noted that some commodity items can mimic PPIs. Physicians will shy away from any item (even if it is a cheap commodity) if there is a problem with it. They may also shy away if the nursing staff does not like it and refuses to cooperate. Physicians may have a preference for a particular commodity item if its use affects any equipment that they use, or if they have a preference for the supplier of that item. Physicians may also have a strong preference for a supposed commodity item if it possesses ergonomic features that they are comfortable with. Research shows that sutures and endome-chanical products—e.g., trocars, clip appliers, staplers, etc.—are not really commodities but actually possess clinical features that differentiate them and foster strong product preference.[81] That is, they act more like PPIs than like commodities. It may be harder to standardize than we realize.

Plurality of Decision-Makers and Influencers

When it comes to the hospital's supply chain, standardization is often pursued in the context of provider fragmentation. For any given product, there can be multiple decision-makers and influencers within a single facility. These decision-makers and their interests include:

- Physicians/surgeons want high-quality products, often based on what they trained in during their residencies and fellowships. Sometimes, these preferences are based on the product's ergonomics. They are not usually based on the product's cost, which physicians may (unfortunately) be unaware of.
- Nurses are often responsible for the set-up of the operating room or procedure rooms, the maintenance of the physicians' preference cards (i.e., what product sets they want in those rooms), and perhaps interaction with supplier representatives (if the latter are allowed into the hospital). Nurses may also have responsibility for hospital-wide quality initiatives such as infection control and quality assurance, and thus may have a stake in what products are utilized.
- Hospital procurement managers, the VPMMs, are tasked with sourcing and procuring the products utilized inside the institution. Unlike the clinicians, they may be more focused on line-item cost, total cost (e.g., for a procedure, for a bundle of products, for an episode of care, etc.), low transaction costs, and meeting budgets set by the Chief Financial Officer. They are also interested in maximizing purchases made under the GPO contract.
- Hospital-level decision-making regarding supplies is often done by committee. Value analysis committees (VAC), value analysis teams (VAT),

new technology committees (NTC), and other clinical committees (e.g., infection control) can make decisions on what products to trial in their hospital, what products they want to buy, and what GPO contracts they want to utilize. These teams draw on physicians and nurses within and across clinical areas (e.g., cardiology, radiology, etc.). VACs and similar committees often do not know which GPO a supplier is affiliated with and whether or not its product is under contract. VACs which prefer a non-contracted supplier can access the product through a local agreement.

- The hospital's "C-Suite" (Chief Executive Officer, Chief Operating Officer, Chief Financial Officer, Chief Medical Officer, Chief Nursing Officer, Chief Resource Officer, etc.) can be motivated by alternative payment models used by public and private insurers to increase quality and/or reduce cost. They are also motivated to ensure patient and provider safety, to ensure physician and nurse satisfaction (to promote retention), to improve population health, and meet the needs of patients. There is some evidence that diverse perspectives on the supply chain exist within the C-Suite, akin to the Akira Kurosawa movie *Rashomon*, that limit systemic agreement on what to focus on. These perspectives differ depending on whether you talk to the System CEO, the System CMO, the Hospital CEOs, and the VP for Business Development.[82]

This plurality of decision-makers gets amplified as hospital facilities band together into multi-hospital systems, IDNs, clinically integrated networks (CINs), and accountable care organizations (ACOs). Variation multiplies in the products used, both within and across hospitals under the same corporate umbrella. Such variation means more stock-keeping units (SKUs), higher transaction costs, higher inventory costs, and likely higher prices paid per product ordered (due to smaller volumes dispersed over more suppliers).

Indeed, GPO executives mention the challenges of working with diverse hospitals and their physicians. As GPOs increase in size, they have more hospitals, physicians, clinical preferences, and thus product needs. This limits their ability to do product standardization and thus their ability to rationalize the number of suppliers used.

The plurality of hospital decision-makers is mirrored (and compounded) by comparable committees at the national GPO level. GPOs form "nursing councils" of clinicians drawn from member hospitals to evaluate alternative suppliers and their products to contract for.

They write up the clinical specifications when bidding out a product to rival suppliers, conduct a weighted analysis of the bids on how well they meet these specifications ("decision criteria award matrix"), and rank the bidding suppliers. Non-financial criteria include clinical acceptability, product line breadth and depth, the supplier's ability to supply and service the product(s), and assistance with product conversion; each of these is weighted by the nursing council to sum to 100%. Data on clinical and financial considerations are combined to identify the "low best bid." This can include a consideration of purchasing scenarios using sole-, dual-, and multi-source contracts; regardless of the range of suppliers allowed, the value equation is paramount. GPO staff act on this information, decide the terms and then award the contract, but do not reportedly overrule what the VACs decide. Price is not really a consideration in VAC deliberations, since the price paid is not yet determined until the total volume to be ordered is calculated.

GPO Limitations

GPOs may be limited or conflicted in their efforts to help hospitals with standardization. Some GPO executives have acknowledged that utilization and standardization efforts have not succeeded because hospitals lacked the resources, staff, and information to do the required analysis and work. The burgeoning consultant staffs of the large national GPOs may help here.

While GPO members want long-term cost reductions, fiscal stringencies orient them to short-term solutions such as contract prices. It is perhaps also worth noting that utilization reduction programs may run counter to the GPO's self-interest. Any reduction in the number of supply items purchased and utilized by member institutions means lower volume flowing through the GPO, and thus lower CAF revenues.

Vendor Resistance to Standardization

Needless to say, PPI vendors resist (and likely resent) contracting with GPOs, because they may not gain any incremental market share. Instead, they feel that they get the same share but at a lower price and with the added cost of CAFs. Moreover, they are concerned about GPO efforts to commoditize their products and blunt their direct marketing campaigns that target clinicians. GPO executives state that PPI contracting remains a problem for them—an issue reaching back at least two decades with little improvement. A survey conducted by one national GPO found that the top three areas for GPO improvement were savings in high-cost device cases, new ideas on pricing to meet surgeon demand, and contracts for PPIs.

Constraints on Standardization Imposed by "All Healthcare Is Local"

One problem is that PPI contracts may be more locally driven than nationally driven. Inside any given hospital, there may be a physician culture that favors one supplier of a specific PPI over others. Suppliers know that if they want to get their products adopted in a local hospital, they need to get the local clinicians on board, and then have them tell the hospital what they want ordered. This game is better played at the local level.

Many medical staff physicians go to professional conferences and/or read professional journals, learn about new technologies from alternate suppliers (not on contract), want to use these technologies, and search for off-contract availability if they are not on the GPO's contract. Such off-contract buying can occur frequently but may require documentation of product performance (e.g., research published in academic journals) to support it. Clinicians do not generally consider whether or not a GPO contract exists when reviewing the products they desire. Off-contract buying using individual agreements is more likely among larger hospitals than smaller hospitals; this is because they have more contracting resources, they have more clout, and they are less compliant in general. Hospitals also resort to off-contract buying when contracted products do not meet their own quality standards and/or the needs of their clinical staff—both of which are idiosyncratic to a hospital. This provides an opportunity for suppliers who lack GPO contracts to pick up additional market share. Historically, off-contract buying could account for a fairly large share of purchases in a given product category (easily 25–30% of medical-surgical items).

Standardization: An Uphill Climb

Several product manufacturers question the success of standardizing efforts in clinical preference areas. First, these efforts require a lot of work for perhaps only small payoffs. Moreover, standardization among a core set of physicians invited in to review and select one supplier may not sway other physicians throughout the GPO's member hospitals. Finally, when physicians have standardized on one supplier and the GPO switches to another supplier, oftentimes the physicians do not follow suit.

As one illustration, some GPOs note that even for simple products like surgical sutures, there can be three SKUs for the same suture based on the length of the suture (for example, 18 inch, 24 inch, and 36 inch). Product SKUs have multiplied here as an effort by manufacturers and hospitals to meet the preferences ("whims") of surgeons; the multiplication of SKUs can lead to product waste. Physicians who prefer the longer length end up using only a portion, throw the rest away, and may not even be aware they could get the same suture in a shorter version.

Such product conversions may also result in lower compliance levels, which decrease CAF revenues flowing to the GPO. Moreover, if the GPO can get a 3% CAF across all of its supplier contracts, there is a clear incentive to go with long-term contracts with large suppliers to minimize their transaction costs (for example, educating members about new contracts). Materials managers at IDNs may likewise be reluctant to shift contracts if these changes threaten compliance levels. Such levels are directly tied to product discounts and rebates, which directly affect their bottom lines.

Conversely, suppliers do not want to lose a GPO contract because of the loss of market share (over the defined contract period), the difficulty in making that share up elsewhere in the short term, and the perceived threat to the supplier's image in the marketplace and its contracts with other buyers. As a consequence of both GPO and supplier consolidation, there is a lot more at stake in losing a GPO contract. Incumbency is a major asset to be protected.

Standardization is an uphill climb, overall. One major hospital system in Texas reportedly utilized 5,200 suppliers. It is impossible to contract for such a large number; contracts existed for less than 25% of these vendors. Another major IDN in the upper northwest spent $1.4 billion on 80,000 SKUs in such areas as medical-surgical, pharmaceutical, and IT items; less than half of that went through contracts struck by its primary national GPO and its business partners. The result is a lot of "off-contract buying." Such purchasing can occur for lots of reasons: the GPO does not contract in that product category, the product category is not yet covered by the GPO contract, the supplier making that product is not under contract, clinicians think there is a better product available off-contract, the product is made by a small supplier with esoteric product clinicians want, the IDN does not want to undergo converting its staff to a product chosen by its GPO, and an equivalent product is available at a lower price that offers a significant savings opportunity. As one VPMM explained it, the goal is not to make every clinician happy but rather to have products that all clinicians can use that are high quality and at a reasonable cost.

Notes

1. Marty Makary. *The Price We Pay: What Broke American Health Care—And How to Fix It* (New York: Bloomsbury Publishing, 2021): p. 208.

2. Chapter 14 summarizes their similarities and differences.

3. Premier has a very strong advocacy group, as does the GPO trade group HSCA. See for example: https://www.supplychainassociation.org/.

4. Marty Makary. *The Price We Pay* (New York: Bloomsbury Publishing, 2019): Chapter 15.

5. GPOs offering private label programs contract directly with manufacturers to manufacture products that are then sold under the GPO's private label brand name. This direct contracting eliminates the need to spend money on sales or marketing, which enable GPOs to offer lower prices on these products. James Scott, John Voorhees, and Melissa Angel. *GPOs: Helping to Increase Efficiency and Reduce Costs for Healthcare Providers and Suppliers* (Alexandria, VA: Applied Policy, October 2014): 10.

6. Edward Zajac, Thomas D'Aunno, and Lawton R. Burns. "Managing Strategic Alliances: Neither Make nor Buy But Ally," in L.R. Burns, E. Bradley, & B. Weiner (Eds.), *Health Care Management: Organization Design & Behavior*. 7th Edition (Delmar Cengage Learning, 2019).

7. Lawton R. Burns and Mark V. Pauly. "Integrated Delivery Networks (IDNs): A Detour on the Road to Integrated Healthcare?" *Health Affairs*, 21(4) (2002): 128–143. David Dranove and Lawton R. Burns. *Big Med: Megaproviders and the High Cost of Health Care in America* (Chicago, IL: University of Chicago Press, 2021).

8. Eugene Schneller. *The Value of Group Purchasing—2009: Meeting the Need for Strategic Savings*. Health Care Sector Advances, Inc.

9. "Since the pandemic began in Q1 of 2020, Premier's contract portfolio has observed a 1.5 percent inflationary increase, whereas off-contract spend increased by 5.2 percent over the same time period – a differential of nearly 3X." Available online at: https://premierinc.com/newsroom/blog/premiers-gpo-contracts-are-a-powerful-tool-in-the-fight-against-inflation.

10. An alternative list of services is provided by James Scott, John Voorhees, and Melissa Angel. *GPOs: Helping to Increase Efficiency and Reduce Costs for Healthcare Providers and Suppliers* (Alexandria, VA: Applied Policy, October 2014): Exhibit 2.

11. Jailendra Singh, Adam Heussner, Carlos Conseugra et al. *Premier Inc.: FY2022 Ahead Across the Board; FY22 Revenue Outlook Raised, EBITDA Unchanged* (New York: Credit Suisse, February 1, 2022).

12. Vizient data courtesy of Chris Callahan.

13. Healthcare Group Purchasing Industry Initiative. *Fourteenth Annual Report to the Public*. February 2020.

14. A fourth GPO (AmeriNet) used to be an alliance among three hospital system shareholders but was then bought out by one of them (Intermountain Healthcare), renamed Intalere, and then subsequently acquired by Vizient.

15. For background on the PPMCs, see: Lawton R. Burns. "Physician Practice Management Companies," *Health Care Management Review* 22(4)

(1997): 32–46. Lawton R. Burns and James C. Robinson. "Physician Practice Management Companies: Implications for Hospital-Based Integrated Delivery Systems," *Frontiers of Health Services Management* 14(2) (1997): 3–35.

16. According to Premier, "Premier has more than 400 member facing FTEs, the majority of which are badged for the hospital they are deployed to and are nearly indistinguishable from the hospitals' supply chain employees".

17. According to Premier, "Premier owns a company called Remitra, which is uniquely focused on invoice processing and AP automation".

18. According to Premier, "We have an ERP system as well as a full suite of technology which covers procure – to – pay and full visibility into the total non-labor expenses enabling them to have the visibility of a system, even if they're using multiple legacy systems".

19. 2010 Hospital GPO Use Survey. *Hospitals & Health Networks*. Survey sponsored by MMHC/AHRMM.

20. John Reese, Amanda Short, and David Gruber. Healthcare Providers Have Spoken: FTI Consulting's 2nd Annual GPO Survey. FTI Consulting, 2021.

21. Hospitals have also engaged in the formation of virtual, local GPOs that take the form of purchasing alliances, networks, or collaboratives. Examples in the past included BJC Collaborative, Dignity Health Network, and Ascension Health Alliance. Such groupings identify specific product segments for which they wish to obtain greater savings by acting "systemically" in the form of standardized purchasing.

22. John Reese, Amanda Short, and David Gruber. Healthcare Providers Have Spoken: FTI Consulting's 2nd Annual GPO Survey. FTI Consulting, 2021.

23. Lawton R. Burns and Allison Briggs. "Hospital Purchasing Alliances: Ten Years After," *Health Care Management Review* 45(3) (2020): 186–195.

24. Arka P. Bhattacharya. *A Comparative Study of Healthcare Procurement Models.* M.S. Thesis, College of Engineering (University of South Florida, October 30, 2007).

25. Jack Curran. *Group Purchasing Organizations.* Industry Report OD5963 (IBISWorld, August 2021).

26. Jack Curran. *Group Purchasing Organizations.* Industry Report OD5963 (IBISWorld, August 2021).

27. Lawton R. Burns and Mark V. Pauly. "Integrated Delivery Networks (IDNs): A Detour on the Road to Integrated Healthcare?" *Health Affairs* 21(4) (2002): 128–143. David Dranove and Lawton R. Burns. *Big Med: Megaproviders and the High Cost of Healthcare in America* (Chicago, IL: University of Chicago Press, 2021).

28. Roger Blair and Christine Durrance. "Group Purchasing Organizations, Monopsony, and Antitrust Policy," *Managerial and Decision Economics* 35(7) (2014): 433–443.

29. Lawton R. Burns. *The Business of Healthcare Innovation.* 3rd Edition (Cambridge, UK: Cambridge University Press).

30. The history here is based on the chronicle found in James Scott, John Voorhees, and Melissa Angel. *GPOs: Helping to Increase Efficiency and Reduce Costs for Healthcare Providers and Suppliers* (Alexandria, VA: Applied Policy, October 2014).
31. Jailendra Singh, Jermaine Brown, and Adam Heussner. *Vizient Management Provides Business & Industry Update, & Shares Views on Some Key Topics* (New York: Credit Suisse Equity Research, December 11, 2020).
32. Lawton Robert Burns. *The U.S. Healthcare Ecosystem* (New York: McGraw-Hill, 2021): Fig. 17–13.
33. Richard Scheffler, Eric Kessell, and Margareta Brandt. "Covered California: The Impact of Provider and Health Plan Market Power on Premiums," *Journal of Health Politics, Policy and Law* 40(6) (2015): 1179–1202.
34. David Dranove and Lawton R. Burns. *Big Med: Megaproviders and the High Cost of Healthcare in America* (Chicago, IL: University of Chicago Press, 2021).
35. Jack Curran. *Group Purchasing Organizations.* Industry Report OD5963 (IBISWorld, August 2021).
36. Jailendra Singh, Jermaine Brown, and Adam Heussner. *Vizient Management Provides Business & Industry Update, & Shares Views on Some Key Topics* (New York: Credit Suisse Equity Research, December 11, 2020).
37. Lawton R. Burns and Allison Briggs. "Hospital Purchasing Alliances: Ten Years After," *Health Care Management Review* 45(3) (2020): 186–195.
38. William Opoku-Agyeman, Robert Weech-Maldonado, Soumya Upadhyay et al. "Hospital Group Purchasing Alliances and Financial Performance," *Journal of Health Care Finance* 46(1) (Summer 2019).
39. The Vizient share combines the shares for Vizient and MedAssets. The Premier share combines the shares of Premier and Yankee Health Alliance. The HealthTrust share combines the shares of HealthTrust and ROi.
40. The Vizient share combines the shares of Novation, MedAssets, and Broadlane. The HealthTrust share combines the shares of HealthTrust and Consorta.
41. Yousef Abdulsalam. "Group Purchasing Organizations: Preliminary Analysis and Results," Unpublished presentation.
42. The exception is Healthtrust Purchasing Group (HPG), which is a subsidiary of the hospital chain HCA Healthcare. HCA hospitals are required to use HPG.
43. U.S. Department of Justice and Federal Trade Commission. *Statements of Antitrust Enforcement Policy in Health Care* (Washington, DC: DOJ and FTC, 1996).
44. Jagdish Sheth and Rajendra Sisodia. *The Rule of Three* (New York: Free Press, 2002).
45. See also: Lawton R. Burns, David Nash, and Douglas Wholey. "The Evolving Role of Third Parties in the Hospital-Physician Relationship," *American Journal of Medical Quality* 22(6) (2007): 402–409.

46. Anonymous source.

47. Government Accountability Office. *Group Purchasing Organizations: Funding Structure has Potential Implications for Medicare Costs.* GAO 15–13 (Washington, DC: GAO, October 2014).

48. James Scott, John Voorhees, and Melissa Angel. *GPOs: Helping to Increase Efficiency and Reduce Costs for Healthcare Providers and Suppliers* (Alexandria, VA: Applied Policy, October 2014).

49. This section relies on Premier Inc. *Form 10-K*. FY 2020.

50. This section relies on Vizient's 2015 debt offering. *Vizient, Inc. Preliminary Offering Memorandum* (Barclays, 2016).

51. As background, in November 2015, Pamplona Capital Management announced it would acquire MedAssets and split the company in two. Pamplona absorbed the revenue-cycle management business and sold its group purchasing, performance-improvement and Sg2 consulting business to Vizient.

52. Jailendra Singh, Jermaine Brown, and Adam Heussner. *Vizient Management Provides Business & Industry Update, & Shares Views on Some Key Topics* (New York: Credit Suisse Equity Research, December 11, 2020).

53. The same did not appear to be true of MedAssets. The offering indicates that of the $445 million in revenue generated by MedAssets in 2014, $291 million (65%) came from net administrative fees (after fee distributions back to shareholders) while $154 million (35%) came from service fees. According to market analysts, MedAssets distributed only 40% of their CAFs to members, but that figure masks a combination of hospital and non-acute organizations.

54. David Cassak. "Vizient and the Role of Group Purchasing in Medtech Today," *MedTech Strategist* (April 2022).

55. Lawton R. Burns, David Asch, and Ralph Muller. "Vertical Integration of Physicians and Hospitals: Three Decades of Futility?" in Mark V. Pauly (Ed.), *Seemed Like a Good Idea: Alchemy versus Evidence-Based Approaches to Healthcare Management Innovation* (Cambridge, UK: Cambridge University Press, 2022).

56. Lawton R. Burns, Eduardo Cisneros, William Ferniany, and Harbir Singh. "Strategic Alliances Between Buyers and Suppliers: Lessons From the Medical Imaging Industry," in Christine Harland, Guido Nassimbeni, and Eugene Schneller (Eds.), *The SAGE Handbook of Strategic Supply Management* (Sage Publications, 2012).

57. Gregory Kruse, Lawton R. Burns, and Ralph Muller. "Health Care Inc," in James Schaefer, Richard M. Mizelle, Jr., and Helen K. Valier (Eds.), *Oxford Handbook of American Medical History*. Chapter 16. Forthcoming 2023.

58. Gregory Kruse, Lawton R. Burns, and Ralph Muller. "Health Care Inc." in James Schaefer, Richard M. Mizelle, Jr., and Helen K. Valier (Eds.), *Oxford Handbook of American Medical History*. Chapter 16. Forthcoming 2023. David Dranove and Lawton R. Burns. *Big Med: Megaproviders and*

the *High Cost of Healthcare in America* (Chicago, IL: University of Chicago Press, 2021).

59. David Dranove and Lawton R. Burns. *Big Med: Megaproviders and the High Cost of Healthcare in America* (Chicago, IL: University of Chicago Press, 2021).

60. Leemore Dafny. "Effects of Cross-Market Combinations: Theory and Evidence from Hospital Markets," Presentation to Federal Trade Commission Health Care Workshop. February 25, 2015.

61. Matt Grennan. Grennan's analogy of what happens in U.S. hospital systems and what happens across nation states in the European Union is a fascinating and tantalizing insight into the tension between centralized buying and decentralized operations. Stuart Craig, Matthew Grennan, and Ashley Swanson. "Mergers and Marginal Costs: New Evidence on Hospital Buyer Power." NBER Working Paper 24926 (August 2018). Available online at: http://www.nber.org/papers/w24926.

62. Lawton R. Burns and Allison Briggs. "Hospital Purchasing Alliances: Ten Years After," *Health Care Management Review* 45(3) (2020): 186–195.

63. "Modern Healthcare's 2012 Survey of Executive Opinions on Supply Chain Issues." *Modern Healthcare* (August 20, 2012): 25ff.

64. Lawton R. Burns and Allison Briggs. "Hospital Purchasing Alliances: Ten Years After," *Health Care Management Review* 45(3) (2020): 186–195.

65. Hospitals and Health Networks. *2010 Hospital GPO Use Survey* (July 2010).

66. Joonhwan In, Randy Bradley, Bogdan Bichescu et al. "Breaking the Chain: GPO Changes and Hospital Supply Cost Efficiency," *International Journal of Production Economics* 218 (2019): 297–307.

67. Jailendra Singh, Jermaine Brown, and Adam Heussner. *Vizient Management Provides Business & Industry Update, & Shares Views on Some Key Topics* (New York: Credit Suisse Equity Research, December 11, 2020).

68. Lawton R. Burns and J. Andrew Lee. "Group Purchasing Organizations (GPOs): Issues and Evidence," *Health Care Management Review* 33(3) (2008): 203–215.

69. These data are unfortunately proprietary and cannot be shared here.

70. Ken Graves and Kevin Grabenstatter. "Time for Medtechs to Rethink GPOs?" *LEK Executive Insights* XX(13): 1–6.

71. Ken Graves and Kevin Grabenstatter. "Time for Medtechs to Rethink GPOs?" *LEK Executive Insights* XX (13): 1–6.

72. Matthew Grennan and Ashley Swanson. "Transparency and Negotiated Prices: The Value of Information in Hospital-Supplier Bargaining," *Journal of Political Economy* 128(4) (2020): 1234–1267.

73. Interviews with supply chain executives at Johnson & Johnson Health Care Systems (JJHCS) during the late 1990s.

74. Lawton R. Burns. *The Health Care Value Chain* (San Francisco, CA: Jossey-Bass, 2002).

75. See, for example: Lawton R. Burns (Ed.), *The Business of Healthcare Innovation—Third Edition* (Cambridge, UK: Cambridge University Press, 2020): Chapters 2 and 5.
76. David Dranove and Lawton R. Burns. *Big Med: Megaproviders and the High Cost of Healthcare in America* (Chicago, IL: University of Chicago Press, 2021).
77. See Lawton R. Burns. *The Health Care Value Chain* (San Francisco, CA: 2002): Chapter 4.
78. Paula DeJohn. "GPO Deals Still Golden: Compliance Is The Key," *Hospital Materials Management* 25(10) (2000): 1, 9–11.
79. David Cassak. "Tenet Shakes Things Up," *In Vivo* (July–August 1998): 41–53.
80. Some of this analysis is borrowed from colleagues: Kathleen Montgomery and Eugene Schneller. "Hospitals' Strategies for Orchestrating Selection of Physician Preference Items," *Milbank Quarterly* 85(2) (2007): 307–335.
81. Lawton R. Burns, J. Andrew Lee, Eric T. Bradlow, and Anthony C. Antonacci. "Surgeon Evaluation of Suture and Endo-Mechanical Products," *Journal of Surgical Research* 141 (2007): 220–233.
82. Lawton R. Burns. "Advancing Proposals to Improve Supply Chain Operations in a Hospital System," Presentation to HealthTrust University 2012.

4

The GPO Chronicle, Part I: 1910–2000—The Players, Market Structure, and Market Conduct

Lawton R. Burns and David Cassak

Introduction

A Challenging Chronicle

There is little documentation on the history of the GPO sector. Most discussions open with a brief (i.e., one paragraph or less) mention of the "Hospital Bureau" in 1909 and then skip to the present day. A lot more happened than this, and one needs to know it. Indeed, as they say, the past is prologue. The patterns of GPO operation over the last two decades—and patterns that have been the subject of recent and intense government scrutiny—were established decades earlier. However, this past is unknown, largely because of the challenge of weaving together all of the separate threads into a coherent picture.[1]

We do not claim to have finally succeeded with that endeavor, but have attempted to push the ball up the hill a bit. This chapter draws on that portion of the trade literature which covered GPOs.[2] It also draws on interviews the lead author conducted over the years with senior executives from product vendors, the GPOs, supply chain consultants, and Vice-Presidents for Materials Management (VPMMs).[3]

Charting the emergence and maturation of the GPO sector resists characterization by time periods, although some have tried to do so.[4] This is because many of the important patterns and characteristics described in Chapters 3 and 6 of this volume evolved over time and show up in more developed form as the decades progress. The chronicle in this chapter focuses

© The Author(s), under exclusive license to Springer
Nature Switzerland AG 2022
L. R. Burns, *The Healthcare Value Chain*,
https://doi.org/10.1007/978-3-031-10739-9_4

on some "big picture" themes: the emergence of the early purchasing vehicles (hospital alliances, shared service organizations), the growing agglomeration of purchasing at broader geographic (local, regional, and then national) levels, changes in regulatory and reimbursement incentives emanating from both the public and private sectors, the impact of investor-owned and nonprofit hospital chains, the rise of integrated delivery networks (IDNs), the development of new contracting strategies and vendor responses, and finally government scrutiny. At the risk of some duplication, the chronicle also takes pains to distinguish the changes in market structure and market conduct. The chapter is organized into three sections: (a) "the players," (b) "the new playing field" caused by GPO mergers and changes in their market structure, and (c) "the new playbook" and changes in their market conduct. The next chapter (GPO Chronicle, Part II) covers the emergence of "new judges" of GPO market conduct: the press, the Senate, and the courts.

The Players

GPO Proliferation Over Time

As noted in Chapter 3, there are no definitive statistics on the current size of the GPO population. There is also little documentation of the growth in their numbers. GPOs began as organizations sponsored and/or supported by local hospital councils starting in the early 1900s, and retained this local character for roughly thirty years (1910–1940). GPOs then entered a forty-year period of more rapid expansion, both numerically and geographically, as (a) local and state hospital associations established what have come to be called "shared service organizations" (SSOs), (b) multi-hospital systems formed following passage of the Social Security Act Amendments of 1965, and (c) a handful of large regional GPOs formed. The decade of the 1980s witnessed further proliferation of regional GPOs, followed by a rash of regional GPO mergers in the 1980s and 1990s that formed national GPOs.

There are also no exact statistics on GPO foundings, only varying estimates. Two studies, for example, classified GPO founding dates as follows:

Period	Study #1[5]	Study #2[6]
Pre-1959	6	7
1960–1969	12	6
1970–1979	22	19
1980–1990	19	22
Total	59	54

The founding dates in these studies are fairly consistent with one another and with other evidence.[7] However, these numbers are likely too low. Long-time analysts of the GPO industry comment that at least 125 GPOs existed in the 1970s, based on attendance at GPO meetings, and at least 400 GPOs by the early 1980s.[8]

One possible way to address the issue is to examine the number of respondents to *Modern Healthcare*'s annual survey of shared services and purchasing groups. We located the published survey results for the years 1981–1998, but variations in survey response rates and how the data are categorized make trend comparisons difficult. For years in which data and response rates seem somewhat consistent, there appears to be a clear upward trend in the number of purchasing contracts and the number of hospital clients. The number of shared service providers in the early 1980s was well over one hundred, but was much lower by the end of the decade (when the magazine began to refer to them as "groups and alliances." They numbered between 50 and 60 for several years into the early 1990s, but then began to drop (possibly due to consolidation). The hunt for better data goes on.

Group Purchasing: An Old Concept

Group purchasing dates back to at least the 18th Century. Benjamin Franklin and fellow fire-fighters formed one of the earliest cooperatives in 1752—the Philadelphia Contributionship for Insurance of Homes from Loss of Fire—as a mutual insurance company to cover property.

During the Industrial Revolution, several small enterprises formed trade associations and guilds in England for their mutual benefit. As one illustration, a group of English weavers banded together in 1844 to form the Rochdale Cooperative and pool their funds to purchase goods at lower costs. In the 1860s, numerous farming purchasing cooperatives (e.g., the Grange Movement) formed in the U.S. to engage in bargaining and negotiation, eventually turning into the American Farm Bureau and National Farmers Union.

The Mesopotamia of Group Purchasing: The Hospital Bureau

The first healthcare GPO was the Hospital Bureau of Standards and Supplies (aka "The Bureau"), founded in New York in 1910. The Bureau initially operated in a local geographic area and then expanded its scope of operations over multiple states. It was particularly active in the Northeast, including New Jersey, Delaware, Connecticut, Rhode Island, and various parts of New York (Long Island, Syracuse, Rochester).

Early in its history, The Bureau focused on furniture supplies. Any furniture that hospitals ordered at that time was not out of a catalogue but rather was custom made; The Bureau marked the first effort to promote standardization. The Bureau also strove to aggregate order volumes across hospitals to permit mass production, much in the same way that the Ford Motor Company manufactured automobiles. Since standardization was not common, purchasing groups struck contracts with particular vendors that could handle the mass production to standardized specifications—in essence, anticipating the sole-source contracts of later years. Such contracts were not controversial then; indeed, product standardization became especially important during World War II due to the need to conserve raw materials (e.g., stainless steel). In this manner, the early large-scale GPOs developed relationships with large vendors (e.g., Corning, Kimball/Owens Illinois) that could undertake mass production for a large, growing national market of hospitals. Such contracts have gained more scrutiny as the number of vendors has dwindled over time.

The Bureau operated as a cooperative buying service, setting up a group purchasing program in a local area, and allowing hospitals to participate at no cost or for a nominal annual fee (initially $5). During the first half of the twentieth century, the Bureau provided local hospitals, hospital councils, and state and local hospital associations with a menu of national and local contracts via a franchise network. The Bureau would employ a local representative in each city, paid for by the local association, to develop a committed volume bidding process (e.g., commit to purchase 500 cases of a product, commit to buy $'000s of product). In this manner, The Bureau developed a revenue model based on fees paid by vendors based on gross sales—as an early version of contract administration fees (CAFs)—that it would then share with the local council. The Bureau also developed shared services beyond product purchasing, some of which (e.g., laundry and linen services) would become controversial (see below). In this manner, The Bureau helped to spawn the shared services programs of state hospital associations.

Foreshadowing later developments, the Bureau would often work with state hospital associations to develop more customized, local programs. As time went on, the Bureau's national contracts diversified to encompass laboratory supplies (beakers, flasks), pharmaceutical products, and multi-source, generically equivalent medical-surgical supplies. Some purchasing areas like food and fuel oil had to be handled locally; others like IV solutions could be handled with a national contract that the local group could elect to utilize. The Bureau thus functioned as a national federation overseeing a sprawling operation of state and local purchasing groups. The Bureau utilized many contracting devices that would become more prevalent in later decades, and draw government scrutiny, such as sole-source contracts, standardization, letters of commitment from hospitals, contracting with large vendors, and vendor fees.

Other Early Entrants: 1916–1940

The Bureau was not alone. The Cleveland Hospital Council formed in 1916 as perhaps the first local hospital association in the U.S., followed shortly thereafter in 1918 with a group purchasing solution (Cooperative Purchasing Service). This evolved into a larger GPO known better as CHAMPS. In New York City, the Federation of Jewish Philanthropies set up the Joint Purchasing Corporation (JPC) in 1922 to assist Jewish hospitals in the city. JPC recruited Charles Auslander to serve as its head from the mid-1940s through the 1970s. Auslander had previously served as purchasing director for laboratory supplies at Michael Reese Hospital in Chicago during WWII and was an early advocate for standardization (e.g., of syringes, bedpans, catheters, etc.) to alleviate shortages of supplies needed for the wartime effort. JPC was one of the first GPOs to issue competitive bids for laboratory supplies with product specifications. JPC members would later join up with the Educational and Institutional Cooperative Buying Service ("E&I Buying Co-op") which reportedly had "the very best steel case contracts in the U.S. for furniture" and which could accommodate the teaching hospital facilities of JPC.[9] The common Jewish background of the JPC members facilitated cohesion and massive purchasing commitment; the Jewish Federation was also a funding arm for many of the JPC hospitals. This became the template for later GPOs, like the Voluntary Hospitals of America (VHA), whereby executives got together to drive cohesion, commitment, and compliance.

Outside Los Angeles, The Hospital Council of Southern California, which began in 1923, developed a shared services division called Council Shared Services (CSS). In Chicago, several hospitals formed the Metropolitan Chicago Healthcare Council (MCHC) in 1935 to improve the local delivery of healthcare services, later establishing standards for blood-bank operations. In 1963, to leverage savings through economies of scale, it developed the Chicago Hospital Council Group Purchasing Service, one of the first pure group-purchasing organizations in the country.

The Rise of Shared Service Organizations (SSOs): 1940s–1970s

During the period from the 1940s–1980s, local and state hospital associations began to develop shared service organizations (SSOs) that could do group purchasing (see below), sometimes partnering with The Bureau, which operated in roughly ten states. Group purchasing was the most widely used among these shared services, with a reported average of 74% non-food hospital supplies mediated by such groups. The SSOs also developed shared services beyond supply purchasing, thus effectively dis-intermediating The Bureau. Some of these early SSOs included[10]:

- The Southwestern Michigan District Hospital Council formed a surgical supply GPO in 1949 called HPS, followed later in 1963 by a warehousing operation and then a multi-state GPO in 1963. HPS was a member-owned and -operated group operating in 31 states. Its diverse, core membership included hospitals, senior living facilities, and schools.
- The Hospital Central Services Corporation (HCSC) was founded in 1967 by the Greater Lehigh Valley Hospital and Health Planning Council, itself founded just a few years earlier in 1964. HCSC offered linen rental and laundry services to nonprofit hospitals and then quickly added centralized supply purchasing.
- The Rochester Regional Hospital Association (RRHA) formed in 1947, and then launched the RRHA Joint Ventures Corporation in 1983 to do group purchasing for goods and brokered services not available through the national GPOs.
- Western Kentucky Hospital Services was founded in 1966. Owned by six hospitals, it began operations as a shared laundry and then added on bulk supplies, IV solutions, paper products, bandages and dressing, pharmaceuticals, and warehousing.
- Carolinas Hospital and Health Services (CHHS) was formed in 1969 by the hospital associations of North and South Carolina and became the forerunner of a regional GPO powerhouse, SunHealth. Ben Latimer, the head of SunHealth, had received his master's degree in industrial engineering from Georgia Tech. Some of the early cost-cutting solutions developed by the SSOs were based on industrial engineering and management engineering techniques—a forerunner of supply chain management. Latimer also recognized the growing competition of the investor-owned hospital chains (like HCA) in the South (covered below).

- Some regions spouted multiple SSOs. In 1946, the Healthcare Council formed in the Mid-Atlantic region as an SSO for providers, schools, and other health-related institutions. It subsequently established a wholly owned subsidiary, ShareSource, to conduct group purchasing. In 1955, local hospital CEOs formed the Hospital Council of Baltimore which then expanded statewide in 1959 to become the Hospital Council of Maryland. The following year, the Hospital Council established a group purchasing program for hospitals throughout the Mid-Atlantic region. Years later in 1979, the Mid-Atlantic Group Network of Shared Services (MAGNET) formed to do group purchasing of specialty products such as capital and small medical equipment. In 1987, MAGNET expanded to become a full-service GPO.

- Similar developments occurred in neighboring Pennsylvania. The Hospital Council of Western Pennsylvania developed a group purchasing subsidiary, Hospital Shared Services (HHS). HHS grew to become a buying cooperative for nonprofit hospitals in 13 states, including almost all of the Hospital Council's 89 local members. HSS became a shareholder and owner of St. Louis-based AmeriNet, one of the nation's largest hospital group purchasing organizations. HSS worked with about 1,000 vendors nationwide who paid an administrative fee to HSS ranging between 0.5 and 3.0 percent of sales. Hospitals saved money by using HSS, not only through discounts on medical products but also from vendor rebates that HHS shared back with its members (hence, "sharebacks").

- In 1977, Derwood Dunbar, then the Vice-President of materials for Columbus-Cuneo-Cabrini, was recruited by the Hospital Council of Central Pennsylvania to serve as Vice-President for shared services and operations. They wanted to start a group purchasing program along the same lines and stature as the HHS. There had been prior attempts to create a purchasing program in the central part of the state, but the obstacles were formidable. "The geography is unusual," said Dunbar, and the area was divided roughly into two distinct population centers. "It was like two separate circles that didn't touch one another."

- In the late 1960s, some Catholic systems noticed an alarming decline in the number of their nuns (who served as both nurses and administrators) and concluded they needed to become more business-like on their supply side. Several Catholic orders formed the Religious Congregation Cooperative Buyers (RCCB) in St. Louis under the auspices of the Catholic Hospital Association. The RCCB suffered from some infighting and was never effective, closing down in less than a decade. Within a decade, it was supplanted by the Catholic Materials Management Alliance (CMMA, in

St. Louis) which later merged with the Sisters of the Sorrowful Mother–
Diversified Health Services (in Milwaukee) in 1998 to form the national
GPO, Consorta.

- Jewish hospital associations also formed in other parts of the country,
  emulating the JPC in New York City and what the Catholic orders had
  done to ensure their survival. In 1983, the Consortium of Jewish Hospitals (CJH) was formed by Alan Weinstein, then Executive Vice-President
  with the Illinois Hospital Association. Weinstein developed CJH into a
  national federation of nearly every Jewish heritage hospital and health
  system around the country. He focused much of its effort on group
  purchasing. To expand its membership, it changed its name to Premier
  Hospitals Alliance in 1986 and then to Premier in 1987.[11]

Legislative and Networking Tailwinds

Group purchasing was initially abetted by the passage of the Non-Profit
Institutions Act (NPIA) of 1938, which granted an exception for nonprofits
to the Robinson-Patman Price Discrimination Act of 1936. The Robinson-
Patman Act stipulated that price savings on quantity purchases must relate to
quantitative differences (e.g., differences in the cost of manufacture, sale, or
delivery) and nothing more. The Act was meant to prevent large buyers from
leveraging their size to extract lower prices from suppliers, and thereby gain a
competitive advantage over their smaller rivals. By contrast, the NPIA allowed
charitable institutions such as hospitals to collectively purchase supplies for
their own use at a lower cost.

As another tailwind, executives from the various hospital associations and
councils formed informal discussion groups without doing any actual group
purchasing. This was the thrust of the Group Purchasing Group formed by
eight executives in 1963. They never discussed product or vendor negotiations; instead, the discussions focused on best practices, such as "how to get
hospitals to commit to utilizing a different brand" or "how to bid a specific
piece of equipment." Hospital members of the GPG and the Bureau also
shared their bid specifications for particular products with one another. They
held an annual meeting and increased their membership from eight (1963) to
50 (1972) to 125 (1987)—validating the observation above regarding GPO
numbers running into the hundreds. In 1997, GPG changed its name to the
Professional Society for Health Care Group Purchasing.

Specifications became increasingly important by the early 1980s as hospitals faced reimbursement pressures on many fronts. Specifications were integrated into product evaluations, value analysis, and therapeutic equivalence

considerations to help guide product decision-making—and which helped to intensify competition among product suppliers. Specifications served as one route to standardization—not necessarily on products but on product features and dimensions. Of course, standardization on one vendor could go in tandem with sole-source contracting if the chosen vendor met the specifications and was preferred.

The Demise of the Hospital Bureau and Ascendance of the SSOs: 1970s–1980s

The Bureau was still active into the late 1970s and 1980 but may have been on its last legs. Starting in the early 1950s, The Bureau in particular and, more generally, SSOs that provided laundry services, faced challenges from the Internal Revenue Service (IRS) regarding their tax status. The IRS referred to these GPOs as "Hospital Service Organizations" or HSOs. The IRS ruled that if two or more tax-exempt hospitals created an entity to perform commercial services for them, that HSO entity was a "feeder organization" and therefore not tax-exempt. The IRS interpretation was challenged and overturned in 1958 (*Hospital Bureau of Standards & Supplies, Inc. v. United States*) in the U.S. Court of Claims on the basis that the cooperative purchasing organization was engaged in a business enterprise which bore a close relationship to the functioning of tax-exempt hospitals and was "an integral part of the operation of its hospital members." The IRS continued to hold its position, prompting Congress to amend the tax code to provide that HSOs qualified for exemption if they performed one of several services, including group purchasing, but without mentioning laundry. Ultimately in 1981, the U.S. Supreme Court ruled that the provision of laundry and linen services to local hospitals by HSOs was not a tax-exempt activity—an event which may have hastened the demise of the Hospital Bureau.

While *Modern Healthcare* referred to The Bureau as the largest purchasing group in 1979, with its CEO reporting $145 million in annual buying and a membership of 1,000 hospitals, the magazine also reported that its CEO was fighting to keep market share from growing regional rivals. The magazine also reported personality conflicts with The Bureau's managers (due to turnover) as well as dissatisfaction with its services. In late 1980, eight regional purchasing groups (all sponsored by state hospital associations) announced their intention to terminate their daily management contracts with The Bureau but maintaining a lesser, affiliated relationship.

In its last years, The Bureau had diversified into energy management, capital equipment, and biomedical engineering—ostensibly in recognition that it had given away its know-how on committed volume purchasing. Observers also stated The Bureau made a serious strategic blunder by failing to coordinate the joint purchasing ventures among the regional purchasing groups—leaving a void that growing buying consortia would now be filling (see below).[12] Moreover, despite targeting furniture as a major effort, much of the Bureau's original purchasing activity in furniture had been appropriated by the E&I Co-op.

Beginning in the early-to-mid-1970s, the more entrepreneurial SSOs had already recognized the opportunity to eliminate the Bureau as a middleman: stop paying any membership fees to The Bureau, hire away The Bureau's local representative, employ that individual in-house, and keep 100% of any vendor fees earned. Supply spending through The Bureau began to plateau in many organizations, as utilization of contracts for multi-source, generically equivalent products became saturated. SSOs began to consider other products to put on group contracts that local hospitals in the association might be willing to purchase.

More purchasing groups developed along with both for-profit and nonprofit multi-hospital systems (covered below) and began to compete for hospital members in what supply chain consultants at the time dubbed "range wars."[13] Hospitals had a plethora of councils, purchasing groups, and GPOs they could join, and often developed multiple affiliations to find contracts covering the specific brands they already used at their facilities. This became known as "cherry-picking" the contracts. While offering access to desired products/contracts, the groups' expanded numbers and contracts did not include conversion to a specific product which might entail greater volume for product suppliers; naturally, suppliers might balk at the contracts and/or not extend favorable pricing.

The financing of purchasing groups began to switch from membership dues, which represented roughly one-tenth of one penny of actual product buys, to CAFs, which represented a small percentage of those buys. This provided substantial funding to increase the purchasing group's infrastructure. Moreover, CAF financing made the GPO "painless" to the hospital and removed the barriers to using the purchasing groups; both of these resulted in higher utilization of purchasing groups.

Multi-hospital Systems: The Forerunner of Regional and National GPOs

Investor-owned hospital systems formed in the late 1960s and throughout the 1970s, quickly followed by nonprofit hospital systems in the 1970s and 1980s. Hospital systems offered unbundled services (such as group purchasing of supplies) to other hospitals as shared service agreements and began to compete with the local hospital councils and state hospital associations. Their emergence marked the beginning of a more widespread regional and (eventually) national purchasing market as the systems themselves expanded geographically. Moreover, with their entry, the group purchasing market began to mushroom and slowly transform into more of an ownership model rather than a shared service model.

Trade magazines began to document this trend starting in 1981, with lots of competitors vying for the same hospitals' business.[14] The 1970s marked the era of group buying as a major market force for suppliers of medical-surgical products; group buying from vendors of pharmaceuticals would commence in the 1980s. By 1996, the percentage of both medical-surgical and pharmaceutical product buys under group purchasing contracts would exceed 80% and sometimes reach as high as 95%.[15]

The Late 1960s and 1970s: Investor-Owned Systems[16]

In 1965, the only major U.S. hospital chain was the Veterans Administration, the public healthcare system for retired military personnel created in 1930, comprised of roughly 125 hospitals. By contrast, the rest of the hospital sector consisted of thousands of mostly independent, community-based hospitals founded in the late nineteenth century to serve their local communities. In 1960, only 331 hospitals, mostly operated by religious bodies that traced their roots back to the 1930s, belonged to a system.

However, 1965 marked the passage of Medicare and Medicaid, which amended the Social Security Act to cover the elderly and poor, respectively. The expansion of insurance coverage to new populations with generous, cost-plus reimbursement provisions (designed to appease and co-opt the hospital and medical associations) prompted the first wave of hospital consolidation. The prospect of greater volume and higher prices (or guaranteed reimbursement for treating patients formerly unable to pay) enticed investor-owned organizations to enter and consolidate the hospital market.

For-profit hospitals had always existed in the hospital industry; however, they were typically small facilities whose numbers dropped precipitously from 2,441 in 1910 (~56% of hospitals) to 852 in 1966 (12%), and even further to 378 (6.3%) by 1975. In the late 1960s, however, several new for-profit (i.e., investor-owned) companies entered the market to establish "chains" of proprietary hospitals and repopulate the for-profit hospital sector. These chains included National Medical Enterprises (NME, formed in 1967),

Hospital Corporation of America (HCA, formed in 1968), and American Medical International (AMI) which formed in 1956 as a medical reference laboratory but diversified into the hospitals it served in the early 1960s. By 1970, there were twenty-nine investor-owned hospital chains that owned 207 hospitals. In 1972, the large investor-owned systems were joined by Humana, which began life in the early 1960s as a nursing home company and quickly switched into the hospital business to take advantage of the Medicare business "gold rush."

The opportunity was instantly recognized on Wall Street. HCA went public in 1969 and saw its stock price rise from $18 to $46 per share on the first day of trading. Other healthcare entrepreneurs, such as David Jones and Wendell Cherry, transformed their Humana chain of nursing homes into a for-profit hospital chain, also going public. Within the first year, the stock's price rose from $8 to $50.

Benefitted by such high market valuations and rich access to capital, the for-profit hospital systems expanded rapidly during the 1970s. Most of this growth occurred through acquisitions of existing, freestanding proprietary hospitals—many previously owned by physicians. Between 1975 and 1984, the number of hospitals belonging to for-profit systems grew from 378 to 878, accounting for over 13% of all U.S. hospitals and roughly 10% of all hospital beds (a near doubling of both). Six of the largest for-profit chains owned 58% of these hospitals (NME, HCA, AMI, Humana, Charter Medical, and Republic Health Care Corporation). In the late 1970s and early 1980s, growth strategies began to include acquisitions of investor-owned systems by larger rivals. Humana acquired American Medicorp in 1978; HCA acquired Hospital Affiliates International (HAI) in 1981; AMI acquired Brookwood Health Services and Hyatt in 1981–82.

Fueled by cost-plus reimbursement, the for-profits saw an opportunity to provide expanded hospital services to the community and also generate sizable financial returns. They thought the key capability missing in hospitals was management, and thus brought in new management approaches to hospital delivery. These approaches included horizontal consolidation of facilities into chains (a.k.a. multi-hospital systems), economies of scale through centralized purchasing and supply chain management, and capital access through the equity markets. The investor-owned systems continued to grow steadily from the 1960s to the early 1980s, earning annual returns on equity averaging nearly 20%.

Two of the first national GPOs were formed by the investor-owned hospital systems, sometimes by the same individual. Gene Burton was the executive director of the SSO in Western Kentucky in 1968, then was recruited by Humana in 1971 as Corporate Director of Purchasing, and then moved to HCA in 1977 as Vice-President of Materials Management (VPMM). These two national groups served as an interesting contrast in contracting, since one employed sole-source contracting while the other used dual-source contracting during the 1970s, respectively. Both chains developed committed, dollar-volume purchasing programs in which the hospitals promised a certain level of sales in exchange for price discounts from vendors. They are briefly profiled below.

Humana

Humana offered the nonprofit industry some early lessons in centralized contracting, centralized purchasing, and mandated compliance based on common ownership and centralized accounts payable. Humana was headed by two attorneys, Wendell Cherry and David Jones; Jones was also a certified public accountant. They personally handled purchasing decisions as to what to buy and at the best price, and then "hoped the hospital liked it." The purchase requisition for any equipment costing more than $2,000 had to go to Gene Burton, who verified the pricing and then consulted a small executive committee that included the two founders every Tuesday morning. Since all invoices for products ordered by hospitals went to the central corporate office to be paid, Burton had monthly reports of suppliers used and which purchases were on (versus off) contract. Burton would notify hospital administrators for any off-contract purchase and ask them to fix it, rather than notifying his bosses, in order to build a relationship with them. But they and their clinicians knew what was company policy and that they really had little choice.

Hospital Corporation of America (HCA)

By contrast, HCA was founded by doctors (Tom Frist Sr. and his son, Tommy Frist) who were more considerate of physician preferences. Burton moved from Humana in Louisville to HCA in Nashville to be VPMM and was tasked with a delicate balancing act between centralized purchasing and listening to hospital medical staffs. Burton populated his department with clinicians (operating room or OR managers, nurses, lab managers, radiology managers) drawn from HCA hospitals. He also set up committees of clinicians (e.g., clinical division representatives, pharmacists) who would come to Nashville, review the contract proposals received from suppliers in a specific product area, and then select two suppliers for every product so that physicians could have a choice. HCA's Regional Vice-Presidents evaluated the products on both a cost and clinical basis—anticipating the value analysis committees (VACs) that would become popular in later decades—but left the final decision to the committees.

The 1970s: Nonprofit Hospital Systems

Initially, nonprofit hospital executives derided the efforts of their investor-owned counterparts. They argued the for-profits cherry-picked patient services with high margins and located in more affluent areas (suburbs) or in the non-unionized southern half of the U.S. But, as they sat on the sidelines, they watched the rise of their for-profit system competitors with increasing alarm. On the one hand, the for-profits spoke a new language of capitalistic profit-making—operating revenues, net income, dividends, shares—rather than community mission and service. On the other hand, the for-profits represented a startling new entrant that had reversed the decline of the independent for-profit hospitals and achieved remarkable success. They had grown quickly by raising long-term debt and issuing equity; when they purchased other hospitals, the latter were subject to immediate financial re-evaluation that allowed additional debt financing and reimbursement for depreciation.

Moreover, these systems were *theorized* to hold several advantages over the nonprofit hospitals.[17] First, they enjoyed scale economies (at least in purchasing), lower operating costs, lower cost healthcare, and thus an advantage in contracting with insurers. Second, systems enjoyed manpower benefits in terms of enhanced recruiting of both clinical and administrative personnel, improved retention, and stronger capabilities in both skill areas. Third, systems enjoyed organizational advantages in terms of growth, survival, and political power.

This alone might have been enough stimuli for nonprofit hospitals to enter the fray and form their own chains. But several other historical forces also propelled them down this path. Due to the passage of the Medicare and Medicaid programs, as well as the earlier Hill-Burton program (1946), hospitals became increasingly dependent on federal and state funding. They also became identified as a major culprit in the rising costs of these programs and viewed as wasteful, duplicative, and inefficient.[18] Given their receipt of public monies, they became subject to increasing federal and state regulation. Several states enacted hospital rate-setting laws in the 1970s to regulate hospital fees. Several states enacted Certificate of Need (CON) programs to curtail capital spending; this was followed by federal legislation, The National Health Planning and Resources Development Act (P.L. 93-641) of 1974, which ushered in national CON requirements. CON made renovation, new construction, and capacity expansion (e.g., new beds and equipment) initially costing more than $150,000 (later, $600,000) subject to regulatory approval by Health Systems Agencies (HSAs). Thus, in order to grow a hospital system, alliances and acquisitions were the preferred route since they did not increase existing bed capacity. In 1977, President Carter's Hospital Cost Containment Act proposed limits on hospital charges to a federally sanctioned ceiling, without controlling the rise in prices hospitals paid for supplies. The latter continued to rise with the rising cost of healthcare. Hospitals saw their supply expenditures climb from 5 to 6% to reach double digits.

Nonprofit hospitals responded to rising cost pressures and the entry of for-profit hospital chains by developing their own regional chains. The number of nonprofit hospitals belonging to systems jumped sharply during this period from 331 (1960) to 472 (1970) and then to 964 (1980). The nonprofit hospital system sector now included more hospitals than the for-profit system sector (795 in 1980) and was typically much larger in size than their for-profit counterparts. The for-profits were more concentrated, however, with a smaller number of systems accounting for the majority of system hospitals. Overall, membership in a system accounted for 30% of all hospitals by 1982.

Nonprofits not only formed their own chains but also developed their own buying groups—at first regionally, and then nationally—to compete with the investor-owned and lower the total cost of ordering supplies and carrying inventories. For example, the Adventist Health Services developed a national purchasing program for its members in the mid-1970s. Their contracts marked the beginning of committed volume and payment contracts with vendors. Likewise, in 1976, the purchasing group for the Sisters of the Sorrowful Mother (SSM) opened the congregation's shared services (including purchasing) to other hospitals to reduce their overhead costs and deal with cost containment pressures. By 1977, the nine Sisters of Mercy provinces organized a national purchasing plan for their 73 hospitals. In that same year, seven nonprofit multi-hospital systems met to develop a national purchasing organization called Associated Hospital Systems.

Many state hospital associations formed group purchasing arms of their own, not necessarily to disintermediate The Hospital Bureau, but to fund their nascent political lobbying to fight state regulations and, in particular, dismantle the HSAs. Group purchasing could also help the finances of their hospital members, reduce the dues their members paid (especially if supplier contracts included rebates to the GPO), and deal with pressures of high inflation and high cost of capital.

The Early GPO Powerhouses

Voluntary Hospitals of America (VHA)

The first national, nonprofit GPO, Voluntary Hospitals of America (VHA) was formed in 1977 with 30 large hospitals and systems invited to participate. VHA formed as a countervailing force to the Federation of American Hospitals (FAH), a trade group representing investor-owned hospitals in Washington D.C. VHA hospital executives feared that passage of the HMO Act of 1973 might propel large employers with a national base of operations to contract with large nationally based, investor-owned hospital chains rather than a cottage industry of small nonprofit hospital systems. The VHA looked at the possibility of national employers contracting with national GPOs as well as national chains of hospitals.

The formation of VHA disrupted the traditional group purchasing industry. VHA's shareholders were large, prominent institutions. Their national purchasing and distribution posed a competitive threat to more locally based hospital councils and state hospital associations. VHA sold hospital memberships as the entry price (estimated to be $250,000) to prominent regional hospitals, who served as "partners," and who then recruited multiple shareholders and affiliates from neighboring cities whose fees paid back the original investing partners.

At that time, VHA's emblem was a circle whose rim included the names of several major vendors that had funded VHA's meetings. These vendors included American Hospital Supply, ServiceMaster, Baxter, and others. While not members or shareholders in VHA, they were sponsors who would become favored supply partners and participants in "prime vendor" relationships and sole-source contracts (covered below). By partnering with major branded products, VHA perhaps aimed to relieve itself and its hospitals of the aggravation of "product conversion"—i.e., getting hospitals and their clinicians to switch to the new contracted vendor. Prime vendor contracts promoted contracting ease and contract breadth, but perhaps at the expense of obtaining lower prices from time-consuming, contract-by-contract negotiations. They also served as a substitute for efficient internal hospital systems run by materials managers and purchasing agents—which may have been valid for the roughly 80% of items that hospitals ordered but which accounted for only 20% of their supply budget. Group purchasing bids and contracts focused instead on the 20% of supply items that accounted for 80% of hospital spending.

Premier

Another regional GPO that formed in the late 1970s and early 1980s included the Jewish Consortium of Hospitals (1978), an alliance of 16 Jewish hospitals. It then expanded its membership to other non-Jewish hospitals and renamed itself Premier Hospitals Alliance (1985). In 1993, it was relabeled as the Premier Health Alliance to reflect the growing representation of hospital systems among its membership. In 1995, Premier was owned by 55 hospitals and health systems, representing 280 hospitals. Organizations like Premier became well-known for their use of vendor fees (CAFs) and exclusive supplier contracts, thereby prompting other groups to follow suit.[19]

University Hospital Consortium (UHC)

About the same time (1984), the University Hospital Consortium (UHC) formed in Chicago around teaching hospitals and academic medical centers (AMCs). Their higher cost facilities looked vulnerable in an HMO environment, and they did not want to be left with just the high-cost tertiary and quaternary services. Moreover, they witnessed some defection of their teaching hospital members to join Premier. So UHC developed a group purchasing wing to fund their growth strategy and political lobbying and did so by partnering with VHA. The new combined purchasing operation was called Novation. Facilitating UHC's formation and cooperation was the fact that many of these AMCs were state-funded. By virtue of receiving state monies, they had to obtain written bids and publish their bids. Instead of doing this individually, they quickly realized they could assemble all of these bids into one national bid. Despite their geographical dispersion, these hospitals represented some of the most prestigious institutions in the country that were attractive to suppliers. But by virtue of being AMCs, they bought from lots of suppliers using multiple GPOs; integrating with VHA would start to tighten the reins on UHC hospital purchasing.

American HealthCare Systems (AmHS)

Finally, multi-hospital systems that were neither Premier members nor AMCs nor religious hospitals (e.g., Jewish, Catholic) had a "FOMO" moment. Nobody was speaking on their behalf, and they felt they might get left behind. A physician and lawyer, Monroe Trout, spotted the need and joined American HealthCare Systems (AmHS), itself a merger of two previous alliances (Associated Health Systems and United HealthCare Systems). As Trout wrote in his autobiography about his start as Chairman and CEO of AmHS in October 1986,

> When I first entered the offices ... my assigned secretary asked if I had come to close the company ... it became obvious to me that the company was on the verge of bankruptcy. We were not self-sustaining and had to rely on dues paid by the individual hospitals. The hospitals were beginning to balk because they saw no advantages coming from the company ... A major purpose of the company was to purchase goods and services for all the hospitals in the consortium. However, the hospitals only randomly complied with the purchasing contracts, which created problems with the suppliers. I decided to change the system. I thought that individual companies would be willing to pay a percentage fee [CAF] if we could guarantee our hospitals would buy under their contracts. We also needed to reduce the number of contracts to a manageable level ... Not only were we asking the companies to reduce their prices for bulk purchases, but also to pay American Healthcare Systems 3 percent of all purchases as a fee for ensuring compliance with the contract ... We established a reward-and-punishment system for the hospitals depending on their compliance. In the first year, we were able to turn American Healthcare Systems totally around and make it self-sufficient ... Since American Healthcare Systems had become self-sufficient with money in the bank, we were able to eliminate all the dues being paid by the individual hospitals...[20]

AmHS developed into a national alliance of 40 shareholders that included multi-hospital systems and launched its own group purchasing function in 1986 as an alternative to VHA and Premier to appeal to non-tertiary hospitals. AmHS' head of purchasing, Lynn Detlor, came from the Adventist system which began its group purchasing program in 1974. Detlor focused on longer-term contracts, contract portfolios and bundles, dual-source contracts involving mandatory compliance, and corporate partnerships. Dual-source contracts were viewed as a compromise or balancing act between (a) committed purchasing and (b) clinician preference and choice. Like Novation, AmHS began to tighten the reins on hospital purchasing and did so by educating the materials managers in its hospitals to focus on contracting and standardizing, working with clinicians inside, and converting a target of 90% of purchases to a single vendor. AmHS also developed compliance programs by the late 1980s that encouraged hospitals to participate at specified levels. Compliant shareholders were rewarded with up to ten percent of annual dividends; noncompliant shareholders were penalized. In 1995, AmHS achieved 90% compliance.

As part of this effort, AmHS and Novation gathered clinical and cost information on products, did in-house clinical analysis, and relayed the information to their clinicians to help make cost-effective purchases. While much of this effort was top-down adherence to GPO-negotiated contracts, it was not viewed as coercive. Rather, hospital administrators viewed it as an opportunity to reduce costs as well as train the materials managers to become more business-like. Knowing they had executive support, materials managers moved to rein in clinician purchasing, rather than allow clinicians to order whatever they wanted.

Some industry observers view the education of VPMMs regarding product conversion and selling contracts to clinicians as a major contribution by the GPOs. This had the unintended effect of also alerting hospitals about how much money their GPOs were making from contracts (and only sharing a portion of it with their members). Hospitals responded in two ways that were not mutually exclusive: they took on more product contracting themselves and asked their GPOs for bigger sharebacks on GPO-negotiated contracts. The number of materials managers began to proliferate; according to one analyst, by 1984, 60 of New Jersey's 100 hospitals had hired such a position.

The example of AmHS showed that GPOs could move market share from one vendor to another. This was not necessarily disruptive to the vendor community, however, as standardization required a vendor that was not only established and known but also acceptable to most clinicians. This made the committed contracts "credible." Like VHA, AmHS also developed a business development program that invested in small vendors and brought their products to AmHS' attention. This investment program was viewed as a way to minimize reliance on hospital membership dues.

Summary: The Fuel Powering Multi-hospital Systems

The historical record highlights some important stimuli to the formation and expansion of the GPO sector. Passage of Medicare and Medicaid in 1965 led to rapid and sizeable increases in national healthcare expenditures (NHE) in a fee-for-service environment. Hospital spending increased considerably since hospitals increased their revenues by providing more services to more enrollees: roughly 40% of NHE was routed through hospitals. A high percentage of a rapidly rising amount of NHE served as a siren song to for-profit investors and nonprofit executives alike to (a) set up chains of hospitals, (b) expand the size and geographic reach of these chains, and (c) develop purchasing arms that could reduce supply expenditures, increase margins, and facilitate system growth.

Hospital revenues also rose due to higher reimbursements pegged to the cost of care and inflation. The hospital sector saw prices rise due to a combi-nation of general inflation in the economy and health sector-specific inflation (e.g., rising prices of supplies), which has consistently outpaced economic growth by 2% in real terms.[21] Part of the price rise was driven by wage and price controls in the early 1970s, which inhibited suppliers from offering multi-year, price-protected contracts for their products. Thus, hospitals bene-fited by expansions in both patient volume and the prices they were paid for their services.

The 1980s: Regulatory, Reimbursement, and Competitive Pressures

Systems faced new regulatory and reimbursement pressures in the 1980s, further increasing the salience of group purchasing as a solution. Passage of Medicare's Inpatient Prospective Payment System (IPPS, 1983) and the rise of managed care organizations (MCOs) in the 1980s and early 1990s increased hospitals' attention to managing their costs, impelled even more hospitals to join purchasing groups, and increased the importance of (and the opportunity for) the GPOs' role. IPPS set fixed, budgeted amounts that hospitals got paid for inpatient admissions of Medicare patients. On the commercial insurance front, MCOs had undertaken their own regional and national consolidation strategy during the 1980s, and now confronted hospi-tals in local markets with a large, organized buyer of inpatient days. Many insurers had adopted two particular MCO forms—the health maintenance organization (HMO) and the preferred provider organization (PPO)—to attract employers and their workers into lower cost plans, channel these higher enrollments to narrow hospital networks, and use the large bargaining power to reduce hospital payments. Such bargaining leverage required hospi-tals to reduce their costs even further. In 1996, the external threat of HMO market penetration reached its zenith, covering roughly one-third of all private sector employees. As in the 1970s, hospitals faced the prospect of fixed or constrained reimbursement without any controls over the rising prices of supplies.

Other public sector legislative actions facilitated GPO growth. The Medicare and Medicaid Patient and Program Protection Act of 1987 (P.L. 100–93) added new provisions to the Social Security Act and its Sect. 1128(b) anti-kickback statute. The Act exempted from the anti-kickback provisions certain payments (contract administration fees) from product vendors to group purchasing organizations acting on behalf of providers rendering services to Medicare and Medicaid patients. The Department of Health and Human Services (DHHS) issued regulations establishing safe harbors in 1991 for purposes of the anti-kickback provisions (see Chapter 3). According to these regulations, the GPOs had to have written agreements with their customer either stating that the fees are to be three percent or less of the purchase price, or specifying the amount or maximum amount that each vendor would pay. The GPO must also disclose in writing to each customer, at least annually, the amount received from each supplier. The Office of the Inspector General (OIG) for DHHS investigated these fees, found that they reduced costs and did not harm patient care quality, and argued that such fees should be allowed.

The 1980s: More Competitors Join the GPO Party

In such an environment, SSOs and GPOs might address some important needs. Shared services such as group purchasing were partly developed to attack rising costs in the face of constrained hospital reimbursement. As governments and payers downstream squeezed hospitals with a mixture of regulatory initiatives, hospitals logically responded by trying to squeeze suppliers upstream and purchase more efficiently. From the beginning, the primary goal of shared purchasing became lower prices and cost savings.

By the end of the 1970s, the U.S. hospital market was threatened with survival, as it began to witness a number of hospital closings and the beginning of a long-term trend from inpatient to outpatient care.[22] Faced with a stagnant inpatient market and growing competition in shared services, systems and groups began to consider one another as customers or potential merger partners in order to protect their market share, grow their business, and increase their purchasing volume. These external threats motivated the remaining nonprofit hospitals to leave the sidelines and join the GPO party. Due to their nonprofit charter, several Catholic hospital systems and other mission-based nonprofit groups had not initially participated in The Bureau, SSOs, or group purchasing—but now expressed interest.[23]

Several more nonprofit regional purchasing groups developed during the late 1970s and early 1980s as alternatives to both the investor-owned systems and VHA. Some alliances—including American HealthCare Systems (1984), Major Catholic Alliance (1984), First Hospitals (1984), Yankee Alliance (1984), Consolidated Catholic Health Care (1985), Hospital Network (1985), Child Health Corporation of American (1985), Pacific Health Alliance (1986), and AmeriNet (1986)—were consortia of local hospitals and hospital systems. Other alliances—MedEcon Services, Health Services Corporation of America (HSCA), Mid America Shared Services, and Mid-Atlantic Group Network of Shared Services—were privately held. Several of these alliances are profiled below.

- MedEcon was formed in 1971 by William Wooldridge, who had worked for Humana/HCA in Kentucky. Wooldridge thought he could do group purchasing on his own. Based in Louisville, MedEcon specialized in building regional buying cooperatives for hospitals in small, rural southern towns. MedEcon charged its members an annual fee and also charged fees to suppliers. MedEcon was sold to Managed Healthcare Associates (MHA), a GPO operating in the alternate site market, in 1998.
- Paralleling MedEcon was Health Services Corporation of America (HSCA), started by Earl and Bob Norman in Cape Girardeau (Missouri) in 1969. HSCA targeted rural facilities, which were underserved by the nascent GPO development. Like MedEcon, it charged supplier fees of roughly one percent based on the volume purchased. Earl Norman also reached out to sign up many Catholic facilities. He also hired representatives to visit the hospital purchasing agents (along with the suppliers' representatives) to try to convince them to move product market shares. This would benefit vendors enormously, who might then pay HSCA more than the one percent fee.
- The MedEcon and HSCA activities got the attention of the hospital associations which, until this time, had negotiated only price discounts from suppliers. They began to imitate MedEcon and HSCA and charge contract fees from one to two percent. Such funds were used to finance other shared services the associations offered.
- Amerinet was formed in 1986 by combining four group purchasing programs: HSCA, Hospital Shared Services of Western Pennsylvania, the Hospital Association of Rhode Island Corporation (HARI Corp), and Intermountain Health Systems. Each of the four founding members was comprised of state hospital associations, local independent GPOs, and investor-owned systems (e.g., Charter Medical). Amerinet sought to combine its national scale to leverage contract negotiation with its local membership base to assist in contract implementation and marketing. It

appealed to smaller hospitals. It also offered the largest contract portfolio which traded off the lowest price for greater access to the products that hospitals and their clinicians wanted. Amerinet thus offered hospitals a choice among GPOs depending on which angle of the iron triangle they wanted to emphasize (e.g., access versus cost). HSCA would eventually depart, leaving Amerinet with three owners. Amerinet quickly aligned with the hospital associations, which had seen their members and purchasing revenues absorbed by the two emerging powerhouses, VHA and Premier. Amerinet made its contract portfolio available to hospital association members to try to ramp up their purchasing volumes and rebates to get good pricing. It also relied on dual-source contracts but nevertheless set up a sole-source program in 1988.

- Amerinet's strategy was copied by a Michigan purchasing group called Hospital Purchasing Service. They approached VHA which acquired them and then used their portfolio to make a secondary offering under the banner Healthcare Purchasing Partners International (HPPI). HPPI ran around the country offering non-VHA and non-UHC hospitals in hospital associations a revenue-sharing deal similar to what Amerinet was offering. HPPI changed its name in 2007 to Provista.

During the 1980s, these burgeoning groups used their size (growing membership) to extract major price concessions from many suppliers, precipitating several price wars in the industry (e.g., over I.V. solutions, standard beds, etc.). Groups expanded the number of hospital members and their access to contracts for commodity supplies; they also revolutionized the hospital supply market for commodity items using national agreements and low prices, and further upgraded the function of materials management and the training of a new managerial group—the director of materials management. While larger in size, the groups were now becoming increasingly diverse in membership, raising internal political problems on how to act in a concerted (e.g., one size fits all) fashion.

Changes in the GPO Playing Field and Market Structure: 1990s Disruption

Competitive Threat Posed by Columbia/HCA

By the 1990s, hospitals were faced with yet another growing threat in their midst: the ascendance of a very large, for-profit hospital chain called

Columbia/HCA. Columbia had modest origins. It began as a two-hospital system in 1988, growing by virtue of acquisitions to ~ 23 hospitals by 1993. That year, Columbia acquired Galen and its 71 hospitals, formerly operated by Humana; the following year, it merged its 94 hospitals with HCA and its 96 hospitals; also in 1994, it acquired 96 ambulatory surgery centers in a stock swap with Medical Care America; and in 1995, it merged again with HealthTrust and its 111 hospitals, which were an ESOP spin-off from the older HCA system which went private in 1987. This series of mergers was one of the watershed events of the 1990s: it fostered greater competition among hospitals and purchasing groups and took hospital purchasing to a whole new level.

Just as the rise of investor-owned hospital systems in the 1970s impelled nonprofit hospitals to form systems, the speed of these acquisitions forced competitor hospitals to follow suit and consolidate. Why was this so? Columbia/HCA's then CEO, now current Florida Senator (and former Florida Governor) Rick Scott, was known for keeping a paperweight on his desk that read, "If you are not the lead dog, the view never changes." Scott's hospital chain, Columbia/HCA, would become known as "the 800-pound gorilla" for its market penetration strategy. Columbia would use its heft to enter a local market, buy up hospitals, consolidate their capacity, then (so the story went) lower their costs, and then offer local HMO and PPO insurance plans lower hospital rates. By doing so, its hospitals would enjoy a competitive advantage in gaining access to payer contracts, especially capitated contracts, and take market share away from nonprofit hospitals. If hospitals wanted to survive, they needed to emulate Columbia/HCA by defensively forming their own systems.

This strategy posed a threat not only to locally based, nonprofit IDNs but also to the purchasing groups and product suppliers. Columbia/HCA's supply chain strategy focused on centralized contracting, sole-source contracts, 95% compliance at the hospital level (with hospital CEOs incentivized to meet such compliance), tiered pricing, standardization, product bundles, corporate contracts, and the biggest discounts and most-favored-nation pricing from suppliers. The system made it clearly known, acquisition by acquisition, that it would rationalize the number of contracted suppliers down to one, instilling fear among the latter they would lose out to competitors. Columbia/HCA subsequently became the "hot contract" to have. Suppliers simultaneously griped and bragged about entering Columbia/HCA's sole-source contracts—griped about the low margins they earned and bragged about the high committed volume.[24]

The irony is that the core HCA was a more decentralized system, run by father and son physicians (the Frists), that focused on local market dominance. The reality was that compliance was a function of execution, not corporate dictates, in which corporate purchasing executives would visit local hospitals, explain the compliance program, develop committees of department reps to provide input in purchasing, and form clinical advisory boards to advise on which products to use, establish a process and measurement of accountability, and ensure that large, market-leading suppliers were available to hospital clinicians—all of which built compliance from the bottom-up. This was not quite the same process observed in other investor-owned hospitals, where materials managers in charge of purchasing programs reportedly ran them as "kingdoms," telling their hospitals what to do and what to buy, based on their common ownership.

One source of Columbia's efficiencies derived from its vendor contracts and huge, purported purchasing leverage. With its new size, centralized control over purchasing, reports that its physicians were willing to standardize, and thus a reputation for compliance, Columbia/HCA began to negotiate a new round of supplier contracts, including several sole-source deals, with pricing not previously seen by the nonprofit groups and alliances. Columbia/HCA accomplished this by combining the contract portfolios of its various merged entities (Columbia, HCA, Galen, etc.), rationalizing the number of suppliers via sole-source or dual-source contracts, and getting member hospitals to purchase through these contracts. The Galen/Columbia/HCA acquisition brought with it Humana's strong purchasing discipline, sophisticated purchasing methodologies and capabilities, and culture of compliance—all of which Columbia sought to extend system-wide. Columbia/HCA also requested that its suppliers bundle their products in order to get better pricing. By virtue of using both sole-source and bundled contracts, it threatened (1) IDNs by its pricing and (2) suppliers by the threat of contract exclusion.[25] Fearing that they might be dropped, suppliers responded with prices and contract terms that neither HCA nor Galen had reportedly seen.

Columbia's cost advantage was attributed to two sources: (1) 15–17% lower costs due to standardization, lower prices, and utilization reductions, and (2) 18–22% lower costs stemming from discounts on renegotiated contracts. Columbia's total savings were reportedly $60 Million out of a $220 Million supply budget. In this manner, Columbia/HCA seemed to have the best of both worlds that the national GPOs struggled to achieve: the 1980s' strategy (large size) and the 1990s' strategy (disciplined purchasing and commitment).

The merger of Columbia, HCA, Galen, and other investor-owned systems at the time shook up the industry. Not only did they control roughly half of all hospital beds in the investor-owned portion of the industry but they also gained new members by virtue of a 1990s trend in hospital owner-ship conversions from nonprofit to investor-owned.[26] The ascendance of Columbia/HCA and its pace of acquisitions served as a wake-up call to the nonprofit hospital systems and the mission-driven systems that had previously eschewed some buying group tactics (e.g., contract fees).

Columbia represented not only a major threat to nonprofit hospitals and their chains by virtue of being the largest multi-hospital system chain. Columbia/HCA also attempted to bolt on several other types of providers (e.g., physicians, ambulatory surgery centers, outpatient rehabilitation centers, home healthcare) to form more of an integrated delivery network (IDN). Such networks became the rage in the 1990s. They would become the next threat to GPOs as well as a customer to target.

IDNs: Yet Another Competitor

Horizontally integrated hospital systems began forming as early as the late 1960s. "Hospital systems" encompass hospitals that have merged, joined multi-hospital systems (with a common ownership base), or joined non-ownership-based networks or alliances.[27] Since the 1960s, there have been several waves of hospital system formation. The 1990s, in particular, marked a spike in systems and mergers set in motion by the consolidation of four investor-owned hospital chains (Columbia, Galen, HCA, and HealthTrust) into one giant chain, Columbia/HCA.

In the early 1990s, the hospital systems were joined by *vertically* integrated delivery networks (IDNs) that combined hospitals, physicians, long-term care facilities, and, sometimes, health plans. The IDNs developed partly in competitive response to managed care organizations (MCOs, such as HMOs) to serve as contracting vehicles to get capitated contracts. The IDNs also developed partly in response to the Clinton Health Plan, submitted to Congress in late 1993, which called for local provider alliances called "accountable health plans."

IDNs mushroomed during the period between 1993 and 1997. Forecasts by groups and consulting firms suggested that IDNs would dominate the future provider landscape. Starting in 1993, UHC and a consulting firm called APM jointly heralded the ascendance of IDNs in the form of their widely disseminated four-stage model of healthcare market evolution.[28] The Advisory Board likewise championed the role of IDNs in their popular 1993 publication, *The Grand Alliance*.[29] The following year, VHA issued a similar forecast in its publication, *Integration: Market Forces and Critical Success Factors*.[30] All of these consulting firm and group reports received confirmation and academic validation in the 1996 publication by health services researchers at the Kellogg Graduate School of Management at Northwestern University.[31]

Regardless of their composition, these combinations were justified on the basis of scale economies, the need for enlarged size to handle capitated risk from payers, and the desire to offer a wider geographic delivery network and continuum of services. Moreover, by virtue of being integrated, IDNs supposedly had three competitive advantages the purchasing groups lacked. First, they could develop better relationships with their clinicians that could drive more committed purchasing. Second, they possessed the ability to do more committed volume purchasing in local markets, similar to the promise of the local/regional hospital clusters. Third, they could integrate the provision of services across a continuum of care and achieve some efficiencies and perhaps both scale and scope economies. Some of these purported advantages, and the threats they posed to GPOs, are explored below.

The Threat Posed by IDNs

Scale Economies

Economies of scale became the mantra of the consolidation movement of the 1990s, mentioned by all players in the healthcare value chain as their rationale for pursuing mergers and acquisitions. Scale economies were very important, especially when the new merged system carried a lot of debt. Scale economies were also important to offset revenue shortfalls from managed care, particularly from the hugely unprofitable multi-year, global risk contracts that IDNs signed with payers in the early 1990s. IDNs inked these contracts in the downward swing of the insurance underwriting cycle, which hit its nadir in 1996. When, as was often the case, IDNs negotiated a percent of premium payment, the fall in the underwriting cycle meant a downward spiral in premium income—and sometimes bankruptcy.[32] Thus, the promise of scale economies served as huge bait to lure hospitals into IDN formation and (hopefully) stabilize/improve their finances.

Internal Efficiencies

Unlike the GPOs which focused on product standardization and lower price, the IDNs focused on increased efficiencies in care provision and utilization reductions. This suggested that product choice may shift to include consideration of the clinical arena in which they are used—concepts that had previously been unlinked or only loosely coupled in group purchasing. This fomented a short-lived trend of risk-sharing agreements (covered below) between suppliers and IDNs that focused on how to best utilize the products acquired upstream.

Vertical integration of different types of providers under an IDN also placed new demands on product distributors to service multiple, diverse ports of call. This helped to further the ongoing consolidation among distributors. By 1994, there were three main distributors of medical-surgical ("med-surg") products: Owen & Minor, Baxter/Allegiance, and General Medical. Distributors were also called upon to help hospitals, systems, and IDNs achieve efficiencies and control rising costs during an era of managed care and the Clinton reform. Consolidation of distributors, which meant fewer intermediaries to carry suppliers' lines of a given product, may have propelled consolidation among manufacturers. Some observers thought this movement might lead to mega-mergers between medical-surgical and pharmaceutical distributors to offer hospitals one common wholesaler platform; these projections proved erroneous due to the totally different nature of the two types of products.[33]

Physician Relationships and Committed Purchasing

Another area where IDNs might enjoy competitive advantage was in the purchase and utilization of physician preference items (PPIs), such as orthopedic implants and cardiovascular devices. The 1980s witnessed a boom in orthopedic surgeries, rising from 30,000 a year to 130,000 a year (1980–1990). This boom reflected the availability of new technologies, training of new surgeons, and the migration of such procedures to community hospitals and ambulatory surgery centers. As much as 40% of the reimbursement and 60% of the cost of hip and knee implant procedures was the implant itself, which naturally focused attention on supply chain management as the key to procedure profitability. Kaiser had developed contracts with specific implant makers in the mid-1980s. The early 1990s witnessed the first wave of GPO orthopedic implant contracts by AmHS and a regional division of VHA, which often included efforts to standardize on one supplier.

A debate developed in the trade literature whether IDNs, by virtue of their integrated relationships with clinicians, could achieve better pricing than GPOs on the more expensive supply items. This emerged as the new frontier in hospital supply cost reductions now that commodity contracts had matured. Consultants and GPO surveys suggested that IDNs not only were engaged in their own contracting but also used GPO-like strategies to reduce costs (e.g., standardization) and achieve more competitive pricing. The rise of IDNs thus threatened the future of GPOs, who now felt challenged to demonstrate their value to hospital members.

To be sure, the degree of integration between IDNs and their physicians was debatable. Many surveys and academic studies conducted during the 1990s demonstrated only lukewarm physician commitment and loyalty to these new hospital systems.[34] An IDN's ability to work with its clinicians on PPIs would depend heavily on the quality of hospital-physician relationships and physician buy-in. Regardless of the reality, suppliers liked the IDNs more than the buying groups due to a perception of greater purchasing discipline (commitment) and competitive advantage in achieving sales targets in local regions where sales executives were accountable. Unlike the GPOs, IDNs also rested heavily on the suppliers' traditional customer, the physician. Suppliers also believed that aggregating the purchases of several dominant, regional IDNs was a more effective way of building market share nationally.

Due to the pressures hospitals faced from (1) rate-setting in the 1970s and (2) DRGs and managed care in the 1980s, they tried to confront the fragmented buying of PPIs and get clinicians to sacrifice their brand preferences for cost savings obtained through group bidding and purchasing. Seasoned supply chain executives commented at the time about the difficulty in getting brand preference out of the picture even for mundane items like toilet paper, and the length of time needed to get a committed volume contract on disposable operating room linens. Part of the problem lay in the oligopolistic structure of the supplier markets in some product areas. In the presence of oligopoly, there was a naturally strong brand preference and no perceived need among suppliers to offer better contracts with lower pricing for products that already enjoyed large market shares. Suppliers responded by selling two levels of product to hospitals: lower cost commodity items (quantity) and higher cost PPI items (perhaps higher quality).

Rationalization of Contracts and GPOs

IDNs begged for integration. Achievement of scale economies required lots of integration and effort, especially in their clinical operations where most of their operating costs lay. But clinical integration with physicians was hard work and took time. A much easier integration target and quicker avenue to savings—and one that did not involve physicians as directly—was the purchasing programs (particularly for commodity medical-surgical items for which clinicians lacked distinct preferences) of the merging hospitals. The net effect of hospital mergers, multi-hospital system building, and IDN formation efforts was a rationalization of supplier contracts: where there were two such contracts prior to the merger, now there was only one. In the likely event that the merging providers contracted with different suppliers, one vendor would be selected to supply the merger while the other would be dropped. This selection was not always straightforward, however: provider mergers might occasion an internal debate over the merits of contracting with one supplier (sole source) or both (dual source). This also represented a clear threat to the incumbent suppliers of the merging providers: which one might get dropped? At the same time, the merging providers also rationalized their respective GPOs which had negotiated the contracts. Thus, where there were two GPOs, now there was just one. With a boom in provider mergers, systems, and IDNs, there was likely to be a shakeout in GPO membership. Purchasing groups would be forced to redouble their recruitment efforts to maintain, let alone gain, market share.

As an illustration, the formation of local IDNs presented a "winner take all" contest for some GPOs. In St. Louis, for example, Barnes Hospital, Jewish Hospital, and Christian Health Services merged to form BJC Health System. Prior to the merger, each hospital had its own GPO (VHA, Premier, and AmHS, respectively). After the merger, BJC studied the three GPO alliances and settled on VHA. Such decisions and GPO consolidation played out across the country. In contrast to the national GPOs, however, IDNs like BJC sought to dominate local markets in inpatient care. The trade literature already carried stories of certain prominent IDNs (e.g., Partners Health Care in Boston, BJC in St. Louis, Continuum Health Partners in New York City) engaging in such strategies, heightening the perceived threat.

Self-Contracting

The IDN threat went further. IDNs formed in great numbers in the 1990s, the same time period as the consolidation of regional GPOs into national GPOs (such as Premier and Novation). Some IDNs engaged in their own purchasing and contracting activities, in effect acting as their own GPOs. There was clearly a trend toward IDNs taking on direct contracting with suppliers, often using sole-source contracts, and sometimes contemplating the establishment of their own in-house GPOs (e.g., the 1997 formation of Continuum Health Partners, the merger of Beth Israel and Roosevelt Hospitals in New York City).

In contrast to the GPOs, the IDNs were based locally or regionally. They thus pursued a local strategy of securing special pricing for hospitals in their local market. Indeed, IDNs had the potential to confront product vendors with a stronger negotiating stance, resist vendor sales terms and programs, and hence drive lower-priced deals than GPOs. The IDNs' ability derived from their smaller numbers (fewer providers to coordinate), greater cohesion (built on local solidarity and common ownership), and closer relationships with clinicians. As high-compliance systems, they did not necessarily wish to subsidize hospital purchasing in GPOs that had a mix of high- and low-compliance members. The potentially greater contracting compliance of IDNs (compared to GPOs) made them more attractive to suppliers, who could drive a greater share in local markets. Their purchasing power also made them somewhat independent of GPOs and their efforts to drive hospital compliance with GPO contracts.

Of course, IDNs needed to conduct their own "make versus buy" analysis regarding whether to (a) take on their own purchasing and distribution, or (b) leave such activities to GPOs and wholesalers. It is not clear whether IDNs actually did the calculus here. If they did, they would need to consider whether or not (1) they could get their clinicians to standardize on certain suppliers, (2) they could afford to invest in more full-time equivalent personnel (FTEs) and information systems needed to do contracting, (3) they could access the same supplies and services outside of a GPO, and (4) their clinicians would use second-tier vendors not on GPO contracts.

The View from the GPOs

Consulting firm and group surveys of IDN executives uncovered several apparent trends that startled the GPO industry. First, IDNs claimed they would shortly centralize the materials management functions across all of their hospital entities, standardize their purchasing, and achieve compliance—thus enabling them to achieve lower levels of pricing, often with the help of suppliers.[35] This would give IDNs competitive advantage in local markets over other hospitals that purchased through the groups. Second, such surveys reported that IDNs would reduce the number of GPOs they use in the near future, thereby increasing GPO competition for members. Third, surveys conducted by SMG Marketing reported a sharp rise in the number of IDNs that qualified as GPOs, that were centralizing their purchasing, and leveraging the GPOs' negotiated prices as benchmarks and ceilings. As a result, IDNs reportedly could purchase more competitively than GPOs.

IDNs thus served as a competitive threat to the regional GPOs and, along with the rise of Columbia/HCA, helped to spur the GPOs' consolidation into a set of national players. The national GPOs had previously pursued a national strategy of "one for all, all for one," and "one size fits all" contracting. They had sought to use their national presence and aggregate their large hospital member purchases to wield negotiating power over suppliers. Such power was based on blended pricing across both high-compliance and low-compliance hospitals.

Now, some IDNs began to limit the number of GPO memberships to just one in hopes of having greater influence over decision-making, greater financial rewards from higher contract compliance, and greater parity with Columbia/HCA. GPOs found themselves confronted with an alternative contracting vehicle that could negotiate equivalent pricing and/or might engage in off-contract buying. Rather than disciplining these hospitals, the GPOs responded by shifting to tiered pricing based on levels of commitment that suited multiple constituents among their members—effectively transforming the GPO into a series of "GPOs within GPOs." The number of pricing tiers they offered possibly suggested the dispersion of buying discipline and compliance within. Many GPOs did not have many other options to deal with noncompliant members, since the latter could be shareholders and were not likely to be kicked out. GPOs also relied on dividends programs to reward compliant hospitals, using a carrot rather than a stick approach.

The ascendance of IDNs and the key role of physicians within them led buying groups to confront physician selection of medical technology and PPIs. GPOs had revolutionized the supply market for commodity products by the early 1980s by virtue of striking national agreements and lower prices with suppliers. The next frontier was non-commodity items like PPIs. PPI contracting reportedly began during the mid-1980s in contracts struck between Ethicon and various hospital systems. Such contracts offered advantages to both parties. Suppliers offered small price discounts and pricing stability; hospitals purchased vendor products in bundles (covered below) and assisted them in gaining access to national accounts (hospitals and systems, not just clinicians).

Buying groups developed "technology forums" in the early 1990s to explore how they might standardize contracting in this product area. Such standardization would require the cooperation of physicians with their hospitals to make joint technology decisions. The forums were largely designed for physician attendees. The buying groups also viewed these forums as an opportunity to take the lead in the burgeoning field of technology assessment and, perhaps, displace the suppliers' sales representatives as the new objective source and filter of data on new products. Physicians' resistance to GPO and hospital compliance programs often rested not on the product selected but on the exclusion of the clinicians from the process and failure to consult them.

Groups also developed a new set of partnerships with small and large vendors in the late 1980s and early 1990s. VHA Supply Company set up a "Technology Development Program" in 1988 to (a) drive some incremental growth in sales (via new products under contract), (b) provide hospital members with early access to new, leading-edge technology and thereby attain some competitive advantage in the local hospital market, (c) enable hospitals to improve their quality of care, and (d) develop the group's capability in research and development. The last objective did not seem far-fetched. Investor-owned hospital systems and some large groups had already developed insurance arms in the mid-1980s as part of a strategy to vertically integrate forward into the payer market; backwards integration into the supplier market seemed equally sensible. Other groups likewise pursued technology partnerships. UHC erected its Technology Advancement Center; both HCA and AmHS established venture capital funds.

National GPO Mergers in the 1990s

By the mid-1990s, the interest in contracting, standardization, and compliance was coupled with a new strategy: mergers to form national GPOs. By 1993, trade journals began writing of a "Darwinian struggle" between the purchasing groups and the emerging IDNs, and argued the industry was ripe for consolidation.[36] All of these competitive forces propelled several of the regional GPOs to merge in the mid-1990s, thereby forming some of the largest purchasing groups in existence today.

These consolidations marked a response to (1) the rise of Columbia/HCA and efforts to duplicate its example, (2) the high purchasing commitment levels demonstrated by AmHS, (3) the threat posed by the IDNs which suggested they could negotiate good contracts with or without a GPO, and (4) hospital executives' calls for better purchasing contracts. Indeed, the hospital members of the GPOs saw all of this as a threat and competitive challenge. They told their GPOs, "we need to do a better job and bring more value to the table," and requested more input in the contract negotiations (i.e., make them more bottom-up rather than just top-down). Hospital mergers, systems building, and IDN formations gave them increased clout with suppliers, forcing GPOs to redouble their efforts and be more responsive.

These consolidations spelled the demise of the state hospital associations and local hospital councils—the seedbed of the early GPOs—and moved them to the purchasing sidelines.[37] Some GPO executives viewed them as an anachronism, "nothing more than an accident of geography." The move away from local hospital councils and associations to IDNs and national GPOs marked the transition from (1) "GPOs as associations" that tried to build consensus among their members and lower their costs to (2) "GPOs as alliances" in which hospitals worked in tandem with the GPOs on strategic issues such as compliance, commitment, and local market share. Some of the emerging national GPO players are profiled below.

Consorta

In 1994, several Catholic organizations (e.g., Daughters of Charity, Holy Cross Health System, Catholic Health Initiatives-Denver) formed a purchasing group called Catholic Materials Management Alliance (CMMA). Four years later, CMMA consolidated with the Sisters of the Sorrowful Mother-Diversified Health Services to form Consorta. Consorta was owned by 13 Catholic healthcare systems and included Catholic Charities USA and more than 900 hospitals. Within two years, it was the third largest GPO in terms of purchasing volume per facility. It was headed by John Strong, who had previously held executive positions at Premier Health Alliance and then Premier and had served as an executive consultant to the Greater New York Hospital Association.

Consorta focused on sole-source contracts with suppliers whenever possible, but otherwise used multi-source contracts. The GPO favored market-leading suppliers for certain contracts, but left supplier choice up to its shareholders whose representatives sat on the GPO's Contracts and Programs Committee. Shareholders promised to use Consorta's contracts exclusively and thereby help the GPO to achieve a high level of compliance. As of mid-1999, the group had negotiated 102 contracts for goods and services, or 60% of its contract portfolio, with goals to increase this to 80% by the end of 2000.

The New Premier

In 1995, Premier merged with American HealthCare Systems (AmHS) and then later that year with SunHealth Alliance—thereby forming "the New Premier." This was a huge organization. The three members of the New Premier consisted of 240 shareholders that represented roughly 700 of the GPO's 1,700 hospitals; the remainder were "affiliates." It had an estimated $10 Billion in annual purchases across the three members, which some analysts equated with one-third of all hospital supply buying. Its combined purchasing volume was three-to-four times greater than that of Columbia/HCA, which posed a profound implication for suppliers (and competing GPOs): anticipated contract concessions from suppliers were of $400–$500 Million annually. Indeed, one consultant opined the savings could approach $800 Million annually.

To reap such savings, Premier's purchasing executive, Lynn Detlor, encouraged the organization to adopt many of the methods he employed at AmHS. Premier challenged its vendors to bring everything they made to the table in a negotiation and get it under contract, thereby reducing both product pricing and variation in product pricing. Bundles thus represented an effort by the GPO to force suppliers to contract and cut prices for items they normally shielded from GPO contracts when they had few competitors. Formation of the New Premier also afforded the opportunity to renegotiate all of the former contracts of the constituent members, have the best product coverage and the top suppliers, develop corporate partners with a small set of manufacturers, and get discounts on previously non-discounted items. Like Columbia/HCA, it also pursued most-favored-nation clauses (tied to hospitals of comparable size and volume) in some of its contracts.

Success with supplier contract concessions rested on contract compliance. AmHS already had a 90% compliance rate, while Premier had launched a program the prior year to get an 80% minimum compliance on select contracts (in exchange for 12% lower prices relative to other Premier contracts). Materials managers at Premier hospitals designed the group's 1994 Committed-Buying program, one of the first among the nonprofit GPOs, that drew on "letters of commitment." The program rewarded hospitals for contract adherence, helped deal with managed care pressures, and competed with the investor-owned systems; the program was not designed to exclude some suppliers. Following Premier, SunHealth also moved to commitment programs and launched ten sole-source contracts in 1995, while VHA responded with its own compliance program ("Opportunity," covered below).

Indeed, consultants told Premier that it could achieve additional savings through larger scale and combined purchasing. In all of these newly merged entities, there was increased emphasis on standardization of vendors, compliance with contracts, use of sole- and dual-source contracts, and use of product portfolios. The impetus for commitment and compliance came largely from Columbia/HCA's announcements and claims of contracting success. In particular, the hospitals located in markets where Columbia/HCA was present pressed their purchasing groups to imitate the investor-owned system.[38]

Success also rested on plans to pursue more sole-source, long-term supplier contracts, as well as corporate partnerships (used previously at AmHS) to develop product bundles with a dozen multi-product vendors that accounted for an estimated 80% of its supply spend. The bundle added a 1–5% further reduction in the price discount achieved by the GPO/IDN, and aimed to add to contracts monopoly items for which suppliers resisted contracts. The New Premier formed a committee of nearly 20 IDNs that provided input on the GPO's contracts and reviewed them prior to awarding the business. The success of the Premier GPO strategy also reportedly rested on the marketplace perception that GPOs obtain competitive contracts, which in turn attracted and retained hospital members, and which required member compliance to support the contracts.

VHA/Novation

In 1996, VHA launched its committed purchasing program ("Opportunity"), which called for 95% compliance with seven suppliers and the use of sole-source contracts in 90% + of VHA's contracts in 13 major supply categories. Compliance was rewarded with lowest pricing and quarterly incentives of 6–8%, and a waiver of annual fees. Opportunity's committed buying was directed at only $2.5 Billion out of $11.2 Billion in overall purchasing, much of it for pharmaceuticals. PPIs were not a focus; rather, VHA focused on products/suppliers where VHA already had a high market share. In 1997, VHA and UHC merged their purchasing to form Novation.

BuyPower/Broadlane

In 1995, National Medical Enterprises (NME) and American Medical International (AMI)—two of the original investor-owned systems that had formed in the late 1960s—merged to become Tenet Healthcare. The two systems had a combined $1.3 Billion in supply and equipment contracts, and a portfolio of 122 med-surg contracts that needed to be either merged or renegotiated; nearly half of those contracts were with competing suppliers. Tenet began a combined purchasing program called BuyPower. Over time, BuyPower would make its contracts available to non-Tenet hospitals. In 1999, the BuyPower GPO was subsumed under Broadlane (a joint venture owned by Tenet and Ventro Corp), which purchased the customer list from Tenet and operated BuyPower as its contracting vehicle. In 2000, Amerinet joined Broadlane to use the same vehicle. Amerinet would own a stake in Broadlane; Broadlane would become a shareholder in Amerinet; and the two would combine their purchasing.

The formation of BuyPower led to supplier rationalization and heightened supplier competition for fewer GPO contracts. BuyPower followed a middle-of-the-road approach to contracting, seeking to combine volume purchasing with a commitment to several suppliers' products, rather than just using sole-source contracts. The latter had potential compliance issues, due to local hospital needs, clinical use, supplier conversion, and pricing. To do so, BuyPower used long-term, sole-source, mandatory compliance contracts for 50 contracts that accounted for roughly 60% of purchases that were non-controversial (large volume commodity items, arcane products). Not all of these contracts were with the market-leading vendor, however; BuyPower sometimes contracted with the number two or three player, if clinicians felt they were superior. Tenet returned 100% of the CAFs earned in these areas to the hospitals. At the same time, Tenet allowed purchasing managers to have flexibility in the other 40% of purchasing that included PPIs (implants, devices, drugs) where standardization and appropriate product use were more difficult to achieve, but yet still worked with hospitals to approve product offerings from several suppliers before awarding any contracts as a process to exert leverage over suppliers.

In the PPI areas, BuyPower was more concerned about product utilization than price or standardization (and getting clinician buy-in on standardizing effective utilization), as well as developing "clinical leaders" in every product category. BuyPower's focus was thus on total cost, not line-item cost, due to the fact that investor-owned systems had supply budgets and spent their own money (which nonprofit GPOs did not). Nevertheless, BuyPower often used price ceilings in orthopedics and the cath lab.

Broadlane entered the market to offer not only group purchasing but also management of the hospital's entire supply chain operation—a function that some of its competitors did not want to assume. One of Broadlane's first customers was Continuum Health Partners in New York City; a second was the Alliance in Cincinnati.

MedAssets

A final GPO profiled here was a dot-com firm, MedAssets Exchange. MedAssets did not start out as a GPO but instead focused on developing creative approaches to supply chain cost reduction and revenue enhancement for members. The company began with an acquisition of Comdisco's equipment refurbishing business (e.g., for imaging equipment) as well as a provider of mobile MRI services. It realized that it would have limited ability to write contracts or create a more efficient procurement model without a GPO solution. Fortunately for MedAsssets, it was venture-backed and enjoyed access to capital to make acquisitions. It soon did so by purchasing two GPOs: InSource Hospital Services (Chatsworth, CA) in 1998 and then Axis Point Health Services (Murietta, CA). Although a startup, MedAssets developed some deep GPO roots through the first of these deals. InSource Hospital Services was the former Purchase Connection, which was the new name for the Council of Shared Services (CSS), the shared services division of the Hospital Council of Southern California. In 2001, MedAssets expanded further by acquiring HSCA in 2001. The company then changed the name of its supply chain business to MedAssets Supply Chain and Business Services Group.

MedAssets was neither hospital-owned nor an owner of hospitals. This allowed it to have a lower cost structure and be more responsive to what its hospital members wanted. For example, MedAssets developed an individual member fee-sharing arrangement with hospitals whereby the shareback CAFs were based on one's own purchases. This allowed it to recruit members from Novation and Premier who were not shareholders and thus did not receive annual dividends on the purchases they made. In contrast to Premier and Novation, MedAssets also adopted a "back to the future," multi-source contracting approach which could accommodate smaller suppliers and could obtain the products that member hospitals wanted. Nevertheless, like AmeriNet, MedAssets developed its own committed purchasing program ("Select") for members who wanted better pricing. Like Broadlane, MedAssets' contract portfolio was thus a hybrid of a core group of national contracts combined with customized local contracts. There was no bundling and no threshold compliance programs. MedAssets also partnered with Aspen Healthcare Metrics to benchmark hospital resource utilization in PPI areas to find the greatest sources of saving opportunities (whether product price or utilization such as lengths of stay and ancillary use).

MedAssets served as a disruptor since it did not have much overhead after its acquisitions and it did not have to split up the revenues obtained from suppliers (since it was private). It also focused on services beyond contracting and group purchasing, prompting incumbent GPOs to expand their service offerings to include consulting and data analytics. So, it too turned to recruit the local hospital councils (e.g., the Metropolitan Chicago Health-care Council, in 2006) and members of those associations, often pulling them away from both Amerinet and HPPI by offering their hospitals a bigger chunk of the revenue sharing.

GPO Merger Impacts

Several of these mergers shook the world, just as the Columbia/HCA deal had previously done. The new GPOs were much larger in size and worked to pursue scale economies in purchasing not previously achieved. Moreover, the newly merged, national GPOs pursued many of the strategies utilized by Columbia/HCA: committed purchasing, compliance, standardization, supplier rationalization using sole- and/or dual-source contracts, product bundles, corporate programs, and centralized control.

The uniformity in strategy across GPOs reflected their common need to compete with Columbia/HCA (which employed them in a seemingly successful manner), to obtain lower hospital prices, and to reduce hospital supply costs. Not only was Columbia/HCA reportedly achieving better supply contracts but it was also utilizing its lower product acquisition and handling costs (estimated to be 30% of a hospital's cost structure) to get more managed care contracts by virtue of offering a lower cost product (i.e., cheaper inpatient costs). Hospital executives reportedly prompted their purchasing groups to merge in order to obtain better contracts.[39] Not surprisingly, hospitals reportedly liked the contracts their groups signed and did not leave. Columbia/HCA became known as the model that other groups needed to imitate due to its competitive advantages. Imitation of the Columbia/HCA model also served to satisfy the dictates of managed care for reduced costs and variability of care.

Competitive and Institutional Isomorphism

The modeling of GPOs upon one another represented an example of (a) "competitive isomorphism"—competing for the same customers and resources, as well as (b) "institutional isomorphism"—defined by sociologists as an imitative process that compels one firm in a population to resemble other firms facing the same set of environmental conditions for normative reasons (i.e., it is the appropriate and acceptable thing to do). There was now less variation among the GPOs; there was also less variability between the GPOs and the IDNs.

Declining GPO Variation

In prior decades, there were several large, national, nonfederal GPOs with a variety of owners. Some, like Columbia/HCA and Broadlane, were formed by investor-owned, multi-hospital systems (HCA and Tenet, respectively) to purchase supplies for their owned (and contract-managed) hospitals. Due to common ownership and centralized accounts payable and information systems, such GPOs achieved higher hospital compliance with their purchase contracts. Another GPO, MedAssets, was initially backed by venture capitalists and served mainly nonprofit hospitals. Membership and/or participation in MedAssets was more voluntary in nature, compared to the investor-owned GPOs. The remaining GPOs (e.g., Premier, Novation, Amerinet, Consorta), all nonprofit in ownership, developed out of two different models. On the one hand, some were shareholder models (Premier, Novation, SunHealth, American Healthcare Systems) in which the GPOs were owned by their hospital members who participated for various reasons. On the other hand, some were pure GPOs (Amerinet, HSCA, MedEcon, JPC) which engaged only in group purchasing, had no hospital members, and received small membership fees from hospitals.

By the 1990s, the lines between these latter two nonprofit GPO models began to blur. In contrast to the investor-owned GPOs and MedAssets, the nonprofit GPOs began to be distinguished by being cooperative networks. The shift to cooperative models was occasioned by the need to deliver more value to shareholders and to confront the growing tide of IDNs now forming. Membership and participation in these GPOs are also voluntary in nature.

Declining Variabililty Between GPOs and IDNs

In addition to the blurring among the GPOs, there was also a blurring of GPOs and IDNs. In 1998, the SMG consulting group reported that 48% of IDNs had established centralized purchasing and were engaged in direct contracting. They also reported an increase in the number of IDNs qualifying as GPOs from 9 in 1990 to 297 by 1998. GPOs accommodated the growing number of IDNs within their ranks by looking the other way when they strayed from national GPO contracts (e.g., AmeriNet's "elite" program), tailoring special offerings for them and helping them strike separate deals with vendors (e.g., AmeriNet's "options" program in which the GPO and the IDN develop the contract together), and developing more regional groupings among their members. These GPOs did a balancing act between national contracts and GPO/IDN-negotiated contracts. The options program allowed suppliers to target specific IDNs without affecting pricing within the rest of the GPO.

Efforts to Differentiate

While the new playing field of national GPOs pursued many of the same strategies pioneered by Columbia/HCA, some nevertheless sought to distinguish themselves from one another (see Chapter 8). As noted above, AmHS utilized dual-source contracts with mandatory compliance; Columbia HCA sought to dominate local hospital markets; VHA pursued a more regional approach but offered value-added services in information systems, clinical improvement, and supply chain management.

Aftermath: Whole Lotta Shakin' Going On

Falling Product Prices

The movement to national GPOs, committed contracts, and sole-source agreements reportedly helped to hold down hospital supply prices by the mid-1990s. This, along with the managed care revolution which prompted many of these changes in purchasing, may have contributed to the deceleration in national health expenditures (NHE) in the U.S. NHE spending increases reached their nadir in 1996. The concomitant movement to risk-sharing contracts with suppliers may also have contributed to (or at least reinforced) the 1990s' trend toward capitated payment.

During the latter half of the 1990s, the economics of contracting (i.e., the need to achieve lower prices and costs) became more important to hospitals and their purchasing groups than did physician preference, brand preference, and product choice.[40] A near-perfect storm swept through the hospital industry, pushing providers in the low-cost direction. HMO penetration reached its zenith in 1996, just as the rate of increase in NHE reached its nadir. HMOs were notorious for sacrificing patient choice of providers for lower costs and premiums. The falling insurance underwriting cycle meant that health insurance premiums were rising at their lowest rates and that providers were negotiating low reimbursement (or even worse, low percent of capitation) rates. The Balanced Budget Act of 1997 further constrained hospital revenues, resulting in negative Medicare margins at many hospitals.

The market witnessed a new wave of price competition among product manufacturers. The New Premier reportedly obtained prices 20–30% lower than those of the premerger partners. Part of the shock was generated by the groups' willingness to change suppliers when contracts were renegotiated following the mergers. By selecting DuPont over Kodak for X-Ray film, and by selecting Mallinckrodt over Nycomed and Bracco for contrast media, Premier reportedly "sent a message" to suppliers that it was willing to contract with non-market-leading suppliers in order to get its members a better deal. In a similar fashion, Tenet contracted with Microsurge for its reusable trocars to send the signal it was willing to contract with non-market leaders. Tenet also competitively bid many of its products following its merger, rather than re-negotiating the existing contract.

Supplier price wars were a two-edged sword for GPOs, however. On the one hand, hospitals received lower prices. On the other hand, vendors faced lower profitability on their GPO contracts; non-contracted vendors cut prices even more to try to wean business away from GPO members. With across-the-board price cutting and "a race to the bottom," GPO contracts became more homogeneous. Moreover, non-GPO hospitals might obtain similar terms on their own.

Of course, it was possible that the low prices hospitals realized in their own agreements were the result of their GPO agreements' past success in keeping prices down. Moreover, the lower prices these hospitals got by going it alone led them to withdraw from GPO competitive bids which then translated into higher prices paid later to suppliers (and perhaps higher prices that suppliers stuck to the GPOs). Alternatively, a single hospital might be able to negotiate a lower price when its GPO had problems with members' commitment to volume thresholds. Such observations potentially explain two important results that would come to light later on: (1) GPOs do not always obtain lower prices compared to hospitals and (2) suppliers may try to make group purchasing ineffective so they can raise prices. GPOs had always encountered troubles with hospital compliance to their contracts since hospitals could cherry-pick other GPO contracts and entertain offers from non-contracted vendors who counter-detailed the incumbent GPO. As a result of such opportunistic behavior, some suppliers became skeptical of GPO and hospital system claims to deliver compliance and either (a) did not renew such contracts and/or (b) did not extend favorable pricing.

This led GPOs to stop announcing prices and to start using rebates and dividends to reward the hospital members of "cooperatives" for their compliance. Such rewards programs had their roots in the 1980s when some GPOs (VHA, Premier) were founded as or switched to cooperatives in order to reward shareholders and affiliates for using their contracts. Starting in 1996, VHA paid out 100% of its net income to members as dividends; in 1999, Premier raised its dividends from 50 to 80%.

Growing Ties and Cohesion Between GPOs and Hospitals

At the same time, the developments over the past decade led to closer relationships between the GPO and its hospital members. For years, hospitals had been on the receiving end of opportunistic supplier pricing—never getting the same price twice, and never getting the same price from hospital to hospital within a given local system. The absence of rational pricing naturally led hospitals into the arms of groups with power to negotiate contracts (that promised) to standardize and stabilize prices. After getting pricing relief, hospitals next realized they needed help in two additional areas: purchased services and professional services (e.g., utilization studies, utilization management). They also needed help with the proliferation of supplies and stock-keeping units (SKUs), and more professional management of materials management and supply chain functions. For example, hospitals could routinely use 60,000 supply items; some institutions used 100,000. This was a tedious and difficult task—and one that did not fit well with the hospital's supposed mission to provide high-quality clinical care. The 1990s suggested that the main goal of the 1980s—large group size to leverage lower prices—was now coming to fruition in the presence of two new elements to the equation: the rise of IDNs rather than small hospitals as GPO members, and the growing acceptance of committed contracts. As noted above, the latter was now actually demanded by the GPOs' membership.

Growing Ties Between GPOs and Manufacturers

The national, consolidating GPOs sought contracts with a smaller number of consolidated, diversified manufacturers. This helped to reinforce the purchasing groups' tendency to contract with market-leading suppliers. Such contracts offered efficiencies that IDNs and groups felt they needed in order to survive. At the same time, groups had to deal with the large diversified manufacturers because the latter offered the products that hospitals and physicians wanted, and the groups could not achieve any level of contract compliance or product coverage with other suppliers.

The name of the game in group purchasing had always been "leverage": by virtue of joining a GPO, hospitals could buy-in volume and leverage suppliers for pricing discounts. However, a new type of leverage now began to emerge (particularly in specific product areas such as PPIs)—that a select group of suppliers enjoyed. The Daughters of Charity switched vendors for wound closure products from Davis & Geck to Ethicon, despite the fact that Ethicon pricing was higher. The system had trouble getting compliance with Davis & Geck's products and swung over to Ethicon which had a dominant market share and strong relationships with its surgeons. This marked an early example of contracting for products with a supplier that most hospitals would comply with (even if the prices might be higher). This new generation of GPO contracts was based on mutual leverage and mutual benefit. Vendor leverage was based on a strong product franchise and physician preference. It showed that GPOs might be better off working with the market-leading suppliers rather than try to "bulk up against them," and that contracting for PPIs may require a win–win between the buying group and the supplier. Finally, according to some heads of purchasing, the group could make more money with a contract that featured higher penetration but a lower discount, compared to a contract with lower penetration and a higher discount. That is, compliance may trump price.

The period witnessed considerable supplier investments in specific GPOs and their contracting requirements—investments that might be hard to unwind. To paraphrase one analyst, vendors realized that if they go to the prom with GPOs, they cannot go home with IDNs. Close relationships between large vendors and large GPOs meant that smaller suppliers might partner with and find business opportunities among IDNs and hospital systems.

Contract compliance was not just a task for investor-owned GPOs with centralized payable systems. Manufacturers had a stake in contract compliance and, thus, increased purchases; they worked with nonprofit GPOs which often lacked centralized systems. Manufacturer sales representatives would often ask hospital managers of the operating room or the cath lab what products/vendors they used; reps would also do some rough calculations regarding the number of procedures that would be conducted in a hospital of that size and calculate their market share. Manufacturers would then feed this information back to the GPOs they contracted with to assist them in calculating hospital compliance, thus viewing the GPOs as their customer. Hospital VPMMs viewed the GPOs as (a) their agents, (b) middlemen and someone to help them reduce the number of full-time equivalent (FTE) employees doing contracting, or (c) both.

Suppliers pursued other strategies to increase the perceived value of their offerings to GPOs and IDNs. Some set up "account managers" to resolve problems that customers had with any product division at a diversified manufacturer. Suppliers also entered the realms of disease management and outcomes studies that (a) placed their products in a broader context relevant to managed care and (b) lessened the role and importance of price discounts. Suppliers also entered the world of capitated healthcare by experimenting with risk-sharing and capitated programs with IDNs. Finally, suppliers switched from "one price fits all" to tiered pricing programs that suited the different needs and capabilities of hospitals within an IDN. This switch suited the growing role of managed care and payer pricing pressures in local markets, which meant that group purchasing needed to switch away from a national approach with a large membership to a localized approach with fewer members. This included efforts to address and serve the "alternate site market"—the physician offices and non-hospital sites that IDNs now accumulated under their roofs. All of this signaled the importance of decentralizing and regionalizing the services offered by the large nationral GPOs, and helping local hospitals with local solutions to their specific problems.

Bigger GPOs, Bigger IDNs ... Bigger Vendors

Buyer consolidation may have fostered the consolidation of suppliers. Purchasing groups and suppliers were ambivalent about each other's consolidation, as well as the emergence of large hospital buyers (systems and IDNs). For suppliers, the consolidated buyers increased the rewards/costs of winning the contract and the risks of losing it. Suppliers both bragged that they could win a contract with Columbia/HCA and resented having to give up major price concessions to win it. On the other hand, if suppliers lost a contract and the group achieved compliance with a competitor, the supplier could lose market share.

For their part, purchasing groups could get more products under contract, develop more value-adding programs for members, and thus earn greater savings for hospital members and greater administrative fees. On the other hand, the existence of long-term contracts with a single vendor could lead to a decrease in the number of smaller players in the product market (e.g., due to acquisition by the larger incumbents or market exit—both occasioned by a loss of share), complacency by the incumbent, reluctance by excluded suppliers to bid in the future for the group's business, and huge costs of conversion if the group ever wished to switch suppliers that might swamp any savings.

Nevertheless, it is unlikely that GPOs fostered oligopolies found in the various manufacturing sectors. Analyses of the consolidation of the pharmaceutical sector reveal little influence of the GPOs: consolidation of the former began years before consolidation of the latter.[41] Consolidation in the medical technology sector was often spurred by manufacturer diversification out of stalled or slower growth product lines into higher growth product lines and the search for innovative products that may not be made in-house (see Chapter 14).

Vendor Choice and PPIs

The impact of GPO mergers, hospital mergers, supplier mergers, distributor mergers, and long-term contracts posed some disquieting issues going forward. Would there be less product choice for clinicians? Would there be less frequent choice? Would clinicians still play a major role in such choice? Would there be fewer opportunities to switch vendors if performance issues arose? And would GPOs become dependent on CAFs as their major revenue stream, which might reinforce the status quo?

Purchasing groups had to walk a tightrope between the need to reduce costs to compete with Columbia/HCA and IDNs, the need to survive under managed care and Medicare reimbursement cuts, and the need to maintain competition among suppliers and allow hospital members some choice. It was always in the groups' interest to foster supplier competition for their business. Getting more vendors on contract meant greater administration fees for the group, more choice for hospitals, and greater access to small suppliers; however, too many vendors under contract undermined the whole point of group buying, i.e., exchanging greater exclusivity for lower prices. Hospitals viewed GPOs and their contracts as a solution to the dilemmas posed by healthcare cost containment, healthcare reform, and supplier competition. The question facing GPOs was where to turn next for efficiencies? Consolidation of the buying groups was potentially reaching its limits.

Perhaps the future lay in helping hospitals reduce costs on their PPIs (20–40% of items that accounted for as much as 60–80% of their costs), in their internal supply chain management, or in the development of a formulary approach to supplies (compare similar products on their therapeutic merits or inter-changeability). Formularies were being utilized by pharmacy benefit managers (PBMs) to manage pharmaceuticals in the retail chain; perhaps GPOs could utilize them in the institutional chain. Formularies held out the potential for savings on price and price changes, reduced purchase orders, reduced inventory, and improved productivity of personnel. Such an approach had been trialed at Group Health Cooperative in working with Becton Dickinson. PPI contracting picked up steam in the latter half of the 1990s as GPOs tackled new product areas such as diagnostic systems, laboratory equipment, spinal implants, and cardiovascular devices (e.g., VHA's clinical markets program).

Vendor Partnerships

The mergers also raised some interesting possibilities going forward. What were once adversarial and arms-length negotiations between buyers and sellers had evolved into more committed "partnerships" and "corporate agreements." The group purchasing arrangements of the 1980s laid the foundation in the 1990s for committed purchasing, private label programs, proprietary distribution, product bundles, and product bundles in specific therapeutic areas and procedures ("clinical markets programs") to serve disease management efforts. In the current (2020s) era of value-based purchasing where suppliers seek to work with providers on utilization of high-value technologies (i.e., that improve quality and lower total cost), such partnerships might prove helpful. Of course, not all GPO executives believed that such partnerships were developing; some opined that GPO-supplier relationships were inherently adversarial, based on different objectives, and had not changed over time.

Some Disquieting Issues Regarding Small Manufacturers

If the "partnership scenario" was valid, where did small vendors with potentially innovative technologies fit into this picture? Some analysts argued that group purchasing naturally lent itself to a "closed marketplace" with large buyers getting lower prices on a range of products made by large sellers. Buyer leverage often rested on minimizing perceived differences among the manufacturers' product offerings in order to have a credible threat of switching; that is, price trumped technological features. Of course, GPOs were not entirely successful in making this argument and exercising this leverage, as evidenced by hospital trials of seemingly generic products (such as sutures and endomechanicals; see Chapter 6). GPOs also did not keep innovative technologies made by small suppliers off of the market; but, due to their small size and sales forces, these suppliers had difficulty getting onto GPO contracts (see Chapters 5 and 6).

It is not clear that GPOs consciously strategized to keep them off contract; rather, GPOs may have focused instead on keeping non-innovative manufacturers making me-too, comparable products off contract. If that is true, then the GPO's function was to keep off contract those products that claimed to be innovative but lacked the evidence to substantiate it.[42] It was perhaps silly to think that GPOs could keep innovative technologies out of the hands of clinicians who wanted to use them in patient procedures, given that an estimated 30–50% of hospital member spend occurred off-contract. Indeed, for PPIs, many large GPOs like Novation created dual- and multi-source contracts, which appear to have grown in utilization over time; by the early 2000s, 90% of Novation contracts for PPIs were multi-source.

GPOs thus indeed did a balancing act between (1) getting more suppliers on contract who made products that physicians and hospital members wanted to use, which would increase CAFs, and (2) limiting the number of suppliers which undergirded the historical rationale for group purchasing and asking hospitals to abide by such constraints in order to induce suppliers to reduce pricing. In practice, this meant contracting with the top two or three vendors, excluding the remaining vendors, but still leaving the door open to small innovative suppliers who delivered higher-value (higher quality and/or lower price) products. To be sure, suppliers that had truly innovative products with no competitors that clinicians wanted to use did not need a GPO contract; GPOs needed competing products in order to be effective. Moreover, GPOs developed "technology breakthrough" programs to locate and contract with product innovators.

The New Playbook and Market Conduct: GPO Contracting Strategies

The preceding section outlines the new GPO market structure: the growing size and concentration among GPO players. It is also important to look at the new market conduct: the contracting strategies and activities the GPOs used to compete. Both would end up being the focus of intense Federal Government scrutiny after 2000 as possibly anticompetitive (topic of Chapter 5). But it is clear that both market structure and (especially) market conduct had roots that went back decades. This section switches from a market structure analysis of the GPO players to a market conduct analysis of GPO contracting strategies. For ease of exposition, we break them out by historical period (1970s/1980s vs. 1990s).

The Emergence of Contract Compliance

1970s/1980s

Starting in the 1970s, compliance with group-negotiated contracts began to be recognized as a legitimate means to lower hospital spending on supplies. National chains of investor-owned hospitals (Humana, HCA) developed committed purchasing contracts with manufacturers on either a sole-source or dual-source basis.

Trade news reports of local hospital councils entering committed volume contracts with suppliers, as well as supplier efforts to avoid such contracts or break them up, became commonplace by the end of the 1970s.[43] Committed volume contracts received an impetus from reports that the Federal Government was using its committed volume purchasing clout to obtain favorable pricing on supplies purchased for its 427 hospitals (Veterans Administration, Department of Defense, Public Health Service) through the General Services Administration, the Veterans Administration supply depot system, and the Defense Supply Agency.[44] Additional impetus came from a General Accounting Office (GAO) report in early 1980 that found that hospitals in the same geographic area paid widely different prices for the same items.[45] The GAO argued that hospitals could save millions of dollars by having an intermediary gather pricing information for them. Following the failure of President Carter's hospital cost containment bill to get through Congress, the Department of Health & Human Services (DHHS) proposed legislation to allow Medicare and Medicaid to pay for certain supplies through group purchasing arrangements and competitively bid contracts, with providers required to obtain supplies from manufacturers under contract with their state or DHHS.[46] Committed contracting "was in the air."

Prodded by their member hospitals, most GPOs developed committed purchasing programs. Many did not succeed to the extent that Columbia/HCA did, due to their much larger membership base, their formation as mergers of regional GPOs, and their initial lack of infrastructure to manage national contracts. While some GPOs (Novation, MedAssets) backed away within a decade, they still maintained "best price arrangements" with some manufacturers whereby they got the best price by buying a certain percentage from them.

As the 1980s and the first round of group-supplier contracts drew to a close, suppliers perceived they had suffered price/profit erosion without any commensurate increase in market share. That is, the existence of contracts with hospital groups did not guarantee any incremental sales volume. Manufacturers of intravenous (IV) products reportedly achieved a 1% increase in market share in return for a 30% drop in their price. Supply chain consultants at the time stated that the purchasing groups were having trouble consistently achieving 50% contract commitment.[47] Contract compliance levels ranged from roughly 30–40% in the pure GPOs to maybe 50–60% in the shareholder models. Suppliers wanted such compliance in their early GPO contracts in exchange for discounting their product prices. Compliance was not yet a major issue for hospitals, however, and would not become so until the rise of larger investor-owned hospital systems in the 1990s.

At the same time, hospital members began to question whether their groups delivered on all of their promises.[48] Not all hospitals were happy with their GPO contracts. In older times, GPOs offered their members standardized pricing irrespective of the amounts purchased off of the GPO's contract. This scheme was designed to offer an even playing field to smaller hospitals who purchased smaller volumes. Larger hospitals, however, felt they were subsidizing the smaller hospitals;[49] they wanted better pricing that reflected their higher purchasing volumes.

Perhaps reflecting the coming shift to regional or local contracting, many groups began to dissolve or fragment. In 1989, one of the four founding members of Amerinet, HSCA, left the group. That same year, three prominent members of VHA left to join rival groups or form their own. In 1990, conflicts over management and regional differences led to a split in the Group Purchasing Alliance/USA group. In 1990, the national Adventist system was also dismantled. In 1991, the purchasing arm of the Greater Cleveland Hospital Association ended its affiliation with MedEcon and joined with Premier.

1990s

By the 1990s, contract compliance began to be viewed by groups as a major strategy to grow their purchasing volume, rather than membership growth, just as contract fees became the major source of GPO cash flow rather than hospital membership fees. Premier, for example, began converting its commodity and specialty contracts with vendor partners to committed contracts. Part of this new perspective was driven by manufacturers' dissatisfaction with the low levels of compliance achieved in first-generation national contracts signed during the mid-1980s. Part of this was also driven by the intense competition among the groups for a declining number of hospitals, and particularly competition with investor-owned groups.[50] Groups sought to attract new members through compliance programs that would lower their costs. Groups also transitioned their organizational models to cooperative structures (e.g., VHA in 1990) that could reward hospital members with cash payments for greater use of group programs.[51] VHA, UHC, and Premier had already been organized as cooperatives; now others such as SunHealth reorganized in this fashion. Cooperative models served the additional purpose of distributing to hospital members the growing contract fees collected from suppliers and thereby responding to growing criticisms that the groups were growing wealthy at their members' expense.

By the end of the 1990s, roughly two-thirds of purchasing groups had developed committed-buying programs.[52] Compliance levels varied considerably across GPO and hospital systems. According to one analyst,[53] vendors could expect compliance levels in the following ranges by account:

• Investor-owned hospital systems	70–95%
• Nonprofit hospital systems	60–85%
• Pure GPOs	35–65%
• Hospital alliances and associations	35–75%
• Government accounts	25–95%

One reason for compliance issues was the structure and composition of the buying groups. Compliance may have required a national accounts program that could adequately serve each affiliate and each geographic segment. Many groups (e.g., VHA in 1987, SunHealth in 1992) felt that regional clusters of hospital members could align their purchases more closely and achieve higher contract compliance levels—mimicking the competitive advantage of IDNs.[54] Suppliers likewise espoused the view that smaller networks of hospitals could deliver market share and reportedly began to give better pricing to such customers.

As a consequence, the earlier strategy of national accounts and corporate partnerships was called into question. Suppliers sought to end the price wars of the 1980s and the discounts offered to groups and sought to raise prices and increase profits. The new round of competition now focused on the groups and their ability to (a) deliver value to the vendors and (b) discipline their hospital members' utilization of contracts.

Nevertheless, it is important to state that contract compliance was not always the main goal. Purchasing groups were more concerned with the use of a GPO contract and less concerned with contract compliance. Compliance benefits accrued to the hospital and the supplier, while contract use benefits accrued to the GPO. GPOs might be indifferent to which supplier the hospital used, as long as that vendor was under contract.

Standardization and Sole-Source Contracting

1970s/1980s

Unlike the nonprofit hospitals, the investor-owned chains standardized on both the branded products they bought (e.g., purchasing from one supplier such as Johnson & Johnson, or J&J) as well as the procedures performed (e.g., utilize one type of dressing applied after surgery). Nonprofit hospitals followed suit, partly as a response to the investor-owned hospitals and partly as a response to the perceived competitive threat of investor-owned contract management hospital companies (which claimed hospital supply cost reductions of 5%).[55] Local groups feared that (a) these contract management firms could reduce hospital supply costs using nationwide contracts, (b) nonprofit hospitals would be lured away from the groups to participate in these firms, and (c) suppliers would support these firms more than the purchasing groups. Letters of commitment to purchase only from contracted vendors (typically using dual-source contracts) were signed by hospital members of the nonprofit Adventist Health Services, a national chain of seventy facilities. Groups also began to put more critical care items out to bid, showing a willingness of their hospital members to sacrifice brand preference for a lower cost. Standardization of supplies was linked to other standardizing management techniques popular at the time, such as standardized hospital design, case-cart systems, and inventory control systems. Standardization was "in the air."

1990s

Standardization efforts targeted at supplies became more common as a method to confront rising supply costs while reimbursements were fixed or reduced. Systems and groups commonly set up committees of clinicians to select specific suppliers for such contracts.[56] More broadly, standardization efforts were oftentimes undertaken system-wide when IDNs and multi-hospital systems faced financial difficulties (e.g., when investor-owned chains like Tenet faced high debt in the late 1990s after its merger and again in 2003 following the fall in its stock price).

There were many pros and cons to standardization. On the plus side, standardization pitted supplier against supplier in competitive bidding wars. It also represented something that hospitals could do on the inside to increase efficiency, once manufacturers and distributors had been squeezed enough on the price and service levels they offered. Standardization also offered another vehicle to cost containment that did not rely on cutting staff, which was heavily nursing-oriented and which impacted the quality of patient care. On the minus side, standardization efforts were challenged by the diversity of participants within a given IDN and their prior lack of collaboration. These participants had never shared data before, let alone medical staff, which made standardization unlikely in the near term. They were further challenged (and distracted) by the 1990s' mantra of developing a seamless continuum of care and aligning with their physicians—tasks that may have been unachievable, particularly because standardization suggested some level of reducing clinician discretion and choice.[57]

The standardization savings potential in healthcare was not as great as in other sectors, according to McKinsey: 5–10% in healthcare versus 20% in manufacturing, 25–35% in automakers, and 35% in electronics.[58] Still, for an average hospital with $50 million in revenues, savings of $2 million provided a big margin boost in the era of managed care. The GPOs' specialty was standardization in commodity items that could lead to cost savings of 5–10%; areas not quite in the GPOs' wheelhouse were PPI items (another 5–10% cost savings potentially) and utilization management (15% cost savings potential). Savings in the latter two areas would rest more on hospital initiative, at least in the short-term; over time, the national GPOs would help hospitals with them.

GPOs noticed one major upside to sole-source contracts. Suppliers that lost out in a GPO's sole-source contracting process reportedly "beat a path" to other GPOs in order to compete for their business. But GPOs were also beginning to notice a major downside of sole-source and bundled contracting: they favored incumbent suppliers and led to a possible decline in competition among suppliers and thus less choice. GPOs realized they may need to spur supplier competition, perhaps through private label programs.

Contract Administration Fees (CAFs)

1970s/1980s

Contract administration fees (CAFs) were not a customary business practice of the early GPOs. The investor-owned hospital systems initially held the view that "we don't charge our other suppliers these fees" and instead viewed contracting as part of their operating costs. Nonprofit buying groups began as shared service, information sharing, and collegial organizations; fees were not part of their business plan. Still other organizations (e.g., mission-based systems) may have viewed the charging of fees as an ethical problem.

Beginning in the 1970s (and perhaps even earlier on a scattered basis) and by the early 1980s, GPOs realized they could get vendors to pay these fees. Although controversial, suppliers viewed them as a cost of doing business with the groups. CAFs became widespread industry practice by the late 1980s. Industry analysts concluded that hospitals consciously chose a system in which GPO funding came from suppliers rather than from hospital membership fees, as hospitals preferred to have external funding of GPO administrative costs rather than contract fees passed onto hospitals in the form of slightly lower product prices. The switch from membership fees to CAFs removed any barriers to hospital use of purchasing groups and encouraged even further utilization of GPO contracts. Moreover, by the 1980s, such fees represented a huge source of income to the buying groups, while hospital membership fees constituted only a token amount. Vendor fees were "in the air."

Not all suppliers paid these fees, however. Buying groups that requested payment of CAFs entered a "game of chicken" with suppliers. Manufacturers of medical-surgical products blinked and paid the fees. By contrast, pharmaceutical manufacturers who sold branded drugs for which there were no product substitutes resisted the fees.

Groups continued to form and diffuse to help hospitals deal with reimbursement (and thus income) pressures from payers, at the same time that they were dealing with the rising cost of supplies. With their members caught in this financial squeeze, hospital associations utilized CAFs paid by suppliers to develop shared services that might benefit members as well as reduce hospital membership fees. Vendor fees arose as a means to finance shared service activities of hospitals (particularly group purchasing of medical-surgical supplies) and relieve hospitals of the rising cost containment pressures they were facing from public and private sector payers.

1990s

CAFs enjoyed several tailwinds as the 1990s began. The DHHS safe harbor permitting CAFs up to three percent was released by 1991. Subsequently, the Department of Justice (DOJ) and Federal Trade Commission (FTC) established an antitrust safety zone for joint purchasing arrangements in 1993 in "Statement 7" of their antitrust guidelines. To fall within the safety zone, GPOs must meet a two-part test: purchases through the GPO account for less than 35% of the total sales of the product in the relevant market, and the cost of the products purchased through the GPO accounts for less than 20% of the total revenues from all products sold by each GPO member.[59] A decade later, the FTC and DOJ elected to maintain Statement 7 after hearings were held on GPO activities in both the Senate and the FTC.[60]

The question naturally arises, why did suppliers pay the CAFs? There are several possible explanations. First, as my economist colleagues like to argue, if they existed and persisted, there must be some value in them. Second, they served as "the entry fee" or a "hunting license" to access a large customer base. Third, they could potentially lower a supplier's selling costs. Fourth, they could potentially increase a supplier's sales and local market penetration.

The Emergence of Product Portfolios and Bundles

1970s/1980s

Many groups engaged in contracts with large, diversified manufacturers for a portfolio of their products ("bundles"). For hospitals, these portfolios performed two cost-saving functions. First, in an effort to gain economies of scope, they reduced the cost of contracting by switching *from* contracts with multiple suppliers for single items *to* contracts with a single supplier for multiple items. Second, in an effort to gain economies of scale, they sought to get as many products that hospitals ordered from suppliers under contract, thereby reducing not only the unit price for the product but also variability in the prices that hospitals within a group or system paid for that product. For hospitals now faced with prospective payment in the mid-1980s, bundled product purchases might serve as a cost-cutting vehicle to deal with the newly bundled DRG payments for inpatient services and perhaps to standardize services.

For suppliers, bundles represented a natural evolution of product line development, product diversification, and technological differentiation. For diversified manufacturers, bundled packages of products might also be useful for selling and managing under bundled payments. Some vendors embarked on a bundle strategy long ago to use their strong market position in one product area to cross-sell products with a lesser market presence. Such efforts often ran counter to hospital preferences for a "best of breed" approach— contract with separate suppliers who made the best products in a given area—rather than a broad portfolio approach.

By the late 1980s, the vast majority (88%) of purchasing groups (GPOs and hospital systems) reported they had agreements with diversified manufacturers and their products which cut across hospital departments. For example, by 1989, Amerinet had signed a long-term (five years) bundled contract with Eli Lilly for multiple categories of drugs. Product bundles were "in the air." Some of the GPO bundling activities and programs are delineated below.

VHA

The earliest bundled portfolios emerged in the late 1970s and mid-1980s. In 1979, VHA signed a corporate agreement with a large manufacturer/distributor, American Hospital Supply (AHS), that rewarded VHA with reduced pricing and rebates based on member hospital purchases from a number of AHS product divisions. AHS had developed as the largest hospital distributor by virtue of offering its hospital customers volume discounts and information systems to help them manage their product procurement, inventory, and distribution activities. Such services were targeted at a new set of customers—hospital managers and executives—rather than the traditional clinician customer of new products. In this manner, AHS helped hospitals manage "the other dollar": for every dollar spent on a product, a hospital spent another dollar on product procurement and logistics.

At the time, AHS had roughly 35% share of the market nationally but was only the number two or three player in many local markets. AHS used its national contracts with GPOs to build its local market share by getting more business with local hospitals. In this manner, AHS helped to underwrite a lot of the local and regional hospital GPOs, which before this time had little revenue.

AHS and Hospital Corporation of America (HCA)

HCA's portfolio strategy developed from its failed 1985 merger (vertical integration) with AHS, a large products distributor. Hospitals used AHS as their prime vendor and were fearful of being held up; AHS was fearful of losing its hospital customers. Baxter blocked the merger because it might lose HCA as a customer, and acquired AHS instead in a $3.8 Billion deal. This began a "divorce settlement" between HCA and AHS. The Baxter-AHS deal included a controversial five-year agreement whereby (a) HCA agreed to purchase a stipulated, graduated dollar volume (estimated at a minimum of $1.2 Billion) of supplies from Baxter over five years (1986–1990), (b) Baxter agreed to pay HCA a multimillion-dollar (4%) rebate for reaching certain annual purchase volume targets to be paid as a bonus in 1991, and (c) Baxter gave HCA an upfront payment of $150 Million to help it continue its diversification efforts into health insurance.

Baxter made IV pumps, IV fluids, and hemodialysis and blood therapy products, while AHS (which became Allegiance) made disposables and custom packs. Following this deal, Baxter developed "corporate programs" with other purchasing groups to distribute a broad array of products under one contract (i.e., single-vendor, multi-product portfolio). According to market analysts, Baxter's ability to contract bid for a broad product range over a long-time period suggested the new power of consolidated firms and the downward price pressure exerted by deals between suppliers and consolidated hospital groups on the supply market. Indeed, as the Baxter deal emerged, AmHS asked for a lower rebid on $50 Million in business it did with AHS, followed by bids from AHS' competitors.

Non-AHS Vendor Efforts in Portfolio Contracting

Other suppliers followed suit in order to compete. Some (e.g., 3M and Kinetic Concepts) collaborated to pool their product lines and develop "corporate alliances" with purchasing groups and thereby counter Baxter's single-vendor, multi-product bundle with a multi-vendor, multi-product portfolio. Such alliances might also offer automated order entry, consolidated product shipments, and centralized customer service. They might soon be joined by additional suppliers to broaden the product suite that was available. All of this served hospitals' burgeoning interest in enhanced distribution capabilities, lower inventories, fewer suppliers, and fewer SKUs.

Other suppliers established "national accounts" to try to deal with purchasing groups through a single corporate contact rather than through multiple, decentralized operating companies. Johnson & Johnson erected its Hospital Services Group (later renamed J&J Health Care Systems, or JJHCS) in 1986 to represent the company's multiple products and operating units to hospital customers with one face (and perhaps achieve some economies of scale). JJHCS would bundle their endomechanical and suture products and ask GPOs to contract for seven of ten products to receive a 3% rebate. Some suppliers likely developed these programs to sell more products and increase sales volume to customers; others developed such programs for defensive reasons to either compete with AHS or to prevent further market erosion due to group purchasing activities. Still others developed these programs to help their hospital customers deal with cost containment pressures by reducing their supply and procurement costs. Finally, some suppliers developed these programs to deal with increasingly consolidated hospital customers. Sometimes, the GPOs would send their own sales forces into hospitals to help them to convert to the bundled contracts.

SunHealth and Other Nonprofit GPOs

SunHealth had similarly initiated portfolio contracts around 1983 with specific distributors (General Medical Corporation) and then specific vendors (Abbott Labs, J&J, DuPont). At SunHealth (as well as its future merger partner, AmHS), the portfolio strategy was pursued in the mid-1980s to get as many non-discounted supply items under discounted contracts as possible, to reduce the number of line-item contracts, to reduce the number of contracts signed annually, to reduce the amount of time spent negotiating contracts, and thereby streamline the contracting process for group executives. In so doing, the group could lower the prices of products for which suppliers held strong market positions and meet hospital members' continuing demands for lower supply costs. A related goal was to leverage the resources of large suppliers to help hospitals reduce their costs and improve their productivity. Not surprisingly, the suppliers with whom the groups contracted were referred to as "corporate partners."

Nonprofit GPOs did not stand by idly; several of them (e.g., Premier, VHA) followed suit shortly and tried to act like HCA. In 1996, VHA launched its "Clinical Markets" program; Premier launched its clinical purchasing program shortly after its merger. These items could be procured from a small number of multi-product manufacturers. In this manner, purchasing groups began to apply the "80–20 rule" to purchasing: standardize the 80% of their medical-surgical supply spending on the 20% of their items to achieve savings and efficiencies. To be sure, however, member hospitals at the nonprofit GPOs chose bundles voluntarily when offered a choice, usually to obtain the 8–10% price discount. They may also have preferred a contract that bundled multiple product categories even when their GPO recommended separate contracts and bids—e.g., in order to standardize suppliers and product training.

1990s

In the new environment of the 1990s, hospital groups and GPOs developed bundled contracts with suppliers for a continuum of products, just as hospital systems and IDNs developed bundled contracts with payers for a continuum of health services. Both were viewed as "integrated care" and a "one-stop-shop" continuum, which received impetus from consulting firms that postulated that healthcare markets were moving through four stages in an inexorable movement from unbundled to bundled payment and delivery systems.[61] It seemed natural to all industry participants that large consolidated payers would contract with large consolidated hospitals and IDNs, and that the IDNs would contract in turn with large consolidated manufacturers for their diverse product portfolios. Indeed, such consolidation across sectors seemed to reflect a domino effect. Suppliers who had consolidated and offered broader product lines not only made contracting with IDNs easier, but also held out the promise of obtaining greater compliance with contracts since more of the physician-preferred items might now be offered under one roof.

Some GPOs (e.g., HealthTrust) likewise embarked on bundling strategies in the 1990s as an early form of committed contracting and effort to generate economic value systemwide that was demonstrable to the marketplace. Part of this reflected their strategy to outperform their nonprofit hospital competitors and, perhaps, attract them away from their GPO or their nonprofit owner. Part of this also reflected the high corporate hurdle rate for supplies inside these investor-owned systems.

The corporate contracting movement hit a speed-bump by the early 1990s as multi-hospital systems, hospital mergers, and IDNs emerged as alternatives to GPOs for group purchasing. This led to a churn in membership and the inability of smaller systems to deliver on volume and compliance, which lessened supplier support for these systems but which also undercut the GPO's committed contracts and corporate agreements. Hospital mergers often meant a change in the hospital's CEO which increased this churn. Suppliers came to question the value of the national accounts in the early 1990s, complaining that it (a) interfered with traditional sales efforts on the ground by regional and local sales reps, (b) failed to deliver on compliance, and (c) failed to justify the CAFs that suppliers had been paying.

Evaluation of Bundles/Portfolios

Like standardization (covered above), there were clearly "pro" and "con" arguments to bundling. On the plus side, bundles could reduce the number of suppliers in the GPO contract, improve stability in the supplier-hospital relationship, increase the involvement of the hospital "C-Suite" in the contracting process, reduce the amount of time spent in contract negotiation, increase the effort spent on compliance and productivity, and reduce overhead costs. Bundles were popular with hospitals and purchasing groups because they held the potential to bring an additional 1–5% savings off the already-discounted price negotiated by the group. Bundles were rarely refused by hospitals if they already utilized that supplier (i.e., the products had a high market share within the group).[62] This minimized the cost of conversion to the bundled contract and increased the likelihood of achieving the additional product discounts.

On the minus side, bundling represented merely a "quick fix" to get a wide range of products on contract, a "lazy man's way" of group purchasing, as well as a strategy of cross-selling that paired higher-priced, non-market-leading items with lower-priced, market-leading items. Such a strategy purportedly served the supplier first, the GPO second, and the hospital third. Bundled contracts were not easy to implement, as research has shown: there is not much widespread support across departments in a hospital for one vendor's products.[63] Conversely, bundles posed problems for diversified manufacturers when their product divisions did not all agree to participate in umbrella programs that restricted their pricing autonomy.

Finally, bundles might increase hospital loyalty with incumbent suppliers and reduce their likelihood of switching. Only a handful of manufacturers possessed the product line breadth and depth to provide a one-stop-shop capability. Smaller suppliers or those with narrower product lines might try to develop an alliance among themselves to simulate this capability. In theory, this might make it easier to offer hospitals the "best of breed" in many product categories; in practice, this would require an alliance among many suppliers. Thus, the pursuit of product portfolios may have increased the incumbency of large suppliers and reduced hospitals' willingness to switch away to other suppliers.

Long-Term Agreements in the 1990s

Toward the end of the 1980s, a new type of contract developed between groups and suppliers. These contracts were longer in term, broader in scope (covering more products), and more exclusive, often referred to as "partnerships." In practice, longer-term contracts meant moving from 1–3 years to 3–5 years. Purchasing directors noted that longer terms were required to consider products under contract, to evaluate and trial products to contract for, and to convert to such products from legacy products; these were costs that the hospital did not want to incur on an annual basis.

Thus began an era of "corporate contracting," marking a new stage in the relationship between GPOs and suppliers, which became a central strategy among such GPOs as Premier and AmHS. Rather than focus on exchanging discounted pricing for higher volumes, the contracts sought to improve the "value" in the supplier-hospital relationship. Hospitals could reduce the number of suppliers they contracted with and the amount of time spent on negotiations to focus more attention on promoting compliance and productivity. This was the essence of the "national accounts" strategy which paired hospitals with large, national suppliers that made the products that clinicians already wanted.

Longer-term agreements over a broader array of products were now seen as a mechanism to lower hospital spending across a wide array of supplies, provide hospitals with protection against price inflation, and deliver more sales to suppliers. More significantly, these agreements were viewed as a platform to foster greater strategic partnerships between hospitals and suppliers in which individual products were only one part. Now, hospitals anticipated that suppliers would help them to lower product utilization, increase hospital productivity, and share risk. Strategic partnerships with suppliers became nearly universal within a decade, according to industry surveys.[64]

These long-term contracts may have had unintended consequences. Such contracts were supposed to incentivize suppliers to reduce their prices in exchange for stable and predictable product volumes which would lower their manufacturing costs. However, these contracts left incumbent suppliers in place for long periods of time, thereby reducing the amount of negotiating taking place between buyers and suppliers. This may have put contracts on "auto pilot," inhibiting price wars between suppliers, and perhaps keeping product prices higher. Further exacerbating these unintended effects, long-term contracts may also have protected the larger incumbents and their chief competitors at the expense of some of the smaller suppliers (e.g., the #5, 6, or 7 player in a product market). Thus, the market shares of the smaller players may have decreased, leading to their acquisition by the larger players and, perhaps, the development of oligopolistic markets. As a result, buying groups ended up with a smaller number of (larger) suppliers to contract with and a situation where they may be less likely to change suppliers. Another consequence was a static shopping list for hospitals with reduced access to newer and potentially more innovative products from smaller suppliers.

New Types of Contracts

Distributor and Prime Vendor Contracting in the 1980s

Traditionally, GPOs and distributors occupied fairly distinct spaces in the healthcare supply chain. GPOs focused upstream on suppliers using purchasing leverage and price discounting, while distributors offered logistical services downstream to hospitals. Some pharmaceutical distributors did offer buying programs during the 1970s but for niche products and non-GPO members. Distributor agreements typically covered high-volume, low-cost generic drugs and small-volume parenterals, items not central to the GPO. But, in the 1980s some GPOs and hospital systems started moving into the distributor space.

The growth in demand for hospital services meant growth in the volume of supplies flowing to hospitals. The growing supply volumes came with higher product prices, however, due to unstoppable price inflation in healthcare. The growing disparity between rising product prices and lower reimbursement rates forced hospitals to look for savings. This was coupled with pressures on reimbursement, starting with rate review in the 1970s and then managed care and prospective payment in the 1980s. Hospitals were now confronted with a multi-pronged threat to their survival, with forecasts of as many as 1,000 closures by 1990.[65] One new area for potential savings was sales handled by product distributors. This was true for both pharmaceutical products as well as medical-surgical ("med-surg") products.

The new role and importance of distribution were quickly evident. When HCA announced its intent to merge with AHS, VHA did not renew its portfolio agreement with AHS (described above). In response, VHA set up its own in-house VHA Supply Company. The company sought to partner with emerging high-tech companies in a technology development program that would provide VHA members with early access to leading-edge technology and improve the quality of care. VHA Supply would also assist the tech companies to conduct clinical evaluation, market research, clinical trials, sales and marketing support, and distribution. The goal was to develop capabilities in research and development, provide incremental sales growth with the new products under contract, and partner with suppliers that VHA thought might have a big impact on the hospital's competitive position in the local market.

VHA Supply moved into a private label program (VHA + Plus) for products such as gloves, alcohol preps, minor procedure trays, and (later) O.R. supplies. VHA + Plus provided a big growth opportunity: while it accounted for only 2.5% of VHA's sales, it accounted for 10% of its operating revenues and offered 10% aggregate savings to its hospital members. One of VHA's partners here was Baxter, as well as several smaller suppliers. VHA's rationale here was that its own marketing clout would trump any brand franchise that smaller suppliers might have, thereby benefitting the latter. By 1985, VHA had established prime vendor contracts with large distributors and a proprietary distribution network for medical-surgical products, including its own private label products. This network included nine regional distribution agents (e.g., Owens & Minor, Stuarts) to exert more control over the distribution system by virtue of VHA now purchasing distribution services on behalf of its members based on cost-plus pricing.

In 1988, VHA Supply announced it would channel over $600 million annually in pharmaceutical purchases through nine wholesalers as part of a series of "authorized distribution agent" (ADA) agreements. VHA Supply sought to pare down the number of its pharmaceutical distributors from 16 to 9, and create efficiencies based on "one truck, one invoice, etc." Such ADAs served to eliminate direct sales and move them to distributor sales, and (in the process) encourage consolidation among distributors to become a prime vendor. VHA then turned to bundled contracts with major product manufacturers who extended discounts across multiple product categories. Sole-sourcing came more from the distributors; bundling came more from the manufacturers.

The 1980s era thus marked a two-fold shift. First, product flow shifted from direct buying from manufacturers to distribution-mediated sales, with distributors becoming more important participants in the healthcare supply chain. Second, increased product flows in the face of reimbursement pressures increased the salience and importance of supply chain management inside the hospital. Management of the internal supply chain—including receipt at storage docks, inventory, re-distribution to hospital floors, etc.—became seen as an important source of logistical efficiencies. Such management required "materials managers" to oversee an operation that could amount to 15% of

hospital operating costs—a figure roughly equal to another 15% of operating costs spent on the products themselves. According to Baxter, for every
dollar that a hospital spent on a product, it spent another dollar to move
it. For products that were commoditized with little room left for further
price discounts, distribution represented the next frontier in supply chain cost
containment.

Thus, the role of GPOs in supply chain management began to widen *from*
what a GPO could contract and pool purchasing for on the outside *to* helping
hospitals and their materials managers with logistical issues on the inside.
Inventory management was not a small issue. According to some suppliers,
hospitals had an average of 3,500–4,000 inventory items in the operating
room alone, with an investment of $2,000 per bed, much of which was
not on contract. The rise of materials management accompanied the shift to
centralized procurement and inventory control and, thus, rationalization in
supply chain management. The rise of materials management did not necessarily diminish the influence of clinicians in product choice as to add another
layer of decision-making and consultative selling to clinicians about selecting
alternative brands that might be comparable and that might be on contract
and/or at a lower price.

New Vendor Contracts in the 1990s

With the rise of managed care and the increasing penetration of health
maintenance organizations (HMOs) into the employer market during the
1990–1996 period, GPOs engaged in several additional strategies to deal with
capitated costs. First, some groups utilized an old concept—of performance-
based contracts—as an incentive for hospitals to buy through groups.[66]
Under this concept, groups offered tiered pricing to hospitals based on levels
of committed purchasing volume. Hospitals could save money through lower
prices and rebates by responding to the incentives and purchasing more
supplies on group contracts. Many groups reported that hospital adherence to
commitment levels and contracts was the most important factor in obtaining
favorable pricing from vendors.[67]

Second, some groups experimented with procedure-based contracts in
which hospitals contracted with a supplier for a bundle of supplies needed in
a given surgical procedure.[68] These bundled contracts between vendors and
hospitals mirrored the bundled episodes of care payment contracts between
the Health Care Financing Administration (HCFA) and hospitals in federally
funded demonstration projects in the early 1990s.

Third, groups entered risk contracts (or capitation contracts) with suppliers, though on a smaller scale. Several hospital systems (Duke University, Allegheny) had already signed innovative risk contracts with Baxter in 1994. Now, such risk-sharing programs were viewed as the appropriate private sector response to deal with capitated payment from private and public sector payers, as well as the anticipated global pricing from payers for bundled hospital and physician services. Risk-sharing agreements with suppliers were seen as a strategy to partner with vendors who might add value in ways beyond lower product pricing—such as lowering unnecessary spending and excessive utilization, and servicing the entire care continuum offered by providers. Capitated supply pacts between groups and suppliers were consonant in their aims with the concurrent strategies of standardization and sole-source contracting.

Fourth, GPOs began to migrate their awarding contracts to suppliers away from competitive bidding, which entailed market studies, member surveys, and vendor meetings. Bidding was replaced by a more efficient mechanism—a quality improvement process known as "vendor certification"—that was found in other industries. This seemed more efficient, particularly for suppliers that were already performing well. Vendor certification was also part of VHA's committed-buying program, which rewarded hospitals for buying more products under certain contracts and was reportedly also used by SunHealth Alliance. Combined with committed buying, vendor certification was viewed as a milestone on the path to strategic partnerships with suppliers—what some analysts called "the Mecca" of supply purchasing. Abbott and 3M participated in these programs in the mid-1990s.

Three other trends at the time added fuel and legitimacy to these new vendor contracts. First, disease management had arisen as a popular provider strategy to integrate care in cost-effective ways for the chronically ill population. Diversified manufacturers offered several of their products bundled around disease states or procedures in a package. Second, value chain partnerships had also developed in the global auto industry as a strategy to reduce costs and improve product quality. McKinsey consultants recommended that hospitals imitate auto and electronics manufacturers' supply chain management techniques by reducing the number of suppliers, forming strategic relationships with a reduced number of suppliers, and investing in long-term capability to manage supply chain costs.[69] Third, certain suppliers had developed entry-order systems and offered them to hospitals to automate their product requisitions. These systems were popular among hospitals, which had historically under-invested in information technology. Using electronic linkages—such as J&J's *Coact* system, Baxter's *ASAP* system, or Abbott's

QuickLink system——suppliers believed they could offer hospitals greater value and efficiency. Such linkages also might increase the percentage of products hospitals purchase from these suppliers and support their corporate marketing programs. These programs were the initial formulation of the product bundling strategies used in subsequent years.

Looking Back: View from the End of the Twentieth Century

By the end of the 1990s, the GPO landscape exhibited an array of contracts that were widely used. According to the annual purchasing survey conducted by *Modern Healthcare*, the majority of surveyed GPO programs utilized committed buying (73%), long-term sole-source contracts (57%), and strategic partnerships with vendors (77%). Such contracts had taken root in prior decades. The GPO landscape also reflected a rich history going back ninety years, to the founding of The Bureau. The GPO chronicle was inextricably intertwined with (in rough historical order): local hospital societies and shared service organizations, favorable federal legislation (e.g., passage of Medicare), the rise of investor-owned and then nonprofit hospital systems, threatening federal legislation (IPPS), threatening federal and state regulation (rate review, CON), the rise of regional and then national GPOs, favorable regulatory treatment (the DHHS safe harbor), the rise of managed care, the rise of IDNs, and then GPO mergers. GPO roles and functions (covered in Chapter 3) must be understood in light of all these historical developments.

As the new millennium began, the GPO sector became the subject of intense scrutiny. This scrutiny never considered the historical path and intertwined development with hospitals, or the contracting strategies pursued to reduce supply costs and keep hospitals afloat—all of which are detailed above. Instead, it focused on one end result (the consolidation of GPOs into a smaller number of national players) and its possible implications (the survival or competitive prospects of smaller product suppliers). It also introduced a new set of "examiners" or "judges" of GPO activity that operated outside of the healthcare industry.

Conclusion

The GPO chronicle of the twentieth century period focused largely (but not entirely) on improving hospital efficiency and then later on ensuring hospital survival. Those developments have been largely ignored in GPO discussions and analyses, likely because no one understood them. This chapter has sought to correct this deficiency. The next chapter focuses on the first decade of the new millennium. During the brief ten-year period from 2000–2010, critics laid several value and performance challenges at the feet of GPOs. GPOs were about to undergo the same scrutiny that physicians and hospitals had begun to endure since the 1970s.[70] This represented a huge disconnect with the preceding nine decades (1910–2000).

Notes

1. This chapter is co-authored by David Cassak. David has studied the GPO sector longer than anyone I know and has published extensively on it. His many publications include: David Cassak. "DRGs and the Changing Hospital Purchasing Environment: The New Jersey Experience," *In Vivo* (June 1984): 33–39. David Cassak and Roger Longman. "Group Purchasing Strategies," *In Vivo* (May–June 1988): 25–28. David Cassak. "The Distribution Revolution," *In Vivo* (July/August 1988): 16–20. David Cassak. "The Revolution in Selling to the Operating Room," *In Vivo* (April 1989): 15–19. David Cassak. "A Boost into the Market for Emerging Companies," *In Vivo* (May 1989): 14–19. David Cassak. "Group Contracting for Specialty Products," *In Vivo* (January–February 1989): 34–38. David Cassak. "A New Kind of Leverage," *In Vivo* (October 1989): 12–16. David Cassak. 1989. "Sun-Health's Corporate Partners," *In Vivo* (December): 13–17. David Cassak. "The New Price Wars," *In Vivo* (October 1990): 13. David Cassak. "Ameri-iNet's Split: When Being Big Isn't Enough," *In Vivo* (March 1990): 4–8. David Cassak. "Orthopedic Implants and the Trend Towards Contracting," *In Vivo* (July/August 1990): 19–24. David Cassak. "American HealthCare Systems Comes of Age," *In Vivo* (October 1990): 18–23. David Cassak. "Measuring Sales: The Big Unknown in National Accounts," *In Vivo* (May 1991): 14. David Cassak. "VHA Supply Co. Finds a Partner in Baxter," *In Vivo* (January 1992): 1–6. David Cassak. "Rites of Succession," *In Vivo* (November 1992): 9–13. David Cassak. "Changing Their Spots: Voluntary GPOs respond to Columbia," *In Vivo* (November 1994): 14–17. David Cassak. "Integrated Systems: Is This a New Kind of Customer?" *In Vivo* (January 1995): 47–56. David Cassak. "Integrated Systems – How Fast the Change?" *In Vivo* (February 1995): 31–40. David Cassak. "Consolidation and Segmentation in Hospital Group Purchasing," *In Vivo* (November 1995): 16–20. David Cassak. "J&J Health Care Systems – Beyond the Supply Chain," *In Vivo* (February 1996): 33–44. David Cassak. "VHA: Testing the Limits in Group Purchasing," *In Vivo* (September 1996): 24–31. David Cassak. "The New Premier: One Year After the Merger," *In Vivo* (July/August 1996): 22–29. David Cassak. "Columbia/HCA: Why Size Matters," *In Vivo*

(April 1997): 41–54. David Cassak. "AmeriNet and Hospital Consolidation's Endgame," *In Vivo* (November 1997): 53–63. David Cassak. "Tenet Shakes Things Up," *In Vivo* (July–August 1998): 41–53. David Cassak. "Ortho- pedic Implant Contracting, Round II," *In Vivo* (October 1998): 5–14. David Cassak. "The New Supply Chain," *In Vivo* (June 1999): 44–57. David Cassak. "The RealPolitik of the Device Industry," *In Vivo* (March 2002): 12. David Cassak. "Is Group Purchasing Broke?" *In Vivo* (December 2002): 27–42.

2. See, for example, prior issues of *Modern Healthcare* and *In Vivo*.

3. In-depth interviews with: Gene Burton, Bill McFaul, Gary Wagner, and Derwood Dunbar.

4. Rick Dana Barlow. "GPO Inc. Demonstrates Heavy, But Precious Mettle," *Healthcare Purchasing News* (February 20, 2017). Available online at: https://www.hpnonline.com/sourcing-logistics/article/13000525/gpo-inc-demonstrates-heavy-but-precious-mettle. Accessed on November 5, 2021.

5. Jean Nollet and Martin Beaulieu. "Development of Group Purchasing: An Empirical Study in the Healthcare Sector," *Journal of Purchasing and Supply Management* 9(1) (2003): 3–10.

6. Mary Wagner. "Purchasing Groups Vie for Control and Clout," *Modern Healthcare* (June 25, 1990): 27–38.

7. The founding dates reported here are consistent with Senate testimony by the CEO of Premier who stated that there were 10 local or regional GPOs by 1962, 40 by 1974, and a tripling of that number by 1977.

8. Such comments were provided to me by seasoned supply chain executives that I interviewed (see Note 3).

9. Again, these quotes were provided to me by seasoned supply chain executives.

10. Going back at least to the late 1970s, *Modern Healthcare* published an annual, lengthy list of SSOs and providers of shared/consulting services. It also included a list of the services they provided and the size of their client base.

11. Premier formed largely in response to the formation of VHA in the late 1970s.

12. Esther Kuntz. "Purchase Groups Leave Hospital Bureau, Inc.," *Modern Healthcare* (December 1980): 13–14.

13. William McFaul. "Can Group Purchasing Survive the 1980s? Part I," *Hospital Purchasing Management* (December 1981): 8–10.

14. Vince DiPaolo. "Shared Service Business Soars 31%," *Modern Healthcare* (October 1981): 68–74.

15. Scott Hensley. "1997 Group Purchasing Survey," *Modern Healthcare* (September 22, 1996): 45–54.

16. This section draws on: Gregory Kruse, Lawton R. Burns, and Ralph Muller. "The Four Waves of Hospital System Formation in the U.S.," in James Schaefer, Richard M. Mizelle, Jr., and Helen K. Valier (Eds.), *Oxford Handbook of American Medical History*. Chapter 16. Forthcoming in 2023.

17. Howard S. Zuckerman. "Multi-Institutional Systems: Promise and Performance," *Inquiry* 16(Winter) (1979): 291–314.
18. Paul Starr. *The Social Transformation of American Medicine* (New York: Basic Books, 1982).
19. Throughout the remainder of this chapter, suppliers are also referred to as "vendors". This is because some of the nomenclature in the healthcare supply chain uses the latter term. Please forgive any confusion.
20. Monroe E Trout. *Winter Galley* (2008): 136–139.
21. David Blumenthal, Kristof Stremikis, and David Cutler. "Health Care Spending — A Giant Slain or Sleeping?" *New England Journal of Medicine* 369 (2013): 2551–2557. See Figure 1.
22. Jeff C. Goldsmith. *Can Hospitals Survive?* (Homewood, IL: Dow Jones-Irwin, 1981).
23. During the 1960s, some Catholic organizations established the"Religious Congregation Cooperative Buyers" group. This early GPO foundered and was later resurrected as CMMA in the late 1980s after the passage of the Prospective Payment System (PPS).
24. Sandy Lutz. *Columbia/HCA: Healthcare on Overdrive* (New York: McGraw-Hill, 1998).
25. Wendy Diller. "Product Standardization in the Lab: Are We Serious Yet?" *In Vivo* (September 1995): 28–35.
26. Lawton R. Burns, Rajiv Shah, Frank Sloan, and Adam Powell. "The Impact of Hospital Ownership Conversions: Results From a Comparative Field Study." *Biennial Review of Health Care Management: Meso Perspectives.* Volume 8 (Bingley, UK: Emerald, 2009): 171–229.
27. Lawton R. Burns and Mark V. Pauly. "Integrated Delivery Networks (IDNs): A Detour on the Road to Integrated Healthcare?" *Health Affairs* 21(4) (2002): 128–143.
28. APM/University HealthSystem Consortium. "How Markets Evolve." *Hospitals and Health Networks* (March 5, 1995): 60.
29. The Advisory Board. *The Grand Alliance* (Washington, DC: The Advisory Board, 1993).
30. Voluntary Hospitals of America. *Integration: Market Forces and Critical Success Factors* (Dallas: VHA, 1994).
31. Stephen Shortell, Robin Gillies, et al. *Remaking Health Care in America: Building Organized Delivery Systems* (San Francisco: Jossey-Bass, 1996).
32. Lawton R. Burns, John Cacciamani, James Clement, and Welman Aquino. "The Fall of the House of AHERF: The Allegheny Bankruptcy," *Health Affairs* 19(1) (2000): 7–41.
33. Lawton R. Burns. *The Health Care Value Chain* (San Francisco, CA: Jossey-Bass, 2002).
34. Lawton R. Burns, Jeffrey Alexander, Stephen M. Shortell et al. "Physician Commitment to Organized Delivery Systems," *Medical Care* 39(7) (2001): 19–29. July Supplement.

35. Premier. 1994–1995. *Integrated System Purchasing Outlook.*

36. Lisa Scott. "Group Purchasing Evolution," *Modern Healthcare* (September 27, 1993): 49–59.

37. Mark Hagland. "Interview with Alan Weinstein and Robert O'Leary," *Hospitals and Health Networks* (September 20, 1995): 46–47.

38. Richard Haugh. "The Leveraged Buy Is Out," *Hospitals and Health Networks* (November 5, 1997): 33–40.

39. Lisa Scott and Jay Greene. "AmHS, Premier to Merge," *Modern Healthcare* (August 7, 1995): 2–3.

40. In Vivo Diarist. "To Bundle or Not to Bundle," *In Vivo* (June 1993): 23.

41. Lawton R Burns, Sean Nicholson, and Joanna Wolkowski. "Pharmaceutical Strategy and the Evolving Role of Mergers and Acquisitions (M&A)." In Lawton R. Burns (Ed.), *The Business of Healthcare Innovation* (Cambridge, UK: Cambridge University Press, 2012). Chapter 3.

42. "A Final Word on GPOs," *In Vivo* (January 2003): 14.

43. Donald Johnson. "Two Committed-Volume Purchasing Groups Reduce Their Members' Costs," *Modern Healthcare* (November 1978): 14–15, 18. Esther Kuntz. "Hospitals Commit to I.V. Contracts," *Modern Healthcare* (May 1980): 45. Esther Kuntz. "Hospitals Play into Hands of Vendors Who Try to Break Group Contracts," *Modern Healthcare* (July 1980): 14–16. Esther Kuntz. "Committed Volume Purchasing Saves Texas Group 7% to 39% on Food Costs," *Modern Healthcare* (November 1980): 44.

44. Sheila Simier. "Feds' Committed Volume Wields Clout," *Modern Healthcare* (June 1980): 30–31.

45. U.S. Government Accountability Office. *Hospitals in the Same Area Often Pay Widely Different Prices for Comparable Supply Items* (Washington, DC: GAO, 1980). HRD-80–35.

46. Sheila Simier. "Inefficient Buying May Spur Controls," *Modern Healthcare* (May 1980): 38.

47. William McFaul. "Evaluating Buying Groups: Sizzle or Steak?" *Hospitals* 61(12) (1987): 101, 105.

48. Jay Greene. "Alliances May Soon Face Their Day of Reckoning," *Modern Healthcare* (December 18, 1987): 24–37.

49. This scenario resembled the predicament facing the old Blue Cross insurance plans that offered uniform community rating to all community residents, regardless of their health status and utilization of health services. Commercial insurers entered the market, offered lower rates to residents with better health status and lower utilization patterns ("experience rating"), and thereby sought to attract away the better risks from Blue Cross plans. The threat forced Blue Cross to abandon community rating.

50. Mary Wagner. "Groups See More Use of Pacts, Target Alternate Sites," *Modern Healthcare* (November 11, 1991): 38–47.

51. Lisa Scott. "Buying Groups Seek Compliance," *Modern Healthcare* (September 26, 1994): 52–62.

52. Scott Hensley. "GPOs Under Pressure to Deliver," *Modern Healthcare* (September 20, 1999): 38–47.

53. John Henderson. "GPO Contracting in the New Health Care Environment: Strategic Implications for Manufacturers," *In Vivo* (January 1994): 8–14.

54. AmHS consisted of 41 shareholders (IDNs) using 1 national GPO; VHA consisted of 67 shareholders organized in 29 regional divisions; SunHealth consisted of 17 hospital clusters; Premier included 50 shareholders and 2 separate alliances (Childrens hospitals, and EENT hospitals). MedEcon was comprised of 11 smaller GPOs, which it used to its advantage: it combined national contracting with regional purchasing cooperatives of 7–23 hospitals, mostly organized around large IDNs, which were better suited to meeting local needs and achieving higher levels of compliance and in the presence of large volume, committed buying. Purchase Connection was comprised of 12 smaller GPOs. Amerinet included 3 major shareholders and had affiliations with 12 other associations.

55. Vince DiPaolo. "Bills Are Lower in Contracted Units," *Modern Healthcare* (January 1978): 13–14.

56. Maria Traska. "More Are Buying Monitors by Committee Decision," *Modern Healthcare* (April 1978): 28–29. Donald Johnson. "Bays Says Hospitals are Buying from Single Vendors to Cut Their Total Costs," *Modern Healthcare* (June 1978): 32, 36.

57. Wendy Diller. "Product Standardization in the Lab: Are We Serious Yet?" *In Vivo* (September 1995): 28–35.

58. Timothy Chapman, Ajay Gupta, and Paul Mango. "Group Purchasing is not a Panacea for U.S. Hospitals," *McKinsey Quarterly* (1) (1998): 160–165.

59. General Accounting Office. *Group Purchasing Organizations: Use of Contracting Processes and Strategies to Award Contracts for Medical-Surgical Products* (Washington, DC: GAO, July 16, 2003).

60. Department of Justice and Federal Trade Commission. *Improving Health Care: A Dose of Competition* (Washington, DC: DOJ and FTC, 2005).

61. Lawton R. Burns, Gloria Bazzoli, Linda Dynan, and Douglas Wholey. "Managed Care, Market Stages, and Integrated Delivery Systems: Is There a Relationship?" *Health Affairs* 16(6) (1997): 204–218.

62. Department of Justice and Federal Trade Commission. *Improving Health Care: A Dose of Competition* (Washington, DC: DOJ and FTC, 2005).

63. Lawton R. Burns, Eduardo Cisneros, William Ferniany, and Harbir Singh. "Strategic Alliances Between Buyers and Suppliers: Lessons From the Medical Imaging Industry," in Christine Harland, Guido Nassimbeni, and Eugene Schneller (Eds.), *The SAGE Handbook of Strategic Supply Management* (Thousand Oaks, CA: Sage Publications, 2012).

64. Scott Hensley. "GPOs Under Pressure to Deliver," *Modern Healthcare* (September 20, 1999): 38–47.

65. Jeff Goldsmith. *Can Hospitals Survive? The New Competitive Health Care Market* (Homewood, IL: Dow-Jones Irwin, 1981).

66. John Henderson. "Emerging Contract Incentives Can Add to Hospitals' Savings." *Modern Healthcare* (October 15, 1990): 38.
67. Government Accountability Office. *Group Purchasing Organizations: Use of Contracting Processes and Strategies to Award Contracts for Medical-Surgical Products.* GAO-03-998 T (Washington, DC: GAO, 2003).
68. Mary Wagner. "Purchase Groups Buy Goods Worth over $15 Billion," *Modern Healthcare* (September 28, 1992): 39–49.
69. Timothy Chapman, Ajay Gupta, and Paul Mango. "Group Purchasing is not a Panacea for U.S. Hospital," *McKinsey Quarterly* (1) (1998): 160–165.
70. Paul Starr. *The Social Transformation of American Medicine* (New York: Basic Books, 1982).

5

The GPO Chronicle, Part II: 2000–2010— New Judges of GPOs: The Press, the Senate, and the Courts

Performance and Value Challenges in the New Millennium

In 1982, Paul Starr published his seminal work on the history of the U.S. medical profession, *The Social Transformation of American Medicine*.[1] The latter half of his book described how physicians (and providers in general) came under attack toward the end of the twentieth century for the cost and quality of the care they rendered. Such attacks came in the form of "performance challenges" (were physicians practicing cost-effective medicine?) and, more importantly, "value challenges" (were physicians acting according to ethical standards and in society's interest?). Such challenges were first leveled in books such as *Medical Nemesis* (1975) and *Doing Better and Feeling Worse* (1977) and then reinforced by managed care pressures in the 1980s and 1990s to reduce costs and improve quality.[2]

By the start of the twenty-first century, the same types of challenges were laid at the feet of group purchasing organizations (GPOs). On the performance side, GPOs were suspected of not obtaining the lowest contract prices and contracting for the highest-quality products for hospital members. On the value side, GPOs were accused of allowing vendors to charge high prices that would generate higher contract administration fees (CAFs) and, thus, higher revenues for the GPOs. That is, GPO contracts were designed to serve the GPOs' financial interests rather than save hospitals money (in the form of lower product prices) and save society money (in the form of lower costs for

© The Author(s), under exclusive license to Springer
Nature Switzerland AG 2022
L. R. Burns, *The Healthcare Value Chain*,
https://doi.org/10.1007/978-3-031-10739-9_5

Medicare and Medicaid patients treated at these hospitals). Moreover, GPO contracts with large suppliers reportedly kept smaller and potentially more innovative suppliers out of the market, thereby reducing market competition and blocking patient access to novel, lifesaving technologies.

There were three big differences in the performance and value challenges of the 1980s versus the 2000s. First, the challenges of the 1980s were leveled at providers; the 2000s challenges were leveled at GPOs. The distinction here was that most people had a personal physician that they trusted; no one had a personal GPO. Second, the 1980s challenges focused on the quality and cost of care rendered by providers; the 2000s challenges also focused on anti-competitive GPO practices. Third, the 1980s challenges were presented in books and academic research articles; the 2000 challenges were advanced in the news media, the U.S. Federal Government, and the courts.

How did the 2000s challenges unfold? The *New York Times* ran a lengthy, multi-year series of articles on GPO contracting practices. These were followed by four Senate Hearings on GPO contracting practices and a series of Government Accountability Office (GAO) reports requested by the Senate. Finally, all of these inquiries were prompted by and may have themselves prompted, several court cases alleging anticompetitive behavior. The press, the Government, and the courts became the "new judges" of the GPO sector. Alerted to these issues, academics began to conduct research on the GPOs during the early part of the new millennium. Proponents and opponents of the GPOs likewise sponsored a series of white papers and expert reports to advance their claims regarding GPO performance and value. This chapter here summarizes what transpired during this tumultuous decade. Chapter 6 summarizes the research findings and reports that followed.

The next three sections of this chapter describe three major salvos fired at the GPO sector between 2000 and 2010. The *Times* articles marked the first salvo in the attack on GPOs. Several of the *Times* articles (March 26, 2002, May 1, 2002) actually heralded the second salvo—the upcoming Senate Hearings, the Senate's investigation into the conflicts of interest noted by the *Times*, and their being "deeply disturbed" by what the *Times* had reported. The *Times* articles quoted many of the executives of small supplier firms that alleged anticompetitive GPO behavior and then testified at the Senate Hearings. Their firms leveled lawsuits at the large, incumbent suppliers, often naming the GPOs as co-conspirators; these lawsuits marked the third salvo.

Press Reports

Beginning in 2002, GPOs came under intense scrutiny, investigation, and criticism. One recurring issue was whether GPOs actually provided better pricing and value to their hospital customers and thereby warranted protection for the fees they charge suppliers under Medicare's safe harbor (covered below). A second issue was the financial relationships (and the potential for conflicts of interest) between the GPOs, large suppliers, and hospital executives. A third recurring issue was whether large GPOs' contracts with large suppliers excluded small supply companies and their innovative products from the market. To date, the discussion has largely been driven by charges of misconduct leveled against the GPOs by small device manufacturers (and their trade group, the Medical Device Manufacturers Association, or MDMA) whose complaints were aired in the media, the Senate, and the courts.

Articles in the *New York Times*

Starting in early 2002, the *New York Times* published a long string of exposé articles on GPOs; most articles appeared that same year but some were published a bit later.[3]

March 4, 2002	"Medicine's Middlemen; 2 Powerful Groups Hold Sway Over Buying at Many Hospitals" By Walt Bogdanich
March 26, 2002	"When a Buyer for Hospitals Has a Stake in Drugs It Buys" By Mary Williams Walsh
April 23, 2002	"Hospital Products Get Seal of Approval at a Price" By Barry Meier
April 27, 2002	"Hospital Group's Link to Company Is Criticized" By Mary Williams Walsh
April 30, 2002	"Hospitals Sometimes Lose Money by Using a Supply Buying Group" By Mary Williams Walsh and Barry Meier
May 1, 2002	"Senate Panel Criticizes Hospital Buying Groups" By Barry Meier and Mary Williams Walsh
June 7, 2002	"A Mission to Save Money, a Record of Otherwise" By Mary Williams Walsh
July 19, 2002	"Questioning $1 Million Fee in a Needle Deal" By Barry Meier with Mary Williams Walsh
August 1, 2002	"Accusation of Conflicts at a Supplier to Hospitals" By Mary Williams Walsh

(continued)

(continued)

August 6, 2002	"Buying Group for Hospitals Changes Ways" By Barry Meier and Mary Williams Walsh
August 9, 2002	"Buying Group for Hospitals Vows Change" By Barry Meier with Mary Williams Walsh
August 15, 2002	"3 Medical Supply Companies Receive U.S. Agency Subpoenas" By Mary Williams Walsh
September 4, 2002	"A Persistent Small Supplier Gets Contract for Hospitals" By Barry Meier
October 8, 2002	"A Region's Hospital Supplies: Costly Ties" By Barry Meier
October 24, 2002	"Ethics Standards Overhaul Urged for Hospital Buying Groups" By Barry Meier
November 23, 2002	"Hospital Network's Switch Is Blow to Novation" By Mary Williams Walsh
December 28, 2002	"More Hospitals Change the Way They Buy Drugs And Supplies" By Mary Williams Walsh
September 15, 2004	"Senate Panel Weighs Tighter Rules for Hospital Suppliers" By Mary Williams Walsh
August 21, 2004	"Wide U.S. Inquiry Into Purchasing for Health Care" By Mary Williams Walsh
September 14, 2004	"U.S. to Address Possible Abuses in Hospital Supply Industry" By Mary Williams Walsh

These articles marked the opening salvo in the attack on the GPO sector.[4] It is unclear what triggered this long string of articles. The upcoming Senate Hearings, GAO reports, and newly emerging court cases in 2001–2002 (see below) are likely suspects. This might explain why the CEOs of the small manufacturers who brought the lawsuits also appeared as witnesses in the earlier Senate Hearings and as sources in the *Times* articles. A media spokesperson, consultant, and advocate for one of these small manufacturers had worked previously as a reporter investigating reckless banking practices.

The *Times* articles claimed that GPO practices exerted several deleterious effects. Here is an extensive laundry list:

- Exclusive, sole-source contracts awarded by GPOs to large incumbent suppliers served to "lock out" smaller competitors (e.g., Masimo Corp.)
- GPOs that awarded these exclusive contracts received "fees" [contract administration fees, or CAFs] from the incumbent suppliers

- Smaller competitors could not afford to pay these fees and did not get GPO contracts
- The innovative medical devices made by these smaller firms did not get into hospitals as a result
- The GPOs had market power and largely determined which products many hospitals bought
- The GPOs were financed not by the hospitals that bought the products but by the suppliers who sold them
- The GPO mission to find the best products at the lowest prices may have been compromised by their financial ties with suppliers
- Big buyer groups (GPOs) creatively nurtured this system
- Some suppliers invested monies in a GPO venture capital fund
- Some GPO officials received stock or options from the suppliers they contracted with
- Such conflicts of interest ("payola") may have led GPOs to not always choose products that were best for patients
- GPOs did not release any public information on how much suppliers paid them
- GPOs became popular more than two decades ago
- In 1986, GPOs convinced Congress that money could be saved if legislators allowed suppliers to finance the GPOs, which led Congress to exempt GPOs from the anti-kickback laws
- Some GPOs invested supplier fees into startup supplier companies—the GPOs lost money on some and steered business to some
- Some GPOs were preoccupied with increasing revenues
- Hospitals slashed their purchasing staffs, leaving them with little expertise to oversee their GPOs or find better deals on their own
- GPOs returned varying amounts (22–68%) of their supplier fees back to their members
- Hospitals that did their own buying saved money.

And that's just from the first article (March 4, 2002)! Subsequent *Times* articles added more allegations, including (a) a "conspiracy" between one company partly owned by a major GPO and a major drug maker to keep a cheaper generic drug off the market (March 26, 2002), (b) GPOs endorsed products for children's hospitals and then helped to market them to member hospitals in exchange for a percentage of sales revenues or shares (April 23, 2002), (c) GPOs did not always lower the costs of supplies for hospitals (April 30, 2002), (d) GPOs struck long-term agreements that locked in price increases over the years, even though at times the product prices may be falling (April 30, 2002); (e) sole-source contracts stifled product innovation and threatened patient safety (May 1, 2002); and (f) GPOs colluded with suppliers (May 1, 2002).

There was a definite *leitmotif* in the *New York Times* series—one that is explicitly stated in nearly every article—that concerns conflicts of interest: GPOs took money from the suppliers that they were supposed to objectively evaluate. This suggests that the GPOs' business model and revenue model were dependent on, influenced, and possibly corrupted by the sellers of products that GPOs contracted with; thus, the GPOs and their product contracts may not have served their hospital members. This message was conveyed so often that the reader likely assumed it was true. The article series made another related, oft-repeated, but unsubstantiated claim: the GPOs lobbied and convinced Congress in 1986 to pass legislation that facilitated the scheme whereby GPOs "accept money from manufacturers that sell products" (May 1, 2002). Many of these claims (and several others listed above as bullet points) are rebutted by the historical chronicle in the preceding chapter. The sub-sections below rebut two of the most oft-repeated claims in detail.

Rebutting Charges of Conflicts of Interest

Contrary to the *Times*, GPOs and their predecessors (SSOs) existed for nine (not two) decades prior to the Senate Hearings, and long ago became popular vehicles for hospitals to save money. Pressures on hospital reimbursement and rising product costs led regional and then national GPOs to promote contracting practices (like sole-source contracts) to help them achieve greater product savings by trading off (balancing) product price and product choice. This is akin to the iron triangle tradeoff mentioned in earlier chapters that confront consumers when they pick health plans: do they want a lower premium or do they want broader provider networks? Sole-source contracts were not new but had existed for decades. Cost pressures also led GPOs to alter their funding mechanism from hospital member fees to supplier fees, a move that hospitals welcomed since it saved them money (no membership dues) and generated extra revenues (sharebacks from supplier fees). Such financing had also existed for decades. Claims that GPOs were agents of the suppliers rather than the hospitals neglected the historical reality that hospitals set up the purchasing cooperatives to work on their behalf.

Another problem with the *Times* allegations concerned the assertion that *GPOs* evaluated the products from suppliers with whom they contract. As delineated in prior and subsequent chapters, clinicians drawn from the GPO's hospital members conduct the clinical assessments of products considered for contracts using a host of clinical criteria. Moreover, the awarding of a GPO contract is no guarantee that any hospital belonging to the GPO will purchase the products on that contract.

Rebutting Charges That GPOs Lobbied for Safe Harbors

To be fair, even GPO critics acknowledge the beneficial role of the nonprofit, cooperative model of GPOs operating throughout most of the twentieth century.[5] They erroneously claim, however, that this beneficial role was then subverted when, in 1986, GPOs lobbied for a safe harbor that allowed them to charge CAFs. What the Times did not understand is that CAFs had been long implemented by shared service organizations (SSOs, see Chapter 4) and local/regional GPOs to reduce membership fees that hospital members paid and alleviate their cost pressures.

In doing so, GPOs followed in the historical footsteps of consumer buying cooperatives that survived by asking their trading partners to fund their activity. Chapter 4 cited the example of the Grange Movement. While that is nineteenth-century history, there was a more recent illustration that observers should have been cognizant of. Beginning in the 1960s, the central procurement office in some state governments switched their funding mechanism from state appropriations or self-funding to the use of administrative fees imposed on vendors doing business with state purchasing agencies. The central procurement office functioned like a GPO on behalf of state agencies (which did the actual purchasing) by collecting a CAF. Like hospitals, states initiated the switch to deal with budget gaps and fiscal pressures. State-imposed CAFs typically consisted of a fixed percentage (e.g., ranging from 0.5 to 2.0%, averaging 1.0%) of every procurement transaction.[6] This system was styled after the General Services Administration (GSA) in the Federal Government, which required commercial vendors to the Federal Supply Schedule (FFS) to remit back an Industrial Funding Fee (IFF) for each transaction. Such fees supported the operating costs of the GSA. A host of other government and industrial sectors (e.g., food service, online marketplaces, consumer credit, hospitality) also used vendor-based fees to reduce costs to their customers.

Hospitals didn't need to push for the safe harbors and the ability to charge CAFs since they had been charging these fees for some time (and without controversy). "Most of the GPOs in existence at that time already had in place everything that was mandated by the safe harbors, i.e., written agreements with healthcare facilities, limits on the amounts of fees, and proper reporting systems back to the healthcare facilities."[7] Moreover, as of 1986–1987, there was no national trade association or advocacy group to lobby on behalf of GPOs. The future advocacy group, the Health Industry Group Purchasing Association (HIGPA), did not form until 1990. At the time of the 1986 legislation, the GPOs were primarily regional organizations that did not possess much market power and/or public sway. The stakeholders who had most to gain from the GPO safe harbor were the hospitals who had formed the regional purchasing cooperatives, served as their shareholders, and attempted to use them to save money. Any "lobbying" efforts made by regional hospital consortia were undertaken to clarify uncertainties in the Medicare laws that might expose them to liability. These uncertainties are explained below.

Moreover, the *Times* articles did not accurately portray the genesis of the safe harbor legislation. The 1972 Amendments to the Social Security Act established penalties for fraud and kickbacks in the Medicare and Medicaid programs—defined as soliciting or receiving bribes, rebates, or kickbacks in connection with furnishing services to publicly-insured patients. This became known as the Anti-Kickback Statute (AKS). Congress' chief concern here was unethical practices to induce patient referrals that would then lead to over-utilization of Medicare services.

Congress amended the law in 1977, broadening the prohibited payments to "any remuneration" and strengthening the capacity of the Government to detect and punish such fraud. AKS violations also transitioned from being misdemeanors to felonies. Some activities were considered exempt from the AKS, including discounts or price reductions that were properly disclosed and properly reflected in the provider's cost reporting. Indeed, the Congressional Committee at the time encouraged providers to seek discounts as a good business practice which would result in savings to Medicare program costs.[8]

Nevertheless, the Office of the Inspector General (OIG) within the Department of Health and Human Services (DHHS) interpreted the law to preclude GPO collection of CAFs from suppliers. This posed a problem for hospitals, hospital systems, and SSOs/GPOs that had switched their funding mechanism from member dues to vendor fees in order to survive financially. More generally, providers were concerned that their emerging commercial arrangements, such as hospital system building and capital pooling which were designed to help them remain competitive and efficient, might be prosecuted. Indeed, the OIG opined that the language of the 1972 AKS was so broad that "providers were uncertain as to what practices were prohibited and what practices were permissible. The consequence of this was that providers were reluctant to engage in many arrangements which were not harmful to the programs and beneficiaries, and which may even have been helpful."[9]

Years later, in 1991, the OIG reiterated that the AKS provision was overly broad:

> The types of remuneration covered specifically include kickbacks, bribes, and rebates made directly or indirectly, overtly or covertly, or in cash or in kind. In addition, prohibited conduct includes not only remuneration intended to induce referrals of patients, but remuneration also intended to induce the purchasing, leasing, ordering, or arranging for any good, facility, service, or item paid for by Medicare or State health care programs. Since the statute on its face is so broad, concern has arisen among a number of health care providers that many relatively innocuous, or even beneficial, commercial arrangements are technically covered by the statute and are, therefore, subject to criminal prosecution.[10]

The OIG was thus of two minds. On the one hand, the OIG acknowledged the CAFs represented a technical violation of the AKS. On the other hand, it also stated that "the prices of items purchased pursuant to [GPO agreements with suppliers] are significantly lower than they would be if each hospital did its purchasing independently because the agent is able to obtain prices based upon large volume discounts."[11]

Moreover, during the 1980s, the OIG was concerned that the AKS and the newly-enacted Inpatient Prospective Payment System (IPPS, 1983) might be working at cross purposes. According to the Inspector General at the time (Richard Kusserow), the OIG wanted to ensure that the GPOs' cost savings were not lost with the passage of IPPS in 1983. The OIG felt that the risks associated with GPOs had been greatly reduced due to IPPS passage, since hospitals had transitioned from fee-for-service to risk-based payments and because variations in provider pricing now had a lessened impact on Medicare's fiscal integrity. Moreover, in tandem with the new payment system, the use of GPO agents by hospitals encouraged competitive marketplace strategies in healthcare. The reimbursement pressures on hospitals would soon increase. Within just two or three years of the IPPS passage in 1983, Congress learned that it had set the Medicare reimbursement rates too high, leading to high hospital profits. What followed was growing political sentiment to cut payments to hospitals, resulting in lower market basket updates for hospitals of 4.5% (1985), 0.5% (1986), and 1.15% (1987).[12] These payment cuts were telegraphed in the forthcoming Medicare legislation profiled below.

It should be noted that the OIG was not a partisan actor in this drama. The OIG had been set up in 1976 and then authorized to act in accordance with the Inspector General Act of 1978, with a mission to protect the integrity of federal programs like Medicare and Medicaid, as well as their beneficiaries.

Richard Kusserow was named to head the office in 1981. He was a former Federal Bureau of Investigation (FBI) agent who took the active stance of "junkyard dog." Under his tenure, the OIG became notorious for prosecuting three main areas of fraud and abuse: submission of false claims, inducements or kickbacks, and self-referrals. Kusserow's high-profile activities led to an expansion of OIG's stature and legislative authority in the 1980s. None of this activity involved GPOs.

What then ensued was a back-and-forth discussion between the OIG and the Department of Justice (DOJ) regarding whether the AKS precluded the collection of CAFs and, thus, whether such activities should be prosecuted. Pending Congressional clarification on this matter, the OIG requested that the DOJ suspend prosecuting such arrangements. In requesting that the DOJ permit GPO activities under the AKS, the OIG noted that DHHS was considering legislation to amend the law to refine the distinctions between permissible and prohibited arrangements, and also set forth its position that GPOs did not add to Medicare program costs:

> The use of volume purchasing through group purchasing agents clearly reduces the costs of purchases by hospitals. Therefore, we would encourage use of such arrangements regardless of the reimbursement methodology. In the case of inpatient hospital care under PPS [Prospective Payment System], any savings which result from volume purchasing accrue to the hospital because Medicare will reimburse a predetermined amount based upon a patient's DRG [Diagnosis Related Group]. In the case of services reimbursed on the basis of cost, the savings from volume purchasing will be passed onto the Medicare program.[13]

The DOJ declined the OIG's request, arguing that this would negate what Congress made criminal. Unable to resolve the impasse, the Executive Branch left the issue to be resolved by Congress. Congress was also of two minds—expressing both support for GPOs and concerns about some specific practices. On the one hand, as noted in the 1985 record of the U.S. House of Representatives Budget Committee[14]:

> Group purchasing organizations (GPOs) purchase goods and services for participating hospitals and other institutions at costs below those which the members would be able to obtain individually. To cover costs, GPO's either charge administrative fees to member institutions, or they require vendors from whom they purchase services or supplies to pay them a fixed percentage of the value of the business that they refer to the vendors. The Office of the Inspector General of the Department of Health and Human Services has

determined that this latter arrangement— the vendor-paid fee — represents a "technical" violation of the anti-kickback provisions.

The Committee believes that GPOs can help reduce health care costs for the government and the private sector alike by enabling a group of purchasers to obtain substantial volume discounts on the prices they are charged. The Committee understands that the amount of the price reductions exceeds the fees the vendors must pay the GPO's. The Committee can see no justification for prohibiting such cost-saving arrangements, and believes that the uncertainty resulting from the Justice Department's position on this issue should be eliminated.

On the other hand, the House was concerned about CAFs that exceeded three percent, and felt that such fees should be modest (three percent or less) and disclosed to hospital members.

In the 1986 Omnibus Budget Reconciliation Act (OBRA, Pub. L. 99-509), Congress finally addressed the issue of coverage of "Group Purchasing Vendor Agreements" under the AKS. An amendment to section 1877 of the Social Security Act established disclosure requirements to increase transparency and exempt certain amounts "paid by a vendor of goods or services to a person authorized to act as a purchasing agent" for healthcare providers furnishing services paid for by Medicare. Under the amendment, "remuneration" under the AKS did not encompass amounts paid by a vendor (supplier) for goods or services to a person authorized to act as a purchasing agent for a group of individuals or entities (e.g., providers) who are furnishing services reimbursed under [Medicare] if two conditions were met: there was a written contract that specified the amount to be paid, and the provider disclosed the amount received. In this manner, Congress expressly permitted GPO arrangements with healthcare providers and vendors as long as the two conditions were met.[15]

This 1986 Act was followed in 1987 by Public Law 100-93, the Medicare and Medicaid Patient and Program Protection Act (MMPPPA), which revised the healthcare fraud and abuse laws and added new provisions addressing the AKS. MMPPPA required the OIG to issue "safe harbor regulations" that would specify various payment and business practices which, although potentially capable of inducing referrals of business under the Federal and State healthcare programs, would not be treated as criminal offenses under the AKS. As noted above, the major thrust in the fraud and abuse laws and subsequent safe harbors was to avoid inappropriate patient referrals and over-utilization of services, both of which increased healthcare costs. Another thrust was to preserve competition. At the same time, however, Congress did not want to thwart legitimate business ventures in healthcare.[16]

Neither the 1986 OBRA nor the 1987 MMPPPA issued the safe harbors; they were promulgated years later by the OIG at the direction of Congress but following Congressional intent. Congress directed the DHHS to solicit input from providers prior to formulating any regulations; in turn, DHHS tasked the OIG to gather this input and then draft the final regulations. These regulations covered eleven practices that would be immune from prosecution under the AKS. One of these eleven areas covered payments to GPOs.

There is no indication that Congress pursued this safe harbor to protect GPO interests. Instead, Congress seemed to try to strike a balance between (a) protecting hospital finances by allowing administrative fees and (b) curbing excesses in these fees and any distortions they might cause by limiting them to three percent. Congress also acted to resolve the impasse between the DOJ and OIG by enacting the statutory clarification for GPOs in 1987. The OIG subsequently codified this provision in the subsequent safe harbors, the net effect of which was to legalize the CAF payments from suppliers to GPOs and legitimate their role in reducing healthcare costs for both public and private sector payers. It should also be noted that, prior to this time, no court had ruled that supplier fees paid to GPOs constituted a "kickback" under the AKS.

An analysis of the stakeholder input solicited by the DHHS revealed no major issues about CAFs and their propriety, and revealed no lobbying by providers or GPOs to obtain them.[17] The issues considered here included:

- Does a nursing home chain that requested percentage payments from laboratories as "GPO fees" in return for the referral of laboratory services from member nursing homes fit the definition of a GPO?
- Is the requirement that the GPO have a written agreement with each individual or entity in the purchasing group that specifies the amount the agent will be paid by each vendor burdensome and expensive? Can this be altered?
- Can the GPO be permitted to specify the range of fees to be paid by the potential vendors instead of the actual amount?
- Can the confusion about the interrelationship of the GPO safe harbor and another safe harbor (dealing with discounts) be clarified?

Thus, there is no historical evidence to support the claim by the *Times* that in the 1986 law "GPOs convinced Congress that money could be saved if legislators allowed suppliers to finance the GPOs, which led Congress to exempt GPOs from the anti-kickback laws." Furthermore, there is no evidence to substantiate the claims of GPO critics that the 1987 law and subsequent issuance of the safe harbors led GPOs to become for-profit entities and to negotiate higher rather than lower prices.[18] For-profit hospital chains had organized the first GPOs back in the early 1970s; if anything, the 1990s period witnessed greater price discounting by-product suppliers who were prodded by GPOs with increasing national scale.

Senate Hearings

The U.S. Senate and its Judiciary Committee's Subcommittee on Antitrust held four hearings on the GPOs between 2002 and 2006. They are summarized below. At times, the Senate requested investigative reports by the Government Accounting Office (GAO)—later known as the Government Accountability Office (also the GAO). These reports are also summarized below.

Senate Hearings April 2002

The Senate began its hearings in April 2002. The hearings focused on whether GPOs inhibited competition and market entry in various medical device markets, negotiated low prices for hospitals, and had financial interests with the suppliers they contracted with.[19] These hearings had a specific spark: The *New York Times* articles, complaints by small suppliers that GPOs were plagued by conflicts of interest, the alleged barriers GPOs posed to new suppliers getting access to hospital markets, and the alleged barriers faced by clinicians and patients getting access to the new technologies offered by these suppliers. As summarized by Senator Herbert Kohl in his opening remarks, the question was one of "agency": did GPOs serve the interests of hospitals and patients? Do they offer a wide choice of products available for purchase at reduced costs, or do they serve their own interests in the form of reduced choice of products (by virtue of discouraging innovation and new supplier firm entry) procured at high costs (that would increase their CAFs)? Such fees were portrayed during the hearings as payments by large incumbent suppliers to GPOs to exclude small, new competitors from the marketplace by virtue of denying them access to GPO contracts.

CEOs of small manufacturers that had brought or would shortly bring lawsuits against large suppliers and their GPO partners submitted written testimony that asserted the following:[20]

- "GPOs have mutated from their intended role as collective bargaining purchasing agents, acting on behalf of hospital members, into sales agents protecting the interest of a select group of large and dominant multi-product suppliers of medical devices" (p. 190)
- hospitals were "compelled to purchase inferior and more costly products from the dominant supplier who could inflict serious economic penalties on the hospitals through a combination of GPO connections and bundling practices" (p. 190)
- small manufacturers have been "prevented from obtaining more than 1 to 2 percent market share … [as] a result of practices that arise from the anticompetitive and exclusionary economic relationships between GPOs and the dominant multi-product vendors" (p. 192)
- "there is no legitimate business justification for bundling the purchase of trocars with sutures" (p. 199)
- "under the current arrangement, in which suppliers pay various fees to the GPOs, there is no incentive for suppliers to reduce prices or for GPOs and hospitals to reduce costs" (p. 263)
- "suppliers, not hospitals, are the GPOs' real customers" (pp. 263–264)
- "the ill-conceived 'safe harbor' from federal anti-kickback statutes that Congress, with the best of intentions, passed in the early 1990's had instead become a 'pirate's cove' for big companies with inferior products seeking to avoid the rigors of fair competition" (p. 264)
- "GPOs are nothing more than shills for the major manufacturers. The GPOs protect them from competition" (p. 266)
- "the presence of yet another high maintenance middleman who is paid by big manufacturers results in higher, not lower, healthcare costs" (p. 267).

Representatives from the National Venture Capital Association went further by claiming GPOs discouraged private investment in medical device firms by virtue of blocking their access to selling products to hospitals. Representatives from the Medical Device Manufacturers Association (MDMA) also opined that most of the innovative products in medical devices, equipment, and diagnostics were developed by small firms, that were systematically blocked from gaining market uptake for their products by (1) GPO contracts with one or two large incumbent suppliers (using sole-source and dual-source contracts) and (2) GPO contracts that bundled multiple products together (which favored large, diversified manufacturers).

Of course, such views ran counter to published evidence that smaller firms with emerging technologies had encountered difficulties ever since the late 1980s due to a constellation of factors. These included: (1) the rising cost of venture capital money had made access to capital difficult, (2) tightening public markets made capital access more difficult, (3) hospital customers were pressuring their systems and GPOs for broader product lines and product bundles, which smaller firms could not satisfy, and (4) rising cost pressures drove hospitals into the arms of GPOs in search of pricing leverage over vendors and higher discipline in product procurement.[21] In response to hospital financial pressures and requests by their members for help, GPOs had developed a definite preference for large vendors and price discounts, two areas where smaller manufacturers with innovative technological features could not deliver or compete.

In response to the hearing, two large GPOs as well as the HIGPA trade association agreed to implement a code of conduct for its members to follow to foster greater transparency, particularly in their purchase of physician preference items (PPIs). According to a HIGPA news release on June 30th of 2002, HIGPA's Code of Conduct Principles were designed to strengthen the delivery of healthcare products and services by creating a set of principles for GPOs to incorporate into their businesses. HIGPA focused on a number of key areas, including:

- Eliminate potential conflicts of interests
- Ensure open communications between members and vendors
- Establish guidelines for the use of contracting tools
- Create a code of conduct certification program
- Appoint a code of conduct compliance officer at each GPO
- Establish reporting & education programs, including surveys to quantify the value of GPOs
- Require full disclosure to members of all vendor payments.

The Code established baseline principles that individual GPOs would adopt to improve group purchasing, while also recognizing that a one-size-fits-all approach would be counterproductive to ensuring a competitive GPO marketplace. Importantly, there were certain issues pertaining to individual GPO business practices—such as the level of CAFs—that HIGPA could not address without being in violation of federal antitrust laws. By establishing baseline principles for all GPOs, the Code recognized that both individual GPOs and the sector as a whole have important spheres of responsibility. Appendix A contains more information about the Code of Conduct.

Senate Hearings July 2003

The next set of hearings in July 2003 followed up on issues from the first hearing—specifically whether the GPOs' voluntary code of ethics was working and what efforts had been undertaken to ensure competition and innovation in product markets.[22] The former issue was characterized as the low-hanging fruit, where some progress had been made; the latter issue was viewed as more critical and with less progress made. These hearings further investigated the contracting process by discussing "bundled sole-source contracts", whereby the GPO negotiated to buy product bundles from one supplier. GPO critics claimed such contracts were anticompetitive by excluding smaller manufacturers who made product lines narrower than the bundle/portfolio negotiated with a single, large, diversified vendor. The hearings also considered the impact of the high purchase commitment levels that hospitals needed to meet to get the best price. By virtue of meeting the high commitment levels on sole-source or dual-source contracts, it was argued, hospitals had little left to spend on purchases from smaller, innovative suppliers not on the GPO contract (what became known as "low headroom").

The GPOs countered during the hearings that (a) they were shifting many of their contracts to multi-source arrangements, (b) they entered high commitment contracts when their hospital members wanted them to, (c) many of the purchases made by their hospital members were not under GPO contracts, (d) such contracts also included an "open tier" where hospitals could buy as much or as little as they desire, and (e) they had reduced the scope of product bundling in several areas.

Senate Hearings September 2004

A third set of hearings held in September 2004 focused on possible legislative remedies if self-regulation and voluntary codes of conduct were deemed insufficient.[23] Senator Kohl discussed the possible need for legislation to mandate and make permanent the voluntary changes undertaken by GPOs once the spotlight of Senate Hearings had been removed. Other experts testified that the reforms they had undertaken were voluntary, non-uniform, reversible, non-enforceable, carried no penalties for non-compliance, and had not in fact worked.

Many of the same criticisms made during the earlier hearings were once again leveled against the GPOs. These included: (a) GPOs erected barriers to market entry by new suppliers, which impeded innovation and raised product prices; (b) GPOs were the agents of large incumbent suppliers; and (c) CAFs facilitated the joint contracting between GPOs and these large suppliers. The hearings also yielded testimony that the GPO code of conduct only applied to PPIs, and not to commodity items where traditional GPO contracting practices (sole-source, bundling) were allowed to continue. Finally, the hearings aired claims that product selection decisions were being taken out of the hands of clinicians and made by non-clinicians (e.g., GPO product committees that could not represent the interests of thousands of doctors and nurses in GPO member hospitals).

The next month, Senators Herbert Kohl and Mike DeWine, the ranking members on the Subcommittee, proposed a new piece of legislation called The Medical Device Competition Act (Senate Bill 2880). This Act would require the DHHS to oversee GPO activities, ensure that GPOs conformed with principles of ethical conduct and competition, and limit the CAFs that GPOs could charge. The Act added a new requirement to the criteria that purchasing agents (like GPOs) had to meet for exemption from criminal penalties for illegal remunerations under the AKS. In addition to a written contract specifying the amount to be paid, and service provider disclosure of the amount received from a vendor, the Act:

(1) directed the DHHS Secretary to promulgate regulations specifying the contracting, business, and ethical practices of an authorized purchasing agent that are contrary to antitrust law and competitive principles, to ethical standards, or to the goal of ensuring that products necessary for proper patient care or worker safety are readily available to physicians, healthcare workers, and patients.
(2) required the purchasing agent be certified to be in compliance with such regulations; and
(3) restricted the amount of fees paid to purchase personnel or GPOs to 3 percent of the purchase price of goods or services provided by contract vendors. It also would have restricted fees to include "only those reasonable costs associated with the procurement of products and the administration of valid contracts" and would not include "marketing costs, any extraneous fees or any other payment intended to unduly or improperly influence the award of a contract based on factors other than the cost, quality, safety or efficacy of the product."

GPOs objected to the calls for regulation and proposed further methods to regulate their own conduct. Specifically, the large GPOs and HIGPA formulated the Hospital Group Purchasing Industry Initiative (HGPII) and a methodology to ensure the changes already being implemented would be sustained and become a permanent way of doing business. HGPII followed three main tenets: promote an "ethical culture of compliance," promote self-governance and commitment to ethical standards by GPO leadership, and share best practices in dealing with issues of ethics and business conduct. To achieve these aims, the GPOs pledged to adhere to six ethical principles (e.g., written code of business conduct, develop a more open and competitive purchasing process free of conflicts of interest), report annually to the public on adherence to these principles via an accountability questionnaire, and participate with other GPOs in an annual best practices forum (see Appendix B). This initiative was launched in May 2005 under the sponsorship of nine large GPOs. To allow this voluntary and self-regulatory approach, Senators Kohl and DeWine held off introducing their proposed legislation.

Senate Hearings March 2006

A fourth set of Senate hearings in March 2006 sought to determine whether such voluntary and industry-led efforts were effective in promoting competition and whether additional steps were necessary.[24] As before, the overall objective of the Hearing (and the Senate Subcommittee) was to ensure competition in the markets connecting product suppliers with hospital buyers that were mediated by the GPOs. As stated by Senator DeWine in his opening comments, the voluntary codes of conduct adopted by each of the major GPOs two years before seemed to have improved the contracting scene and improved market access for small suppliers. But were the industry's own voluntary reforms undertaken to date sufficient? Had the HGPII initiative been successful? Or were other steps needed to reinforce them? Such steps included passage of the Medical Device Competition Act, the proposed Ensuring Competition in Hospital Purchasing Act which would have repealed the safe harbor for GPOs and their collection of CAFs, and the proposed Hospital Group Purchasing Act which would have imposed new ethics and best practices on GPOs and created a federal compliance office to oversee them. In the end, a solution was needed to balance access by the public and clinicians to new innovative technologies with the need for cost containment using GPOs.

During the Hearings, the HGPII Coordinator stipulated the initiative was off to a successful start with the enthusiastic support of the GPOs, as evidenced by the public accountability process (GPO posting of questionnaires and visits to these websites). By contrast, MDMA's Executive Director testified the GPOs had not corrected their practice of exclusionary contracts—e.g., using bundles of unrelated products, using long-term sole-source contracts, awarding of no-bid contracts, collecting high CAFs, and preferring large incumbent suppliers that excluded small innovative suppliers. Evidence to support such claims was limited to anecdotal testimony from an antitrust case in the courts and a GAO report (see below) that GPOs kept a portion of their CAFs rather than distribute them all back to their hospital members. A third witness testified that the HGPII effort failed to meet rigorous standards for industry-developed codes of conduct and compliance with ethical practices, and thus that there were no real objective means to monitor and verify GPO practices.[25] A fourth and final witness, a hospital CEO from Senator DeWine's home state of Ohio, testified that GPOs saved her hospital money on product purchases. She also stated that the portion of the CAFs retained by the GPO goes toward supplier contracting efforts that helped her hospital reduce its operating costs (e.g., staffing levels). Finally, she stated her GPO accounted for nearly two-thirds of its supply spending, leaving more than one-third of that spending done by the hospital based on clinician preferences (and without any GPO mediation). Whether or not a small vendor can convince the hospital to contract for its product rested on how well it convinced clinicians in vendor fairs.

By far, the most surprising portion of the Hearing was the statement made by Senator Charles Schumer (NY-D). Echoing the OIG's assertions from 1985 (see above), Senator Schumer recast the role of GPOs *from* "agents of suppliers" *to* "agents of hospitals" who help them to negotiate with the wealthy manufacturers. One of the few things hospitals can do to save money is to band together to buy supplies in bulk, and GPOs played an instrumental role in this process. Unfortunately, Congress did not allow Medicare to bargain in the same way with pharmaceutical manufacturers, which cost the public money. The idea that hospitals would want to pay more money for supplies to feather the nest of the GPOs made no sense. Finally, he suggested the self-regulatory approach undertaken by the GPOs was working, that the HGPII made sense, and that a large number of organizations were participating in it. Senator Schumer stated he would need evidence to the contrary before supporting any of the regulatory and legislative approaches to reforming GPO practices.

GAO and OIG Reports

The U.S. General Accounting Office (GAO) submitted several reports between 2002 and 2004 in testimony before the U.S. Senate Judiciary

Committee and its Subcommittee on Antitrust, Competition, and Business and Consumer Rights. These reports were accompanied by three additional reports prepared during roughly the same period (2002–2005) by the Office of the Inspector General (OIG) inside DHHS. Years after the Senate Hearings had been completed, the new Government Accountability Office (GAO) prepared five additional reports on the GPOs between 2010 and 2014. These reports are listed below in chronological order:

April 30, 2002	*Group Purchasing Organizations: Pilot Study Suggests Large Buying Groups Do Not Always Offer Hospitals Lower Prices* (GAO-02-690T)
February 2003	*Review of Compliance with Conditions of the Group Purchasing Organization Safe Harbor, Premier Purchasing Partners, L.P.* (OIG, A-05-01-00092)
July 16, 2003	*Group Purchasing Organizations: Use of Contracting Processes and Strategies to Award Contracts for Medical-Surgical Products* (GAO-03-998T)
May 2004	*Contract Management: Impact of Strategy to Mitigate Effects of Contract Bundling on Small Business is Uncertain* (GAO-04-454)
January 19, 2005	*Review of Revenue from Vendors at Three Group Purchasing Organizations and Their Members* (OIG, A-05-03-00074)
May 19, 2005	*Review of Revenue from Vendors at Three Additional Group Purchasing Organizations and Their Members* (OIG, A-05-04-00073)
January 19, 2010	*Group Purchasing Organizations: Research on Their Pricing Impact on Health Care Providers* (GAO-323R)
August, 2010	*Group Purchasing Organizations: Services Provided to Customers and Initiatives Regarding Their Business Practices* (GAO-10-738)
September 2010	*Empirical Data Lacking to Support Claims of Savings With Group Purchasing Organizations* (Minority Staff Report—Senate Finance Committee)
January 2012	*Lack of Price Transparency May Hamper Hospitals' Ability to be Prudent Purchasers of Implantable Medical Devices* (GAO-12-126)
March 30, 2012	*Group Purchasing Organizations: Federal Oversight and Self-Regulation* (GAO-12-399R)
October 2014	*Group Purchasing Organizations: Funding Structure Has Potential Implications for Medicare Costs* (GAO-15-13)

Coincident with the first Senate Hearings, the GAO released the first of its many reports on April 30, 2002.[26] William Scanlon, Director for Health Care Issues, testified regarding a GAO pilot study of hospital purchases of two types of medical devices—pacemakers and safety needles—in one metropolitan area. The study found that a hospital's use of a GPO contract did not guarantee the hospital saved money since GPO-negotiated prices were not always lower than the prices that hospitals could negotiate on their own. Larger hospitals were more likely to obtain lower prices on their own, while smaller and medium-sized hospitals were more likely to obtain lower prices using GPO contracts.

Less than one year later, prior to the second set of Senate Hearings, the OIG released its first report.[27] The report was an audit of one GPO, Premier Purchasing Partners, and whether or not it complied with the safe harbor regulations that pertained to notifying and disclosing to its members the CAFs received from suppliers during the 1999–2000 period. The OIG found that among 107 hospital members sampled, 26 members that were subject to the safe harbor reporting requirements did not receive an advance written agreement or after-the-fact disclosure of vendor fees; 8 members did not receive a report showing actual, after-the-fact payments. The breakdown in information transmission was occasioned by Premier's reliance on its purchasing partners and group affiliates to convey the information. In a follow-up letter to the OIG in August 2003, Premier promised to implement policies to assist in the conveyance.

In July 2003, the GAO released its second report on seven GPOs' use of contracting processes and strategies to award contracts for medical-surgical ("med-surg") items.[28] All seven GPOs used sole-source contracts for varying amounts of these purchases; the percentage of med-surg product volume procured using such contracts ranged from 2 to 46%. All seven GPOs also used bundled contracts, which could assume one of three forms: bundles of complementary products, bundles of unrelated products from the same vendor ("corporate agreements"), and products from multiple vendors whereby customers are required to purchase a minimum percentage from product categories to earn discounts. One large GPO routed 40% of its med-surg volume using corporate agreements; another large GPO routed 20% through the multi-vendor bundle. The GAO also reported that most CAFs met the maximum 3% threshold, with a modal fee of 2%. Private label manufacturers paid higher fees (5%). Finally, the GAO reported that (a) the most important driver of product selection in GPO decision-making were "customer requests," (b) that one-third of newly awarded contracts in 2002 went to non-incumbent vendors, with a range of 16–55% across the seven GPOs, (c) customer commitment and volume purchasing were the major determinants of obtaining favorable pricing, and (d) most GPOs used three-year contracts but the two largest GPOs used 5-year contracts.

In May 2004, prior to the third set of Senate Hearings, the GAO released a third report on (a) the use of bundled contracts by Federal Agencies in their FY 2002 procurement, and (b) the effects of such contracts on small business vendors.[29] The GAO found that bundled contracting was found in 24 contracts used by 4 of 23 agencies studied. They also reported there was no information or metrics available to assess the impact of contract bundling on small businesses. The report did not mention GPOs, but its relevance to the Senate's GPO inquiries warrants its inclusion here.

In January 2005, the OIG released its second audit of GPOs, this time focusing on the revenues received from vendors by three GPOs.[30] Over a 4- or 5-year period (depending on the specific GPO), the three GPOs collected a total of $1.8 Billion in CAFs, which incurred $0.5 Billion in operating expenses, and reported total net revenues of $1.3 Billion. Of this amount, $898 Million was distributed back to members, while $415 Million were retained earnings (68% vs. 32%). There was varying accuracy in how hospital members reported these distributions as revenue offsets on their Medicare cost reports (54–92% offset rates). In May 2005, the OIG issued a follow-up audit of three additional GPOs and their vendor revenues.[31] The split between member distributions and retained earnings was slightly higher (79% vs. 21%). Moreover, 7 hospital systems received 57% of the distributions; nearly all of these distributions were correctly reported by the systems as revenue offsets on their Medicare cost reports.

In January 2010, the GAO (now known as the Government Accountability Office) sent a three-page letter to Senator Charles Grassley and ranking member of the Senate Finance Committee on the impact of GPOs on pricing.[32] The GAO was tasked with reviewing the literature on GPOs' impact on pricing for hospitals and other healthcare providers. The GAO located only one peer-reviewed study: my 2008 article in *Health Care Management Review*.[33] According to my study, which surveyed hospital Vice-Presidents of Materials Management (VPMMs), GPOs reduced product prices and transaction costs for hospitals, as well as increased their revenues. A decade later, I published a follow-up study in the same journal replicating the results from this study.[34]

Later in August 2010, the GAO issued another report on the services that GPOs provided to their customers and how they were funded, as well as new initiatives undertaken by the GPOs since 2002 (the time of the first Senate Hearing).[35] All six GPOs queried offered custom contracting, new technology assessment, clinical evaluation, and product standardization. Five of the six provided e-commerce and benchmarking data services. Funding for such services was accomplished using CAFs or charging hospital customers on a fee-for-service basis. CAFs ranged from 1.22 to 2.25% of customer purchases. As for new initiatives, the GPOs reported they had revised their codes of conduct and set up a voluntary membership association (HGPII, see below) to promote best practices and public accountability among member GPOs, and enunciate a code of ethics and business conduct.

The next month, in September 2010, the Senate Finance Committee issued a Minority Staff Report questioning whether there was any evidence that GPOs led to hospital savings.[36] The Report was notable for its reliance on some of the 2002 *New York Times* articles and (a) their erroneous citation of 1986 Congressional legislation providing a GPO safe harbor, (b) their erroneous claim that GPOs convinced Congress to pass this legislation, (c) their suspicions that GPOs serve the interests of vendors who pay the CAFs and thus have serious conflicts of interest, and (d) allegations by small device vendors that filed lawsuits against GPOs and/or incumbent suppliers that GPOs are really anticompetitive. The Minority Staff Report also summarized some of the prior GAO and OIG reports (reviewed above). The Report concluded that there were no data to evaluate whether the safe harbor for GPOs had helped to reduce healthcare costs, and that Congress should consider legislation to increase OIG oversight of the sector.

More than a year later, the GAO issued a report on the lack of price transparency for implantable medical devices (IMDs), which may hamper hospitals' ability to be prudent shoppers.[37] As noted in prior chapters of this volume, IMDs are classic examples of PPIs—products that both GPOs and IDNs have trouble including and managing in their supplier contracts. The GAO report documented the wide variation in prices that hospitals paid for IMDs, and noted that a major driver of pricing variation was physician preference and influence over hospital purchasing. Other factors were supplier competition in the specific IMD market and the hospital's market share. All together, these three factors undermined a hospital's ability to negotiate lower IMD prices from suppliers and led to pricing variation. Research on IMDs showed that hospitals pay suppliers based on their bargaining skills, and what they can bargain with suppliers for is affected by what they can negotiate with their own medical staff.[38] The GAO study interviewed GPOs for their input. The Report indicated that GPOs' ability to help hospitals achieve lower product prices and thus savings was oftentimes driven by factors inside the hospital as well as the external market structure for the supplier's product.

Two months later in March 2012, the GAO sent another letter to Senator Grassley (ranking member on the Senate Judiciary Committee) and Senator Kohl (Chairman of the Senate Special Committee on Aging) on Federal Oversight and Self-Regulation of the GPOs.[39] This letter seemed to respond to the Minority Staff Report of 2010, as well as to a request by the two Senators. The letter described (1) oversight of GPOs by DHHS, the DOJ, and the

FTC; and (2) efforts at self-regulation undertaken by HGPII. With regard to the first issue, none of the three agencies had imposed administrative penalties on any GPO since 2004, undertaken any enforcement action against a GPO since 2004, or routinely requested disclosures from GPOs on the CAFs they collect. With regard to the second issue, the GAO stated only the following:

> The voluntary GPO association—HGPII—has continued its activities for GPOs to self-regulate their business practices, and also added some new activities since our 2010 report. HGPII members are required to follow a set of principles of ethics and business conduct. HGPII members continue to be required to have a written code of business conduct, be accountable to the public by completing an annual public accountability questionnaire, and share best practices through an annual best practices forum. Subsequent to our August 2010 report, HGPII officials told us that the association formed an ethics advisory council in 2010 to provide advice to its steering committee and member GPOs on best practices and other HGPII activities. In addition, to address the concerns of vendors, HGPII implemented a vendor grievance process in 2010 that allows complaints to be reviewed by a third party provided by the American Arbitration Association.[40]

Academic researchers subsequently conducted a lengthy analysis of HGPII and self-regulation in general. They concluded that "the annual reporting mechanism established by HGPII and attention to compliance through an annual questionnaire, available to the public, suggests that the code of conduct has established a footing for government and the GPO industry itself to assess GPOs…the trail of behavior documented by the code of conduct acts as a demonstration of citizenship via a code of conduct or purchasing social responsibility."[41]

The GAO issued a final report in October 2014 on the funding structure of GPOs and its potential implication for Medicare costs.[42] The report outlined the three-phase contracting process that GPOs use and revealed that the majority of GPO contracts are dual- or multi-source, that such contracts are typically three years long, and that GPOs do not bundle together unrelated products. The report also noted that CAFs represent anywhere from 83 to 98% of GPO revenues and that GPOs funnel 70% of CAFs back to their hospital members. Interviews with industry experts conducted by GAO staff showed wide variability in the potential impacts of GPO funding via CAFs (e.g., on product prices or Medicare payment rates), with little empirical data on such effects.

In summary, the multiple GAO and OIG reports issued between 2002 and 2014—like the articles in the *New York Times*—represented more smoke than fire or, as the Germans might alternatively say, less *Sturm* (storm) and more *Drang* (stress). The reports informed the discussions at the Senate Hearings but did not prompt any changes to the AKS, the MMPPPA legislation passed in 1987, or the safe harbors. The title (but not the plot) of Shakespeare's play comes to mind: *Much Ado About Nothing*.

Court Actions

There have also been a wave of legal actions taken by small medical device manufacturers against large product suppliers; most of these involved GPOs in various ways but did not always name them as defendants. Often-times, the GPOs were un-named co-conspirators. The first of these actions occurred early on in 1995; the remainder began in 2001–2002 and ensuing years, many coincident with the Senate Hearings. The small manufacturers included Kinetic Concepts (maker of specialty beds), Retractable Technolo-gies Inc. (maker of safety needles), Masimo Corporation (maker of pulse oximeters), Applied Medical Corporation, ConMed Corporation (makers of trocars and clip appliers), and Rochester Medical (maker of specialty catheters). Several of their executives testified in the Senate hearings. The chronicle of such actions includes[43]:

1995	*Kinetic Concepts, Inc. v. Hillenbrand Industries, Inc*
2001	*Retractable Technologies, Inc. v. Becton Dickinson & Co*
2002	*Masimo Corp. v. Tyco Healthcare Group*
2003	*Applied Medical Resources Corp. v. Johnson & Johnson, Inc*
2003	*ConMed Corp. v. Johnson & Johnson, Inc*
2004	*Rochester Medical Corp. v. C.R. Bard Inc*
2004	*Genicon, Inc. v. Ethicon, Inc*
2005	*Spartanburg Regional Healthcare System v. Hillenbrand Industries*
2005	*Daniels Sharpsmart, Inc. v. Tyco International, US Inc*
2005	*Natchitoches Parish Hosp Service District v. Tyco International*
2007	*Allied Orthopedic Appliances v. Tyco Health Care Group*
2009	*Freedom Medical v. Premier Purchasing Partners*
2007	*Retractable Technologies Inc and Thomas Shaw v. Becton Dickinson*
2009	*Southeast Missouri Hospital and Saint Francis Medical Center v. C.R. Bard*
2010	*Freedom Medical v. Universal Hospital Services*

The disposition of these cases was decidedly mixed. Some resulted in a victory for the plaintiff; some settled either before trial or before formal entry of judgment; and some were dismissed. Of course, even this is not conclu-sory, since many of these cases have been litigated over time (even up to the last few years!) with changes in the court's decisions. Many of the early cases

(*Kinetic Concepts, Retractable v. Becton Dickinson, Masimo*) awarded financial damages to the plaintiffs, which may have encouraged the filing of the later cases; however, the later cases were less successful. This latter observation could suggest that the later cases were more copy-cat in nature, with less substance and merit; alternatively, defendants learned from their setbacks in the early cases and "upped their game" in the later cases; or, perhaps both. Partly supporting this view is the fact that some of the settlement amounts were small, suggesting the weakness of the lawsuit claims. More tellingly, these cases appear to have subsided over time.

This chapter does not review each of these cases; many have already been catalogued elsewhere in some detail.[44] Instead, this section outlines some of the commonalities in argument across the cases. It then draws on (and, in some cases, expands upon) the content of the prior chapter to discuss the relative merits of the arguments and outlines some reasons why the later cases failed.

Commonalities in Case Arguments

One common set of issues, which served as key issues in the original case (*Kinetic Concepts v. Hillenbrand Industries*), included "exclusive dealing", "product bundling", "market foreclosure," and "conspiracy." These issues are outlined below.

The defendant supplier is usually accused of tying discounts on the purchase of one product to the hospital's agreement to utilize another of the supplier's products. Usually, the complaints argue that the tied products are in separate markets, are unrelated, and do not really belong together. But, by bundling these different products, the defendant suppliers create disincentives for hospitals to buy from the plaintiffs who may have a superior product in one market but lack a product in the other. Oftentimes, this tying arrangement involves sole-source and/or committed purchase contracts, such that (a) other suppliers are excluded and (b) hospital members of the GPO are dis-incentivized to shop with other suppliers. GPOs are the named or un-named co-conspirators in such instances because they negotiated these contracts with the large suppliers on behalf of their hospital members. Some expert witnesses involved in these cases further alleged that an accumulation of exclusionary agreements (struck by multiple defendants) cause market-wide foreclosure—what became known as "aggregation theory."[45] In some court cases (like *Masimo*), the Integrated Delivery Networks (IDNs) were also involved in these schemes.

A second related issue is that the GPO defendants would "penalize" their hospital members by forcing them to pay higher product prices if they did not adhere to the bundled, committed, and/or sole-source contracts. As a result, hospitals would be forced to buy more products from the incumbent supplier (the defendant) and, to avoid the financial penalties, forego the use of the plaintiff's product. The latter product might be of higher quality and lower cost, thereby harming patients. Such actions would block market entry by the plaintiff.

A third common issue is "market foreclosure." Here, the exclusive dealing locks the plaintiff out of the market by virtue of the defendant supplier creating a monopoly. The suppliers have such large market shares that effectively limit any competition from small players (i.e., the plaintiffs). In some cases (e.g., *Rochester Medical Corp. v. C.R. Bard*), GPOs are named as co-defendants. Such activities that limit competition have several negative downstream effects. These include increased healthcare costs, increased hospital costs, increased harm to patient quality and safety, and reduced product innovation—all of which harm public welfare.

A fourth common issue is "conspiracy" between the defendant supplier and its GPO partner(s) to keep small, more innovative startups from selling their products—thereby allowing the defendants to monopolize the market. Indeed, some of these cases (e.g., *Retractable Technologies v. Becton Dickinson*) state the GPOs are middlemen whose goal is to funnel large market shares to incumbent suppliers in exchange for substantial fees. In such cases, the GPOs are named as co-conspirators and as co-defendants, whose conspiratorial actions are facilitated by kickbacks and bribes (usually in the form of CAFs).

When GPOs were included in these court cases, they purportedly played several nefarious roles that facilitated everything described below. Rather than developing volume-based and/or committed purchasing contracts in exchange for lower prices, they were instead characterized as developing "customer loyalty contracts." Moreover, these contracts were "enforced" by the GPO, rather than being hospital-driven or hospital-motivated. In addition, the GPOs "penalized" their members for not adhering to these contracts and/or utilizing products from competing suppliers, and did not allow any freedom of choice or product selection among their members. The GPOs also deliberately excluded the plaintiffs from accessing GPO contracts that would enable them to compete; they did so by virtue of specific contracting practices such as bundling, sole-source contracting, and committed purchasing—all of which the GPOs brokered to their singular benefit. The fact that the GPO market was concentrated allegedly posed entry barriers that kept other potential GPO entrants out. Finally, they foreclosed the plaintiffs from the market, reduced the output they could sell, prevented them from achieving economies of large-scale production, and prevented their expansion and growth. The net effect of all this was higher market prices, lower quality products, and lower quality care.

Illustration: *Applied Medical Resources (AMR) v. Johnson & Johnson*

Applied Medical Resources (AMR) was a recent startup (1987) in the medical device field. In September 2003, it filed a complaint against Johnson & Johnson (J&J) and two of its product divisions—Ethicon and Ethicon Endo-Surgery (EES)—that made sutures and endomechanical devices, respectively. The suit also named Novation and Premier as co-defendants. AMR made trocars and clip appliers used in minimally invasive laparoscopic surgery. In such procedures, endo-mechanical instruments are introduced into the body by means of a trocar, which avoids opening up the abdomen and allows passage of instruments and faster sealing of the abdomen.

According to the complaint, J&J leveraged the market power of Ethicon (which made sutures) to increase its share of the market for EES (which made trocars and clip appliers) and thereby illegally expand its monopoly. It did so through a series of exclusive contracts with both GPOs and IDNs. This had the effect of (1) shutting AMR out of the endo market, even though its products were reportedly of the same or higher quality than EES and carried lower prices, and (2) increasing EES' market share since the late 1990s to 65–75%. By contrast, AMR's market share was only 1–2%, even though its trocar and seal technology were reportedly one of the best on the market.

According to the complaint, J&J designed exclusive contracts with the GPO that centered around (a) product bundling of sutures and endo supplies, (b) commitment to purchase such supplies from Ethicon/EES at 80–90% levels, and (c) payments of CAFs that gave J&J leverage. These GPO contracts "governed" hospital purchases of endo products. Hospitals had to abide by terms consistent with those contracts; non-compliance with those terms would expose hospitals to financial penalties in the form of higher prices. J&J "induced" and "hijacked" the GPOs to enter such agreements by paying them CAFs and other forms of remuneration (e.g., rebates on committed purchases), and thereby erected entry barriers to competitors such as AMR. AMR stated it could not afford to pay the same level of fees. It also stated that the contracts prohibited hospitals from evaluating competitors' products, which reportedly led some GPO members to even refuse to speak to AMR's sales representatives ("reps"). As a result of J&J's alleged anticompetitive agreements, (1) AMR was foreclosed from the endo market and could only sell a small amount of product; (2) the number of endo competitors fell, harming market competition; (3) hospitals who would have preferred AMR's products could not obtain them; and (4) hospitals were forced to buy lower quality or less innovative products at a higher price.

Three years later, in August 2006, the Court ruled against AMR and dismissed its suit. Testimony provided in the case documented several facts that undermined AMR's arguments.[46] First, percentage commitment contracts were used by buyers in multiple industry segments to obtain lower prices and increase supplier competition; the same held for bundled contracts, sole-source contracts, exclusive contracts, and quantity discount contracts. Second, in a similar vein, large intermediaries such as the GPOs served beneficial functions such as (a) reducing opportunistic pricing by suppliers and (b) posing a countervailing force by virtue of aggregating buyer demand. GPOs also rendered suppliers into closer substitutes (via bundling of products where one supplier might be stronger in product A but another supplier might be stronger in product B), increased supplier competition to win GPO contracts, and reduced prices. Third, AMR was not precluded from competing to sell its products in the marketplace, for several reasons: (a) J&J's competitor Tyco was an alternative supplier of both sutures and endo products which had successfully negotiated GPO contracts; (b) Tyco had fewer GPO contracts than J&J and still managed to compete in both product markets; and (c) AMR had potential "headroom" in terms of market share that J&J had not captured, but was unable to capitalize on this opportunity.

Some Inconvenient Truths from the Court Cases

There are several reasons why firms such as AMR failed to gain traction in the marketplace. Those reasons lie within the companies themselves rather than in the alleged anticompetitive practices of their external competitors. One set of reasons deals with product quality, clinician acceptance, and brand reputation (reflected in peer-reviewed empirical research); another set of reasons deals with sales and marketing support for the company's products. According to some suppliers, market leadership is a joint function of one's products, clinical trials of these products, and dedicated sales forces that can promote the products. AMR may have suffered deficiencies on all of these fronts.

According to researchers, product innovation and product commercialization represent the "twin pillars" of medical device success.[47]

Product Quality and Brand Reputation

During the period of the AMR case, one GPO that was not implicated in any of the J&J/EES cases (listed above) commissioned an empirical study to gauge the quality (as rated by physicians) of suture and endomechanical products (e.g., trocars, clip appliers) made by different manufacturers. These were the products at the center of some of the litigation discussed above.[48] The GPO followed this course in order to make an evidence-based, contract award to the most appropriate product supplier. The study evaluated five categories of suture and endo-mechanical products from eight suppliers.[49] A panel of general and urological surgeons who routinely used such products developed a list of criteria on which to do head-to-head supplier comparisons about the quality and performance of their respective products. The measures included ergonomics, functionality, overall performance, and clinical equivalence. The actual product evaluation was conducted by local surgeons operating on animal subjects in animal labs at academic medical centers around the country, none of which had an affiliation with the GPO. The surgeons utilized different suppliers' products in different product categories as they operated, relaying to reviewers their numerical assessment of the functionality and performance of each device.

The analyses showed that the supplier receiving the top performance rating in most product categories was the supplier with the largest market share (J&J/EES); this finding held even after controlling for the surgeon's prior training and vendor preference. The analyses also suggested that product brand was typically more powerful in explaining the variation in physician evaluations than were individual physician preferences (e.g., due to anatomical differences). While AMR's products were rated favorably compared to several other suppliers, they were ranked lower than those made by EES in different product categories. This contradicted the claims in AMR's complaint about the superiority of its products.

The study also found that products made by ConMed and Genicon—who had also brought lawsuits against J&J/EES—were clearly rated as inferior by physicians. The ConMed case was settled out of court in 2007, with Johnson & Johnson paying $11 Million; the Genicon case was dismissed by the court that same year. The fact that these plaintiffs all made comparable products led to the development of the "aggregation theory" noted above. This theory implied (but never proved) that foreclosure could occur cumulatively through the joint (but uncoordinated) actions of independent firms—not all of whom were considered by plaintiffs as monopolists.

Similar issues regarding the quality of products made by small suppliers surfaced in other cases cited above. Some issues dealt with product malfunctioning and FDA recalls of their devices; others dealt with the companies' failures to discuss these issues and recalls with their customers, as well as company (mis)steps to address product performance. Such occurrences reportedly led to customer vows not to use their products again. Questions about the quality of products made by small manufacturers could also arise because of the companies' lack of time or financial resources to conduct trials and evaluations of its products across multiple hospitals—which could prove crucial to convincing local clinicians to adopt. Such studies might be used to publish results in clinical journals. Clinicians might want to see such studies to validate the supplier's claims of product performance and superiority.

One problem here was the inability of small startups to document the advantages of their products using empirical studies that might persuade clinicians to convert to a different supplier. Any manufacturer that wants to promote its technology to physicians and nurses needs published clinical studies that show the superiority of its products to interest physicians. This documentation must be physically brought into the hospital and then shown to both the purchasing department as well as the various clinician stakeholders. Sales rep visits and meetings with clinicians are needed to prompt the latter to undertake product reviews and trials at the hospital. One problem is that physicians oftentimes treat patients in their offices and are not at the hospital during the time that sales reps visit. Moreover, product trials can last 4–5 months and require significant investments of the sales reps' time as well as free products to be used during the trials. Small suppliers may lack the resources to make such investments, as well as investments in clinical trials with rival (established) suppliers in head-to-head comparisons. All of this suggests that the time and cost burden to document product superiority rests with the startup supplier. In at least one of the court cases listed above, the plaintiff claimed to offer breakthrough technology; however, that claim was weakly supported by a single study referenced on the plaintiff's website without any peer-reviewed publication to substantiate it.

Sales and Marketing Support

Research shows that success in the medical device field rests not only on product research & development (R&D) but also on market commercialization.[50] Evidence from several of the other court cases itemized above substantiates the point and illustrates several problems with sales and marketing support at smaller startups. One problem is the small number of staff responsible for following up with potential hospital customers after an initial phone call. A related issue is the small number of staff who can follow up with product complaints made by hospital customers, leading to untimely responses and problem resolution. Small sales forces (e.g., 5–15 reps) are unable to cover the entire U.S. across all customer segments, which can mean less dependability on the part of the supplier. Hospitals comment they rely on the sales force to cover all three shifts of the nursing staff, to assist in staff training with the product, and to handle multiple hospitals and care sites within the same system or IDN. New product suppliers often have problems with product supply and product support; the latter can be critical if there is any sophisticated technology that involves clinician instruction. Small sales forces also mean limited channels to relay product concerns from customers back to the manufacturer. Another related problem is the small number of "clinical sales specialists" with clinical training who can answer customer questions about the product's performance.

A second problem is the lack of the hospital's familiarity with the supplier's sales rep—e.g., the difficulty in recalling the rep's name or the last time they visited. Small sales forces mean less frequent visits to hospital customers and less contact with clinician adopters: the difference between a large supplier and a small supplier is customer contact once a week versus once a quarter. Startup manufacturers often assign one sales rep to cover many states. According to hospital VPMMs, vendor success is often a function of "seeking to gain the business weekly"; this is often necessary due to the busy schedule of clinicians who may not be available on the one day the rep visits. Few reps also mean the less likely are visits to the multiple "ports of call" inside a hospital that all have a stake in the product.

A third related problem is the relative inability of small manufacturers—who have small sales forces, narrow geographic coverage, and perhaps limited manufacturing capacity—to handle sole-source contracts and/or assist hospitals in converting from an incumbent supplier to the small startup. Such conversion efforts require not only sales force effort but also the clinical acceptance of the product. Sales rep visits allow the supplier to promote the solutions offered by its products, to educate clinicians on best practices in patient care, to conduct clinical projects with the hospital, and to assist in quality improvement.

A fourth problem is a lack of product knowledge, prior healthcare experience, or understanding of hospital clinicians on the part of a startup's few sales reps, as well as their (in)ability to know the hospitals in their territory and/or distinguish hospitals that are members of particular GPOs. Part of this may stem from financial constraints at the small manufacturer that preclude it from paying higher or more competitive salaries to attract the sales reps it needs, or inhibit it from funding hospital trials of its products. This can also reportedly lead to high turnover rates in the sales force, some of whom may not be replaced.

Fifth, and perhaps most telling, sales reps at small startup manufacturers may not even know why the hospitals they do call on do not buy their products. And, yet, they are the most knowledgeable people on the ground to understand the outcomes of a sales call.

All of these issues can undermine the small manufacturer's brand awareness in the marketplace. They can also retard clinicians' familiarity with the company's technology and, thus, their willingness to consider it. Such problems are further exacerbated by narrow product lines (i.e., "fewer things in the bag" to interest physicians), and by commensurately low budgets for marketing. Small manufacturers with low budgets for sales and marketing may also have less latitude in pricing, be unable to offer pricing pegged to different commitment tier levels, and may in fact be selling at a premium price to support the firm. Some manufacturers report that once they get on a GPO contract and generate greater sales, they can afford to hire more sales reps; the logic here may be "chicken-and-egg." Any contract that does not include the supplier(s) that member hospitals want will not be utilized and will not generate any sales for anybody. The supplier's current market share may thus be a better reflection of hospital preference for its products. Alternatively, small manufacturers could outsource their sales effort to third-party distributors who may have GPO access and provide greater clinician coverage—but such distributors may not have expertise in that given product line.

Indeed, plaintiffs who file lawsuits alleging anticompetitive behavior on behalf of a large supplier (Supplier #1) may then use third parties to help it distribute products to hospital customers. They will then sign a marketing/distribution agreement with another large supplier (Supplier #2). Some of these plaintiffs may subsequently file lawsuits against Supplier #2, this time alleging that the latter failed to market its products. This means that plaintiffs accuse both suppliers of causing its lack of product sales, but for completely different reasons. The secondary lawsuit may not implicate the GPOs or any competitors. In fact, their subsequent annual reports sometimes suggest that low sales reflected market competition and the initially higher price of its product, both of which hindered product adoption by clinicians.

Some Bigger Lessons

This analysis has several important implications. First, small manufacturers may be "leaving money on the table." Hospital VPMMs routinely mention the amounts of products that they buy from non-contracted suppliers, ranging as high as 30–50% of medical-surgical items. They do so routinely when contracted vendors' products do not meet their own quality standards or the specific needs of their medical staff. According to VPMMs, many new innovative products enter the hospital in the hands of "clinical champions" who have experience with the product, or who have been approached by the sales rep, and want to try it out in-house. They also state that their GPO does not penalize them in any way for doing so and, in fact, may assist them in negotiating such purchases. GPOs turn a blind eye to off-contract purchases that are below the GPO agreement, and give the hospital a waiver that allows them to remain on any committed price tier. Waivers are granted by both lower commitment nonprofit hospitals as well as higher-commitment investor-owned hospitals. This renders the GPO contract as an established price list for hospital members that want to use it; even in the presence of a contract, VPMMs can and will pursue local contracts with non-contracted vendors when the hospital insists on it.

Second, small manufacturers engage in a game of rationalization to explain their lack of market success. Instead of looking inward to identify the source of their troubles, they externalize the problem and accuse the GPOs of blocking their access to the market. When they exhaust that line of attack, they then accuse other trading partners of "not doing their job." Years ago, psychologist Daniel Kahneman called attention to the cognitive biases of CEOs who attributed their companies' failures to external events outside of their control, while failing to take account of competitors, limited internal resources, and their own over-optimism.[51]

The overall issue facing small startups is not the presence of GPOs but the vulnerabilities of the startup firms themselves. There are numerous reasons why new medical device firms succeed or fail, but group purchasing is rarely considered to be one of them. Empirical research on entries and exits from the medical device industry highlights the important role played by the startup's age and size, its access to sufficient venture capital, the acquisition experience of the firm's venture capital partners, and the number of competitors it faces.[52] The role of GPOs is rarely mentioned as a considerable threat in the trade literature or by venture capitalists who fund these companies. Thus, new or small firms do not need GPO contracts to increase sales. What they need is an innovative product and the ability to garner the attention and enthusiasm of clinicians.

Other Inconvenient Truths

Hospitals (Not GPOs) Purchase Products and *Not* Based on CAFs

Another flaw in the AMR argument was that GPOs do not purchase products; their hospital members do. Hospitals often use a group process for decision-making on new products to use in clinical areas. For urological products, this can include (a) a clinical services product review committee composed of up to 15 people, mostly nurses; (b) an infection control committee composed of 10–15 people, with input from the hospital's chief medical officer; and (c) the director of purchasing who usually defers to these clinical committees and accepts their product recommendations (regardless of whether the product is on or off the GPO contract). It should be noted that the purchasing directors do not conduct the research on new products to utilize in the hospital; they are already responsible for overseeing the purchasing of $40–50 Million in medical-surgical items. Instead, the search for new products begins with the vendor's sales rep bringing their new product to the attention of the hospital's clinicians, communicating the unmet clinical need that the new product satisfies, prompting the clinicians to conduct trials of the new product and inform the purchasing department of what product they want to use. Even products that are under a GPO contract require internal promotion; there are no automatic sales.

Moreover, the hospitals do not purchase products based on any CAFs that might be generated through GPO-mediated contract sales that ultimately result in rebates back to the hospitals. That is because: (1) hospitals do not know what the rebates are; (2) the rebates returned to the hospital are not broken down by product category; (3) the hospital may not get the rebate check from its GPO until several months later, and perhaps in a different fiscal year; and (4) clinicians order many of these products, not the hospital or its VPMM, and oftentimes the product decisions are made by a committee of clinicians. The hospital's GPO affiliation rarely enters the picture. Moreover, hospital purchasing directors state that the CAF for any particular product is a tiny, insignificant portion of the hospital's spend in that clinical area; for example, catheters may cost the hospital $700,000 a year, but the rebated CAFs amount to only 1–2% of that. On a bigger scale, the total amount of CAFs received pales in comparison to the total spending on supplies.[53] Finally, there is no incentive for the hospital to pay higher prices up front to receive higher CAFs on the back end. Indeed, according to purchasing directors, if product prices rise, the hospitals don't buy, and the GPOs earn lower CAFs—so everyone loses.

GPO Contracts Do Not Guarantee Product Sales

GPOs not only do not purchase products used by their hospitals, but the presence of GPO contracts does not guarantee that hospitals will purchase products off of them. Purchasing directors uniformly state that hospitals buy "off contract" on every single day—by definition. According to one director, the hospital used 5,200 suppliers but only 28% of them were on the GPO's contract. Off-contract buying occurred even if the GPO had developed a contract for that product area and that contract brought a lower price. Clinician preference and product quality routinely trump a product's cost and its on-contract status. Product sales occur because clinicians want to use the product. The presence of a GPO contract not only does not trump quality, it also does not trump sales rep coverage, sales rep services, and product innovation.

The "Real" Problem at New Start-Up Manufacturers

The real problems for start-up firms are what management researchers label "the liability of newness": newer firms lack business legitimacy and established cooperative patterns with other firms, and face stiff competition from large incumbent companies. The risk of firm failure is highest at the earlier stages of a firm's life cycle. Some surmise the liability of newness masks another related problem, "the liability of smallness": the relative lack of resources and capabilities to compete, and thus greater vulnerability to economic pressures in the environment. It is no secret that most new ventures fail. According to the Bureau of Labor Statistics, 20% of new businesses fail during the first year of operation, 30% during the first two years, 50% during the first five years, and 80% within the first ten years.[54] The odds of survival are not great.

As for the small device vendors who typically bring the lawsuits listed above, they may face even higher risks of failing since they are dealing with (a) PPI items that (b) require clinician acceptance and thus (c) product trials and evaluations, as well as (d) continuing and extensive sales support. A key issue is whether the new start-ups have the capital resources to do all this. In the biopharma space, new firms discover new products but cannot afford to commercialize these products themselves. Instead, they need to undertake some "business development" to find larger partners to work with (e.g., in a strategic alliance) or an exit strategy (e.g., merger and acquisition, or M&A).

Some of the plaintiffs above had known financial problems prior to filing their lawsuits (e.g., negative cashflows, negative operating margins). One plaintiff received a 510(k) approval for its product in year 1 and began its full year of selling it in year 2 to both the acute care hospital market and the post-acute care alternate site market. The firm was not able to hire many sales reps and had trouble covering the "multiple ports of call" in both market segments on a national scale at the same time. To do any marketing necessitated cutting expenditures on product development and clinical testing—activities needed to convince clinicians and thereby support the sales effort. The plaintiff was, not surprisingly, losing millions of dollars annually for several years. One conclusion is that the lawsuits represented an effort to capitalize on the negative sentiment generated about the GPOs and their trading partners by the *New York Times* articles and during the Senate Hearings and thereby "re-capitalize" the firm.

Difficult Markets for Small Vendors

Many of the plaintiff startups chose to compete in the medical device market where large competitors often had a dominant market share. Although it is entirely possible for a truly innovative company to succeed in such a market, startups faced the following inherent challenges:

Fragmentation: Supplies are sold to individuals, hospitals, health systems, IDNs, and nursing homes. There are over 5,000 acute care facilities, 16,500 nursing care facilities, and over 20,000 centers of community and residential care for the elderly. None of these customer groups is highly concentrated in ownership, requiring firms to target tens of thousands of different purchase points for the sale and after-sales service of their products. For small startups with small sales forces, each salesperson would have thousands of potential target clients.

Mature market with well-capitalized competitors: Many of the incumbent suppliers released their products decades ago. New entrants offer fewer products and face competition in all product and customer segments without any first-mover advantage.

Economies of scope and scale: Larger firms tend to enjoy scale economies with respect to production, distribution, ease of ordering for customers and advertising/marketing. For multi-product vendors selling complementary products, scope economies may be available and supported by brand loyalty. Startups may thus be at a disadvantage.

Not first to market: Startups entering a mature market often pursue the lower cost and faster route to approval by the Food and Drug Administration (FDA). They do so by applying for a 510(k) approval, indicating that their products are substantially equivalent to incumbent (predicate) devices already on the market. This signals that the technology in question does not constitute a "breakthrough" therapy.

Unable to establish a dominant presence in the market niche: Because the start-up's product is not a pioneering application but, rather, an alternative to an existing product, the firm cannot grow its franchise value by establishing dominance in a niche category.

Failure to build a strong clinical evidence base: The most important strategic task for an innovation-driven startup in the medical technology field is defining its clinical superiority. Most startups fail to invest in clinical trials and publishing results from those trials—both of which need to demonstrate superiority. This severely hampers the firm's ability to enlist physicians as allies for clinical trials or purchase, especially given the decision to charge a significant price premium for the product. The lack of a clinical evidence base may contrast sharply with that developed by larger incumbent suppliers who likely have funded numerous peer-reviewed, published studies to demonstrate their products' efficacy.

Failure to build a product assortment that more closely addressed customer needs: Small competitors can create a strong niche by tailoring their product closely to expressed customer needs—surgical kits that matched specific patient types/procedures. Startups may be hampered by narrow product lines that leave gaps in such kits, however.

Highly competitive market: Startups face numerous competitors in each of the market segments in which they choose to play.

Increasing Difficulty of These Markets for Small Vendors

Industry observers have long noted the difficulties facing small vendors, many of which were evident by the late 1980s—years before the major wave of purchasing group consolidation. Access to capital became more difficult for small firms with new technologies as venture capital became more expensive and the public markets tightened. In 1990, The Safe Medical Devices Act altered the pre-market approval process for the majority of devices falling under the 510(k) category, increasing the reporting burden for vendors and lengthening product approval times by the FDA.[55]

Moreover, by the late 1980s, a reported 84% of hospitals began to restrict the access of the vendors' sales representatives to the end-user departments in their facilities. This restricted access was initiated by the hospitals, not the purchasing groups, in order to control their inventory and inventory costs, to reduce buying without a purchase order, and to allow hospital materials management departments to exert some control over vendor activities.[56] Part of this control is intended to help the hospital know what is being used and whether or not the staff know how to use it; materials staff assert that clinicians need proper in-service education prior to trialing a new product. Part of this control is that hospitals "don't want just anybody running around" the facility; instead, hospitals are preoccupied with patient safety and want to limit the non-clinician traffic flow on patient floors. With several hundred sales reps visiting a large hospital and calling on physicians and nurses on a given day, this is understandably an issue. The goal has been to reduce prices and cut costs, not limit access to new technology or firms without a contract. Hospitals are also concerned that unfettered vendor access can take clinicians away from patient care, diminish clinical productivity (and revenue), and undermine contract compliance.[57]

Some purchasing group activities likely made it more difficult for small vendors to get their products in front of hospitals and their clinicians, and thus to compete. The use of corporate portfolios, standardization, and longer-term contracts may have impeded access to technology from non-contracted vendors. In the same vein, purchasing group efforts to minimize technological differences among vendors may have differentially affected small vendors whose strategies focused on technological superiority rather than sales and marketing. Moreover, the development of risk-sharing contracts and one-stop-shopping may have precluded the participation of small vendors in partnerships with IDNs.

New or small firms do not require a group contract to order to increase sales. What they need is the opportunity to get the attention and enthusiasm of clinicians. Materials management staff uniformly state that the vendor needs to provide published, peer-reviewed clinical studies that (1) demonstrate the superiority or advantages of its products and (2) back up the supplier's claims. It is well known that physicians can be persuaded by credible clinical data. Some of the most credible data are head-to-head comparisons of the products made by rival manufacturers; other credible data come from a trial of the product on the hospital's own patients. Suppliers also need to curry the physicians' interest in their products through such venues as conferences, symposia, trade shows, and office visits. Supplier sales reps also need to be well-versed in their firm's clinical research to explain the published results, savvy in terms of their sales skills, persistent in opening up new accounts, and diligent to provide product support, education, and in-service training. Suppliers may also need to be willing to discount their product in order to be competitive and get hospitals to try it.

However, the major barriers confronting small suppliers may have been their own small size and the growing scale and concentration of their industry due to mergers and acquisitions (M&As). Due to their size, small suppliers could not invest as much in research and development (R&D) and sales, general, and administrative (SG&A) costs. Thus, they had fewer innovative products to show clinicians and fewer sales reps to detail them. Moreover, their low market share made it difficult for any purchasing group to justify the effort of contracting with them and trying to convert clinicians to utilize their products.

Suppliers began their trend toward consolidation around the same time as did hospitals and purchasing groups in the early to middle 1990s. The common timing of M&A across sectors of the healthcare industry is partly due to a rising stock market, which made acquisitions of publicly traded firms easier to do using one's higher stock price. M&A in the pharmaceutical and device industries may have also been spurred by slowdowns in FDA approvals and a diminution in the pipeline of new innovation coming out of larger firms. Finally, suppliers (like the purchasing groups) may have been prompted to consolidate as they saw their hospital customers and distributors consolidate. Rather than the purchasing groups creating supplier oligopolies, the groups were attracted to serve the supplier oligopolies due to their large market share.[58]

The consolidation trend resulted in an oligopolistic market structure in many product markets. Larger suppliers swallowed up smaller firms to access their innovative technology, which provided an exit strategy for many new startups, as well as to diversify their product lines.

More generally, new startups and small firms in the medical device industry face a host of competitive challenges to their survival.[59] These include:

- Finding a profitable niche in the market where large, diversified incumbents do not operate
- The ability to develop and sustain incremental product innovation on a 19–24 month cycle

- The need to develop predictable revenues and profits to attract investors and secure an IPO
- The need for long-term, sustained funding from venture capitalists and other sources
- The need for experienced management
- The need for a strong business plan
- The need for a planned exit strategy: new startups outnumber successful exits by 3-to-1 or 4-to-1
- The need to develop a broader product line rather than just a single technology
- The need to bring physicians and clinicians into the product development process early on to gain their input, enthusiasm, and support
- The need to plan for and secure insurance reimbursement
- The need for FDA approval
- The need for clinical trials by providers, and funding for these trials
- The need to market and sell the product to end-users
- The need to avoid hype and over-enthusiasm that can lead to investor disillusionment and abandonment (e.g., the medical device IPO class of 1996).

This list identifies the major contributors to new medical device firm success or failure. The role of purchasing groups is rarely mentioned as a considerable threat in the trade literature or by venture capitalists (VCs) who fund these companies. The notion, advanced in the Senate hearings cited above, that the emergence of large purchasing groups is tied in some way to diminished VCs' interest and investment in medical devices ignores the major reason for VC disinterest: the "nuclear winter" of medical device startups beginning in 1998 after the widespread failure to perform by the much-hyped IPO class of 1996.

Moreover, there are lots of reasons why small firms in this industry are unable to grow sales and market share. Competition in this industry is a function of several forces—including the number of competitors, the concentration of the industry, the size dispersion and heterogeneity of the firms, the price sensitivity of customers, the availability of capital, the firm's pipeline of new technology, the ability to interest physicians in that technology, etc. All of these factors describe conditions within the device industry itself. The existence and activities of outside purchasing groups are likely tangential or irrelevant.

Summary

During the first decade of the new millennium, GPOs took a public relations "smack-down" from a series of judges often acting in concert. In forty years of research, I cannot personally recall many other healthcare sectors taking (and withstanding) such a pounding—with the possible exception of (1) the investor-owned hospitals during the 1970s and 1980s regarding the quality of care they rendered and (2) the health maintenance organizations (HMOs) and managed care in general during the 1990s. In those instances, time and research evidence have jointly demonstrated that industry fears were unfounded. Today, the suspicions regarding the investor-owned hospitals and HMOs have been transferred to private equity firms involved in healthcare delivery; there is little evidence here so far. As the next two chapters seek to demonstrate, fears about the GPOs were also unfounded.

Appendix A: 2002 HIGPA Code of Conduct Principles

The HIGPA Code of Conduct Principles addressed the three major concerns that Senator Kohl expressed at the April 30, 2002, Senate Judiciary Antitrust Subcommittee hearing: conflicts of interest, contracting practices, and cost savings.

- Prohibiting employees who are in a position to influence the GPO contracting decisions from accepting any gifts, entertainment, favors, honoraria, or personal services payments (other than those of nominal value) from any participating vendor.
- Prohibiting employees who are in a position to influence the GPO's contracting decisions from having an equity interest in any participating vendor.
- Requiring GPO non-employees, officers, directors, or advisors who are in a position to influence the GPO's contracting decisions to disclose any gifts, entertainment, favors, honoraria, or personal services payments they receive from participating vendors and be recused from any negotiations or decisions relating to such participating vendor.
- Requiring GPO non-employees, officers, directors, or advisors to disclose any equity interests in any participating vendor and be recused from any negotiations or decisions relating to such participating vendor.

- Prohibiting a GPO from having a corporate equity interest in any participating vendor of clinical products or services, unless the acquisition of the equity interest demonstrably benefits the GPO's members by creating a source of a clinical product or service where there is no other source or very limited sources.
- Requiring each GPO to permit its members to (a) communicate directly with all vendors (b) assess products or services provided by all vendors and (c) purchase clinical preference products or services directly from vendors that do not contract with the GPO.
- Requiring that, to the extent contracting tools are used, either alone or in combination, in contracting arrangements, each GPO consider a set of specific factors—such as the occurrence of innovation in the product category and the market share of relevant vendors—to achieve a high quality of care and competitive pricing.
- Requiring each GPO to implement a contracting process that (a) informs potential vendors of the process for seeking and obtaining contracts with the GPO and (b) provides all interested vendors with the opportunity to solicit contracts.
- Requiring each GPO to individually engage in, or otherwise participate in, processes, and programs that routinely evaluate, and provide opportunities to contract for, innovative clinical products or services.
- Requiring each GPO to adopt policies and procedures that endeavor to address vendor grievances related to access to innovative clinical products or services.

HIGPA's Code of Conduct Principles addressed the issue of the cost savings GPOs provide by:

- Committing to support the production of authoritative surveys and studies that will provide the public with reliable and up-to-date information on the value of GPOs.

In addition, the Code addressed other issues, including some of those advanced by other healthcare trade associations, such as:

- Requiring GPOs to appoint a compliance officer who will be responsible for overseeing compliance with the Code and the fulfillment of the GPO's reporting requirements.
- Requiring each GPO member of HIGPA to certify annually to HIGPA that it is in compliance with the principles. HIGPA will publish an annual

report identifying those HIGPA members that have certified their compliance. This certification shall constitute a requirement for membership in HIGPA.

- Creating and supporting a web-based directory where vendors can post product information, including information about products that the vendors consider to be new and innovative.
- Requiring full disclosure to a GPO's members of all vendor payments, including those payments that are not allocable to the actual purchase of a member.
- Requiring GPOs to offer or participate in programs that promote diversity among vendors to include women and minority-owned vendors.

One GPO developed a web-based "Technology Forum" where suppliers could upload information on their new products for hospitals to consider, regardless of whether or not they had a GPO contract, as well as submit bids electronically.

Appendix B: 2005 HGPII Code of Conduct[60]

HGPII sought to assure ongoing adherence to ethical conduct and business practices, and to hold the confidence of the public and the Government in the integrity of the industry. For purposes of the antitrust laws, however, it is critical to distinguish between competitive bidding practices that result in certain vendors failing to win contracts and exclusionary practices that result in foreclosure of an entire market in which a particular product is sold, thereby reducing consumer welfare. In somewhat different terms, while GPO contracting practices may result in commercial disappointment for certain vendors, it is important that in most instances they do not injure competition.

Members of HGPII pledge to:

1. Establish a process for the industry to improve and monitor its ethical and business conduct practices through significant transparency and to sustain a high level of trust with the public.
2. Follow the six core ethical and business principles:

    a. have and adhere to a written code of business conduct. The code establishes high ethical values and sound business practices for the signator's group purchasing organization.

b. train all within the organization as to their personal responsibilities under the code.

c. work toward the twin goals of high-quality healthcare and cost effectiveness.

d. commit itself to work toward an open and competitive purchasing process free of conflicts of interest and any undue influences.

e. have the responsibility to each other to share their best practices in implementing the Principles; each Signatory shall participate in an annual Best Practices Forum.

f. be accountable to the public

3. Report annually on adherence to these principles using an Annual Public Accountability Questionnaire.

4. Participate in the Annual Best Practices Forum to discuss best ethical and business conduct practices with other GPO representatives and interested parties. For instance, the 2011 forum included sessions on expanding business opportunities for small, disadvantaged, and diverse vendors, trends in organizational ethics, current healthcare policy and legislative issues, and compliance programs. This forum also included a panel of representatives from six vendors who spoke about their experiences with GPOs.

The Initiative also formed an independent Advisory Council, with participants from outside the GPO industry, to provide a source of independent advice and counsel to a steering committee charged to build trust with the public and promoting legal compliance and high ethical standards and achieving accountability. The principal mechanism for accountability is the annual accountability questionnaire that is available to the public and "used by the Initiative Coordinator to compile a summary report on the adherence of those signing to participate to the Principles and a report on evolving Best Practices in fulfillment of the Principles." The questionnaire requests that each GPO describe:

1. The key components of the GPO's written code of business ethics and conduct. (Please provide a copy and describe any changes since the last submission.)

2. The GPO's policies and procedures that address conflicts of interest for all employees and clinical advisory members in a position to influence contracting decisions and for all other employees and members of the Board of Directors and/or the GPO's governing body.

3. The GPO's policies and procedures that address activities, including other lines of business of the GPO and the GPO's parent company or

affiliates, that might constitute conflicts of interest to the independence of its purchasing activity.

4. The GPO's policies with regard to disclosing to customers money or value received from vendors, whether in the form of administrative fees, marketing fees, partnership incentives, equity, or any other form.
5. If it discloses to each customer all fees, in any form, paid to the customer organization?
6. The GPO's policy with regard to whether all responsible vendors are eligible to compete and receive a contract award under the criteria.
7. The GPO's publicly available policy and procedure dealing with vendor rights, including a procedure for vendor grievances.
8. The GPO's policy and process to evaluate and provide opportunities to contract for innovative clinical products and services.
9. The GPO's program or activities encourage contracting with small, women-owned, and minority businesses.
10. Whether and in what manner the GPO distributes its written code of business ethics and conduct to all applicable employees, agents, contractors, clinical advisory committees, and others involved in group purchasing activity.
11. How new employees involved in group purchasing are provided an orientation to the written code of business ethics and conduct.
12. The nature and content of the GPO's annual employee refresher training on the written code of business ethics and conduct.
13. The mechanism (e.g., a corporate review board, ombudsman, corporate compliance, or ethics officer) for employees to report possible violations of the written code of business ethics and conduct to someone other than one's direct supervisor, if necessary.
14. The mechanism the GPO utilizes to follow up on reports of suspected violations to determine what occurred and who was responsible and to recommend corrective and other actions.
15. How the GPO employees' compliance with its written code of business ethics and conduct is measured in their job performance.
16. The processes the GPO utilizes to monitor, on a continuing basis, adherence to the written code of business ethics and conduct, and with applicable federal laws.
17. How the GPO fulfilled its obligation to participate in the most recent Best Practices Forum.

18. How the GPO reports to the company's Board of Directors or its Audit or other appropriate committee on the GPO's ethics and compliance program and its commitment to the Initiative's Principles.
19. The senior manager assigned responsibility to oversee the business ethics and conduct program.

Notes

1. Paul Starr. *The Social Transformation of American Medicine* (New York: Basic Books, 1982).
2. Ivan Illich. *Medical Nemesis* (London, UK: Calder & Boyars, 1975). John Knowles. *Doing Better and Feeling Worse: Health in the United States* (New York: W.W. Norton, 1977).
3. This list is taken from: https://www.masimo.com/company/news/media-room/nyt-series/. Accessed on November 16, 2021.
4. Walt Bogdanich, Barry Meier and Mary Williams Walsh. "Medicine's Middlemen: Questions Raised of Conflicts at 2 Hospital Buying Groups," *New York Times* (March 4, 2002). Walt Bogdanich, Barry Meier and Mary Williams Walsh. "When a Buyer for Hospitals Has a Stake in Drugs It Buys," *New York Times* (March 26, 2002).
5. Philip Zweig. "A Cost Analysis of the 1987 Medicare Anti-Kickback Safe Harbor for Group Purchasing Organizations and Pharmacy Benefit Managers" (October 20, 2018). White Paper.
6. National Association of State Procurement Officials. *Administrative Fees: Creative Funding for Central Procurement in Difficult Economic Times.* Research Brief (September 2009).
7. "HIGPA: Derwood Dunbar on GPOs," *Journal of Healthcare Contracting* (n.d.). Available online at: https://www.jhconline.com/higpa-derwood-dunbar-on-gpos.html. Accessed on November 20, 2021.
8. H.R. Report 95-453 95th Congress 1st Session (1977).
9. Letter from Richard P. Kusserow, Inspector General, DHHS, to Stephen S. Trott, Assistant Attorney General, Criminal Division, U.S. Department of Justice (April 17, 1985).
10. Richard P. Kusserow. "The Medicare & Medicaid Anti-Kickback Statute and The Safe Harbor Regulations—What's Next?" *Health Matrix: The Journal of Law-Medicine* 2(1) (1992): 49–70.
11. Letter from Richard P. Kusserow, Inspector General, DHHS, to Stephen S. Trott, Assistant Attorney General, Criminal Division, U.S. Department of Justice (April 17, 1985).
12. George Chulis. "Assessing Medicare's Prospective Payment System for Hospitals," *Medical Care Research & Review* 48(2) 1991: 167–206.

13. Letter from Richard P. Kusserow, Inspector General, DHHS, to Stephen S. Trott, Assistant Attorney General, Criminal Division, U.S. Department of Justice (April 17, 1985).

14. "Legislative History of Titles I-XX of the Social Security Act." Available online at: https://archive.org/stream/legislativehisto00unit_16/legislativehist o00unit_16_djvu.txt. Accessed on November 18. 2021.

15. Richard P. Kusserow and Thomas E. Herrmann. *Activities and Perspectives of the Office of Inspector General in the U.S. Department of Health and Human Services Regarding Group Purchasing Organizations (GPOs)* (Alexandria, VA: Strategic Management Services, 2013).

16. Durin Rogers. "The Medicare and Medicaid Anti-Kickback Statute: Safe Harbors Eradicate Ambiguity," *J.L. & Health* 8 (1993–1994): 223–244.

17. Department of Health and Human Services. Office of Inspector General. 42 CFR Part 1001. RIN 0991-AA49. Medicare and State Health Care Programs: Fraud and Abuse; OIG Anti-Kickback Provisions. Monday, July 29, 1991 (56 FR 35952). Available online at: https://oig.hhs.gov/fraud/docs/safeharbo rregulations/072991.htm. Accessed on November 21, 2021.

18. Philip Zweig. "A Cost Analysis of the 1987 Medicare Anti-Kickback Safe Harbor for Group Purchasing Organizations and Pharmacy Benefit Managers" (October 20, 2018). White Paper.

19. United States Senate Committee on the Judiciary, Subcommittee on Antitrust, Competition, and Business and Consumer Rights, "Hospital Group Purchasing: Lowering Costs at the Expense of Patient Health and Medical Innovation?" (April 30, 2002).

20. Page references are to the Senate Hearings.

21. David Cassak. "A Boost into the Market for Emerging Companies," *In Vivo* (May 1989): 14–19.

22. United States Senate Committee on the Judiciary, Subcommittee on Antitrust, Competition, and Business and Consumer Rights, "Hospital Group Purchasing: Has the Market Become More Open to Competition?" (July 16, 2003).

23. United States Senate Committee on the Judiciary, Subcommittee on Antitrust, Competition, and Business and Consumer Rights, "Hospital Group Purchasing: How to Maintain Innovation and Cost Savings" (September 14, 2004).

24. United States Senate Committee on the Judiciary, Subcommittee on Antitrust, Competition, and Business and Consumer Rights, "Hospital Group Purchasing: Are the Industry's Reforms Sufficient to Ensure Competition?" (March 15, 2006).

25. See S. Prakesh Sethi. *Group Purchasing Organizations: An Evaluation of Their Effectiveness in Providing Services to Hospitals and Their Patients* (New York, NY: International Center for Corporate Accountability, 2006).

26. General Accounting Office. *Group Purchasing Organizations: Pilot Study Suggests Large Buying Groups Do Not Always Offer Hospitals Lower Prices.* GAO-02-690T (April 30, 2002).

27. Office of the Inspector General. Department of Health and Human Services. *Review of Compliance with Conditions of the Group Purchasing Organization Safe Harbor, Premier Purchasing Partners, L.P.* OIG, A-05-01-00092.

28. General Accounting Office. *Group Purchasing Organizations: Use of Contracting Processes and Strategies to Award Contracts for Medical-Surgical Products.* GAO-03-998T.

29. Government Accounting Office. *Contract Management: Impact of Strategy to Mitigate Effects of Contract Bundling on Small Business Is Uncertain.* GAO-04-454.

30. Office of the Inspector General. *Review of Revenue from Vendors at Three Group Purchasing Organizations and Their Members.* OIG, A-05-03-00074.

31. Office of the Inspector General. *Review of Revenue from Vendors at Three Additional Group Purchasing Organizations and Their Members.* OIG, A-05-04-00073.

32. General Accounting Office. *Group Purchasing Organizations: Research on Their Pricing Impact on Health Care Providers.* GAO-323R (January 19, 2010).

33. Lawton R. Burns and J. Andrew Lee. "Group Purchasing Organizations (GPOs): Issues and Evidence," *Health Care Management Review* 33(3) (2008): 203–215.

34. Lawton R. Burns and Allison Briggs. "Hospital Purchasing Alliances: Ten Years After," *Health Care Management Review* 45(3) (July/September) (2020): 186–195.

35. General Accounting Office. *Group Purchasing Organizations: Services Provided to Customers and Initiatives Regarding Their Business Practices.* GAO-10-738 (August 2010).

36. *Empirical Data Lacking to Support Claims of Savings with Group Purchasing Organizations* (Minority Staff Report—Senate Finance Committee) (September 2010).

37. Government Accountability Office. *Lack of Price Transparency May Hamper Hospitals' Ability to be Prudent Purchasers of Implantable Medical Devices.* GAO-12-126 (January 2012).

38. Mark V. Pauly and Lawton R. Burns. "Price Transparency for Medical Devices," *Health Affairs* 27(6) (2008): 1544–1553. Government Accountability Office. *Medicare: Lack of Price Transparency May Hamper Hospitals' Ability to Be Prudent Purchasers of Implantable Medical Devices.* GAO-12-126. (Washington, DC: GAO, 2012). Mark V. Pauly and Lawton R. Burns. "When Is Medical Care Price Transparency a Good Thing (And When Isn't It)?" in Jennifer Hefner and Mona Al-Amin (Eds.), *Advances in Health Care Management—Transforming Health: A Focus on Consumerism and Profitability.* Volume 19 (Emerald Press, 2020): pp. 75–97.

39. Government Accountability Office. *Group Purchasing Organizations: Federal Oversight and Self-Regulation.* GAO-12-399R (March 30, 2012).

40. Government Accountability Office. *Group Purchasing Organizations: Federal Oversight and Self-Regulation.* GAO-12-399R (March 30, 2012): p. 4.

41. Bushra Rahman, Eugene Schneller, and Natalia Wilson. "Integrity and Efficiency in Collaborative Purchasing." In Gabriella Racca and Christopher Yukins (Eds.), *Integrity and Efficiency in Sustainable Public Contracts: Balancing Corruption Concerns in Public Procurement Internationally* (Bruxelles: Bruylant, 2014). Chapter 3.

42. Government Accountability Office. *Group Purchasing Organizations: Funding Structure Has Potential Implications for Medicare Costs.* GAO-15-13 (October 2014).

43. This list of lawsuits is not meant to be exhaustive.

44. David Balto. "Recent Medical Device Antitrust Cases" (December 2009). Available online at: http://www.dcantitrustlaw.com/assets/content/documents/Medical%20Device%20Antitrust%20Cases.pdf. Accessed on November 17, 2021. See also: S. Prakesh Sethi. *Group Purchasing Organizations: An Evaluation of Their Effectiveness in Providing Services to Hospitals and Their Patients* (New York, NY: International Center for Corporate Accountability, 2006): Appendix C.

45. Frank Hinman and Brian Rocca. "The Aggregation Theory: A Recent Series of Decisions in Bundled Discounting Cases Threatens to Expand Section One into Unchartered Territory," *The Antitrust Source* (February 2007).

46. Parallel and relevant arguments are presented in: Keven Murphy, Edward Snyder, and Robert Topel. "Competitive Discounts and Antitrust Policy," George J. Stigler Center for the Study of the Economy and State, University of Chicago. Working Paper No. 250 (2013).

47. Lawton R. Burns. *The Business of Healthcare Innovation,* 3rd Edition (Cambridge, UK: Cambridge University Press, 2020). Lawton R. Burns. *The U.S. Healthcare Ecosystem* (New York: McGraw-Hill, 2021).

48. Lawton R. Burns, J. Andrew Lee, Eric T. Bradlow, and Anthony C. Antonacci. "Surgeon Evaluation of Suture and Endo-Mechanical Products," *Journal of Surgical Research* 141(2007): 220–233.

49. The five product categories included: clip appliers, internal mechanical and endoscopic-mechanical staplers, trocars (bladed and non-bladed), sutures and needles, and endoscopic specimen retrieval devices. The eight vendors included two market leaders (J&J/EES, Tyco/US Surgery) and six smaller players (AMR, ConMed, Genicon, Teleflex, Neosurg, Aesculap).

50. Lawton Burns. *The Business of Healthcare Innovation,* 3rd Edition (Cambridge, UK: Cambridge University Press, 2020). Prior editions in 2005 and 2012.

51. Dan Lovallo and Daniel Kahneman. "Delusions of Success: How Optimism Undermines Executives' Decisions," *Harvard Business Review* (July 2003).

52. Lawton Burns, Michael Housman, and Charles Robinson. "Market Entry and Exit by Biotechnology and Medical Device Companies Funded by Venture Capital." *Health Affairs*. Web Exclusive (December 2008).
53. For example, $4–5 Million in CAFs versus $1.4 Billion in total supply spend.
54. U.S. Bureau of Labor Statistics—Business Employment Dynamics. Available online at: https://www.bls.gov/bdm/us_age_naics_00_table7.txt. Accessed on March 12, 2022.
55. Gordon Schatz. "The Impact of the Safe Medical Devices Act of 1990," *In Vivo* (April, 1991): 27.
56. David Cassak. "Revolution in Selling to the O.R.," *In Vivo* (April, 1989): 15–19.
57. "GPO Contracting in the New Health Care Environment: Strategic Implications for Manufacturers."
58. "In GPO Battles, A Pyrrhic Victory for Suppliers," *In Vivo* (September, 2002).
59. David Cassak. 2006. Presentation to The Wharton School.
60. This section is taken verbatim from Bushra Rahman, Eugene S. Schneller, and Natalia Wilson. *Integrity and Efficiency in Collaborative Purchasing* (Brussels: Bruylant, 2015).

6

GPO Performance: A Review of the Literature

Overview

It is difficult to summarize the performance of GPOs and group purchasing. As noted in prior chapters, there is no national database on the GPO sector and no readily available and comparable information to analyze. The same holds true for supply chain management in hospitals. These are all rather opaque areas. The extant literature consists of a handful of academic field studies (which have been turned into texts), a larger number of industry-sponsored reports (either pro-GPO or anti-GPO), analyses by the Government Accountability Office (GAO) chronicled in the previous chapter, and a host of trade magazine and newspaper articles. In 2014, the American Hospital Association and its Association for Healthcare Resource and Materials Management (AHRMM) awarded me a grant to conduct (a) a national survey of the hospital members of GPOs and (b) a review of the literature.[1] This chapter presents evidence from that survey and updates the review.

This review first summarizes the results of the academic research and industry-sponsored studies that speak to the issues and arguments raised in the Senate Hearings. It then summarizes the evidence base on GPOs as it speaks to the performance and value challenges laid at the feet of the GPOs (described in Chapter 5).

The review limits itself to U.S.-based academic research and industry-sponsored studies on GPOs utilized by hospitals. I do not consider physician-owned GPOs, which have existed for more than two decades and have become quite controversial.[2,3] I also readily acknowledge that group

© The Author(s), under exclusive license to Springer
Nature Switzerland AG 2022
L. R. Burns, *The Healthcare Value Chain*,
https://doi.org/10.1007/978-3-031-10739-9_6

purchasing is a global phenomenon that is not confined to the U.S. (covered later below). Finally, my review seeks to avoid any tendency to homogenize the GPOs or treat them as a monolithic group. Indeed, research highlights the diversity in GPO structure and function (i.e., their history, formation, ownership, governance, contracting practices, etc.), the variability in their performance and member satisfaction, and the variability in their customers.[4,5] Such variability is often forgotten and neglected in the GPO debate.

GPO Operations and Strategy

Just prior to the first Senate hearing in 2002, Wharton School researchers published a field study of the U.S. healthcare industry that included a discussion of the role of GPOs in the supply chain, as well as GPO operations and strategy.[6] The analysis was thus not colored by the issues and rhetoric that prevailed during the Senate hearing and in the *New York Times* articles.

The analysis considered the relationships GPOs have with suppliers upstream and hospitals downstream, as well as GPO efforts to develop strategic capabilities in clinical standardization, product (stock-keeping unit, or SKU) rationalization, product bundling, and reductions in both costs and utilization. The latter efforts met with only mixed success. Utilizing a mixture of interviews and case studies, the study offered an objective view of how GPOs functioned and how well they served the welfare of their hospital members. The Wharton study suggested that while GPOs sought to serve the hospitals' interests, their national scope and size limited their ability to represent the interests of their numerous, diverse members. Their performance was also constrained by the tendency of hospital systems and integrated delivery networks (IDNs) to contract with suppliers on their own. In light of the criticisms leveled at the GPOs during the Senate hearings, the analysis concluded that GPOs are not as good as they think they are but are certainly not as bad as their critics say they are.[7]

Four years later, researchers at Arizona State University (ASU) published a second field study of the supply chain in healthcare.[8] The authors argued that GPOs served as an important partner in hospitals' efforts to manage their procurement processes, reduce their cost of operations, and improve the clinical outcomes of their patients. The study was also quite clear in stating that GPOs served the interests of hospitals, not the suppliers. Hospitals had very measured strategies for utilizing their GPOs and often engaged suppliers in the marketplace on their own for both GPO-contracted and non-GPO-contracted products. They identified four types of GPO engagement by hospitals:

Type 1—GPO-dominated purchasing: high GPO involvement in product selection and high use of GPO contracts.

Type 2—Strategic outsourcing of contracting: low GPO involvement in product selection and high use of GPO contracts.

Type 3—Strategic manipulation of purchasing: high GPO involvement in product selection and low use of GPO contracts.

Type 4—Hospital/IDN dominated purchasing: low GPO involvement in product selection and strategic sourcing and low use of GPO contracts.

The existence of these four different types of engagement rested on the heterogeneity in both the GPOs and their hospital members. Hospitals chose GPOs on the basis of fit with their needs and capabilities, including the possible presence of GPO demands for committed contracting. The ASU analysis recast the debate from how GPOs behaved (the focus of the rhetoric in the press and Senate hearings) to how hospitals behaved in their use of GPOs.

Supply Prices

Accompanying and supporting the first Senate hearing was a report released by the General Accounting Office (GAO) on the GPOs' contract prices obtained for 18 hospitals in one geographic market for medical devices (e.g., pacemakers).[9] The April 2002 report compared the prices obtained by GPOs with the prices that hospitals negotiated on their own.[10] The report found that the use of GPO contracts did not always guarantee the lowest prices for their hospital members, although the pattern varied by product category. For some pacemakers, hospitals beat the GPO price by 39%; for other pacemaker models, the GPO contract prices outperformed hospital-negotiated contract prices by 26%. Price savings had no relationship to GPO size; large GPOs with large volume purchases did not always get lower prices. Savings were related to hospital size, however: larger hospitals (500 + beds) could negotiate lower prices on their own, while smaller hospitals were more likely to obtain lower prices using GPO contracts.

The GAO report found that the use of group contracts by small-size (less than 200 beds) and medium-size (200–499 beds) hospitals led to price savings by hospitals.[11] This finding is important since the vast majority (94%) of hospitals in the U.S. fall into these two bedsize categories. The GAO found that group contracts for large hospitals with 500 beds or more did not produce savings. This says less about the effectiveness of groups and more about the documented tendency among large hospitals to engage in self-contracting. The Lewin Group found that large hospital systems and IDNs were less likely than smaller and independent hospitals to utilize purchasing group contracts.[12] While 75% of hospitals overall used the contracts, only 69% of IDNs and hospital systems did. Moreover, the larger the hospital system, the less the system used the group's contracts.

A July 2003 GAO report specified some of the factors involved in obtaining lower pricing.[13] For the five smaller GPOs queried, hospital adherence to contract commitment levels was the most important factor in obtaining favorable supplier pricing; for the two large GPOs queried, volume was the most important factor.

A 2009 report issued by academic researchers at ASU suggested one reason why GPO prices were not always the lowest price that hospitals could obtain.[14] In a survey of 429 hospitals in 55 hospital systems, 35% of hospitals and 42% of systems indicated they used the GPO contract as a starting point (e.g., price ceiling) in their negotiations with manufacturers from which they negotiated the price downward. Indeed, supply chain executives at large IDNs and hospital systems stated their goal was to leverage the group's price and renegotiate it even lower ("enhance the group's contracts"). This percentage varied for different types of products, being less likely for pharmaceuticals (29–35%) and commodity items (33–44%) and more likely for capital equipment (40–52%) and physician preference items (PPIs, 50–57%). These percentages reflected the fact that respondents did not perceive GPO prices as being the lowest prices across all product categories. When asked to rate the GPO's role in obtaining the lowest price using a five-point Likert scale (1 = not at all important, 5 = extremely important), respondents gave the GPO the highest rating for commodity items (4.9) and pharmaceuticals (4.9), but lower ratings for PPIs (3.6). Within the PPI category, hospitals utilized GPO contracts and GPO pricing to greater or lesser degrees depending on the sub-category of products. GPO contracts were more heavily utilized for stents (29%) than for orthopedic implants (19%) or pacemakers (16–17%); hospitals were more likely to use the GPO price as a "reference price" for orthopedic implants (15%) than for stents and pacemakers (8%), and more likely to use GPO price as a "benchmark" for orthopedic implants (23%) than for stents or pacemakers (20–21%).

A 2003 report by The Lewin Group, conducted for the Health Industry Group Purchasing Association (HIGPA, the GPO trade association), surveyed materials managers about the financial benefits offered by their GPOs.[15] The Lewin study found that small hospitals using the group's contracts achieved 1–6% lower prices than did other small hospitals contracting on their own. Using group contracts in three product areas (pharmaceuticals, medical-surgical, laboratory) saved 17% compared to self-contracting; using the group's best price (tied to volume) saved 26%. The average value provided by the group to the hospital, measured as a percentage of purchases, was 10.4%; the majority of the savings (7.7%) came from the lower prices negotiated by the group.

As suggested by the ASU research, the Lewin Group found that 82% of respondents perceived GPO prices as "benchmarks" or price ceilings, below which hospitals might negotiate even lower prices. Price discounts on product purchases represented the majority of these benefits, accounting for 7.7% savings on purchases; an additional 1.8% savings was provided by dividends received from GPOs, along with another 0.8% savings on labor staffing. When asked what would happen if GPOs were absent, 90% of hospitals responded that prices would rise; 7% said there would be no change in prices, and another 2% were unsure. Qualitative remarks suggested that hospitals felt suppliers would increase their negotiating power and that products might revert to (higher) list prices. Hospitals also felt they would have to add staffing to compensate for the functions performed by the GPOs.

Most of the literature on price savings obtained through GPO contracts is based on survey responses from hospital purchasing managers and anecdotal reports. Only two of the studies were peer-reviewed.[16,17] Moreover, many of the studies reporting high or low savings were funded by the GPO industry itself or by critics of the GPO industry (e.g., Medical Device Manufacturers Association).

To ascertain the quality of the evidence base, members of Congress requested the GAO to review the literature regarding the impact that GPOs exerted on pricing.[18] The GAO located only one peer-reviewed study published in the academic literature. That study conducted a national survey of hospital vice-presidents of materials management (VPMMs), who reported that GPOs saved them money on product prices, reduced transactions costs, and improved revenues through rebates and dividends.[19] That study received subsequent validation by another national survey of hospital managers (chief financial officers, directors of materials management, etc.) in 2010 that indicated high satisfaction with GPOs for their pricing and savings.[20] Nevertheless, a Minority Report from the U.S. Senate Finance

Committee emphasized, as did the GAO study, the lack of empirical data to substantiate claims that GPOs helped their hospitals to save money.[21]

In a more recent effort to investigate this issue, two consultants (and critics of the GPO industry) analyzed 8,100 after-market transactions for capital equipment in which the winning GPO price was put up for bid after the initial GPO auction.[22] On average, hospitals achieved 10–14% savings over the period 2001–2010, suggesting that GPOs did not secure the best pricing for their hospital members. The paper is consistent with the evidence reviewed above that hospitals could often obtain better pricing than their GPOs, particularly when using the GPO price as the ceiling or benchmark from which to negotiate additional discounts. However, the paper did not study GPO prices but rather the discounted pricing from auctions—which was comparable to what hospitals obtained when negotiating on their own. The fact that auction prices were lower than GPO prices failed to address what GPOs did (or did not) achieve for their members. Moreover, the paper suffered from a methodological flaw of commingling several different product categories that have greater or lesser degrees of GPO market penetration.

An interesting set of case studies conducted as part of a Master's Degree thesis compared the costs of product procurement across three models: self-procurement by hospitals, use of a national GPO, and a hybrid approach that combined use of a national and a regional GPO. The study found that the use of the national GPO outperformed hospital self-contracting, but that a hybrid approach led to additional savings. Similar findings were reported for the breadth of products and the presence of products with innovative features.[23]

Finally, several recent government and academic studies shed further light on why hospitals and their GPOs vary in their ability to obtain lower pricing for medical devices (the subject of the April 2002 GAO report). A 2012 GAO report found that hospitals paid widely varying prices for cardiovascular and orthopedic implants.[24] The GAO concluded that a major source of the variation rested with the hospitals' ability to manage their relationships with physicians. The hospital's ability was a function of the number of specialists whose preferences needed to be considered, the dollar volume each specialist accounted for and the referral volume each specialist generated, the specialists' ties to the suppliers, and the presence of confidentiality clauses imposed by suppliers on the hospitals which prevented the latter from sharing price information with physicians. Researchers at the University of California reported similar results on pricing variations due to physician-hospital relationships.[25] Both studies were consonant with the theoretical arguments outlined in an earlier academic paper as to why pricing variations existed and why mandated price transparency would not reduce them.[26]

There is a nascent base of empirical academic research on this issue. It has often found no impact—either positive or negative—of national GPO membership on supply costs.[27] Other researchers have found savings on specific supply categories (medical devices) in small purchasing cooperatives.[28] One problem is that some studies do not make GPO membership or contract utilization their focus.[29] The focus instead is on the effect of physician employment on supply costs; GPO membership is often a control measure. Another problem is the use of binary measures of GPO membership (e.g., member vs. non-member) or GPO utilization (route more or less than 60% of purchases through GPOs).[30] Such measures leave little variation in their dependent measures to explain. A third problem is the reliance on measures of national GPO membership, ignoring the growing use of regional and local GPOs, as well as self-contracting, to extract further price discounts. While some researchers do measure membership in regional/local alliances, they do so using a binary indicator; they find no effect on supply costs.[31]

One recent study surmounts many of these issues by using better data. As the predictor, it uses the percentage of hospital supply spending in 2014 routed through national, regional, and local GPO alliances—taken from a national survey of hospitals. The dependent variable is hospital expenditures on a variety of supply items (PPIs, medical supplies, pharmaceuticals, non-clinical supplies) taken from the American Hospital Association. The measure of supply expense is adjusted by the hospital's case-mix index (CMI) and logarithmically transformed. The study found that, relative to either spending off-contract or spending through self-negotiated agreements, GPO-mediated spending exerts a downward but insignificant effect on supply costs. However, GPO-mediated spending does exert a significant downward effect on supply costs for smaller hospitals.[32] This latter finding has been consistently reported (see above).

Value of Group Purchasing

Favorable Evidence

One issue related to best pricing is whether or not GPOs deliver value in the aggregate to their hospital members. Such "value" is often measured in terms of the overall savings that GPOs can provide.

Arizona State University (ASU) Studies

One early report conducted at ASU utilized case study evidence collected by Novation, the GPO contracting for hospitals in the University Hospital Consortium (UHC) and Voluntary Hospitals of America (VHA). The case studies were based on interviews with and data collected from department managers in 55 hospitals in ten hospital systems. The report compared the cost of self-contracting by hospitals with the cost of GPO contracting.[33] Hospital-led efforts incurred a cost of $3,116 per contract compared to GPO-led efforts of $1,749 per contract, suggesting a savings of $1,367 per contract when hospitals outsourced this activity to their GPOs. Taking into account the total cost of contracting for a base of 340 contracts, the researchers concluded it would cost a hospital $353,147 to perform the functions performed by the GPOs; by using the GPOs, the hospital avoided $154,927 in cost. To further substantiate their conclusions, the researchers cited evidence from a prior 1997 survey of UHC/VHA hospitals. The survey found that the higher the level of hospital participation in the GPO's contracts, the lower the total supply expense per adjusted discharge.

A 2009 follow-up study by ASU researchers pursued the same topic as the Novation study using a larger sample of 429 hospitals in 28 hospital systems.[34] The study reported that these hospitals routed 72.8% of their purchases in four product categories (commodities, pharmaceuticals, PPIs, and capital equipment) through their GPOs and achieved an estimated 18.7% in savings. Overall industry savings amounted to $36 Billion in price savings and another $2 Billion in human resource savings. The percentage of purchases routed through GPOs (and the savings achieved) varied by product category: general medical-surgical items = 82% (19% savings), inpatient pharmaceuticals = 89% (15% savings), and PPIs = 34–48% (15–17% savings). Respondents indicated that the absence of a GPO led to an increase in acquisition cost of 3.1% at the hospital level and 19.7% at the system level; the absence of a GPO also led to a workforce increase of 9 additional full-time-equivalents (FTEs) needed at the hospital level and 15 FTEs at the system level.

Muse & Associates Studies

Muse & Associates conducted a parallel set of studies. In a 2000 report, Muse reported results from interviews conducted with purchasing and accounting managers in 221 hospitals across the country.[35] Respondents indicated that hospitals utilized GPOs for 72% of their non-labor purchases and that GPOs helped them to achieve 10–15% savings on their supply purchases in 1999 (with overall industry savings of $19–33 Billion annually). Respondents also reported that GPO contracting (a) helped them to reduce provider staff time involved in product purchasing, (b) supplied them with product information they would otherwise have had to compile on their own, and (c) helped them to standardize product purchases. Utilizing the 72% statistic as a lower bound along with the 80% metric suggested by the GPO industry as an upper bound, Muse then computed the aggregate national savings in product purchases obtained by GPOs. They computed this by identifying national health expenditures (NHE) on hospitals and nursing homes using data from the Centers for Medicare and Medicaid Services (CMS), taking the proportion of those expenditures that are non-labor expenses (44.6% for hospitals, 25% for nursing homes), and then applying the percentage of non-labor costs that GPOs mediate using the upper and lower bound statistics. They then applied the various savings rates in GPO contracts reported in the literature (10%, 15%, 18%) to derive the national savings due to GPOs.

In a 2002 report meant as a HIGPA/industry response to the first Senate hearing, Muse & Associates updated these findings utilizing more recent NHE data.[36] The same benchmark statistics from the earlier report were applied to the updated NHE figures. The report emphasized the additional spending on products that hospitals would bear if restrictions were placed on their utilization of GPOs (e.g., elimination of contract administration fees or CAFs, reduction in GPO savings), and the impact on societal costs due to increased spending on Medicare, Medicaid, and Veterans Administration (VA) patients. In June 2005, Muse & Associates released a third report updating the findings from the prior two.[37] Muse estimated that the GPOs generated up to 15% supply savings for a hospital and aggregate savings of $38.7 Billion.

The Healthcare Supply Chain Association (HSCA, formerly known as HIGPA) commissioned Locus Systems in 2009 to update the findings through 2007 and 2008.[38,39] The aggregate savings to the industry for 2008 ranged from $29–64 Billion. Finally, in 2014, HSCA commissioned a consulting firm to update the 2009 report to estimate GPO savings for 2012 and projected savings over five and ten-year periods.[40] Savings for 2012 ranged from $25–55 Billion.

Lewin Group Studies

The Lewin Group likewise conducted an analysis of the value provided by GPOs. In a 2003 report prepared for HIGPA, Lewin surveyed 79 purchasing managers representing 183 hospitals.[41] Similar to the studies above, they reported that hospitals purchased 75% of their supplies via GPO contracts. However, the larger the hospital, the smaller the percentage of supply purchases routed through GPOs: hospitals with less than 500 beds routed 80–83% of purchases through GPOs, while hospitals with 500+ beds routed only 63% of their purchases through GPOs. Moreover, the larger the hospital system, the smaller the percentage of purchases routed through the GPO: freestanding hospitals utilized GPOs for 79.6% of purchases, 3-hospital systems utilized GPOs for 70.2% of purchases, 6-hospital systems utilized GPOs for 58.3% of purchases, and 13-hospital systems utilized GPOs for only 50% of supply purchases. In other words, hospital reliance on GPOs diminished as hospitals grew larger in bed size, joined a hospital system, and developed larger systems. This reflected the ability of larger hospitals and systems to negotiate the same or better pricing as GPOs, as well as their ability to offer vendors greater market penetration, higher levels of contract compliance, and greater product standardization in exchange for lower unit pricing.

Similar in vein to the ASU analysis, the Lewin Group report documented the variation in hospital compliance with GPO contracts across product areas. The percentage of hospitals with compliance levels of 60% or more was highest for commodity items (89.1%) and pharmaceuticals (84.9%), but much lower for PPIs (32.4%) and capital equipment (19.9%). Overall, hospitals reaped 17% savings in their utilization of GPO contracts across three product categories (medical-surgical, pharmaceuticals, and laboratory).

Other Studies

Several literature reviews conclude that GPOs save their hospital members money via contracts and prices negotiated with product suppliers, value-added services, and reduced labor staffing.[42] Hospitals themselves routinely reported that their national GPOs save them money in these ways. In one earlier national survey, GPOs fostered demonstrable cost savings and margin improvement, lower prices, sharebacks of CAFs, and information technology.[43] In a later national survey, the researchers found a significant increase in hospitals reporting savings in many of these same areas: sharebacks, information technology, and centralized staffing economies via GPO use.[44] There was a slight decrease in hospitals reporting savings from demonstrable cost savings and margin improvement, but the overall level of agreement on such savings remained very high.

While some reports suggest that GPOs fail to save hospitals money, other reports that base their findings on what hospitals tell researchers provide a different perspective. One survey of hospitals reported that 30% of hospitals reported hard-dollar savings of 0–4%, 31% reported savings of 5–8%, 26% reported savings of 9–14%, and 13% reported savings of 15% or more (see Table 6.1).[45] These survey data also compared the hard-dollar savings that hospitals achieve through their combined GPO purchases versus what they earn on their own outside of GPO contracts. Table 6.1 shows that more hospitals report higher savings earned through GPOs than on their own via self-contracting

Another national survey reported the percentage of hospitals that affirm the cost-saving role of their primary national GPOs across multiple dimensions.[46] These savings are depicted in Table 6.2. Hospitals also report value derived from non-price services, such as benchmarking data, data analytics, and data on clinical outcomes. These findings are important as they suggest customer satisfaction with many of the newer initiatives pursued by the national GPOs (see Chapter 3).

One consulting group estimated that GPOs generated aggregate cost savings for 2016 in the amount of $34 Billion, based on a set of parameters roughly consistent with other figures cited here: 30% + of national health expenditures accounted for by hospitals, 30% non-labor expense in hospitals, roughly 60% GPO-mediated spend in a sample of hospitals, and a 13.1% GPO savings rate.[47]

Academic research shows that, between 2004 and 2014, the percentage of U.S. hospitals using GPOs rose from 72.9 to 75.2%. The research suggests one reason for the increase: the use of GPOs is associated with higher hospital

Table 6.1 Estimated percentage of hard dollar savings realized annually using combined GPO purchases versus outside GPO contracts

% Savings	Use GPO contract (%)	Outside GPO contract
0	3	5
1–2	8	21
3–4	19	23
5–6	17	16
7–8	14	10
9–10	14	12
11–12	9	4
13–14	3	1
15 or more	13	7

Source 2010 Hospital GPO Use Survey. Hospitals & Health Networks. Survey sponsored by MMHC/AHRMM

Table 6.2 Percentage of hospitals reporting satisfaction with savings from national GPO efforts

Savings from lower prices	88%
Demonstrable cost-savings and improvement	86%
Savings from contract standardization	84%
Savings from providing the market price point	73%
Savings from rebating CAFs back to hospital	67%
Savings from information technology	64%
Savings from economies of centralized staffing	57%
Savings from shareholder dividends	39%

operating margins.[48] Academic research also suggests that hospitals are more likely to add a GPO affiliation in a given year (14.5%) than to drop an affiliation (8%). Whether affiliations are added or dropped seems to be partially driven by how many affiliations the hospital currently has: those with fewer affiliations add, while those with many affiliations drop. Adding affiliations does not increase a hospital's supply chain efficiency but dropping an affiliation exerts a harmful effect. Hospitals that switch their national GPO affiliation without either adding or dropping total affiliations also experience higher supply chain efficiency.[49]

Unfavorable Evidence

Lynn Everard issued two rebuttals to the above claims regarding GPO value. In a 2003 white paper, Everard argued that historically, GPOs delivered value by obtaining price discounts for their members.[50] But such savings accrued more to smaller hospitals with low negotiating power and for mostly commodity items. Over time, with greater product commoditization (and thus, presumably, more competition among suppliers that would lower prices), the GPO value to hospitals has diminished. The value offered to suppliers—in the form of easier market access, control over a large block of hospital purchases, and lower selling costs which allowed suppliers to keep their prices steady—thus now exceeded the value to hospital members. He also opined that GPOs did not really act as agents of the hospital for several reasons:

- Low hospital compliance with GPO contracts
- Multiple hospital GPO memberships
- Hospital systems' use of GPO prices as benchmarks or leverage
- Lack of hospital input into GPO policy

- Inability of hospitals to evaluate or oversee GPO decision-making
- Historical hospital dependence on GPOs
- GPO fees paid by the suppliers

In a second white paper, Everard challenged the studies reviewed above regarding their findings on GPO cost savings.[51] He correctly observed there were no empirical studies substantiating the savings that GPOs help hospitals reap; the results were entirely based on opinion surveys. There was no definition of "cost savings" and no clear demarcation of "savings off of what." He also argued that the CAFs charged by GPOs and distributed back to hospitals were not really savings, since suppliers purportedly covered the cost of the CAFs through higher prices and limits on the discounts they offered.

Hal Singer similarly criticized the studies reviewed above regarding the aggregate value provided by GPOs, contending they compared savings from GPOs with an unrealistic scenario of purchasing without GPOs present.[52] By contrast, Singer argued that GPOs did not pass along all of the CAFs they collected from suppliers (estimated to be 68–79% according to two 2005 OIG-DHHS reports—see below). He suggested, as did those testifying in the Senate hearings, that GPOs suffered from agency problems in their relationships with hospitals by virtue of their receipt of CAFs from suppliers. He further suggested that removal of the safe harbor exemption for GPOs would not increase governmental spending on healthcare for the Medicare, Medicaid, and VA populations; instead, hospitals would capture a greater share of the CAFs now paid to the GPOs.

GPO Contract Fees

This section and the next deal with perhaps the two most contentious topics surrounding GPOs: contract fees and contracting practices. These sections reiterate some of the findings reported by the GAO and OIG-DHHS reported in Chapter 5.[53]

A July 2003 GAO report focused on the business practices followed by GPOs in contracting for commodity items and medical devices. The report found that CAFs generally conformed to the 3% safe harbor guideline (but not always); the modal fee was 2 percent, while the highest fees were typically achieved in contracts with private label manufacturers.[54] The report mentioned that having to pay these CAFs, along with the lower prices negotiated by the GPOs and their slow contracting processes, could pose a barrier for small suppliers.

In January 2005 and then again in May 2005, the Office of the Inspector General within the Department of Health and Human Services (OIG-DHHS) audited the history of CAFs collected by the GPOs.[55,56] The January 2005 report examined two large GPOs from 1998–2002 and a third from 1999–2002. The CAFs they collected amounted to $1.8 Billion, while GPO operating expenses amounted to $487 Million; this left the three GPOs with net revenues of $1.3 Billion. Of this surplus, $898 Million was distributed back to hospital members, while the residual $415 Million was kept by the GPOs as retained earnings. The government also investigated whether the hospitals that received these revenue distributions fully accounted for them on their Medicare cost reports. For the 21 hospitals examined, $200 Million of the $255 Million distributed by the GPOs was correctly offset.

The May 2005 audit of three additional (and large) GPOs examined CAFs collected during the 2001–2003 period. Here the CAFs amounted to $513 Million, with $238 Million in operating expenses and $275 Million in net revenues. Of the $275 Million, $217 Million was distributed back to members and $58 Million was kept as retained earnings. Among the hospitals receiving these distributions, seven systems (comprising 38 hospitals) received 57% of the total ($123 Million out of $217 Million); $115 Million of this $123 Million amount was correctly offset on the hospitals' Medicare cost reports.

On a related note, the OIG-DHHS audited one of the large GPOs (Premier) to ascertain whether it was complying with the GPO safe harbor conditions by notifying and disclosing to its hospital members the CAFs it received from suppliers.[57] Of the 107 hospitals belonging to Premier that responded to a survey, 70 received an advance agreement indicating that the GPO would receive a CAF from vendors based on the hospital's volume of purchases, while 37 did not. Of these 37, 26 were subject to the safe harbor reporting requirements (they were affiliates of rather than owned by Premier's partners). Of the 107 respondents, 72 received a report showing actual supplier payments to Premier, while 35 did not; of the latter, only 8 were subject to the safe harbor reporting requirements. According to the OIG, part of the problem reflected Premier's reliance on its partners and group affiliates to disseminate information to its hospital members.

A 2010 GAO report stated that the average CAFs paid by suppliers to GPOs in 2008 ranged from 1.2% to 2.2% of purchases, weighted by purchasing volume.[58] The lower level of fees received, compared to earlier levels reported above, reflected the new codes of conduct: four GPOs reported they no longer received CAFs in excess of three percent. Suppliers similarly reported to the GAO that they were paying lower CAFs to the GPOs.

Finally, national survey data from 2014 indicate that CAFs exerted a relatively unimportant influence on hospitals' buying decisions. Instead of CAFs, the most important influence was the value of the product contract negotiated by the GPO.[59]

GPO Contracting Practices

The July 2003 GAO report stated that seven GPOs used sole-source contracts to achieve lower product prices.[60] Five of the seven GPOs queried used sole-source contracts for anywhere from 2–46% of their medical-surgical supply dollar volume; the two largest GPOs used sole-source contracts for 19% and 42% of this dollar volume, respectively. Use of sole-source contracts varied by commodity item versus PPIs for smaller and larger GPOs: among smaller GPOs, commodity items represented 62–91% of the dollar volume purchased using such contracts, whereas in one of the two largest GPOs, PPIs represented 82% of the dollar volume purchased through such contracts.

The 2003 GAO report also identified three types of bundled contracts used by the GPOs: bundles of complementary products from one supplier, bundles of unrelated products from the same supplier, and bundles of products from multiple suppliers whereby hospitals were required to purchase a minimum percentage across product categories to receive discounted pricing. Six of the seven large GPOs used some form of bundling. According to the GAO, four GPOs used the first type of bundled contract; such bundles were included in a small percentage of the GPO's contracts. Three GPOs used the second type of bundled contract; one of the two large GPOs used the second type of bundled contract for 40% of its medical-surgical supply dollar volume. Four GPOs used the third type of bundled contract; one large GPO used this type of bundled contract for 20% of its volume. The seventh GPO did not report using bundled contracts.

The GAO report also noted that GPO use of bundling was possibly declining. Data supplied by one GPO showed a decline in one type of bundled contract between 2001 and 2003. This trend was consistent with comments made by industry stakeholders. One manufacturer and two medical-surgical product distributors reported that GPOs were "less interested in bundling different manufacturers together," "GPOs have fewer bundling arrangements," and "some bundles were pulled apart."

Moreover, in 2002 (the year of the first Senate hearing), nearly one-third of contracts were signed with new suppliers who did not previously hold GPO contracts. Across the seven GPOs studied, 16–55% of all contracts were with new, non-incumbent suppliers. This represented evidence of a leveling in the contracting process and greater access to GPO contracts by new suppliers. The most important parties consulted and making decisions on vendors to contract with were customers (e.g., clinicians) who requested those suppliers' products.

The July 2003 GAO report noted that the two largest GPOs typically awarded five-year contracts, while the other five GPOs typically used three-year awards. The GAO also found the GPOs had taken steps to address concerns about their contracting practices, but it was too early to evaluate their efforts. The GAO noted there were variations in GPO efforts to address business practices (e.g., variations in their codes of conduct and the practices specified in those codes).

Finally, national survey data from 2014 indicate that there had been little change in hospital use of, or satisfaction with, bundled contracts since 2004—using either a single vendor or multiple vendors to construct the bundle. There was also no change in physician attitudes toward these contracts. This may help to explain why bundled contracts are still offered by GPOs and why hospitals continue to utilize them.[61]

National surveys indicate that hospitals are satisfied with several of these contracts offered by their primary GPOs, and have been so over time. As depicted in Table 6.3, hospitals assert they obtain excellent pricing through standardization and compliance with both sole-source and dual-source contracts. The data also show the majority of hospitals believe there is value in committed contracts for multi-vendor product bundles as well as committed contracts for single-vendor product bundles. Finally, the same survey data indicate that three-quarters of hospitals report their national GPO offers single- and multi-vendor bundled contracts and that hospitals sometimes use them.

It is worth noting that some of the disputed practices discussed above— such as group purchasing, product bundles, sole-source contracts, and committed purchasing contracts—are widely used in other industries. A report issued by the Center for Advanced Purchasing Studies at ASU documented that purchasing consortiums like GPOs constitute a long-standing form of buying behavior that helps buyers to achieve cost savings of 13.4%.[62] A Rand Corporation report noted the increased interest in the bundling of services supplied to the U.S. Department of Defense and the improvements in supplier performance and product cost associated with bundling.[63]

Table 6.3 Percentage of hospitals reporting value in use of single- and multi-vendor bundled contracts

GPO committed contracts for multi-vendor multi-product portfolios are valuable	66%
GPO committed contracts for single-vendor multi-product portfolios are valuable	55%
GPO gets excellent prices through standardization and compliance to sole-source contracts	57%
GPO gets excellent prices through standardization and compliance to dual-source contracts	56%

GPO Customer Service

Another review by the GAO found that GPOs render a range of services to their hospital members.[64] The six largest GPOs offered custom contracting, clinical evaluation and product standardization, and new technology assessment. Five of the six GPOs also offered e-commerce and benchmarking data services. These services were funded by the CAFs collected by the GPOs or through charges to the hospitals themselves. As my Wharton economist colleagues typically say, if hospitals are paying for these services they must be getting some value from them.

GPO Clinical Review Processes

In addition to how GPOs contract with suppliers, research has also examined how GPOs clinically review the contracted products hospitals use in patient care. On behalf of HIGPA, the Lewin Group surveyed five hospital systems and six GPOs during 2002 to ascertain how products considered for contracting were clinically reviewed.[65] Lewin reported that hospital systems and GPOs utilized committees of clinical experts and administrators to review products, drew upon independent technology assessments (e.g., ECRI) and literature reviews (e.g., MEDLINE), monitored breakthrough technologies, and employed mechanisms to incorporate them into the process of product review, and had ongoing reviews of technologies and sometimes a perpetual review of new technologies. They also reported that GPOs helped to facilitate clinical trials of new products by their member hospitals. Product review mechanisms included value analysis committees and product evaluation committees (for medical-surgical devices), pharmacy and therapeutics committees (for drugs), and capital committees (for capital equipment).

A subsequent review by the GAO confirmed that the six largest GPOs they studied offer clinical evaluation of products and assessments of new technology.[66] Clinical evaluation was conducted through clinical advisory committees comprised of clinicians from member hospitals. Reviews of innovative technologies were also bolstered by GPO codes of conduct and newly instituted mechanisms to support the inclusion of innovative products on GPO contracts.

GPO Oversight, Codes of Conduct, and Self-Regulation

One ongoing, contentious issue during the Senate hearings was the oversight of GPO activities. The Senate followed up on this issue several times through GAO investigations. In 2003, the GAO reported that selected GPOs had adopted codes of conduct or revised their existing codes to respond to criticisms about their business practices.[67] Due to the recent nature of the codes, the GAO could not evaluate their impact; however, it did state that two suppliers and two distributors had noticed improvements in contracting practices, and that one supplier had received several GPO contracts compared to none previously. The GAO also noted variations across the GPOs in their conduct codes addressing specific issues such as: caps on CAFs, limits on use of sole-source contracts for PPIs, and restrictions on using bundles for unrelated products and for PPIs.

The Senate subsequently asked the GAO to review the various oversight activities aimed at GPOs conducted by DHHS, the Department of Justice, and the Federal Trade Commission since 2004, as well as the GPO's own self-regulatory approach exercised through the HGPII effort (see Chapter 5, Appendix II).[68] The report noted that GPOs were subject to various laws that the three federal agencies were supposed to enforce, but the agencies did not routinely exercise this authority. The OIG-DHHS reported it had not imposed any administrative penalties on GPOs since 2004, while the FTC reported it had not undertaken any enforcement actions against GPOs since 2004. For its part, the HGPII has continued to monitor the business practices of its GPO members and added some new activities (an ethics advisory council for best practices) between 2010 and 2012.

At the same time, a national survey of hospital VPMMs reported that 75% had reviewed the Senate-approved code of ethics for GPOs and 82% felt the code of ethics was strong. Moreover, on a scale of 1–5 (never-always), VPMMs ranked their own GPO's compliance with the code as 4.44.[69]

Shortly thereafter, two former OIG-DHHS officials submitted a white paper to the Healthcare Supply Chain Association (HSCA) on the history of OIG oversight regarding the GPOs.[70] Their report summarized the OIG-DHHS' historical stance that the CAFs collected by the GPOs from suppliers should be permitted and that the safe harbor for GPOs remained viable. They concluded that "any risks associated with GPOs are addressed through the current statutory and regulatory requirements for disclosure, reporting and transparency. The mandated disclosure and reporting of cost savings that healthcare providers achieve through the use of GPOs ensures that Federal healthcare programs also benefit from lower costs."

An additional GAO report stated that the GPOs' codes of conduct had varied impacts across GPOs, hospitals, and suppliers. The GPOs informed the GAO that their codes had altered their contracting processes (limits on the use of sole-source contracts, greater use of multi-source contracts, limits on the use of product bundles), selection of innovative products, CAFs, potential conflicts of interest, and the transparency and accountability of their business practices. Some hospitals and suppliers noted there were more vendors available to contract with via multi-source contracts, although this resulted in higher product prices. To obtain lower pricing, the hospitals resorted to direct contracts with the supplier and used the GPO price as their starting point in price negotiations. Some hospitals also resorted on their own to employing prior GPO-hosted practices of sole-source contracts, product bundles, and committed purchasing contracts. Some hospitals and suppliers echoed the improvement in transparency, while others did not offer any comments regarding the impact of the codes on the addition of innovative products to GPO contracts.[71]

When confronted by negative findings or allegations concerning the behavior of its members, an industry sector often develops mechanisms to both improve its image and buffer itself against both criticism and intervention (formal regulation).[72] Codes of conduct have served as a key mechanism to achieve this goal. The 1987 American Society of Association Executives survey revealed that 43% of industry associations had promulgated a code of conduct; 78% of the top 1,000 organizations had drawn up such a code.[73] Most attempts at industry self-regulation have involved national trade associations as well as professional associations (representing processors, manufacturers, and service industries) in a joint effort to advance the business practices of their industry members.[74]

HGPII has released an annual report to the public on its members' adherence to its six principles and their efforts to promulgate and enforce a code of ethical conduct.[75] The HGPII initiative has since expanded from nine to eleven large GPOs, and in recent years has added a random site visit by an independent coordinator to review the GPO's policies regarding supplier agreements, vendor forums, and CAFs.

In 2014, ASU researchers analyzed the HIGPA code of conduct and its embrace by GPOs and their hospital members. They concluded the annual reporting mechanism and questionnaire established "a footing for government and the GPO industry itself to assess GPOs." They also concluded that the Code responded to "concerns regarding administrative fees, market maintenance, product positioning and the behavior of individuals working within GPOs," and served as a "demonstration of citizenship" and "purchasing social responsibility."[76]

Competitive Market for National GPOs

One issue permeating the GPO literature is whether or not the GPO marketplace is competitive. This issue is important because rivalry can spur GPO efforts to achieve lower pricing and greater customer service for their hospital members. Despite the consolidation movement in the 1990s, vigorous competition exists within the group purchasing sector.

In an early statement on this issue sponsored by HIGPA, Law Professor Herbert Hovenkamp argued that the GPO market was competitive by virtue of several facts: (1) the national GPOs faced competition from regional GPOs and hospital systems that handled their own contracting (see next section), (2) no one GPO controlled more than 10–15% of the market, (3) hospitals belonged to multiple GPOs and thus had divided loyalties to any one GPO, and (4) there were no entry barriers to the GPO market (as evidenced by the entrance of MedAssets in the late 1990s). Hovenkamp also inferred that the GPO sector met both conditions in the FTC/DOJ antitrust safety zone for GPOs[77]: the purchases of any one GPO were less than 35% of total sales of the purchased product/service in the relevant market, and the cost of products/services purchased jointly was less than 20% of the total revenues from all products/services sold by each competing supplier in the joint purchasing arrangement.[78]

As further substantiation for this argument, academic researchers examined the Herfindahl–Hirschman Index (HHI)—a standard measure of competitiveness—for the GPO market.[79] Hovenkamp computed an HHI for the GPO marketplace for the top ten purchasing groups of 410–450, clearly in the range of high competition. His estimate of each group's share was based on the group's contracted sales figures as a percentage of supply and equipment purchases made by healthcare institutions. Such calculations correctly took into consideration the fact that contracted sales within a group only penetrate roughly 50–80% of the purchases made by the group's hospital members; in the larger, nonprofit groups like Novation and Premier, this penetration rate is not at the higher end of the scale. If, instead, one used only the reported purchasing volumes of the top purchasing groups and calculated market shares based on that, one would derive an HHI approaching 1,800—which is borderline between moderately concentrated and concentrated—but clearly not an oligopoly like the ones observed in many local hospital and payer markets.

In testimony presented to the Federal Trade Commission, another researcher noted that the large share of total GPO volume accounted for by the top GPOs provided a misleading view of the sector's concentration. This was especially so, given that (1) hospitals often bought products directly from suppliers, and (2) GPO-mediated purchases averaged only 72% across hospitals and varied greatly across product categories.[80]

This point countered claims by another researcher that the GPO marketplace was highly concentrated and oligopolistic in nature because a handful of GPOs controlled over 80% of the supplies purchased through such buying groups.[81] The researcher's other claim that similarities among GPOs left them no incentive to compete with one another was similarly wrong. The fact that GPOs (a) offered the same services, (b) vied for the same supplier and hospital customers, and (c) vied with equally large GPOs, suggested the presence of Michael Porter's conditions for competitive rivalry as expressed in his "Five Forces" framework.[82]

Indeed, looking across each of these five forces, there are signs of strong competition. First, there is considerable internal rivalry among the purchasing groups, due to the sheer number of groups, the low HHI, the differentiation among the groups in terms of their ownership and size, their overlapping membership, and their different service offerings. Second, there exist substitutes for the purchasing groups—namely IDNs that purchase on their own. Third, there are few barriers to entry to the purchasing group industry, as witnessed by the late entrance of MedAssets in 1999 which grew quickly to rank among the top seven groups nationally. Fourth, the buyers (hospital customers) exert power over the groups due to the fact they voluntarily join the groups, can and do switch from one group to another, and are quite price sensitive. Fifth, the suppliers (vendors) can have countervailing power relative to the groups, particularly if the vendors make the products that hospitals and clinicians want (vendor preference) and/or the providers cannot obtain them from another vendor (vendor monopoly). The GPO market is thus highly competitive.

Moreover, while purchasing groups have consolidated at the national level, there has been considerable variation at the local market level in terms of the percentage of hospitals affiliated with the largest nonprofit groups. In some markets, regional and local purchasing groups and smaller national groups may have a stronger presence.

Additional academic research has considered the possible concerns over GPO monopsony power and concluded that GPOs exert pro-competitive effects.[83,84,85,86,87,88,89,90] In general, researchers found that GPOs help providers to lower their total purchasing costs, and that CAFs exert little impact on these costs. Moreover, many of the questioned practices employed by GPOs (e.g., volume-based discounts, sole-source contracts) may serve to reduce input prices for hospital members. One study argued that GPO contracts not only helped to reduce supply prices, but also that the loss of GPO contracts prompted suppliers to counter-detail these contracts, maintain a presence in the hospital accounts, and thereby further increase pricing pressures.[91] One of the studies did suggest that GPOs dampened the innovation incentives of suppliers, however. Another study echoed allegations raised in the Senate hearings that GPOs limited market entry by new suppliers and engaged in exclusive (and thus exclusionary) contracts.[92] It should be noted, however, that all of these studies were typically based on modeling exercises and theoretical arguments rather than empirical analysis. Their results also run counter to the observed positive effects exerted by the GPO codes of conduct.

Articles and white papers by several attorneys attacked GPOs and their contracting practices based on their alleged anticompetitive effects.[93,94,95] These papers typically argued that GPO contracts with large and diversified suppliers foreclose the market for small niche (and innovative) suppliers. Such foreclosure operates through the use of the contracting practices analyzed above: sole-source contracts, market share discounts, product bundles, and CAFs (labeled "kickbacks" by GPO critics).[96] By contrast, articles and white papers by other attorneys supported the pro-competitive view of GPOs: i.e., GPOs promote rivalry among suppliers and lower input prices for buyers.[97,98,99] They cautioned, however, that antitrust agencies ensure that the two FTC/DOJ guidelines for GPO safety zones be strictly monitored and enforced.

Growing Competition from Regional GPOs, Local GPOs, Virtual GPOs, & IDNs

More recently, a number of hospital systems developed what researchers describe as "captive GPOs" to serve their own members and increasingly like-minded hospitals and systems within their region.[100] These are variously known today as regional aggregation groups, regional purchasing coalitions, regional purchasing alliances, and custom supply chain networks. They are referred to here as regional GPOs.

The regional GPOs pool the purchasing of non-related hospitals, hospital systems, and IDNs that typically share a common locality, and may even belong to the same national GPO. The members work together to optimize their GPO portfolio contracts, in the belief that "everyone believes they can do better" regarding product pricing. They appear to focus less on developing tighter cost controls (e.g., through better management of product utilization) and more on obtaining supplemental savings from additional contracts. They offer hospitals yet another vehicle to get providers to work together on purchasing. This may lead to more intimate efforts to work on contract commitment which may help hospitals get to a higher tier of committed purchasing than they could do on their own or with their national GPOs. The theory is that it is easier to get agreement among a smaller number of hospitals to commit a high percentage (e.g., 85%) of purchases through the regional GPOs. This is one reason why the national GPOs could not consistently obtain the lowest prices.

As noted in Chapter 3, the existence of the regional GPOs serves as recognition that national GPOs cannot perform several functions well. The regional GPOs also constitute an effort to combine and balance the scale of large purchasing groups with the nimbleness of small hospital networks. They are also rooted in the belief that smaller groups have greater alignment and shared goals when it comes to purchasing and committed contracting. Finally, they exist to complement national GPOs and add local savings to national savings. As such, national GPOs may actually partner with and support them; in such cases, the regional GPOs may be affiliates of the national GPOs but are not required to use national GPOs. This creates another layer of purchasing with suppliers and, of importance, utilizing national GPO contracts as ceilings from which to begin negotiations. It remains to be seen if the hospital trend to insource key supply chain functions (e.g., contracting, strategic sourcing, logistics) will result in what has been described as fully integrated supply chain companies (FISCOs), competing directly with national GPOs and distributors.[101]

In addition to the regional GPOs, there has been a recent rise in "virtual GPOs" using alliance models. Examples include Ascension Health Alliance, CHA Shared Services Program, BJC Collaborative, MNS Supply Chain Network, Dignity Health Purchasing Network, and Shared Clarity. These models look quite similar to the local and regional purchasing groups and shared service organizations started by state hospital associations in the 1960s, suggesting a "back to the roots" movement in group purchasing.

As a consequence, it has become more evident that hospitals do not see themselves as being held captive by their GPOs. Hospitals frequently belong to more than one GPO and, increasingly, have developed regional alliances to engage in collaborative purchasing. This lends credence to the idea that hospitals make their own decisions about how to engage the marketplace and see the GPO as only one of several channels (covered below). One recent analysis found that 37% of hospitals engage with two or more GPOs and/or regional GPOs.[102] The largest regional GPOs, according to this analysis, are MAGNET Co-op and Capstone Health Alliance. Another 58% of hospitals source their purchasing through only one GPO—most of these (88%) through one of the three largest national GPOs (Vizient, Premier, HealthTrust).

There also exists considerable competition between purchasing groups and IDNs. Groups compete for hospital and IDN members, which can switch group affiliations. IDNs are not only periodically approached by other groups to join them but will also actively take a look at them. Thus, the threat of switching by hospital customers is clearly present. Groups also face competition from some IDNs which seek to act as their own groups. Hospitals can elect to purchase from vendors through group contracts, through independent agreements negotiated by their IDN, or off contract entirely.

The historical narrative in Chapter 4 indicates that purchasing groups have consistently competed with each other, with hospital systems (both investor-owned and nonprofit), and with IDNs to grow their hospital membership base. Competition is likely augmented by the diversity of groups and group strategies that have developed. The major competitive strategy has been, and continues to be, the pricing negotiated with suppliers.

At this time, there is no systematic study of the consequences of the proliferation of local, regional, and virtual group purchasing alliances—including those that are independent of national GPOs or those supported by national GPO contracts and augmented by local contracts. There is also no systematic research on the proliferation of e-commerce platforms for purchasing or the consequences of hospital access to pricing by independent price analytic services (e.g., Broadjump). Such developments suggest that the marketplace in which GPOs currently operate is becoming increasingly competitive. All of these factors allow suppliers that fail to secure national group contracts with alternative avenues for selling their products at the local hospital level.[103]

Nevertheless, in a recent national survey, VPMMs were asked to rank-order their national, regional, and local GPOs in importance. They ranked the national GPOs as #1, followed at a distance by regional GPOs (#2) and local GPOs (#3). They were also more likely to agree that the role and impact of the national GPOs had grown over the preceding five-year period, compared to the role of regional and local alliances. They were neutral regarding the competitive impact of the regional and local alliances on their national counterparts. This suggests that despite the proliferation of alliances at different geographic levels and the re-routing of some purchases to regional and local GPOs, the role and impact of the national GPOs has not diminished.[104]

GPOs' Alleged Exclusionary Agreements and Anticompetitive Practices

A major bone of contention in the GPO debate has been the alleged presence of anticompetitive GPO practices and supplier-GPO agreements that serve to exclude small and potentially more innovative manufacturers from the marketplace. A leading proponent of this view was Law Professor Einar Elhauge (referenced above). Given the prominence of his writings in the GPO literature, Senate hearings, and GPO litigation, it is worthwhile to review his opinions in some detail.

Elhauge advanced several arguments regarding GPO activities. First, GPOs engaged in anti-competitive strategies with large incumbent manufacturers to establish and maintain their monopoly power in supplier markets. Second, these suppliers used their GPO contracting partners to erect entry barriers that inhibit new innovative suppliers from entering the market. Third, suppliers induced GPOs to enter these anti-competitive contracts by paying CAFs to the GPOs, which amounted to hijacking them. Fourth, GPOs acted in the suppliers' interests, forcing their hospital members to buy products they may not prefer and imposing contracts on them that governed and regimented their purchases. Fifth, the low market shares held by small and innovative suppliers reflected these anti-competitive agreements which (a) were designed to foreclose the product market and (b) generated the "low headroom" hospitals had available to them to buy from alternate suppliers. Sixth, the specific tactics used by the suppliers to effect foreclosure included bundled contracts, sole-source and dual-source contracts, and share-based discounts (lower prices for higher committed levels of products purchased). Seventh, incumbent suppliers exercised their market power to obtain these contracts and then pressured GPOs and hospitals to conform to them by threatening higher prices if they did not.

According to Elhauge, these practices restrained sales by small suppliers, denied them the opportunity to increase their production levels to achieve scale economies and efficiencies (at which point they could sell their products more cheaply and be more competitive), limited their expansion, and thus foreclosed the product market. As a consequence, hospital customers faced a product market with higher product prices and lower product quality (due to the absence of the small and presumably more innovative suppliers). Hospitals were thus unwitting stooges in the contracts between incumbent suppliers and the GPOs.

Other law and business school professors seriously challenged Elhauge's arguments regarding the anti-competitive effects of product bundling and quantity-linked discounts.[105,106] Some of their points rested on the widely acknowledged tradeoff that buyers have to make between lower cost and broader access/choice. Thus, if buyers commit to purchasing higher volumes of a single specific product from one supplier, they can obtain that product at a lower cost; if buyers want to exercise choice among alternate suppliers of rival products, they can purchase smaller amounts of each at a higher price. This happens because buyers promise higher volumes to the supplier, which can then plan its manufacturing runs accordingly, achieve production economies, and pass along some of the efficiencies to buyers in the form of lower prices.

Some of their points also rested on the widespread use of bundled discounts and committed purchasing contracts in other industries—which have the effect of lowering prices and increasing competition among suppliers to win these contracts. Additional points included the role that large intermediaries (like GPOs, pharmacy benefit managers or PBMs, health insurers) play in healthcare to counteract the power of suppliers and reduce their pricing opportunism. This is in essence what Senator Schumer argued in the 2006 Senate hearings. Finally, these professors noted that the presence of sole-source contracts did not inhibit hospital buyers from using alternative suppliers not on contract. The presence of sole-source contracts also did not reduce the survival prospects of smaller or larger competitors who could still successfully (a) compete for GPO contracts in the next round of bid contracting, or (b) compete for individual hospital contracts in the interim via counter-detailing the GPO contract.

In a follow-up report prepared for HIGPA, Professor Hovenkamp took issue with Professor Elhauge's assertion that GPO contracts with large suppliers had the intent and impact of excluding small and innovative suppliers from the marketplace.[107] Hovenkamp argued that suppliers, GPOs, and hospitals were all independent of one another with little vertical integration to assure suppliers of dedicated purchases by hospital members.[108] Not only did each GPO have low market share, but hospitals could and did join different GPOs over time and switched their purchases from one GPO to another. Even in the presence of a sole-source contract, only 20% of the market was potentially closed to a small supplier, leaving 80% of the remaining market to pursue product sales. The largest GPO might account for no more than 15% market share for a given device, leaving an unconcentrated market for suppliers to contest for. In sum, GPOs were neither monopolists nor monopsonists (controlling markets upstream or downstream).

Access to Innovative Technology

Several bits of evidence counter criticisms that GPOs impeded (a) market entry by innovative suppliers and (b) hospital access by their sales reps. While group purchasing argues for a closed marketplace and by nature is exclusionary, groups have not kept innovative technology from coming to the hospital market. Trend data at the start of the new millennium showed a healthy flow of venture capital (VC)-backed device firms and initial public offerings (IPOs) over the prior 10–15 years.[109]

Second, an analysis of the entry and exit rates of new startups in the medical device sector revealed no slowdown in market entry by entrepreneurial startups during the period that spanned the 1990s and early 2000s—the same period when GPOs grew.[110] Major drivers of market entry by new device firms included the number of entries in prior years, prior merger and acquisition activity in the firm's sector, the number and valuation of prior initial public offerings for firms in that sector, the amount of VC funding invested in firms in that sector, and VCs' views of rival investments in biotechnology.

Third, industry analysts argue that, had it existed, the presence of group contracting for innovative products would have discouraged investors in VC-backed start-up firms.[111] Long-term businesses are built upon technologically-advanced products and PPIs that can withstand the need to contract with purchasing groups.[112] The single biggest deterrent to new

IPOs has not been purchasing groups but the inflated expectations and disappointing earnings of these companies, which serve to dampen investor interest going forward. These earnings themselves are not influenced by purchasing groups but by the new firms' failure to attend to both of "the twin towers" of innovation: develop breakthrough technology that clinicians need and want and market the technology to end-users.[113]

Fourth, surveys indicate that hospital VPMMs generally disagree with the contention that their GPOs had blocked their access to innovative devices and the manufacturers that made them.[114] However, there has been a slight increase in VPMMs reporting this issue. When asked in 2004 if their primary national GPO brought innovative products to their attention, materials managers gave their GPO a score of 3.64 (using a Likert scale ranging from 1 – 5, where 5 expressed the highest level of satisfaction); in 2014, VPMMs gave their GPOs a lower score (3.50). They gave slightly lower ratings (score of 3.24) of their GPO's ability to increase their knowledge of innovative devices and manufacturers; that rating did not change during the 2004–2014 period.

Fifth, GPOs such as Premier have hosted annual meetings where medical product innovators can network and share their innovations with clinicians from the GPO's member hospitals. Such meetings not only help innovative firms get their products in front of clinicians but also provide feedback from clinical customers for product iterations. Premier also hosted a program called "SEEDS" (Sourcing Education and Enrichment for Diverse and Small Suppliers) that provided mentoring and coaching to small manufacturers to help them scale their businesses.[115]

A major issue in nearly all of these cases was the anti-competitive nature of bundled, sole-source contracts.[116] Plaintiffs typically alleged that such contracts unfairly excluded them and restricted hospital access to their technology. Defendants countered (successfully in later cases) that the small manufacturers had ample opportunity to sell their products, that the contracts in question allowed for considerable "headroom" for hospital purchasing of new technology, that the GPOs did not mandate what products clinicians had to buy, and that the technology of the small manufacturers may not have been as claimed. In support of this last assertion, sales figures for the small manufacturers barely rose when they were finally added to GPO contracts. This suggested that GPOs were not that adept in moving market share for those vendors it contracted with and, conversely, they did not pose a sales barrier to those vendors they did not contract with. This also suggested that the products made by the small manufacturers might not have been desired by clinicians: even when offered on GPO contracts, clinicians still did not order them.

Continued Hospital Use of and Satisfaction with GPO Services

Hospitals are clearly the major customer of the GPOs. The historical record demonstrates that hospitals and their state hospital associations were instrumental in forming the GPOs through the 1960s, and are once again active in establishing virtual GPOs.

According to the late management sage, Peter Drucker, the best way to assess a firm's performance is to ask its customers how satisfied they are with the company. Hospitals have demonstrated their satisfaction with their GPOs in at least four important ways. First, studies conducted over time show that the vast majority of hospitals (90–98%) still have GPO memberships. Second, studies show that hospitals still belong to only a small number of GPOs (1.6–2.6 memberships). Third, studies over time show that hospitals still route the majority (66–72%) of their supply purchases through GPOs. Fourth, research shows that hospitals' routing of a greater share of PPI purchases through their national GPO is associated with several benefits: excellent contract pricing, contract currency/customization/conversion, value from sole-source contracts, and price optimization and contract fees.[117] Fifth, panel data show that hospitals have not changed the percentage of purchases of certain product categories (commodities, purchased services) routed through their national GPO over time (2004–2014). Indeed, they have increased such GPO-mediated purchases in two other categories (PPIs, capital items); the only category exhibiting lower GPO mediation is pharmaceuticals.[118] Sixth, as noted below, studies over time have repeatedly reported high hospital satisfaction levels with their GPOs, particularly with GPO pricing and cost savings.[119,120,121,122,123]

An early survey of hospital materials managers in 2005 found that 49% of hospitals and 65% of hospital systems were "very satisfied" with their primary GPO relationship; another 42% of hospitals and 24% of hospital systems were "satisfied." The percent of hospitals and systems stating they were dissatisfied was only 9 and 12%, respectively.[124]

In another national survey conducted in 2004, hospital VPMMs assigned their national GPO highest ratings (5 = very satisfied, 1 = very dissatisfied) on several summary scales: low pricing (3.92 out of 5.00), contracting convenience (3.92), multi-source contracts (3.91), and experience sharing and networking (3.92).[125] GPOs received more modest ratings on supply chain analysis and improvement (3.51), product bundles and portfolios (3.50), hospital input and voice in decision-making (3.50), benchmarking, product selection, and product conversion (3.49), and clinical improvements (3.48). GPO services received lower (but still positive) assessments regarding pricing information tools (3.32), outsourcing (3.31), and education (3.26). The only GPO service receiving a negative assessment was information system tools (2.89), although the provision of a web-based contract catalog was very highly rated (4.06). Despite these variations, the research found that managers were quite satisfied with their GPO overall (4.06).

In 2004, VPMMs' satisfaction with their GPO was significantly and positively correlated with: (1) utilization of the GPO (i.e., the level of hospital spending routed through the GPO) on 12 of the 13 summary scales; (2) the use of single-vendor bundled contracts (9 of 13 scales); and (3) use of multi-vendor bundled contracts (8 of 13 scales). In 2014, VPMMs' satisfaction with their GPO was significantly and positively associated with utilization of the GPO, use of single-vendor bundled contracts, and use of only one national GPO on all 3 of 3 summary scales (satisfaction, savings, product standardization), but was associated with the use of multi-vendor bundled contracts on only 1 of these 3 summary scales.

The 2014 survey also queried VPMMs about the value they derived from their national GPO on five dimensions: revenue cycle, purchased services, data analytics, benchmark data, and clinical outcomes data. The degree of value derived from their GPO was significantly and positively associated with utilization of the GPO, use of only one national GPO, and use of single-vendor bundled contracts on all 5 measures; and use of multi-vendor bundled contracts on 4 of the 5 measures.

A 2009 ASU survey similarly revealed that hospitals had a high overall level of satisfaction (5 = highly satisfied, 1 = highly dissatisfied) with their GPO (4.1 out of 5.0), which was again correlated with greater utilization of the GPO's contracts. However, hospitals and systems had relatively high levels of expectations for GPO performance that were not always met. The variability in met expectations was higher for GPO pricing than for GPO contracting. Expectations were met more for "lowest pricing" on pharmacy products (3.9 out of 5.0), commodity items (3.9), and medical-surgical products (3.8), but not for physician preference items (2.7). Expectations were also largely met for "financial returns" via disbursed CAFs (3.7) and "managing supplier items and conditions" (3.6), and somewhat for "high guaranteed savings" (3.4). When pricing expectations were not met, hospitals and systems were likely to engage in self-contracting.[126] The degree to which hospital expectations regarding GPO contracting were met exhibited a narrow range of variation: "breadth of portfolio" (3.9), "contract flexibility" (3.7), "contract management support" (3.6), and "identify new products" (3.5).

A 2010 national survey of hospitals' use of and satisfaction with their GPOs reported that GPOs received "very satisfied" ratings from 30% of respondents and "satisfied" ratings from another 60%.[127] On specific items, hospitals expressed fairly uniform levels of satisfaction: "pricing/savings" (36% very satisfied, 53% satisfied), "clinical/consulting" (24% very satisfied, 54% satisfied), and "customer service/responsiveness" (37% very satisfied, 51% satisfied).

In the eyes of Professor Elhauge, hospitals may be the unwitting dupes of GPOs; alternatively, in the eyes of Professor Drucker, hospitals may simply be satisfied customers. Of course, as shown above, hospital satisfaction with their GPOs is not unqualified or absolute.

Longitudinal data indicate that hospitals express changing levels of satisfaction with their national GPOs.[128] They reported growing levels of satisfaction in seven areas: clinical improvement, clinical expertise, and data support for value analysis, consulting services, direct input into product/service selection, auditing for procurement of device implants, assistance with contract conversion for physician preference items (PPIs), and item master maintenance. By contrast, hospitals reported declining levels of satisfaction with their primary GPO in four areas: safety improvement initiatives, bringing innovative products to their attention, access to innovative technologies, and multi-source contracts for PPIs. For all other performance dimensions, there was no significant change in hospital satisfaction with their GPO.

Other, recent surveys provide a more nuanced picture. FTI's 2nd Annual GPO Survey reveals that while hospitals report generally high levels of overall satisfaction with their GPOs (ranging from 62–68% in 2020–21), they report varying levels of satisfaction with specific products: commodities (70%), pharmaceuticals (59%), pharmaceutical services (54%), purchased services (35%), and PPIs (33%).[129] Satisfaction ratings are inversely related to member size and, thus, dependence on national GPOs. The FTI results are based on only 40 respondents, however.

Finally, hospitals are more or less equally satisfied with their national GPOs and do not pick a clear winner. In a 2004 national survey, hospital VPMMs rated the national GPOs on a variety of performance dimensions. Satisfaction levels across the seven major GPOs were quite similar. Cooperatively based GPOs tended to receive slightly lower evaluations than those not organized as cooperatives; the magnitude of the differences was small and often statistically insignificant, however.[130] The data suggested that the national

GPOs were not strongly differentiated from one another, at least in terms of their member evaluations. Such findings are important for two reasons. First, the GPOs have striven to gain a competitive advantage over others by developing distinctive capabilities and differentiating their offerings; such efforts had not yet paid off by 2005–2006.[131,132] Second, such lack of differentiation is likely associated with rivalry among the GPOs and thus competitive market conditions. Chapter 8 examines this issue in greater detail.

GPOs and Drug Shortages

Over the past decade or so, long-time GPO critics have blamed the GPOs for the shortages of prescription drugs experienced by hospitals and physician offices between 2005 and 2012.[133] GPOs allegedly propelled the shortage by squeezing supplier margins, awarding sole-source contracts, and pursuing other strategies that reduced the number of suppliers making the needed products. The majority of the drugs in short supply were sterile injectables (74% of the drug shortage in 2010), particularly for oncology. Some analysts discussed the possibility of linkages between these drug shortages and GPO sales practices. The argument here was that the heavy use (60%) of sole-source contracts for sterile injectable molecules and the resulting tendency for a small number of suppliers to have these contracts contributed to a concentrated market that left few alternative sources of supply and lower market access to new entrants—all of which might exacerbate shortages.[134]

By contrast, the literature on the drug shortages points to many other causes beyond GPOs. These include manufacturing difficulties, shortages of raw materials, imbalances in supply and demand, FDA oversight and enforcement actions, the impact on generic drug pricing by the Medicare Modernization Act, activities in the secondary drug distribution marketplace, and other unknown reasons.[135,136,137] The Healthcare Supply Chain Association (HSCA) commissioned two reports in 2014 on the causes of the shortages and the roles played by GPOs to alleviate them.[138,139] The GAO also issued its own report in 2014, which concluded that:

> The immediate cause of drug shortages can generally be traced to a manufacturer halting or slowing production to address quality problems, triggering a supply disruption. Other manufacturers have a limited ability to respond to supply disruptions due to constrained manufacturing capacity. GAO's analysis of data from the Food and Drug Administration (FDA) also showed that quality problems were a frequent cause. GAO also identified potential underlying causes specific to the economics of the generic sterile injectable drug

market, such as that low profit margins have limited infrastructure investments or led some manufacturers to exit the market.[140]

Product quality and manufacturing issues are thus the leading causes of product shortages. Such problems rest with the pharmaceutical manufacturers, not the GPOs. Other problems rest with (1) the concentration of the manufacturers of specific drugs, such that the decision by one to discontinue production can cause shortages; (2) manufacturing delays or capacity issues; (3) the unavailability of raw materials or components to these drugs; (4) natural disasters which affect drug manufacturing plants; and (5) increased product demand. Combined, these explanations cover 97% of the drug shortages investigated.

It should be emphasized that the majority (62%) of the drugs in short supply were generics. Generic drug manufacturers obtained a growing number of abbreviated new drug approvals (ANDAs) during the periods 2010–2012 and 2014–2017.[141] Such ANDAs were made possible by the Hatch–Waxman Amendments to the Food Drug and Cosmetic Act of 1984 that were designed to speed up generic entry. The steady increase in ANDAs led to increased entry and competition among generic manufacturers and their products, which subsequently led to lower and lower generic drug prices. This hurt the financial performance of generic manufacturers and may have occasioned their market exit, leaving fewer alternative suppliers. This helps to explain the constrained capacity at generic manufacturing plants.

GPOs may have played some role in fostering some of this price competition and falling margins among generic manufacturers. As noted in Chapter 3, any GPO monopsony power may compel price discounts which then prompts product manufacturers to restrict output. To the extent it exists, however, the GPO effect is exerted only in the institutional side of the pharmaceutical supply chain, where drugs are sold to hospitals and (perhaps) some of their employed physicians and alternate site facilities. GPOs do not mediate drug purchases in the retail market.

In 2018–2019, several parties issued additional analyses of U.S. drug shortages—which reiterated many of the arguments listed above and identified some new drivers.[142] These included price competition among generic manufacturers and their "race to the bottom", more market exits than entries in generic manufacturing, consolidation of drug manufacturers (leading to sole-source suppliers), concentration of generic manufacturers, concentration of ANDAs in a small percentage of ANDA "sponsors", problems with good manufacturing practices, regulatory challenges facing manufacturers to respond to disruptions in supply, the lack of incentives for high-volume buyers (GPOs, hospital chains, chain pharmacies) to buy from more reliable and higher-quality manufacturers (even if at a higher price), increased demand for generics, lack of transparency as to what manufacturer makes which drug at which production site—which inhibits planning by buyers, long-term contracts struck by GPOs (which disincentivizes market entry), and longer/more complex/less flexible drug supply chains. GPOs may have played a role, but clearly, GPOs were not the key driver.

Group Purchasing in International Contexts

There is a growing literature on "collaborative procurement" and public procurement (with a focus on healthcare) outside the U.S.[143,144,145,146] This literature emphasizes the benefits (e.g., scale economies, buying power, pooling of expertise) of collaborative procurement for both suppliers and contracting authorities. At the same time, the fragmentation among purchasing bodies (national government vs. local government vs. organizational) allows for contractual autonomy and individual procurement.[147] Several studies compare healthcare procurement in the U.S. and the United Kingdom (UK).[148] The UK's National Health Service (NHS) established the Purchasing and Supply Agency to coordinate contracting at the national level; the latter, however, encouraged the formation of regional cooperatives to foster local level initiatives in supply purchasing.

Much of the attention focuses on purchasing in the public sector and, within the European Union (EU), on the role of both the EU and sovereign governments in purchasing. Group purchasing is clearly an international phenomenon that is often conducted by the public sector. By contrast, healthcare group purchasing in the U.S. tends to take place within the context of private sector organizations (both not-for-profit and investor-owned systems) as well as public healthcare delivery systems (including some public academic health centers) participating in GPO purchasing arrangements as permitted by state procurement statutes.

Summary of the Evidence on GPO Performance: What Have We Learned?

Beginning in 2002 with the *New York Times* exposé and the Senate hearings, GPOs have been accused of engaging in many harmful business practices and exerting anti-competitive effects in supplier markets. Over the next few years, a host of reports were issued in support of and in response to these allegations. Many of these reports were underwritten or otherwise sponsored by opponents and proponents of the GPOs. These included the trade associations for small suppliers and the GPOs. Some reports were produced as part of the testimony presented in the Senate hearings; others were prepared as expert witness reports used in litigation involving the GPOs and the large suppliers with which they contracted.

Following these early articles, reports, and testimony, there has been a small but growing volume of academic analyses of GPOs and group purchasing. Most of their analyses are based on economic theory and models; a few include survey data on GPO performance. A handful of academic texts have also analyzed the GPOs in terms of their business models, business practices, and strategies in working with suppliers and hospitals.

The sections above attempt to outline the allegations and issues concerning GPO performance, and then review the evidence base that exists to address them. Overall, the preponderance of the evidence, such as it is, does not support the anti-GPO allegations. Most of these allegations rest on anecdotal evidence (e.g., reports in the *New York Times*), case evidence that surfaced in litigation, and small-scale surveys of GPO pricing and practices (e.g., by the GAO). These allegations and (to the extent it exists) any supporting evidence stem mainly from the early 2000s. Indeed, many of the stories in the *New York Times* critical of the GPOs date from 2002 (see Chapter 5).

To be sure, most of the evidence refuting these allegations similarly rests on small-scale studies and a handful of large-scale survey research studies. However, the evidence base resting on survey research findings and academic analyses has been growing steadily and is more recent in origin. The findings are consistent with the two academic texts (based on field studies) that appeared earlier.[149] Together, they suggest (more or less consistently) that GPOs act as agents for and serve the interests of their hospital customers in ways these customers value. There are no empirical studies that even hint that hospitals are dissatisfied with their GPOs, and several studies that document how well GPOs meet their needs. A report issued by the former head of the DHHS-OIG further suggests that the GPOs serve societal interests by helping hospitals to lower their purchasing costs, and thus warrant continued protection by the safe harbor and exemption from the anti-kickback statute.

The disjunction between the early allegations and negative press versus the later research and more positive evidence may partly reflect the GPO industry's efforts to change. Undoubtedly, the voluntary code of conduct effort was prompted by the negative press and Senate hearings and constituted an attempt at self-policing that would avoid external regulation.

Moreover, academics have acknowledged that such voluntary efforts are imperfect, difficult to evaluate and enforce, and continually subject to skepticism. Nevertheless, the voluntary industry effort met with some positive though preliminary assessments by the GAO (in its 2003 and 2010 reports), which noted changes in GPO contracting practices. The GAO reports also mentioned the positive assessments made by the GPOs' stakeholders. The HIGPII Code of Conduct has continued to operate without controversy; federal watchdog agencies have not undertaken any enforcement actions; defendants prevailed in many of the later litigation cases brought against the large suppliers and their GPO contracting practices; and the incidence of such cases appears to have subsided. The trail of behavior documented by the Code of Conduct may well demonstrate GPO citizenship and purchasing social responsibility.

It is worth noting that the Code of Conduct constituted a response to a Senate inquiry that in many ways was stirred by criticisms from small suppliers who felt excluded from the GPO marketplace. The Code was not prompted by criticisms from the GPOs' customers (i.e., hospitals and healthcare systems).

Finally, much of the GPO criticism came without attention to the changing landscape of healthcare purchasing. The purchasing environment has become much more competitive. In recent years, suppliers have witnessed a noticeable diversification in the array of local, regional, and virtual GPOs—as well as self-contracting by hospitals. These alternative sources of contracting both complement and compete with national GPO contracts which small suppliers once decried and which have been the only subject of inquiry. Simply having a contract with a national GPO does not guarantee sales to GPO-contracted suppliers. Regional and other alliances also enter into local contracts for their hospital customers. Thus, off-contract suppliers that lack a national GPO point of access nevertheless have multiple avenues to secure business on the basis of pricing or clinically differentiated products. If anything, the evidence suggests that GPOs are pro-competitive rather than anti-competitive, and thus serve societal interests as well as hospital interests.

Likewise, much of the GPO criticism came without attention to the changes in hospital finance. Hospitals have faced a string of reimbursement cuts under Federal payment programs such as Medicare and Medicaid. These included payment-to-cost (PCR) ratios of 92% and 93% for these two programs in 2010, respectively.[150] They also included cuts from the Sequestration, cuts in Medicaid disproportionate share hospital payments, the 3-day window cut, the two-midnight offset, and MS-DRG coding offsets. Beginning October 1, 2013, CMS began to reduce payments to 2,225 hospitals in

49 states (except Maryland) as part of the Hospital Readmissions Reductions Program.

In addition to these cuts, hospitals have yet to generate efficiencies and savings from the formation of multi-hospital systems and vertical integration efforts with physicians.[151,152,153] As a result, hospitals have few (if any) avenues left to generate savings to deal with reduced reimbursement. Group purchasing and, more generally, improvements in hospital supply chain management represent perhaps their best hope for the future.

This is especially critical given that supplies and logistics account for up to 30% of a hospital's cost structure, second only to labor.[154] This is also important because responsibility for procurement and supply management is dispersed across multiple departments inside the hospital. The supply chain thus remains perhaps the last area of hospital operations without comprehensive and professional management. There is growing recognition of the importance of supply chain management for increasing the efficiency of the healthcare system, but very little evidence for its effects.[155,156,157,158]

Notes

1. Lawton R. Burns. *The Performance of Group Purchasing Organizations (GPOs) in the Health Care Value Chain: A Literature Review* (Philadelphia, PA: Wharton Center for Health Management & Economics, 2014).
2. John Jones, "Benefits of Physician-owned Group Purchasing Organizations," *Physician's News Digest* (October 2005). Available online at: http://www.physiciansnews.com/2005/10/13/physician-owned-group-purchasing-organizations/.
3. United States Senate. *Physician Owned Distributors (PODs): An Overview of Key Issues and Potential Areas for Congressional Oversight*. An Inquiry by the Senate Finance Committee Minority Staff (June 2011).
4. Booz and Company. *GPO Market: Abstract of Findings*. (New York, NY: Booz, June 2008).
5. For example, see "The Premier Healthcare Alliance Emerges," in Linda Swayne, W. Jack Duncan, and Peter Ginter, *Strategic Management of Health Care Organizations* (San Francisco, CA: Jossey-Bass, 2008).
6. Lawton R. Burns. *The Health Care Value Chain: Producers, Purchasers, and Providers* (San Francisco, CA: Jossey-Bass, 2002).
7. Lawton R. Burns. Presentation to U.S. Senate and House of Representatives Staffers (January 2013).
8. Eugene Schneller and Larry Smeltzer. *Strategic Management of the Health Care Supply Chain*. (San Francisco, CA: Jossey-Bass, 2006).

9. Effective July 7, 2004, the GAO's legal name was changed from the General Accounting Office to the Government Accountability Office. The GAO acronym applied to each.

10. U.S. General Accounting Office. *Group Purchasing Organizations: Pilot Study Suggests Large Buying Groups Do Not Always Offer Hospitals Lower Prices*. GAO-02-690 T (April 30, 2002).

11. U.S. General Accounting Office. *Group Purchasing Organizations: Pilot Study Suggests Large Buying Groups Do Not Always Offer Hospitals Lower Prices*. GAO-02-690 T (April 30, 2002).

12. The Lewin Group. *Assessing the Value of Group Purchasing Organizations* (Washington, DC: Lewin Group, May 2003).

13. General Accounting Office. *Group Purchasing Organizations: Use of Contracting Processes and Strategies to Award Contracts for Medical-Surgical Products*. GAO-03-998 T (July 16, 2003).

14. Eugene Schneller. *The Value of Group Purchasing – 2009: Meeting the Need for Strategic Savings* (Tempe, AZ: Arizona State University, 2009).

15. The Lewin Group. *Assessing the Value of Group Purchasing Organizations* (Washington, DC: Lewin Group, May 2003).

16. William Cleverly and Paul Nutt. "The Effectiveness of Group Purchasing Organizations," *Health Services Research* 19(1) (1984): 65–81.

17. Lawton Burns and Andrew Lee. "Hospital Purchasing Alliances: Utilization, Services, and Performance," *Health Care Management Review* 33(3) (2008): 203–215.

18. Government Accountability Office. *Group Purchasing Organizations: Research on Their Pricing Impact on Health Care Providers*. Letter to Senator Charles Grassley (January 29, 2010).

19. Lawton Burns and Andrew Lee. "Hospital Purchasing Alliances: Utilization, Services, and Performance," *Health Care Management Review* 33(3) (2008): 203–215.

20. Chris Serb. "Does Your GPO Deliver the Goods?" *Hospitals and Health Networks Magazine* (July 2010).

21. United States Senate. *Empirical Data Lacking to Support Claims of Savings With Group Purchasing Organizations*. Minority Staff Report, Senate Finance Committee (September 24, 2010).

22. Robert Litan and Hal Singer. "Do Group Purchasing Organizations Achieve the Best Prices for Member Hospitals? An Empirical Analysis of Aftermarket Transactions," Unpublished manuscript.

23. Arka Bhattacharya. *A Comparative Study of Healthcare Procurement Models*. Masters Degree Thesis, College of Engineering, University of South Florida (2007).

24. Government Accountability Office. *Lack of Price Transparency May Hamper Hospitals' Ability to Be Prudent Purchasers of Implantable Medical Devices* (January 2012).

25. James Robinson, Alexis Pozen, Samuel Tseng, and Kevin Bozic. "Variability in Costs Associated with Total Hip and Knee Replacement Implants," *Journal of Bone and Joint Surgery* 94(18) (2012): 1693–1698.

26. Mark Pauly and Lawton R. Burns. "Price Transparency for Medical Devices," *Health Affairs* 27(6) (2008): 1544–1553.

27. Gilbert Nyaga, Gary Young, and E. David Zepeda. "An Analysis of the Effects of Intra- and Interorganizational Arrangements on Hospital Supply Chain Efficiency," *Journal of Business Logistics* 36(4) (2015): 340–354. Gary Young, Gilbert Nyaga, and E. David Zepeda. "Hospital Employment of Physicians and Supply Chain Performance," *Health Care Management Review* 41(3) (2016): 244–255. Yousef Abdulsalem, Mohan Gopalakrishnan, Arnold Maltz, and Eugene Schneller. "The Impact of Physician-Hospital Integration on Hospital Supply Management," *Journal of Operations Management* 57 (2018): 11–22. Daniel Walker, John McAlearney, Luv Sharma et al. "Examining the Financial and Quality Performance Effects of Group Purchasing Organizations," *Health Care Management Review* 46(4) (2021): 278–288.

28. Pricivel Carrera, Sukran Katik, and Fredo Schotanus. "Cooperative Purchasing of High-risk Medical Devices by Dutch Hospitals: What are the Actual Price Savings, Perceived Non-monetary Advantages, Disadvantages and Impediments?" Unpublished manuscript (2017).

29. Gary Young, Gilbert Nyaga, and E. David Zepeda. "Hospital Employment of Physicians and Supply Chain Performance," *Health Care Management Review* 41(3) (2016): 244–255. Yousef Abdulsalem, Mohan Gopalakrishnan, Arnold Maltz, and Eugene Schneller. "The Impact of Physician-Hospital Integration on Hospital Supply Management," *Journal of Operations Management* 57 (2018): 11–22.

30. Gilbert Nyaga, Gary Young, and E. David Zepeda. "An Analysis of the Effects of Intra- and Interorganizational Arrangements on Hospital Supply Chain Efficiency," *Journal of Business Logistics* 36(4) (2015): 340–354.

31. Gilbert Nyaga, Gary Young, and E. David Zepeda. "An Analysis of the Effects of Intra- and Interorganizational Arrangements on Hospital Supply Chain Efficiency," *Journal of Business Logistics* 36(4) (2015): 340–354.

32. Allison Briggs and Lawton R. Burns. "Do Group Purchasing Organizations (GPOs) Help Hospitals to Reduce Supply Costs?" Paper presented to Annual Meeting of Academy of Management (Boston, MA: August 2019).

33. Eugene Schneller. *The Value of Group Purchasing in the Health Care Supply Chain* (Tempe, AZ: Arizona State University, 2000).

34. Eugene Schneller. *The Value of Group Purchasing—2009: Meeting the Need for Strategic Savings.* (Tempe, AZ: Arizona State University, 2009).

35. Muse & Associates. *The Role of Group Purchasing Organizations in the U.S. Health Care System* (Washington, DC: Muse & Associates, 2000).

36. Muse & Associates. *The Role of Group Purchasing in the Health Care System and the Impact on Public Health Care Expenditures if Additional Restrictions are Imposed on GPO Contracting Processes* (Washington, DC: Muse & Associates, 2002).

37. Muse & Associates. *A Cost Savings and Marketplace Analysis of the Health Care Group Purchasing Industry* (Washington, DC: Muse & Associates, 2005).

38. Locus Systems. *A 2007 Update of Cost Savings and a Marketplace Analysis of the Health Care Group Purchasing Industry* (Laurel, MD: Locus Systems, January 2009).

39. David Goldenberg and Roland "Guy" King. *A 2008 Update of Cost Savings and a Marketplace Analysis of the Health Care Group Purchasing Industry* (Laurel, MD: Locus Systems, July 2009).

40. Allen Dobson, Steve Heath, Kevin Reuter, and Joan DaVanzo. *A 2014 Update of Cost Savings and Marketplace Analysis of the Health Care Group Purchasing Industry* (Vienna, VA: Dobson DaVanzo & Associates, July 7, 2014).

41. The Lewin Group. *Assessing the Value of Group Purchasing Organizations* (Washington, DC: Lewin Group, 2003).

42. Dan O'Brien, Jon Leibowitz, and Russell Anello. *How Group Purchasing Organizations Reduce Healthcare Procurement Costs in a Highly Competitive Market* (The Antitrust Source: 2017). Retrieved January 3, 2018, from https://www.davispolk.com/files/antitrust_source_how_group_purchasing_organizations_reduce_leibowitz_anello.pdf. Dan O'Brien, Jon Leibowitz, and Russell Anello. *Group Purchasing Organizations: How GPOs Reduce Healthcare Costs and Why Changing their Funding Mechanism Would Raise Costs* (The Antitrust Source: 2017). https://www.supplychainassociation.org/wp-content/uploads/2018/05/Leibowitz_GPO_Report.pdf Allen Dobson, Steve Heath, Kevin Reuter, and Joan DaVanzo. (2014). *A 2014 Update of Cost Savings and Marketplace Analysis of the Health Care Group Purchasing Industry* (Vienna, VA: Dobson DaVanzo & Associates, 2014). James Scott, John Voorhees, and Melissa Angel. *GPOs: Helping to Increase Efficiency and Reduce Costs for Healthcare Providers and Suppliers.* (Alexandria, VA: Applied Policy, 2014).

43. Lawton Burns and Andrew Lee. "Hospital Purchasing Alliances: Utilization, Services, and Performance," *Health Care Management Review* 33(3)(2008): 203–215.

44. Lawton R. Burns and Allison Briggs. "Hospital Purchasing Alliances: Ten Years After," *Health Care Management Review* 45(3) (2020): 186–195.

45. 2010 Hospital GPO Use Survey. *Hospitals & Health Networks.* Survey sponsored by MMHC/AHRMM.

46. Lawton R. Burns and Allison Briggs. "Hospital Purchasing Alliances: Ten Years After," *Health Care Management Review* 45(3) (2020): 186–195.

47. Allen Dobson, Steve Heath, Phap-Hoa Luu et al. *A 2018 Update of Cost Savings and Marketplace Analysis of the Group Purchasing Industry* (Vienna, VA: Dobson/DaVanzo & Associates, April 16, 2019).

48. William Opoku-Agyeman, Robert Weech-Maldonado, Soumya Upadhyay et al. "Hospital Group Purchasing Alliances and Financial Performance," *Journal of Health Care Finance* (Summer 2019). Available online at: http://healthfinancejournal.com/index.php/johcf/article/download/180/184.

49. Joonhwan In, Randy Bradley, Bogdan Bichescu et al. "Breaking the Chain: GPO Changes and Hospital Supply Cost Efficiency," *International Journal of Production Economics* 218 (2019): 297–307.

50. Lynn Everard. *The Impact of Group Purchasing on the Financial Prospects of Health Systems: Changing Value Perceptions and Unintended Consequences* (V.I.P.E.R. Group, 2003). Available online at: https://nebula.wsimg.com/c1d7456a5a119322ee0a72dd4092f658?AccessKeyId=62BC662C928C06F7384C&disposition=0&alloworigin=1.

51. Lynn Everard. *Defining and Measuring Product-Based Cost Savings in the Health Care Supply Chain.* Available online at: http://www.medicalsupplychain.com/pdf/Defining%20and%20Measuring%20Product%20Based%20Cost%20Savings.pdf. Accessed on July 3, 2014.

52. Hal Singer. *The Budgetary Impact of Eliminating the GPOs' Safe Harbor Exemption from the Anti-Kickback Statute of the Social Security Act* (Washington, DC.: Criterion Economics, 2005).

53. I beg the reader's forgiveness. These empirical findings from the GAO/OIG reports were summarized in Chapter 5 in serial (historical) fashion. Here, in Chapter 6, they are summarized by topic.

54. Government Accounting Office. *Group Purchasing Organizations: Use of Contracting Processes and Strategies to Award Contracts for Medical-Surgical Products* (2003).

55. Department of Health & Human Services. *Review of Revenue from Vendors at Three Group Purchasing Organizations and Their Members.* A-05–03-00,074 (Washington, DC: Office of the Inspector General, DHHS, January 2005).

56. Department of Health & Human Services. *Review of Revenue from Vendors at Three Additional Group Purchasing Organizations and Their Members.* A-05–04-00,073. (Washington, DC: Office of the Inspector General, DHHS, May 2005).

57. Office of the Inspector General. *Review of Compliance with Conditions of the Group Purchasing Organization Safe Harbor, Premier Purchasing Partners, L.P., Oak Brook, Illinois.* A-05–01-00,092. (Washington, DC: Department of Health and Human Services, February 2003).

58. Government Accountability Office. *Group Purchasing Organizations: Services Provided to Customers and Initiatives Regarding Their Business Practices.* (Washington, DC: GAO, August 2010).

59. Lawton R. Burns and Allison Briggs. "Hospital Purchasing Alliances: Ten Years After," *Health Care Management Review* 45(3) (2020): 186–195.

60. Government Accounting Office. *Group Purchasing Organizations: Use of Contracting Processes and Strategies to Award Contracts for Medical-Surgical Products* (Washington, DC: GAO, 2003).

61. Lawton R. Burns and Allison Briggs. "Hospital Purchasing Alliances: Ten Years After," *Health Care Management Review* 45(3) (2020): 186–195.

62. Thomas Hendrick. *Purchasing Consortiums: Horizontal Alliances Among Firms Buying Common Good and Services—What? Who? Why? How?* (Tempe, AZ: Center for Advanced Purchasing Studies, Arizona State University, 1996).

63. Laura Baldwin, Frank Camm, and Nancy Moore. *Federal Contract Bundling: A Framework for Making and Justifying Decisions for Purchased Services* (Santa Monica, CA: RAND, 2001).

64. Government Accountability Office. *Group Purchasing Organizations: Services Provided to Customers and Initiatives Regarding Their Business Practices* (Washington, DC: GAO, 2010).

65. The Lewin Group. *The Clinical Review Process Conducted by Group Purchasing Organizations and Health Systems* (Washington, DC: Lewin Group, April 2002).

66. Government Accountability Office. *Group Purchasing Organizations: Services Provided to Customers and Initiatives Regarding Their Business Practices.* (Washington, DC: GAO, 2010).

67. Government Accounting Office. *Group Purchasing Organizations: Use of Contracting Processes and Strategies to Award Contracts for Medical-Surgical Products* (Washington, DC: GAO, 2003).

68. Government Accountability Office. *Group Purchasing Organizations: Federal Oversight and Self-Regulation.* Letter to Senators Herbert Kohl, Charles Grassley, and Tom Coburn (March 30, 2012).

69. Lawton Burns and Andrew Lee. "Hospital Purchasing Alliances: Utilization, Services, and Performance," *Health Care Management Review* 33(3) (2008): 203–215.

70. Richard Kusserow and Thomas Herrmann. *Activities and Perspectives of the Office of Inspector General in the U.S. Department of Health and Human Services Regarding Group Purchasing Organizations (GPOs)* (Alexandria, VA: Strategic Management Services, March 2013).

71. Government Accountability Office. *Group Purchasing Organizations: Services Provided to Customers and Initiatives Regarding Their Business Practices.* (Washington, DC: GAO, 2010).

72. Bushra Rahman, Eugene Schneller, and Natalia Wilson. "Integrity and Efficiency in Collaborative Purchasing," in Gabriella M. Racca and Christopher R. Yukins (Eds.), *Integrity and Efficiency in Sustainable Public Contracts* (Brussels: Bruylant, 2014): p. 295.

73. American Society of Association Executives. *1987 Policies and Procedures in Association Management* (Washington, DC: 1987). Quoted in Bushra Rahman, Eugene Schneller, and Natalia Wilson. "Integrity and Efficiency in Collaborative Purchasing," in Gabriella M. Racca and Christopher R. Yukins (Eds.), *Integrity and Efficiency in Sustainable Public Contracts* (Brussels: Bruylant, 2014): p. 295.

74. *National Directory of Trade and Professional Associations.* (Washington, DC: Columbia Books, 1991).

75. Philip English, Byron Dorgan, and Robert Bennett. *Healthcare Group Purchasing Industry Initiative: Eighth Annual Report to the Public* (Arent Fox LLP, 2013).

76. Bushra Rahman, Eugene Schneller, and Natalia Wilson. "Integrity and Efficiency in Collaborative Purchasing," in Gabriella M. Racca and Christopher R. Yukins (Eds.), *Integrity and Efficiency in Sustainable Public Contracts* (Brussels: Bruylant, 2014).

77. U.S. Department of Justice and Federal Trade Commission. *Statements of Antitrust Enforcement Policy in Health Care* (August 1996). Available online at: http://www.justice.gov/atr/public/guidelines/1791.htm#CONTNUM_12. Accessed on July 14, 2014.

78. Herbert Hovenkamp. *Competitive Effects of Group Purchasing Organizations' (GPO) Purchasing and Product Selection Practices in the Health Care Industry* (Washington, DC: HIGPA, April 2002).

79. The HHI measures the concentration of a market. It is computed by squaring the market shares of each firm in the market and then summing these squared terms. Markets with HHIs below a level of 1,000 are assumed to be un-concentrated and therefore competitive.

80. Lawton R. Burns. Testimony to Federal Trade Commission. FTC Health Care and Competition Law and Policy Workshop. Panel 3: Hospital Group Purchasing Organizations (Washington, DC: September 10, 2002).

81. S. Prakesh Sethi. *Group Purchasing Organizations: An Evaluation of Their Effectiveness in Providing Services to Hospitals and Their Patients* (New York, NY: International Center for Corporate Accountability, 2006).

82. Michael Porter. *Competitive Strategy* (New York, NY: Free Press, 1980).

83. Roger Blair and Christine Durrance. "Group Purchasing Organizations, Monopsony, and Antitrust Policy," *Managerial and Decision Economics* (2013). Available online at: http://onlinelibrary.wiley.com/doi/10.1002/mde.2633/abstract. Accessed on July 3, 2014.

84. Qiaohai Hu and Leroy Schwarz. "Do GPOs Promote or Stifle Competition in Healthcare-Product Supply Chains?" Regenstrief Center for Healthcare Engineering, Purdue University (August 2008).

85. Qiaohai Hu, Leroy Schwarz, and Nelson Uhan. "The Impact of Group Purchasing Organizations on Healthcare-Product Supply Chains," Regenstrief Center for Healthcare Engineering, Purdue University (May 2011).

86. Qiaohai Hu and Leroy Schwarz. "The Controversial Role of GPOs in Healthcare-Product Supply Chains," *Production and Operations Management* 20(1) (2011): 1–15.
87. Carl Johnson and Curtis Rooney. "GPOs and the Health Care Supply Chain: Market-Based Solutions and Real-World Recommendations to Reduce Pricing Secrecy and Benefit Health Care Providers," *Journal of Contemporary Health Law and Policy* 29(1) (2012): 72–88.
88. Howard Marvel and Huanxing Yang. "Group Purchasing, Nonlinear Tariffs, and Oligopoly," *International Journal of Industrial Organization* 26 (2008): 1090–1105.
89. James Dana. "Buyer Groups as Strategic Commitments," Kellogg School of Management (2003).
90. Rajib Saha, Abraham Seidmann, and Vera Tilson. "The Impact of Custom Contracting on the Key Information Roles of Group Purchasing Organizations (GPOs) in the Healthcare Supply Chain," Simon Business School, University of Rochester, and Indian School of Business.
91. Arnold Celnicker. "An Economic and Antitrust Analysis of the Distribution of Medical Products," *American Journal of Law and Medicine* 16(4) (1990): 499–523.
92. L. Weinstein Bernard. "The Role of Group Purchasing Organizations (GPOs) in the U.S. Medical Industry Supply Chain," *Estudios de Economia Aplicada* 24(3) (2006): 789–802.
93. Einar Elhauge. *The Exclusion of Competition for Hospital Sales Through Group Purchasing Organizations*. Report to the U.S. Senate (2002).
94. Einar Elhauge. *Antitrust Analysis of GPO Exclusionary Agreements*. Comments Regarding Hearings on Health Care and Competition Law and Policy. Statement for DOJ/FTC Hearing on GPOs (2003).
95. David Balto. *The Effects of Regulatory Neglect on Health Care Consumers*. Testimony before the Consumer Protection, Product Safety and Insurance Subcommittee of the Senate Committee on Commerce, Science and Transportation (July 16, 2009).
96. Most of these papers and reports were supported by either the opponents of GPOs or the GPO trade association HIGPA/HSCA, and thus were often written by individuals who served as expert witnesses in antitrust cases brought by small suppliers who felt they were foreclosed by GPO contracts.
97. Michael Lindsay. "Antitrust and Group Purchasing," *Antitrust* 23(3) (2009): 66–73.
98. Robert Bloch, Scott Perlman, and Jay Brown. *An Analysis of Group Purchasing Organizations' Contracting Practices Under the Antitrust Laws: Myth and Reality*. (Washington, DC: Mayer, Brown, Rowe and Maw, n.d.). Available online at: https://silo.tips/download/an-analysis-of-group-purcha sing-organizations-contracting-practices-under-the-an.
99. William Kolasky. *Group Purchasing Organization (GPO) Contracting Practices and Antitrust Law*. Report prepared for HIGPA (November 2009).

100. Bushra Rahman, Eugene Schneller, and Natalia Wilson. "Integrity and Efficiency in Collaborative Purchasing," in Gabriella M. Racca and Christopher R. Yukins (Eds.), *Integrity and Efficiency in Sustainable Public Contracts.* (Brussels: Bruylant, 2014): p. 302.

101. Yousef Abdulsalan, Mohan Gopalakrishnan, Arnold Maltz and Eugene Schneller. "Investigating Supply Chain Shared Service Organizations in Healthcare," Unpublished Manuscript (Under review at *Journal of Business Logistics*).

102. Yousef Abdulsalam. "Group Purchasing Organizations: Preliminary Analysis & Results," Unpublished presentation.

103. Gary Appel and Chris Lee. "The Importance of Local Market Analysis to Sales and Marketing," *In Vivo* (July/August 1997): 33–40.

104. Lawton R. Burns and Allison Briggs. "Hospital Purchasing Alliances: Ten Years After," *Health Care Management Review* 45(3) (2020): 186–195.

105. Daniel Crane and Joshua Wright. "Can Bundled Discounting Increase Consumer Prices Without Excluding Rivals? A Comment on Tying, Bundled Discounts, and the Death of the Single Monopoly Profit by Einer Elhauge," *Competition Policy International* 5(2) (2009): 209–220.

106. Kevin Murphy, Edward Snyder, and Robert Topel. "Competitive Discounts and Antitrust Policy," Working Paper No. 250, George J. Stigler Center for the Study of the Economy and the State, The University of Chicago (2013).

107. Herbert Hovenkamp. *Group Purchasing Organization (GPO) Purchasing Agreements and Antitrust Law* (Washington, DC: HIGPA. April 2004).

108. There is considerable variation in GPO ownership. In the early 2000s, when much of this controversy surfaced, two GPOs (HealthTrust Purchasing Group, Broadlane) were housed within investor-owned hospital chains (HCA and Tenet, respectively). Two other GPOs (Premier, Novation) were organized as cooperatives with hospital system shareholders and affiliates. Amerinet was a strategic alliance of three hospital systems/groups. There was thus some degree of linkage with hospitals in some of the GPOs. However, in almost all cases, there was no linkage between the GPOs and the physicians and clinicians who ordered products.

109. In Vivo Diarist. "A Final Word on GPOs," *In Vivo* (January 2003): 14.

110. Lawton R. Burns, Michael Housman, and Charles Robinson. "Market Entry and Exit by Biotech and Device Companies Funded by Venture Capital," *Health Affairs* Web Exclusive (December 2, 2008).

111. David Cassak. "Is Group Purchasing Broke?" *In Vivo* (December, 2002): 27–42.

112. David Cassak. "IDNs and GPOs: Changing the Leopard's Spots," *In Vivo* (July 2001): 32–44. https://scrip.pharmaintelligence.informa.com/IV0 01708/IDNs-and-GPOs-Changing-the-Leopards-Spots.

113. Lawton Burns and Steve Sammut. "Healthcare Innovation Across Sectors: Convergences and Divergences," *The Business of Healthcare Innovation* (Cambridge, UK: Cambridge University Press, 2005): Chapter 8.

114. Lawton Burns and Andrew Lee. "Hospital Purchasing Alliances: Utilization, Services, and Performance," *Health Care Management Review* 33(3) (2008): 203–215. In response to this survey item, managers assigned their national GPO a score of 2.29 using a Likert scale that ranged from 1 (strongly disagree) to 5 (strongly agree).

115. Tom Groenfeldt. "$40 Billion Hospital Supplier Links Health Innovators with Clinicians," *Forbes* (July 7, 2014).

116. For example, see R. Laurence Macon. *Bundling and GPOs – Antitrust Lessons Learned From Kinetic Concepts v. Hill-Rom.* Akin Gump Strauss Hauer & Feld LLP. Report to 408th District Court, Bexar County, TX.

117. Lawton Burns and Andrew Lee. "Hospital Purchasing Alliances: Utilization, Services, and Performance," *Health Care Management Review* 33(3) (2008): 203–215.

118. Lawton R. Burns and Allison Briggs. "Hospital Purchasing Alliances: Ten Years After," *Health Care Management Review* 45(3) (2020): 186–195.

119. Lawton Burns and Andrew Lee. "Hospital Purchasing Alliances: Utilization, Services, and Performance," *Health Care Management Review* 33(3) (2008): 203–215.

120. Robert Neil. "From the Buyer's Perspective," *Materials Management in Health Care* (September 2005): 18–25.

121. *2010 Hospital GPO Use Survey.* Hospitals and Health Networks (2010).

122. *Modern Healthcare's 2012 Survey of Executive Opinions on Supply Chain Issues* (Chicago, IL: 2012).

123. L.E.K. Consulting. *The Hospital Purchasing Shift: Strategic Hospital Priorities Study* (LEK, 2012).

124. Robert Neil. "From the Buyer's Perspective," *Materials Management in Health Care* (September 2005): 18–25.

125. Lawton Burns and Andrew Lee. "Hospital Purchasing Alliances: Utilization, Services, and Performance," *Health Care Management Review* 33(3) (2008): 203–215. Table 2.

126. Eugene Schneller. *The Value of Group Purchasing—2009: Meeting the Need for Strategic Savings.* (Tempe, AZ: Arizona State University, 2009).

127. *Materials Management in Health Care.* Abstract of findings available online at: http://insidehsca.blogspot.com/2010/07/hospital-survey-finds-gpos-save-money.html. Accessed on July 15, 2014. (No longer available).

128. Lawton R. Burns and Allison Briggs. "Hospital Purchasing Alliances: Ten Years After," *Health Care Management Review* 45(3) (2020): 186–195.

129. FTI's 2nd Annual GPO Survey.

130. Lawton R. Burns. "Hospital Purchasing Alliances: Customer Ratings of GPO Performance," Presentation to HIGPA, Orlando (October 2008). Presentation based on findings presented in Lawton Burns and Andrew Lee. "Hospital Purchasing Alliances: Utilization, Services, and Performance," *Health Care Management Review* 33(3) (2008): 203–215.

131. Mark Thill. "GPO Differentiation: The Real Deal," *Journal of Healthcare Contracting* (May/June 2006). Available online at: https://www.jhconline.com/gpo-differentiation-the-real-deal-2.html.

132. Mark Thill. "What Makes a GPO Stand out From the Others?" *Journal of Healthcare Contracting* 15(3) (March/April 2008): 30–44.

133. Margaret Clapp, Michael Rie, and Phillip Zweig. "How a Cabal Keeps Generics Scarce," *New York Times* (September 2, 2013).

134. Diana Moss. *Healthcare Intermediaries: Competition and Healthcare Policy at Loggerheads?* (Washington, DC: American Antitrust Institute, May 2012).

135. C. Lee Ventola. "The Drug Shortage Crisis in the United States," *Pharmacy & Therapeutics* 36(11): 740–757 (2011).

136. Department of Health and Human Services. *Economic Analysis of the Causes of Drug Shortages* (Washington, DC: U.S. DHHS, October 2011).

137. Food and Drug Administration. *A Review of FDA's Approach to Medical Product Shortages* (Washington, DC: USFDA, October 2011).

138. Healthcare Supply Chain Association. *Group Purchasing Organizations (GPOs) Work to Maintain Access to Product Supply for America's Health Care Providers* (Washington, DC: HSCA, n.d.). Available online at: https://www.supplychainassociation.org/wp-content/uploads/2018/05/gpo_drug_shortage_paper.pdf.

139. Healthcare Supply Chain Association. *The Vital Role of Group Purchasing Organizations in Alleviating Drug Shortages in the United States.* (Washington, DC: HSCA, 2014). Available online at: https://www.supplychainassociation.org/wp-content/uploads/2018/05/avalere_hsca_gpo_drug_shorta.pdf.

140. Government Accountability Office. *Drug Shortages: Public Health Threat Continues, Despite Efforts to Help Ensure Product Availability.* GAO-14–194 (Washington, DC: GAO, 2014).

141. Lawton Burns. *The U.S. Healthcare Ecosystem* (New York: McGraw-Hill, 2021): Chapter 21.

142. Duke University Margolis Center for Health Policy. *Identifying the Root Causes of Drug Shortages and Finding Enduring Solutions* (Durham, NC: Duke University, 2018). American Hospital Association. *Drug Shortages as a Matter of National Security: Improving the Resilience of the Nation's Healthcare Critical Infrastructure* (2018). Available online at: https://www.aha.org/topics/drug-shortages. Accessed on March 14, 2022. U.S. Food and Drug Administration. *Drug Shortages: Root Causes and Potential Solutions* (Washington, DC: FDA, 2019).

143. Gabriella Racca and Gian Luigi Albano. "Collaborative Public Procurement and Supply Chain: The European Experience," in Christine Harland, Guido Nassimbeni and Eugene Schneller (Eds.), *The SAGE Handbook of Strategic Supply Management.* (London, UK: Sage, 2013): 178–213. Chapter 8.

144. Christine Harland, Jan Telgen and Guy Callender. "International Research Study of Public Procurement," in Christine Harland, Guido Nassimbeni

and Eugene Schneller (Eds.), *The SAGE Handbook of Strategic Supply Management.* (London, UK: Sage, 2013): 372–399. Chapter 16.

145. Gabriella Racca. "Collaborative Procurement and Contract Performance in the Italian Healthcare Sector: Illustration of a Common Problem in European Procurement," *Public Procurement Law Review* 8 (2010): 119–33.

146. Gabriella Racca. "Professional Buying Organizations, Sustainability and Competition in Public Procurement Performance," *Proceedings of 4th International Public Procurement Conference* (Seoul: August 26–28, 2010).

147. Gabriella Racca and Gian Luigi Albano. "Collaborative Public Procurement and Supply Chain: The European Experience," in Christine Harland, Guido Nassimbeni and Eugene Schneller (Eds.), *The SAGE Handbook of Strategic Supply Management.* (London, UK: Sage, 2013): 178–213. Chapter 8.

148. Eugene Schneller, Christine Harland, Helen Walker and Samantha Forest. "Systems of Exchange: Cooperative Purchasing in the UK and US Health Sectors," in Christine Harland, Guido Nassimbeni and Eugene Schneller (Eds.), *The SAGE Handbook of Strategic Supply Management.* (London, UK: Sage 2013): pp. 214–238. Chapter 9.

149. Lawton R. Burns. *The Health Care Value Chain: Producers, Purchasers, and Providers.* (San Francisco, CA: Jossey-Bass, 2002). Eugene Schneller and Larry Smeltzer. *Strategic Management of the Health Care Supply Chain.* (San Francisco, CA: Jossey-Bass, 2006).

150. American Hospital Association. *Underpayment by Medicare and Medicaid Fact Sheet 2012* (Chicago, IL: AHA).

151. Lawton R. Burns, Jeffrey McCullough, Douglas Wholey, Peter Kralovec, Gregory Kruse, and Ralph Muller. "Is the System Really the Solution? Operating Costs in Hospital Systems," *Medical Care Research and Review* 72(3) (2015): 247–272.

152. Lawton R. Burns, Jeff Goldsmith, and Aditi Sen. "Horizontal and Vertical Integration of Physicians: A Tale of Two Tails," in *Annual Review of Health Care Management: Revisiting the Evolution of Health Systems Organization.* Advances in Health Care Management. Volume 15 (Emerald Group Publishing, 2013): 39–119.

153. Lawton R. Burns, David Asch, and Ralph Muller. "Vertical Integration of Physicians and Hospitals: Three Decades of Futility?" in Mark V. Pauly (Ed.), *Seemed Like a Good Idea: Alchemy versus Evidence-Based Approaches to Healthcare Management Innovation* (Cambridge, UK: Cambridge University Press, 2022).

154. Lawton R. Burns. *The Business of Health Care Innovation.* (Cambridge, UK: Cambridge University Press, 2012). Figure 1.3.

155. National Academy of Engineering and Institute of Medicine. *Building a Better Delivery System: A New Engineering/Health Care Partnership.* (Washington, D.C.: National Academies Press, 2005).

156. John Agwunobi and Paul London. "Removing Costs from the Health Care Supply Chain: Lessons From Mass Retail," *Health Affairs* (September/October, 2009): 1336–1342.
157. Kenneth Boyer and Peter Pronovost. "What Medicine Can Teach Operations: What Operations Can Teach Medicine," *Journal of Operations Management* 28 (2010): 367–371.
158. Heather Nachtmann and Edward Pohl. *The State of Healthcare Logistics: Cost and Quality Improvement Opportunities* (Little Rock, AR: Center for Innovation in Healthcare Logistics, University of Arkansas, July 2009).

7

Summary: GPOs' Pro-competitive and Welfare-Generating Benefits

Introduction

Chapters 3–6 have analyzed (in turn) the roles played by GPOs, their historical development, their recent controversies, and their performance track record. This chapter draws on much of the preceding material to articulate the GPOs' pro-competitive and welfare-generating benefits. The chapter makes several bold, declarative statements that speak to the issues raised in Chapter 5, particularly the court litigation. The chapter thus serves as the counterpoint to the mostly negative allegations and GPO assessments found in the litigation literature.

It is more than just counterpoint, however. Unlike the litigation literature (which rested heavily on ideology), the argument in this chapter cites the relevant research and historical record to substantiate these declarative statements.[1] A perusal of the references at the end of this chapter reveals that the relevant research and evidence base already existed prior to the articles in the *New York Times*, the Senate hearings, and the court cases. This evidence base was definitely not consulted or cited, and perhaps was ignored.

This chapter is organized around the following themes (declarative statements):

- First, GPOs have long played an important role in pooling the supply purchases of hospitals. As illustrated in Figure 2.1, the GPOs occupy an intermediary position between hospital providers and product suppliers.

L. R. Burns, *The Healthcare Value Chain*, https://doi.org/10.1007/978-3-031-10739-9_7

- Second, GPOs are powerful intermediaries that act as the hospitals' agents to neutralize the historical power of large suppliers dealing with small, fragmented hospital buyers. They are thus a major countervailing force. Moreover, GPO consolidation during the 1990s augmented this bargaining power and helped them to exert influence over suppliers. The major effect they exerted was to lower the prices of products supplied to the hospitals.
- Third, GPOs are responsive and accountable to their hospital members. Hospitals established the GPOs to work on their behalf for lower prices to improve their fiscal health, be more efficient, and (later) satisfy external demands for cost containment (see Chapter 4). The particular contracting strategies that GPOs employed toward this common objective were also driven by the requests of their members. In this manner, the GPOs benefited their members while also accommodating their diverse needs and interests. GPO membership and contract utilization is voluntary, driven by hospitals, and under the control of hospitals. There is no coercion or penalties imposed by GPOs on their members.
- Fourth, GPO contracts and strategies not only serve the interests of their hospital members. These contracts and strategies also serve to promote competitive healthcare markets and improve public welfare.
- Fifth, GPO contracts and strategies are compatible with competitive supplier markets. Indeed, GPOs want more (rather than less) competition among suppliers. GPO contracting practices can spur supplier competition.
- Sixth, GPOs perform only moderately well in getting hospitals to comply with their contracts. This moderate level of performance allows suppliers considerable "headroom" to compete for market share and, thus, avoids any market foreclosure.
- Seventh, like their hospital members, GPOs embrace smaller suppliers and the new technologies they bring to the attention of providers. They have done so historically and continue to do so through private label programs. At the same time, they do not see their mission as supporting small suppliers.
- Eighth, GPOs do not select the products, vendors, and technologies used by providers; the providers do. There are multiple criteria that providers use in product and vendor selection that have nothing to do with GPOs.

GPOs' Historical Role in Pooling Hospital Purchases

A GPO is an organization whose primary function is to develop purchasing contracts that its hospital members can access. A GPO operates as a pooling alliance that brings together hospitals and pools their resources (i.e., purchasing dollars) to exert leverage over suppliers in order to obtain lower prices and thereby lower hospital costs—i.e., buying in bulk to obtain a price discount. Joint purchasing of supplies and equipment offers hospitals one potential avenue to achieve (purchasing) economies of scale and generate savings on the products they purchase. Hospitals have found these scale economies elusive using other strategic avenues, such as multi-hospital systems and hospital networks.[2] Hospitals established GPOs for this purpose. Perhaps they deserve some credit here.

The history of group purchasing reveals the long-standing, widespread involvement of hospitals, hospital systems, local and state hospital associations, and other groups in supply purchasing. As early as the late 1980s, consulting firm estimates of hospital membership in purchasing groups was at least 90%; by the early 2000s, the estimate was 96%.[3] These figures, combined with the historical narrative, suggest that hospital participation in some form of group purchasing is north of 90%. The Health Industry Group Purchasing Association (HIGPA) claimed that 96–98% of hospitals belonged to purchasing groups in 2014.

This suggests that hospital support for GPOs is both widespread and enduring. During the 2003 Senate hearings, a series of hospital executives filed statements affirming the value provided to their institutions by their purchasing groups. The group provided lower cost commodities via private label contracts, helped hospitals to avoid the costs of hiring contracting staff, financed the needed activities of contracting and product evaluation, evaluated new technologies and devices, helped hospitals to standardize on commodity products to improve patient safety, and provided one-stop-shopping convenience for a wide range of products.

GPOs Are Powerful Intermediaries That Confront Suppliers[4]

GPOs Seek to Neutralize Suppliers and Product Differentiation

As pooling alliances, groups aggregate individual hospital purchases into volume purchasing. Such alliances pool and exchange a critical mass of purchase volume by buyers for price discounts by sellers.[5] This is one powerful intermediary function. Moreover, the group blends different product and vendor preferences of individual buyers into common preferences to channel volume to particular suppliers. This is a second powerful intermediary function. In this manner, the group aims to minimize supplier product differences in the eyes of hospital buyers.[6] The goal is to commoditize products, render them more substitutes in the eyes of hospital buyers, and thereby lower prices. Groups can try to persuade hospital members to switch suppliers and shift market shares in order to gain price discounts on what are now perceived to be similar products.[7] The group strategy works to the extent it can demonstrate to its hospital members that the price discounts it can obtain through standardizing preferences are more important and relevant than any quantitative or qualitative differences in the technologies or products offered by different suppliers.[8]

Groups Serve as a Countervailing Force to Suppliers

Groups are, thus, not the sales agents or marketing arms of large suppliers, contrary to claims repeatedly made by the critics of purchasing groups during the Senate hearings. Instead, groups serve as a countervailing force to suppliers, and reverse the historical situation for most of the last century where larger suppliers confronted smaller hospital buyers in the marketplace. Suppliers could exploit (a) differences in supplier versus buyer size and (b) variation in hospital and clinician preferences for products and product features, and as well as charge prices consistent with this differentiation.

One reason for the emergence of group purchasing was thus the "pricing opportunism" of suppliers in earlier decades. Hospitals commonly reported that not only did suppliers and supplier competition establish prices, but their prices were set capriciously to increase their margins.[9] Suppliers charged varying prices to the same hospital or different prices to hospitals within the same hospital system or integrated delivery network (IDN)—i.e., never paying the same price for the same product. This was exacerbated by "maverick buying" or "spot buying" by individual departments or clinicians, in which case suppliers took further advantage of hospitals and increased their prices.[10] As executives say, suppliers raise prices "because they can."

Such pricing behavior drove hospitals to purchasing groups, whose contracts (and particularly longer-term contracts) with suppliers could bring some stability to product pricing. Hospitals then made their suppliers go through their purchasing groups. By forming groups, hospital buyers could organize and deal with a relatively more concentrated supplier market on a more equal footing, and thereby induce suppliers to bid and price their products more aggressively. By aggregating purchases (and product preferences) across hospitals and clinicians, groups could also render the suppliers closer substitutes, increase supplier competition, and thereby achieve lower pricing. The suppliers' goal was to make purchasing groups ineffective or irrelevant; the groups' goal was to counterbalance the suppliers' leverage based on technological features and physician preference with its own leverage based on group volume and minimization of brand differences between suppliers.[11]

Groups' Consolidation Augments Their Countervailing Power

The historical narrative reveals that purchasing groups have consolidated over time, with a smaller number of groups accounting for a larger percentage of group purchases. They now constitute an even larger intermediary between product suppliers and their hospital customers.

As noted in prior chapters, supplier concentration in some sectors preceded group consolidation; in other sectors, they went in tandem; finally, consolidation in group purchasing led to increased competition among suppliers for the business of a smaller number of large buying groups and thus a relationship based on leverage. This situation set the stage for big price discounts and price wars among the suppliers (e.g., new pricing obtained by Columbia HCA and Premier in the mid-1990s for film and IV solutions). Sometimes these price wars were set in motion by the groups' willingness to disrupt any complacency among incumbent manufacturers by awarding contracts to non-market leaders. This also set the stage for further supplier consolidation: e.g., suppliers perceived weakness in their ability to compete for large customers.

Columbia/HCA is recorded as having been "extremely aggressive with suppliers," offering its business to the supplier that offered the best deal.[12] Suppliers who got the business reportedly both griped about it (lower profit margins) and bragged about it (they got a high-profile contract).[13]

Consolidation of purchasing groups also increased the rivalry among suppliers as merging groups rationalized their contract portfolios. For example, if two groups—each with dual source contracts for a given product—combined, they could continue to offer a dual source contract for that product. But if their contracted suppliers did not fully overlap, there would necessarily be a reduction in the number of suppliers with contracts from the combined group—akin to a game of musical chairs. The slimming down of the group's list of contracted suppliers took place irrespective of any sole-source contracting strategy.

Not surprisingly, suppliers view groups as *obstacles to the marketplace* and *gatekeepers to their hospital customers.*[14] Groups also foster *more work for their sales representatives.*[15] Suppliers feel they are *forced* to pay contract administration fees (CAFs) to get access to their hospital members. They also feel that groups *extract* lower prices from them for their services.[16] Suppliers pay these fees because they feel they *need access* to a critical number of purchasing groups, particularly those with high compliance.[17] All of this language sounds like GPO leverage in action.

Purchasing Groups Wield Influence Upstream over Product Suppliers

Groups bring suppliers to the contracting table through both a carrot and stick approach. As the carrot, suppliers that succeed in getting a group contract have the promise of higher sales volume. As the stick, suppliers that do not succeed in getting a group contract face the threat of losing sales to the competitor who does get the contract, and thus higher future expenses in terms of trying to regain any lost sales. This results in a "game of chicken" between the supplier and the group to see which side needs the other's business more.[18]

According to both manufacturers and groups, the relationship between them is adversarial.[19] The two parties have opposing objectives and non-aligned contracting philosophies. Suppliers seek to sell more products to hospitals at the highest price possible and exploit pricing differences between hospitals. The groups' mission is to obtain lower prices for hospitals and reduce the pricing variances among them through the development of contracts and hospitals' adherence to them. Groups also want to get as many of the products that hospitals purchase on contract as they can—but are not interested in having their hospitals purchase more products in the aggregate. Suppliers want annual price increases, while groups push for price-protected agreements. Suppliers want contract extensions, while groups want periodic requests for proposals (RFPs). Suppliers want facility-based letters of commitment on which to ground compliance agreements, while groups want hospital system-based or IDN-based letters of commitment. Suppliers argue for "value beyond price," while groups want "best price" relative to other groups and competitive pricing for sole awards. Finally, suppliers want contract limits on coverage of new technology, while groups want access to new technology and compliance "carve-outs" for such technology.

Groups employ negotiating tools and strategies to counteract supplier power and obtain better prices and terms than hospitals could do on their own. These tools and strategies include:

- *RFPs*: requests for proposals and invitations to competitively bid for the group contract pit supplier against supplier.
- *Vendor reduction*: sole-source contracts reduce the number of suppliers under contract, which increases the winner-takes-all stakes for suppliers.
- *Market share compliance agreements*: sole-source contracts offer hospitals share-based discounts for reaching a given percentage level in their product purchases from that supplier with the sole-source contract. Share-based discounts have several advantages. First, they allow smaller hospitals to obtain lower prices that might otherwise only be available to larger hospitals based on just the volume purchased. Second, the buyer's willingness to commit to one supplier is what generates competition among suppliers, not the volume purchased. For a single hospital buyer with known demand for a given product, share-based and volume-based discounts function in an equivalent manner. But for a group negotiating for many differently sized hospitals at the same time, the share-based discount generates the best competition for the aggregate business. Empirical studies show that committed purchasing generates greater savings for the hospital than does volume-based purchasing.[20]
- *Bundling of products*: portfolios of bundled products level the differences between a supplier's higher-preference and lower-preference products, reduce prices on high-cost items in markets where a supplier enjoys a monopoly, increase product comparability across suppliers, and thereby increase supplier competition.
- *Value analysis teams (VATs)*: VATs verify competing supplier claims regarding product performance and superiority, allow clinicians to define the relative clinical value of supplier products, shape physician consensus on a small list of approved suppliers, and reduce variation in individual physician preferences.

- *Control over timing of bidding*: groups time the bid to allow all suppliers in, as well as to minimize buyer distractions with bids on other products.
- *Duration of contract*: longer-term contracts increase the stakes (winner take all) for suppliers engaged in bidding and increase price stability.
- *Reputation of the group and/or hospital*: it is prestigious for the supplier to gain the contract of high-profile customers and purchasing groups.

Historical Evidence of Groups' Influence over Suppliers

Suppliers would prefer not to contract with purchasing groups, since they (1) counterbalance and thus challenge the suppliers' relative market power over disaggregated hospital buyers, (2) force them to lower prices, and (3) pose a hurdle to their traditional marketing efforts targeting clinicians. Suppliers also view group contracts as "empowering an intermediary" that reduces prices in the short-term, constrains price hikes over the longer term, and commoditizes the value of their products. Indeed, suppliers elect not to contract with groups when they do not have to—as in the case where they enjoy a monopoly. When there is no competition among suppliers, there is no contracting with groups, and suppliers sell directly to hospitals.[21] This is the situation with branded pharmaceuticals for which there is no therapeutic equivalent.[22] For this reason, groups want to maintain some degree of competition among suppliers. Without any competitors, there is little likelihood that a group can get a contract with a supplier and thus any price discounts for the group's hospitals. When there are competitors, then hospitals have a choice, can use the group's contract, and lower their product costs.

Since their advent, groups have successfully pursued their mission of obtaining lower prices from suppliers on the bulk of items purchased through them. Suppliers have reportedly seen both their prices and revenues fall. In the early days of group purchasing, hospital buyers reported they paid 40% higher prices for surgical dressings prior to group bids. The historical narrative above illustrates the fact that group contracting precipitated a succession of price wars among suppliers. Suppliers reportedly would prefer to return to the era where national groups did not wield influence, they could randomly price their hospital customers, and they only had to focus on the clinician customer.

Beginning in the mid-1980s and picking up steam in the early-to-middle 1990s, purchasing groups tried to extend their contracting efforts from commodity, medical-surgical items to branded pharmaceuticals and physician preference items (PPIs), such as orthopedic implants and cardiovascular devices. This effort marked the "new price wars" between suppliers and groups in the 1990s.[23] The early contracts were not successful overall, as some market-leading suppliers balked at signing group contracts.[24] In some instances, the group did not work with clinicians or supplement the efforts of suppliers' sales reps in ways to augment sales and market share.[25] In all cases, the group's attempt to exert leverage competed with the supplier's leverage based on the product's technological advantages, physician preferences, and market share.

In several cases, however, groups were successful in negotiating contracts for PPIs. Suppliers might agree to contract out of fear of losing share to rivals, to build commitment or stem any erosion of share likely to occur due to a new entrant, or, conversely, to try to take share away from rivals. Suppliers might contract with the goal of gaining access to under-penetrated hospital accounts or enhance their traditional sales and marketing efforts targeting clinicians. Suppliers might contract due to hospital demands for lower-cost products or economic value to deal with cost reimbursement pressures. Suppliers might contract due to a slowdown in product innovation or growth, and thus seek to shift from technology to marketing as a source of competition.[26] Finally, suppliers might contract in consideration of a broader relationship they have with the group, or because they wish to develop a closer relationship with both the administrators and clinicians of member hospitals or simply just to reduce their selling costs into hospitals.[27]

Common Group Objective: Lower Product Prices

One reason why groups have lowered the prices paid by their hospital customers is that this pricing strategy is their major, common objective. Purchasing groups have historically competed with one another in terms of their ability to achieve lower pricing. As part of the new price wars of the early 1990s, groups competed for the lowest price in order to attract hospital members. During this period, and throughout much of their history, group pricing has been very close. Another reason why groups lowered prices is that reduced pricing and product savings have consistently been the main goals hospitals have in affiliating with groups. Groups have been able to maintain their hospital membership because (a) price is the most visible and measurable feature of supplier contracts, and (b) groups have served to lower the prices that hospitals paid. Suppliers have tried to avoid lowering their prices, or at least tried to mask how much they have had to lower them, by offering post-sale rebates to hospitals. In this manner, they have sought to slow down or prevent the price discounting spiral instigated by purchasing groups.

In other industries, purchasing groups achieve average price savings for their members of 13.4%.[28] In the hospital industry, groups are reported to have achieved price savings for their hospitals of anywhere from 10–26%.[29] This upper bound was confirmed in the GAO's own initial pilot study, although the GAO also found that hospitals could contract for even lower prices than the group.[30]

Groups Respond and Are Accountable to Their Hospital Members

Groups are not the agents of suppliers. GPOs serve as the purchasing agents of their hospital members and owners. This agency role has several features, summarized below.

Group Strategic Objectives Reflect Hospital Member Needs and Demands

The historical narrative in Chapter 4 reveals that the strategies of purchasing groups have been largely driven by the needs and demands of their hospital members. For example, the conversion of several nonprofit groups to cooperative status was partly driven by the need to demonstrate a tangible financial return and contribution to their members' fiscal health.

Due to state rate review, prospective payment, and managed care, hospitals faced revenue constraints (lower increases in reimbursement) from both public and private sector payers at the same time that they faced rising health supply costs. Hospitals turned to their groups to focus on product prices and thereby achieve needed savings.[31] Group member surveys repeatedly found that "savings" are the most valuable service provided by the group.

Hospital Vice-Presidents for Materials Management (VPMMs) state that their top expectation for purchasing groups is to achieve the best price and leverage suppliers.[32] This expectation has been shaped and driven over the past several decades by relentless pressures on hospitals (in the form of public sector regulation and competitive initiatives) for cost containment. These pressures explain the increase in purchasing groups over time.[33] Hospitals are convinced that groups have delivered lower prices than what they could have achieved on their own. Likewise, hospital CEOs state that the most valuable service offered by their groups is the savings from their national purchasing programs. Member hospitals judge their purchasing group on the latter's ability to deliver discounted prices, and they participate on that basis.

Groups compete for hospital members based on the lower (not higher) prices they can negotiate from suppliers. This is their mission—a mission which is consistent with the decades-long pressure on hospitals to deal with cost containment. This competition is the basis for the "range wars" between purchasing groups (and between the purchasing groups and the IDNs, investor-owned hospital systems, and contract management firms) noted in the earlier historical review. Groups thus exist to negotiate better product and pricing deals for their hospital members.

Groups Accommodate Interests of Their Diverse Membership

During the 1990s, purchasing groups witnessed the increase in hospital system affiliations, hospital mergers via horizontal integration, and the formation of IDNs via vertical integration. Hospital systems and IDNs could operate as "islands unto themselves." They might also try to compete with investor-owned systems like Columbia/HCA and seek to dominate local healthcare markets. In this manner, IDNs could serve as a possible substitute for and competitive threat to purchasing groups, since they could achieve higher levels of compliance and standardization on local supplier contracts than could groups with their national contracts. Groups learned they had to accommodate the rising market power of hospital systems and IDNs, and to balance the interests of the national membership and group contracts with the interests of local systems and IDNs and their individual interests.

How did groups manage this balancing act?[34]

1. Groups looked the other way when their hospital system and IDN members strayed from national contracts and programs.
2. Groups might sign clauses that allowed a supplier to pursue "exception pricing" (price below the group price) with certain hospital members that devote more business to the supplier. In the absence of such clauses, groups might not challenge IDNs for their exception pricing, which could undermine national contracts. Premier did not enforce its "most favored nation" (MFN) pricing when it discovered exception pricing offered to its hospital members. Moreover, suppliers might not inform the group if they violated MFN pricing by offering its hospitals better prices.
3. Groups used "price tiers" to accommodate hospital systems and IDNs that wanted to comply with national contracts at different levels. Hospitals could tell the group that they wanted more tiers. Indeed, price tiers were a signal that group members have diverse preferences for compliance with

a contract. In hospitals' eyes, price tiers were not penalties or disincentives imposed on them for non-compliance, but rather part of a normal contract structure where you need to purchase higher volume in order to get better prices.

4. Groups developed tailored programs where hospitals that wanted to make more commitment in exchange for better pricing could enter one program, while hospitals that wanted more supplier choice could enter another program. This is what AmeriNet did when it established its sole-source contracting program Elite, and what VHA sought to accomplish in its segmentation strategy.

5. Groups offered hospitals more latitude in order to minimize hospital defections to rival groups.

6. Groups transitioned some of their sole-source (or dual-source) contracts to become dual-source (or triple-source) contracts to create flexibility for their larger shareholders and accommodate clinician preferences.

7. Groups developed regional strategies and clusters to accommodate the varying preferences of their hospital members.

8. Groups recognized that accommodating hospital systems, IDNs, and their diverse interests was just another service to be offered to group members.[35]

Group Contracting Strategies Reflect Member Needs and Demands

One major set of related vehicles that IDNs and hospital systems believed would help with cost containment in the mid-1990s included product standardization, sole-source contracts, and prime supplier contracts. IDN executives expected standardization to occur in many product areas.[36] IDNs also thought they could obtain better pricing than their primary purchasing group. These factors may explain why groups pushed so hard on standardizing and sole-source contracting.

Sole-source contracts developed by groups in the mid-1990s were often "pulled down" by hospital members who were facing (1) financial difficulties due to reimbursement issues with payers and (2) competition with other local hospitals that belonged to rival groups that pursued sole-source contracts.[37] These hospitals wanted their groups to offer programs not tied to the volume that would create additional savings. The competitive pressures fostering such contracts may have been particularly acute for hospitals in markets with high managed care penetration and/or with a higher presence of investor-owned hospitals (particularly Columbia/HCA).

The consolidation of the GPO industry was, in large measure, a response to hospital members' clamor for better product contracts and pricing that could help them to better compete with investor-owned hospitals in their local markets.[38] Larger groups were viewed as vehicles that could help nonprofit hospitals obtain contracts and pricing similar to investor-owned hospitals operating in their markets. The newly merged groups often developed contracting programs (e.g., compliance) based on requests from their member hospitals and designs of the materials managers at their member hospitals. Compliance programs were also initiated at local and regional purchasing cooperatives based on their members' input.

Groups developed sole-source contracts, compliance-based contracts, and packaged discount contracts that hospitals preferred. Indeed, Premier was surprised by how few of its members left after it began these programs.[39] Hospital members remained in the group to take advantage of what these contracts offered, including 95% participation in the group's committed compliance program.[40] Groups that developed any other contracting strategies that hospitals preferred would have come to dominate the market.

In fact, when IDNs departed groups to develop their own purchasing programs, they often retained the packaged discount contracts that their former groups had developed. In other cases, when the nonprofit groups began to migrate away from committed contracts and packaged discount programs in the early 2000s, investor-owned groups targeted their members for recruitment into their own committed purchasing programs.

Group Contracts Benefit Hospitals

VPMMs offer many reasons why group contracts benefit their institutions. First, the group can do a better job than a hospital or IDN in negotiating contract prices for commodity items by virtue of aggregating the spending of many hospitals and concentrating it on a few suppliers. Second, hospitals get access to lots of contracts without having to negotiate them or to manage price files or price changes. This allows hospitals to re-deploy staff to higher-value areas. Third, groups help the hospitals to lower their cost of business by virtue of reducing inaccurate information and transaction errors. Group contracts also reduce the total delivered cost of products, which helps the hospital's budget and increases the hospital's margin to fund indigent care. Fourth, the groups keep their eyes on suppliers and supplier agreements, and thereby avoid supplier "price creep" and pricing opportunism. Fifth, group contracts help hospitals to standardize their products and reduce variations that might harm patient care. Sixth, group contracts help hospitals to negotiate even lower prices on their own, often with the assistance of their purchasing group. Seventh, groups provide services that some hospitals desire (e.g., product training, networking, education).

Hospital Participation in Most Groups and Group Contracts Is Voluntary

Hospitals join purchasing groups on a voluntary basis. Hospitals have the freedom to decide whether or not to belong to a purchasing group, which purchasing group (or groups) to belong to, and whether or not to use the group's contracts.[41] In fact, hospitals formed most GPOs on their own initiative.

Hospitals either form or self-select into the type of group and its purchasing philosophy that they feel comfortable with. Hospitals that want committed contracts (e.g. sole-source) might opt to join one GPO, while hospitals that want supplier and product choice might opt for another GPO. Different groups will then offer their hospital members those types of contracts that the hospitals are looking for: e.g., sole-source versus dual-source.[42]

The hospital membership base of groups is not static. It is not uncommon to find hospital systems and IDNs switching group memberships. Groups can have good times and bad times, and go in and out of vogue with hospital members based on their contracts and other offerings.[43] Groups can disband or fragment due to the inability of group members to collaborate on purchasing. Groups can also suffer defections as hospital members engage in mergers and system formations, both of which can lead to supplier and contract rationalization. Groups can also suffer membership losses when their system members divest facilities and sell them to other systems that participate in other groups. Hospitals often switch group memberships due to changes in their Chief Executive Officers (CEOs) who want to use their previous hospital's group or merely the desire to test the waters and work with another group. Such changes in group membership can be one source of problems with contract compliance and commitment.

Similarly, hospitals participate in group contracts on a voluntary basis. According to the Lewin Group, 91% of hospitals in their study voluntarily participated in compliance, sole-source, and/or a package discount program to earn bigger price savings.[44] If hospitals join groups on a willing, voluntary basis, and use their contracts on a voluntary basis, then the group and its contracts must be serving their members' self-interests. Case evidence indicates that hospitals participating in one large GPO's contracts at Tier

3 pricing were not required to use that contract, were not forced to buy anything under the contract, and were not prevented from buying from other suppliers.

Groups Sign Supplier Contracts That Hospital Members Want

Groups sign contracts with the suppliers that its hospital members want. According to VPMMs, purchasing groups sign with the "A" players in the supplier community (i.e., the most popular suppliers in the eyes of clinicians). It is a contradiction in terms for a group to sign a preferred supplier contract with a supplier that is not preferred by the group's hospital members. The group would be faced with too much supplier conversion effort that is hard and expensive to do, and which a group would rather avoid. Groups that sign with "B" and "C" players typically find that their hospital members do not utilize those contracts.

Overall, groups would prefer to sign contracts of convenience with suppliers that their hospitals want (e.g., dual- and multi-source contracts) whereby the physician and hospital can get the product they want, the group can generate its fee off of the hospital's on-contract purchase, and the group doesn't have to engage in a lot of hard work to get hospitals to comply with a given contract and/or convert to a new product supplier. This is why the bulk of a group's contracts are dual- and multi-source contracts. But if the group gets too many suppliers on contract for the same product, there is much less likelihood that any one supplier will witness an increase in market share, and thus no incentive to give the group a reduced price. This explains why the group must impose some constraints on supplier choice.[45]

For the same reasons, it is in the group's interest to contract for any new innovative technologies that member hospitals and their clinicians want: members get the products at a lower (contracted) cost and the group generates administrative fees. However, if the suppliers with truly innovative technologies/products have no competitors, they do not and will not need to contract with groups.

Groups Are Unlikely to Sign Deals That Do Not Serve Hospitals

Purchasing groups are unlikely to sign deals that do not serve the interests of their members or require hospitals to trade off rebates for higher supply prices. Why is this so?

- Hospital members would not use the group's contracts, and thus the group would lose the contract administration fees
- Members would exit the group and join a rival group
- The group has the incentive to get the best deal it can for its members since it is competing with other groups trying to get the best deal for their members
- Groups can discern prices/deals that are not beneficial for their hospitals and are powerful enough to say "no" to the supplier.

Large Suppliers' Failure to Coerce Hospitals into Accepting Anti-competitive Contracts

There are several instances in prior decades when large suppliers tried to get groups to accept packaged discount contracts and the groups refused to do so and dropped the supplier.

(a) Premier dropped Beckman-Coulter when the supplier tried to package its contracted items with some other items not on contract.[46]
(b) VHA dropped DePuy for the same reason: it refused the supplier's demand to bundle across product segments (both contracted and non-contracted).[47]
(c) Hill-Rom offered a packaged discount contract to American Health-care Systems (AmHS), but AmHS refused due to a prior supplier commitment.
(d) Johnson & Johnson (J&J) offered VHA a portfolio agreement covering not only suture and endo products already on contract, but also other J&J product lines. VHA refused the corporate product portfolio.[48]

Sometimes the hospital members of purchasing groups will complain to the groups about dropping these suppliers, and the group will later re-instate them. For example, prior to the formation of the "new Premier" in 1995 (see

Chapter 4), some hospitals had contracts with Beckman-Coulter, which were then terminated. Premier was pressured into re-instating Beckman-Coulter a few years later by these hospitals.[49]

Hospitals Hold Groups Accountable

As noted above, hospitals have the freedom to decide whether or not to belong to purchasing groups, which purchasing group to belong to, and whether or not to use the group's contracts.[50] There has been only a slight decrease over time in the average number of purchasing group affiliations that a hospital maintains. Hospitals thus prefer to maintain alternatives, and thereby play one group off against another. This forces groups to compete with one another on product prices and product range. This makes it unlikely that purchasing groups can impose contracts containing over-priced and/or under-valued products on their hospital members.[51]

The published membership numbers of the purchasing groups far exceeds the number of hospitals in the U.S. My examination of their actual membership rosters from two national surveys (2004, 2014) revealed that this is due to overlapping memberships. Indeed, the past rosters of some of the largest groups overlapped considerably: e.g., AmeriNet and Novation, MedAssets and Novation, and Premier and Novation. Hospitals often belong to multiple groups (each with a unique set of contracts) in order to have access to a contract (from whichever group) for products their clinicians want. Data from SMG Marketing suggested that hospitals belong to 2+ groups on average; Professor Hovenkamp estimated the average number of memberships was even higher.[52] Multiple group affiliations permit hospitals to "cherry-pick" the contract they want from whatever group has it. Hospitals also use the group contract's price as their ceiling and work to negotiate their own deals off of it.

Investor-owned purchasing groups (e.g., HealthTrust, Broadlane) are members of investor-owned hospital systems (HCA and Tenet, respectively). Unlike the nonprofits, these groups are spending their own money and thus are accountable for the supply budgets of their hospitals (not just a contract portfolio).

Groups Do Not Sanction Hospital Members

The only real downside for a nonprofit hospital that does not comply with its purchasing group's committed contract is that it has to buy products at list price or market access price (the price tier offering the smallest discount). Hospital members that do not comply with group contracts are infrequently sanctioned in any other way. The assertion that groups "threaten" to terminate noncompliant members actually suggests how little power and influence the groups have over their members to get them to do what the group wants. The most notable shareholder termination from Premier for non-compliance was the Methodist system in Houston in 1997. Methodist, however, was running its own purchasing program and reportedly never participated in Premier's program. Thus, there was little lost by this sanction on either side.[53]

In reality, groups do not want to terminate their members. One reason is that groups compete on the basis of membership size. Defections and terminations also reduce the group's aggregate purchasing volume and revenues generated from administrative fees. Another reason is that the group loses money by doing so. A simple illustration shows why. A hospital member of a group that buys $10 Million in supplies through the group's contracts earns the group a contract fee of 2–3% of the purchases (or $200,000–300,000). Assume the hospital is noncompliant on one contract that accounts for $2 Million, and instead buys off contract. The group loses $40,000–60,000 in fees. But if the group kicks out the hospital for being noncompliant on the one contract, the group also loses the (much larger) balance of the fees that the hospital's purchases generated for it. What the group would prefer to do is not terminate the hospital for non-compliance with its contract, but rather develop a different, customized contract for that noncompliant hospital whereby the group can generate its fee.

In some of the court complaints chronicled in Chapter 5, Plaintiffs argued that the defendant manufacturer engaged in anti-competitive behavior by imposing "penalty prices" on hospitals that did not adhere to compliance contracts and bundled contracts. Neither argument is correct. With regard to compliance contracts, the only real downside for a hospital that does not comply with the commitment level it has chosen under a GPO contract is that it potentially may have to buy products at list price, market access price, or negotiate a price of its own. This is not a "penalty" (as alleged in the press) but, rather, a reversion back to the status quo prior to GPO contracting. Moreover, hospitals that elect not to comply often negotiate local independent agreements with the supplier at prices lower than both list price and the GPO-negotiated price. Case evidence indicates that GPOs may actually help their hospitals to negotiate these separate agreements, waive the hospital's responsibility to comply with the group's contract, and ensure that the hospital remains on its current price tier. Hence, there is no penalty and no penalty price.

With regard to bundled contracts, hospitals elect to participate in such agreements when they already purchase a high percentage of the products in the bundle from the manufacturer offering that bundle. Given hospitals' difficulty in getting clinicians from multiple departments and specialties to agree on a given supplier for all of their product needs,[54] hospitals engage in bundled agreements only when they need to convert perhaps one or two product lines to the contracted supplier. All other product purchases in the bundle are unaffected. Hence, any difficulty hospitals experience in achieving compliance with a bundled contract is limited to one or two products, and thus any contract non-compliance potentially leads to reversion back to list price or market access price only for those items. Hospitals retain the price discounts for all other product categories in the bundle for which they already purchase a high percentage of their items.

Some industry analysts suggest that the distribution of hospital compliance with specific GPO contracts roughly resembles a bell-shaped curve.[55] Thus, with regard to prior VHA committed contracts, 20% of hospital members were fully committed, 60% were partially committed, and 20% exhibited no commitment at all. This explains why contract compliance rates of 50–60% in the GPO industry are considered "normal" (in statistical terms) and "good." These figures are congruent with case evidence that hospitals negotiate off-contract buys (e.g., use independent agreements) for roughly 30–50% of their purchases. Overall, purchasing groups (and their member hospitals and IDNs) intermediate anywhere from 45 to 66% of hospital purchases of medical-surgical supplies and equipment.[56] Some small-scale surveys place the figure as high as 72%.[57]

Group Contracts with Suppliers Are Pro-competitive and Welfare-Enhancing

Sole-source contracts, share-based discounts, packaged discount contracts, and share-based packaged discount contracts are commonly used across several industries to achieve lower prices. Packaged discount contracts have also been used by the Department of Defense in dealing with its contractors to achieve cost reductions and supplier performance improvements.[58]

Such contract strategies are not only desired by GPO hospital members but also serve their interests. In healthcare, sole-source contracts (and packaged discount contracts to some degree) evolved as part of the hospital industry's strategy to deal with cost containment pressures and lower prices. Such contracting practices were commonly utilized by groups and could be applied to either a narrow or wide range of products to help hospital buyers achieve lower prices.[59] During the 1980s and 1990s, such contracts were not controversial. In some product categories (laparoscopic/endomechanical), they became the norm by 1994. These contracts were popular among hospitals that asked their groups to develop them. Few hospitals reportedly left Premier because of its compliance requirements.[60] One reason why they were popular is that they were oftentimes designed after assessing what member hospitals were already purchasing or what they needed to have. For example, when applied to hospitals acquired via mergers and acquisitions (M&As), sole-source contracts and contract tiers were tied to the acquired hospitals' usage of the products prior to their acquisition. Because the products were already being used, hospitals could generate additional savings without incurring any costs of supplier or product conversion, or any disruptions to patient care. Thus, rather than being imposed on hospitals, they (already) met hospital needs and demands for certain suppliers. One GAO report found that all seven purchasing groups studied use sole-source contracts; six of the seven used them primarily for commodity products rather than PPIs.[61]

Similarly, hospital executives that testified at the 2003 Senate hearings stated that "hospitals choose to standardize" because multi-source contracts that sacrifice price discounts are wasteful—a view also shared by clinicians, purchasing groups, and suppliers. Standardization also allows hospitals to create uniformities in the process of patient care. Exclusive (e.g., sole-source) and near-exclusive (e.g., dual-source) contracts for medical products generate efficiencies by virtue of having one seller for products (lower transaction costs, scope economies). They also permit hospitals to obtain products at lower prices, focus their contracting activities in areas where their groups had no contracts (roughly 30–35% of their purchases), and to reduce utilization—all of which could reduce hospital costs (and enhance public welfare).

Sole-Source Contracts with Suppliers Have Pro-competitive Effects

Sole-source contracts at the group level and share-based discounts at the hospital level are not anti-competitive in nature or design. In fact, they can have several pro-competitive effects:

1. *Intense Competition for GPO Contracts.* With the emergence of sole- and dual-source contracts, suppliers were required to vigorously compete for these contracts, as opposed to the past when they exclusively competed for the individual hospital or clinician's product choice. This introduced a new, second stage of the competition: compete for the contract, and then compete for the individual hospital's business. This intensified the competition among suppliers.

   Suppliers feared that the loss of contracts would lead not only to a loss of market share (which would be expensive to regain), but also a loss of image (failure to successfully contract with a large group). The fear and uncertainty over losing contracts created greater competition among suppliers; each group contract became another individual competition that the supplier tried to win. Groups reportedly boasted when they were successful in obtaining such contracts.

   Suppliers reportedly reacted to the initial wave of sole-source contracts sought by Columbia/HCA with prices and contract terms that predecessor investor-owned groups had not seen.[62] Premier, which formed shortly after and in competitive response to Columbia/HCA, likewise pursued sole-source contracts and reportedly set off another wave of fierce price competition among suppliers and a new tier of pricing.[63] Other investor-owned and nonprofit groups did not want to be at a competitive disadvantage, followed the lead of Columbia/HCA and Premier, and embarked on sole-source contracts to achieve comparable pricing.

   Given the number of hospital sales that are potentially at stake, suppliers compete vigorously to obtain these contracts. Suppliers that are unable to obtain the GPO contract will often try to undercut the discounted GPO contract price even further in order to gain a share of the hospital's business. Such competition leads to lower pricing. Such competition resembles the competition among pharmaceutical manufacturers to obtain contracts with pharmacy benefit managers (PBMs, covered in Section III).

2. *Competition to Retain GPO Contracts.* Suppliers report that the potential loss of contracts (whether sole-source or dual-source) has fostered much competition with their rivals. Suppliers that were selected for sole-source contracts had to work hard to keep them sole-source by means of good prices and clinical advantages. Without these contract and product features, they were forced by GPOs into (at least) dual-source (or multi-source) contracts. Thus, even in the presence of a sole-source contract, suppliers still had to compete on price. Conversely, suppliers without

a sole-source contract competed on price to try to get on the contract and make it at least a dual-source contract. Suppliers with a dual-source contract report their concern that the group might make the contract sole-source and go with its rival. This threat is especially pronounced when the rival has contracted with another GPO on a sole-source basis.

3. *Competitors' Incentives to Improve.* Sole- and dual-source GPO contracts can motivate those suppliers that do not win them to undertake several competitive strategies. First, they can find ways to improve their product, reduce their costs, and sell their products elsewhere. Second, they can offer the same or a lower price than that offered by the contract winners. This competition at the price level can take place at the hospitals that have the group contract, as well as at other hospitals in other groups. This strategy is often pursued and financed by using the contract fees that would have been paid to the group (had the contract been won) to subsidize the sale of products to the group's hospital members at the contracted price. An equally efficient supplier that does not win a sole-source contract can thus capture market share by agreeing to sell at the same (or lower) price than the price offered under the contract. In this manner, sole-source contracts can initiate price wars among suppliers at multiple purchasing groups.[64] Even in the presence of sole-source contracts, incumbent suppliers and their sales representatives continually have to defend their market share against rivals coming into the hospital on a weekly basis. Incumbent suppliers could lose business when a rival comes in with a lower price (even without a contract) and/or a product that the clinician wants.

4. *Periodic Renegotiation.* The intense competition fostered by the competitive bidding process is further enhanced by the fact that group contracts come up for periodic renegotiation. During each period of renegotiation, competing groups have the opportunity to (and do) attempt to win over hospitals' business by offering terms and pricing that are more favorable.

5. *Competition Following Hospital M&As, IDNs, and GPOs.* GPO sole- and dual-source contracts also can augment competition among suppliers by providing opportunities for suppliers to compete for large blocks of new business following the merger and acquisition (M&A) of IDNs and GPOs and the rationalization of their contracts. The formation of Columbia/HCA in the early 1990s spawned huge competition among suppliers seeking to be the ones to secure contracts with this new, large investor-owned hospital system. Similarly, the merger of several regional GPOs to form Premier in 1995 led to 20–30% lower prices than those obtained by the regional GPOs.[65]

6. *Reduced Transaction Costs.* Such contracts also reduce transaction costs for both parties by aggregating greater volume in fewer contracts. The presence of national contracts means that suppliers do not have to negotiate individual local terms and prices with each hospital. This frees up time for sales representatives (reps) to focus on the provision of other value-adding services to hospitals. The presence of a GPO contract, however, does not reduce the need for sales reps to sell the supplier's products; suppliers typically do not cease their sales effort inside hospitals once a contract is signed. Salesforce economies lead to lower costs and, thus, the supplier's ability to lower prices.

7. *Production Economies for Suppliers.* In testimony before the Senate in 2003, one supplier executive stated that the group contracts enabled his firm to reduce its costs by reducing the number of employees needed for bidding and sales, as well as improve the efficiency and efficacy of its marketing, sales, and service functions. When accompanied by hospital compliance, such contracts also lower the supplier's selling costs and increase supplier efficiency. Such contracts yield economies of production and research and development (R&D) for suppliers by ensuring some measure of future demand, which allows them to forecast future sales and schedule production, lower their inventory costs, as well as produce larger volumes at lower costs.

8. *Economies of Consumption for Hospitals.* Sole- and dual-source GPO contracts can yield economies of consumption on the buyer side in terms of increased asset utilization (fewer inventory items and dollars, faster inventory turns, fewer space requirements—particularly in the high-cost operating room), reduced operating expenses (reduced inventory obsolescence, reduced order processing, improved logistics, improved storeroom and loading dock productivity, fewer line items managed, lower cost of handling), and improved system quality (improved invoice accuracy and product availability, improved fill rates, easier in-service training). They thus improve operating efficiency and augment revenues by reducing turnaround time in the operating room.

9. *Improved Hospital Care.* Sole- and dual-source contracts can also serve to improve the quality of hospital care by improving item inspection and handling, managing and selecting a product from a smaller number of stock keeping units (SKUs), improved accuracy and quality of documentation, increased consistency and safety in product use, and lower cost of education and training regarding the product.

They can also standardize supplies across hospital units and across hospitals within an IDN, which increases staff familiarity and improves consistency of care as nursing staff float across units and hospitals. All of these help to lower the costs of errors. Such contracts can also yield network effects for hospital buyers by virtue of standardized education and maintenance activities, increased staff familiarity with one supplier's product, potential learning curve advantages, and possible positive impacts on care quality.

10. *GPO Competition*. Sole-source contracting and standardization programs constitute a vehicle for purchasing groups and their hospitals to compete with one another, as well as deal with managed care pressures to contain costs. Even in the earlier days of group purchasing, groups were commonly compared and ranked in terms of their contract compliance.[66] Historically, groups have had difficulty achieving or maintaining compliance rates in excess of 80%.[67] This leaves a minimum of 20% and a ceiling as high as 40–50% of a group's purchases that can be competed for by other groups. Sole-source contracts are not exclusive deals given the headroom allowed above the compliance levels and the low compliance levels achieved in many groups. Rather, these contracts are incentive arrangements that encourage hospitals to buy more products through the group.[68]

Packaged Discount Contracts with Suppliers Have Pro-competitive Effects

One GAO report (see Chapter 5) found that all seven purchasing groups studied utilized packaged discounts (otherwise known as bundled contracts). According to academic evidence, over eighty percent (80%) of U.S. hospitals report that their national GPO offers single-supplier multi-product contracts in which hospitals sometimes participate.[69] Packaged discount contracts can also have several pro-competitive effects:

1. *Expand Supply Items Under Contract*. Groups pursued an early version of packaged discount contracts in the 1980s called "corporate partner" agreements. Such agreements served to get more of a supplier's product under contract. Prior to the portfolios, hospitals often purchased products without a contract, at much higher prices, and variable prices across a system.

2. *Improved Pricing*. Packaged discount contracts had two beneficial outcomes. First, the contract reduced the price of a given product; second, the existence of a contract reduced the variability in prices paid by hospitals within the same system for that product.[70] Accordingly,

hospitals often pressured their suppliers to bundle their products and pressured their GPOs to develop these portfolios.[71] Other groups that pursued bundling (e.g., Columbia/HCA) and requested product portfolios from suppliers did so because they reportedly obtained better pricing from two or more product lines.

3. *Improve Hospital Efficiency.* Hospital supply chain managers report such portfolios bring their hospitals the best pricing, financial incentives and returns from their cooperatives, and additional savings through standardization. Product portfolios can offer scope economies by virtue of the fact that they derive from the same catalogue, are detailed by the same sales representatives, are used by the same surgeons, are used in the same procedures, are delivered by the same distributor, and have the same purchase order.

4. *Persuade Suppliers to Offer Discounts When They Didn't Want To.* In general, groups requested packaged discount contracts in order to force suppliers to discount products that they previously did not (and did not want to) discount. Often, the firms that did not discount their products were those with dominant positions in their product markets who faced no competitive threats. Hospitals saved money if they bought a specified range of products in the package. The savings could be large since the portfolio contracts were signed with a small number of large diversified suppliers that supplied the majority of the hospital's medical-surgical supplies.

5. *Render Supplier Product Portfolios More Comparable and Substitutable.* Sometimes the portfolio strategy is driven by a desire to commingle the more preferred product #1 of supplier A (where it has a leading or dominant position) with the less preferred product #2 of supplier A (where it doesn't have a dominant position). The goal is to find another supplier that has complementary products: less preferred product #1 of supplier B with the more preferred product #2 of supplier B. By virtue of commingling the two types of products, groups can make the respective portfolios of products #1 and #2 offered by suppliers A and B more substitutable and closer competitors—in effect, canceling out the advantages of each supplier in its dominant product market. The result is more intense price competition and the ability to get each supplier to discount its dominant product.

6. *Promote Supplier Competition.* In the mid-1990s, Hill-Rom offered to Premier a packaged discount contract for standard beds (where it was dominant) and therapy/specialty beds (where it was less dominant). While there was no other supplier that made beds in both markets,

Premier executives tellingly sought to get Stryker (a leading supplier of standard beds) to joint-venture with Kinetic Concepts (KCI, a leading supplier of therapeutic beds) to develop a rival packaged discount contract. KCI itself signed a long term, product portfolio agreement with American HealthCare Systems.[72]

Product portfolios thus became a source of competition among suppliers as well as groups. Bard reportedly sought to build a portfolio across its product divisions to "meet the bundling challenge" of Kendall. Following the rise of American Hospital Supply (AHS) and the development of Baxter's program with HCA (see Chapter 4), J&J aggressively followed with its Hospital Systems Group, and Abbott and 3M developed their "Corporate Alliance" to mimic the broad product lines of Baxter and J&J. Similarly, Bard tried to develop a corporate alliance with Guidant/Cook and erect a virtual portfolio to compete with Medtronic and Boston Scientific. In many instances, suppliers competed with one another to offer supply chain and distribution improvements to their hospital customers.[73]

7. *Risk-Sharing and Global Pricing.* Product portfolio agreements between groups and suppliers developed during the 1990s at the same time as capitated, risk-sharing arrangements developed between hospitals and payers. Both were viewed as illustrations of global package pricing that stimulated lower pricing for services. Product portfolios also developed as suppliers consolidated and diversified to fill gaps in their product lines and offer more of a one-stop-shopping service to hospitals that sought to economize on their transactions costs with suppliers. Bundled purchases allow suppliers to increase product volume, lower their manufacturing costs, and pass along the savings to hospitals via lower prices.

8. *Platform for Supplier-Provider Partnerships.* Product portfolios served as a platform that allowed suppliers and hospitals to explore various strategic partnerships that could add value. Hospitals hoped that these partnerships would include the transfer of knowledge from suppliers on more efficient supply chain management, productivity management, and product utilization.

9. *Motivate Supplier Reorganization.* Product portfolios required radical changes in the suppliers' sales and marketing organizations. To service a large hospital system or IDN or purchasing group with a diverse array of products, diversified suppliers had to develop national accounts teams or dedicated personnel to cover these customers, as well as to coordinate price and product offerings across product divisions.[74] This had

the potential to reduce duplicative activities across product divisions and provide one face to the customer.

10. *Packaged Discounts Foster Pro-competitive Pressures in Hospitals.* Bundling strategies pursued by suppliers foster pressures and counter-pressures among hospitals that promote competition. Hospital buyers of bundled products want the "best of breed" across product categories. No clinician wants to use inferior products, thus forcing hospitals and GPOs to contract for products that are superior or equivalent across product categories. Thus, hospitals pressure the suppliers and GPOs to include the best, premium-priced products within the bundles at discounted prices.

Purchasing Groups and Supplier Competition Are Compatible

Groups Want Competitive Supplier Markets

Purchasing groups do not desire monopolistic supplier markets. As noted earlier, suppliers in such markets have no incentive to contract with groups and discount their products. Instead, monopolist suppliers enjoy high pricing and pricing freedom. Groups and their hospital members may like that supplier's products but not its pricing.

When confronted with such markets, or markets with one dominant supplier, groups oftentimes seek to award contracts to a second supplier (in addition to the market leader) in order to promote competition and level the playing field. Groups will look to contract with suppliers with opportunities for market growth—i.e., those suppliers that might broadly appeal to their hospital members—and try to give them some market share. In this manner, the group tries to (1) identify the best possible countervailing force to a dominant supplier and develop them into a legitimate rival, and (2) prepare the next round of future contracts when, by virtue of having given a rival supplier some business, the group can use the rival's rising market share as bargaining leverage over the market leader.

One way in which groups try to foster this exercise in leveling the playing field is through competitive bidding. Bidding helps to lower the prices of suppliers by creating uncertainty about what is a winning bid. Moreover, the supplier is typically not informed why it lost a contract, which heightens the uncertainty over the process.

Industry analysts add that "large groups have always insisted on the viability of small manufacturers as potential supply partners"—whether to contract with them, to keep incumbents honest, or to avoid the appearance of excluding small firms from the bidding process.[75] One GAO report found that nearly one-third of the suppliers involved in new contracts negotiated by purchasing groups in 2002 had not previously been under contract. Across all seven groups studied by the GAO, the percentage of new suppliers contracted ranged from 16–55%.[76]

Groups are aware that driving out competitors in the supplier market can undermine their own efforts to exploit competition among suppliers and thereby secure price discounts. The existence of competitors is what motivated suppliers to contract with groups in the first place. Thus, it is contrary to the groups' self-interest to have few suppliers or to create anti-competitive conditions in supplier markets. According to the executives of hospital systems, groups have a responsibility to keep more suppliers than just the market leaders in business.[77] Group and hospital welfare are maximized when supplier markets are as competitive as possible.[78]

Loss of Group Contracts Can Spur Supplier Competition

Suppliers that did not secure contracts with one group on a given round of contracting often target rival groups for the same kinds of contracts during the same round, thereby intensifying competition for those other group accounts. Alternatively, suppliers that did not secure contracts with one group on a given round might compete more vigorously on the next round of contracting with that group. Finally, suppliers that did not secure these group contracts might also target large IDNs willing to develop independent agreements.[79] Such IDNs have more contracting resources than smaller hospitals and are less compliant with group contracts. Contracts based on independent agreements may not require the payment of administration fees; this allows the supplier to lower their price, which can spur more competition and the loss of market share for the supplier with the contract.

Frequently, suppliers that succumb to one group's pressure to discount prices do not wish to extend that same level of low pricing to other groups. The latter groups may then switch the suppliers on their national accounts and move market share. For example, after the new Premier contracted with Mallinckrodt for contrast media, AmeriNet asked the supplier for the same contract terms. When it was refused, AmeriNet switched to Bracco.[80]

Low Levels of Compliance Allow Supplier Competition for Market Share

Low Compliance

In court cases, plaintiff's experts argued that a supplier's use of sole-source and dual-source contracts constituted anticompetitive behavior by virtue of committing GPO hospital members to buy from contracted suppliers to the exclusion of rivals. The claim lacks face validity, given the low contract compliance rates achieved historically by GPOs. Since the 1980s, groups have had difficulty achieving contract compliance.[81] Awards of dual- and triple-source contracts were signs of compliance difficulties, as was the presence of multiple price tiers in a given contract. Investor-owned groups had a reputation for higher compliance, which was reflected by the small number of tiers; conversely, nonprofit groups had a reputation for lower levels of compliance, reflected in a larger number of price tiers.

Case evidence indicates that contract compliance at Novation, one of the two largest GPOs, was only 50–60%. In 2002, the CEO of Novation testified before the Senate that for 75% of the hospital items that are under group contracts, member hospitals utilized the contracts for only 55% of their purchases. Overall, hospitals thus utilized the nonprofit group for only 40% of its purchases. According to recent academic evidence, many hospitals do much of their purchasing outside of national GPO contracts. Hospitals route 70% of supply spending through their GPOs. For commodity medical-surgical items, 48% of hospitals route less than three-quarters of purchases through GPOs; for PPIs, 70% of hospitals route less than half of their purchases through GPOs.[82] This suggests that rival manufacturers compete for sizeable hospital spending outside of GPO contracts and, thus, are not foreclosed.

Surveys of suppliers show similar results. The level of hospital purchasing through group contracts varies widely across the major groups. On average, only 18.5% of suppliers report they realized 50% or more of the sales volume promised by groups. Across the seven largest groups, the percentage ranged from a low of 2.1% (AmeriNet) to a high of 28.3% (HealthTrust). Consonant with the pattern noted above, the investor-owned groups were accorded higher scores than most of the nonprofits.[83] Supplier sales figures show that compliance levels among the nonprofit groups in the late 1990s ranged from 30–70%, with very little upward trend in the decade.

Compliance Problems

One source of difficulty in achieving compliance in large purchasing groups is the group's composition. Due to their formation through M&As, some large groups were philosophically, organizationally, and geographically diverse assemblies of subgroups (e.g., AmeriNet, Novation).[84] Such a structure sometimes forced these groups to separate contract negotiation at the national level from contract implementation and marketing at the regional and local level. These groups focused their standardization efforts at the level of hospital clusters or regions, thus fostering variability in compliance across the entire group.

Another source of difficulty is the composition of physicians at the level of the individual hospital member. The hospital's medical staff is composed of lots of physicians; some are independent solo practitioners, some are members of group practices, and others yet may be employed by the institution. This diversity poses two problems for standardization. First, through historical forces, training differences, and possible economic relationships with suppliers, these physicians will likely have developed preferences for different suppliers' products. Second, due to their different working arrangements, the hospital lacks uniform control over their behavior. Third, since the hospital relies on its physicians for admissions and referrals, it often adopts the attitude of trying to make them all happy. For all of these reasons, a sole-source contract can be nonsensical. What happens instead is that hospitals sign "primary source" contracts with one or a limited number of suppliers, which the physicians may or may not uniformly use. Seen through this lens, compliance or standardization with any contract is more a function and job of the supplier in trying to persuade physicians to shift from another supplier to use its products.

According to McKinsey, groups had little impact on supplier rationalization and product standardization in the 1990s.[85] Of course, groups did not necessarily have strong incentives to enforce compliance. Enforcing compliance and promoting conversion to new suppliers under contract entailed a lot of hard work for groups, with much of the rewards accruing to the hospitals. Groups preferred to have multi-source contracts that their members preferred, that did not require lots of enforcement, and that freed up the group's time to pursue other contracting opportunities. Such contracts (1) offered hospital members easier access to desired suppliers and products and (2) offered groups the convenience of easy contract administration and guaranteed contract administration fees. Indeed, groups earned higher fees and hospital members generated greater savings when they contracted with preferred suppliers at slightly discounted prices than with non-preferred suppliers at sharply discounted prices. This is because the former contracts would be utilized while the latter contracts would not.[86]

Finally, compliance may be less a function of the ownership of the group, the type of enforcement mechanism, or the quality of the data, and more a function of the contract execution. That is, compliance is more a function of supplier and group process than of group structure. Case studies in the trade literature illustrate how processes of participation, deliberation, motivation, and accountability promote compliance within a group.[87] Other analyses point to the important role of manufacturer follow-up on contract implementation, and the degree of coordination between the manufacturer's national accounts office and sales representatives.[88]

IDN Exceptionalism

IDNs that are faced with contracts (including packaged discount contracts) that they do not wish to use are not forced to do so. Indeed, suppliers can be forced into independent contracts with IDNs that do not want the portfolio, and thus have to offer choice to the customer. Groups are more concerned that IDNs buy off of some negotiated contract than they are with forcing IDNs to buy off a particular contract. Thus, groups are not that interested in enforcing compliance with any contract. This attitude is likely reinforced by the historically moderate levels of compliance that the groups (mostly nonprofit) have achieved with their hospital members (ranging from the high teens to the low fifties).

In nonprofit groups, IDNs commonly negotiate independent agreements with suppliers, using the group's contract price as a ceiling, to develop better pricing. Some observers claim this practice "happens every day," has always been the case, and is never really a struggle.[89] Group contracts for PPIs are particularly ineffective, since physicians utilize the products they want to use regardless of a contract. Thus, many of these purchases are locally driven and based on direct marketing to physicians.

Particularly in those cases where they are prominent players in local healthcare markets, IDNs can force suppliers to un-bundle contracts negotiated by their group and obtain pricing similar to the packaged discount price. IDNs can also utilize rival groups and their contracts. In both the nonprofit and the investor-owned groups, hospitals can exit the group contracts and buy direct from the supplier without a contract or utilize regional group contracts. Indeed, clinician trade publications have published articles encouraging their readers to do so.[90] Finally, group contracts may include clauses that allow

(a) the IDN to access a carve-out supplier without impacting its compliance levels, and (b) the group to abrogate the contract if significant technological advances render covered products obsolete. As IDNs become larger in size and more prevalent in the market, groups are forced to solicit their input on contracting and reflect IDN preferences in supplier selection decisions.

License to Sell

It is commonly noted in the industry that the presence of a purchasing contract does not guarantee any purchases, just as the lack of a contract does not prevent hospitals from making purchases. Indeed, it is commonly recognized that a contract is merely a "license to sell."[91] Even in the presence of a contract, hospitals and their clinicians still have to elect to use it and find value in it. This may be a function of the supplier's ability to market and service the product inside the institution. Hospitals report they do not push their physicians to use products just because they are under contract. Similarly, suppliers do not demand or threaten hospitals to comply with contracts, or raise prices on noncompliant hospitals, since they risk alienating their clinical customers and losing their current business. Instead, they see contract use and compliance as a sales process (which is their job). They state that clinicians are always looking for the product that will give them the best outcome and good patient care—aspects of product quality and service that are not trumped by the existence of any contract. That is why, despite having a contract, a supplier's sales reps are continually inside their hospital accounts trying to detail their products, and having to compete daily with reps from other suppliers with and without a contract.

Even when enforced, contract compliance still leaves hospitals a lot of room to maneuver. In many groups, the contracts are signed by systems/IDNs and entail compliance measured at the system/IDN level (i.e., across several hospitals). This leaves room for individual hospitals within the system/IDN to purchase products from the contracted supplier at low compliance rates and acquire products from rival suppliers without losing the price discount. Moreover, groups can allow hospital members to negotiate whatever deal they want, as long as the products are on contract and the group can still earn administrative fees.

Measurement Issues

This, of course, begs the question of whether compliance can be reliably measured at all, let alone enforced. Some group executives claim that their data on what hospital members buy are not very thorough or accurate. Typically, such data come from the supplier and not the GPO. GPOs reportedly have no one monitoring contract compliance at member hospitals. To the extent they do monitor hospitals' off-contract buying, it is to inform the hospitals of savings opportunities. If the group's data come from contracted suppliers, then the group only knows what the hospitals were buying on contract (not off contract) from that supplier. Group executives report that there are "significant data issues" with 70–75% of its suppliers, sometimes due to suppliers using an unrecognized hospital identifier. This can lead them to credit the hospital system rather than the hospital. In the presence of multiple group memberships, it is not surprising that suppliers also have difficulty in assigning the sales to the particular group that a hospital belongs to. If the group's data come from self-reports from its hospitals, then the data may be subject to favorable response bias. Moreover, the group can be at the mercy of its hospitals' materials management information systems, which historically have been underdeveloped. Indeed, some supply chain management consultants argue that, with so many contracts and purchases, hospitals may not even know if they are compliant with their group's contracts. It is this lack of clean and accurate data that prompted many of the groups to develop business-to-business (B2B) technology solutions in the late 1990s and early 2000s.

In a similar vein, suppliers report that measuring compliance is an art rather than a science. Suppliers may try to estimate compliance in terms of how much hospitals should be spending based on their bed size or on observed deviations in sales numbers. A compliance level of 90%, for example, is a "moving number" that can fluctuate with the hospital's patient census or the process of product conversion. It is also unclear what are the potential sales for a hospital account against which to measure actual purchases. The suppliers themselves are at the mercy of the data supplied to them by their sales reps, which can be based on a series of subjective judgments such as: (a) checking store rooms for inventory, (b) walking hospital floors, and (c) prodding purchasing managers regarding what products are being used. The sales rep also may have a bias in reporting favorable compliance rates. The numbers they report to the supplier may include any number of exceptions and exclusions (e.g., the purchase of specific products carved out of the data because the supplier does not make them). Not surprisingly, these data often do not match benchmark data obtained from vendors (e.g., IMS); indeed, suppliers are not even sure these data are accurate. As a result, suppliers commonly note that it is difficult for them to determine the difference between compliance levels of 80, 85, and 90%.

Off-Contract Buying

IDNs that are faced with group contracts that they do not prefer have options to "exit" those contracts. That is, group members have the freedom to buy products "off contract" without any repercussions and face no mandatory requirement to buy products using their group's contracts. Off-contract buying occurs so frequently because hospitals can and do negotiate prices lower than the GPO contract price. Case evidence suggests that hospitals can obtain "enhanced pricing" on up to 50% of their GPO agreements. This is because the GPO price represents a ceiling ("the minimum a supplier can do for the hospital") that the supplier may lower for hospitals that choose to negotiate.

Why does off-contract buying occur and occur so frequently? One major reason is that hospitals do not contract for every item or product category they utilize. A large hospital system, for example, reportedly uses 5,200 suppliers but has contracts with only 28% of them. It is impractical to devote resources to contracting with lots of suppliers for small amounts of items. In many cases, these small amounts of items will be purchased from small suppliers. In addition, there is considerable turnover in the suppliers used ("products come and go all the time from many manufacturers"), such that it may not be economical to develop contracts with them until the supplier's sales reach a certain minimum threshold (e.g., several hundred thousands of dollars). Alternatively, it may be the technology is too new to be under contract.

Clinical demand also drives off-contract purchasing. Oftentimes off-contract buying happens because physicians want a product and demand that it be trialed or purchased. That is, physicians "pull" the product into the hospital. Physicians will do this when they perceive the product solves some problem, meets some clinical need, performs better than the product currently under contract, or works better ergonomically to suit their taste. Physicians appear to have a great deal of discretion and exercise some degree of subjectivity in deciding which supplier's product to utilize. Finally, it is likely the case that contracts and compliance are issues that are invisible and relatively unimportant to clinicians, who don't see them as part of their responsibility.

Moreover, GPO contracts often contain terms allowing GPOs to add a supplier's products that qualify as new technology under contract, even when the GPO has a sole-source contract with a different supplier. For example, one supplier's sole-source contract with a large GPO allows that GPO to unilaterally add a new supplier to its contract if it determines that the new supplier's product provides incremental patient care benefits and/or incremental safety benefits over the technology currently sold under the supplier's sole-source contract. Thus, sole-source contracts are never truly guaranteed to be sole-source, as a GPO may add a new supplier at any time if the supplier comes forward with a product that incrementally benefits patients.

Absence of Coercion and Control

Perhaps the biggest misconception about purchasing groups is that they can coerce their member hospitals and physicians to use products from contracted suppliers that they do not want. For commodity items where there is (by definition) no physician preference, the issue is moot. There is no coercion because hospitals and physicians are typically indifferent between suppliers' products, and one product can be easily substituted for another. For PPIs, the group's contracting office located far away in another state or region of the country cannot hold sway over the local hospital and clinical decision-making. This results in a logical as well as geographical disconnect between local physician behavior and national contracting for PPIs.[92] The farther away a party is from the point of care, the less influence that party has on what product gets utilized. Following the ancient Chinese proverb, "The mountains are high, and the Emporer is far away." This goes for both groups and suppliers. In the end, the clinicians in the hospital setting exert great sway over the products and suppliers selected, and are basically unchallenged by groups. The adage "all healthcare is local" thus holds for the purchase of PPIs.[93]

Supplier market surveys of decision-making for PPIs repeatedly demonstrate that physicians exert the primary influence. Nurses and materials managers run a distant second or third in influence. The physicians' influence is historically rooted in the hospital's dependence on their admission of paying patients and referrals to hospital-based specialists, their ability (and sometimes threat) to take their business to a competitor hospital, their relatively higher level of training, their greater knowledge of the products and technologies involved, and their contractor status (i.e., non-employees) in the hospital. Hence, no lay party or group can legislate the use of products in a clinically-driven environment.

Larger hospitals tend to have lots of clinicians doing lots of procedures and ordering lots of supplies. In such settings, there is little likelihood that (1) all of these clinicians would agree on one supplier, and (2) anyone could force them to accept one supplier. Clinicians are both adept and accustomed to ordering the products they want for their patients from whichever supplier they select. Groups exert little control over them. Moreover, the suppliers of PPI items reportedly do not want exclusive contracts, recognizing the clear need for physicians to have a choice. They are thus comfortable with non-exclusive agreements. All they want is to limit the number of suppliers they have to compete with.[94]

There is a host of evidence showing that PPIs are not highly subject to group contracting or contract compliance. During the 2002 Senate hearings, the CEO of Premier testified that of the 377 contracts his group had negotiated for clinical use products and PPIs, only 20 (5%) were sole-source contracts. His counterpart at Novation stated that while his group developed contracts for 75% of the items his hospitals purchase, the 25% that are not on contract are partly comprised of new technology products like PPIs. Consonant with their remarks, The Lewin Group found that PPIs and devices have compliance levels of only 32.4%.[95]

GPOS Are Not Inimical to New Technology or Small Suppliers

Purchasing Groups Have Not Blocked Hospital Access to New Technology

Industry analysts argue that purchasing groups are irrelevant for the majority of device firms that have developed innovative technology. Such firms do not need purchasing groups to sell their products to clinicians; the products' technology does this job. They also do not want to contract with groups and discount their innovative products if they do not have to. Suppliers themselves admit this is why some of their product divisions elect not to go through purchasing groups.

In commodity markets, the suppliers of new products are frequently too small to reach the size threshold for group contracting, to supply all of the product needs of a large group, to devote the resources needed for contract implementation, to educate clinicians about the technology and its proper use, and to provide service and support. For PPIs, by contrast, many of these obstacles diminish. This is because the suppliers of PPIs (a) target niche markets where manufacturing capacity is not an issue, and (b) are known for their innovative capability. Thus, while market share in commodity markets may be influenced by the presence of a group contract, for PPIs market share is an indicator of who has the leading-edge technology and who has a pipeline of such technology.

PPI manufacturers recognize that clinicians will require their hospitals to buy any such items that they feel are necessary for quality care. This is one major explanation for why purchasing groups have not been able to achieve high levels of compliance on PPIs: they are the products and technologies that physicians prefer. This also explains why groups have had to resort to dual-source and multi-source contracts for PPIs, and why hospitals have lots of off-contract buying. Compliance is not a controversial issue when purchasing groups lack control over what physicians and their hospitals want to buy.

Groups Historically Allied with Small Suppliers to Serve Hospital Members

Starting in the 1980s, purchasing groups developed a variety of strategic alliances with suppliers to monitor the pipeline and ensure the flow of new technology desired by hospital members and their physicians. Early access to leading-edge technology could help increase the quality of hospital care and augment the competitive advantage of the group's hospital members in local markets. Such alliances could take the form of venture capital funds, cash investments, or equity stakes in suppliers with new technology, product exclusivity agreements, or licensing fees exchanged for helping new firms market their products to clinicians. These alliances were typically struck with small, unknown suppliers making PPIs or with small firms seeking to compete in a crowded market with large incumbents. Illustrations of the latter include AmHS's investments in (1) Kinetic Concepts International (and its refurbished beds) to compete with Hill-Rom, (2) Immunex (and its colony-stimulating factor product) to compete with Sandoz/Schering, and (3) Criticare Systems (and its pulse oximeters) to compete with Nellcor.

These programs did not suffer from conflicts of interest since the technology programs were kept separate from group purchasing programs. Moreover, it seemed unlikely that member hospitals would purchase any technology involved in an alliance if the supplier did not first satisfy the cost, quality, and service needs of the hospital.

Some groups like VHA developed private label programs in 1986 using smaller suppliers as well as some large suppliers (e.g., Baxter). As with the business development programs above, private label programs represented a strategy of diversification by the purchasing groups into the manufacturing side of the industry. They also constituted an attempt to maintain competition among suppliers of the products supplied under private label agreements. In such cases, the brand became the purchasing group's label; the specific supplier of the product could be interchangeable.

Private label programs brought lower prices and increased savings to group members, increased the group's control over product availability and increased the group's administrative fees and operating revenues. In return, the programs guaranteed specified purchasing levels to new or smaller firms and enabled them to lower their prices to group members without having to lower them to hospitals in other groups.[96] Thus, the private label programs required small firms to yield up control over their brand in exchange for enhanced market access and guaranteed sales.

Purchasing groups thus afforded small suppliers with several forms of access to their members via these alliance programs. Alternatively, small suppliers could and did join strategic alliances of suppliers that collectively could pool their products and offer a portfolio to purchasing groups that resembled that of larger, diversified suppliers.

Groups Do Not See Themselves as the Protector of Small Suppliers

Although groups desire to have competition among suppliers, they do not see themselves as the saviors of small suppliers. As noted above, the groups' major common interest is developing contracts with suppliers that bring its members lower prices and higher savings. These contracts are likely to be struck with market leaders and preferred suppliers. In such cases, the contracts serve to lower the prices of products that carry more premium prices and that are already purchased by member hospitals in large quantities. Here the savings to the hospitals can be sizeable, along with the administrative fees generated for the group that can support its contracting and other activities.

Conversely, if a contract is struck with a firm that few hospital members use, even if the price is the lowest in the market, the product will not be purchased in any quantity by the hospitals and their clinicians. Consequently, the hospitals will not see any price savings (since the preferred products are not on contract), the group will not receive any administrative fees that can support its contracting and other activities, and the group will not have served its members. To correct this, the group would have to spend a lot of resources on "conversion"—i.e., convincing hospitals and their physicians to buy the small supplier's product. But groups are not that successful in building market positions for suppliers. Nor do groups view this as their role. According to one group executive, "I'm puzzled why companies think we can do something they've been unable to do."[97]

Some Necessary Background: Competitive Strategy and Market Entry

Michael Porter, a leading authority on corporate strategy, identified two primary strategies for firms to pursue: focusing on the unique value and asking a higher price (differentiation) or focusing on low cost (cost leadership).[98] Product differentiation in this marketplace would be based on establishing a strong base of scientific evidence as well as attracting testimonials from leading physicians. Cost leadership would be based on setting up efficient factories and quickly growing a base of business through competitive pricing and aggressive distribution and sourcing arrangements. Startups typically lack the capital to do either and, thus, appear to be strategically "stuck in the middle."

Adopting a differentiation strategy would be visible in a company's R&D spending, sales spending, and willingness to fund clinical trials to prove the value of its intellectual property. Yet, all too often, as documented in Chapter 5, the startup's product was neither the first to market nor backed by clear, peer-reviewed clinical data. As a result, startups try to achieve high growth through the sale of a product that lacks differentiation. The problem is often compounded by reliance on private label manufacturing, sales, and distribution—all of which dilutes brand image and foregoes the opportunity to develop close ties with clinicians in acute care hospitals where startups historically lack recognition and presence.

Similarly, a "cost leadership" is difficult to sustain due to low sales volumes and the resultant inability to gain scale economies in production. These problems hamper any effort to compete on price or reliability. New startups often lack the financial capital to undertake a significant price war to grab market share and instead fall back and rely on market prices.

New startups also have limited manufacturing capacity relative to their main competitor(s) in the product market. The geographic concentration of their manufacturing in one plant site raises customer concerns about their ability to meet production obligations as sales volumes increase. Geographic concentration of plant and limited redundancy in their own supply chains (e.g., few or one supplier) exposes it to increased risks which could temporarily or expensively interrupt supply. These risks include natural disasters and more minor issues such as unanticipated employee absenteeism, mechanical issues, loss of electricity, severe weather, and access to the facility, which large incumbent manufacturers mitigate by load-balancing between redundant facilities.

Finally, while startups typically raise funds early on to start operations, they often suffer from several problems in the acquisition and deployment of capital down the road. As they mature and expand operations, they can incur significant operating expenses and negative cash flow. This leads, in turn, to failure to invest heavily in functions that allow it to grow and generate greater cash flows from operations. Instead, management often resorts to significant cuts to selling, general, and administrative expenses (SG&A), with the majority of the pain felt by the sales and marketing function. Decreases in sales and marketing expenses do not usually lead to significant increases in revenues in subsequent years, and cash flows from operations again are not significant to make meaningful investments in R&D or the sales organization.

A common scenario is an oligopolistic marketplace where there are a handful of large suppliers that hospitals commonly use and a number of small suppliers with low market shares. These oligopolies have developed in many product segments as a result of M&A trends. Purchasing groups are faced with the issue here of which and how many suppliers to contract with. If the group contracts with too few suppliers, it risks alienating important hospital members who have traditionally purchased from an excluded supplier; if the group cannot convert these members to the contracted supplier, the members pay higher (i.e., non-contract list) prices for the products and the group earns no fees. If the group contracts with too many suppliers, hospital members enjoy a full choice of products but at higher prices, since suppliers will not discount their prices without some promise of exclusivity. In such instances, while the suppliers could conceivably earn higher administrative fees because all products purchased by their members are on some contract, they are unlikely to because the members end up paying higher prices and thus are unlikely to use the contracts. Instead, hospital members may negotiate their own contracts or cherry-pick another group's contracts to obtain the preferred supplier's products at lower cost.

To resolve this dilemma, groups have typically contracted with one or a small number of preferred suppliers. The choice of which and how many suppliers is determined by surveying where hospital members currently buy from. That is, there is a bias to use incumbent suppliers. Groups some-times also employ a dollar purchase volume threshold to determine which suppliers to contract with. Thus, at some groups, contracts are struck only with suppliers that a group does $100 Million or more in annual business. In this manner, the group rationalizes the number of contract negotiations it enters into. Groups need to do this because contract negotiations are long, protracted, and time-consuming exercises. Groups view these contracting exercises in terms of the opportunity costs of foregoing other partnerships where they could be investing their time. Again, this creates a bias of contracting with large suppliers that do a large volume of business with the group's hospitals.

The result is that groups do not contract as frequently with smaller suppliers as they do with larger suppliers. This contracting pattern is not designed to exclude small suppliers from the marketplace or abet the competitive advantage of larger suppliers. On the contrary, the groups have an interest in maintaining competition in product markets and ensuring the flow of new technology for their hospital members to access on favorable terms. Groups have tried to maintain a balance here in several ways: through the technology investment programs they created in the past, through web-based technology forums that allow suppliers to post information on their products regardless of whether or not they are on contract, and through the formal "breakthrough technology" programs they developed in their contracts in the late 1990s (Premier) or early 2000s (AmeriNet). AmeriNet suspended its program in 2002, due to a lack of interested suppliers.[99]

Groups have also observed the trend toward M&A in the medical device industry, where much of the innovation has been developed by smaller firms which have then been acquired by larger firms. Group executives reason that access to proven, valuable technology will come from their large trading partners via their new acquisitions.[100]

Clinicians Select the Technologies They Use (Not the GPOs)

Clinicians, not purchasing groups, select the technologies they use. Perhaps the biggest misconception about GPOs is that they convince their member hospitals and physicians to use products from contracted suppliers that they do not want. In the end, the clinicians in the hospital setting exert great sway over the products and suppliers selected and are basically unchallenged by groups.[101]

More generally, it is nonsensical to believe that purchasing groups can prevent their member hospitals and their clinicians from getting access to critical new technology. There are too many forces lined up to push and pull new technology into the clinical setting for any purchasing group to resist, even if they wanted to. The suppliers' sales reps have historically enjoyed closer relationships with physicians than have the hospitals, materials managers, and purchasing groups.[102]

On any given day (until recent years), there could be hundreds of supplier sales reps in a large hospital detailing their products to physicians.[103] Physicians are well known for desiring the latest technology to serve the clinical needs of their patients, and historically have exerted much sway over hospitals in terms of the acquisition of new technology and equipment. They are also free to present and evaluate any product they want. New products thus get introduced via the efforts of clinicians who champion them.

The U.S. spends billions of dollars on R&D, partially funded through the National Institutes of Health (NIH) and partially conducted in academic medical centers (AMCs).[104] AMCs, IDNs, and other hospital systems all compete for physicians and their patients through their offering of technological services. There is mounting evidence for societal benefits of increased spending on technology. All of these forces contribute to a century-long trend in healthcare roughly paraphrased as a "technological imperative."[105]

Purchasing groups have been more effective in contracting with suppliers in competitive product markets for more routine products and technologies than they have for PPIs. Groups have not challenged physician decision-making for PPIs.[106] As a result, multi-source contracts for PPIs are the norm in most groups. Moreover, group contracts do not even exist for 50% or more of PPI items; instead, PPIs lend themselves to customization and segmentation strategies, rather than standardization.

Indeed, the presence of a group contract can suggest that the purchasing group has been able to persuade not only the supplier but also the hospital/physician buyer that the value of a price discount on the supplier's product is more important than any qualitative differences between that supplier's product and that of competitors. That is, the presence of a group contract may help to differentiate commodity products from PPIs. Purchasing groups thus serve an important function for their hospital and physician customers by evaluating some of the suppliers' claims that their products have innovative features. They serve as a "check and balance" that offsets the marketing efforts of suppliers. Analysts argue that groups do not serve as gatekeepers for innovative technology, but rather serve to ensure that hospitals pay less for routine technology and to keep non-innovative products off group contracts.[107]

Criteria Used by Providers in Selecting Suppliers

Hospital VPMMs offer uniform descriptions of the criteria they seek in a supplier with which to do business. These criteria include (in no particular order):

1. the supplier's reputation: ability to meet commitments, respond to hospital problems and needs, a good partner to work with
2. the size of the supplier's sales force: ability to service multiple hospital sites in an IDN
3. the dependability of the supplier's sales force: provide staff training, ability to cover three hospital shifts, deal with issues in the hospital's clinical areas
4. the knowledge of the sales force
5. the supplier's capacity to manufacture enough product to prevent back-orders
6. the supplier's ability to contract with the IDN's prime distributor
7. the existence of peer-reviewed clinical studies on the supplier's product
8. the ability of the supplier to send a clinical nurse specialist into the hospital to help conduct an evaluation of the product on site
9. the clinical acceptability of the product
10. the product's cost
11. the size and breadth of the supplier's product line
12. assistance with product conversion

These are staff-intensive, time-intensive, and cost-intensive services. Small startups may lack the resources to perform such functions.

Hospital and Physician Roles in Supplier and Technology Selection

Hospitals conduct their own technology evaluations of products based almost exclusively on the products' impact on patient care.[108] These evaluations are a group process composed primarily of clinicians (physicians and nurses) at the hospital (not the purchasing group) level. Hospital-based trials are more credible since they provide evidence of the product's performance on patients typically seen in that institution. Hospitals also rely on their own literature reviews rather than those conducted by purchasing groups. Such reviews are designed to verify any claims made by the manufacturer using peer-reviewed evidence.

The deliberations of these committees are driven primarily by a clinical analysis of the product, not the product's price. Price is often unknown anyway, since it is set by the manufacturer based on volume purchased. Purchasing and materials management staff must defer to the decisions of these committees since the former lack clinical backgrounds. Purchasing groups likewise do not influence these deliberations. Product reviews are conducted in a consistent manner regardless of the existence of a contract.

The evaluations are typically initiated by physician requests to trial a product for possible use in the hospital. Other initiators include nurses and value analysis teams. Physicians trial products when they feel strongly about them and are willing to push forward. Due to the large number of products that must be acquired, purchasing and materials staff may not have the time to conduct their own independent research on new suppliers for possible contracts, and thus must rely on the initiative and push of their clinicians. Physicians reportedly initiate trials on a regular basis—as many as 22 times in a six-month period at one hospital system. This is one vehicle by which hospitals can switch away from contracted to non-contracted suppliers. It should be noted that hospitals report that current group contracts and product prices are not considered by physicians when evaluating these products. Nor do clinicians need the approval of purchasing or materials staff to conduct these evaluations.

In sum, the hospital's technology review process is quite involved. It begins with a physician's request to trial a product. This is followed by literature review and an in-house product trial, and then by committee deliberations and possible review by the hospital's risk management personnel—all before a decision is reached and the purchasing and materials staff are asked to procure the product. This indicates that selling a new product in the hospital first requires marketing to clinicians to get them interested. It also shows that the process can be drawn out, often for as much as a year, as data on many patients are collected and analyzed, and as various stakeholders are consulted. Due to the expense involved, suppliers are typically expected to help fund these in-house trials, which can be quite expensive—another hurdle facing small startups. Hospitals and groups naturally want to avoid incurring the expense and length of time needed to conduct the evaluations on an annual basis, and thus look for longer-term contracts with suppliers.

Starting in the 1980s and developing during the 1990s, IDNs and groups increasingly recognized the value of hospital member and clinician input into the product and supplier selection process. Groups assembled committees from across their members to review products and contracts before they were awarded. Hospital members and clinicians thus achieved "voice" in the selection process. These committees are called "Clinical Councils" in some groups. Such councils evaluate new products on four broad dimensions: clinical acceptability of the product, product breadth and depth of supplier, the ability of the supplier to supply and service product, and conversion assistance and value-adds. Hospital representatives to these councils state that the group defers to their deliberations on new technology and has not trumped their decisions. They also state that, at the hospital level, the group requires that the supplier bear the burden of documenting its claims for its product.

One GAO report found that hospital customers were the most important source consulted by groups in making supplier and product decisions, and were most important in deciding which products to place on contract. The CEO of Novation testified during the Senate hearings that when his group contracts for PPIs with 75%+ compliance levels, it is at the request of its members and with the approval of product councils whose representatives come from group member hospitals.

Indeed, the Lewin Group's analysis of the clinical review process (CRP) of technologies found that CRP can be conducted at the group level or the hospital system level.[109] Most hospitals use a decentralized approach for identifying products and technologies for review. The process can be initiated by centers of excellence, departments, or specialty areas within the hospital system. The important thing to note is that the process starts with the end-users and their requests to review the product or technology. Lewin noted that hospitals also have several other mechanisms beyond the purchasing group to evaluate and acquire new technology. These can include technology assessment firms such as ECRI and the Health Technology Center, as well as the Advisory Board.

Conclusion: Groups Balance Access to Technology with Cost Reduction

There is a common dilemma facing purchasing groups and their members, just as there are facing the U.S. healthcare ecosystem. This dilemma has been described as "the iron triangle."[110] In this triangle, there are three vertices: cost, quality, and access. The dilemma derives from the fact that efforts to reduce cost oftentimes impose restrictions on access/choice. Insurance companies have developed options that allow their enrollees to choose between lower cost premiums versus greater provider choice: health maintenance organization (HMO) plans versus preferred provider organization (PPO) plans. The reality here—which few GPO critics bother to acknowledge, but which economists commonly note—is that tradeoffs are inevitable and everywhere.

In the realm of supply purchasing, group efforts to reduce the prices their hospital members pay for supplies oftentimes entail some diminution in the choice of contracted suppliers that hospitals can deal with. Without some restrictions on supplier choice and channeling of purchases to a subset of suppliers, there are no incentives for suppliers to contract with groups and offer their members lower prices. The restricted choice is thus one price hospitals pay (and willingly pay) for lower supply costs. By adding more suppliers to a contract to satisfy their critics (e.g., suppliers not on the contract) or to satisfy every clinician's preference, the groups end up sticking their hospital members with higher prices that have to be paid.

If a GPO gets too many suppliers on contract for the same product, there is much less likelihood that any one supplier will witness an increase in market share; thus, suppliers have no incentive to give the group a reduced price. For example, as the group moves from sole-source to dual-source contracts, the incumbent supplier loses exclusivity, sees its sales volume fall, and raises its price. This explains why suppliers are willing to offer GPOs more advantageous pricing under sole-source contracts than under dual or multi-source contracts.

Hospital members recognize the tradeoffs and balancing acts. A hospital CEO testified during the 2003 Senate hearings that hospitals want and value clinical innovation, but have to balance it with their finances. If groups bend to every clinician's preference and go with multi-source contracts, the hospitals end up paying higher prices. Some members (especially large IDNs who have the resources to contract) will exit the group's contract and negotiate an independent agreement with the supplier for a better price, leaving the smaller hospitals in the group to pay perhaps even higher prices (since the group's total purchased volume can drop) as well as earn lower rebates.

Groups have recognized the iron triangle dilemma and constructed different programs to allow those hospital members who value choice to have access to a broad range of contracted suppliers, while those members who want lower costs and greater savings can opt to utilize their committed purchasing programs. Moreover, the large purchasing groups have differentiated themselves over time in terms of their emphasis on product access versus purchasing efficiencies. This differentiation has allowed hospitals to self-select themselves into the type of group that matches their purchasing disposition and that of their clinicians. Groups thus engage in balancing acts with their members by trying to simultaneously promote contract compliance (to achieve savings) and allow members latitude (to promote access).[111] One mechanism they have developed are breakthrough technology programs in which members are asked to comply with sole- or dual-source contracts but are allowed a safety valve if a smaller supplier enters the market with clinically superior technology. In this manner, hospital members can have the best of both worlds: product standardization and product innovation.[112]

Purchasing groups thus trade off lower hospital pricing for fewer suppliers on contract. Contrary to statements made during the 2003 Senate hearings, groups do not trade off lower pricing for less competitive supplier markets. The competitiveness of supplier markets, and the survival of small firms and new entrants in those markets, are driven by forces generally unrelated to the presence and activities of purchasing groups.

Notes

1. The literature that this chapter relies on includes the many articles written by David Cassak over the years (see Footnote #1 in Chapter 4 for an itemized list). Some of these are repeated below when I have quoted from them. I rely on additional articles David has written; they too are included in the references below.
2. David Dranove and Lawton R. Burns. *Big Med: Megaproviders and the High Cost of Healthcare in America* (Chicago, IL: University of Chicago Press, 2021).
3. Jay Greene. "Alliances May Soon Face Their Day of Reckoning," *Modern Healthcare* (December 18, 1987): 24–37.
4. Lawton Burns. *The Health Care Value Chain* (San Francisco: Jossey-Bass, 2002). In Vivo Diarist. "A Final Word on GPOs," *In Vivo* (January 2003): 14.
5. Edward Zajac, Thomas D'Aunno, and Lawton Burns. "Managing Strategic Alliances," in Stephen Shortell and Arnold Kaluzny (Eds.), *Health Care Management: Organization Design and Behavior*, 4th Edition (Albany, NY: Delmar, 1999): pp. 307–329.
6. "Hospital, Healt Thyself," *In Vivo* (October 2001): 15.
7. *In Vivo* Diarist. "A Final Word on GPOs," *In Vivo* (January 2003): 14.
8. *In Vivo* Diarist. "A Final Word on GPOs," *In Vivo* (January 2003): 14.
9. *In Vivo* Diarist. "A Final Word on GPOs," *In Vivo* (January 2003): 14.
10. Maverick buying and spot buying are terms used in the industry.
11. For smaller suppliers dealing with large groups, this leverage was less important. For a group doing billions of dollars of business per year, a smaller supplier with only $100 Million or less in sales did not possess the capability to coerce a purchasing group.
12. Robert Kuttner. "Columbia/HCA and the Resurgence of the For-Profit Hospital Business." *New England Journal of Medicine* (August 1, 1996): 362–367.
13. Sandy Lutz, Woodrin Grossman, and John Bigalke. *Med Inc.* (San Francisco: Jossey-Bass, 1998).
14. "In GPO Battles, A Pyrrhic Victory for Suppliers," *In Vivo* (September 2002): 12.

15. John Henderson. "GPO Contracting in the New Health Care Environment: Strategic Implications for Manufacturers," *In Vivo* (January 1994): 8–14.

16. Lawton Burns. *The Health Care Value Chain* (San Francisco: Jossey-Bass, 2002). In Vivo Diarist. "A Final Word on GPOs," *In Vivo* (January 2003): 76.

17. John Henderson. "GPO Contracting in the New Health Care Environment: Strategic Implications for Manufacturers," *In Vivo* (January 1994): 8–14.

18. David Cassak. "AmeriNet and Hospital Consolidation's Endgame," *In Vivo* (November 1997): 53–63.

19. "In GPO Battles, A Pyrrhic Victory for Suppliers," *In Vivo* (September 2002): 12. David Cassak. "IDNs and GPOs: Changing the Leopard's Spots," *In Vivo* (July/August 2001): 32–44.

20. William Cleverly and Paul Nutt. "The Effectiveness of Group-Purchasing Organizations," *Health Services Research* 19(1) (1984): 65–81.

21. Lawton Burns. *The Health Care Value Chain* (San Francisco: Jossey-Bass, 2002).

22. Lawton R. Burns. *The Health Care Value Chain* (San Francisco: Jossey-Bass, 2002).

23. David Cassak. "The New Price Wars," *In Vivo* (October 1990): 13.

24. David Cassak. "Winds of Change in Orthopedic Implants," *In Vivo* (October 1992): 1–8.

25. "National Contracting Comes to Cardiovascular Devices," *In Vivo* (May 1999): 1–5.

26. Around the Industry. "Novation Signs a Spinal Implant Agreement," *In Vivo* (January 2000): 4.

27. David Cassak. "Novation's Play in Physician-Preferred Products," *In Vivo* (July/August) 2005: 29–36.

28. Thomas Hendrick. *Purchasing Consortiums: Horizontal Alliances Among Firms Buying Common Goods and Services: What? Who? Why? How?* (Tempe, AZ: Center for Advanced Purchasing Studies, 1997).

29. William Cleverly and Paul Nutt. "The Effectiveness of Group-Purchasing Organizations," *Health Services Research* 19(1) (1984): 65–81. Lawton R. Burns. *The Health Care Value Chain* (San Francisco, CA: Jossey-Bass, 2002). *The Role of Group Purchasing Organizations in the U.S. Health Care System* (Washington, DC: Muse & Associates, 2000). *Group Purchasing Organizations: Use of Contracting Processes and Strategies to Award Contracts for Medical-Surgical Products* (Washington, DC: GAO, 2002). GAO-02-690T. The Lewin Group. *Assessing the Value of Group Purchasing Organizations* (Washington, DC: Lewin Group, May 2003).

30. General Accounting Office. *Group Purchasing Organizations: Pilot Study Suggests Large Buying Groups Do Not Always Offer Hospitals Lower Prices.* GAO-03-998T (Washington, DC: GAO, 2003).

31. Jean Nollet and Martin Beaulieu. "Development of Group Purchasing: An Empirical Study in the Healthcare Sector," *Journal of Purchasing and Supply Management* 9(1)(2003): 3–10.

32. Eugene Schneller. *The Value of Group Purchasing in the Health Care Supply Chain* (Tempe, AZ: School of Health Administration and Policy, 2000).

33. Jean Nollet and Martin Beaulieu. "Development of Group Purchasing: An Empirical Study in the Healthcare Sector," *Journal of Purchasing and Supply Management* 9(1) (2003): 3–10.

34. David Cassak. "IDNs and GPOs: Changing the Leopard's Spots," *In Vivo* (July/August 2001): 32–44. Wendy Diller. "GPOs Rethink Diagnostics," *In Vivo* (September 1999): 46–56.

35. David Cassak. "IDNs and GPOs: Changing the Leopard's Spots," *In Vivo* (July/August 2001): 32–44.

36. Voluntary Hospitals of America. *Standardization: A Guide to Reducing Variations to Improve Outcomes* (VHA, 1994). Premier. *Integrated System Purchasing Outlook* (Charlotte, NC: Premier, 1994–1995).

37. David Cassak. "The New Premier: One Year After the Merger," *In Vivo* (July/August 1996): 22–29.

38. Lisa Scott and Jay Greene. 1995. "AmHS, Premier to Merge," *Modern Healthcare* (August 7): 2–3.

39. Richard Haugh. "The Leveraged Buy Is Out," *Hospitals and Health Networks* (November 5, 1997): 33–40.

40. Scott Hensley. "Exceeding Expectations," *Modern Healthcare* (February 10, 1997): 20–21.

41. U.S. General Accounting Office. *Group Purchasing Organizations: Use of Contracting Processes and Strategies to Award Contracts for Medical-Surgical Products.* GAO-03-998T (Washington, DC: GAO, 2003).

42. Lawton R. Burns. *The Health Care Value Chain* (San Francisco, CA: Jossey-Bass, 2002). David Cassak. "IDNs and GPOs: Changing the Leopard's Spots," *In Vivo* (July/August 2001): 32–44.

43. David Cassak. "GPO Realignment—The Hidden Dynamic in National Account Contracting," *In Vivo* (May 1991): 8–11.

44. The Lewin Group. *Assessing the Value of Group Purchasing Organizations* (Washington, DC: Lewin Group, May 2003).

45. In Vivo Diarist. "A Final Word on GPOs," *In Vivo*. David Cassak. "Reforming Group Purchasing: How Far Is Enough?" *In Vivo* (January 2003): 52–55.

46. Around the Industry. "Talking Back to Premier," *In Vivo* (July/August 1999): 4.

47. David Cassak. "Orthopedic Implant Contracting, Round II," *In Vivo* (October 1998): 5–14.

48. David Cassak. "AmeriNet and Hospital Consolidation's Endgame," *In Vivo* (November 1997): 53–63.

49. Around the Industry. "Premier Listens to Members," *In Vivo* (July/August, 2000): 4.

50. General Accounting Office. *Group Purchasing Organizations: Use of Contracting Processes and Strategies to Award Contracts for Medical-Surgical Products.* GAO-03-998T (Washington, DC: GAO, 2003).

51. Herbert Hovenkamp. *Competitive Effects of Group Purchasing Organizations' (GPO) Purchasing and Product Selection Practices in the Health Care Industry* (April 2002).

52. Herbert Hovenkamp. *Competitive Effects of Group Purchasing Organizations' (GPO) Purchasing and Product Selection Practices in the Health Care Industry* (April 2002).

53. Richard Haugh. "The Leveraged Buy Is Out," *Hospitals and Health Networks* (November 5, 1997): 33–40.

54. Lawton R. Burns, Eduardo Cisneros, William Ferniany, and Harbir Singh. "Strategic Alliances Between Buyers and Suppliers: Lessons From the Medical Imaging Industry," in Christine Harland, Guido Nassimbeni, and Eugene Schneller (Eds.), *The SAGE Handbook of Strategic Supply Management* (Sage Publications, 2012).

55. David Cassak. Personal communication.

56. Herbert Hovenkamp. *Competitive Effects of Group Purchasing Organizations' (GPO) Purchasing and Product Selection Practices in the Health Care Industry.* Prepared for The Health Industry Group Purchasing Association (Washington, DC: HIGPA, April 2002).

57. Muse & Associates. *The Role of Group Purchasing Organizations in the U.S. Health Care System.* Prepared for HIGPA (March 2000).

58. Laura Baldwin, Frank Camm, and Nancy Moore. *Federal Contract Bundling* (Santa Monica: Rand, 2001). Competition for contracts is also common in many markets that use intermediaries (such as purchasing groups, distributors, and pharmacy benefit managers).

59. General Accounting Office. *Group Purchasing Organizations: Use of Contracting Processes and Strategies to Award Contracts for Medical-Surgical Products.* GAO-03-998T (Washington, DC: GAO, 2003).

60. David Cassak. "The New Premier: One Year After the Merger," *In Vivo* (July/August 1996): 22–29.

61. General Accounting Office. *Group Purchasing Organizations: Use of Contracting Processes and Strategies to Award Contracts for Medical-Surgical Products.* GAO-03-998T (Washington, DC: GAO, 2003).

62. David Cassak. "Columbia/HCA: Why Size Matters," *In Vivo* (April 1997): 41–54.

63. David Cassak. "Tenet Shakes Things Up," *In Vivo* (July/August 1998): 41–53.

64. Lisa Scott. "Price Battle Leaves Premier Wary," *Modern Healthcare* (August 19, 1996): 13.

65. David Cassak. "Amerinet and Hospital Consolidation's Endgame," *In Vivo* (November 1997): 53–63.

66. "FAH Systems Conference," *In Vivo* (May–June 1998).

67. John Henderson. "GPO Contracting in the New Health Care Environment: Strategic Implications for Manufacturers," *In Vivo* (January 1994): 8–14.

68. Herbert Hovenkamp. *Competitive Effects of Group Purchasing Organizations' (GPO) Purchasing and Product Selection Practices in the Health Care Industry.* Prepared for The Health Industry Group Purchasing Association (Washington, DC: HIGPA, April 2002).

69. Lawton R. Burns and J. Andrew Lee. "Group Purchasing Organizations (GPOs): Issues and Evidence," *Health Care Management Review* 33(3) (2008): 203–215.

70. David Cassak. "Group Purchasing Group Meeting," *In Vivo* (January–February 1989): 12–14.

71. David Cassak. "A Boost into the Market for Emerging Companies," *In Vivo* (May 1989): 14–19. David Cassak. "The Corporate Alliance," *In Vivo* (September 1989): 14–18. David Cassak. "American HealthCare Systems Comes of Age," *In Vivo* (October 1990): 18–23.

72. David Cassak. "Kinetic Concepts and the New Capital Equipment Market," *In Vivo* (May 1993): 23–30.

73. David Cassak. "The Distribution Revolution," *In Vivo* (July–August 1988): 16–20.

74. Lawton R. Burns, Eduardo Cisneros, William Ferniany, and Harbir Singh. "Strategic Alliances Between Buyers and Suppliers: Lessons From the Medical Imaging Industry," in Christine Harland, Guido Nassimbeni, and Eugene Schneller (Eds.), *The SAGE Handbook of Strategic Supply Management* (Sage Publications, 2012).

75. David Cassak. "The New Supply Chain," *In Vivo* (June 1999): 44–57.

76. General Accounting Office. *Group Purchasing Organizations: Use of Contracting Processes and Strategies to Award Contracts for Medical-Surgical Products.* GAO-03-998T (Washington, DC: GAO, 2003).

77. David Cassak. "GPO Realignment—The Hidden Dynamic in National Account Contracting," *In Vivo* (May 1991): 8–11.

78. Herbert Hovenkamp. *Group Purchasing Organization (GPO) Purchasing Agreements and Antitrust Law* (Washington, DC: Health Industry Group Purchasing Association, January 2004).

79. Lisa Scott. "Price Battle Leaves Premier Wary," *Modern Healthcare* (August 19, 1996): 13.

80. David Cassak. "AmeriNet and Hospital Consolidation's Endgame," *In Vivo* (November 1997): 53–63.

81. Wendy Diller. "GPOs Rethink Diagnostics," *In Vivo* (September 1999): 46–56.

82. Lawton R. Burns and J. Andrew Lee. "Group Purchasing Organizations (GPOs): Issues and Evidence," *Health Care Management Review* 33(3) (2008): 203–215.

83. Cinda Becker. "What Suppliers Think," *Modern Healthcare* (July 14, 2003): 7, 15.

84. David Cassak. "Novation's Debut," *In Vivo* (January 1998): 23–26.

85. Timothy Chapman, Ajay Gupta, and Paul Mango. "Group Purchasing Is Not a Panacea for U.S. Hospitals," *McKinsey Quarterly* (Winter 1998).

86. David Cassak. "A New Kind of Leverage," *In Vivo* (October 1989): 12–16. David Cassak. "Staking Ground in Orthopedics," *In Vivo* (April 1995): 3–9.

87. David Cassak. "Columbia/HCA: Why Size Matters," *In Vivo* (April 1997): 41–54.

88. John Henderson. "GPO Contracting in the New Health Care Environment: Strategic Implications for Manufacturers," *In Vivo* (January 1994): 8–14.

89. David Cassak and Roger Longman. "Group Purchasing Strategies," *In Vivo* (May–June 1988): 25–28. David Cassak. "AmeriNet and Hospital Consolidation's Endgame," *In Vivo* (November 1997): 53–63.

90. Kathy Malloch. "What's Your GPO IQ?" *Nursing Management* 32(6) (2001): 11.

91. Lawton R. Burns. *The Health Care Value Chain* (San Francisco, CA: Jossey-Bass, 2002).

92. David Cassak. "Novation's Play in Physician-Preferred Products," *In Vivo* (July/August 2005): 29–36.

93. Lawton R. Burns. *The U.S. Healthcare Ecosystem* (New York: McGraw-Hill, 2021).

94. David Cassak. "Novation's Play in Physician-Preferred Products," *In Vivo* (July/August 2005): 29–36.

95. General Accounting Office. *Group Purchasing Organizations: Use of Contracting Processes and Strategies to Award Contracts for Medical-Surgical Products.* GAO-03-998T (Washington, DC: GAO, 2003).

96. David Cassak. "VHA Supply's Private Label Program," *In Vivo* (January 1990): 1–4.

97. David Cassak. "AmeriNet and Hospital Consolidation's Endgame," *In Vivo* (November 1997): 53–63.

98. Michael E. Porter. *Competitive Strategy* (New York: Free Press, 1998).

99. Cinda Becker. "In Search of a Breakthrough," *Modern Healthcare* (August 5, 2002): 28–31.

100. David Cassak. "AmeriNet and Hospital Consolidation's Endgame," *In Vivo* (November 1997): 53–63.

101. David Cassak. "The New Supply Chain," *In Vivo* (June 1999): 44–57.

102. Lawton R. Burns, Michael Housman, Robert Booth, and Aaron Koenig. "Implant Vendors and Hospitals: Competing Influences over Product

Choice by Orthopedic Surgeons," *Health Care Management Review* 34(1) (2009): 2–18.

103. Timothy Chapman, Ajay Gupta, and Paul Mango. "Group Purchasing Is Not a Panacea for U.S. Hospitals," *McKinsey Quarterly* (Winter 1998).

104. Lawton R. Burns. *The U.S. Healthcare Ecosystem* (New York: McGraw-Hill, 2021): Chapter 20.

105. Lawton R. Burns. *The Business of Healthcare Innovation*, 3rd Edition (Cambridge, UK: Cambridge University Press, 2020): Chapter 1.

106. David Cassak. "The New Supply Chain," *In Vivo* (June 1999): 44–57.

107. David Cassak. "The RealPolitik of the Device Industry," *In Vivo* (March 2002): 12. *In Vivo* Diarist. "A Final Word on GPOs," *In Vivo* (January 2003): 14.

108. David Cassak. "GPOs Cry Foul Following Senate Hearings," *In Vivo* (May 2002): 4, 6, 8.

109. The Lewin Group. *The Clinical Review Process Conducted by Group Purchasing Organizations and Health Systems* (Washington, DC: Lewin, April 2002).

110. William Kissick. *Medicine's Dilemmas* (New Haven: Yale University Press, 1994).

111. Wendy Diller. "GPOs Rethink Diagnostics," *In Vivo* (September 1999): 46–56.

112. David Cassak. "Reforming Group Purchasing: How Far Is Enough?" *In Vivo* (January 2003): 52–65.

8

GPOs: Differentiated or Commoditized?

Allison D. Briggs and Lawton R. Burns

Introduction

The preceding chapter makes the case for the pro-competitive and welfare-generating impacts of GPOs. As stated earlier, "GPOs are certainly not as bad as their critics say they are." This chapter makes a different point. GPOs are intermediaries in the healthcare value chain performing contracting and supply chain functions. Such functions are largely "back office" and opaque. Like other intermediaries—such as insurers and product distributors—it is hard to get excited about the GPOs. Moreover, given their back-office role, it is hard to distinguish one from another and talk about excellence. The point here is that "GPOs may not be as good as they think they are." Perhaps Larry David had it right: curb your enthusiasm.

Surveys of hospital Vice-Presidents of Materials Management (VPMM) conducted over time consistently suggest positive evaluations of GPO performance. Satisfaction levels with GPOs are fairly (and consistently) high on several dimensions.[1] Yet, the satisfaction scores are not whopping and not consistently high across all measures of performance. Prior research shows the satisfaction levels across the different GPOs may not be all that different.[2] This runs counter to stories in the trade press that GPOs seek competitive advantage over one another and attempt to stand out from one another.[3] Like most intermediaries in healthcare (e.g., insurers, wholesalers), GPOs may have difficulty documenting their distinctiveness.

© The Author(s), under exclusive license to Springer
Nature Switzerland AG 2022
L. R. Burns, *The Healthcare Value Chain*,
https://doi.org/10.1007/978-3-031-10739-9_8

Comparative Effectiveness

Demonstrating the distinctive advantage(s) of one's product or service is a common objective of many healthcare suppliers and a key to success in the institutional supply chain. Branded drugs undergo randomized clinical trials to demonstrate absolute efficacy relative to placebo; less commonly they are evaluated in terms of relative efficacy—i.e., compared to older drugs and standard therapies. Some medical devices (e.g., those undergoing PreMarket Approval, or PMA) are compared to existing therapies. Results from these studies are usually published in the peer-reviewed, scientific literature in order to convince clinicians to adopt them. Outside of clinical trials to gain Food and Drug Administration (FDA) approval, however, there are much fewer comparative, head-to-head analyses of competing products; they are even fewer analyses of competing service providers.[4]

In business-to-business (B2B) markets, comparative evaluations of competing healthcare companies and their products are often performed by contracted market research firms. Such evaluations rank the performance of one company's products against another on dimensions that are important to customers. These evaluations are often commissioned by one of the competing firms to benchmark their own performance and suggest avenues for improvement. Their results may also be selectively distributed to customers and made public through marketing materials. Otherwise, the evaluations are usually limited to internal use. They are infrequently published and rarely conducted by academic researchers.

These evaluations have been important for nearly two decades due to the growing interest in comparative effectiveness analysis (CEA); they have become much more salient in the current era of value-based purchasing (VBP), cost containment, and quality improvement where the quality and cost of products and services need to be jointly assessed. They have also become more important in an era of data transparency to inform consumer choice.

An analysis of U.S. national healthcare expenditures reveals that hospitals are the largest category ($1,270 Billion, or 30.8% - 2020 data) of spending and are projected to increase at a compound average growth rate (CAGR) of 5.6% from 2017–2026. Of these $1,270 Billion in expenditures, an estimated $380 Billion are non-labor expenses and, among these, $228 Billion are subject to purchases (potentially) mediated by technology assessment and procurement firms, otherwise known as GPOs.[5] Based on the reported 13.1% savings from this mediated spend, researchers suggest that GPOs have the potential to save hospitals (at least) $25–30 Billion annually, and thereby can play a major role in helping hospitals reduce costs and manage the current value-based environment.

Most hospitals are free to join any GPO, and most belong to at least one GPO. There are two exceptions: (a) freestanding hospitals that join a multi-hospital system typically switch to the GPO used by the system; (2) hospitals owned by a specific for-profit system can be mandated to use the system's in-house GPO, and perhaps on an exclusive basis as well. At present, however, hospitals lack comparative data or any rigorous evidence base on GPO performance to (a) make an informed decision regarding GPO membership and (b) "benchmark" performance under their GPO. Benchmarking helps to understand how one's organization compares with similar organizations, as well as to identify areas, systems, or processes for improvements.

There are several barriers to gathering data that can be used to benchmark GPOs. The GPOs are quite guarded about their internal operations—and for good reason. As documented in Chapter 5, they have been subjected to withering criticism about their purchasing practices and assessment (and acceptance) of new technologies. And, like the pharmacy benefit managers (PBMs) covered in Section III of this volume, they have been tarred as unnecessary "middlemen" that contribute to the rising costs of healthcare, charge high fees without rendering any commensurate benefits, and need to be eliminated.[6] As a result, they rarely make their membership rosters available to the research community, let alone the public. Moreover, the "customers" of the GPOs—the Vice-Presidents of Materials Management (VPMMs) in their member hospitals—have no real national association where such a membership roster might be obtained. The closest thing to such an association is the Association for Health Resource and Materials Management (AHRMM), a society hosted by the American Hospital Association; but their membership list contains a more diverse set of interested stakeholders. Finally, as I have experienced first-hand, surveys of VPMMs about their GPO's performance suffer from notoriously low response rates.

There are also barriers to utilizing such comparative data, even if they are gathered and made public. One reason is the low response rate (typically less than 5%) of VPMMs to surveys that seek to assess GPO performance. Studies that rely on these data rarely assess the representativeness of their sample, an issue that restricts the study's utility. Oftentimes, these surveys are based on convenience samples (e.g., VPMMs in attendance at a conference). Another reason is the perception that such data are not really useful. There is a widespread perception that the GPOs are "commodities," i.e., are interchangeable in terms of their contracts, products, and services due to a lack of differentiation in the eyes of customers. The process of commoditization is usually accompanied by a "race to the bottom," competition over unit pricing, and the view that all competitors are generic. Commodification in healthcare has traditionally been discussed in terms of hospital purchases of such basic products as generic drugs, housekeeping supplies, drapes, and gowns. In recent years, analysts have suggested the process is penetrating the higher-end, medical technology (medtech) space such as surgical instruments and implantable devices. The threat of commodification is now also applied to the intermediaries in healthcare—such as health insurers, PBMs, wholesalers, and GPOs—who are perceived to be at survival risk due to the entrance of "tech" start-ups (e.g., Oscar Health, Amazon).[7]

This chapter draws on a large national and representative sample of hospitals to present data on GPO performance on dimensions rated by their hospital VPMM customers. Such data allow hospitals and VPMMs to benchmark their GPO against other GPOs. The chapter addresses the question of whether GPOs are commoditized or, alternatively, whether some GPOs perform consistently higher than others, and on what dimensions. It addresses whether GPOs add value in their roles as intermediaries or middlemen—partly in terms of their levels of VPMM satisfaction, and partly in terms of observed differences in VPMM satisfaction levels compared to earlier surveys using the same items. Answers to these questions may help hospitals improve their decision-making on GPO membership. If meaningful differences exist in GPO performance, and if GPOs do indeed drive hospital cost savings from their contracts and other services, then the analyses may promote greater competition in the GPO sector and greater hospital efficiency.

Commoditization: Reality or Fiction?

The labeling of a product as a "commodity" is by no means clear-cut. What should one expect to see if an economic sector and its products/services are commoditized? There is no science here to guide us, but the following characteristics seem likely:

- Low brand preference
- Low brand loyalty
- Few differences in product/service quality
- Low willingness to pay for product enhancements
- Low switching costs

- High switching behavior
- High likelihood of being on group purchasing contracts
- Inter-changeability and uniformity

There is a growing divergence of opinion in the literature regarding the commoditization of medical technology ("medtech") products. On the one hand, recent reports suggest that this process is now underway in medtech.[8] This process typically reflects the slowdown in product innovation, which has beset medtech over the past two decades.[9] It can also reflect the growing unwillingness of customers to pay a premium for that technology, whether due to more iterative than innovative technology, reimbursement pressures from payers, calls for value-based purchasing, the decreasing voice of physicians in the procurement of high-end products (known as physician preference items, or PPIs), the rise of product formularies, increased presence on GPO contracts, or increased consumerism.

On the other hand, empirical research documents that supposedly commoditized products (such as sutures, surgical staplers, and orthopedic implants) are decidedly differentiated in the eyes of their physician customers on a host of product features.[10] These products appear to have enduring attributes that make them preferred and "sticky," which help to explain their stable market shares.

Group Purchasing Organizations

The issue of commoditization has arisen regarding the GPOs that evaluate and procure these medtech (and other) products for hospitals. GPO critics assert they are not only unnecessary but indeed harmful intermediaries. They do not add value for their members but, rather, put their own interests first. Reports issued by The Government Accountability Office (GAO), reviewed in Chapter 5, focus on their failure to reduce prices and costs and their lack of differentiation. For example, a 2010 GAO Report described the range of services offered by the six largest GPOs. According to the GAO, all six provided the following services: custom contracting, clinical evaluation and standardization, and technology assessments; five of the six commonly offered supply chain analysis, electronic commerce, benchmarking data services, and continuing medical education.[11] The only services that were provided by a minority of the GPOs studied were relatively unimportant functions such as warehousing, equipment repair, and insurance services.

Academic research provides mixed findings regarding the degree of GPO commoditization. On the one hand, the research presented above documents the frequency with which hospitals add GPO affiliations (14.5%) or drop GPO affiliations (8%) in a given year, as well as the multiple reasons why hospitals switch GPOs. On the other hand, earlier (unpublished) research found few differences in the VPMMs' satisfaction and performance ratings of the top eight GPOs in 2004.[12]

Background on Healthcare Intermediaries

GPOs are "intermediaries" in the healthcare value chain, situated between (a) the manufacturers of supplies and equipment and (b) the hospitals, hospital systems, and integrated delivery networks (IDNs) that use them in patient care. The former are the sellers located upstream; the latter are the downstream buyers (see Fig. 2.1). Intermediaries do not make innovative medical products or deliver critical medical services to patients. To survive, intermediaries need to develop a cost-efficient platform in a two-sided market that links the sellers and buyers. Sellers and buyers must find that it is too expensive not to use the intermediaries due to high transaction costs (finding trading partners, negotiating contracts, etc.).

GPOs differ from other intermediaries like health insurers working for fully-insured employers, which use monies collected from the buyers. Instead, GPOs collect much of their revenue from the sellers in the form of CAFs, although some are now collecting more fees from hospital members who purchase their services. GPOs may also collect membership fees from their hospital customers (the buyers), but such fees are much smaller in magnitude. Unlike the insurers, the GPOs also do not pay the sellers for the products their hospitals purchase.

The "theory" of how GPOs work to reduce supply costs is based on the cost-efficiency of their platform. As argued throughout this volume, it heavily rests on exchanging higher volumes channeled to suppliers for lower prices given to buyers. By virtue of consolidation, GPOs achieve national scale and coverage—but perhaps not as much as product suppliers. Using their scale as leverage, GPOs contract aggressively with suppliers of medical devices, drugs, capital equipment, commodity items, and other products/services to extract large, item-line price discounts and contract administration fees (CAFs, often 1–3% of the product price) in exchange for market access to a large customer base. The primary advantage is thus lower product costs aggregated across lots of product contracts.

The large national GPOs address the heterogeneity of product needs and demands among their members by differentiating contract offerings that move beyond scale to gain additional price discounts. Such offerings represent a menu of options that GPOs allow their hospital members to choose from in order to select the particular "iron triangle" tradeoff they prefer: product access versus product cost. These differentiated offerings include:

- "committed contracts" (hospitals exchange a guaranteed percent of purchases for a given product from the vendor)
- "commitment tiers" (higher levels of hospitals' committed purchases through a vendor lead to higher discounts)
- "sole-source contracts" and "dual-source contracts" (hospitals receive more favorable pricing for using one or two vendors exclusively) and
- "bundled contracts" (hospitals receive more favorable pricing by agreeing to buy a certain level of products from a vendor across multiple product categories).

In addition to lower unit prices and differentiated contracts, national GPOs have expanded their service offerings to include supply chain support (e.g., maintain the hospital's item master and benchmark costs with peer institutions), general management support (e.g., operational improvements, technology assessment), clinical and safety improvement initiatives, and consulting services. These additional services support both cost containment and quality improvement efforts by their members. They also obviate the need for hospitals to hire more personnel in such areas, thereby lowering their human resources costs.

Despite the differentiation of contract types and diversification of service lines, national GPOs face a dilemma between centralized supply procurement (pooled purchasing contracts) and decentralized focus to respond to individual member needs. Hospital members have increasingly rejected the national one-size-fits-all alliances which cannot adequately accommodate the interests of diverse members and serve local hospital interests. Hospitals have formed regional and local alliances, either on their own or (more commonly) with the help of the national GPOs, to negotiate local customized contracts. For contracts negotiated through non-national GPOs, hospitals utilize national GPO-contracted pricing as a benchmark or ceiling to extract further pricing concessions. In addition, hospitals increasingly have made supply chain management and self-contracting a strategic priority, thereby pressuring the national alliances to be more competitive.[13]

Not everyone subscribes to the theory of GPOs. Indeed, as noted above, the national GPOs have been squeezed on two fronts. Externally, they have faced 1–2 decades of scrutiny and criticism from the U.S. Senate, the Government Accountability Office, the courts, and some researchers who assert they provide no value, they may actually cause harm to competition and product innovation, they increase prices and spending, and they are all the same. Internally, they have faced growing demands for customized service from their hospital members, who have increasingly (a) pushed for regional and local GPOs to better serve them and (b) initiated self-contracting to act as their own GPO. This chapter investigates whether some GPOs have been more successful than others in dealing with such pressures and thereby distinguished themselves. It also identifies the GPO functions where such differentiation can be achieved.

Empirical Methods

Study Population

Data for this study come from a 2014 survey of the members of the top five national GPOs that represented most hospitals at that time: Amerinet, HealthTrust, MedAssets, Novation, and Premier. Prior evidence shows that hospitals route the bulk of their purchases through one national GPO. For this reason, we utilized the membership in the five national GPOs as our population to study.[14] The survey was sponsored by the American Hospital Association (AHA) as part of an effort to track GPO performance over time. Details on the survey administration, hospital population, and response rate (23%) have already been published, and thus are not covered here.[15]

GPO Performance Measures

The survey collected data to measure GPOs on a host of performance dimensions important to their customers (*benchmarking* issue), the variation in that performance across GPOs (*commoditization* issue), the degree to which GPOs provided functions that their members were satisfied with (*intermediary* issue), and the degree to which GPOs provided assistance to and served as a strategic partner with their hospital members (*agency* issue). There were four sections in the survey:

> The first section of the survey identified the hospital's memberships in national, regional, and local alliances. Hospitals also reported their tenure (number of years) with each alliance, their shareholder status in the primary national alliance, and the rank order in importance that each alliance played in the healthcare supply chain.

The second section asked about the hospital's utilization of purchasing alliances. VPMMs estimated the percentages of their total supply spending routed through national, regional, and local purchasing alliances, supplemented by self-negotiated contracts and off-contract purchases. They also estimated the percentage of purchases mediated through the primary national alliance in eight categories: commodity items, physician preference items (PPIs), pharmaceuticals (both generic and brand), capital items, purchased services, dietary, and information technology.

The third section asked about the hospital's perceived savings that flowed from various aspects of their primary national GPO's contracting. It also asked about the hospital's evaluation of the GPO's contracting for physician preference items (PPIs).

The fourth section asked about the value derived from five services offered by alliances: revenue cycle management, purchased services, data analytics, benchmarking data, and clinical outcomes data. These services constitute newer areas of capability that GPOs have sought to develop.

The fifth section asked VPMMs to evaluate their national alliance's performance. This encompassed the ability to generate demonstrable cost savings as well as economic savings on seven dimensions: lower prices, CAFs shared back with the hospital, GPO providing the market price point, standardized contracts, centralized staffing, shareholder dividends, and information technology. It also solicited their overall level of satisfaction with the national alliance and satisfaction with 20 specific alliance functions. These functions spanned the following areas: clinical services, safety improvements, benchmarking with other hospitals, consulting services, operational improvements, assessment of new technology, strategic partnership, and pricing (cost). VPMMs also evaluated the alliance's success with contracting for PPIs on twelve different dimensions, including pricing, CAFs earned, exposure to innovative products, contract standardization and compliance, and use of differentiated contract offerings.

Analytic Approach

We present the means for the survey measures for hospitals in each of the five national GPOs. While the identities of the five GPOs are blinded, we provide information to help understand any observed differences between them. We also test for significant pairwise differences among these GPO means using Tukey–Kramer tests.[16] In Tables 8.1–8.5, the second column from the right indicates whether there are any significant differences among the five GPOs; the far right column indicates which pairs of GPOs are significantly different. For purposes of anonymity, we have labeled the GPOs by number rather than by name.

Results

Purchasing Alliance Memberships

By definition, all of the hospitals in our sample belong to at least one national GPO. Table 8.1 examines the characteristics of hospitals belonging to each national GPO and their pattern of GPO participation.[17] There is considerable variation in the acute care bedsize of hospitals across the five GPOs: hospitals in GPO 1 are the smallest on average, while hospitals in GPO 3 are the largest. There is also considerable variation in the percentage of hospitals that are shareholders in the GPO: GPO 3 has the lowest percentage, while GPO 4 and GPO 5 have the highest percentage. Membership in regional and local GPOs differs. Hospitals in two of the five GPOs (GPO 4, GPO 5) are significantly more likely to also have both regional and local GPO affiliations compared to the other GPOs. There are no differences in the hospital tenure with these regional and local GPOs. Hospitals in GPO 1 and GPO 4 tend to have longer (15+ years) tenure with their national GPO.

Table 8.1 Characteristics of hospitals belonging to national GPO and level of GPO participation—by national GPO

	GPO					ANOVA significance level	Tukey–Kramer pairwise comparisons
	1	2	3	4	5		
Number of hospitals	62	120	157	396	362		
Hospital characteristics							
Total acute beds	101	192	250	219	237	<0.001	1 < 3, 4, 5
Percent hospitals are GPO shareholders	52%	53%	11%	65%	70%		3 < 1, 2, 4, 5; 1, 2 < 5
Survey item						<0.001	
Member of:							
Regional GPO	52%	49%	43%	69%	75%	<0.001	2, 3 < 4, 5
Local GPO	41%	21%	35%	39%	48%	<0.005	2 < 4, 5
# years member in:							
National GPO (primary)	15.14	9.74	8.06	15.23	10.64	<0.001	1, 4 > 2, 3
Regional GPO	13.20	11.32	7.26	9.33	8.97	n. s	
Local GPO	9.50	8.87	8.96	7.86	9.17	n. s	

GPO Utilization

Table 8.2 compares how the members of the different GPOs route their national, regional, and local GPO purchasing. Hospitals that belong to GPO 2 are significantly more likely to route supply purchases through GPOs of any kind, and are significantly more likely to route these purchases through their national GPO. They are significantly less likely to route these purchases through regional GPOs, local GPOs, and self-negotiated contracts. By contrast, hospitals that belong to GPO 1, GPO 4, and GPO 5 are more likely to route purchases through regional GPOs. There are few differences across GPOs in routing purchases through local GPOs or purchasing supplies off-contract.

Similar patterns are observed in the routing of purchases for specific types of products. Hospital members of GPO 2 are significantly more likely than the others to route a higher percentage of purchases through their national GPO for all measured items: PPIs, commodities, branded drugs, generic drugs, capital items, purchased services, and information technology. There are few significant differences among the remaining GPOs in terms of how they route such purchases.

Sources of Savings from the National GPO

Table 8.3 examines whether the national GPOs differ in terms of the sources of savings they provide to hospital members. Two particular sources are evident: (a) demonstrable cost savings and margin improvement, and (b) savings from standardized contracts. Members of GPO 2 are significantly more likely to report such savings than hospital members of the other GPOs. Members of that GPO are also likely to report savings from lower prices, but only in comparison with one other GPO. Overall, the GPOs are comparable in their hospital members reporting savings across the other sources of savings.

Table 8.2 Hospital purchasing routed through national, regional, and local GPOs—by national GPO

	GPO					ANOVA signifi-cance level	Tukey–Kramer pairwise comparisons
	1	2	3	4	5		
Percent of purchases made through:							
Any GPO	67.41	80.77	68.99	67.11	70.10	<0.001	2 > 1, 3, 4, 5
National GPO	46.72	76.39	58.86	48.75	52.03	<0.001	2 > 1, 3, 4, 5; 3 > 1, 4, 5
Regional GPO	16.38	3.14	3.84	11.57	12.46	<0.001	1, 4, 5 > 2, 3
Local GPO	4.31	1.24	6.29	6.78	5.61	<0.08	2 < 4, 5
Self-negotiated contracts	21.52	8.61	21.75	23.13	19.68	<0.001	2 < 1, 3, 4, 5
Off-contract purchases	11.07	10.61	9.26	9.77	10.21	n.s	
Percent of supplies purchased off-contract for which GPO contract exists	18.15	15.61	16.34	17.73	16.84	n.s	
Percent of purchases in following product areas mediated by primary national GPO*							
PPIs	1.93	2.97	2.03	1.86	2.11	<0.001	2 > 1, 3, 4, 5
Commodities	3.17	3.80	3.36	3.22	3.48	<0.001	2 > 1, 3, 4, 5; 5 > 4
Branded drugs	2.83	3.55	2.96	3.04	3.09	<0.001	2 > 1, 3, 4, 5
Generic drugs	2.93	3.66	3.05	3.13	3.14	<0.001	2 > 1, 3, 4, 5
Capital items	2.24	2.96	1.89	1.79	1.94	<0.001	2 > 1, 3, 4, 5
Purchased services	1.93	2.59	1.69	1.63	1.81	<0.001	2 > 1, 3, 4, 5
Dietary	2.93	3.42	2.46	2.40	2.84	<0.001	2 > 3, 4, 5; 5 > 3, 4

(continued)

Table 8.2 (continued)

	GPO					ANOVA signifi-cance level	Tukey–Kramer pairwise comparisons
	1	2	3	4	5		
Information Technology	2.03	2.91	1.81	1.65	1.90	<0.001	2 > 1, 3, 4, 5; 5 > 4

*Rating Measure : 1 = 0–24%; 2 = 25–49%; 3 = 50–74%; 4 = 75–100%

By contrast, Table 8.3 suggests no differences among the national GPOs in terms of their contracting for PPIs, PPI pricing, collection of administrative fees, knowledge of innovative suppliers, access to innovative suppliers, contract conversion for PPIs, and various types of PPI contracts. Members of GPO 2 are more likely to report their purchasing group gets excellent prices in dual-source contracts but not in sole-source contracts.

Sources of Value from Other GPO Services

Table 8.4 investigates the value added by the relatively newer services offered by GPOs: revenue cycle, purchased services, data analytics, benchmarking data, and clinical outcome data. There are virtually no significant differences and no definite patterns in the handful of significant pairwise comparisons. Hospital members of GPO 3 suggest their purchasing group does slightly better than the others in purchased services; members of GPO 2 and GPO 3 suggest their group does better on clinical outcomes data. The provision of data analytics and benchmarking data seem to be comparable across the GPOs. Other data reveal that hospitals derive the most value from benchmarking data (mean = 3.51 out of 5.00) and data analytics (3.39), but less value from clinical outcomes data (3.16), purchased services (3.07), and revenue cycle management (2.85).[18]

Table 8.3 Sources of savings national GPOs provide to hospital members—by national GPO

	1	2	3	4	5	ANOVA significance level	Tukey–Kramer pairwise comparisons
Level of agreement regarding primary national GPO							
GPO provides demonstrable cost savings and margin improvement	1.93	2.77	1.88	2.01	2.23	<0.001	2 > 1, 3, 4, 5
Savings flow from information technology	2.24	2.26	2.03	2.12	2.21	n.s	
Savings flow from shareholder dividends	2.45	2.38	2.57	2.25	2.30	n.s	
Savings flow from lower prices	2.00	2.59	2.10	1.95	2.25	<0.05	2 > 4
Savings flow from administrative fees shared back with hospital	2.14	2.20	2.08	1.78	2.11	<0.06	5 > 4
Savings flow from GPOs providing the market price point	1.90	2.43	2.00	1.87	2.02	n.s	
Savings flow from standardizing contracts	2.07	2.84	1.95	2.03	2.08	<0.001	2 > 1, 3, 4, 5
Savings flow from economies of centralized staffing	2.31	2.53	2.21	2.14	2.24	n.s	

(continued)

Table 8.3 (continued)

	1	2	3	4	5	ANOVA significance level	Tukey–Kramer pairwise comparisons
Level of agreement regarding primary national GPO contracts for PPIs							
GPO gets excellent prices overall	2.10	2.73	2.23	2.31	2.18	n.s	
GPO gets excellent prices through standardization and compliance to dual-source contracts	2.03	2.83	2.36	2.15	2.09	< 0.003	2 > 1, 4, 5
GPO collects high administrative fees on national contracts for these items	2.86	2.35	2.42	2.37	2.45	n.s	
GPO has increased our knowledge of innovative medical devices & manufacturers	2.38	2.35	2.59	2.20	2.43	n.s	
GPO actively involved in helping us convert to the contract for these items	2.07	2.37	2.44	2.38	2.47	n.s	
GPO gets excellent prices through standardization and compliance to sole-source contracts	2.24	2.61	2.23	2.25	2.12	n.s	

(continued)

Table 8.3 (continued)

	1	2	3	4	5	ANOVA significance level	Tukey–Kramer pairwise comparisons
Hospital/system can get better prices for preference items than those obtained through the GPO contract	2.66	2.83	2.65	2.78	2.46	n.s	
GPO provides assistance negotiating local custom contracts	2.17	2.57	2.28	2.52	2.42	n.s	
Our physicians dislike sole-source contracts for PPIs	2.41	2.46	2.61	2.64	2.38	n.s	
GPO committed contracts for multi-vendor multi-product portfolios are valuable	1.93	2.14	1.95	1.98	1.96	n.s	
GPO has blocked access to innovative medical devices & manufacturers	2.86	2.94	2.88	2.70	2.93	n.s	
GPO committed contracts for single-vendor multi-product portfolios are valuable	1.76	2.31	2.13	1.98	1.95	n.s	
Our physicians prefer dual/multi-source contracts for these items	2.31	2.14	2.49	2.23	2.11	n.s	

Rating Measure = 1 = Strongly Disagree; 2 = Disagree; 3 = Neither Disagree Nor Agree; 4 = Agree; 5 = Strongly Agree

Table 8.4 Perceived value of newer services offered by GPOs—by national GPO

	GPO					ANOVA significance level	Tukey–Kramer pairwise comparisons
	1	2	3	4	5		
Revenue cycle	2.76	2.88	2.91	2.71	2.75	n.s	
Purchased services	2.66	2.19	2.79	2.35	2.35	<0.06	3 > 2, 4, 5
Data analytics	2.52	2.51	2.40	2.25	2.25	n.s	
Benchmark data	2.21	2.56	2.56	2.27	2.18	n.s	
Clinical outcomes data	2.66	2.80	2.79	2.44	2.31	<0.014	2, 3 > 5

Rating Measure: 1 = Strongly Disagree; 2 = Disagree; 3 = Neither Disagree Nor Agree; 4 = Agree; 5 = Strongly Agree

Satisfaction with GPO Services

Table 8.5 examines the level of hospital satisfaction with their national GPO across a variety of services provided. Members of GPO 2 express higher overall satisfaction with their purchasing groups. This general evaluation carries over to relatively superior evaluations on several specific GPO services: multi-source contracts for PPIs, multi-source contracts for commodities, lowest price in GPO contracts, group purchasing, and price discounts. That same particular GPO scores significantly higher than two of the other GPOs on three other services: clinical improvement initiatives, local clinician input on PPIs, and services supporting prevention and personalized medicine. GPO 5 also receives higher evaluations relative to two other GPOs on the following services: clinical improvement initiatives, and multi-source contracts for PPIs. For many other items, there is only a single significant pairwise comparison in satisfaction scores.

However, just as one particular GPO scores consistently higher than the others on many dimensions, so also do two GPOs (GPO1, GPO 4)

Table 8.5 Hospital satisfaction with national GPO across variety of services—by national GPO

	GPO					ANOVA significance level	Tukey–Kramer pairwise comparisons
	1	2	3	4	5		
Overall, I am satisfied with primary national GPO	2.41	2.89	2.14	1.89	2.29	<0.001	2 > 3, 4, 5 5 > 4
Clinical improvement initiatives	2.14	3.20	2.81	2.44	2.99	<0.001	2, 5 > 1, 4
Consulting services	3.07	2.93	2.94	2.42	2.67	<0.02	1, 2, 3 > 4
Clinical expertise & data support for value analysis	2.83	3.34	3.13	2.59	3.03	<0.002	2, 3, 5 > 4
Direct input to product & service selection	2.82	2.96	3.01	2.32	2.57	<0.002	2, 3 > 4
Group purchasing and price discounts	3.52	4.09	3.49	3.15	3.57	<0.001	2 > 3, 4, 5 > 4
Implant procurement auditing of costs/units used	2.24	2.76	2.39	2.10	2.20	<0.10	2 > 4
Local input from clinicians for preference items	1.90	2.73	2.45	2.06	2.41	<0.01	2 > 1, 4
Multi-source contracts for commodity items	2.83	3.67	3.15	2.90	3.14	<0.001	2 > 1, 4, 5
Operational improvements	2.24	2.71	2.29	2.01	2.39	<0.04	2 > 4

(continued)

Table 8.5 (continued)

	GPO					ANOVA significance level	Tukey–Kramer pairwise comparisons
	1	2	3	4	5		
Technology assessment and advisory services	2.14	2.76	2.63	2.11	2.31	<0.02	2, 3 > 4
True strategic partnership with hospital	2.93	3.27	3.03	2.50	2.85	<0.002	2, 3, 5 > 4
Services to support prevention, personalization of medicine	1.69	2.49	2.14	1.76	2.02	<0.010	2 > 4 1 < 2
Predictive analytics to make better decisions around cost, quality and outcomes	2.48	2.93	2.84	2.43	2.82	<0.05	5 > 4
Multi-source contracts for PPIs	2.24	3.70	2.96	2.68	3.02	<0.001	2 > 1, 3, 4, 5 5 > 1, 4
Member's control and input on alliance direction	3.10	2.70	2.82	2.18	2.49	<0.001	1, 2, 3 > 4
Item master maintenance	2.10	2.72	2.35	2.03	2.25	<0.09	2 > 4
Benchmark with peer hospitals and hospital systems	2.96	2.83	2.81	2.82	2.91	n.s	
Bring innovative products to our attention	2.96	2.99	2.75	2.35	2.69	<0.02	2 > 4
Safety improvement initiatives	2.55	2.84	2.47	2.26	2.49		

(continued)

Table 8.5   (continued)

	GPO					ANOVA significance level	Tukey–Kramer pairwise comparisons
	1	2	3	4	5		
Lowest price in GPO contracts	2.66	3.94	2.89	2.72	3.02	<0.001	2 > 1, 3, 4, 5

Rating Measure: 1 = Very Dissatisfied; 2 = Somewhat Dissatisfied; 3 = Neither Dissatisfied Nor Satisfied; 4 = Somewhat Satisfied; 5 = Very Satisfied

score significantly lower than other GPOs on some dimensions. This is evident for the following services: clinical improvement initiatives, multi-source contracts for PPIs, and (to some extent), technology assessment and lowest price in GPO contracts.

Tables 8.3 and 8.5 also address the GPOs' agency role in acting on behalf of their hospital members. There are few reported differences among the national GPO being named as a "strategic partner" with their members (see Table 8.5). Data from the 2014 survey show that, overall, there was a slight increase in hospitals reporting such partnerships with their GPO.[19] There are also no differences among GPOs in actively helping their members with contract conversion and local customized contract negotiation (see Table 8.3). In sum, the data suggest that all GPOs serve as the hospital's agents.

Discussion

The findings presented here address the topics raised in the chapter's introduction. First, they present national data on GPO performance measures that are of interest to their hospital customers and that can be used for benchmarking purposes. Second, they include tests of significance as to whether or not GPOs differ in their performance on these dimensions. Third, they include head-to-head assessments of the level of satisfaction hospital members express about their GPO.

The findings clearly speak to the issue of "commoditization." One GPO (GPO 2) stands out favorably on many performance dimensions. Most of the other GPOs are bunched together on performance, while one or two GPOs are occasional laggards. Overall, one GPO is distinguished, while the remaining four are fairly similar.

What might explain this? First, the differences in the size of the hospitals in the standout GPO may play a role. The hospitals are smaller; they likely derive a greater benefit from contracting through the national GPO as opposed to contracting on their own (where they might have less bargaining clout due to their smaller size). Second, these hospitals have a particular ownership structure that may exert greater command-and-control over their purchasing behavior. The GPO may have different requirements regarding contract adherence and utilization: the hospitals route a higher percentage of purchases through this national GPO across all product categories. Purchases are likely routed through the national GPO and away from regional and local GPOs (to which they are less likely to belong to). The (slightly) higher performance of GPO 2 suggests that hospitals and GPOs might mutually benefit (in terms of satisfaction and savings) from exerting greater centralized control over purchasing.

That said, there is much less to differentiate the remaining four national GPOs. Tables 8.2–8.5 are startling in terms of how few significant differences there are—either overall or between specific pairs of GPOs. There are not many significant differences among GPOs in terms of PPI contracting and pricing, the value provided by newer-generation GPO services, the types of savings generated by the GPO, and satisfaction levels with many GPO services. One should remember, however, that these data were gathered in 2014. Since that time, the GPOs have developed more extensive service offerings (see Chapter 3) that account for an increasing share of their revenues. The fact that hospitals are purchasing these services suggests the services add value and may serve as differentiators.

So, to return to the title of this Chapter, are GPOs differentiated or commoditized? The answer may be "yes." Or, as the late comedian George Carlin would say, "definitely no yeah." Moreover, these results seem stable. Similar results were obtained over a decade ago.[20]

The evidence here provides mixed, and somewhat contradictory evidence on the possible measures of "*commoditization*" proposed at the beginning of this chapter. On the one hand, hospitals exhibit long tenure with their national GPO, suggesting perhaps brand loyalty. On the other hand, they exhibit long tenure with their regional and local GPOs too, so they are brand loyal to multiple groups.[21] Moreover, this multi-brand loyalty is still consistent with hospitals adding or dropping GPO affiliations on a regular basis.

The findings also speak (at least indirectly) to the issue of "*disintermediation*." There are several supporting threads of evidence to support the conclusion that this threat is not imminent. The data in Table 8.1 show that GPO affiliations have long tenures, suggesting the membership is "sticky." Moreover, hospitals still route a high level of purchases (~70%)

through their GPOs, although in recent years some of that GPO-mediated spending has shifted to regional and local alliances. However, these regional and local alliances are typically affiliates of the national GPO, thus keeping most of the spending "in-house" while simultaneously providing a modicum of contracting flexibility to members. Third, other data show that VPMMs' levels of satisfaction with their GPO have not altered much over a decade; on some performance dimensions, satisfaction has actually increased.[22]

Finally, the findings speak to the issue of *"agency"* raised in Chapter 2. The survey findings from 2004 and 2014 consistently indicate hospitals believe that (1) they have a strategic partnership with their national GPO, (2) their GPO acts in their interests, and (3) they are satisfied with their GPO's performance. Conversely, there is no evidence from the survey or from the historical chronicle that GPOs serve the suppliers or act as their agents.

Notes

1. Lawton R. Burns and Allison Briggs. "Hospital Purchasing Alliances: Ten Years After," *Health Care Management Review* 45(3) (2020): 185–195. Lawton R. Burns and Andrew Lee. "Group Purchasing Organizations (GPOs): Issues and Evidence," *Health Care Management Review* 33(3): 203–215. 2008.
2. Lawton R. Burns. Presentation to the Health Industry Group Purchasing Association Annual Meeting. October 2008.
3. Mark Thill. "GPO Differentiation: The Total Package," *Repertoire* (April 2006): 50-58. Mark Thill. "GPO Differentiation: The Real Deal," *Journal of Healthcare Contracting* (March/April 2006, May/June 2006). Available online at: http://www.jhconline.com/?s=gpo+differentiation+real+deal. Accessed on April 13, 2020. Mark Thill. "What Makes a GPO Stand Out From the Others?" *Journal of Healthcare Contracting* (March/April 2008): 30–42.
4. Lawton R. Burns, J. Andrew Lee, Eric T. Bradlow, and Anthony C. Antonacci. "Surgeon Evaluation of Suture and Endo-Mechanical Products," *Journal of Surgical Research* 141 (2007): 220–233. Lawton R. Burns, Michael Housman, Robert Booth, and Aaron Koenig. "Implant Vendors and Hospitals: Competing Influences over Product Choice by Orthopedic Surgeons," *Health Care Management Review* 34(1) (2009): 2–18. Lawton R. Burns, Michael Housman, Robert Booth, and Aaron Koenig. "Physician Preference Items: What Factors Matter to Surgeons? Does the Vendor Matter?" *Medical Devices: Evidence and Research* 11 (2018): 39–49.
5. Allen Dobson, Steve Heath, Phap-Hoa Luu et al. *A 2018 Update of Cost Savings and Marketplace Analysis of the Group Purchasing Industry* (Washington, D.C.: Dobson DaVanzo Associates, April 16, 2019).

6. David Balat."Middle Men in Healthcare Creating High Costs"(2018). Available online at: https://davidbalat.com/middle-men-in-healthcare-creating-high-costs/. Accessed on March 25, 2022. Pricewaterhouse Coopers. *Top Health Industry Issues of 2018* (PwC Health Research Institute, 2017).

7. If the threat of disruption by tech start-ups is true, then comparative performance data on one GPO versus another GPO might be viewed as anachronistic. However, the threat of disruption in healthcare has been overblown for decades.

8. "Report: Medtech Industry Must Differentiate to Avoid Commoditization." Available online at: https://www.odtmag.com/contents/view_breaking-news/2014-10-09/report-medtech-industry-must-differentiate-to/. Accessed on March 25, 2022.

9. Kurt Kruger and Max Kruger. "The Medical Device Sector," in Lawton R. Burns (Ed.), *The Business of Healthcare Innovation—Third Edition.* (Cambridge, UK: Cambridge University Press, 2020). Chapter 6.

10. Lawton R. Burns, J. Andrew Lee, Eric T. Bradlow, and Anthony C. Antonacci. "Surgeon Evaluation of Suture and Endo-Mechanical Products." *Journal of Surgical Research* 141 (2007): 220–233. Lawton R. Burns, Michael Housman, Robert Booth, and Aaron Koenig. "Implant Vendors and Hospitals: Competing Influences over Product Choice by Orthopedic Surgeons." *Health Care Management Review* 34(1) (2009): 2–18. Lawton R. Burns, Michael Housman, Robert Booth, and Aaron Koenig. "Physician Preference Items: What Factors Matter to Surgeons? Does the Vendor Matter?" *Medical Devices: Evidence and Research* 11 (2018): 39–49.

11. United States Government Accountability Office. *Group Purchasing Organizations: Services Provided to Customers and Initiatives Regarding Their Business Practices.* GAO-10-738 (Washington, D.C.: GAO, August 2010): Table 2, page 9.

12. Lawton R. Burns. Presentation to Health Industry Group Purchasing Association (HIGPA), October 2008.

13. Alan Cherry. "Understanding Purchasing Coalitions and Current Trends," *The Journal of Healthcare Contracting* 14(5) (2017): 12–19. Rick Conlin. *The Unprecedented GPO Environment and its Impact to your Supply Chain.* Advisory Board Webinar. Ken Graves, Kevin Grabenstatter, and Jonas Funk (2017). "Time for Medtechs to Rethink GPOs?" *The MedTech Strategist* (October 2017): 38–43.

14. To be sure, hospitals can simultaneously (a) belong to one or more national GPOs, (b) belong to regional and/or local GPOs (often affiliated with their national alliances), and (c) contract on their own. However, there are no known databases of national, regional, or local alliances. We acknowledge that reliance on the national GPO can introduce bias in the performance measures reported (issue addressed later in chapter).

15. Lawton R. Burns and Allison Briggs. "Hospital Purchasing Alliances: Ten Years After," *Health Care Management Review* 45(3) (2020): 186–195.

16. Tukey-Kramer tests are conducted in tandem with analysis of variance (ANOVA). ANOVA tests discern whether there are any significant differences among the GPOs. Tukey tests are based on the studentized range distribution (t-tests) to discern which GPOs are different from which other GPOs in a head-to-head comparison of means. In conducting these significance tests, we employ the Bonferroni correction for multiple comparisons. The means scores are adjusted using AHA data on the hospital's characteristics.

17. We have excluded data on hospital ownership/governance (e.g., nonprofit versus for-profit) since that would help to identify the specific GPO.

18. Lawton R. Burns and Allison Briggs. "Hospital Purchasing Alliances: Ten Years After," *Health Care Management Review* 45(3) (2020): 186–195.

19. Lawton R. Burns and Allison Briggs. "Hospital Purchasing Alliances: Ten Years After," *Health Care Management Review* 45(3) (2020): 186–195.

20. Lawton R. Burns. Presentation to the Health Industry Group Purchasing Association Annual Meeting. October 2008.

21. Lawton R. Burns and Allison Briggs. "Hospital Purchasing Alliances: Ten Years After," *Health Care Management Review* 45(3) (2020): 186–195. See Table 1.

22. Lawton R. Burns and Allison Briggs. "Hospital Purchasing Alliances: Ten Years After," *Health Care Management Review* 45(3) (2020): 186–195.

Part III

Pharmacy Benefit Managers (PBMs)

9

PBMs and the Ecosystem of Prescription Drug Benefit Contracting

Introduction

Chapters 3–8 dealt with the role of GPO intermediaries in the *institutional* supply chain—i.e., the channels that lead from product manufacturers down to the institutions the provide healthcare (e.g., hospitals). These products include medical-surgical supplies, medical devices and other physician preference items, and certain types of pharmaceuticals (e.g., drugs that deal with sepsis, large molecule biologics that must be infused). This chapter and Chapters 10–13, by contrast, deal with the role of pharmacy benefit manager (PBM) intermediaries in the *retail* supply chain—i.e., the channels that lead from product manufacturers down to retail pharmacies, mail-order pharmacies, and big-box retailers. This chain involves a narrower range of products—primarily small-molecule pharmaceuticals that are taken orally by patients, large molecule drugs that are infused or injected, and (more recently) specialty pharmaceuticals.

These latter chapters deal with a broader and more diverse set of players. Like Chapters 3–8, these include the product manufacturers and wholesalers; unlike Chapters 3–8, they also include insurers (managed care organizations, or MCOs), employers, and pharmacies. As a result of the greater number of players, there are also more intermediaries to consider. There are buying intermediaries serving not only the MCOs, but also the employers and the pharmacies. Hearkening back to the preceding section of this book, these intermediaries function much in the same way as GPOs: aggregate the

L. R. Burns, *The Healthcare Value Chain*,
https://doi.org/10.1007/978-3-031-10739-9_9

volume of drugs purchased and channel the specific drug products selected to negotiate lower prices.

Like the GPOs, the PBMs are at the center of these supply chains. Also like the GPOs, the PBMs do not act as buyers, handlers, or purchasers of any products; instead, they are contracting entities serving as agents for others downstream (e.g., the MCOs and employers). Thus, contracts and contracting strategies are key topics to be addressed. Like the GPOs, the PBMs are also shrouded in mystery and secrecy. This is partly a function of the complex ecosystem that characterizes the retail chain; it is also partly due to the large number of contracts struck between the large number of players. Finally, paralleling the GPOs, the PBMs have been the subject of considerable scrutiny by the U.S. Government (in the form of Congressional hearings and Federal reports), growing suspicion, and accusations by certain stakeholders.

To understand PBMs, one needs to first understand the ecosystem in which they operate.[1] This chapter first outlines the two players for which PBMs often act as agents (the employers and the MCOs) and the two sets of benefits offered to employees (health plan enrollees): medical and pharmacy. The discussion then turns to the key elements of prescription drug benefit plans and the functions that PBMs perform here. Given the rising utilization and cost of pharmaceuticals, the chapter next considers the role of all three players in cost-sharing with health plan enrollees.

Given the complexity of the retail supply chain and the abundance of technical terms used to capture it, the shaded insert below provides some helpful definitions. Such terminology populates the technical literature and legal proceedings often brought against the PBMs. Some of these terms derive from legislation concerning the Employee Retirement Income Security Act (ERISA, 1974).

Definitions of Terms

- *ERISA Plan Sponsor*: defined in Sect. 3(16) of ERISA as (i) the employer in the case of an employee benefit plan established or maintained by a single employer, (ii) the employee organization in the case of a plan established or maintained by an employee organization, or (iii) in the case of a plan established or maintained by two or more employers or jointly by one or more employers and one or more employee organizations, the association, committee, joint board of trustees, or other similar group of representatives of the parties who establish or maintain the plan.
- *ERISA-Covered Health Plans*: health benefit plans sponsored by employers that provide insurance coverage for employees (ERISA plan participants, see below), including coverage for prescription medications.

- *ERISA Plan Participants*: the employees covered under the employers' ERISA plans.
- *ERISA Fiduciary*: According to the U.S. Department of Labor, ERISA protects a plan's assets by requiring that those persons or entities who exercise discretionary control or authority over plan management or plan assets, anyone with discretionary authority or responsibility for the administration of a plan, or anyone who provides investment advice to a plan for compensation or has any authority or responsibility to do so, are subject to fiduciary responsibilities. Plan fiduciaries include, for example, plan trustees, plan administrators, and members of a plan's investment committee.[2]
- *Health Insurers*: third-parties that underwrite and/or administer health insurance plans on behalf of ERISA Plans sponsored by employers, who pay premiums and/or administrative fees to the insurers to do so.
- *Deductibles*: a fixed dollar amount that a health plan participant must pay out-of-pocket annually for medical and/or prescription drug costs before the participant's plan will issue healthcare reimbursements.
- *Percentage Coinsurance Payments*: a fixed percentage of the cost of a healthcare service or drug provided that the plan participant must pay. For a prescription drug, the amount is a percentage of the list price or the rate negotiated between the PBM and the pharmacy.
- *Out-of-Pocket Payments*: the payments for deductibles and coinsurance (whether flat or percentage) that ERISA plan participants are responsible for making when filling a prescription at a pharmacy.
- *PBMs (pharmacy benefit managers)*: third-party administrators that manage the pharmacy and prescription drug benefits on behalf of various entities that provide healthcare benefits, including ERISA Plan Sponsors and health insurers.
- *Clients*: those who contract with the PBMs, including: ERISA Plan Sponsors (employers), health insurers, and unions (also referred to collectively as "plans").
- *Rebates*: percentage discounts on a drug's list price (usually wholesale average cost, or WAC) negotiated by a PBM on behalf of clients (employers, health plans) and payable to the PBM by the manufacturer on a periodic basis, based on each prescription filled over a certain period of time (usually three months). Such rebates are explicated more fully later on in this chapter.
- *Fees*: Payments paid by manufacturers to PBMs in addition to rebates. These include: (a) administrative fees for administering the rebate program, also calculated as a percent of a drug's list price; (b) price protection payments, i.e., the amount by which the actual WAC price increases set by manufacturers exceed a stipulated, allowed ("base") WAC price increase negotiated by the PBM; and (c) other fees for formulary access, market share performance, provider education, research, data access, and other purposes. Such fees are described more fully later on in this chapter.
- *Formularies*: list of drugs covered by health plans, and used to manage the utilization of drugs by ERISA plan participants and control the drug costs borne by the ERISA plans and/or insurers.
- *List Price*: the price set directly and published by the manufacturer for a drug, usually based on wholesale average cost (WAC).

- *Net Price*: The price that results from subtracting the invoice (benchmark) price set by the manufacturer and the rebates it pays to the PBM.
- *Plan Design & Administration*: establishing and maintaining the varying benefit designs that plan sponsors choose. Plans differ according to their benefit levels, drug coverage, copayment and coinsurance amounts, and the number of drug tiers.[3]
- *Contractual Framework*: In legal proceedings, this framework usually encompasses the common contracts, contract amendments, contract features and structures, rebates, and fees that pharmaceutical manufacturers negotiate with each PBM.

Variation Reigns

Not only are there multiple players in the retail supply chain, but these players are quite diverse. Each of the various entities—the ERISA Plan Sponsors, ERISA plan participants, the health insurers, the PBMs, the pharmaceutical manufacturers, the retail pharmacies—have contractual relationships that are highly differentiated and highly individualized across their membership. For example, the ERISA Plan Sponsors differ in the weights (importance) they assign different objectives in healthcare benefit coverage provided to participants, including balancing the goals of *cost*, *quality*, and *access*. The different weighting of these objectives manifests itself in the types of health plans offered to their employees. The ERISA Plan Participants (employees) also differ in the weights (importance) they assign to the goals of cost, quality, and access—which manifests itself in the types of health plan choices they make.

The contracts between the ERISA Plan Sponsors, health insurers, and ERISA plan participants can and do vary in terms of the benefits offered, the amounts contributed by the employer to coverage, and the degree of cost-sharing borne by the ERISA plan participants. The dyadic contracts between ERISA Plan Sponsors, health insurers, and PBMs can and do vary in terms of their prescription drug benefit designs, formulary development and management, and the degree to which rebates negotiated by the PBM with the manufacturer are passed down to the ERISA Plan Sponsor. Moreover, the health insurers and PBMs develop several proprietary formularies—which regulate *access* to specific drugs, as well as determine employee *cost*-sharing—to meet the specific needs and preferences of their ERISA Plan Sponsors. Health insurers and PBMs make independent drug evaluations and formulary coverage decisions based on their specific insurance plans and the needs of ERISA Plan Sponsors. They typically develop and manage several different formularies to meet different clients' needs.

In sum, there is enormous (a) variability in health plan options offered to participants by ERISA Plan Sponsors, (b) variability in choice among these health plan options by participants, (c) variability in premium and cost-sharing levels associated with participants' choices of health plans, and (d) variability in the large number of ERISA Plan Sponsors and the large number of health insurers engaged in contractual networks with a given PBM. Moreover, these sources of variation themselves vary (change) over time and over players in the drug channel. Given this variation, there is likely to be enormous variability in the amounts paid by ERISA plan participants for a given drug.

Why is all of this important? Such variation makes it difficult, if not impossible, to draw broad generalizations (and thus conclusions) regarding PBMs and their contractual strategies. Such variation also makes it difficult to lump together all PBMs, all ERISA plans, and/or all ERISA participants into one homogeneous group with common interests. Nevertheless, class action lawsuits filed against the PBMs attempt to show that all plaintiffs (e.g., ERISA participants, independent pharmacies) have been harmed in the same way by the PBMs and their trading partners (e.g., pharmaceutical manufacturers).[4]

Understanding Employer Health Coverage

To attract more and better-qualified labor, employers offer prospective employees a combination of salary and benefits. Together, salary and benefits are considered the employee's total compensation and the employee's money.[5] Employer payments for health insurance premiums ultimately come out of what would otherwise have been paid to workers as money wages. In the mid-1990s, consultants estimated that 88% of premiums were offset by money wage reductions; others reported a range of 56–90% depending on the industry.[6] Thus, it is the employee and not the employer who is paying for the health insurance premium. For workers who obtain insurance coverage through their workplace, the employers basically act as the employees' insurance agent. How well they play that role is another issue.

Employees have the discretion to accept the total compensation package in return for contributing their labor. However, it is financially disadvantageous for employees to forego the health insurance coverage since their wages would not rise, they save on their income and payroll taxes, and they would have to spend more on their own to obtain coverage without the group discount.[7] Employees also have discretion in determining the mix of the total compensation going to the various components of the benefit package. Employer decisions on the benefit packages they offer and the wage-benefit tradeoffs partially reflect the preferences of their employees. Employees offered a wider choice via a flexible "cafeteria-style" plan of compensation pay for this wider choice via higher (e.g., 10%) insurance premiums. In general, employee choice of benefits is financed by lower take-home pay, less generous health insurance benefits, and/or reductions in other benefits.[8]

Following ERISA, the employee's benefit package can be simply summarized here as a mix of retirement plan benefits and "health and welfare plan" benefits.[9] The latter center on the provision of group health plans that provide medical care benefits for ERISA plan participants or their dependents.[10] The latter can also include not only medical and drug insurance coverage, but also life, disability, and long-term care insurance, as well as other types of health coverage (dental, vision).[11] According to data from the Bureau of Labor Statistics, insurance benefits represented 7–9% (depending on firm size) of total worker compensation in 2016.[12] Employers typically segment the specialists who set the employees' compensation (as applied to cash wages) from the specialists who set benefits policies.[13] The result is a lack of coordination between the two types of compensation.

Variation in Employer Financing of Health Plan Coverage

Employers may sponsor their health insurance plans in two ways: (a) offer a fully-insured plan whereby the employer purchases coverage from a health insurer who then bears the risk, or (b) offer a self-insured plan where the employer bears the risk and the insurer serves as a third-party administrator (TPA) that administers the benefits, processes and pays the claims, and assembles the provider network under "administrative services only" (ASO) contracts. Between 2007 and 2019, a higher percentage of covered workers were employed by firms that self-insured and offered their own "self-funded plans" (see Fig. 9.1).[14]

Medical and Pharmacy Benefit Contracting by Employers

Regardless of whether they are fully- or self-insured, employers can arrange for the management of drug benefits in two different ways. First, they can

Percentage of Covered Workers Enrolled in a Self-Funded Plan, by Firm Size, 1999-2019

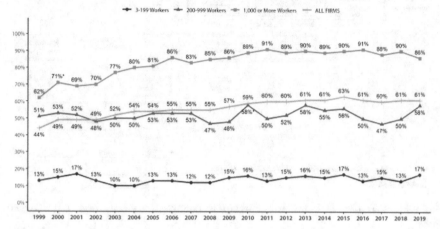

* Estimate is statistically different from estimate for the previous year shown (p < .05).
NOTE: Figure includes covered workers enrolled in partially or completely self-funded plans. Overall, 61% of covered workers are in a partially or completely self-funded plan in 2019. Due to a change in the survey questionnaire, funding status was not asked of firms with conventional plans in 2006; therefore, conventional plan funding status is not included in the averages in this figure for 2006. See the glossary at the end of Section 10 for definitions of self-funded, fully-insured, and level-funded premium plans.
SOURCE: KFF Employer Health Benefits Survey, 2018-2019; Kaiser/HRET Survey of Employer-Sponsored Health Benefits, 1999-2017

Fig. 9.1 Percentage of workers in self-funded employer plans

assign the management of both benefits to a health insurer; the insurer usually manages the medical benefit and contracts with a PBM for the drug benefit (see Fig. 9.2). Second, employers can contract with health insurers for the medical benefit and contract separately with PBMs for the pharmacy benefit—this arrangement is referred to as a "carve-out" (see Fig. 9.3). In both cases, health insurers act as agents of the employer, while the PBMs act as agents of the insurers (see Fig. 9.4).

A majority (81%) of smaller employers (less than 1,000 employees) contract for both benefits with their health insurer; a near majority of medium-sized employers (1,000–5,000 employees) contract for both benefits with their health insurer; a majority (59%) of large employers (5,000+ employees) contract separately and directly with a PBM for the pharmacy benefit (data for 2017).[15]

Some large insurers have kept the PBM function in-house or vertically integrated to acquire a PBM. This is evident from the recent mergers of (a) CVS with Aetna and (b) Express Scripts with Cigna (see Chapter 13). Many larger insurers perform several PBM functions in house (e.g., formulary management) while outsourcing others.

There is thus, considerable variability among ERISA Plan Sponsors in the degree to which they contract with health insurers and PBMs for the

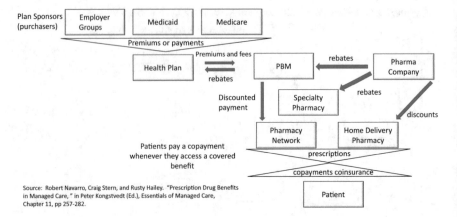

Fig. 9.2 "Carve-in" drug benefit coverage to health plan, which then contracts with PBM

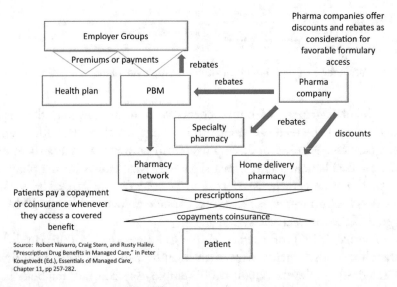

Fig. 9.3 "Carve Out" drug benefit coverage directly to PBM

Fig. 9.4 Agency relationships in the retail pharmaceutical supply chain

medical and pharmacy benefits offered to employees. Some of this variability is detailed in the breakout section below.

It is important to note that the above discussion of medical and pharmacy benefits applies to enrollees with commercial insurance coverage. There is a somewhat parallel separation of medical and pharmacy benefits in the Medicare population. Part B of Medicare (enacted in 1965) covers the medical benefit, which includes most physician-administered drugs that are infused or injected; Part D of Medicare (enacted in 2003) covers the pharmacy benefit, which covers most self-administered drugs taken orally. Due to the growth in the Medicare population and their use of drug therapies, Part D spending now accounts for roughly one-third of all retail drug expenditures.[16] While these two parts (benefits) are administered separately for those with fee-for-service Medicare coverage, they are combined in Medicare Advantage plans.

Variation Among ERISA Plan Sponsors in Insourcing/Outsourcing PBM Contracting

One of the basic building blocks of drug benefit design is deciding whether, and how to integrate drug benefits with the medical benefit. When the drug benefit is carved-in, the employer contracts directly with their health plan for both medical and drug benefit management and administration. The drug benefit may be administered directly by the health plan-owned PBM, or the health plan contracts with a PBM to handle the drug benefit administration. Conversely, when the drug benefit is carved out, the employer contracts with the PBM to administer the drug benefit, either directly or via their health plan, but under a separate contract. While employers may contract with more than one medical insurance plan in a carve-out model, they typically require all of them to use one PBM (thereby preventing enrollee selection on the basis of drug formularies or pharmacies).

According to the 2018 PBM Customer Satisfaction Report conducted by the Pharmacy Benefit Management Institute (PBMI),[17] the majority of employers (72%) contract with their PBM directly, and 75% reported having a self-insured plan. Self-insured employers have more financial risk and responsibility and usually play a more active role in the day-to-day management of their pharmacy benefit programs. Insurance carriers and managed care organizations hold most of the financial risk for fully insured pharmacy benefit plans.

A majority (63%) carved out the drug benefit. That is, the management of the drug benefit is separate from the management of the medical benefit, using two different entities or two separate contracts to administer the benefits. Irrespective of whether employers chose a carved-in or a carved out drug benefit, one thing is clear—most respondents had no plans to change their carve-in or carve-out status. Large employers were more likely to carve out pharmacy benefits than were smaller employers (74% and 56%, respectively). However, there were no differences by employer size in plans to make changes to what was currently in place.

A majority (60%) of employers reported carving out their pharmacy benefit to a different vendor from their medical benefit; the remaining 40% said that they procure pharmacy and medical benefits from the same vendor. Additionally, most (74%) offered a specialty drug benefit managed by the same PBM that provides traditional pharmacy benefit management services.[18]

According to PBMI, consultants are rated by 26% of employers as being the most influential in evaluating drug benefit design. This represents a small decline over the last few years of consultants being reported as most influential (36% in 2016, 30% in 2017). There is no discernible pattern in others that might be gaining or losing influence. There are differences in the most influential group by employer size. Large employers more frequently reported consultants, their PBM, their health plan, and employee benefits committee as most influential when compared to smaller employers. Smaller employers were more likely to report brokers, senior management, and finance as influential.

Regardless of whether pharmacy benefits are "carved into" the health plan or "carved out" separately to a PBM, the goals of the ERISA Plan Sponsor are the same: reduce overall cost, improve quality of care, and increase access to services. These are the three goals of the "iron triangle." However, different ERISA Plan Sponsors may weigh these goals differently and may design health plan options that assign different weights to these goals. As outlined below, some health plan options for the medical benefit may focus on broader access to providers but with higher costs to enrollees; other health plan options may narrow provider network access but lower the costs to enrollees. The same tradeoff may be found in the pharmacy benefit. Some sponsors may try to limit access to certain drugs and increase enrollee cost-sharing in order to reduce expenditures, while other sponsors (e.g., unions) may broaden access to more drugs and limit cost-sharing while incurring higher expenditures.

Since the advent of managed care in the 1980s and 1990s, ERISA Plan Sponsors and health insurers have focused much of their efforts on cost containment. Both parties seek to manage drug expenditures using two similar techniques: manage supply costs both upstream and downstream, and manage utilization demand downstream. The former includes the negotiation of product discounts/rebates with pharmaceutical manufacturers upstream, and the negotiation of dispensing fees and reimbursement of the drug's cost with retail pharmacies downstream. Utilization management involves cost-sharing mechanisms for ERISA plan participants, including deductibles, coinsurance, and high-deductible health plans (HDHPs) which may be accompanied by a savings option (HDHP-SO); these represent the major changes in pharmacy benefit design over the past two decades.

Pharmacy benefit management activities have grown in importance as the percentage share of national healthcare expenditures paid out-of-pocket by consumers has decreased and the share paid by third-party payers (both public and private insurers) has increased. Moreover, ERISA Plan Sponsors implement and enforce the pharmacy benefit design using a host of additional techniques, including Pharmacy and Therapeutics (P&T) Committees and formulary development and management practices. For example, the advent of expensive specialty pharmaceuticals has led some employers to delay placing them on their formularies (until their PBM partners can vet them), while others—particulary the self-insured employers—have purchased "stop-loss" insurance to protect against catastrophic financial losses.[19] However, the implementation of these pharmacy benefit management techniques differs across ERISA plan sponsors and the health insurers and PBMs with whom they partner—depending on the tradeoffs they wish to make in cost, quality, and access.[20] These variations are documented in detail below.

The Flow of Products and Payments for Branded Drugs in the Retail Channel

Figures 9.2 and 9.3 provide some introduction to two of the three flows in any supply chain: the flow of products and the flow of money. The former is much easier to understand than the latter. This section explicates these flows and the manifold prices charged in this channel (see Fig. 9.5).

Product Flow

As in the institutional channel where GPOs operate, products sold to the retail channel originate with the (pharmaceutical, in this case) manufacturers. They often sell their products indirectly through wholesalers, who then re-sell and distribute the drugs to the pharmacies and other locations; they can also sell directly to chain and "big box" retailers. Wholesalers take delivery

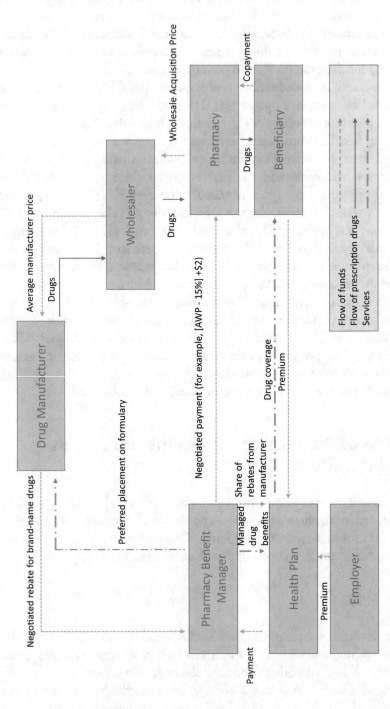

Fig. 9.5 Flow of products and money for branded drugs in the retail channel

and physical possession of these products and house them in large, auto-mated warehouses. During the last twenty-five years of the twentieth century, the number of drug wholesalers coalesced from approximately 200 down to 50. Such mergers involved the physical consolidation and automation of warehouses to gain scale economies.[21] As with the GPOs, these mergers were partly occasioned by increasing pressures to reduce healthcare costs and provide other efficiencies to trading partners downstream. Additional consolidation at the turn of the millennium resulted in three main players (McKesson, Cardinal, and AmerisourceBergen). They then deliver to retail (and institutional) channels downstream on an as-needed ("just in time") basis. For most players downstream, including the mail-order pharmacies operated by PBMs, the wholesalers act as an inventory buffer. ERISA plan beneficiaries who purchase their drugs at pharmacies and other retailers serve as the final link in the product chain. All of this activity is portrayed using the solid lines on the right side of Fig. 9.5.

Money Flow

The dashed lines on the right side of Fig. 9.5 depict the flow of money among these participants. For simplicity, these flows are broken out as follows:

Pharmaceutical manufacturers establish the list prices for their drugs, given the absence of price controls in the U.S. These prices reflect expected consumer demand, projected marketing costs, future competition, etc.

In the retail channel, list price is referred to as "wholesale acquisition cost," or **WAC**. The WAC price, a term defined by federal law, captures the price to be charged to wholesalers downstream before any discounts or rebates. It is akin to the sticker price on a new automobile or the invoice price to wholesalers at their loading dock, rather than any transaction price. WAC is the most commonly used benchmark in drug purchasing.

Wholesalers pay manufacturers what is known as the "average manufacturer price," or **AMP**. AMP is another term defined by federal law (Omnibus Budget Reconciliation Act of 1990) to calculate rebates for Medicaid patients and set the federal upper limit price. AMP reflects the net sales price the manufacturer receives from the wholesaler or another direct purchaser after subtracting the discounts and rebates. The discounts can cover prompt-payment incentives as well as volume buying incentives. So, AMP is calculated as WAC less a discount. This is an average of transaction prices paid for drugs distributed to retail pharmacies.

The "average sales price", or **ASP**, has become the gold standard for reim-bursing drugs that are administered in physicians' offices. The ASP is the weighted average of all non-federal sales to wholesalers net of discounts and rebates. In 2003, the Medicare Modernization Act changed the basis for reimbursement of drugs covered under the Part B medical benefit from AWP to ASP.

The list price paid by pharmacies and other retailers who purchase the drugs from wholesalers is known as "average wholesale price", or **AWP**. AWP was established by California's Medicaid program in the 1960s to standardize drug reimbursement.[22] Like AMP, AWP is a benchmark or reference price that is an average, non-discounted price—like a suggested retail list price. It is often estimated as 120% of WAC. This is a price that manufacturers report to various parties (e.g., Redbook, Medi-Span). The joke in the industry is that AWP is neither an average nor what is paid (i.e., "ain't what's paid"). Nevertheless, the AWP has two main purposes: (1) it serves as the base price in negotiations between manufacturers and private sector purchasers (e.g., insurers, PBMs, self-insured employers); and (2) many insurers (both public and private) base their reimbursement to pharmacies for branded drugs on AWP.

AWP is not the actual price that pharmacies pay. Instead, pharmacies pay wholesalers a discount off of AWP (usually WAC—16.7%). The AWP amount is also computed as WAC plus a percentage markup (e.g., WAC * 1.2). The discount can be based on volume sales and/or market share. After purchase, pharmacies assume responsibility for drug storage and dispensing to consumers. ERISA plan beneficiaries then pay the pharmacy whatever cost-sharing amounts (copayment, coinsurance) that are contained in their pharmacy benefit plan design.

Pharmacies are the point where prescription drug claims are generated. PBMs then "adjudicate" these claims for their sponsors (the insurers/MCOs). Adjudication involves verification of the patient's insurance coverage, formulary restrictions, drug interactions, and cost-sharing. PBMs contract with networks of pharmacies for drug reimbursement and dispensing, and then determine what the insurers and enrollees will pay them. For branded drugs, the pharmacies are paid (reimbursed) by PBMs based on a percentage off of AWP plus a flat drug dispensing fee; for example, with a branded drug, the formula can be calculated as AWP—15% + \$2. The PBM bills the insurer for the drug, a drug administration fee, and a dispensing fee. Any difference in the amount that the PBM bills to the sponsor and pays to the pharmacy is known as the **spread**. Spread pricing is most commonly observed in the dispensing of generic drugs, due to the large price discounts offered by manufacturers. There is considerable tension in the PBM-pharmacy relationship based on lower pharmacy reimbursement compared to government payers, declining dispensing fees, increasing discounts off AWP, added administrative duties when filling a prescription for a PBM client, and differences in payments to pharmacies for branded versus generic drugs.[23]

For generic drugs, PBMs reimburse pharmacies in two ways, depending on the competitiveness within a generic drug class. For less competitive classes, reimbursement may be determined in the same way as a brand drug. For more competitive classes, pharmacies are reimbursed using a schedule known as "maximum allowable cost", or **MAC**.[24] This schedule sets the maximum amount (price ceiling) the PBM will pay for each drug. The schedule may not necessarily be disclosed to insurers, allowing for spread pricing here as well.[25] MAC prices are established at the state level in order to control spending in the Medicaid program.

Drug manufacturers pay rebates to those parties who adjudicate the pharmacy claim. These rebates, which are discounts off of WAC, represent payments to "steer utilization" of the manufacturer's drug—whether measured by predetermined sales volume targets or market shares. Such rebates are paid retrospectively based on PBM performance. They can include price discounts based on inclusion/exclusion from the insurer/PBM formulary, formulary tier placement which can entail lower patient cost-sharing, and use of specific clinical programs that emphasize certain drugs. Rebate amounts are based on the contracts negotiated between the plan sponsor, the PBM, and the manufacturer. They are influenced by the number of competitors in that therapeutic class, as well as the formulary tier on which they are based (see Chapter 13).

The rebates received by the PBMs from the manufacturers can be passed along downstream to the insurer and perhaps the employer. Their contracts may permit the PBM to retain a portion of the rebate in return for developing the formulary and negotiating with the manufacturer.

Finally, fully-insured employers pay the health plans a premium to cover the costs of their employees. If the plan only includes copayments, the co-pay is independent of the total reimbursement to the pharmacy; if the plan includes coinsurance, the coinsurance amount is pegged to the pharmacy's reimbursement. The ERISA plan participants may also pay a percentage of this premium on their own.

Complexity in the Money Flow

To paraphrase the late rock n'roller Jerry Lee Lewis, "there's a whole lotta pricing going on." There is nothing unusual about different sets of prices. When you buy a new car, you are confronted with the manufacturer's suggested retail price (MSRP), the dealer invoice cost, the sticker price attached to the car's window, and then the retail price you pay. There is considerable variation in some of these prices as you go from dealer to dealer. But, ultimately the price you pay is pegged to one of these prices. What sets the drug channel apart is the sheer number of parties involved, the diversity in the price negotiations that take place among them, the variation in the bargaining leverage among these parties and thus the prices struck, and the lack of consumer transparency into these—not to mention the three-letter acronyms (TLAs). Thus, prices vary based on transactions between wholesaler with pharmacy, pharmacy with insurer, and PBM with manufacturer.

Another way to explain all of these prices is the multitude of "agents" involved in the transactions to get prescription drugs from manufacturers to ERISA plan participants (Fig. 9.4). Manufacturers do not sell their drugs directly to patients; nor do they sell them directly to most pharmacies. Instead, the products are physically routed through wholesalers and paid at prices negotiated by the PBMs working on behalf of ERISA plan sponsors and their insurers. Economists explain that the presence of all of these agents occasions a variety of *ex post* reconciliations and "true ups" of flows of funds[26]:

> One of these is the chargeback. It arises because … few brand manufacturers sell directly to providers, instead distributing their products primarily via wholesalers. Suppose that a manufacturer negotiates with a third party payer ("TPP") or group purchasing organization ("GPO"), which does not take title to the product, a discounted price that is below the price the manufacturer charged the wholesaler. Pharmacies contracting with the TPP or members of the GPO purchase from the wholesaler at the contractually agreed on TPP/GPO price. The chargeback is the difference between the manufacturer's price charged the wholesaler and the manufacturer's contract price with the TPP/GPO and makes the wholesaler whole. Typically the wholesaler submits chargeback requests to the manufacturer on a regular basis, and the manufacturer transfers the invoiced chargeback to the wholesaler via electronic data interchange.
>
> In addition to chargebacks, various forms of rebates are common in pharmaceutical transactions. Manufacturers contracting with TPPs/GPOs and PBMs often have market share or absolute number/dollar provisions that provide financial incentives for the TPPs/GPOs/PBMs to meet certain targets: e.g., a 10% of WAC rebate if brand X attains 40% of all dispensed prescriptions in a given, well-defined therapeutic class, and 15% if it attains 50%. Depending on the extent to which targets are attained or exceeded, manufacturers pay these organizations rebates. Since whether such target thresholds have been reached can typically only be determined retrospectively, these rebates (or at least a portion of them) are paid *ex post* at regular intervals. PBM contracts with network pharmacies often contain similar rebate provisions, as do PBM contracts with TPPs.

One exception to this myriad set of agents is Kaiser Permanente, which streamlines the drug procurement and distribution process by purchasing from the manufacturers and dispensing in their own on-site pharmacies.

There is nothing unusual about the presence of rebates and volume incentives in the retail pharmaceutical channel. Part II of this volume details their widespread use in the institutional channel that serves hospitals.

The irony here is that plan sponsors (whether self-funded employers or fully-insured employers along with their insurers) are contracting not only for drug coverage but actually for administration and management of the drug supply chain depicted in Fig. 9.5. As a result, the plan sponsor's total spend on pharmaceuticals is determined by the cumulative actions of many players in Fig. 9.5, not to mention the behaviors of their employees and their eligible dependents (i.e., the patients). To the degree the plan sponsors wish to more closely manage this spending, they can resort to managing the drug benefit design (what it will or will not pay for), which includes deductibles, coinsurance, out-of-pocket maximums, etc., as well as the reimbursement levels negotiated with the many players. The plan sponsor bears the entire financial risk. PBMs may assume some form of performance risk in the contracts they strike with plan sponsors, including: clinical quality measures (e.g., enrollee drug adherence, inappropriate medications), cost management (e.g., generic utilization), and customer service.

Prescription Drug Benefit Design in ERISA Health Plans

Nearly all (99% +) covered workers today are at firms that provide prescription drug coverage in their largest health plan. Many employer plans have increasingly complex benefit designs for prescription drugs, as employers and insurers expand the use of formularies with multiple cost-sharing tiers as well as other management approaches. Cost-sharing tiers generally refer to a health plan placing a drug on a formulary or preferred drug list that classifies drugs into categories that are subject to different cost sharing or management.[27]

Drug benefit plans include several fundamental services. These include:[28]

- Plan design and administration
- Formulary development and management
- Rebate negotiation
- Enrollment and member services
- Utilization management
- Claims adjudication
- Reporting

These services can be performed by several parties within the drug channel that spans ERISA Plan Sponsors, health insurers, and PBMs. PBMI refers to a subset of these activities as "core PBM functions." These include: account management, claims processing, eligibility data management, mail-order pharmacy, member services, plan implementation and changes, retail network options, utilization management programs, and the hosting of a member website. Other activities are labeled "noncore PBM services": benefit design consulting, clinical consulting, consumer education tools, formulary management, management reports, medication adherence programs, medication therapy management, trend management programs, and rebates.[29] These services represent the PBM's "bundling" strategy offered to employers and insurers.

Some of these activities—e.g., formulary development and management, rebate negotiation—are covered separately in detail below. The prevalence of utilization management tools to manage drug costs has increased over time.[30] Examples of utilization management protocols common within drug formularies include:

- **Coverage Restrictions**—Determines the medications that are included within a formulary. Formulary exclusions block access to specific products.
- **Step Therapy**—More expensive drugs are not authorized unless patients do not respond to less expensive therapeutic alternatives.
- **Drug Utilization Review (DUR)**—Ongoing review of the prescribing, dispensing, and taking of medications.
- **Therapeutic Interchange Programs**—Encourages patients to use preferred formulary products. Pharmacists may substitute one brand-name drug for another only with prior physician authorization.
- **Narrow Pharmacy Networks**—Encourages or requires patients to use designated pharmacies or dispensing channels instead of allowing them to select from an open network of pharmacies.
- **Quantity Limits**—Establishes limits on the amount of medication a patient may receive during a designated period or in a single refill, such as a 30, 60, or 90-day supply.
- **First Fail Protocols**—Requires a demonstration that a generic drug, lower level of treatment, or lower cost drug fails to work for the patient before a health plan will approve a more expensive medication or treatment.
- **Prior Authorization Criteria**—Requires the submission and approval through the telephone, an online portal/website, or written coverage request for the health plan to cover the drug.

- **Mail-Order Criteria**—Requires a higher co-pay if the patient obtains the drug from a retail pharmacy versus the PBM's mail-order pharmacy.

Drug Benefit Design

Drug benefit design typically starts with the ERISA Plan Sponsor and its team of human resources and benefits professionals. They are responsible for developing and managing employee benefits that make their firm an employer of choice as well as one that provides for the health needs of its workforce. Most of these professionals juggle drug benefit design and management with their other job responsibilities. According to 2018 survey data gathered by PBMI,[31] 62% of respondents reported that 25% or less of their job was focused on designing and managing the drug benefit.[32]

Although the process of designing and evaluating drug benefits differs by employer, the basic components include collaboration with key influencers and advisers, determination of benefits funding, and deciding whether to purchase stop-loss insurance. Most employers rely on experts to help them design and purchase drug benefits. According to PBMI, 83% use a benefits consultant, up from 76% in the prior year. Use of benefits consultants is virtually identical for large and smaller employers (86% large; 81% smaller).

Of those using a consultant, 66% use the same person to evaluate and design the medical benefit. Here differences by employer size are more striking. Smaller employers are much more likely to use the same person to design both pharmacy and medical benefits (75%) than large employers (53%). 62% of employers reported that the drug benefit and medical benefit are designed in concert.

Designing the drug and medical benefit together does not imply that the drug benefit is carved into the medical benefit plan. Rather, the designs on both benefits are done together but may ultimately fall under separate contracts and perhaps through different vendors. Given that smaller employers are more likely to use the same consultant to design both pharmacy and medical benefits, it is not surprising that they are also more likely to report designing both benefits together (66% compared to 56% of large employers).

Employers must also decide how to fund medical and pharmacy benefits. The clear majority (83%) of employers self-insure both pharmacy and medical benefits. Self-insured plans take on more financial risk but may have lower overall costs when they manage benefits effectively.

Prescription Drug Formulary Overview

A prescription drug formulary is a list of approved drugs that a health plan, often through the help of a PBM, has agreed to cover. The formulary defines the prescription drug benefit. The purpose of using a drug formulary is to provide high-quality care using the most "cost-effective" medications. That is, the formulary performs a balancing act between clinical effectiveness considerations (i.e., the drug's therapeutic value) and financial considerations (i.e., the drug's economic value or cost relative to other competing drugs). This balancing act is illustrated below.

Typically, a drug formulary is developed by physicians, nurses, and pharmacists using clinical evidence. The development process may begin with a Therapeutic Assessment Committee (TAC) inside the PBM that conducts an internal clinical review by pharmacists and physicians who prepare a monograph on the drug. The PBM next forwards the monograph for review to a Pharmacy and Therapeutics (P&T) committee. The P&T Committee consists of an outside group of independent physicians and pharmacists tasked with establishing the clinical parameters for the drug: e.g., add the drug to the formulary, exclude the drug from the formulary, or make the drug optional. The P&T Committee deliberations are supplemented by recommendations made by a Value Analysis Committee (VAC) which evaluates the financial aspects of the drug. The P&T Committee selects the medications included within a formulary based on a joint assessment of the clinical and financial considerations. In general, formularies look for situations where there are multiple, branded drugs in a therapeutic class that are clinically interchangeable and equivalent. The P&T committee develops, reviews, and updates the formulary so it reflects the most current clinical guidelines, FDA-approved prescribing protocols, published literature, and clinical trial results. Although the design of the cost-sharing tiers is typically left up to the health plan sponsor or insurer, the information submitted by the P&T committee is valuable in determining the final formulary structure.

The P&T committee recommendations extend beyond the drugs to be included in the formulary. They are also responsible for designing and implementing formulary policies that address utilization and access to medications. These policies aim to promote appropriate use, enabling patients to receive necessary services while limiting over-utilization of medical resources.

A drug formulary usually consists of two to five groups of drugs—called tiers—with different levels of copayments or coinsurance by tier.[33] The drugs in the lowest tier will have the smallest patient cost-sharing, while the drugs in the highest tier will have the highest patient cost-sharing. Brand drugs occupying lower tiers will thus be cheaper and hopefully gain greater sales volume and market share than drugs on higher tiers; pharmaceutical manufacturers compete with one another to gain these more favorable formulary positions by paying higher rebates to the PBMs. In essence, they are trading off lower price for higher volume and greater patient access. Generic drugs—medications that are essentially copies of brand-name drugs with similar dosage, intended use, and side effects—are often assigned to the lowest tiers, with brand name and "specialty" drugs (i.e., high-cost drugs for small patient populations) occupying the higher tiers. There are some scattered instances where the branded drug may occupy a lower tier than the generic drug, a controversial topic taken up later.

Variation in Formulary Decision-Making

Formulary decisions are an important aspect of drug benefit management, from the perspective of both rebate contracting (i.e., rebates may influence or be influenced by formulary placement) and member cost-sharing. Plan sponsors can choose to use the PBM's standard national/preferred formulary, develop a custom formulary, or use some other formulary such as that developed by their health plan. According to PBMI, 70% used the PBM's national/preferred formulary while 27% had a custom formulary. A small percentage (3%) used formularies developed by their health plan or medical third-party administrator (TPA).

To provide some insight into the decision-making process to choose either the PBM's national/preferred formulary or to use a custom formulary, the PBMI Survey asked an open-ended question on why the employer chose the formulary they did. Common responses from plan sponsors choosing the PBM's national/ preferred formulary included:

- "We prefer to have a formulary that is consistent, and we can follow recommendations/changes of that formulary made by the PBM."
- "Recommendation by consultant."
- "It was the easiest choice and we feel very comfortable with their formulary development methodology."
- "We do not have the expertise to customize the formulary. That is one of the reasons we hire a PBM."

Among those choosing a custom formulary, reasons included:

- "Better control of costs."
- "Greater flexibility and autonomy."
- "Flexibility combined with a focus on clinical outcomes/efficacy first and foremost."
- "Being a faith-based institution, some of the drugs on the standard formularies need to be included or excluded. The result is a custom formulary, although it's not very different."

The practice of excluding specific drugs from the formulary ("formulary exclusions") has emerged as a powerful tool used by PBMs to gain bargaining leverage over pharmaceutical manufacturers. PBMs leverage manufacturers of therapeutically comparable drugs to offer larger rebates to (1) avoid exclusion from the formulary and (2) gain more favorable position (i.e., lower tier) on the formulary. Such exercise of leverage is a major factor behind the growth in the "gross-to-net discounts" in the price of branded drugs (covered below).[34]

These formulary exclusions influence the national formularies recommended by the PBMs to the ERISA Plan Sponsors and insurers they contract with. These are recommendations, not requirements or mandates. Plan Sponsors and insurers that adopt the recommendations earn higher rebates and face lower plan costs; those that do not adopt the recommendations earn lower rebates and face higher plan costs. ERISA Plan Sponsors, thus like their employees and health insurers, face a tradeoff between access and cost. However, a drug's presence on a given formulary does not mean that consumers are denied access to that drug. Employers are constrained in their use of formulary exclusions by the dissatisfaction of their own employees with such exclusions. Nevertheless, the threat of exclusions leads manufacturers to offer steeper rebates.[35] The number of drugs on PBM formulary exclusion lists has grown steadily since 2013–2014 (see Fig. 9.11 below).[36] According to Adam Fein, the top three PBMs excluded 1,156 unique drugs in 2022, up from 899 in 2021, 846 in 2020, and 390 in 2018.[37]

ERISA Plan Sponsors' Management of Drug Rebates

Rebates are percentage discounts off the manufacturer's list price granted to the PBMs. While manufacturers rarely (if ever) lower their list prices, they do offer increased rebates or discounts in order to gain access to the PBM's formulary for their drugs. These rebates and their percentage levels are typically based on three "access" considerations: (1) placement of the drug on the PBM formulary, (2) more favorable placement (i.e., lower cost tier) on the formulary, and (3) exclusive placement on the formulary (i.e., comparable drugs made by a competing manufacturer are either not on formulary or placed disadvantageously on a higher cost tier)—see Chapter 13 for an explanation of the contracting dynamics. These arrangements essentially trade volume for price, and serve to reduce the actual price of the drugs for employees with drug coverage and enhance their access to them.

Rebate terms for employers vary based on how their PBM contract is written. Contracts may guarantee a flat dollar amount or a percentage share of rebates (with or without minimum guarantees), on a "per prescription," "per rebatable drug," or brand and generic utilization basis. The payment of rebates is often conditioned on the volume of drugs purchased through PBM-negotiated contracts and the latter's ability to move market share for the drug manufacturer paying for formulary access. To be clear, however, PBMs (like GPOs) do not purchase drugs; providers (hospitals, physicians, pharmacies) do.

Rebates are typically negotiated as part of formulary contracting agreements; depending on the contract, some or all of the savings are passed on to the health plan and/or employer. Longitudinal data (covered below) suggest a growing majority of rebates are passed along from PBMs to health plans and employers. Recent data indicate that 75%+ of the commercial clients of Express Scripts received all of the rebates, up from <50% prior to 2018.[38] Some employers are concerned that insurers and PBMs may not be passing on all of the rebates they collect. Data from the Kaiser Family Foundation (see Fig. 9.6) indicate the percentage of rebates received back by the ERISA plan sponsor (employer) among larger firms. One-quarter of large employers report they receive "most" of the rebates; another third report they receive "some" of the rebates. More specific data on the rebates passed along to ERISA plan sponsors are collected by PBMI, which found that 83% of respondents reported that they received rebates on traditional (non-specialty) drugs. The most frequent arrangement was 100% of rebates being passed through to the employer, either with a minimum guarantee (31%) or with no guarantee (27%).

According to PBMI, rebate arrangements are more common for large employers, with 87% reporting receiving rebates versus 80% of smaller employers. Differences by employer size are also seen when looking at receipt of 100% of rebates. Large employers were more likely to receive 100% of rebates with a minimum guarantee than were smaller employers (39 vs. 26%), whereas smaller employers were more likely to receive a flat dollar guaranteed amount (17 vs. 7%).

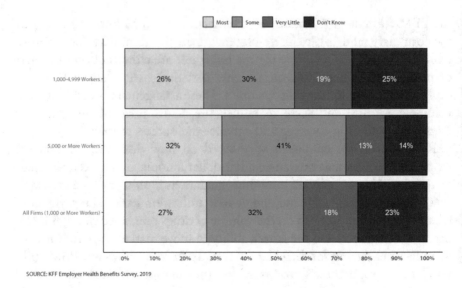

Fig. 9.6 Percent of PBM rebates passed on to employers

Price protection provisions are sometimes included in PBM contracts as a way to provide some cost stability. These are construed by some analysts as additional rebate mechanisms. The provisions put a ceiling or cap on the amount manufacturers can increase the cost of a medication during the life of the rebate contract with the PBM, without incurring additional rebates. According to PBMI, 31% of respondents reported that they had price protection (inflation cap provisions) in their PBM contract. Large employers were more likely than smaller employers to have price protection provisions (38% vs. 26%, respectively). Of those with such provisions, 98% reported that the revenue from them gets passed back to the plan. Nearly all surveyed employers (87%) felt that their plan benefits from price protection provisions.

Retail Pharmacy Contracts and Reimbursement

PBMs also contract with a network of retail pharmacies where employees can get their prescriptions filled at the negotiated price. PBMs may assemble a large pharmacy network to increase patient access and convenience, or a smaller network to reduce the price paid at the pharmacy counter by extracting further discounts from the dispensing pharmacy. The latter is akin to the preferred provider model of MCOs.

PBM contracts with pharmacies may include either traditional markup (often called "spread" pricing) or pass-through pricing. In traditional/spread pricing, PBMs pass along some of the savings negotiated with manufacturers to plan sponsors, retaining some of these savings as compensation for PBM services. The "spread" is the difference between the amount charged to the plan sponsor by the PBM and the amount the PBM pays the pharmacy that dispenses the drug to the consumer. On the other hand, pass-through pricing passes all pharmacy pricing (including discounts, rebates, other revenues) negotiated by the PBM on to the plan sponsor; the PBM is paid an administrative fee by the plan sponsor for its services. That is, there is no difference in the amount paid by the plan sponsor to the PBM and the amount paid by the PBM to the pharmacy: the pharmacy is paid what the client is billed. Smaller PBMs are more likely to contract based on pass-through pricing.[39]

According to Drug Channels Institute data from 2017, 41% of employers reported using spread pricing while 59% of employers reported using pass-through pricing. Similar data are reported in the PBMI 2018 Survey: 37% of respondents indicated that they received traditional/spread pricing, and 63% reported pass-through pricing. The use of pass-through pricing has increased slightly from last year. Large employers were more likely to report pass-through pricing (71%) than were smaller employers (57%). Discounts on drug ingredient costs are typically expressed as a percentage off the Average Wholesale Price (AWP), a list price benchmark for many drug transactions. According to PBMI, 77% reported a guaranteed discount applied to all generic medications, and 56% reported a guaranteed discount applied to all brand medications. Guaranteed discounts are those that the PBM is contractually obligated to provide to the plan. Other discounts may also be offered but are not guaranteed. The average discount off AWP varied by channel. For generic drugs, average AWP discounts ranged from 56% at retail to 63% for mail-order in the 1980s. Discounts on brand-name drugs were much lower with averages between 19 and 25% depending on channel.[40]

Cost-Sharing for Drugs

Cost-Sharing Data from Kaiser

The vast majority of covered workers (91%) are in a plan with tiered cost-sharing for prescription drugs; 84% of covered workers are in a plan with 3+ tiers of cost-sharing for prescription drugs (see Fig. 9.7).

HDHP/SOs have a different cost-sharing pattern for prescription drugs compared to other plan types. Enrollees in HDHP/SOs are more likely to be in a plan with the same cost-sharing regardless of drug type (10% vs. 3%) or

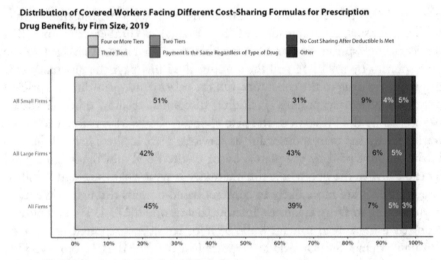

Distribution of Covered Workers Facing Different Cost-Sharing Formulas for Prescription Drug Benefits, by Firm Size, 2019

Tests found no statistical difference between Small Firm and Large Firm distributions (p < .05).
NOTE: Small Firms have 3-199 workers and Large Firms have 200 or more workers. Number of tiers include any tiers specifically for specialty drugs.
Excluding tiers specifically for specialty drugs, 64% of covered workers with prescription drug coverage are enrolled in a plan with four or more tiers, 12% have three tiers, 5% have two tiers, 4% have the same cost sharing regardless of the drug, and 1% have no cost sharing after the deductible is met. For more information on the definition of specialty drugs and how this survey defines drug formulary tiers, see Section 9.
SOURCE: KFF Employer Health Benefits Survey, 2019

Fig. 9.7 Percent health plans with cost sharing tiers

in a plan that has no cost-sharing for prescriptions once the plan deductible is met: 9% vs. 1% (see Fig. 9.8).

For covered workers in a plan with 3 + tiers of cost-sharing for prescription drugs, copayments are the most common form of cost-sharing in the first three tiers, with coinsurance as the next most common. These percentage distributions vary by size of the employer and by whether the plans are HDHP/SOs. The average copayments are $11 for first-tier drugs, $33 for second-tier drugs, $59 for third-tier drugs, and $123 for fourth-tier drugs; the average coinsurance rates are 18% for first-tier drugs, 24% for second-tier drugs, 34% for third-tier drugs, and 29% for fourth-tier drugs. 12% of covered workers are in a plan with two tiers for prescription drug cost-sharing (excluding tiers covering only specialty drugs). For these workers, copayments are more common than coinsurance for first-tier and second-tier drugs. The average copayment for the first-tier is $11 and the average copayment for the second-tier is $31. Five percent of covered workers are in a plan with the same cost-sharing for prescriptions regardless of the type of drug (excluding tiers covering only specialty drugs). Among these workers, 25% have copayments and 75% have coinsurance. The average coinsurance rate is 22%.

Coinsurance rates for prescription drugs often include maximum and/or minimum dollar amounts. Depending on the plan design, coinsurance maximums may significantly limit the amount an enrollee must spend out-of-pocket for higher cost drugs. These coinsurance minimum and maximum

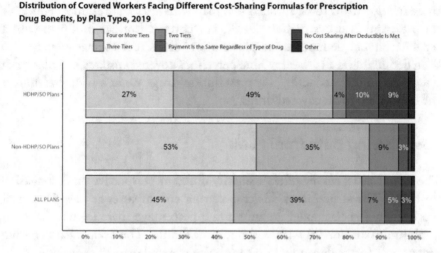

Distribution of Covered Workers Facing Different Cost-Sharing Formulas for Prescription Drug Benefits, by Plan Type, 2019

Tests found no statistical difference between HDHP/SO Plan and Non-HDHP/SO distributions (p < .05).
NOTE: Number of tiers include any tiers specifically for specialty drugs. Excluding tiers specifically for specialty drugs, 64% of covered workers with prescription drug coverage are enrolled in a plan with four or more tiers, 12% have three tiers, 5% have two tiers, 4% have the same cost sharing regardless of the drug, and 1% have no cost sharing after the deductible is met. For more information on the definition of specialty drugs and how this survey defines drug formulary tiers, see Section 9.
SOURCE: KFF Employer Health Benefits Survey, 2019

Fig. 9.8   Cost sharing tiers in HDHP/SO plans

amounts vary across the tiers. Among covered workers in a plan with coinsurance for the first cost-sharing tier, 16% have only a maximum dollar amount attached to the coinsurance rate, 6% have only a minimum dollar amount, 18% have both a minimum and maximum dollar amount, and 58% have neither. For those in a plan with coinsurance for the fourth cost-sharing tier, 40% have only a maximum dollar amount attached to the coinsurance rate, 2% have only a minimum dollar amount, 13% have both a minimum and maximum dollar amount, and 43% have neither.

Many plans allow enrollees to fill prescriptions through the mail. In some cases, there may be a financial incentive, such as lower cost-sharing for enrollees to use this process. In 2019, a very small share of workers (2%) were in plans that only covered prescription drugs provided through the mail and 4% were in plans which only covered some prescriptions through the mail. For these workers, the plan would generally not pay anything for a prescription if the enrollee visited an actual pharmacy. Among workers at firms with 50+ employees that offer coverage for prescription drugs, 58% have a financial incentive for enrollees to fill some or all prescriptions through a mail-order pharmacy.

Among covered workers in a plan with coverage for prescription drugs, 13% are enrolled in a plan that has a separate annual deductible that applies only to prescription drugs. Covered workers in small firms are less likely than those in large firms to be enrolled in a plan with a separate annual deductible for prescription drugs (9% vs. 14%). For covered workers in a plan with a separate annual deductible for prescription drugs, the average prescription drug deductible is $194. Sixty nine percent of covered workers in a plan with a separate annual deductible for prescription drugs are in a plan that applies the deductible to all covered drugs.

Cost-Sharing Data from PBMI

The PBMI 2018 survey offers a slightly different perspective on cost-sharing for drugs. The structure of this cost-sharing encompasses at least 5 types of mechanisms—a flat dollar amount and a percentage share (a) with/without a minimum and/or (b) with/without a maximum. The average cost-sharing amounts can vary depending on the choice of retail or mail-order fill.

Employer plans also vary in their use of drug deductibles and whether they are combined (shared) with the medical deductible. Finally, employers report that the biggest influence on the cost-sharing decision is exerted by consultants and brokers, claims history, recommendations by health plans and PBMs, and a host of corporate factors and industry benchmarks.

The Brouhaha over the Gross-to-Net Price Disparity

Over the past few years, observers have noted not only the rise in drug list prices but also the growing disparity between gross and net prices for pharmaceutical products. As a percent of drug price growth, rebates accounted for only 6–9% during 2011–2012 but then accounted for 57–77% during 2013–2015 (see Fig. 9.9). The disparity has continued. More recent data published by IQVIA show that between 2015 and 2018 branded drug invoice price grew between 5.5 and 11.2%, while branded drug net price grew between 0.3 and 2.9%; between 2018 and 2021, branded drug invoice price grew between 4.3 and 6.6%, while net price either fell or grew only modestly (−2.9 to +1.7%).[41] The latter data indicate that net brand prices are growing less than the annual average growth in the consumer price index, and that manufacturer rebates are partly responsible. Some health economists argue that rebates are roughly the difference between list price and net price.[42]

Indeed, a recent report by a small, provider-owned PBM (Navitus Health Solutions) shows that per-member-per-month (PMPM) drug spending for its plan sponsor clients grew only 1.5% during 2021. This low growth rate was driven by higher utilization (9.1% for specialty drugs, 1.3% for nonspecialty drugs) and not by unit cost (−4.8% for specialty drugs, −2.2% for nonspecialty drugs).[43] Another recent report by Milliman estimates that manufacturer rebates reduced total per-capita healthcare costs by 6% ($397) in 2022.[44]

Some observers believe that the rise in list prices is partly caused by the higher rebates (and other payments made by manufacturers to PBMs), which are represented by the gap between gross and net price. In their view, the facts that (1) higher rebates and other fees account for a higher percentage of the drug's list price increase and (2) the rebate size increases with list price are evidence of causation. The theory behind this presumed causality is that the PBMs benefit from higher rebates, and that this may encourage manufacturers to hike their list prices which leads to a win-win situation: the PBM earns more rebates, and the higher rebates earn the manufacturer a more favorable position on the formulary where they can achieve higher sales volume. They nevertheless admit that the lack of granular data on PBM rebates and drug prices (due to confidentiality clauses) renders this causal assertion uncertain. For example, some economists state that to the degree that PBMs retain rebates (rather than pass them along to health plans) "a higher list price *might* generate more revenue for PBMs" [italics added].[45]

The flaw in this causal logic is shown by several pieces of evidence. Drug manufacturers raise prices several times a year, whereas PBMs negotiate contracts and rebates every two to three years, with the rebates remaining

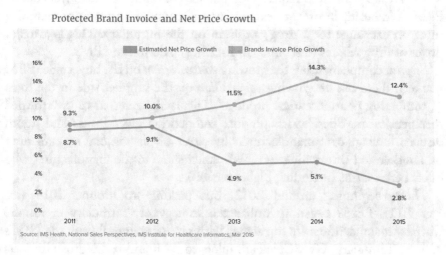

Fig. 9.9 Growing divergence between gross sales price & net sales price

constant during the duration of each contract. Moreover, drug manufacturers raise prices in anticipation of losing patent protection (and thus market share), in the event of filing patent lawsuits against competitors (potentially gaining share), in anticipation of a generic product entering the market (losing market share), in anticipation of new competitors entering the market (and thus losing market share), or in the event that an existing competitor pulls their product from the market (gaining market share). In general, drug manufacturers raise prices because they can—e.g., when they enjoy more of a monopoly position in their therapeutic category, when they have superior marketing, when their product is a physician preference item (PPI), and when their product has brand preference among patients. Most health economists acknowledge that drug manufacturers control list price.

Multiple factors have contributed to the growing spread between gross and net drug prices (known as the gross-to-net disparity). *First* is the growing consolidation of the PBM sector. PBM consolidation was legitimated by the Federal Trade Commission's (FTC) sign-off on Express Scripts' (ESI) acquisition of WellPoint's Next Rx in-house PBM in 2009, and the market valuation placed on Next Rx's business.[46] This consolidation accelerated in the 2012–2015 period (see Fig. 9.10), led by ESI's acquisition of Medco (2012), Catamaran's acquisition of ReStat, and TPG's acquisition of EnvisionRx (both in 2013), and then Optum's acquisition of Catamaran (2015). By 2017, the top three PBMs commanded 71% of the market (measured in scrips): CVS (25%) ESI (24%), and Optum (22%). The top 7 PBMs controlled 95% of the market. This market concentration of buyers allows PBMs and health insurers to extract large discounts in price from manufacturers in exchange for a drug's position on the formulary. This is a major driver of drug rebates (discounts on list price) paid to the PBMs.

Second, complementing the growing *concentration* on the buyer side (PBM market), there can be growing *competition* on the supplier side in the form of competing pharmaceutical products. This is also referred to as "crowded therapeutic categories." Such product competition gives PBMs and health insurers leverage over manufacturers by virtue of playing one manufacturer off another and threatening to move market share to the manufacturer who offers better terms (including higher rebates).

Third, beginning around 2012, but picking up around 2014 (see Fig. 9.11), PBMs began to utilize the strategy of "formulary exclusion" whereby manufacturers are threatened with product removal from the PBM's national formulary. CVS/Caremark removed 34 brand-name drugs from its standard national formulary in January 2012, and added another 17 drugs to

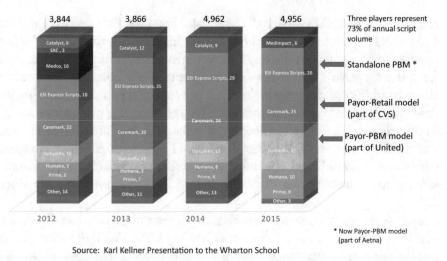

Source: Karl Kellner Presentation to the Wharton School

Fig. 9.10 The PBM industry has consolidated to 3 key players, each with a unique model in the healthcare value chain

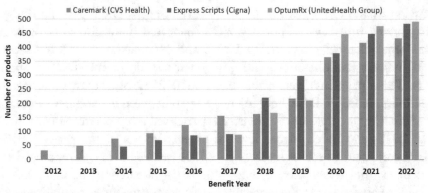

Source: Drug Channels Institute analysis of company reports; Xcenda. Note that some data have been restated due to midyear additions to exclusion lists. Express Scripts did not publish exclusion lists before 2014. OptumRx did not publish exclusion lists before 2016. Note that PBMs may exclude many of the same medications, so certain products may appear on multiple lists.

Fig. 9.11 Number of products on PBM formulary exclusion lists, by PBM, 2012 to 2022

the exclusion list in 2013; ESI followed CVS' example in 2014. Both PBMs have added more drugs to the list over time. Optum, Prime Therapeutics, Aetna, and Cigna embraced drug exclusions by 2016.

Such a strategy works in the presence of therapeutically comparable brand-name drugs. In 2016, more than 50% of the commercial market was covered by plans with formulary exclusions. Note that exclusions block access to specific products on a PBM's recommended national formulary; they are thus suggestions rather than mandates. ERISA Plan Sponsors and health insurers can ignore the PBM's national formulary, but then face reduced rebates and/or higher plan costs. They, thus, tradeoff higher access to drugs for higher costs incurred—much in the way that formularies financially reward patients for selecting generic and lower-tier drugs with lower costs, while allowing access to additional drugs on higher tiers but requiring patients to face higher costs via higher copays or coinsurance. Nevertheless, the prospect of exclusion leads manufacturers to offer larger rebates. A precipitating event here was the introduction of AbbVie's Hepatitis-C drug Viekira Pak to compete with Gilead's Sovaldi and Harvoni. The number of products on the formulary exclusion lists for two PBMs (CVS and ESI) has grown steadily since 2012.[47]

Fourth, statutory rebates are another large driver of gross-to-net discounts. The Patient Protection and Affordable Care Act (PPACA 2010) increased the mandatory rebates that pharmaceutical manufacturers must pay under the Medicaid program. For single-source (non-generic) drugs, the Unit Rebate Amount (URA) increased from 15.1% of a product's average manufacturer price (AMP) to 23.1% of AMP. It also required manufacturers to provide rebates in the Medicare Part D coverage gap. The Bipartisan Budget Act, signed into law in February 2018, increased these discounts. Rebates and other channel discounts to PBMs and pharmacies constitute "Direct and Indirect Remuneration" (DIR) payments made to Part D Plan Sponsors. These payments were stable from 2010–2012 but began to accelerate beginning in 2013. DIRs help to create a gap between list and net prices.

Fifth, the pharmaceutical industry experienced steep patent cliffs in 2012 and 2015, and much higher level of patent expiries in the period 2013–2019 compared to earlier levels (e.g., 2010) (see Fig. 9.12). Attending these patent expiries was a wave of new generic drugs entering the market. The advent of biosimilars in the biotechnology market constituted a parallel development, but on a smaller scale. Research shows that drug prices decrease markedly after patent expiration.[48] In 2017, the generic dispensing rate—the percentage of drug prescriptions dispensed with a generic drug instead of a branded drug—was 90%. The rise in generics and generic dispensing rates occasioned a slowdown in the price growth of branded drugs.

Sixth, the same increase in rebates has been observed in Medicare Part D. Between 2006 and 2020, Part D drug rebates as a percentage of total drug costs rose from 8.6% to 27.0%.[49] This is relevant since PBMs, which administer the drug benefit, retain less than 1% of these rebates and thus do not benefit. Instead, analysts point out that the growing Part D rebates are tied to competition among manufacturers within a given drug class to get on the formulary.[50] Research by Milliman shows that, among drugs with rebates covered under Part D, rebates as a percentage of gross drug costs reached 39% in the presence of direct brand competition. Rebates reached 34% when there were 3+ competitors including a direct generic substitute, 27% when there were 1-2 competitors with a direct generic substitute, and only 23% in the absence of direct brand competition or a generic substitute.[51]

Seventh, the growth in the gross-to-net difference observed over time has been driven not by commercial rebates but instead by Medicare Part D rebates and 340B discounts (covered in Chapter 11). According to Adam Fein, the gross-to-net difference in the price of branded drugs reflects a declining share in commercial rebates (22% of difference in 2021, down from 27% in 2017), a rising share in Part D rebates (23% of difference in 2021, up from 19% in 2017), and a sharply rising share in 340B discounts (20% in 2021, up from 10% in 2019).

PBM critics counter by asserting that PBMs are not the only drug channel parties with an incentive for higher prices under Medicare Part D. Since 99%+ of the manufacturer rebates flow to the health plans, there may be an incentive for the health plan sponsors to favor higher list prices. The prescription drug plans (PDPs) which administer the Part D benefit earn a portion of their profits from DIR payments. Manufacturer rebates comprise the vast majority (92%) of DIR payments, which are paid to plans to get favorable placement on their formularies.[52] Critics have expressed concern that this remuneration structure may lead health plans to favor higher-priced brand drugs (which come with rebates) on their formularies over lower-cost generics (which do not come with rebates).

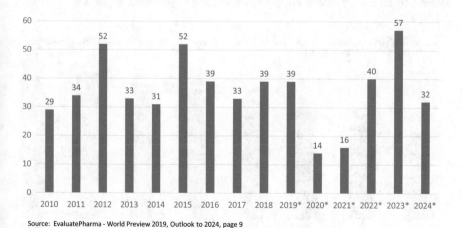

Source: EvaluatePharma - World Preview 2019, Outlook to 2024, page 9

Fig. 9.12 Worldwide total prescription drug revenue at risk from patent expiration from 2010 to 2024 (in billion U.S. dollars)

As evidence, researchers examined 57 unique drug formularies across all 750 stand-alone PDPs in 2016, focusing on 935 drugs that were "multi-source" (brand and generic both available).[53] They found that 12.8% of multi-source drugs did not have generics covered in any formulary; they also found that 72% of formularies placed at least one branded product in a lower cost-sharing tier than the generic. When they examined 222 multi-source drugs covered in all formularies that had both brand and generic products covered in at least one formulary, they found that brand products were placed in a lower cost-sharing tier than the generic for 5% of these drugs. If there is a problem, the low percentages suggest it is limited in scope. Additional evidence from other researchers confirms this.[54] A recent analysis of Medicare Part D plans with matched pairs of brand and generic drugs found that branded drugs are rarely covered when generics are available. Most of the time (84%), only generics were covered; some plans might cover both brand and generic products (15%). In the few instances where branded drugs had preferential formulary placement, beneficiary and Medicare prices were generally low for both products.

All of these factors contribute to gross-to-net discounts. These discounts accelerated from 2014 through 2019 (See Fig. 9.13). Industry analysts estimate that roughly two-thirds of these discounts are attributable to rebates paid to public and private payers; another quarter of these discounts reflect contract administration fees, discounts to wholesalers and pharmacies, discounts to providers under the 340b Drug Pricing Program (see Chapter 11), and other off-invoice discounts; the remainder reflect patient assistance and copayment support, which are covered later (see Fig. 9.14).

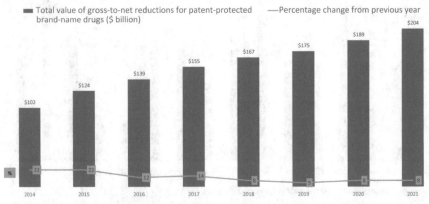

Source: Adam Fein. *The 2020 Economic Report on U.S. Pharmacies and Pharmacy Benefit Managers*, Drug Channels Institute, 2020. Used by permission.

Fig. 9.13 Total value of pharmaceutical manufacturers' gross-to-net reductions for brand-name drugs, 2014–2021

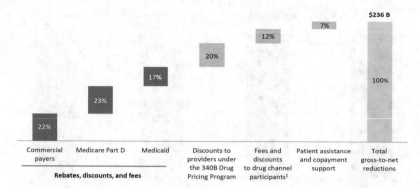

Fig. 9.14 Total value of pharmaceutical manufacturers' gross-to-net reductions for brand-name drugs, by source, 2021

The majority of these gross-to-net discounts were not realized by PBMs and other drug channel participants such as wholesalers and pharmacies, but rather were realized by public and private payers (62%). Researchers estimate that pharmacies capture the bulk (15%) of the remainder, with PBMs (5%) and wholesalers (2%) capturing much less (see Fig. 9.15).[55]

This means that ERISA Plan Sponsors and the health insurers they contract with realized large discounts off of drug list prices, which accounts for the majority of the growing gross-to-net disparity. This is reflected in data

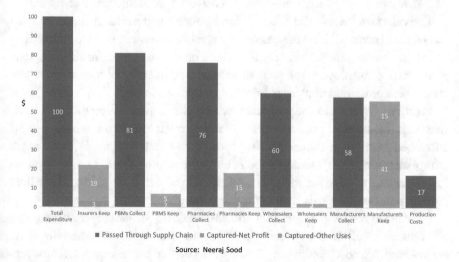

Fig. 9.15 Flow of a hypothetical $100 expenditure on prescription drugs covered under private insurance through the U.S. retail distribution system

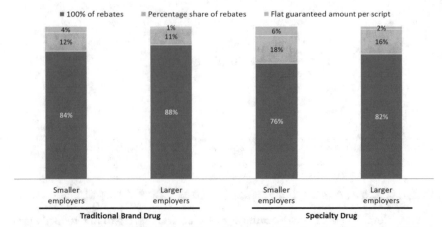

Smaller employers = 5,000 or fewer covered lives; Larger employers = More than 5,000 covered lives. Number of covered lives includes employees and dependents.
Source: Drug Channels Institute estimates

Fig. 9.16 PBM rebate arrangements for traditional and specialty medications in employer-sponsored plans, by employer size, 2021

for both small and large employers that capture the rebates flowing back to the ERISA Plan Sponsors in 2021 (see Fig. 9.16).

The data indicate that a growing percentage of both smaller and larger employers are receiving 100% of the rebates negotiated by their PBMs. Among larger employers, the 100% pass-through is by far the most common rebate arrangement; a majority of smaller employers also received 100% pass-throughs, but nearly one-quarter receive a percentage share of rebates.

The question is what did ERISA Plan Sponsors and health insurers do with the rebates (savings)? The rebates can be used in a number of ways, according to insurance executives.[56] First, they can be used to offset the healthcare costs generated by employees (or plan members) and thereby reduce their insurance premiums; this approach benefits everyone. Second, they can be used to fund employer wellness programs, which also benefit all members. Third, they can be used to finance patient engagement programs which extend enhanced benefits to those choosing more cost-effective plans or those more compliant with their medications. Alternatively, the rebates can be used to lower patient copays for members using specific drugs or reduce the prices paid at point-of-sale; this benefits specific members.

PBMI survey data suggest that the vast majority of employers (68%) use the rebates to offset the overall plan costs to the employer, especially their own spending on drugs.[57] By contrast, a smaller percentage of employers (11%) use the discounts to reduce the premiums of their employees (11%), a strategy that benefits all workers. A small percentage of employers (15%) split the savings with employees, or reduce employee out-of-pocket costs at the point-of-sale (4%). This means that employers use the discounts generated by their employees with more severe illnesses that require expensive drugs (which earn higher rebates) to cover their overall health expenditures rather than benefit the employees who generate the rebates. The irony, according to industry analysts, is that the employees' actual out-of-pocket costs are set by their insurer and ERISA Plan Sponsor. It is not the PBMs, but rather the Plan Sponsors and health insurers who elect not to share the rebates directly with employees.[58]

Over time, employers' drug benefit designs have shifted out-of-pocket spending from flat copayments to deductibles and coinsurance arrangements. By 2019, more than half of all consumer out-of-pocket spending on prescription drugs was for coinsurance or deductibles, both of which are tied to list price.[59] A comparison of Figs. 9.17 and 9.18 shows the decline in cost-sharing using copayments and the rise in cost-sharing using coinsurance when employer plans include high deductibles, by drug tier. Figure 9.19 shows the dollar amount of cost-sharing by drug tier for both copayment and coinsurance.

Moreover, over time, the percentage of ERISA Sponsor Plans with pharmacy benefit deductibles has risen (see Fig. 9.20). These deductibles can be separate from or combined with the medical deductible.

A recent survey of large employers by the National Business Group on Health suggests some change in employer sentiment here. In 2019, 18% of employers reported having a point-of-sale rebate program in place; 2% said they were implementing a program in 2020, and another 40% were considering such a program for 2012–2022.[60] Such programs pass the rebates

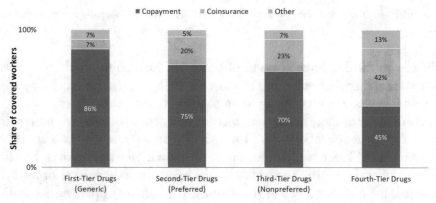

Source: Drug Channels Institute analysis of *2021 Employer Health Benefits Survey*. Data presented for covered workers (1) with three or more tiers of prescription cost sharing and (2) who do not have a high-deductible health plan with a savings option (HDHP/SO).

Fig. 9.17 Type of cost sharing for prescription drug benefits, employer-sponsored plans without high deductibles, by benefit tier, 2021

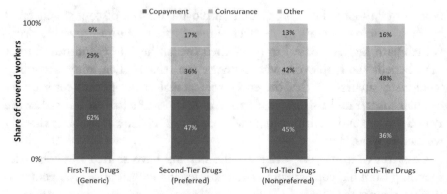

Source: Drug Channels Institute analysis of *2021 Employer Health Benefits Survey*. Data presented for covered workers (1) with three or more tiers of prescription cost sharing and (2) who have a high-deductible health plan with a savings option (HDHP/SO).

Fig. 9.18 Type of cost sharing for prescription drug benefits, employer-sponsored plans with high deductibles, by benefit tier, 2021

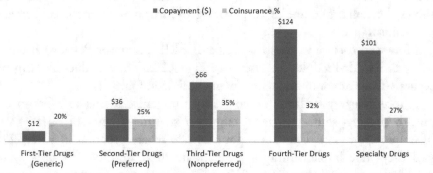

Source: Drug Channels Institute analysis of company reports; Xcenda. Note that some data have been restated due to midyear additions to exclusion lists. Express Scripts did not publish exclusion lists before 2014. OptumRx did not publish exclusion lists before 2016. Note that PBMs may exclude many of the same medications, so certain products may appear on multiple lists.

Fig. 9.19 Average cost sharing by prescription drug tier, employer-sponsored plans, 2021

directly to the employee at point of purchase. Such point-of-sale programs are most appropriate when the employee is filling a prescription during the deductible phase of coverage or when paying a coinsurance.

As industry analysts make clear, this decision about point-of-sale programs is at the discretion of ERISA Plan Sponsors and the health insurers they contract with. These two parties choose the overall prescription drug benefit that is offered to plan participants, which can include: which drugs are covered, the different levels of cost-sharing, the number of pharmacies available to participants, and the incentives for using certain network pharmacies. As far back as 2011–2012, PBMI survey data indicate that ERISA Plan Sponsors, their benefits consultants, and their insurers shoulder the responsibility

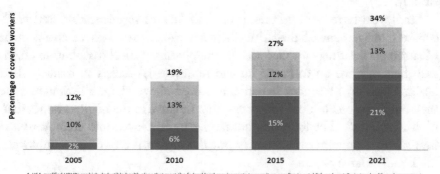

1. HSA-qualified HDHPs are high-deductible health plans that meet the federal legal requirements to permit an enrollee to establish and contribute to a health savings account (HSA). Enrollees are subject to the general annual deductible amounts for all services, including prescription drugs.
2. Includes plans with a separate annual deductible that applies only to prescription drugs.
Source: Drug Channels Institute analysis of *Employer Health Benefits Survey*, various years; Drug Channels Institute estimates

Fig. 9.20 Percentage of covered workers with pharmacy benefit deductibles, employer-sponsored plans, 2005–2021

for pharmacy benefit designs offered to employees.[61] These choices reflect the tradeoffs that ERISA Plan Sponsors and health insurers make between access, quality, and cost. These two parties then contract with PBMs to <u>administer</u> their prescription drug plans and <u>implement</u> the choices made by Plan Sponsors. This means the PBMs process and pay prescription drug claims, secure discounts and rebates from manufacturers, and manage networks of retail, mail, long-term care, and specialty pharmacies. Even in cases of self-funded employers outsourcing their drug plan coverage to PBMs, the PBMs "can provide advice and guidance as pharmacy benefits experts," but ERISA Plan Sponsors retain control.[62]

This has been true for some time. Data from 2012–2013 indicate that HMO plans, the most widespread plan option across public and private insurers, rarely adopt a PBM's formulary even though they increasingly outsource pharmacy benefit management services to the PBMs. According to survey data, 80% of HMOs create proprietary formularies rather than adopting the PBM's formulary; only 14% rely on the PBM's formulary.[63] Beyond the PBMs, ERISA Plan Sponsors rely on a host of pharmacy benefits consultants to help them analyze PBM relationships, advise on PBM contracting, and assist with the negotiations. Such consultants can include business groups on health as well as employer coalitions (e.g., the Health Transformation Alliance).[64] Such coalitions represent large buying hubs that aggregate their purchasing power to extract contract concessions from the PBMs as well as the drug manufacturers they contract with (see Chapter 13). Depending on the firm's size, anywhere from 3–10% of firms contracted for pharmacy benefits using a coalition or collaborative agreement among employers.[65]

Employers have been criticized for their lack of sophistication and inadequate management of their drug benefits plans, their lack of engagement with the parties they contract with in the pharmaceutical distribution chain, and their reliance on in-house human resources specialists to manage their health care and pharmacy benefits, as noted above.[66] One reason may be their emphasis on employee compensation (relative to the market) rather than health benefits.[67] The following quotations by employers and employer business group representatives squarely put the responsibility on the employers, the ERISA Plan Sponsors.

> The majority of employers are still using HR specialists to do negotiations and manage health care plans. Formularies are mostly based off of cost savings, not clinical outcomes, and most employers don't know how to ask the PBM the right questions. Contracts need to be reworded. What does it really say? How is it helping my business/member? Employers should not engage in contracts they do not understand.
>
> Our 'suppliers' don't share contracts or disclose fees. Employers are starting to notice and wonder why they are paying so much. We need to ask intermediaries what they are paying each other and how they spent the money.
>
> We don't talk to employers about the concept of fiduciary responsibility; in this health care environment, employers will have to make ethical decisions about which drugs to cover that will require making difficult choices.
>
> As a fiduciary, an employer is responsible for reviewing the quality of its vendor and its products; they need to gather information, compare data points among vendors, document the process, and why they made the decision.
>
> Employers haven't felt there is a problem (with pharmacy benefits) and have been told by consultants and partners that everything is under control and they are getting the best deal possible. We want to trust our partners, but don't know what questions to ask or what to include in the RFP. Employers need help!
>
> Manufacturers can tell you what they charge the wholesaler but they can't talk about rebates with the PBM because of required confidentiality clauses between the two.
>
> When you pay a PBM a PMPM fee, any revenue or rebate derived by adjudicating your formulary should get passed back to you. PBMs have lots of ways to hide revenue streams so it doesn't always happen.
>
> Transparency standards have been in place for a long time but you still need to negotiate with suppliers. Today, employers are not allied and have no common agenda (to drive change). The people you're buying benefits from know it. You have to stand up and ask (your vendors) for accountability.

Include questions in your RFP that ask intermediaries what they have been paid by partners in the supply chain (and indicate they will be audited – you have a fiduciary duty).

Don't accept the status quo. There is a lack of willingness to change and employers need disruption and transformation. The easiest way to do this is through pharmacy benefits. If one PBM doesn't want to play, there are others waiting.

The Pharma Manufacturers Strike Back

Pharmaceutical manufacturers have not sat by idly and watched PBMs, health plans, and employers engage in all of the strategies above to manage the cost and utilization of drug benefit coverage. In general, manufacturers have historically resisted discounting the prices of their drugs and have engaged in various efforts of their own. Three of these efforts are briefly detailed below.

Cooptation of the PBMs via Ownership

When manufacturers realized that the price discounting by PBMs was a fact of life, they decided to co-opt the PBMs by owning them or allying with them (see Chapter 10). The 1993–1994 period witnessed three large-scale mergers of pharmaceutical companies and PBMs: Merck-Medco, Eli Lilly-PCS Health Systems, and GlaxoSmithKline-Diversified Pharmaceutical Services. One strategic intent here (there were others) was to ensure favorable formulary access on the PBM's formulary for the manufacturer's drugs. The FTC stepped in and made the manufacturers construct a "firewall" between the two operations. The firewall stipulated that the manufacturer would not have access to confidential pricing information on its rivals, would not be able to unduly influence the formulary of its (now) in-house PBM, and would allow competing manufacturers access to the same formulary. This put the "kibosh" on such mergers. Two of the three mergers unwound within five years, with the manufacturers selling off their PBMs at a huge loss; the third dissolved years later.

Disease Management

A second strategy was to avoid paying discounts and ensure formulary access by partnering with health plans on disease management programs for the plans' enrollees (see Chapter 13). In such programs, the manufacturer stated that it would go "at risk" with the plans, guarantee the clinical benefits of its drugs, and pay back any savings not realized if the drugs did not work—IF the plan formularies included the manufacturer's drugs. As one prominent example, Pfizer struck such a deal with the State of Florida and its Medicaid program in the early 2000s. Disease management programs in general, and the Pfizer-Florida experiment in particular, did not demonstrate positive results.

Use of Coupons and Patient Assistance Programs

Drug manufacturers operate or fund programs to reduce the costs of prescriptions for patients. Some are aimed at lower income or uninsured patients, while others assist people with coverage who still may face high out-of-pocket costs. Some drug manufacturers provide coupons (also known as co-pay cards) to patients who are prescribed their drugs. Coupons are discounts that prescription users can present at the pharmacy that reduce their cost sharing liability. They can have multiple effects: they increase patients' access to high-cost drugs, they decrease competition between drugs based on price, they limit insurers' ability to discourage utilization of higher cost drugs on higher formulary tiers, they thus blunt health plan efforts of patient cost-sharing (by reducing patient out-of-pocket costs), and they can increase drug spending, utilization, and insurance premiums.

The provision of coupons has accelerated rapidly since their introduction in the early 2000s. Research suggests that the share of branded drug spending with a coupon increased from 26 to 54% between 2007 and 2010.[68] Data from 2017–2019 suggest that manufacturers offer coupons on roughly half of all branded drugs.[69] When offered, patients presented coupons in 16–17% of transactions. Payers are concerned that coupons and some patient assistance programs affect the incentives employees otherwise may have to use lower cost drugs. Medicare bans the use of coupons on the grounds that they are kickbacks that induce utilization, but they are commonly used by commercially-insured enrollees. Coupons and patient assistance programs have increased in absolute monetary value in recent years, rising from $10.7 Billion in 2017 to $16.5 Billion in 2021; as a percentage of the gross-to-net differences, such payments have maintained a small, stable share (7%).

Economists have studied the impacts of coupons on spending and utilization. One research team recently reported that coupons increase quantity sold by 21–23% for commercial insurers but do not differentially impact net-of-rebate prices, at least in the short-run. They also estimate that coupons raise negotiated prices by 8% and result in just under $1 Billion in increased U.S.

spending annually.[70] Another team found that coupons increased the total mean cost per patient but not out-of-pocket cost.[71]

Summary

The pharmaceutical supply chain depicted here is easily the most complex and least understood portion of the U.S. healthcare ecosystem. It is worthy of an entire volume, or at least half a volume. The drug benefits covered by health insurance that are managed by this chain are becoming increasingly important, particularly as more and more of the population receives coverage under HDHPs. The rebate portion of this supply chain has prompted many policymakers to subject the PBMs to greater transparency or eliminate the rebates they charge. Subsequent chapters take up these issues.

Notes

1. This chapter borrows heavily from Chapter 16 in my recent introductory textbook, *The U.S. Healthcare Ecosystem: Payers, Providers, Producers* (New York: McGraw-Hill, 2021). I thank McGraw-Hill for allowing me to reproduce much of this chapter here (and a bit in Chapter 10).
2. U.S. Department of Labor. Fiduciary Responsibilities. Available online at: https://www.dol.gov/general/topic/retirement/fiduciaryresp. Accessed on January 28, 2020.
3. Drug Channels. *The 2018 Economic Report on U.S. Pharmacies and Pharmacy Benefit Managers*: p. 107. Available online at: https://www.drugchannels.net/2018/02/new-2018-economic-report-on-us.html.
4. One lawsuit is briefly profiled at the end of Chapter 12.
5. Mark V. Pauly. *Health Benefits at Work* (Ann Arbor: University of Michigan Press, 1997).
6. Lewin-VHI. *The Financial Impact of the Health Security Act* (Fairfax, VA: Lewin-VHI, 1993). See also: Linda Blumberg. "Who Pays for Employer-Sponsored Health Insurance?" *Health Affairs* 18(6) (1999): 58–61. There is considerable debate among economists on these figures. See: Laurel Lucia and Ken Jacobs. "Increases in Health Care Costs are Coming Out of Workers' Pockets One Way or Another: The Tradeoff Between Employer Premium Contributions and Wages," UC Berkeley Labor Center. January 29, 2020. Available online at: https://laborcenter.berkeley.edu/employer-premium-contributions-and-wages/. Accessed on June 1, 2022.
7. Mark Pauly. *Health Benefits at Work* (Ann Arbor: University of Michigan Press, 1997): p. 9.

8. Dana Goldman, Neeraj Sood, and Arleen Leibowitz. *The Reallocation of Compensation in Response to Health Insurance Premium Increases.* RAND Health Working Paper WR-107 (March 2003). Michael Morrissey. "Price Sensitivity in Health Care: Implications for Health Care Policy." Presentation to the National Association of Business Economists (September 2005).

9. U.S.Department of Labor. Fact Sheet: What is Erisa? Available online at: https://www.dol.gov/agencies/ebsa/about-ebsa/our-activities/resource-center/fact-sheets/what-is-erisa.

10. U.S. Department of Health. Health Plans. Available online at: https://www.dol.gov/general/topic/health-plans.

11. Anthem BlueCross BlueShield. *Trends in Health Benefits* (2018). Available online at: https://ga.beerepurves.com/news/carriernews/anthem/bcs2018NationalHealthBenefitsStatisticsTrendsReport.pdf. Accessed on January 26, 2020.

12. U.S. Bureau of Labor Statistics. *Economic News Release. Table B. Private Industry, by Establishment Employment Size* (March 2017).

13. Mark Pauly. *Health Benefits at Work* (Ann Arbor: University of Michigan Press, 1997): p. 35.

14. Unless otherwise specified, all "Kaiser Figures" reproduced in this report are taken from the following source: Kaiser Family Foundation. *Employer Health Benefits 2019 Annual Survey.* Available online at: https://www.kff.org/health-costs/report/2019-employer-health-benefits-survey/. Accessed on January 20, 2020. I thank them for permission to reproduce their figures here.

15. Drug Channels Institute. *The 2018 Economic Report on U.S. Pharmacies and Pharmacy Benefit Managers.*

16. William Feldman, Benjamin Rome, Veronique Raimond et al. "Estimating Rebates and Other Discounts Revieved by Medicare Part D," *JAMA Health Forum* 2(6) (2021): e210626.

17. The 2018 survey respondents included 466 plan sponsors representing more than 85 million Members. Not all respondents provided demographic information, but results are reported for those who did complete this section of the survey. As shown in Fig. 40, employers constitute 68% of the respondents, followed by health plans (26%), and union groups (6%). For respondents reporting group size, the median size group represented in the survey was 8,100 members, with a mean of 184,540 (minimum = 5; maximum = 5 million). PBMs with more than 20 million lives have a significantly higher mean number of lives (231,769) compared to PBMs with 20 million or fewer lives (25,249). Respondents represented a range of job titles, including Pharmacy Benefits Director (26%), Pharmacy Benefits Manager (15%), and Vice President (12%). The primary source for this research was the proprietary database of drug benefit decision makers developed and maintained by PBMI. This database was supplemented with client lists voluntarily provided by PBMs who chose to participate in the sampling process. PBMI conducted its PBM customer satisfaction survey of employers June 11–July 9, 2018.

PBM employees, as well as brokers and consultants, were excluded from the survey. The survey sample included 466 benefit leaders representing employers providing drug benefit coverage for more than 85 million covered members. As in past years, results for PBMs with more than 20 million reported members and PBMs with 20 million or fewer reported members are presented separately.

18. Employers may also choose to work with a coalition or other group purchasing organization. Coalitions and group purchasing organizations are entities that leverage group purchasing and contracting to obtain better pricing and terms than an individual member of the coalition/group might be able to secure on their own. They may be employer-led, consultant-led, or organized by common interest, industry, or geography. As shown in PBMI Fig. 5 (data not presented here), 27% reported that they purchase their PBM services via one of these organizations. This is an increase from the 21% reporting use in 2017. No differences were seen by employer size. Other data suggest that the percentage of employers using such coalitions is smaller (10% or less), with greater use by large employers (5,000 + workers). Drug Channels. *The 2018 Economic Report on U.S. Pharmacies and Pharmacy Benefit Managers*. Exhibit 73: 108.

19. Ed Silverman. "Employers are Planning How to Blunt the Cost of Gene Therapies, Pricey New Specialty Drugs," *Stat+* (August 27, 2020).

20. Drug Channels. *The 2018 Economic Report on U.S. Pharmacies and Pharmacy Benefit Managers*: 106.

21. Lawton R. Burns. *The Health Care Value Chain* (San Francisco: Jossey-Bass, 2002). Adam J. Fein. *Understanding Evolutionary Processes In Non-Manufacturing Industries: Empirical Insights From The Shakeout In Pharmaceutical Wholesaling.* (Philadelphia, PA: Pembroke Consulting, 1998). ISBM Report 3–1998.

22. According to Ernst Berndt and Joseph Newhouse, "Following Congressional passage of the federal Medicaid enabling legislation in 1965, the various states were required to develop beneficiary and reimbursement practices, subject to approval from the Health Care Financing Administration ('HCFA,' now the Centers for Medicare and Medicaid Services). At that time, numerous small wholesalers existed, and while prices of prescription drugs were very low by current standards, they varied enormously. Large third party payers were coping with how to reimburse pharmacies for prescription pharmaceuticals they acquired and dispensed. Around the same time, in 1967 the United Auto Workers reached a precedent-setting agreement with Ford Motor Company enshrining drug insurance benefits as part of Ford employees' benefit package. In both the private and public sectors, therefore, insurance covering prescription pharmaceuticals was becoming an increasingly important benefit. California Medicaid program designers, who were conceiving a formula to facilitate reimbursement to pharmacies for costs incurred in dispensing prescription drugs to beneficiaries, focused on a total

or aggregate reimbursement that consisted of a dispensing fee plus a reimbursement of acquisition costs." The reimbursement was termed the AWP. MediCal was the country's largest third party drug benefit program; Blue Shield was the largest drug benefit program in the private sector. Over time, various parties published information on the actual prices that pharmacies paid to wholesalers. These included Drug Topics' *Red Book* in 1970 and then the *Blue Book*. Over time, the prices listed in these publications became known as the AWP. Source: Ernst Berndt and Joseph Newhouse. "Pricing and Reimbursement in US Pharmaceutical Markets," In Patricia Danzon and Sean Nicholson (Eds.), *The Oxford Handbook of the Economics of the Biopharmaceutical Industry* (Oxford University Press, 2012). https://www.sciencegate.app/document/10.1093/oxfordhb/9780199742998.013.0008. Chapter 8.

23. Ernst Berndt and Joseph Newhouse. "Pricing and Reimbursement in US Pharmaceutical Markets," In Patricia Danzon and Sean Nicholson (Eds.), *The Oxford Handbook of the Economics of the Biopharmaceutical Industry* (Oxford University Press, 2012). https://www.sciencegate.app/document/10.1093/oxfordhb/9780199742998.013.0008. Chapter 8: Tables 8–3. For branded drugs, the drug cost constitutes roughly 95% of reimbursement, while the pharmacy retains only 5%. For generic drugs, pharmacies retain over two-thirds of the reimbursement, while the drug's cost constitutes only one-third.

24. For reference, MAC (maximum allowable cost) pricing constitutes the pharmacy's revenue; the pharmacy's expense is based on NADAC, the average national drug acquisition cost (or rough invoice price) paid by pharmacies to acquire the drug. The NADAC is reported at the National Drug Code (NDC) level.

25. This spread amount can be substantial. In Ohio, two PBMs reimbursed pharmacies for $2.3 Billion while billing Medicaid $2.5 Billion for both generic and branded drugs. Ohio Department of Medicaid. *Report on MCP Pharmacy Benefit Manager Performance* (State of Ohio, June 15, 2018).

26. Ernst Berndt and Joseph Newhouse. "Pricing and Reimbursement in US Pharmaceutical Markets," In Patricia Danzon and Sean Nicholson (Eds.), *The Oxford Handbook of the Economics of the Biopharmaceutical Industry* (Oxford University Press, 2012). https://www.sciencegate.app/document/10.1093/oxfordhb/9780199742998.013.0008. Chapter 8.

27. It is common for there to be different tiers for generic, preferred, and non-preferred drugs.

28. Drug Channels. *The 2018 Economic Report on U.S. Pharmacies and Pharmacy Benefit Managers*: 107.

29. Pharmacy Benefit Management Institute. *Pharmacy Benefit Manager Customer Satisfaction Report 2018*. Available online at: https://www.globenewswire.com/news-release/2018/09/18/1572689/0/en/PBMI-Research-shows-Overall-PBM-Satisfaction-Score-Reaches-All-Time-High-of-8-0.html. Accessed on May 10, 2022.

30. Drug Channels. *The 2018 Economic Report on U.S. Pharmacies and Pharmacy Benefit Managers*. Exhibit 74: 111.

31. The PBMI survey respondents encompassed 273 benefit leaders representing an estimated 61.6 million covered lives. Respondents included employers, unions, or the person designated to provide responses on their behalf, such as their health plan representative. All respondents offer prescription drug benefits for active employees. To qualify for the survey, respondents had to report being responsible for the organization's prescription drug benefit. Respondents reporting retiree only, workers' compensation, and publicly covered groups (i.e., Medicare, Medicaid) were excluded from this survey. All 273 respondents of this year's Trends in Drug Benefit Design report stated that they were responsible for managing the drug benefit for their organization. This group of primarily human resources (HR) professionals manages the challenging job of working through both the strategic considerations and budget implications of an ever-changing drug benefit landscape. More than three-quarters (76%) reported they worked directly for the employer who sponsored the drug benefit. The remaining 24% were employed by the employer's health plan (21%) or by a union, union health fund, broker, coalition or group purchasing organization, consulting company, or TPA.

32. Pharmacy Benefits Management Institute. *Trends in Drug Benefit Design 2018* (Plano, TX: PBMI, 2018).

33. As discussed in Chapter 10, the initial drug formularies were simple plans with one tier: the manufacturer's drug was either covered (on contract) or not (off contract).

34. Drug Channels. *The 2018 Economic Report on U.S. Pharmacies and Pharmacy Benefit Managers*.

35. Drug Channels. *The 2018 Economic Report on U.S. Pharmacies and Pharmacy Benefit Managers:* 126.

36. Drug Channels. *The 2018 Economic Report on U.S. Pharmacies and Pharmacy Benefit Managers*. Exhibit 85: 127.

37. Adam Fein. "Drug Channels News Roundup," Drug Channels (June 2022). Available online at: https://www.drugchannels.net/2022/06/drug-channels-news-roundup-june-2022.html. Accessed on July 12, 2022.

38. Three Axis Advisors. *Understanding the Evolving Business Models and Revenue of Pharmacy Benefit Managers* (PBM Accountability Project, 2021). Available online at: https://www.3axisadvisors.com/projects/pbm-accountability-project-report-120221. Accessed on July 12, 2022.

39. Drug Channels. *The 2018 Economic Report on U.S. Pharmacies and Pharmacy Benefit Managers:* 135.

40. Another pricing metric is the Maximum Allowable Cost (MAC) price. MAC prices represent the maximum payment amounts for generic medications. Because they provide consistent pricing for generic drugs of the same strength and dosage made by multiple manufacturers (e.g., multi-source generics), MAC prices offer an important source of discounts for plan sponsors. PBMs

generally consider their MAC lists to be proprietary, and it is common for PBMs to use different MAC lists within their book of business. Like AWP, there is no standard definition for MAC.

41. IQVIA Institute. *The Use of Medicines in the U.S.* 2022. Available online at: https://www.iqvia.com/-/media/iqvia/pdfs/institute-reports/the-use-of-med icines-in-the-us-2022/iqvia-institute-the-use-of-medicines-in-the-us-2022. pdf. Accessed on July 12, 2022.

42. Gerard Anderson. Remarks to "Understanding the Role of Rebates in Prescription Drug Pricing," Conference sponsored by Alliance for Health Policy (December 28, 2018). Available online at: https://www.allhealthpolicy.org/11282018-publicbriefing-transcript/. Accesssed on July 12, 2022.

43. Adam Fein. "Drug Channels News Roundup," Drug Channels (June 2022). Available online at: https://www.drugchannels.net/2022/06/drug-channels-news-roundup-june-2022.html. Accessed on July 12, 2022.

44. Mike Gaal, Paul Houchens, Dave Liner et al. *2022 Milliman Medical Index*. Available online at: https://www.milliman.com/-/media/milliman/pdfs/2022-articles/2022-milliman-medical-index.ashx. Accessed on July 12, 2022.

45. Ge Bai, Aditi Sen, and Gerard Anderson. "Pharmacy Benefit Managers, Brand Name Drug Prices, and Patient Cost Sharing," *Annals of Internal Medicine* 168(6) (2018): 436–437. A similar admission regarding the circumstantial evidence for causality is stated by Christine Buttorff, Yifan Xu, and Geoffrey Joyce. "Variation in Generic Dispensing Rates in Medicare Part D," *American Journal of Managed Care* 26(11) (2020): e355–361.

46. Andrew Ross Sorkin and Michael J. de la Merced. "Drug Benefit Unit in $4.7 Billion Deal "(April 13, 2009). Available online at: https://www.nyt imes.com/2009/04/14/business/14deal.html. Accessed on February 3, 2020.

47. Drug Channels. The 2018 Economic Report on U.S. Pharmacies and Pharmacy Benefit Managers. Exhibit 85: 127.

48. Gerard Vondeling, Qi Cao, Maarten Postma et al. "The Impact of Patent Expiry on Drug Prices: A Systematic Literature Review," *Applied Health Economics and Health Policy* 16 (2018): 653-660.

49. *The 2022 Annual Report of The Boards of Trustees of The Federal Hospital Insurance and Federal Supplementary Medical Insurance Trust Funds*. June 2022. Table IV.B8.

50. Jack Hoadley. Remarks to "Understanding the Role of Rebates in Prescription Drug Pricing," Conference sponsored by Alliance for Health Policy (December 28, 2018). Available online at: https://www.allhealthpolicy.org/11282018-publicbriefing-transcript/. Accesssed on July 12, 2022.

51. Nicholas Johnson, Charles Mill, and Matthew Kidgen. *Prescription Drug Rebates and Part D Drug Costs*. Milliman Research Report (July 16, 2018).

52. William Feldman, Benjamin Rome, Veronique Raimond et al. "Estimating Rebates and Other Discounts Revieved by Medicare Part D," *JAMA Health Forum* 2(6) (2021): e210626.

53. Mariana Socal, Ge Bai, and Gerard Anderson. "Favorable Formulary Placement of Branded Drugs in Medicare Prescription Drug Plans When Generics Are Available," *JAMA Internal Medicine* 179(6) (2019): 832–833.

54. Stacie Dusetzina, Juliette Cubanski, Leonce Nshuti et al. "Medicare Part D Plans Rarely Cover Brand-Name Drugs When Generics Are Available," *Health Affairs* 39(8) (2020): 1326–1333.

55. Neeraj Sood, Tiffany Shih, Karen Van Nuys et al. *The Flow of Money Through the Pharmaceutical Distribution System* (Los Angeles: University of Southern California, Leonard D. Schaeffer Center for Health Policy and Economics, 2017).

56. Linda Etemad. Presentation to Understanding the Role of Rebates in Presciption Drug Pricing Conference. Sponsored by Alliance for Health Policy (December 28, 2018).

57. Pharmacy Benefit Management Institute. *2017 Trends in Drug Benefit Design* (Plano TX: PBMI, 2017).

58. Drug Channels. *Employers are Getting More Rebates Than Ever—But Sharing Little With Their Employees* (January 18, 2018). Available online at: https://www.drugchannels.net/2018/01/employers-are-getting-more-rebates-than.html. Accessed on February 1, 2020.

59. IQVIA. "Patient Affordability Part One" (May 18, 2018). Available online at: https://www.iqvia.com/locations/united-states/library/case-studies/patient-affordability-part-one. Accessed August 4, 2020.

60. Drug Channels. *Employers Slowly Warm to Point-of-Sale Rebates - - But Most Move Faster for Insulin (rerun)* (September 19, 2019). Available online at: https://www.drugchannels.net/2019/09/employers-slowly-warm-to-point-of-sale.html. Accessed on February 1, 2020.

61. Drug Channels. *More Formulary Exclusions for Many Drug Therapies.* Available online at: https://www.drugchannels.net/2011/10/more-formulary-exclusions-for-many-drug.html. Accessed on February 2, 2020.

62. Drug Channels. *If Employers are so Unhappy with Their PBMs, Why Can't They Change the Model?* (November 15, 2017). Available online at: https://www.drugchannels.net/2017/11/if-employers-are-so-unhappy-with-their.html. Accessed on February 1, 2020.

63. Drug Channels. *A New Peek at HMO-PBM Relationships* (December 5, 2012). Available online at: https://www.drugchannels.net/2012/12/a-new-peek-at-hmo-pbm-relationships.html. Accessed on February 3, 2020.

64. Health Transformation Alliance. Available online at: http://www.htahealth.com. Accessed August 4, 2020.

65. Drug Channels Institute. *The 2018 Economic Report on U.S. Pharmacies and Pharmacy Benefit Managers.*

66. Midwest Business Group on Health. *Drawing a Line in the Sand: Employers Must Rethink Pharmacy Benefit Strategies.* No date. Available online at: http://specialtyrxtoolkit.0470c2a.netsolhost.com/wp-content/uploads/SP-Line-in-the-Sand-Final-4.pdf. Accessed September 6, 2022.

67. *Health and Well-Being Touchstone Survey Results 2019* (PriceWaterhouseCoopers, June 2019). Available online at: https://www.pwc.com/us/en/services/hr-management/assets/pwc-touchstone-2019.pdf. Accessed on February 3, 2020.

68. Leemore Dafny, Christopher Ody, and Matt Schmitt. "When Discounts Raise Costs: The Effect of Copay Coupons on Generic Utilization," *American Economic Journal: Economic Policy* 9(2) (2017): 91–123.

69. So-Yeon Kang, Aditi Sen, Joseph Levy et al. "Factors Associated with Manufacturer Drug Coupon Use at US Pharmacies," *JAMA Health Forum* 2(8) (2021).

70. Leemore Dafny, Kate Ho, and Edward Kong. "How Do Copayment Coupons Affect Branded Drug Prices and Quantities Purchased?" NBER Working Paper # 29735 (February 2022).

71. So-Yeon Kang, Aditi Sen, Joseph Levy et al. "Factors Associated with Manufacturer Drug Coupon Use at US Pharmacies," *JAMA Health Forum* 2(8) (2021): e212123.

10

The PBM Chronicle in the Twentieth Century

Lawton Robert Burns, David Cassak, and Roger Longman

Chapter Introduction and Overview

Depicting the rise of the PBMs is not easy, given the paucity of historical accounts. This explains why I recruited two co-authors who had already done a lot of the early analysis.[1,2] This also explains why the volume needed two chapters, this one and the next, to (hopefully) do the job. Just chronicling the history in the twentieth century entails this very long chapter. We beg the reader's indulgence: it is a long-winding road full of twists and turns. To organize the chapter, we have divided it into two main sections (one shorter, one longer). The shorter section sets the stage for PBMs by examining five historical forces that occasioned the rise of drug benefits; the longer section analyzes the rise of the PBMs in four historical periods.

Rise of Prescription Drug Benefits

Until the 1980s, drug coverage was not a distinct benefit in employer-based health insurance. Instead, when it was offered, it was included in major medical plans. Such plans were developed by the commercial insurance companies in the late 1950s to compete with Blue Cross and Blue Shield (which covered the services of hospitals and physicians, respectively). Major medical plans served as the start of "catastrophic coverage," reimbursing up to $10,000 in expenses which were not restricted to specific categories of

© The Author(s), under exclusive license to Springer
Nature Switzerland AG 2022
L. R. Burns, *The Healthcare Value Chain*,
https://doi.org/10.1007/978-3-031-10739-9_10

hospital or physician expense (i.e., they could include drugs).[3] Coverage was usually subject to an overall deductible for all services and to the same coinsurance amounts (usually 20%) that applied to all medical care.[4] It was thus a limited feature of private insurance plans.[5]

In 1960, spending on prescription drugs constituted roughly 10% of national healthcare expenditures (NHE) (see Fig. 10.1).[6] This is not too different from today.[7] However, the biggest difference is that 1960 spending was out-of-pocket spending for the most part, since drugs were not covered by third-party payers, either private or public; only 4% of the population enjoyed such a benefit. Third-party expenditures on drugs as a percentage of total drug expenditures were basically zero (see Fig. 10.2) and, not surprisingly, out-of-pocket spending on drugs constituted 20% of all out-of-pocket spending on healthcare (see Fig. 10.3).

Five factors fomented massive change in the emerging landscape of drug benefits in the 1980s and 1990s: (1) the rise of the pharmaceutical sector (e.g., drug introductions, large-sized firms), (2) the expansion of insurance benefits to cover drugs, (3) the increased urgency among employers to address issues with their health plans and designs and the rise of managed care and managed care organizations (MCOs) to help both employers and public payers, (4) the need to contain the cost of the new drug benefit, and (5) the shift from inpatient to outpatient care. These five factors occasioned the rise of pharmacy benefit managers (PBMs).

These factors evolved simultaneously in symbiotic fashion. The rise of the pharmaceutical sector was tied to its development of more innovative products, which both physicians and patients wanted. This, in turn, created

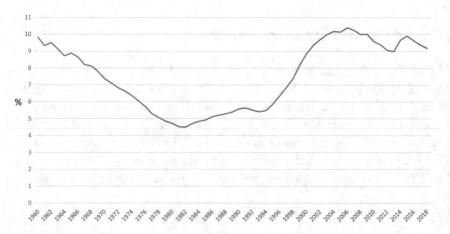

Fig. 10.1 Total prescription drug expenditures as a % of total national health expenditures

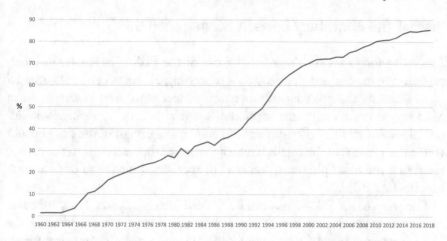

Fig. 10.2 Health insurance expenditures as a % of total prescription drug expenditures

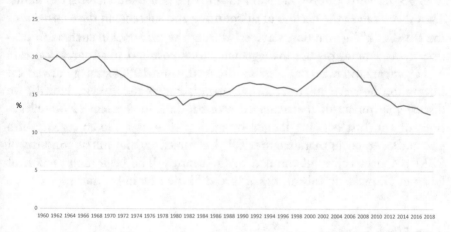

Fig. 10.3 Out of pocket spending on drugs as a % of total out of pocket expenditures

demand for insurance coverage to cover more products for more people (rising quantity). Innovative drugs carried more expensive price tags (higher prices and cost). Rising utilization and costs called for new organizations to manage this growth on behalf of private and public sector payers. Both sectors called on MCOs to (1) oversee the expansion of pharmacy benefits and then later (2) manage the costs of the pharmacy benefit. As part of the MCO strategy, care shifted from more expensive inpatient settings to less expensive outpatient settings. This included retail drugs and community pharmacies, the sites where the new prescription benefits were accessed by patients.

Rise of the Pharmacy Benefit Managers (PBMs)

These five forces set the stage for the rise of the PBMs. Advances in information systems enabled the electronic processing of claims generated at retail pharmacies by the growing number of enrollees with drug coverage. Most MCOs had traditionally managed the "medical benefit" covering hospitals and physician services; they did not integrate management of the drug benefit with management of the medical benefit. Instead, they outsourced the task of managing the new "pharmacy benefit" to specialized managers of pharmacy benefits (the PBMs).

The story of the PBMs' rise can be divided into four parts. First, we cover their emergence during the *1960s–1980s*, along with a description of the "1st generation services" they offered: identification cards, claims processing, and pharmacy networks. Second, we analyze their subsequent growth in the *early 1990s*, with a heavy focus on formularies and manufacturer discounts. Third, we analyze the decline of discounting and subsequent development of the PBM's "2nd generation services" during the *mid-1990s*, such as utilization management, disease management, total cost and pharmaceutical care management, and big data. We also discuss the mid-1990s strategy of vertical integration between pharmaceutical manufacturers and PBMs. Fourth, we discuss the impact of the managed care backlash in the *late 1990s*, allegations of antitrust conduct lodged by retail pharmacies, the emergence of a safe harbor to cover manufacturer-PBM contracting, and initial concerns of PBM practices voiced at the end of the century. The beginning section of Chapter 12 picks up this historical thread in the new millennium.

The Five Forces

1. The Rise of the Pharmaceutical Sector

The history of the pharmaceutical sector and innovative drug therapies has been described elsewhere.[8] Between 1960 and 2000, manufacturers introduced a variety of new drugs into the market,[9] drawing on several scientific and technological advances. This marked the shift from traditional drug discovery based on natural materials (e.g., plants) to laboratory- and industry-based research—what some call the gradual transformation from empirical drug discovery to rational drug design. Other advances included the rise of synthetic organic chemistry and cell biology, the resultant establishment of the chemical and biological foundations of pharmacology, and the introduction of powerful new techniques (e.g., molecular modeling, combinatorial chemistry, and automated high-throughput screening).

Two statistical trends reflect these advances. First, the number of investigational new drug applications (INDAs) accelerated from 1975 to 1986.[10] Second, the rate of FDA approval of new molecular entities (NMEs) steadily increased from the early 1970s through the remainder of the century.[11] The rate of approvals (along with expenditures on them) particularly accelerated in the 1980s and 1990s with the advent of "blockbuster" drugs (i.e., drugs with peak annual global sales over $1 Billion),[12] many targeting widespread, chronic conditions. As one illustration, Squibb discovered and marketed the first angiotensin-converting enzyme (ACE) inhibitor, *Capoten*, in 1975, to treat high blood pressure. *Tagamet* and *Zantac* hit the market in the late 1970s and 1980s to treat ulcers and gastrointestinal problems. IMS Health reported that the drug industry had introduced 101 drugs, each with more than $1 Billion in worldwide sales in 2006.[13] Perhaps the single most important advance in terms of new products created was the development of the monoclonal antibodies (MAb) to target specific mutations and defects in protein structure and expression in a wide range of diseases and conditions. The MAb was first generated in 1975 and then licensed in 1986, and was vastly more expensive than virtually any of the small-molecule drugs then available.

Manufacturers' development of the new technologies and new drugs was one major driver. Another was their ability to commercialize these drugs through the expansion of sales forces. Manufacturers hired thousands of sales representatives ("reps") to call on physicians in their offices and detail the new products. Drug advertising and promotion by manufacturers became a major key to compete for market share and thus a major expense, sometimes reaching as high as 20% of total sales. The vast majority of this expense (75%) went to drug detailing by sales reps.[14]

Oftentimes, manufacturers leveraged these two "twin towers" of innovation—drug discovery/development (adoption) and commercialization (diffusion)—using corporate strategy such as mergers and acquisitions (M&A). An early exemplar was the 1989 combination of Bristol Myers and Squibb to form Bristol Myers Squibb (BMS). Squibb brought Bristol a great cardiovascular franchise and a strong research orientation, while Bristol brought Squibb the salesforce firepower to help commercialize the drug (and better compete against Merck's *Vasotec*, which had stalled *Capoten*'s market share with its introduction).

The combined impact of the twin towers was impressive. Drug manufacturers expanded their forces of sales reps to market their new blockbuster products to physicians. With growing insurance coverage, patients were shielded from their cost. Pharmaceutical manufacturers were not yet threatened by generic drugs, and were not yet challenged by any large, organized buyers. It was thus an era of high demand and high supply, and a period of high inflation in prices for both new and existing drugs.

2. Rising Insurance Coverage for Drugs

These new pharmaceutical therapies offered considerable health benefits to patients, helping to increase life expectancy and reduce mortality rates, particularly for cancer (even though the absolute improvements were small).[15] The new medications also reduced patients' disability from chronic conditions, and made these drugs more popular with physicians and patients alike, thereby stoking demand.[16] But such new products were costly and less affordable compared to over-the-counter treatments (and the remaining patent medicine remedies) that patients were used to buying. The dramatic clinical benefits of the new innovative products occasioned coverage by insurance benefits. Between 1960 and 1993, the percentage of the U.S. population with a drug benefit rose from 4 to 50%.[17] The gains were particularly strong during the period from 1972 to 1995, when third-party coverage of outpatient drugs rose from 20 to 60% of retail drug spending.

An early contributor was public sector coverage of drug benefits. Most of the uptake came from the Medicaid program (Title XIX of the Social Security Act) passed in 1965. Compared to Medicare, the Medicaid program ended up providing far more comprehensive drug coverage in the late 1900s, including outpatient prescription drug coverage as an optional benefit, which all the states elected to offer when they set up their Medicaid programs.[18] Following passage, Medicaid spending (as well as enrollment) rose exponentially—more than double what was forecasted. This resulted from failure to anticipate expanded coverage by states of optional eligibility groups and services. There were also several program changes in the early 1970s that further increased enrollments, services, and (thus) spending.[19]

Uptake was slower in the Medicare program (Title XVIII of the Act), also passed in 1965. The opportunity to cover Medicare beneficiaries for the costs of outpatient prescription drugs failed because the benefit was not seen as a high enough priority when compared to the far less predictable and potentially more devastating burden on retirees of hospital costs. Medicare did cover prescription drugs administered in a physician's office (under the Part B benefit) in order to keep doctors from hospitalizing patients who needed the drugs, but did not include coverage for outpatient drugs that were self-administered by the patients.[20]

Insurance coverage spurred sales of the new drug products, since insurance reduced elasticity of demand and made patients less price-sensitive.[21] Insurance coverage also spurred further investments in research and development (R&D) by the pharmaceutical manufacturers, which led to more and more expensive products to cover. Economists described this process as "the healthcare quadrilemma": (1) expanded insurance coverage induced (2) more investments in R&D, which led to more innovation, which created (3) higher-quality products which patients and physicians desired, but which were (thus) higher cost products which (4) begged for greater insurance coverage.[22] Private and public payers obliged by offering such coverage, thereby increasing access to these innovative products and thus greater demand. This formed a "virtuous cycle" of innovation, spending, quality, and access. This explained the growing preoccupation with "the iron triangle" of healthcare: trying to simultaneously balance the tradeoffs among access, quality, and cost.

The healthcare quadrilemma has been likened to a "flywheel," which is a mechanical device that efficiently stores kinetic energy.[23] While it takes considerable effort up front to get the flywheel rotating, the flywheel eventually picks up speed and gains momentum—momentum that eventually becomes nearly unstoppable due to the accumulation of effort applied in a consistent direction to get the wheel moving. Given growing momentum, the flywheel increasingly resisted any effort to slow it down.

There is evidence that this flywheel picked up momentum as the millennium came to a close. Statistics on drug spending show that the percentage of personal health expenditures (PHE) on drugs rose from 1984 to 1994, and especially from 1994 to 2002. Research by health economists showed that, from 1997 to 2000, higher prices accounted for roughly 22% of this growth while larger percentages of PHE growth were due to higher utilization of existing drugs (32%) and new drugs (46%).[24] Before 1980, the percentage change in drug prices fell below the percentage change in spending on hospital and physician services; after 1980, the situation was reversed.[25]

One particular feature of the pharmaceutical manufacturers' business model, which supported this flywheel, "begged" for disruption. Manufacturers had traditionally relied on their sales forces (supplemented by articles and advertisements in medical journals, and presence at medical conferences) to detail drugs to office physicians. Physicians were largely brand loyal to a particular manufacturer and, in a fee-for-service environment, not very price-conscious. In a market where drugs were now increasingly covered by insurers, patients were likewise not very cost conscious. Drug prices were, thus, not a issue (except for the elderly, who generally lacked insurance coverage of medications). However, the advent of managed care (covered below) introduced new intermediaries that would disrupt this marketing channel. Payers, both private and public, would look to such intermediaries to serve as gatekeepers for the rising expense tab; they would find these in MCOs and PBMs.[26]

3. The Rise of Managed Care and Drug Benefit Management

Rise of HMOs

Private sector coverage of drugs historically preceded public sector coverage under Medicaid, but such coverage was limited to certain geographic and provider settings (e.g., prepaid group practices, covered below). At the same time that manufacturers were bringing their new drugs to market, new types of provider organizations were being developed to (at least initially) incorporate these drugs into their therapeutic regimens. The forerunners of these organizations had existed for decades since the late 1920s in the form of prepaid group practices, sometimes called consumer-sponsored health plans. These were the forerunners of the Kaiser plans and health maintenance organizations (HMOs). Their philosophy centered on "comprehensive care services": all types of providers, all family members, and both therapeutic and preventive services. A comparison with Chapter 4 reveals the parallel between the early HMOs and the early GPOs: local, voluntary, cooperatives designed to reduce input costs.

These early plans (e.g., Group Health Association of Washington, the Community Hospital of Elk City, OK) included drug coverage because the advent of sulfas and antibiotics in the first half of the twentieth century meant inordinately expensive products compared to what patients were used to paying (usually for patent medicines in the non-prescription market). Moreover, the prescribing of these drugs went hand-in-hand with physician office visits to obtain them, compounding the cost of care. Many of these early prepaid group practice plans included an on-site pharmacy to dispense them for members at economical rates.[27] The focus was not so much on the *insurance* of these services as the *assurance* they would be covered.

Nevertheless, anticipating trends observed later in the century, these early prepaid plans sought to be prudent purchasers of these drugs, since the plans operated on a capitated basis (rooted in annual enrollee premiums) with a fixed budget. The plans tried to effect their own iron triangle solution:

balance access to the new technologies with cost savings through selective purchasing of drugs from manufacturers and the establishment of formularies (circumscribed lists of drugs to use that were agreed upon by plan physicians and pharmacists). The formularies allowed providers to limit the varieties of a particular drug to be stocked, and to limit the number of drug combinations for the complete management of illness. This helped the pharmacies reduce the cost and inventory of drugs that would satisfy all of the physicians.

In essence, similar to what the GPOs were doing on the inpatient side, the pharmacies inside the prepaid plans engaged in standardization and bulk buying from a reduced set of drug vendors on the outpatient side. The most extensive drug coverage was provided by Group Health Cooperative (GHC) of Puget Sound. GHC's Director argued that drug coverage was economically feasible in the presence of (1) a formulary, (2) strict adherence to that formulary, (3) volume buying from manufacturers, (4) prepackaging of frequently-used drugs, and (5) filling prescriptions within the limits of the GHC contract.[28] The early plans and HMOs also developed new managed care techniques that later HMOs and PBMs would emulate: combine the drug and medical benefits to encourage substitution of the former for the latter, and lower copayments to encourage patients to use their medications.[29]

The early prepaid group practice plans such as Kaiser and GHC did not multiply or spread widely beyond the West Coast. One limiting factor was the small number of group practices in the country around which one could build such plans. Moreover, the prepaid plans were anathema to organized medical societies, who opposed both prepayment and group practice. These societies actively opposed and boycotted them until the courts enjoined them from doing so in the 1940s and 1950s.

Spread and Growing Legitimacy of HMOs
The early 1970s helped to confer greater legitimacy—both political and professional—on such plans. Paul Ellwood, who had grown up in Kaiser's backyard in California, served as an advisor to President Nixon, who was looking for a private sector strategy to contain healthcare costs that would counter Democratic Party proposals for national health insurance. Ellwood recast the prepaid group plans as "health maintenance organizations" (HMOs), which called out the positive nature of maintaining one's health. Passage of the 1973 HMO Act legitimized HMOs, provided some initial funding for planning, and overrode many state regulations impeding their formation. Indeed, Kaiser was singled out in the HMO Act as the best health plan model to emulate. The HMO Act stipulated a set of basic health services that must be provided by the HMO to its enrollees, as well as supplemental health services that the HMO could optionally offer and members

could contract for at an additional fee. The latter services included drugs prescribed by the HMO physician.

However, the medical society boycotts that were legally enjoined during the 1940s and 1950s exerted lasting effects. At the national level, enrollment was still limited. During the 1970s, the largest HMOs were Kaiser (3.5 million enrollees), Health Insurance Plan of Greater New York (750,000 enrollees), GHC (250,000 enrollees), and the Group Health Association (110,000 enrollees).[30] As late as the 1970s, HMOs operated in only ten states and enrolled only 6 million people—3% of the insured population. Physician opposition to HMOs, along with the HMO Act's requirement to offer comprehensive benefits (basic services), slowed down the efforts of the Blue Cross/Blue Shield plans to develop their own such plans and expand insurance coverage for drugs.

Nevertheless, HMOs gained a foothold during this epoch due to some organizational compromises. Organized medicine objected to the Kaiser plans for their reliance on groups and salaried employment. In 1954, Kaiser expanded into the San Joaquin Valley in central California. Local physicians responded by developing the San Joaquin Foundation for Medical Care. This model accepted consumer prepayment but allowed physicians to remain independent, practice in their own offices, and still receive fee-for-service payment from the health plan. These plans became known as "Independent Practitioner Associations," or IPA-models of HMOs. The IPAs held several competitive advantages over the earlier staff-model HMOs. First, they proved wildly popular with physicians who could retain their traditional style of solo, fee-for-service practice and yet capture a few managed care patients. Second, the larger size of the IPA network meant that panel physicians were widely distributed geographically (rather than in one central location) and thus more convenient and accessible to patients. Third, the large panel size also meant the IPAs contained the personal physician of most patients, as well as free choice of any physician in the IPA network. Fourth, the distributed network meant that any HMO pharmacy was also not geographically centralized but accessible at a variety of neighborhood locations, which fit well with the pharmacy distribution networks used later by PBMs. The IPA model enjoyed steady growth. Indeed, the San Joaquin IPA grew to 180,000 enrollees, making it one of the largest HMOs in the country.

Variegated MCO Landscape

In general, the shift to variegated MCO health plans represented what some observers called a "contractual archipelago."[31] Once the MCO model deviated from its historical roots as a staff-model HMO with an employed physician group at one physical site, MCOs relied on contractual networks of physicians, hospitals, utilization management companies, and other outsourced providers (e.g., pharmacy, mental health). The PBM as an outsourced provider of pharmacy benefits would fit well with such a siloed model.

Many of the newer, non-staff, and non-group model HMOs (such as the IPAs and Networks) contracted with outside pharmacies. They were also less likely to mandate use of the few generic drugs that existed (18.6% of dispensed units in 1984),[32] drug utilization review, formularies, and therapeutic substitution. Observers also suggest they maintained separate budgets for drugs and medical care; this is consistent with the fact that most HMOs (74%) did not manage the drug benefit along with the medical benefit but separately as a rider agreement (covered below). This may have weakened them as rigorous price negotiators and/or cost controllers (e.g., unable to spend more on the drug side to reduce utilization on the medical side)—thereby abetting the rise and role of the freestanding PBMs.

Employer Interest in Managed Care
Beyond the 1973 HMO Act, another major impetus came from employers and their increasing engagement in managed care. Employers had financed much of the rise in healthcare costs generated after the passage of Medicare. Part A of Medicare was mostly financed through payroll taxes paid by employers and employees; Part B was partly financed by corporate taxes; and employers who initiated healthcare coverage during the 1940s now found themselves paying directly for the healthcare costs of their elderly retirees. Some pundits quipped that the cost of insurance coverage for autoworkers exceeded the cost of steel used in Detroit automobiles.[33]

Those employers looking for a solution to their rising healthcare outlays found it in the HMOs that had already staked a place in their markets. Employers enlisted the help of their insurance carriers to develop new HMO plans and either pushed employees (via reduced choice) or enticed employees (via lower premiums) to join them. Between 1984 and 1996, the share of employees in large firms enrolled in HMO plans jumped from 8 to 33%.[34] Total HMO enrollment increased rapidly between 1980 and 2000 (see Fig. 10.4). These HMO plans either employed their own providers in centrally located groups (staff-model HMOs) or contracted with a select subset of providers using independent group practices (group model HMOs), independent solo practitioners (IPA model HMOs), or combinations of independent groups and solo physicians (network model HMOs) in the local marketplace. Provider selection was presumably based on their quality and lower cost; in reality, providers were promised more enrollee (patient) volume in exchange for accepting lower rates of reimbursement. This was the

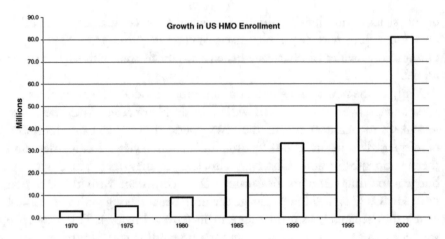

Fig. 10.4 Growth in U.S. HMO enrollment

employer's and MCO's version of trading volume for price—a strategy GPOs were already using, and which some analysts suggest may be the only clearly demonstrated comparative advantage of managed care.

One particular issue that energized employers was a change in accounting regulations.[35] In March 1993, the Health Care Financing Administration, the precursor to the Centers for Medicare & Medicaid Services (CMS), issued the Financial Accounting Standards Board Statement Number 106 (FASB 106). The standard required employers to book expenses for the medical costs of their retirees and accrue these liabilities by the time workers actually retired for all future use. As a result, employers now had to look at the medical services and expenditures of active workers, early retirees, and their Medicare eligibles.

At that time, employers were the largest source of drug benefits for the Medicare population due to their coverage of retiree health benefits; in 1996, 32% of Medicare beneficiaries had drug coverage. While drug costs accounted for only 9% of the health spending by employers overall, drugs accounted for 35% of retiree spending. Employers realized they had to manage their drug costs in order to manage their own bottom lines or face the prospect of eliminating coverage for retirees or asking retirees to bear the future costs. Employers turned to MCOs and their PBMs for help—not just to manage the costs of the drugs utilized but also the prices paid for them. PBMs thereby entered the role of manager of pharmacy benefits and costs.

Legislative Tailwinds & The Rise of the PPOs

The Employee Retirement and Income Security Act (ERISA) of 1974 provided further impetus to MCOs. ERISA meant that self-insured employers could avoid state insurance taxes and mandated benefits. Employers embraced the MCO models because it allowed them to directly receive provider discounts while avoiding costly state regulations.

Employers then found a new managed care option. An alternative MCO, called the preferred provider organization (PPO), took off in the 1980s— largely due to the regulatory changes and the arrival of selective contracting.[36] During the 1980s, states dropped decades-old regulations that required insurers to reimburse all licensed providers. California helped to lead the way by passing legislation permitting the use of selective contracting to relieve the financial stress imposed by rising Medicaid expenditures on state budgets and taxpayers.

Selective contracting had already been utilized by staff-model HMO pharmacies to generate competition among drug manufacturers. Now, the central objective of selective contracting was to foster greater competition among providers. The legislation allowed the use of selective contracting by private sector insurers. Insurers responded by creating PPOs whose central feature was a network of contracting providers. In California between 1983 and 1987, the number of PPO plans nearly tripled from 25 to 70; the percentage of the non-elderly population enrolled in PPOs skyrocketed from 1% to nearly 50%. HMO penetration grew likewise between 1980 and 1987: from 32 to 49 plans, and from 17 to 26% of the total population.[37] The PPOs (as well as HMOs) provided enrollees financial incentives—such as lower premiums and lower cost-sharing—to utilize physicians and hospitals in the smaller networks ("stay in network"); these incentives were financed (offset) by providers accepting discounts off of their rates.

Patients paid substantial out-of-pocket costs if they ventured outside the network, which meant that out-of-network providers (physicians and hospitals) could lose enormous market share. Insurers used this threat to negotiate discounts off of providers' usual charges. Most providers preferred to be in network at a discounted price than out-of-network at full price, so most PPO networks ended up including most providers. Able to obtain lower cost coverage without surrendering access, enrollees flocked to PPOs nationally. Starting from essentially zero in 1983, the number of PPO enrollees rose to 28 million in 1987 and to 50 million by 1995. Large corporate employers were especially eager to build their health benefits packages around PPOs, since such plans allowed for freer provider choice to employees and fewer complaints from employees.

The rapid penetration of PPOs and HMOs contributed to a period of near zero inflation-adjusted growth in private healthcare spending, something the U.S. has not achieved before or since. The savings may have been one-time-only savings achieved when employers transitioned workers from indemnity into MCO plans. Both indemnity and MCO plans experienced similar levels of cost inflation thereafter. By the end of the 1990s, roughly 70% of employees with employer-based health insurance were enrolled in either an HMO or PPO plan.

MCOs and Drug Benefits

Like Medicaid, the HMOs offered a distinct drug benefit with minimal deductibles and copayments. The drug benefit could be included as part of the basic benefit package (23% of HMOs in 1989) or in a rider typically purchased as part of a supplemental services package (74% of HMOs in 1989).[38] The HMOs offered such coverage to reduce (i.e., substitute for) more expensive, downstream care in hospitals and emergency departments (EDs), and thereby manage the capitated payments they received. For other MCOs (especially the HMOs not relying on a staff-model), the emphasis was tilted more to hospital and physician (medical) benefit management; they tended to outsource drug spend to PBMs who filled the void.

Employer contracting efforts with MCOs served as a strong tailwind to the prescription drug coverage already underway in the public sector. Third-party insurance coverage for drug benefits expanded rapidly during the 1990s (see Fig. 10.5). In 1996, 55% of the commercial population and 67% of the non-Medicare population had drug coverage. Moreover, this coverage had quickly shifted from non-managed care (indemnity) to managed care.[39] While non-managed care/private-office physicians accounted for 60% of pharmaceutical sales in 1986, that percentage fell to 43% by 1992. Conversely, the share of drug sales accounted for by HMOs and PPOs combined rose from 7% in 1986 to 22% in 1992. HMOs, in particular, had more extensive drug coverage than other plans due to their low levels of cost-sharing (no deductibles, low co-pays); they also integrated the drug and medical benefits to encourage substitution of the former for the latter. In 1995, IMS Managed Care Services reported that managed care accounted for 52.5% of total pharmaceutical sales. In the early 1990s, it was estimated that about half of PPOs had a prescription benefit program, with over 90% of HMOs having some kind of prescription drug plan, either as a basic benefit or (more commonly) as a rider typically purchased with the basic benefit.

The shift from indemnity to managed care had a profound impact on both insurers and pharmaceutical companies. In the physician-controlled environment, price was rarely an issue: insurers just paid for the price of

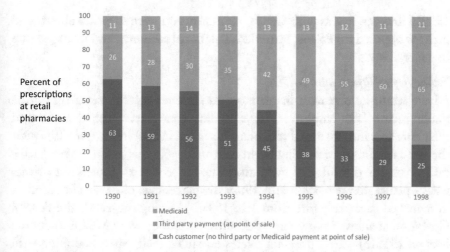

Fig. 10.5 Growth in third-party coverage for drugs (*Source* IMS Health Retail Method-of-Payment Report, 1999)

prescriptions. Under managed care, by contrast, HMOs were at financial risk; they depended on cost control for both profitability and survival. MCOs began to use their purchasing power to secure discounts on drugs, medical products, physician services, and hospital services. MCOs also began to shift some of the risk to patients (in the form of cost-sharing) and drug manufacturers (in the form of discounts). They might employ therapeutic substitution or interchange in which a lower-priced drug was used instead of a more expensive one if it were of similar efficacy; they might also employ generic substitution, using either their formularies or incentive contracts with pharmacies.[40] Indeed MCOs' preference for generic substitution was the major reason that generic's share of total prescriptions had risen from 18.6% in 1984 to 42.6% in 1996.[41] This was facilitated by (1) liberalized state laws passed mostly during the 1970s that allowed generic substitution by pharmacists, and (2) Federal law (the 1984 Drug Price Competition and Patent Term Restoration Act, aka the Hatch-Waxman Act) relaxing entry by generics manufacturers in the early 1980s.

The new MCOs joined the GPOs in introducing new marketing channels that diametrically opposed the manufacturers' traditional, decentralized marketing to individual physicians. The MCOs redirected marketing using "national accounts," which interposed an economic customer between the manufacturer and its clinical customer.[42] SmithKlineBeecham (SKB) was one of the earliest pharmaceutical manufacturers to embrace the national accounts strategy in 1986, developing a contract for a bundle of drugs with a GPO, Voluntary Hospitals of America (VHA), and then developing 30 more by

1990. However, just as with GPOs, manufacturers were skeptical about (and perhaps opposed to) PBMs, formularies, national accounts, and managed care in general.

Public Sector Efforts with MCOs

Private sector involvement in managed care exerted a feedback effect on the public sector. Like employers, state Medicaid programs pushed or nudged their enrollees into managed care plans (usually HMOs) in the early 1990s for the same reason: control rising healthcare outlays. In this manner, state Medicaid programs transitioned away from fee-for-service to contracted private MCO plans. Between 1983 and 1993, the percentage of Medicaid enrollees in managed care plans rose from 1 to 15%.[43] During the 1980s the Federal Government allowed states more flexibility, including use of MCOs under the Section 1915(b) waiver program. States expanded their experimentation with these plans during the mid-1990s. By the end of 1996, more than 24 states accounting for over 60% of Medicaid spending had demonstration projects that were either approved or pending.

Medicare moved more slowly toward managed care, propelled by the Tax Equity and Fiscal Responsibility Act (1982) and the Balanced Budget Act of 1997; Medicare managed care would gain momentum in the new millennium under the Medicare Advantage program.[44] Medicare coverage of drugs was primarily limited to drugs dispensed in physician offices and outpatient settings (Part B). Coverage of retail drugs was limited to enrollees of Medicare managed care plans and those with employer-based supplemental drug coverage; both groups had their drug benefits managed by PBMs. InterStudy data from early 1998 suggested that 4 million Medicare beneficiaries enrolled in HMOs were served by PBMs; half of these were covered by HMOs with their own in-house PBM, while the other half were covered by external PBMs with which the HMOs contracted. Another 10 million Medicare beneficiaries had employer-sponsored supplemental drug coverage which could also be benefits managed by the PBMs.

4. The Common Sense of Urgency: Contain the Cost of the Drug Benefit

PBM Coverage, Savings, & Penetration

No insurer was immune from the need for cost containment. Between 1988 and 1995, Blue Cross saw its prescription drug expenditures rise faster (21% annually) than its total benefit expenditures (12% annually). Blue Cross turned to two PBMs, Medco and PCS, to manage its mail-order transactions and retail network transactions, respectively. The Blues estimated that the two PBMs saved it over half a billion dollars in pharmacy benefit costs in 1995.[45]

PBM savings derived largely (50+%) from retail and mail-order pharmacy discounts, with savings also coming from negotiated discounts with manufacturers (20%), maximum allowable cost restrictions (14%), and utilization review (12%). These figures are consistent with government estimates of the savings achieved by staff-model HMOs and PBMs during this era: 50–70% savings from pharmacy discounts, compared to only 2–21% savings from manufacturer discounts.[46]

In anticipation of such successes, payers covering prescription drug benefits embraced HMOs and their cost containment mechanisms. Shifts in the sales of pharmaceuticals were immediately apparent. Between 1986 and 1992, the percentage of sales through non-managed care channels and private physician offices fell from 60 to 43%; sales through hospitals similarly fell from 20 to 11%. These declines were offset by increased sales through HMOs (from 2 to 7%), PPOs (from 5 to 15%), and mail-order (from 2 to 10%).[47] Sales of drugs through non-managed care channels nevertheless continued, since managed care penetration in the country (both HMO and PPO) was only 47% in 1993.

Needless to say, as both third-party insurance coverage and MCOs expanded in the 1990s, so did the number of people covered by PBMs. In 1990, PBMs covered approximately 60 million lives; by 1998, the number of covered lives exceeded 125 million and may have reached 140 million. During this time interval, the biggest gains were observed among the HMOs, with enrollees growing from 10 to 60 million. The next largest gains were observed in employer pharmacy carve-out programs (using outsourced PBMs), rising from just over 20 million lives to 50 million lives. The number of covered lives in indemnity PPOs with a PBM remained flat overall, rising from 30 to 40 million and then falling back to 30 million. HMO pharmacy departments began to mimic PBM techniques; insurers and claims processors developed their own PBMs. Compared to less than 25% market penetration in 1989, PBMs now administered pharmaceutical benefits to over 50% of the population. This gave them greater leverage in the marketplace.

While the PBMs exerted some moderating impact on drug prices, drug volume was a different matter. During the period 1992–2002, the expansion in drug coverage (as well as the rise of blockbuster drugs for chronic conditions) led to a massive 74% increase in prescription volumes, a 59% increase in prescriptions filled per person, and a tripling in aggregate U.S. spending on drugs. Price hikes accounted for only 29% of the increase in spending.[48] As a percentage of NHE, retail prescription drug costs rose from 6% in 1990 to 9% by 2000 and 10% by 2005. The consumer price index (CPI) for prescription drugs outpaced the CPI for all medical care and the CPI for all items.

Health insurance costs were much more volatile than the costs of benefits and the cost of wages/salaries. Part of the problem may have stemmed from the loosely-coupled management of medical and pharmacy benefits, as well as the lower utilization of cost containment measures by non-group and non-staff HMO plans. Part of the volume increase was due to HMOs' substitution of drugs for medical services and lower use of drug cost-sharing.

PBM Contracting and Functions

As noted earlier, managed care plans succeeded in managing costs by virtue of their strategy of "selective contracting": i.e., exchanging discounts in provider reimbursement for network inclusion of providers. The early HMO prepaid group plans (and then PPOs) employed this strategy in developing their physician networks; the HMOs also utilized this in managing their pharmacies in terms of their formularies, the drugs to be stocked, and the manufacturers to use. Selective pharmacy networks were the major source of savings.

The PBMs took on a series of functions during the 1980s and 1990s that borrowed from and extended the MCOs' strategy. They developed their pharmacy networks and mail-order delivery networks to obtain retail discounts downstream. Beyond providers, however, PBMs helped to achieve lower drug costs via generic substitution, brand name substitution using a lower cost equivalent, formulary management, and negotiating lower drug prices with drug manufacturers upstream to access their formularies. In this manner, the PBMs acted as group buyers for drugs on behalf of (a) self-insured employers or (b) health insurers contracting with fully-insured employers, offering scale economies in drug purchasing.

A full-service PBM thus emerged with responsibility for the design, implementation, and administration of the pharmacy benefit program. The PBM had four defining characteristics: claims processing and adjudication, pharmacy network management, formulary development and management for clients, and rebate negotiations with pharmaceutical manufacturers. Later in the 1990s, PBMs took on additional functions that sought to improve the effectiveness and efficiency of drug prescribing via disease management programs, medication therapy management, physician profiling, and drug utilization review. The evolution of PBM services is depicted in Fig. 10.6 and explicated in the remainder of this chapter.

5. The Shift from Inpatient to Outpatient Care

A key component of the MCO cost containment strategy was to substitute more outpatient care for inpatient care. Outpatient care was covered by both

PBM Service Mix by Era

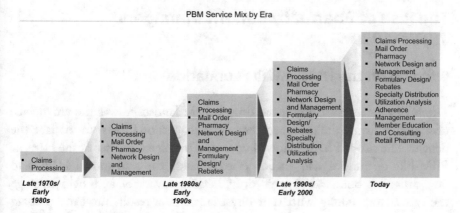

Fig. 10.6   Progression of PBM service offerings

Medicare and Medicaid, allowing public enrollees to be treated in the rising number of hospital outpatient departments, which handled roughly 16% of physician visits in 1960. Private sector insurance coverage of outpatient care facilitated some of the shift away from inpatient care. Between 1968 and 1978, Blue Cross enrollees used 18.6% fewer inpatient days and 137.6% more outpatient visits. Still, by the late 1970s, only 30% of U.S. hospitals had outpatient departments.

Ambulatory and outpatient care received a huge boost in the early 1980s. Changes in federal reimbursement of hospitals beginning with the Inpatient Prospective Payment System (IPPS 1983) capped institutional payments but left outpatient payments untouched and, thus, still reimbursed on a fee-for-service basis. Hospitals and other providers responded to the new financial incentives by migrating patients from the inpatient to the outpatient setting and developing new outpatient services (e.g., outpatient rehabilitation and cardiac care programs).

Technological advances and organizational innovations had already made such substitution clinically feasible. The technological advances included minimally-invasive surgical techniques. The organizational innovations included ambulatory surgery centers, chains of retail pharmacies, and the pharmacy benefit managers (discussed below)—all roughly following the rise of hospital chains. Chains of MCO plans, themselves strongly rooted in primary and ambulatory care, also took off in the 1980s. Moreover, outpatient care emphasized the importance (and perhaps centrality) of medication therapy and pharmacy network management—central features of the PBMs.

The Rise of Pharmacy Benefit Managers: 1960s–1980s

Building on the HMO/MCO Foundation

The final event transforming the drug benefit landscape was the emergence of specialist firms (the pharmacy benefit managers or PBMs) to manage the benefit. The rise of PBMs followed upon and paralleled the rise of the HMOs. PBM-like operations had already existed inside the staff-model HMOs to buy drugs in bulk, administer drug benefit coverage, and help manage the formularies (along with staff physicians). As a result, the early prepaid group practice plans were a combination of MCO, PBM, and (medical group-based) GPO. Staff-model HMO physicians and pharmacists developed formularies to standardize the drugs clinicians would prescribe, and then focused on selective contracting with a reduced number of pharmaceutical suppliers to reduce inventories and gain volume buying discounts. Such plans and in-house capabilities were not prevalent. Outsourcing was also not yet widespread; only 23% of HMOs utilized outside PBMs for their formularies or other clinical programs.[49]

Over time, the PBM model inside the staff-model HMOs was adopted by other HMOs, other MCOs (e.g., PPOs), and a variety of public and private payers who utilized HMOs and MCOs. New PBMs originated as the internal pharmacy departments of MCOs, subsidiaries of insurers, or, like Diversified Pharmaceutical Services (DPS), as external contractors with HMOs on a national or regional basis.[50] Some observers labeled the PBMs as part of the "rapidly growing new managed care technology" that included new "purchasing techniques" to help payers and employers.[51]

Administrative Solutions

The initial, immediate problem was one of numbers and complexity: there were a lot of small dollar claims (relative to hospital bills) to be managed. The PBM's basic, initial advantage was that, unlike indemnity insurance carriers, PBMs could reap scale economies in pharmacy claims processing and pharmacy benefit coverage. These conferred some of the PBMs' "1st generation benefits"—administrative simplication—that the wide healthcare ecosystem has been seeking (see Insert below).

Going beyond administrative simplification, PBMs emerged as a new class of organization to help various parties in the value chain manage the growing number and cost of these prescriptions—which were a function of the growing insured population with either private sector and public sector (e.g., Medicaid) drug coverage and the growing array of new drug therapies that physicians could order. Looking downrange, the next frontier would be cost control and utilization management. Like the MCOs that confronted providers, some observers viewed PBMs as a countervailing force to large pharmaceutical manufacturers and the latter's ability to set high prices and engage in continual price hikes that exceeded inflation.[52] They might also address issues with drug utilization. Finally, PBMs might take the MCO effort of formularies and utilization management to a higher level than that achieved by the most stringent MCO, the health maintenance organization. Compared to retail pharmacies, HMOs paid 20% below the average invoice price for branded drugs; the problem was that HMOs accounted for only 2.7% share in the sales of the 100 top-selling branded drugs in the mid-1990s.[53]

Commenting on their growing role in proactive pharmaceutical management rather than passive distribution, one PBM executive remarked, "With the evolution toward managed care, there has been more interest on the part of payors in finding intermediaries who serve as gatekeepers to monitor how care is delivered, influence practice patterns, and negotiate with doctors and hospitals to improve the quality of care. What we're doing in pharmacy benefits is a microcosm of that."[54] These developments are covered in the sections below.

Advances in Information Systems and Processing

The PBM sector was founded as a set of administrative simplification solutions using both computer hardware and software. Computers enabled batch processing of pharmacy claims that were previously handled manually and stored on data tapes. In 1976, industry stakeholders developed a universal claim form that all insurers could use. In 1977, data standards organizations (i.e., the National Council of Prescription Drug Programs) created and promoted standards for the electronic transfer of healthcare transactions. In short, these developments represented an early version of "big data," "connectivity," and "standardization." Within a decade, further electronic linkages would transform the processing and adjudication of pharmacy claims into an online, point-of-service system. Software engineers working at the fledgling PBMs worked with pharmacies to get the formularies of insurers into the pharmacies' computer systems. According to analysts, this was a key factor enabling the PBMs' growth (along with managed care). Such electronic linkages of pharmacies and PBMs were partly spurred by new forthcoming legislation, the Medicare Catastrophic Coverage Act of 1988, which required pharmacists to submit their claims electronically.

The rise of information systems enabled the electronic processing of claims generated by the growing number of enrollees with drug coverage. These early claims processing functions would serve as the basis for occupying an intermediary role between payers on the one hand and pharmaceutical manufacturers and pharmacies, on the other. Over time, this intermediary role became one of "network centrality" and the ability to "fill structural holes" in those networks between parties who needed to be interdependent.[55] As central network actors, the PBMs would charge fees to these parties—first to pharmacies downstream (discounted charges), and then to manufacturers upstream (discounts off list price). These would become the PBMs two revenue streams; those PBMs that operated a mail-order pharmacy developed a third source.

Claims processing has historically been associated with third-party administrators (TPAs) and pharmacy service administrative organizations (PSAOs), organizations sponsored by either groups of independent pharmacies or a state pharmacy in a local region.[56] While many of the early PSAOs only contracted as a network for dispensing medications, some evolved by the 1990s to provide everything from claims administration and eligibility verification to drug utilization review and formularies—basically indistinguishable from PBMs.

1st Generation PBM Benefits: Identification Cards, Claims Processing & Pharmacy Networks

Outside staff-model HMOs, the PBM sector began as prescription drug claims processors and administrators to help the array of third-parties (HMOs, private insurers, Medicaid programs, employers) now offering drug coverage. Estimates suggested that PBM customers were one-third self-insured employers, one-third HMOs, and one-third PPOs and indemnity insurers.[57]

The PBM industry got its start in the late 1960s when one company (Pharmaceutical Card Systems, or PCS)—with financing by the drug wholesaler McKesson—developed a plastic drug benefit identification card. The card plan was occasioned by collective bargaining between the "Big Three" automakers and the United Auto Workers. PCS allowed employers to offer a new benefit to their unionized employees that facilitated the processing and payment of their drug claims. Formerly, employees had to pay cash for the prescription at the pharmacy, send their receipt to the insurer, and then wait to get reimbursed. Now, with the PCS card, workers could get their medications at retail pharmacies which verified their insurance coverage and charged them only a small, fixed dollar, copayment amount (without having to fill out any insurance forms or keep any receipts to get reimbursed later). Moreover, the card could be used at any participating pharmacy.

PCS served as the TPA, setting both the reimbursement formula (discounted price on the drug) and an agreed-upon dispensing fee for the pharmacy (rather than letting the pharmacy set its own prices). These discounted, per-prescription reimbursements were roughly 10–15% below the average wholesale price index (AWP, see Chapter 9), thereby contributing to lower healthcare costs. Competition among retail pharmacies also reduced their dispensing fees. The pharmacies gathered up the receipts, mailed them into PCS which processed them in batches, and received bi-weekly payments for the TPA-negotiated amounts not paid by patients. PBMs then charged plan sponsors a transaction fee per prescription for processing prescription drug claims as well as a fee to cover the pharmacies' dispensing costs.

The card marked an advance beyond the major medical coverage plans developed years earlier which (1) failed to capture detailed prescription data, (2) required the patient to pay for the drug at the pharmacy and wait to be reimbursed, and (3) contained no proactive methods to reduce costs. Patients liked the convenience and the low out-of-pocket payment; payers liked it because the low copayment incentivized patients to be compliant with their prescriptions; payers further liked it because it reduced the complexity of claims transactions; pharmacies liked it (at least initially) because they received regular, guaranteed payments; and employers liked it because it provided accurate recording and report analysis, as well as improved relationships with employees (and organized labor). Working on behalf of their customers, typically employers and/or their MCOs, the PBM's goal was congruent with efforts to solve the iron triangle: reduce cost, maintain quality, and optimize the use of medications.

Under a master contract, pharmacies could choose to accept or reject involvement and, depending on the employer's size, such contracts could be regional or national. This allowed the new PBM to aggregate demand across beneficiaries on the retail side. The emphasis was on volume purchasing of pharmacy services and wide pharmacy access.[58] These pharmacy networks would serve as the first source of the PBMs' fee revenues: pharmacies that agreed to be in the networks accepted discounted reimbursement, much in the manner of selective contracting. The growing purchasing power and size of the PBMs gave them more leverage over the independent pharmacies and, thus, a foothold to subsequently extract bigger discounts. Such leverage would diminish the pharmacies' enthusiasm for the card plans and increasingly generate animosity between them.

Early Spread of Card Plan PBMs as Outside Contractors to Payers

In 1973, McKesson bought PCS and offered it as a new service to retail pharmacies it supplied as a wholesaler, providing them with quick reimbursement. The popularity and advantages of the PCS approach did not go unnoticed. Another PBM, National Pharmacies, entered the market in 1983; in 1984, after an IPO, National Pharmacies became Medco Containment Services. Medco had originated as a mail-service pharmacy but diversified to offer retail and claims processing functions through its acquisition of PAID Prescriptions in 1985. Medco provided plan subscribers with a prescription drug card that allowed them to purchase drugs at discounted prices from a network of 40,000 drugstores, who then billed the plan sponsors. It was the first PBM to integrate mail-order with claims processing, marking an extension beyond the McKesson/PCS model. Medco dedicated most of its efforts to switching patients from brands which had lost exclusivity to generics, thereby taking advantage of the rising use of generic drugs. After that, PBMs like Medco and health plans would turn their attention to therapeutic substitution (lower cost brand for a higher cost brand) and formulary restrictions where preferred brands paid huge rebates to be preferred.

The card system engendered several first-order and second-order effects that conferred several efficiencies and pro-competitive benefits. It marked a departure from indemnity insurance coverage of drugs under the major medical plans to an administered network relying on TPAs. Writing fewer checks and paying fewer pharmacies minimized administrative costs. The initial efficiency benefit from administrative simplification was further enhanced during the 1970s and 1980s with data standardization and electronic connectivity between the PBM and the pharmacies in its network. In 1987, PCS established the first online, real-time, two-way drug claims processing link with its pharmacies—similar to using a credit card swipe at the point-of-service. This replaced the manual batch processing system used initially by PCS. The technology allowed the pharmacist to send patient information to the PBM and receive back data to immediately confirm the patient's eligibility, whether the drug was on the PBM's formulary, and the amount of the patient's copayment. This was an enormous advance, given that a PBM might contract with 40,000+ retail pharmacies. Over time, as information technology advanced, the pharmacy links included not only claims data but also clinical information. The entire claims adjudication process became paperless.

This advance yielded an extremely valuable tool for PBMs—a massive computer database of prescription records. The national spread of the card plan PBMs and their computer networks allowed PBMs to gather information on consumer prescription drug spending and sell that information to the nation's largest health plan sponsors. The national spread of TPA contracting also facilitated national data on pricing as benefits managers consulted employers on their purchasing decisions. Such national competitive price data engendered national competitive price pressures, which temporally coincided with the managed care pressures to reduce costs. Market forces now confronted the cost of medications. Contracting emphasis shifted from administrative simplification to cost management and improved service.[59]

For example, under the card system, the TPA used an open network approach that allowed patients to use any participating pharmacy. The open-model TPAs would soon give way to "closed-model TPAs" where negotiations with the pharmacy covered price discounts and business volume, as well as included monitoring of pharmacy performance and quality assurance. This newer version TPA model would give way, in turn, to the PBM model which, in the 1990s, got more involved in clinical decision-making to influence physician prescribing and patient utilization.[60] This transition was fueled by the rise in drug expenditures and the need for cost containment.

Calls for Integrated Care and Managed Care Discounts

We should point out that the managed care revolution underway at this time—reflected in the rise of both MCOs and PBMs—was supported by the mantra of "integrated care," which entailed "the right drug/product/service delivered at the right place at the right time to the right patient." This mantra was advanced by policy advocates, embraced by payers and their use of capitation (which might financially benefit from adoption of more cost-effective therapies and non-hospital sites of care), and adopted by the provider community (as they jumped on the integration bandwagon and sought to obtain capitated contracts from payers).

The manufacturers of pharmaceutical and medical products, on the other hand, may have been late to this party. The drug and medical products sectors struggled mightily with this new mantra and these new managed care organizations, largely in opposition to the latter's efforts to reduce product costs and prices on behalf of their clients and the latter's view that was now more hostile than friendly or welcoming. To be sure, some manufacturers quickly discounted their prices and accepted discount contracting as a given. But many if not most of these companies had to be dragged kicking and screaming to the party. Manufacturer executives assigned to "national accounts"—contracting with the new, consolidating managed care and hospital buyers—were now perceived as the enemy, lowering the company's prices, giving away margins, and subverting long-standing marketing relationships with clinician customers.

These dynamics played out differently in the pharmaceutical and medical supplies sectors. But the underlying dynamics were the same. First, manufacturers commonly believed they made physician preference items that did not warrant price discounts, since such discounts did not move market share. Second, and more generally, manufacturers did not believe that the advent of managed care should mean their abandonment of their traditional strategy of marketing directly to the physician. That explains why any PBM or GPO contracting that occurred was largely defensive in nature, and why it met with manufacturer skepticism and hostility.[61]

Mail-Order Benefit

A second-order effect was the rise of mail-order pharmacies that could capitalize on automation allowing high-volume and high-productivity dispensing. Some pharmacies had long used the U.S. Post Office to deliver drugs to residents in rural areas. The Veterans Administration expanded its mail-order pharmacy program in 1946 to deal with the large volume of veterans returning home after World War II. The Veterans Administration was followed by the National Retired Teachers Association in 1959, and then the American Association of Retired Persons (AARP). Other organizations involved in mail-order pharmacy early on included some HMOs (Health Insurance Plan of Greater New York) and organized labor (United Mine Workers). The private sector joined during the 1970s and then more fully in the 1980s. The 1980s saw the most rapid growth of the mail-order pharmacy industry with revenues soaring from $100 Million to $1.5 Billion. The percentage of manufacturer total sales revenues fulfilled via mail-order rose from 6% in 1991 to 10% in 1996.

Mail-order benefits focused on branded (and generic) drugs prescribed for the chronically-ill poor and elderly who might benefit from the convenience of home delivery, particularly since they offered 90-day maintenance medications (rather than the traditional 30-day supply). This not only improved service, but also helped to reduce the customer's copayments (once for 90 days versus thrice for 30 days). The mail-order benefit could be added onto the major medical or comprehensive health plan, or it could be integrated with the card plan as an option to the retail pharmacy network. Enrollees were incentivized to use the mail-order benefit by having their deductibles waived or their copayments reduced (e.g., to $2). The mail-order pharmacy could purchase drugs directly from the manufacturer (rather than through wholesalers) and aggregate prescription fills at high-volume centers in order to further reduce the price of the drug (usually 25% below retail price). Plan sponsors faced lower mail-order service prices of 5–15% compared to retail. Most importantly, fulfillment via mail-order allowed the PBM pharmacist a two-day window to contact the prescribing physician to switch to a lower cost brand (therapeutic substitution)—a time luxury the retail pharmacist did not enjoy. PBMs and other payers could extract higher discounts/rebates where there existed a higher number of competing brand drugs as well as available generics.

Generic Substitution

As noted above, Medco dedicated most of its efforts to "generic substitution": substitute an off-patent brand (which had lost exclusivity) with a generic equivalent. PBMs like Medco were abetted by the generic substitution rules stemming from the Hatch-Waxman Act. PBMs parlayed this advantage in the 1980s into exchanging price discounts from generic manufacturers for inclusion on their formularies. Unlike branded drugs, the competition among the generic manufacturers was all about being the lowest price product—not about product efficacy; formularies were mostly about branded drugs. The mail-order pharmacies helped PBMs to sharpen their competences in developing and managing these formularies. With a growing share of drugs sent through the mail being generics, PBMs gained experience in substituting one generic over another. By the early 1990s, they extended this strategy to branded drugs and negotiating discounted prices and formulary inclusion with branded manufacturers whose drugs faced several competitors in their therapeutic areas, particularly those who were laggards in these therapeutic areas. Many of these developments are illustrated by the rise of Express Scripts (covered below). Consulting firms like McKinsey fed the frenzy over generic drugs during the mid-1990s by developing a formulary designed to cover all of the main therapeutic areas and meet 95% of current drug needs.[62] The formulary contained only 247 drugs, 70% of which were already generic and projected (optimistically but erroneously) to rise to nearly 90% by 1998.

What is not as clear, however, is the degree of MCO and PBM success in leveraging the growing use of generic drugs. Journalists following the industry at that time recall issues with generic substitution rates, physician loyalty to brands, physician compliance with formularies, patient acceptance of any formulary restrictions, physician and consumer distrust of generics as truly effective substitutes, and manufacturers' resistance to discounting generally. The success of generics at this time likely depended on whether the affected brand drug was new or had been on the market for a long time, whether the drug was a market leader or a market laggard, the degree of brand competition, and drug company policies about pricing and discounting. Research suggests the key agency role of physicians in determining whether their patients received brand-name or generic drugs.[63] In particular, physicians targeted by drug manufacturers' via marketing and detailing were much less likely to prescribe generics.[64]

History of Express Scripts (ESRX)[65]

ESRX was launched in St. Louis in 1986 as a joint venture between a large retail pharmacy chain (Medicare Glaser) and Sanus Health Systems, a New York HMO. The company provided mail-order and network pharmacy benefit management services. The initial aim was not to manage drug costs but to take advantage of the expanding market for pharmaceuticals and get into the drug distribution business. ESRX focused on claims processing; its innovative automation reduced cost of processing a claim from $3–4 to $.50. Automation of claims processing also allowed ESRX to monitor the completeness and accuracy of prescriptions at the point-of-service (rather than retrospectively) which could address clinical issues such as drug interactions, refills, and duplicate therapies.

In 1989, ESRX was acquired by another insurer (New York Life, or NYL). NYL then soured on the mail-order business due to its low profitability and its low growth prospects under NYL: other insurers did not want to sign on for ESRX's mail-order business in order to avoid helping a competitor. In 1992, NYL spun off ESRX as a separate public company.

ESRX had weak presence in the group insurance market, which its competitors Medco (13 million lives) and PCS served; the latter PBMs lacked a mail-order business, however. ESRX became one of the first PBMs to offer integrated claims processing, a mail-order service, and a retail network. It built its PBM business via strategic alliances with MCOs and GPOs (e.g., Premier). For one client, ESRX designed an information system to help the staff-model HMO's pharmacies capture prescribing and dispensing data in retail settings, as well as an inventory replacement program for their mail-service business, and helped convert network scripts that could be converted to mail-order in order to cut costs.

In 1995, ESRX founded Practice Patterns Science (PPS) to analyze clusters of diagnostic codes that combined medical claims data with prescription data using hundreds of thousands of decision rules. PPS sought to demonstrate how use (and non-use) of drugs might influence other medical costs. The data were not the key; rather, it was the ability to make informed clinical decisions based on the data and then influence physicians and patients to change their behaviors.

In 1998, Columbia/HCA sold off the PBM (ValueRx) it had acquired the prior year, likely due to the legal problems it faced with its hospital holdings. ESRX picked up ValueRx as an opportunistic buy. By doing so, it doubled its mail-order volume and increased its network prescription claims by 75%. It also acquired DPS. It was now the #3 player in the PBM sector (behind Medco and PCS) and the largest independent, pure-play PBM.

Summary: 1st Generation PBM Benefits

In sum, during the 1970s and 1980s, the PBMs offered valuable administrative functions. These included (1) claims processing, payment to pharmacies, and record keeping and reporting to clients; (2) developing and maintaining pharmacy networks, along with negotiated prices, payment terms, and contracts; (3) developing mail-order pharmacies, and (4) managing drug formularies. These functions improved the efficiency of the growing ecosystem of retail pharmacy utilization, with retail pharmacies taking a financial hit. Prior to the development of PBMs, retail pharmacies purchased drugs from wholesalers at an 18-20% discount off of AWP, but then were reimbursed by payers at a rate above AWP. However, with managed pharmacy networks that traded off negotiated discounts (lower reimbursement rates) from pharmacies in exchange for network inclusion, retail pharmacies now found they were reimbursed below the AWP index. They also began to lose market share in the dispensing of generic drugs.

Subsequent PBM Growth and Success: *The Early 1990s*

As the 1980s progressed, cost pressures built throughout the ecosystem that called for more than administrative simplification. The PBMs' ability to develop competences in formulary design and management, which originated in their more humble origins of patient cards, claims processing, and generics dispensing, now served them well.[66] As the early PBMs got good at developing these solutions targeting administrative simplication, they were able to offer such services to other clients (such as insurers and self-insured employers). This provided them with exposure to their clients' formularies and formulary management techniques, which they developed into their next service offering: managing pharmacy benefits, plan designs, and formularies for brand drugs (including patient co-pays). This, in turn, gave them the ability to aggregate patients and their pharmacy utilization data. Finally, these service additions could be used to obtain price discounts from manufacturers for both generic and branded drugs, and develop formulary designs (using co-pays) that would trade higher price discounts for formulary inclusion and the promise of higher drug sales.

The early 1990s witnessed perhaps the greatest growth in the PBM sector. In early 1994, one analyst summarized the changes as follows[67]:

- 70 million people covered in a 5-year period
- 150–170 million covered by 1994
- Annual growth rate of 20%+
- 25+ PBMs served the market

Pharmacy Networks and Use of Generics

The success of PBMs during this period was due to multiple factors. The PBMs' use of narrow pharmacy networks, preferred generic drugs, lower patient cost-sharing, and pricing contracts and financial incentives paid to pharmacies led to higher generic substitution. In staff-model HMOs, payers/PBMs held great sway over formularies, drug coverage, and physician decision-making. For drugs dispensed outside of staff-model HMOs, PBMs utilized several mechanisms to spur generic use: (1) educational efforts targeting the physician, patient, and pharmacist; (2) lower prices to patients; (3) negotiated reimbursement to pharmacists (MAC payment provisions); and (4) price discounts to manufacturers to get on the PBM formulary.[68] Closed formularies provided no reimbursement for drugs not on the formulary. PBMs that relied more on mail-order pharmacies had a greater opportunity to shift market share in the absence of financial incentives by virtue of their ability to phone the physician.

Formularies for Branded Drugs

As another success factor, PBMs designed formularies to help their clients control drug utilization and drug expenditures on branded drugs. This encompassed several mechanisms:

- encourage the use of formulary drugs through compliance programs that informed physicians and enrollees about which drugs were on the formulary;
- limit the number of branded drugs a plan covered; and/or
- develop financial incentives that encouraged the use of lower-cost brands on the formulary

To develop the formulary, PBMs and/or their clients used pharmacy and therapeutic (P&T) committees, comprised of physicians and pharmacists, to analyze the safety, efficacy, and substitutability of prescription drugs.[69] Based on the recommendations of these committees, the PBM and/or client developed a formulary containing drugs that gave physicians a number of treatment options. To get their drugs on formulary, manufacturers had to discount their prices. These formularies took three different shapes:

- *Open formularies* covered and reimbursed all drugs, regardless of formulary status. They did not penalize enrollees if their physicians prescribed non-formulary drugs. Such formularies were used by the overwhelming majority of PBMs. They were akin to open-network indemnity plans for physicians and hospitals.
- *Incentive-based formularies* reimbursed the enrollee for non-formulary drugs, but required the enrollee to pay a higher copayment. These formularies were akin to PPO models of health coverage.
- *Closed formularies* limited payment to formulary drugs only, unless a physician determined that the non-formulary drug was medically necessary for the patient. These formularies were akin to closed-model HMO plans.

Manufacturer Discounts

Introduction

Formularies called for discounts, but price discounting by pharmaceutical manufacturers was not widespread in the mid-1980s. Many manufacturers hid behind a "one-price policy" to deny discounts to big customers: according to this policy, "we make a drug, it costs this much if you want it, and we're not allowing any wiggle room on this." Only a handful of large, staff-model HMO plans (e.g., Kaiser) succeeded in extracting price discounts. Manufacturers held considerable pricing discretion due to patent protection and (thus) the limited number of new entrants in a therapeutic category. Differentiated oligopolies—where a handful of competitors competed on product differences—were more common than monopolies in many therapeutic areas. Government reports indicate the high degree of concentration within therapeutic areas in the early 1990s. Of 66 drug classes studied (representing 70% of total retail drug sales during 1991–1994), the Congressional Budget Office found that the top three innovator drugs accounted for 80%+ of sales in more than half of the classes. Conversely, in only 9 of these classes did the top three innovator drugs make up less than 50% of sales.[70]

Pricing rivalry among manufacturers was further blunted by manufacturers' "respect for oligopolistic interdependence"[71]—manifested in their reluctance to cut drug prices in one therapeutic area due to likely competitor retaliation in another area—and their preference to compete on product differentiation. Manufacturers wanted to compete on the basis of product performance and differentiation, not prices (which were almost a taboo subject). That formed the basis of their one-price policy. The drug manufacturers' spending on sales, general, and administrative (SG&A) costs, exercised through marketing and their sales representative forces, all served to reinforce this.

Following in the GPOs' Footsteps

The GPOs had already (1) pioneered their own version of drug product formularies in their pharmacy departments and (2) exchanged manufacturer price discounts for placement on their formularies. They, too, relied on discounted pricing to change hospitals' buying, just as PBMs tried to influence physicians' prescribing. But, the GPO effect was muted for several reasons. First, these drugs did not include branded products with a monopoly in their therapeutic area; manufacturers did not have to enter

GPO contracts, since there was no competitive alternative. Second, for some drugs, the hospitals may not have routed their purchases through their GPOs if such purchases were managed by the hospital pharmacy rather than materials management—somewhat similar to separating the management of the drug and medical benefit. Third, hospital GPOs were relatively insignificant customers of pharmaceutical manufacturers. According to David Cassak, hospital sales constituted only 15% of pharmaceutical sales.[72] Moreover, GPOs only intermediated roughly half of those hospital sales (7.5%); any one GPO represented only one-fifth of that (1.5%), affording it very little leverage over suppliers. SmithKlineBeecham, which launched its first national account for a bundle of drugs, only did so in 1986.

Moreover, the GPO phenomenon played out slightly differently for retail pharmaceuticals than for medical supplies. The retail/institutional ratio was reversed for these two products: 75–25% for retail drugs, and 25–75% for hospital supply. Culturally, the hospital pharmacist was seen as a professional with a legitimate voice in product selection, while the hospital materials manager was often promoted from the warehouse, didn't have the same professional cachet and authority when weighing in on product selection/preference issues, and was assigned an office located near the loading dock. Hence if the hospital pharmacist was reluctant to use a product on contract, he/she was less likely to be challenged; by contrast, the materials manager sometimes ran into opposition from the physicians/surgeons/nurses who were being asked to use the products offered on the contract and who had more support/sway within the institution.

The inpatient drug formularies used by hospitals helped to stimulate formularies on the outpatient side, developed initially by HMOs/MCOs, to foment competition among manufacturers, gain price concessions, and tackle the bigger problem of outpatient drug spending. The only headwind facing these formularies, other than manufacturer dislike, was physician acceptance and compliance. Physicians in IPA-model HMOs saw only a few managed care patients and thus did not earn much from the incentives employed by MCOs and PBMs (e.g., a withhold for cost-effective prescribing). Physicians' primary concern was with the quality, not the cost, of prescription medication. Nevertheless, physicians who observed the inpatient formularies may have grown more accustomed to their presence on the outpatient side.[73]

PBM Replication of GPO Traction

The situation began to change before the end of the 1980s. The rise of large GPO buyers on the inpatient side was now accompanied by the rise of large

PBM buyers on the retail side. The PBM programs of large MCOs began to exercise the same influence as the GPOs, or at least try to employ the same tactics. Analysts like David Cassak recognized that what was happening with medical supply GPOs could be replicated in the world of retail drugs and PBMs—but had trouble convincing opinion leaders such as John Wilkerson or even his colleague, Roger Longman. Cassak and Longman, two of this chapter's co-authors, represented the views of PBM advocates and skeptics, respectively. According to Longman, "David wasn't right then, but he became right over time: everyone knows PBMs are huge powerbrokers today." GPOs and PBMs both pursued aggregated buying, both sought to win price discounts, and both sought to influence physician product selection or prescription behavior. But the PBMs utilized more management strategies that were less national and more customized to local markets. These strategies included:

- Help MCO plans manage pharmacy use and work with their P&T committees on issues of therapeutic equivalence, compliance rates, side effects, and local community standards
- Create a different type of customer for the national account teams of manufacturers that tried to: manage pharmacy benefits (not just volume buys at the lowest unit price), focus on local community practice standards and customized formularies (no national formulary), balance the need to reduce costs via reducing duplication and limiting the number of drugs in a therapeutic area with the clinical value of having a well-stocked formulary
- Maintain an open formulary but recommend to physicians what drugs to use based on cost-effectiveness by designating each drug's relative cost (number of $$ signs)
- Utilize aggressive generic substitution programs, already instituted in the late 1970s (e.g., 40% generic usage at DPS vs. 27% nationally), promoted by coverage policies (formularies make explicit when generics should be prescribed) rather than exclusion of brands
- Encourage use of the formularies via MAC reimbursement to pharmacies that set limits on how much the HMO will pay for a prescription

Shift to Discounting

The shift to outpatient discounting was much less passive mimicry of the GPOs than active PBM strategy to exploit the weakening of manufacturer market power. While the drug buyers were consolidating, drug suppliers were facing increased competition within therapeutic areas due to their introduction of more "me-too" drugs: drugs that were slightly differentiated in their chemical formulation (where the patent lay) but used the same basic mechanism to treat an illness and thus were functionally similar.[74] Two therapeutic areas—beta-blockers and statins—quickly flooded with me-too drugs due to the rapid demand for these products.

Aggressive HMOs and PBMs began to challenge the old order in the mid-to-late 1980s by using formularies.[75] Listing on HMO formularies was becoming critical to drug sales, since there were more competing drugs in a given class and there were an increasing number of HMOs whose formularies could be either closed or incentive-based. HMOs recognized this and began tough negotiations with manufacturers. An HMO would seek a price discount from the weakest manufacturer, and then threaten the others with removal from formulary and subsequent movement of their share to the price discounter if they did not follow suit. Not surprisingly, manufacturers lacking a strong brand made similar price concessions. As noted by Federal Court Judge Arthur Kocoras, who presided over the 1996 antitrust suit brought by retail pharmacists (covered at end of chapter), one manufacturer committed the "original sin" of granting the first discount.[76]

Many (but not all) manufacturers quickly abandoned a one-price policy and recognized the need for pricing differentials. They entered contracts with discounted prices for several reasons: (1) the era of managed care was at hand, (2) managed care's emphasis on cost threatened to commoditize the manufacturers' product offerings and brand image that had been carefully nurtured over time with physicians, (3) manufacturers thought it worth the risk to discount in order to potentially gain new business, (4) manufacturers feared they might lose business and market share if they did not enter price discounting contracts, (5) manufacturers faced growing competition within therapeutic areas, and (6) there was the potential threat that many managed care plans with open formularies (that did not restrict brand choice) might tighten them.

We might make two qualifications to the foregoing argument. First, the uptake and degree of contracting clearly suggests that manufacturers were becoming more receptive to discounting, but not without much internal angst and debate. Some drug manufacturers adopted the stance of defensive contracting. This tact was designed more to appease PBMs and hold market positions than to drive new business; it may have been used more for well-established products than for promising new blockbusters. It was a curious phenomenon for the pharmaceutical industry that the rise of managed care largely coincided with the rise of the blockbuster drug in the mid-1990s. Pharmaceutical CEOs were challenged with an ambidextrous task. On the one hand, they had to find the next blockbuster on which rested the company's soaring stock valuation; on the other hand, they were told they had to reckon with the new reality of managed care and price discounting.

Second, adding to the resistance of manufacturers, the notion of a "contract" in the PBM/GPO world had a different meaning than in other areas of business: simply put, it wasn't binding. Executives of drug companies would routinely say, "I would be more supportive if we offered discounts/rebates that actually drove business, but that's not always what happens."

More generally, they offered such discounts to MCO/PBM customers on the assumption that long-standing class of trade distinctions would safeguard them from any requirement to offer the same prices to the much more lucrative retail sector.[77] To be sure, manufacturers preferred not to grant discounts to those with buying power. "It was much more important, however, to retard the development of that power in the first place."[78] That is why manufacturers granted discounts to HMOs and mail-order pharmacies (i.e., those who could influence physicians) but not to the retail pharmacies or their buying groups (PSAOs).[79]

Indeed, there are some reports that the PBMs did not always initiate ("pull down") the use of discounts; rather they were pushed down by manufacturers in efforts to gain better formulary status and thereby market share. Manufacturers may have also entered such contracts because other private payers, as well as public payers such as Medicare and Medicaid, were still paying undiscounted prices. Drug prices more than tripled the inflation rate between 1981 and 1988, perhaps making discounts paid to PBMs affordable.

Finally, MCOs and PBMs appeared to be new central players in the ecosystem that served to link up multiple, interdependent participants: physicians, patients, pharmacies, manufacturers, and insurers. By the early 1990s, there were signs that smaller, more restrictive, and even closed formularies would take off. HMO and PPO models were now on the upswing in terms of their numbers and the size of employee enrollments: managed care penetration soared from 26% in 1988 to 61% by 1995.[80] As HMO and PPO enrollments swelled in the late 1980s and early-to-mid-1990s, evidence emerged of shifts in market shares within a given HMO as well as spillover effects from HMO to less restrictive MCO plans (e.g., IPAs).

Discounting Dynamics

By the early 1990s, the landscape had dramatically changed. PBMs negotiated with the drug manufacturers to obtain discounts for a variety of plan sponsors (employer, insurer, or MCO). Nearly all HMOs (89% in 1992) offered their enrollees an outpatient prescription drug benefit and utilized their market power to leverage manufacturers. Such HMO benefit designs increasingly included formularies: from 39% (1989) to 49% (1991) and then to 66% (1992). Formulary use was still most prevalent in staff-model HMOs (90%) but were nevertheless heavily utilized by their IPA counterparts (59%).[81] Manufacturers who balked at discounting demands were relegated to unfavorable formulary positions and lost sales. The threat of lost sales led manufacturers to grant discounts.

The size of the discount depended on several factors: the degree of manufacturer competition in that therapeutic area, the number of lives covered by the PBM (aggregated purchasing volume), formulary policy, and demand for that manufacturer's drug. High-selling brand drugs might bring only a small discount if there were no or few competitor products to which the PBM could switch. Sometimes the PBM might earn a discount if it was willing to include a bundle of the manufacturer's products on its formulary that included both the popular brand drug along with less favored drugs. Such efforts at bundling had to be careful not to violate tying arrangements and the Robinson Patman Act (which blocked offering different prices to different customers).

According to the Boston Consulting Group,[82] the average discounts from manufacturers' list prices rose from 4% in 1987 to 16% in 1992, due to the rising percentage of drugs sold through MCOs. Favored purchasers like HMOs got discounts based on the <u>promise</u> to increase sales of drugs from their formularies, which induced price competition among manufacturers.[83] The HMOs also used their market power to leverage pharmacies. HMOs obtained 18–25% discounts off the average invoice prices paid by retail pharmacists; some HMOs or hospitals got 50% discounts off WAC for 32% of all single-source drugs.

Price discounts took several forms. One was a flat rebate (constant percentage of drug price, e.g., 10%) that was used when there were only a limited number of competitors. Another was an access rebate (also based on a constant percentage) that was used to gain a foothold in the PBM's formulary or just prevent being blocked by the PBM. A third type was a market share or tiered rebate, which pegged the percentage of the drug's market share sold through the PBM compared to its competitors for a given drug class. This was used when there were multiple competitors in the therapeutic area. In all cases, rebates were captured by the PBM at the end of a calendar quarter; the information was then submitted to the manufacturer who validated it and then paid the PBM 3–6 months later.[84,85]

Public Payers and Discounting

Rebates were soon pursued by public payers seeking to contain one of their fastest growing public expenditures. The Medicare Catastrophic Coverage Act of 1988 intended to cover outpatient prescriptions for the elderly but base prescription drug prices at AWP—far higher than the retail rate. The plan was quickly repealed, especially when Congress learned the drug benefit would quickly run a deficit. Subsequent Congressional hearings identified a major problem in rising drug prices. The Medicaid program then picked up the banner to make drugs accessible at lower prices. Up until this time, states did not receive drug discounts but rather paid near-retail prices, even though Medicaid was the largest purchaser of drugs.

The Medicaid Prescription Drug Rebate Program (MDRP), embodied in the Medicaid Prudent Pharmaceutical Purchasing Act (itself part of Omnibus Budget and Reconciliation Act, or OBRA, 1990) and sponsored by Senator David Pryor—was designed to save money for state/federal Medicaid programs. It gave Medicaid "most favored nation" (MFN) status, guaranteeing that manufacturers sell their drugs to Medicaid at the lowest price available to any other purchaser. The program was phased in over three years and included a minimum rebate of 12.5% of AMP in 1991 and 15.1% in 1992; after that, rebates were driven by the best price a manufacturer offered its customers. Generic manufacturers got a flat rebate of 10% of AMP (and then 11%). In exchange for these rebates, Medicaid guaranteed open-access and coverage of all of the manufacturer's drugs with no use of formularies. To qualify for coverage, manufacturers had to sign agreements to pay rebates on all drugs. Medicaid rebates likely fostered support for MCO contracting and rebates which, in turn, fostered the use of PBMs. By 2004, 550 pharmaceutical manufacturers participated in the program. The program reportedly horrified drug company executives (and some politicians) who hated the idea that the federal government would use its size and clout to get into price negotiations. Yet, difficulties in the states' monitoring of their "best prices" may have limited the success of the MDRP. Between 1990 and 1997, Medicaid expenditures on outpatient prescription drugs increased 14.8% annually; between 1997 and 2000, they increased 18.1% annually.[86]

Ironically, the strategy of price discounting by Medicaid in the public sector may have curtailed the success of brand drug discounting in the private sector. To protect themselves against high Medicaid rebates, many pharmaceutical manufacturers ceased paying price discounts in the private sector; others began to retract or alter their contracts with PBMs; most were wary of offering big discounts to any one insurer greater than the 15.1% threshold in

Medicaid (in 1992).[87] According to health economists, OBRA also induced pharmaceutical "cost-shifting." By requiring rebates paid to State Medicaid programs for retail drugs based on "best prices" charged to other customers, manufacturers responded with higher prices charged to HMOs and GPOs. Indeed, GAO reports[88] suggested that the purchaser with the greatest market power (Medicaid) forced manufacturers to cost shift to those with less market power (payers in the private sector). This was evident from data between 1991 and 1993 showing that the best price discount obtained by HMOs and GPOs for outpatient drugs fell[89]:

	HMOs	GPOs
1991	24.4%	27.8%
1992	18.4%	22.1%
1993	14.2%	15.3%

There was also the question whether the mandatory discounts in Medicaid (12.5% and then 15.1%) now served as *de facto* price ceilings (or, alternatively, discount floors) which vitiated more substantial discounts some PBMs had negotiated (estimated at 25–30% for the largest HMOs). This may have had the effect of dampening price competition among manufacturers. Manufacturers may also have engaged in defensive pricing strategies by hiking list prices in their commercial business before the rebates kicked in as part of a cost-shifting approach.

Another reason for the slow uptake and impact of price discounting may have been the small size of PBMs relative to pharmaceutical manufacturers. Even though all PBMs used tools such as formularies, drug utilization review (DUR, covered below), and generic substitution, the MCO sector which contracted with them was quite fragmented and disorganized, precluding any PBM from exercising enough clout to extract pricing discounts. Other reasons included the continuing prevalence of open formularies and manufacturer reluctance to discount for fear of alienating retail druggists.

Shift to 2nd Generation of PBM Services: *Mid-1990s*

As the 1990s progressed, discounts appeared to have limited ability to hold down prescription drug costs; more was obviously needed. Therapeutic substitution and price discounting began to give way to outcomes research and utilization-driven approaches (e.g., DUR). What motivated this shift?

Demise of Discounting

One possible explanation came from "the sell side." The rise of the initial formularies prompted pharmaceutical manufacturers to offer big price discounts to get listed on formulary. But manufacturers grew increasingly skeptical that price discounts drove sales. Manufacturers wanted evidence that formulary inclusion would alter physician prescribing patterns and thereby lead to shifts in market share. Many pharmaceutical firms reportedly signed contracts but did not witness any changes in market share, perhaps due to the prevalence of open formularies. Indeed, in order to generate market share changes, PBMs had to induce changes in prescriptions to the drugs under their contracts; to do so, however, required the cooperation of physicians, patients, clients' P&T committees, and maybe pharmacists.[90] As Spencer Johnson's famous book of the era suggested, "that was a lot of cheese to move."[91] As market share increases failed to materialize after one round of contracting, pharma manufacturers became more cautious in offering rebates in the second round. There were three relevant issues here: (1) the stance of defensive contracting which offered smaller discounts just to secure a spot on the formulary; (2) the "hunting license" nature of so-called contracts, which did not guarantee sales; and (3) the implicit bias among physician customers (prescribers) to favor entrenched market leaders. The market leaders had large sales forces that dwarfed those of smaller, non-market leaders. The latter could, in theory, have offered deeper discounts to gain business but didn't have the commercial infrastructure to support conversion to a non-market-leading brand.

Pharmaceutical firms realized that only a minority of MCO health plans (e.g., staff-model HMOs) exerted influence over physician prescribing to manage drug utilization. The implication was simple: no influence over market share meant no discount. Plans now had to "earn their discounts" by delivering gains in market share. The more effective MCOs now received even deeper discounts to secure their preferred status, while smaller or less effective plans saw their discounts eliminated.[92] Plans and PBMs focused on actively managing prescriptions with the highest dispensing volume and highest cost. They also shifted to therapeutic substitution as a better approach, which fit with their prior strategy of generic substitution.

Another explanation came from "the buy side." PBMs had two different customers that differed in what they wanted from them. MCO customers wanted their PBM subcontractors to support the MCOs' own programs. That meant contracts that maximized rebates, systems that helped MCOs to manage their investment in the drugs they covered (e.g., therapeutic substitution, use of drugs to offset physician and hospital expenditures), and help with analyzing data to facilitate drug switches. By virtue of high patient turnover in managed care plans (who worked on behalf of fully-insured employers), MCOs wanted to manage costs over the shorter-term. By contrast, employers (especially those who were self-insured) found the rebates helpful but were also attuned to access and service issues. Employees wanted access to preferred drugs and pharmacies. Access was implicit in the pharmacy network and claims processing functions offered by the PBMs. It also included "member support": answering the phone when enrollees called, taking calls 24/7, and having a broadly distributed (geographically) pharmacy network to service lots of scattered employee sites. These employers also wanted to manage the healthcare costs of their employees over the longer-term, since employees might stay with them longer than with their health plans and because employers might have assumed responsibility for healthcare costs of employees post-retirement.

Yet another possible explanation was that the volume-driven, price discounting contracts suffered from other weaknesses. Such contracts reportedly had escape clauses that were too easy for manufacturers to exercise. It may also have been the case that all manufacturers offered discounts, but that such discounts did not yield enough price differentials to benefit one drug over another. Alternatively, there may have been weak employer resolve to push workers into closed plans and closed formularies. For example, three-tier co-pays were viewed as a less disruptive effort to achieve some cost savings but allow patient choice and access to desired drugs. This was an essential part of defensive contracting. David Cassak also recalls from his conversation with large employers in the mid-1990s how they viewed their management of the drug spend:

> We're really focused on managing the medical care portion of our health costs; drugs are a cost, but relatively minor. The last thing we want to do is to alienate hard working employees who get very nervous when we ask them to switch drugs (true in some cases about generics as well as branded). I don't want my Human Resource (HR) department's voice messaging system filled on Monday morning with a lot of employees complaining that they used to take a round white pill and now they have to take a red tablet. It makes them nervous, can be alienating, and is not worth the hassle.
>
> [According to David] "I don't know how widespread that sentiment was at the time, but several people mentioned that. Now, there was some selection bias - - I was talking to employers who were active and aggressive when it comes to managing health benefits. Maybe other employers would have a different perspective. But I definitely heard, "it's just not worth it" when it came to

aggressive therapeutic and generic substitution. It's also possible that another factor was the tendency of many MCOs to have separate budgets for drugs and medical care as well as the perception in some circles that the greater use of Rx could help reduce the medical component by keeping people healthy."[93]

Shift to Utilization Management

Prodded by their clients, PBMs shifted away from closed networks and price discounting to a second generation of PBM services focused on the clinical side as well as the economic side of managed care. While some clients wanted PBM formularies to drive bigger savings, most employers did not want to alienate their employees. Employers did not want to be in the position of forcing employees to choose one drug brand over another, and were somewhat agnostic about the specific brands on formulary due to concerns over patient confidentiality and privacy. The HR staff at employers also did not want to field complaints from both workers and physicians; they already had enough on their hands by pushing or influencing workers to join HMOs and PPOs. Employers just wanted to manage their aggregate drug expenditures and leave the details of formulary management to their benefits consultants, their MCO, the PBM, and their P&T committees. This was important since the choices about which drugs to cover, even in closed formularies, were made by the client and the P&T committee, not by the PBM.

After 1996, the HMO movement stalled and the employer market shifted to more open-access plans such as PPOs and point-of-service (POS) plans. Even some staff-model HMOs (like Kaiser) followed suit to compete by moving away from totally closed networks to embrace IPA panels and non-employed MDs. Manufacturers saw the demise of closed formularies as part of the larger failure of the PBMs and MCOs to deliver on promised greater market share in return for rebates.

If the PBMs were to exert influence and move market share, it would not be through price discounting. An alternate path was to reduce drug utilization (volume) while leaving employees with choice. This ushered in patient cost-sharing and tiered networks, rather than closed formularies. These efforts initially targeted lower cost products (e.g., generics or brands offering rebates). Like PPOs, employees retained freedom of choice but faced higher cost-sharing if they selected non-preferred drugs. As patients' freedom of choice was restricted, so too was physician influence over drug choice. To effect this shift, PBMs engaged in patient education and drug co-pays. This served as a precursor to efforts that focused initially on finding the most cost-effective therapy rather than the cheapest product, and then later on shifting from volume to value. This had the virtue of getting at least some buy-in from manufacturers and reducing the hostility and resistance that discount contracting engendered. Once manufacturers recognized that some form of utilization review was coming, they figured it was better (at least optically) to be on the side of proper medical care than fight against it in the name of opposing price cuts.

Managed care approaches to drug coverage also entailed DUR to improve quality and reduce cost. OBRA included a regulatory requirement for real-time DUR. This requirement entailed screening for therapeutic duplication, drug disease contra-indications, drug interactions, incorrect dosage or duration of drug treatment, drug allergy interaction, and clinical abuse or misuse. The needed clinical services helped spur growth in the PBM sector.

More generally, utilization review for acute care services took one of three forms: retrospective, concurrent, and prospective. Utilization review for drugs consisted of just the first two types. In *retrospective DUR*, PBMs analyzed drug utilization practices to identify possible inappropriate drug prescribing and consumption. In such cases, the PBM contacted the prescribing physician about better and potentially more cost-effective treatment options. *Concurrent DUR* took place at the point of dispensing. The pharmacist utilized the computer linkage to the PBM to review the prescription and identify if there was a generic or formulary alternative. The system also analyzed whether the prescription duplicated an existing prescription or whether it adversely interacted with another medication taken by the patient. If a non-formulary, duplicate, or potentially harmful drug was identified, the pharmacist was notified on the computer screen.

Over time—as with managed care health plans, P&T committees, and formularies in general—physicians became more accustomed to these control mechanisms and, perhaps, more cost conscious in their prescribing. Studies conducted during the 1990s indicated that managed care practices of physicians "spilled over" to their non-managed care patients, once they reached a certain threshold of MCO patients in their panel.[94] Moreover, many physicians saw them not as control mechanisms but as advisory services and less objectionable than mandates to prescribe drugs just because they were cheaper. Throughout the last two decades of the twentieth century, perhaps as an acceptance of small area variations research (e.g., The Dartmouth Atlas), there was an interesting uptake in physician acceptance of data, benchmarking, and controls.

Disease Management

During the 1990s, managed care plans also developed disease management programs to target the utilization and cost incurred for specific conditions.[95] These conditions were typically for chronic illnesses such as asthma and diabetes. Because drug therapies were a major part of the physician's armamentarium for dealing with chronic illness, managed care plans and PBMs borrowed this approach to manage the small percentage of enrollees that had each condition but which contributed a disproportionate share of their care costs. PBMs evaluated treatment options from existing medical research and identified a program of treatment that would hopefully result in better therapy management and lower cost.

When the management program was developed, the PBM then educated both plan enrollees and their physicians about the more cost-effective treatment program and monitored the rate of compliance. For example, PBM pharmacists would contact the physician to (1) inform the physician that his/her patient should be taking its drug, (2) make sure the patient with that condition was prescribed the appropriate medication, and (3) likewise contact the pharmacist and patient to close the loop. Disease management technologies also included outcomes reporting and cost effectiveness studies. David Cassak provides one illustration.[96]

> The treatment of diabetes was a major focus for PBM's disease management programs. For example, research showed that better glycemic control and management could reduce the complications associated with diabetes by as much as 60%. Moreover, significantly better glucose control could be achieved simply by improved patient self-management and adherence to the acknowledged standards of care. In a fully functional disease management platform a PBM could identify those patients that met specific criteria based on the prescriptions both written and filled by mining its pharmaceutical claims database. The PBM could then design a two-pronged education campaign targeted both at the patient and the prescriber. The patient was contacted and given a newsletter, an 800 number information hotline, counseling, diabetes education referrals, and a primary assessment report. Similarly, the physician received a newsletter, an information hotline, and a primary assessment report, and worked with patients to better control their disease.

Other players in the healthcare value chain began to focus on managing disease, perhaps as part of the ongoing 1990s movement toward integrated healthcare. Some hospital systems that vertically integrated into their physician markets (e.g., by employing primary care physicians) and/or entered risk contracts with payers now sought to gain control over outpatient spending, including retail drug spend. Retail drugs were the larger share of drug costs, and represented costs the hospitals were now responsible for under capitated contracts. There were several illustrations:

American Healthcare Systems (AmHS), which operated its own GPO (see Chapter 4), entered a joint venture with a PBM, Express Scripts, to develop a joint formulary, merge volume buying, and give AmHS access to the PBM's information systems and disease management approach.[97] AmHS was motivated by the integration mantra of managing the continuum of care, which included the ambulatory (and thus retail) market.

AmHS was not alone. Another PBM, Caremark, was acquired by a physician practice management company, Mullikin, to gain access to its pharmaceutical prescribing information to develop its own disease management program.[98]

Three other deals between hospital systems/GPOs and PBMs were inked during the same time period. In 1994, Premier and Express Scripts signed a 10-year agreement, possibly to help Premier's new physician practice management company (PPMC). In 1996, VHA struck an alliance with a PBM, Advance ParadigM, largely because some of VHA's largest hospital members had their own HMOs which might use the PBM's services. In early 1997, Columbia/HCA acquired Value Health and its subsidiary PBM, ValueRx (where 70% of its revenues lay).

The new "holy grail" of pharmacy management was to link inpatient and outpatient formularies so that patients started on a drug in the hospital were not forced to switch to another drug for in-home therapy after discharge.[99] Disease management also held out the hope of a higher-margin business by virtue of allowing the PBM to capture a portion of the MCO's savings on the 93% of spending. This looked more attractive than the traditional fixed, low-margin fee charged per transaction.

But disease management was not without its problems. First, in the traditional model, the PBM made money by using more of a pharmaceutical manufacturer's drugs. In disease management, the PBM made money by sharing in the savings generated for MCO clients by reducing spending on patients with specific conditions; if the pharmaceutical manufacturer did not have drugs in this therapeutic area, there was little basis for partnership. Second, successful disease management was more about classes of therapy, not specific pharmaceutical brands (which had always been the preoccupation of large manufacturers).

Total Cost, Pharmaceutical Care Management, and Big Data

A related PBM initiative included data capture and management—perhaps a forerunner to "big data." On the clinical side, PBMs amassed aggregated (non-identifiable) and longitudinal patient data characterizing drug prescribing, utilization, and expenditure. These data were superior to the information available to pharmaceutical manufacturers, which encompassed prescriptions, the prescribing physicians, and prescription frequency. Longitudinal data on large patient populations might allow PBMs to address appropriate drug use, improve population health, and tackle healthcare costs. PBMs used such data to provide their clients with reports that highlighted enrollee compliance with medications. In this manner, PBMs could link multiple interdependent parties (e.g., pharmacies, patients, payers, PBMs, and physicians), convey information regarding disease management and therapeutic interchange, and help foster integrated healthcare.[100]

Indeed, as a result of these efforts, the enhanced PBMs presented themselves to payer clients as "integrated pharmacy services" that spanned claims administration, adjudication, mail-order, and clinical oversight—all to improve quality and reduce cost. This was reminiscent of, and coincident with, the integrated delivery networks (IDNs) being developed at exactly the same time by providers. Indeed, Dr. Roy Vagelos, CEO of Merck, commented, "We could see that the power of the buyers was growing: through their formularies, PBMs were changing the competitive dynamic of our marketplace by bringing together the person who chooses the drug and the person who pays for the drug." In effect, this looked just like the prepaid group model HMOs of the 1970s and 1980s that integrated financing and care.[101]

Medco joined this integration movement by first combining its two businesses (mail-order and claims processing) into a comprehensive PBM program that Fortune 500 clients found attractive. Then, in 1991, Medco launched its "Prudent Prescriber Program" to steer physicians to the drugs it considered cost-effective using education in its mail-order program; it extended this to its retail prescription drug business as well. Both were designed to drive volume. In early 1993, Medco rolled out a closed formulary in several therapeutic areas but allowed most formularies to remain open with incentives (co-pay differentials) to steer patients to drugs on the formulary. Medco's "Prescribers Choice" program contracted with ten pharmaceutical companies to cover 32 drugs in 10 therapeutic areas on a discounted price basis, which encompassed a base discount with 2–3 tiers.[102] These plans replaced earlier plans that included only a base discount on branded products.

One issue confronting Medco was the mismatch in the capacity of its two businesses. By 1992, only 7 million of Medco's 29 million covered lives partook of the integrated offering; 22 million participated in just the mail-order business (where Medco had market share of 50%+). Medco believed that the client sponsors of the latter wanted a integrated program which could impose managed care controls and capture information on drug utilization and cost. Medco also launched its formularies in early 1993; most were open formularies but some clients experimented with closed formularies.

This was not so much a new model of integrated pharmaceutical care, but perhaps rather a strategy of vertical integration into the information business. The emphasis was no longer on just selling pills but also selling pharmaceutical care management. The new theory was that manufacturers could make more money by saving money for MCOs via prescription medication therapy management (MTM) than by getting physicians to prescribe more pills.

According to this theory, greater attention to the 7% of drug spending on these high-risk patient groups might contribute to lower spending and reduced utilization of hospitals and physicians (the other 93% of spending). This was the essence of disease management. It re-defined the value of a drug within a broader healthcare cost containment context and sought to combine drug treatment with guidelines and utilization protocols. The focus now broadened to "episodes of care" and looked at how substitution of lower cost drug therapies might supplant higher cost acute care services. The goal was to link drug usage with data on acute care utilization, provide a more holistic view of physician prescribing and treatment choices, as well as their impact on patient health status and outcomes, and thereby change physician prescribing behavior. In this new environment, drugs were not a commodity item but rather a powerful and unique contributor to the patient's health status. In some respects, this represented an integrated approach to employee health benefits. Rather than carve out the pharmacy benefit, it needed to be coordinated with the medical benefit.

But this strategy too, like disease management, faced some serious headwinds. Larger MCOs were more likely to invest in technology upgrades to their medical information systems (the medical benefit side) than their pharmaceutical information systems (the pharmacy benefit side); a main reason was the latter benefit had been traditionally outsourced. Moreover, MCOs and their sponsors (the employers) may not have been convinced about the strategy of substituting lower cost drugs for higher cost hospital and physician services. Indeed, economists are not unanimous about the success of such substitution efforts.

Thus, at a macro level, the pendulum swung from the cost angle of the iron triangle to the access (and quality) angle of the iron triangle. The *cost angle* encompassed price discounts, commoditization via generic use, and (increasingly) commoditization via therapeutic substitution (when there were several alternative drugs in a class). All pharmaceutical manufacturers offered discounts which led to some fall in prices, but the cost differentials were not big enough to benefit one drug over another. As a result, there was little movement in market share and, thus, waning manufacturer interest in discounting. By contrast, the *access angle* focused on the differentiation (rather than commoditization) of the drug and its ability to manage the outcomes of specific groups of patients, particularly those with chronic conditions that entailed a large chunk of drug spending.

Vertical Integration with Manufacturers

Background: Playing Defense

Analysts characterized the historical relationships between pharmaceutical manufacturers and MCOs/PBMs as "difficult."[103] In the past, Merck had resisted MCO/PBM discounting pressures by insisting on a one-price policy and a product line that MCOs could not substitute against. Merck felt it had little need for PBMs. However, manufacturers who had decided not to discount their drug prices to PBMs may have underestimated the speed at which PBMs were changing their business.

For example, Merck elected not to contract with Medco in therapeutic areas like cholesterol-lowering drugs that contributed heavily to Merck's sales. BMS, by contrast, agreed to aggressive price discounting and won the Medco contract for its drug *Pravachol* in a "price-based formulary win" that showed the power of therapeutic substitution. It also won a lot of major payer accounts based on its lower, discounted price. The price gap that now existed between *Pravachol* and Merck's *Mevacor* led Medco pharmacists in their regional distribution centers to call physicians and urge them to prescribe BMS's drug or use generics rather than Merck.[104] Medco pharmacists reportedly made 2 million phone calls a year to educate physicians in this manner—all of which accelerated price competition among manufacturers.[105] Merck's top-selling cholesterol drug immediately began to stagnate in sales (2% growth 1992–1993) and lose market share. One Merck executive commented that, "The degree to which Medco was able to shift market share away from *Mevacor* was unthinkable. One day it was all quiet on the western front, and the next day it was war."[106] This posed a huge threat to Merck, which had added 700 sales representatives in the prior few years to market these drugs.

According to industy analysts, the biggest fear of pharmaceutical manufacturers was price competition. A corollary threat was the ascendance of managed care that might energize and galvanize the efforts of price-sensitive clients to spur such competition. MCOs and PBMs exploited the weakening market power of manufacturers. By the early 1990s, over 90% of drugs on patent had competitors with similar benefits, although drug classes were still largely oligopolies. According to an analysis by the Boston Consulting Group, there were 3 + drugs that shared similar clinical profiles in 15 of the 20 major therapeutic classes.[107] This nevertheless signaled to manufacturers the importance of getting physicians to try their drug first over one's competitors. In therapeutic classes with substitutes, the first drug to be tried was successful 60–70% of the time, yielding 60–70% market share. Thus, competition for the formulary became key. The entry point to the formulary was price discounting.[108] This resembled the two-stage competition among suppliers developing on the inpatient hospital side to deal with GPOs: compete for the contract and then compete for product sales within that contract. To slow down this train, some pharmaceutical executives felt that using class of trade distinctions—i.e., offering discounts to the large PBMs and GPOs—would shelter them from having to offer the same lower prices to the more lucrative retail sector.[109] Pricing differentials might also be used for the manufacturer's more vulnerable product lines to protect the more franchise drugs.

PBM Cooptation

In response to market share losses on *Mevacor*, Merck's CEO Roy Vagelos urged executives to negotiate with PBMs to get the company's products into preferred positions on PBM formularies. Merck had already witnessed the 1980s' success of GPOs in obtaining discounts on commodity items for hospitals, and their initial 1990s' foray into obtaining similar discounts on physician preference items (PPIs), the corollary to pharma's brand-name drugs.[110] There were already industry reports that the PBM programs inside the large MCOs were beginning to wield the same influence on the outpatient side that GPOs had done on the inpatient side using the same strategies: aggregated buying to extract price discounts, using national accounts teams, and formularies. Supporting this view, Medco had successfully negotiated price discounts based on moving prescription volumes in its mail-order business by getting physicians to switch to drugs covered by a Medco contract. Statistics at the time suggest that PBMs like DPS had 75% of the branded drugs they covered under contract.[111] Some analysts quoted Joseph Stalin, who dwelt on the number of tanks Russia had: "quantity has a quality all its own."[112]

Merck went one step further. It not only yielded to price discounting requests by PBMs; in 1993, it paid $6 Billion to acquire the PBM (Medco) that gave it so much trouble. This reflected a capitulation to the new sales strategy going forward. The following year, it formed the Merck-Medco U.S. Managed Care Division that included two units: one to help market its drug products to MCOs, the other to market its in-house PBM services (Medco) to health plan sponsors. Merck articulated the following post-hoc rationale for the deal[113]:

- PBMs could help Merck increase volumes to offset falling prices.
- Managed care rather than individuals would determine drug choice. As a result, MCOs will want to negotiate with a one-stop-shop for all their pharmaceutical products and services rather than contract with lots of drug firms.
- PBM computers could pinpoint MCO plan members who have failed to renew important prescription medications as well as those who need additional drugs prescribed.
- The PBM channel constituted an opportunity to cut marketing costs expended on sales representatives who call on physicians. Pharma marketing and administrative expenses accounted for roughly 30% of sales.
- PBM data could prove the value of Merck's drugs (i.e., worth the high price) and communicate this to payers.
- Merck could integrate Medco data and its own pharmacy management programs to use as weapons to avoid discounting.

It is worth noting that the 1993 Merck-Medco merger paralleled the earlier 1985 merger of Baxter Travenol with American Hospital Supply (see Chapter 4). In both cases, the product manufacturer sought out a service provider when it lost faith in the power of brand-name technologies to maintain market share while commanding premium prices.[114] The acquired service business looked better as a source of top-line sales growth and as a vehicle to sell more products—e.g., get PBMs to sell more of a manufacturer's drugs and gain market share.

The Merck-Medco merger was quickly followed by two other manufacturer-PBM mergers. In 1994, SmithKlineBeecham (SKB) acquired Diversified Pharmaceutical Services (DPS) from United Healthcare for $2.3 Billion; that same year, Eli Lilly acquired PCS for $4.1 Billion. The deals were premised on the theorized ability of MCOs/PBMs to substitute therapeutically equivalent drugs to gain and leverage formulary status. So, the logic went, let pharmaceutical manufacturers buy the companies who set the formularies and thereby influence what drugs get on formulary.

Like Merck, Eli Lilly had been reluctant to contract with PBMs. Lilly executives did not want to abandon their traditional marketing focus on prescribing physicians—a focus they had spent their careers building. As of 1992, Lilly had only one discounted pricing contract with Kaiser. But then Lilly decided to embrace MCOs, PBMs, and PCS in particular. The abrupt shift was occasioned by several events, including: a change in its top management team, stalled productivity in its R&D pipeline, its first quarterly loss in 31 years (reported in 1992) and first year of lower earnings, patent expiration of *Ceclor*, increased competition from other antibiotics, the merger of Merck-Medco in 1993, the firm's exposure to *Prozac* (26% of sales in 1993, with 61% of those sales in the U.S.), and the incipient threat to *Prozac* from fast followers and competition coming in from SSRI drugs (especially *Paxil* and *Zoloft*).

Merck, SKB, and Lilly recognized the same shift in sales strategy. PBMs had the opportunity and perhaps the capability to move share via therapeutic substitution; manufacturers were vulnerable to this growing buyer leverage and their own high fixed costs. Moreover, in just a few years, the PBM contracts had begun to penetrate the market. In 1990/91, PBM formularies controlled only 4% of the market, reflecting manufacturers' influence with physicians. However, armed with their new online adjudication capabilities, PBM formularies soon controlled 12–15% of the market by 1993/94, with scary estimates that such control might reach as high as 60% in two years and 90% by 2000. These merger deals were not so much a revolution undertaken by the PBMs as they were manufacturer exercises to diversify, develop channel influence, achieve a national distribution channel for their drugs, and ensure their drugs were on the PBM formulary.

A New Path to Disease Management?

Vertical mergers between manufacturers and PBMs also offered a different approach to disease management, selling to MCOs, and outcomes research. SKB's acquisition of DPS provides an illustration. At least 50% of DPS' 50 million covered lives came from HMOs. All of these lives were formulary lives, which offered an opportunity to move market share—and hopefully to SKB's products. The theory was, at least initially, that "only formulary lives count."[115] That theory gave way to a new promise of using the acquired PBM as a data manager by tapping the patient database developed by United (the former owner of DPS) and combining it with the pharmacy claims data at DPS and the diagnostic database inside SKB's Clinical Labs division. The entire package might then be sold to employers and other payers.

This helped animate the early push into "big data" and "informatics"— i.e., stitching together the different databases of drug manufacturers and PBMs into a useable whole—and the early disease management program partnerships between the manufacturers and the MCOs/PBMs. One stumbling block to such programs was whether there were specific diagnosis codes to help correctly identify the patients who needed to be more intensively managed. Moreover, the claims processing systems inside PBMs tracked only about 8 disease parameters; by contrast, one might need to track 50 parameters in order to do disease management. The only alternative was to dredge through data on millions of covered patient lives to develop algorithms. Another stumbling block was that most patients remained with their insurer for five years or less, limiting the medication history available to payers for particular patients. The high patient turnover also limited the incentives to insurers to invest in disease management programs. Not surprisingly, due to patient turnover, PBMs were likewise reluctant to adopt strategies (like disease management) that would be successful in the long term but costly in the short term, believing that the money they spent today would yield benefit for the patient's next PBM.

The Government Kibosh on Manufacturer-PBM Combinations

There was another, bigger downside to the manufacturer-PBM mergers, however. Government regulators recognized the likely restraint of trade, just as other critics recognized the inherent conflict of interest between selling one's own drugs versus serving customers. This led to a government backlash to the three manufacturer-PBM mergers undertaken in 1993–1994. The Federal Trade Commission (FTC) scrutized these mergers in terms of what they might do to the formularies and the drug options offered to patients. Up until this time, the PBM industry was moving toward smaller, restricted, and closed formularies. In early 1995, the FTC reviewed the Lilly-PCS merger to ensure there was a competitive process in place that determined how drugs got onto the PBM's formulary. In a subsequent consent agreement, the FTC required that (1) PCS maintain an open formulary, (2) PCS appoint an independent P&T committee composed of non-Lilly and non-PCS professionals to oversee the formulary, (3) Lilly and PCS establish safeguards to ensure each from sharing non-public information concerning other drug manufacturers' and other PBMs' bids, and (4) PCS accept all discounts or other concessions offered by manufacturers and reflect them when determining the rankings in their open formulary. The FTC did not want the formulary to favor the PBM parent (the acquiring manufacturer), but rather wanted the formularies to be open to include drugs made by other manufacturers.

As a consequence, two of the three manufacturers quickly spun off their PBMs for huge losses: Lilly sold PCS to Rite Aid for $1.5 Billion, while SKB sold DPS for $700 Million. Neither manufacturer reportedly could generate any incremental drug sales from its in-house PBM, which served as a drag on their corporate earnings. That left Merck as the only manufacturer still operating a PBM, perhaps "only because Merck remains profitable, rather than for any integral value to its main drug business," or perhaps because the combination of Medco's strengths in mail-order and Merck's pipeline made their fit stronger than the other two deals.[116]

These vertical mergers were supposed to have two anticipated impacts: (1) the opportunity for drug manufacturers to co-opt the managed care threat posed by PBMs and bring it inside the firm to better control the process; and (2) harness the ability of managed care organizations to move market share. Like the strategy of disease management, neither really worked out that well.

More generally, the divestitures and abandonment of PBM integration were perhaps an admission that the anticipated impact of managed care on manufacturers did not materialize, and that pharmaceutical manufacturers were still trying to accurately gauge and then cope with changes in the marketplace. Analysts pointed to the evidence trail supporting this latter conclusion: drug prices were not lower, PBMs found it nearly impossible to shape formularies that put an end to blockbuster drugs and product differentiation, PBM clients had waning enthusiasm to impose customer restrictions or prohibitions on access to branded drugs, and PBMs and manufacturers had trouble leveraging disease management programs to become providers of "integrated" or "coordinated" pharmaceutical care. Moreover, direct-to-consumer (DTC) advertising reinforced the traditional manufacturer reliance on and perceived importance of brand identity. As a consequence, the rationale to own a PBM vanished.[117]

Moreover, the migration of HMO models from closed panel staff plans to more open-panel IPA plans vitiated the push for closed formularies. The resultant loss of wind to the sails of price discounting may have motivated pharmaceutical manufacturers to actually raise prices. With escalating expenditures on prescription drugs, the focus shifted back to pure-play PBMs to manage the problem. PBMs were clearly back on their heels; the entire sector underwent a shakeout as the millennium ended. Several divestitures occurred, with some of the divested plans picked up by other PBM incumbents (e.g., Express Scripts). Merger and acquisition (i.e., horizontal integration) seemed poised to replace the vertical integration efforts of the 1990s.

To be sure, vertical integration with pharmaceutical manufacturers did not engulf all PBMs. Caremark had begun as an in-house, mail-order pharmacy to serve Baxter employees. Caremark entered the PBM market via its Prescription Service Division (PSD) in 1985 when payers encouraged its to do so in order to leverage its background in distribution and pharmacy operations. Then, in 1991, it acquired PHS to develop true pharmacy benefit management capabilities. In 1992, Baxter spun off its Caremark PBM and its non-hospital, home infusion therapy business. Caremark forged strategic alliances with Pfizer and BMS. Large retail pharmacy chains formed their own PBM (Pharmacy Direct) to compete with the larger PBMs.

Back to the Future in *the Late 1990s*

Weakening of MCO/PBM Efforts

The late 1990s witnessed the "managed care backlash" and the declining popularity of closed-model HMOs with their smaller provider networks and penalties for going outside those networks.[118] Within the HMO sector, plans had migrated away from closed-model staff HMOs (which accounted for less than 1% of all drug spending in the first six months of 2001) to open-model IPA and network HMOs. The problem with the latter was that such networks might contain physicians who had contracts with 6 or more MCOs. This gave each MCO less leverage over that physician's prescribing behavior. Moreover, HMO market share fell while open-access PPO market share rose.

The demise of closed panels of providers was mirrored by the demise of closed formularies and steep discounting pegged to drug restrictions. By mid-1995, closed formularies had a reportedly low prevalence of only 10–20%. Employers did not necessarily embrace them because they limited employee choice; and the clients' P&T committees often made the choice about formulary design, not the PBMs they contracted with. In short, as the MCOs backed off their aggressive strategy of closed panels and formularies in favor of patient choice, so did their PBM agents.

This retreat coincided with the rise of consumerism, which often meant shifting costs from the plan to the enrollee using co-pays, deductibles, and three-tiered formularies (rather than the two-tier plans used in the early-mid-1990s). These formularies were not closed (as in the staff-model HMOs) but rather managed. These benefit design changes moved the iron triangle tradeoff of access versus cost from the MCO model to the enrollee. But such tiered plans only covered 16% of enrollees. Many insurers also used tiered copayments, but the copayments were modest and flat ($5–12), suggesting to payers that they needed to either increase the flat co-pay amount to get consumers' attention or shift to co-pays as a percentage of drug costs.[119]

To be sure, restrictive formularies and therapeutic substitution also suffered from clinical issues, such as variation in the physiological effects of the drugs covered. For drugs in certain therapeutic areas (e.g., proton pump inhibitors or anti-ulcer drugs), there was some consistency in their effects on patients, which allowed one to restrict formulary choice. For drugs in other therapeutic areas, particularly antidepressants and oncology, there was much greater variation in patient response; this required physicians and patients to have greater choice among alternatives.[120]

More importantly, with a healthy U.S. economy and tight employment market, employers were now reluctant to squeeze healthcare benefits or cajole employees into closed-model plans. PPO plans took off in popularity, quickly outrunning the HMOs in terms of market share. Capitation had also failed to spread beyond the West Coast; risk-sharing arrangements among providers were on the wane. In tandem with open-model networks and less risk, MCOs and PBMs took a more physician-friendly and patient-friendly approach. This included more customer-friendly formularies (e.g., 3-tier co-pays) and fewer restrictions on physicians' clinical decision-making. In addition to consumerism, PBMs and their clients pivoted to tinkering with plan designs and generic substitution—areas which could move market share and generate bigger savings with a lot less effort.

The Empire Strikes Back

In such a relaxed environment, pharmaceutical utilization and costs accelerated. Drug prices rose 16.8% in 1998 and another 17.4% in 1999, the highest rates of increase in the prior three years. This largely reflected price increases on products already on the market, and not so much new drug introductions. Of the 17.4% increase between 1998–1999, only 1.8% was attributable to new drugs introduced in prior year, which were often priced higher than drugs already on market. The pure price increase for existing drugs (net of inflation) was roughly 5%—continuing a long-standing trend of price hikes above inflation.[121]

Moreover, community-based physicians were prescribing new and more expensive therapies as they become available, similar to their colleagues' use of physician preference items (PPIs) inside the hospital. On the retail drug side, insurers found their own version of PPIs (proton pump inhibitors) as their #1 drug expense item. Drug categories with high generic usage also saw double digit price increases.[122] Generics offered little price protection for payers. By the time a brand went off-patent, the entire therapeutic category had moved to another class of drugs (Zantac went off-patent, but everyone used PPIs instead).[123]

It is likely that the optics of pharmaceutical manufacturers may have shifted during this period of blockbuster drugs, many and oftentimes meaningful new product introductions, and direct-to-consumer (DTC) advertising. Their image changed from "bad guys" with high-priced drugs to "good guys" developing important new therapies. This may have emboldened their price-setting strategies.

Armed with insurance coverage and more friendly cost-sharing arrangements, consumers became less price sensitive. Escalation in prescription drug costs outpaced medical costs. Pharmaceutical manufacturers also went on the offensive in promoting their products "direct to consumer," now permitted by federal law in 1997. As a result of the Prescription Drug User Fee Act (PDUFA) in 1997, a new bolus of drugs received FDA approval and flooded the market. While in the past, providers had only 1–2 new extraordinary drugs to deal with each year, now there were 3–5 blockbusters a year. The impact of newer, costlier drugs became felt in subsequent years: for example, drugs introduced in 1992 accounted for 40% of drug costs in 1999 (suggesting that it takes 5–6 years for a drug to hit its peak).[124]

In Search of Relief

Both private and public payers returned to the pooled purchasing strategy to look for price and cost relief. Some employers formed their own PBM. The National Business Coalition on Health sponsored a PBM called "National Prescription Administrators" in which 24 regional and local business coalitions participated.[125] States now got into the act of joining prescription drug purchasing pools to negotiate volume discounts. Governor Howard Dean of Vermont launched the Pharmacy Discount Program (PDP) for eligible state residents. Other states used First Health Services Corp as the fiscal intermediary to pool their purchasing power. Such pools could either negotiate directly with manufacturers or use PBMs.[126] Many states began to contract with PBMs to rein in the rapid growth of health plan prescription drug spending on their public employees and Medicaid beneficiaries.[127] Medicaid drug spending was a small portion of overall Medicaid services (9.1% in 2001) but had experienced 20% annual growth rate, the highest rate among all Medicaid services.[128] This posed budgetary problems for the states. They looked to their Medicaid programs, which represented their #1 or #2 expense, to try to close their budget gaps.

Federal law prohibited the states from using the 3-tiered co-pay systems found in the private sector in order to protect the low-income population, whose co-pays were limited to $3. Instead, the states focused instead on "quantity limits" (number of prescriptions a beneficiary could fill monthly or annually) and preferred drug lists (PDLs). The latter relied on using outside experts to review all therapeutic categories to identify drugs that required prior authorization. States began to use PDLs to extract price discounts, which represented supplemental rebates over and above Medicaid guaranteed "best low price" obtained by pharma's most preferred customer.[129]

Antitrust Issues

Finally, the PBMs' traditional reliance on contracts to obtain price discounts from manufacturers got disrupted by a major antitrust case filed in 1994. The disruption did not come from the PBMs or pharmaceutical manufacturers, however. Instead, it originated with independent retail pharmacies and a pooling of lawsuits filed against drug manufacturers and wholesalers that came to be known as the "Brand Name Prescription Drugs Antitrust Litigation." As described by the Institute for Clinical and Economic Review,[130]

> Prior to 1996, manufacturers offered discounts to health plans and PBMs for their drugs, while charging an undiscounted list price to wholesalers and pharmacies. Wholesalers would then bill the manufacturer for the difference between the amount they purchased the drug for from the drug manufacturer, and the amount they were reimbursed for the drug, as determined by the discounted rate negotiated by the health plan. This was known as a *chargeback*. Pharmacies, however, had no direct relationship with drug manufacturers and could not negotiate similar discounts, or chargebacks. As a result, pharmacies paid the wholesale price for the drug to the wholesaler, while all other parties achieved discounts by directly negotiating with drug manufacturers. Chain pharmacies attempted to negotiate directly, and as part of a collective, but were denied discounts by all drug manufacturers.

The independent pharmacists alleged a conspiracy to fix retail prices and keep them artificially high using a dual pricing system whereby retail pharmacies paid a higher price while MCOs were given lower prices via discounts and rebates. The Federal Court, however, affirmed the implicit trade-off of market share for rebates/discounts that formed the basis of much contracting between manufacturers and MCOs/PBMs, and that discount pricing may actually promote competition. Instead, the court ruled that discounts must be based not on the buyer's status but on the buyer's ability to affect market share. Differential pricing was legitimate and competitive, but it must be based on demonstrated ability to move market share. The ruling preserved the right of manufacturers to incentivize (using lower prices) those MCO/PBM buyers who can increase market share, but extended the same right to the pharmacists if they could do so too. Of course, it was not clear that independent pharmacists had the same ability as MCOs/PBMs to influence which products were sold. Indeed, community pharmacies paid higher average invoice prices precisely because they could not affect volume or move market share like the MCOs and PBMs.[131] The settlement put pressure on MCOs and PBMs to prove they could deliver market share, and thus to develop performance-based contracts. This all occurred at the same time that MCOs, and managed care in general, came under fire for their limited ability to control costs.

The 1996 settlement's longer-term impact was a movement away from (a) up-front price discounts offered by manufacturers to get on the PBM's contract to (b) back-end rebates offered to PBMs for demonstrated changes in market share for that manufacturer's products. The new regime preserved volume-based discounts but now for demonstrated shifts in purchasing, not just promises. Such rebates could be a percentage discount on drug quantities purchased and/or formulary placement which would affect the quantity demanded. PBMs were confronted with a dilemma: accept lower discounts (now back-end rebates), figure out another set of incentives to promote formulary compliance, or figure out another way to earn the discounts. PBMs were faced with average manufacturer rebates of 5–6% and rebates per prescription that were quickly falling: from $1.25 (1995–1996) to $1.04 (1996) to $0.96 (1997).[132]

PBMs still retained more discretion and leverage to move market share in their mail-order business, however, since they had more time to contact physicians to switch to lower cost brands, and they may have a better ability to promote generic substitution (compared to community pharmacists). It did not hurt that the mail-order generic business was the PBM's most profitable business line: profit margins on generic scripts were four times higher than on retail pharmacy scripts.[133] It was also the least costly option for both payers and patients. The GAO provided confirmation here: PBM savings on branded drugs were 27% in the mail-order side (versus 18% on the retail side) and 53% on generic drugs in the mail-order side (versus 47% on the retail side).[134]

Finally, it should be noted that the resolution to this antitrust litigation was a negotiated settlement. It did not carry the weight of federal legislation or legal case precedent, and instead faced expiration in 1999. Nevertheless, it did rest on two antitrust laws (Robinson-Patman Act, Sherman Act) which reinforced the back-end rebate, which remained in place for over two decades.[135] The Federal Government would revisit this settlement in 2019, when the Office of the Inspector General (OIG) of the Department of Health & Human Services (DHHS) issued a proposed rule to curtail the payment of back-end rebates in exchange for formulary placement, and replace it with up-front discounts or fixed payments (see Chapter 12).

The Safe Harbor Comes to the Retail Channel

Moreover, as part of the shift away from discounted pricing, the OIG-DHHS revised the discount safe harbor in 1999 to explicitly treat a rebate as a permissible discount, thereby shielding drug companies' rebate contracts from the implications of the Anti-Kickback Statute (AKS)—just as it had done for the GPOs several years earlier.[136] The revised regulation defined a "rebate" as a discount which is fixed and disclosed to the buyer at the time of the initial purchase to which the discount applies, but which is not given at the time of the sale. As such, a rebate was granted after the sale had concluded and was applied retrospectively.[137]

The OIG's issuance of the safe harbor may have reflected an earlier OIG report in 1997 that was based on a 1996 national survey of all HMO plans. The survey data revealed that three-quarters of responding HMOs contracted with PBMs, a tripling over the three-year period 1993–1996. HMOs increasingly covered three main population segments: commercial, Medicaid, and Medicare. The latter two (public) programs utilized HMOs in their managed care plans: 39% of Medicaid enrollees and 12% of Medicare enrollees. These public sector enrollees were the largest share of the outpatient drug market. According to plans, the main benefit of using HMOs was to control the costs of drugs. They also had the potential to improve health outcomes by influencing physician prescribing, pharmacist dispensing, and patient compliance. According to one HMO, the actual savings from using PBMs ranged from 10–25%. Nevertheless, HMO plans did not cede control to PBMs for many important clinical activities: 76% of HMOs used their own P&T Committee to review their PBM's programs, and 62% of HMOs conducted their own DUR analyses. PBMs were used to contract for Medicare (45% of plans) and Medicaid (48%), while nearly all (95%) used PBMs to contract for commercial lives.

The OIG's issuance of the safe harbor may also have reflected an earlier 1996 GAO report on the role of PBMs in the Federal Employee Health Benefits Program (FEHBP). The GAO studied the largest of the FEHBP plans, operated by the Blue Cross/Blue Shield Association, which represented 9 million (or nearly 20%) of federal employees. The Blues used Medco for mail-order prescriptions and PCS for retail prescriptions. The GAO found that the PBMs saved the Blues 20–27% (over half a billion dollars) in their annual pharmacy benefit costs, with little evidence of reduced access to desired drugs. Of these savings: 50%+ came from pharmacy discounts, 20% came from manufacturer discounts, 14% came from MAC restrictions in the retail network, while the remaining 12% came from DUR and other clinical intervention programs. The OIG safe harbor may also have reflected the fact that while some consolidation was taking place among the PBMs, the PBM market was still considered competitive (see below).

Aftermath

By the end of the millennium, a majority of all outpatient prescriptions were now covered by some form of managed care, thereby transforming the delivery of pharmaceutical services. PBMs, whether freestanding or sponsored, were already playing a major (and growing) role. The overriding goal was to contain rising expenditures on prescription drugs, which seemed to increase relentlessly throughout the 1990s. They were not only central players but also in high demand to deal with these expenditures. If there was a "bad apple" in the ecosystem, it seemed to be the pharmaceutical manufacturers and their continuing drug price hikes. Criticism of their practices had begun as early as 1991 in hearings held before the Senate Special Committee on Aging. Analysts commonly noted that manufacturers and PBMs were "adversaries."

This is not to say that PBMs did not have their own critics prior to the new millennium; rather, like the GPOs, the volume of criticism was more muted. During the 1990s there was scattered murmuring about PBMs. James Sheehan, Associate United States Attorney in Philadelphia, earned headlines for investigating potential mail-order fraud, transparency in PBMs' dealings with manufacturers when advocating drug switches, kickback payments from manufacturers, and breach of fiduciary duty. This took place at the same time that the government was scrutinizing other PBMs for similar practices, resulting in a handful of consent decrees. In addition, public interest groups also called attention to some of the PBMs' activities (such as therapeutic substitution) as they impacted patients.[138] Another major critic of PBMs, the independent pharmacists, continued to complain about the increasing discounts that PBMs charged them as well as the loss of business to the mail-order pharmacies that the PBMs ran. They called on state legislators to increase their oversight of the PBMs, but at a time when the states were looking to the same PBMs for relief in helping them control their Medicaid expenditures.[139] Government remedies would have to wait—at least until the next century (see Chapter 12).

However, at this time, the PBMs were not major targets for antitrust behavior. One reason was that the PBM sector was still quite competitive, with many new market entries occasioned by the rising demand for PBM services. There were an estimated 40+ for-profit PBMs providing client services in 1995; a directory issued the following year by Managed Healthcare listed 79 PBMs. Such estimates were, not surprisingly, all over the map given differences in how a PBM was defined. Some of the newer entrants were formed by health plans as well as by each of the five largest retail pharmacy chains. According to some observers, the latter were particularly well positioned to serve local businesses by virtue of having more localized PBMs and lacking the historical PBM-pharmacy antagonism. Moreover, the decade of the 1990s was less about the horizontal consolidation among PBMs as it was about vertical partnerships with drug manufacturers. Another factor augmenting PBM competition was their heterogeneity in sponsorship (stand-alone, MCO-affiliates, drug store-affiliates, employer-affiliates) as well as geographic scope (national versus regional). This latter observation paralleled the growing regional activity of GPOs.

The 1995 DHHS/OIG survey also revealed that 43% of HMO plans changed their PBM between 1993 and 1995, suggesting lots of switching behavior by payers in choosing their PBM partners. Moreover, by the early 2000s, the PBM sector was not highly concentrated but rather still fragmented. Data published by Goldman Sachs suggested a Hirschman–Herfindahl Index (HHI) ranging from 2,132 to 2,708, depending on whether or not one included captive PBMs (see Fig. 10.7).

HHI calculations rested on firm market shares; the computation of those shares varied depending on whether one used prescription volumes, covered lives, or annual drug spend. Data published early in the new millennium

Top pharmacy benefit management companies by number of covered lives

PBM	Lives Covered Ownership	2003	2002	2001	2000
1 Advance PCS (a)	Advance Paradigm	75.0	75.0	75.0	83.0
2 Medco Health Solutions	Merck & Co.	62.0	65.0	69.0	69.0
3 Express-Scripts (b)	Express-Scripts	50.0	46.0	48.5	43.0
4 WellPoint Pharmacy Management	WellPoint Health Networks	36.0	31.0	26.0	15.5
5 Caremark - Prescription Service Div.	Caremark Rx	25.0	24.0	10.0	10.0
6 Argus Health Systems	DST Systems	23.0	23.0	NA	NA
7 Medimpact Healthcare Systems	Medi-Impact Healthcare	20.0	20.0	12.0	12.0
8 Health Net Pharmaceutical Services (c)	Health Net	14.0	14.0	14.0	14.0
9 Aetna Pharmacy Management (d)	Aetna	12.0	12.0	5.0	5.0
10 PharmaCare Management Services	CVS Pharmacy	12.0	12.0	10.0	NA
11 Pharmacy Services Corp.	PSG - PBM	11.0	11.0	NA	NA
12 First Health Services Corporation	First Financial Management	9.4	9.4	10.4	8.0
13 CIGNA Pharmacy Services	CIGNA Healthcare	8.7	8.7	8.3	5.2
14 Benecard Services	Benecard	7.5	7.5	7.5	7.5
15 Scrip Pharmacy Solutions	MIM Corporation	7.0	NA	NA	NA
16 Prescription Solutions	PacifiCare Health Systems	5.0	5.0	5.0	5.0
17 Anthem Prescription Management	Anthem	4.9	4.9	NA	2.5
18 Rx America	Longs Drug Stores Corporation	4.7	4.7	6.4	3.5
19 Prime Therapeutics	BCBS of NE, MN, ND and WY	4.0	4.0	NA	NA

(a) Formerly PCS Health Systems PBM with lives covered under Rite Aid Corp during 2000.
(b) Pro forma for 1999 acquistions of Diversified Pharmaceutical Services and National Prescription Administrators.
(c) Pro forma for Foundation Health acquisition.
(d) Pro forma for 1999 acquisiton of Prudential Pharmacy Services.

Fig. 10.7 PBM market shares 2000–2003 (*Source* HDMA Fact Book, Verispan, Company reports, Goldman Sachs Research)

showed that the choice of market share metric used drove the rankings of the PBMs' relative market shares. Indeed, a comparison of the top three PBMs on these three metrics illustrates the variability (see Fig. 10.8). Some of the available metrics were even more complex than many realized. For example, "covered lives" could vary based on the contracts struck between the employer, MCO, and PBM. They could include pharmacy network lives, lives that were under self-insured ASO contracts, and lives that were under fully-insured risk contracts. This led to possible double counting if the sponsor had multiple PBM service contracts.[140] Double counting could also occur if PBMs outsourced their claims processing to other PBMs.

Nevertheless, as discussed in the next chapter, the consolidation movement among the PBMs was already underway. The merger of purchasing bodies on the retail side followed the similar merger of purchasing bodies on the inpatient side (the GPOs) which, in turn, had followed the merger of hospitals and (before them) the merger of health insurers. Like mergers, the use of formularies had migrated from hospitals to MCOs and then to PBMs. And, of course, all of this was interspersed with efforts to strike vertical deals among all of these parties in the value chain. Some of these deals were actually "turduckens": a hospital chain that started its own health plan that

Advance PCS
- 16% of covered lives
- 18% of Rx/year
- 22% of annual drug spend

Merck-Medco
- 14% of covered lives
- 22% of Rx/year
- 24% of annual drug spend

Express Scripts
- 11% of covered lives
- 12% of Rx/year
- 14% of annual drug spend

Fig. 10.8 Comparison of top three PBMs on 3 metrics (*Source* Chris Nee. "Uncovering the Mysteries Behind Rebates", Drug Cost Management Report [June 2002])

then signed strategic alliances with PBMs. Horizontal and vertical integration strategies were the *Zeitgeist* of the last two decades of the millennium. All of these movements, however, were strategic efforts to combat suppliers upstream and their high prices. As analysts noted, "PBMs have historically positioned themselves as drug industry antagonists."[141] Such antagonism was fueled by the fact that the PBMs' clients (MCOs and employers) likewise did not see much value in "Big Pharma"—particularly in light of the massive spike in drug spending as the millennium ended and manufacturers' rush into DTC marketing. The battle lines were pretty clearly drawn: managed care and PBMs (like the GPOs) were countervailing forces to the market power and the differentiated oligopolies of big suppliers.[142] Winners and losers in these tough negotiations and bargaining games were determined by one's relative market power. Analysts expected a shakeout in the PBM sector as the millennium came to a close, particularly as they anticipated a slowdown in industry growth. PBMs would need to shift gears in the next two decades to change their position. They would also need to respond and confront any further consolidation among their client MCOs, any further expansions in insurance coverage, and any future changes in new drug approvals—all of which occasioned their rise (as chronicled at the outset of this chapter).

Notes

1. David Cassak has spent much of his career studying and writing about the PBMs. Here is a list of articles (in chronological order) he authored for *In Vivo* that this chapter draws upon. David Cassak. "Inside Selling— The New Sales/Marketing Mix for Rx Companies," *In Vivo* (January 1990): 12–16. David Cassak. "DPS and the Managed Care Revolution," *In*

Vivo (May 1991): 17–22. David Cassak. "From Mail Service to Managed Care," *In Vivo* (January 1993): 37–44. David Cassak. "McKesson's Push into Managed Care," *In Vivo* (December 1993): 23–31. David Cassak. "Caremark's Bet on Physicians," *In Vivo* (July–August 1994): 25–33. David Cassak, "Listening to Prozac: Lilly in Managed Care," *In Vivo* (September 1994): 23, 30–36. Roger Longman, "Lilly's Industrial Policy," *In Vivo* (September 1994): 22, 24–29. David Cassak. "Pharmacy Benefit Management's Second Generation," *In Vivo* (July 1995): 48–57. David Cassak. "PBM's Second Generation: From Formularies to Triggers," *In Vivo* (September 1995): 38–48. David Cassak. "Unsettled," *In Vivo* (October 1996): 10–17. David Cassak. "Express Scripts' Friendly Data Play," *In Vivo* (May 1997): 39–50. David Cassak. "Managing Physicians, Managing Prescriptions," *In Vivo* (April 1998): 37–47. David Cassak. "Express Scripts—Back to Basics, Only Bigger," *In Vivo* (October 2000): 15–30.

2. Like David, Roger Longman has spent much of his career studying and writing about the PBMs. Here is a list of articles (in chronological order) he authored for *In Vivo* that this chapter draws upon. Roger Longman. "Are Pharma Sales Forces Too Big?" *In Vivo* (September 1990): 4–8. Roger Longman. "Merck-Medco: Defining a New Pharmaceutical Company," *In Vivo* (September 1993): 29–36. Roger Longman. "The Club of Three," *In Vivo* (July/August 1994): 1–6. Roger Longman, "Lilly's Industrial Policy," *In Vivo* (September 1994): 22, 24–29. Roger Longman. "SmithKline's Data Challenge," *In Vivo* (January 1995): 41–46. Roger Longman. "Alliances with PBMs: Experiment in Progress," *In Vivo* (September 1995): 3–8.

3. Robert Cunningham III and Robert Cunningham Jr. *The Blues: A History of the Blue Cross and Blue Shield System* (De Kalb, IL: Northern Illinois University Press, 1997).

4. Office of the Assistant Secretary for Planning and Evaluation. *Report to the President: Prescription Drug Coverage, Spending, Utilization, and Prices* (Washington, DC: ASPE, 2000).

5. Thomas Oliver, Philip Lee, and Helene Lipton. "A Political History of Medicare and Prescription Drug Coverage," *Milbank Quarterly* 82(2) (2004): 283–354.

6. Prescription drug spending represented just over 11% of personal healthcare spending (PHS).

7. This is a gross generalization. Drug spending as a percentage of national health expenditures fell and then rose again during the remainder of the twentieth century. There are a lot of dynamics at play here that explain this fall and rise—some of which are covered in this chapter.

8. See, for example, Jon Northrup. "The Pharmaceutical Sector," in Lawton R. Burns (Ed.), *The Business of Healthcare Innovation*, 1st Edition (Cambridge, UK: Cambridge University Press, 2005): Chapter 2.

9. Ralph Landau, Basil Achilladelis, and Alexandre Scriabine, editors. *Pharmaceutical Innovation: Revolutionizing Human Health* (Philadelphia, PA:

Chemical Heritage Press, 1999). Walter Sneader. *Drug Discovery: A History* (Chichester: Wiley, 2005).

10. Congressional Budget Office. *How Increased Competition From Generic Drugs Has Affected Prices and Returns in the Pharmaceutical Industry* (Washington, DC: CBO, July 1998): Table 3.

11. Lawton Robert Burns. *The U.S. Healthcare Ecosystem* (New York: McGraw-Hill, 2021): Fig. 21–15.

12. The definition of a blockbuster drug and the sales threshold may have changed over time. The $1 Billion figure is the most commonly-cited benchmark. Historical analyses of blockbuster drugs have put the threshold at lower levels ($500 Million or less) in earlier years.

13. Stacy Lawrence. "Billion Dollar Babies—Biotech Drugs as Blockbusters," *Nature Biotechnology* 25(4) (2007): 380–382.

14. Congressional Budget Office. *How Increased Competition From Generic Drugs Has Affected Prices and Returns in the Pharmaceutical Industry* (Washington, DC: CBO, July 1998).

15. Frank Lichtenberg. "The Effect of New Cancer Drug Approvals on the Life Expectancy of American Cancer Patients, 1978–2004," *Economics of Innovation and New Technology* 18(5) (2009): 407–428.

16. David Cutler, Allison Rosen, and Sandeep Vijan. "The Value of Medical Spending in the United States, 1960–2000," *New England Journal of Medicine* 355 (2006): 920–927. Jason Schnittker and George Karandinos. "Methuselah's Medicine: Pharmaceutical Innovation and Mortality in the United States, 1960–2000," *Social Science & Medicine* 70 (2010): 961–968.

17. Anita McGahan. "Industry Structure and Competitive Advantage," *Harvard Business Review* (November–December 1994): 115–124.

18. Thomas Oliver, Philip Lee, and Helene Lipton. "A Political History of Medicare and Prescription Drug Coverage," *Milbank Quarterly* 82(2) (2004): 283–354.

19. Co-author David Cassak was a close observer. According to David, it was not until the end of the century that Congress would attempt to rein in drug spending, particularly in the Medicaid program. Senator David Pryor of Arkansas led the charge to reign in Medicaid drug costs, a battle that highlighted tensions between the suppliers and government payers. Most pharmaceutical manufacturers opposed and lobbied against the Pryor legislation. Merck, however, supported it, albeit by trying to enforce across-the-board discounts on all drugs, rather than therapeutic substitution. Merck's strategy was an obscure effort that went nowhere, but it highlighted some of the interesting challenges that arose when a drug industry that, until this point had never faced questions about high drug costs, suddenly had a new reality to deal with. It was, in an oblique way, a precursor to the PBM battles they would soon face.

20. Medicaid, by contrast, did not make drug reimbursement mandatory but all states elected to include outpatient drug coverage. Private insurers tended

to follow the lead of Medicaid in setting their own drug coverage policies. Kathleen Gondek. "Prescription Drug Payment Policy: Past, Present, and Future," *Health Care Financing Review* 15(3) (1994): 1–7.

21. Later on, managed care organizations (MCOs) and pharmacy benefit managers (PBMs) would try to re-introduce price elasticity into the demand for drugs using a variety of techniques—explained in this chapter.

22. Burton Weisbrod. "The Healthcare Quadrilemma: An Essay on Technological Change, Insurance, Quality of Care, and Cost Containment," *Journal of Economic Literature* 29(2) (1991): 523–552.

23. Lawton Robert Burns. *The U.S. Healthcare Ecosystem* (New York: McGraw-Hill, 2021): Chapter 2.

24. Ernst Berndt. "The U.S. Pharmaceutical Industry: Why Major Growth in Times of Cost Containment," *Health Affairs* (March–April 2001).

25. This was true except for the period from 1993–1997 when the proposed Clinton Health Plan led manufacturers to limit their price increases.

26. David Cassak opines that this cycle would later give rise to a controversy between drug manufacturers and PBMs. Drug companies would argue that they needed high prices to afford high costs of research and development (R&D), especially in light of the high project failure rates in R&D. PBMs and others that posed market access challenges to drugs that made it to market began to challenge that story line. They pointed out that the sales, general and administrative (SG&A) costs of pharmaceutical companies were rising in tandem with their R&D costs as drug companies invested more in sales forces to promote the sale of drugs that had already made it to market.

27. William MacColl. *Group Practice & Prepayment of Medical Care* (Washington, DC: Public Affairs Press, 1966).

28. William MacColl. *Group Practice & Prepayment of Medical Care* (Washington, DC: Public Affairs Press, 1966).

29. Congressional Budget Office. *How Increased Competition From Generic Drugs Has Affected Prices and Returns in the Pharmaceutical Industry* (Washington, DC: CBO, July 1998).

30. Enrollment figures are taken from: Harold Luft. *Health Maintenance Organizations: Dimensions of Performance* (New York: Wiley, 1981).

31. J.D. Kleinke. "Just What the HMO Ordered: The Paradox of Increasing Drug Costs," *Health Affairs* (March–April 2000).

32. Congressional Budget Office. *How Increased Competition from Generic Drugs Has Affected Prices and Returns in the Pharmaceutical Industry* (Washington, DC: CBO, July 1998).

33. Both economic theory and empirical research show that it is, in fact, employees who bear the brunt of rising health spending. As health benefit costs increase, wages fall almost dollar to dollar. For the general theory see Janet Currie and Brigitte C. Madrian, "Health, Health Insurance and the Labor Market," *Handbook of Labor Economics* 3, ed. Orley C Ashenfelter and David Card (Amsterdam: Elsevier Science, 1999): pp. 3309–3416.

For the most convincing evidence, see Jonathan Gruber, "The Incidence of Mandated Maternity Benefits," *The American Economic Review* 84(3) (1994): 622–641. Katherine Baicker and Amitabh Chandra, "The Labor Market Effects of Rising Health Insurance Premiums," *Journal of Labor Economics* 24(3) (2006): 609–634.

34. Kaiser Family Foundation. *Employer Health Benefits Annual Survey* (San Francisco: Kaiser Family Foundation, various years).

35. Robert Navarro and Albert Wertheimer. *Managing the Pharmacy Benefit* (Emron, 1996).

36. The history of selective contracting has been told elsewhere, so a thumbnail sketch will suffice. See David Dranove, *The Economic Evolution of American Health Care: from Marcus Welby to Managed Care* (Princeton: Princeton University Press, 2009).

37. Glenn Melnick, Jack Zwanziger, and Alicia Verity-Guerra. "The Growth and Effects of Hospital Selective Contracting," *Health Care Management Review* 14(3) (1989): 57–64.

38. Marsha Gold, Mark Joffe, Timothy Kennedy et al. "Pharmacy Benefits in Health Maintenance Organizations," *Health Affairs* 8(3) (1989). Available online at: https://www.healthaffairs.org/doi/full/10.1377/hlthaff.8.3.182. Accessed online August 4, 2020.

39. What follows is adapted from the Harvard Business School Case # 9-598-091: *Merck-Medco: Vertical Integration in the Pharmaceutical Industry* (1998).

40. Congressional Budget Office. *How Increased Competition from Generic Drugs Has Affected Prices and Returns in the Pharmaceutical Industry* (Washington, DC: CBO, July 1998).

41. Congressional Budget Office. *How Increased Competition from Generic Drugs Has Affected Prices and Returns in the Pharmaceutical Industry* (Washington, DC: CBO, July 1998).

42. Lawton R. Burns. *The Health Care Value Chain* (San Franciso, CA: Jossey-Bass, 2002).

43. Source: Health Care Financing Administration, as reported in Kaiser Family Foundation. *Medicaid and Managed Care—Policy Brief* (Washington, DC: Kaiser Family Foundation, May 30, 1995).

44. Today, one in three Medicare beneficiaries is in a private HMO or PPO. Gretchen Jacobson, Anthony Damico, Tricia Neuman, and Marsha Gold. *Medicare Advantage 2017 Spotlight: Enrollment Market Update* (Washington, DC: Kaiser Family Foundation, June 6, 2017). https://www.kff.org/medicare/issue-brief/medicare-advantage-2017-spotlight-enrollment-market-update/.

45. John Hansen. "A Perspective from the General Accounting Office," *Journal of Pharmaceutical Marketing and Management* (1998): 51–54.

46. Congressional Budget Office. *How Increased Competition from Generic Drugs Has Affected Prices and Returns in the Pharmaceutical Industry* (Washington, DC: CBO, July 1998).

47. Government publications on channel use yielded similar estimates for the 1993–1994 period: 49% via retail pharmacies, 15% via food and mass merchandisers, 26% sales via hospitals and managed care, and 10% via mail-order. Congressional Budget Office. *How Increased Competition from Generic Drugs Has Affected Prices and Returns in the Pharmaceutical Industry* (Washington, DC: CBO, July 1998).

48. Elizabeth Dietz. "Trends in Employer-Provided Prescription-Drug Coverage," *Monthly Labor Review* (August 2004): 37–45.

49. Robert Rubin, Anne Hawk, and Elisa Cascade. *PBMs: A Purchaser's Perspective* (CRC Press, 1998).

50. Helene Lipton, David Kreiling, Ted Collins et al. "Pharmacy Benefit Management Companies: Dimensions of Performance," *Annual Review of Public Health* 20 (1999): 361–401.

51. Lynn Etheredge. "Pharmacy Benefit Management: The Right Rx?" Sponsored by the Health Insurance Reform Project of George Washington University, with funding from the Robert Wood Johnson Foundation (April 1995).

52. Congressional Budget Office. *How Increased Competition from Generic Drugs Has Affected Prices and Returns in the Pharmaceutical Industry* (Washington, DC: CBO, July 1998).

53. Congressional Budget Office. *How Increased Competition from Generic Drugs Has Affected Prices and Returns in the Pharmaceutical Industry* (Washington, DC: CBO, July 1998).

54. David Cassak. "From Mail Service to Managed Care," *In Vivo* (January 1993): 37–44.

55. Lawton R. Burns, Ingrid Nembhard, and Stephen Shortell. "Integrating Network Theory into the Study of Integrated Healthcare," *Social Science and Medicine* (2022). https://doi.org/10.1016/j.socscimed.2021.114664.

56. S. McEachern. "PSAOs: Fewer, But Stronger," *Managed Care Pharmacy Practice* 2(2) (1995): 33–36.

57. Harvard Business School Case # 9-598-091: *Merck-Medco: Vertical Integration in the Pharmaceutical Industry* (1998).

58. Craig Stern. "The History, Philosophy, and Principles of Pharmacy Benefits," *Journal of Managed Care Pharmacy* 5(6) (1999): 525–531.

59. Craig Stern. "The History, Philosophy, and Principles of Pharmacy Benefits," *Journal of Managed Care Pharmacy* 5(6) (1999): 525–531. Quote from page 528.

60. It is not entirely clear whether this transition focused more on driving down drug costs, as opposed to more effective therapy strategies.

61. There were two ramifications according to David Cassak. First, while medical product companies signed national contracts, their local/regional

sales forces often gave better terms to big customers in major markets as part of a regional sales strategy. This served as a major spur to the "integrated delivery networks" (IDNs, profiled in Chapter 4) and their independently negotiated non-GPO contracts. The companies did not mind giving a local discount to a large IDN, especially if it secured their business on a regional level, but they resented making that price available to smaller providers in less urban communities, whose volumes didn't warrant a big discount. Admittedly, this may have been more true on the medical product side (because of its strong institutional profile) than the retail pharmaceutical side, but the sentiment was the same for both. Companies strongly felt that "we make valuable products that clinicians want, and we resent offering price discounts if and where we don't need to and/or they aren't really earned." A second ramification was the rise of defensive contracting. Given how difficult it was to achieve product conversion at individual hospitals and the fact that hospitals weren't really obligated to use GPO contracts, most major market share leaders offered discounts much smaller than non-market leaders and small companies were willing to offer, confident that the effort to get both doctors and nurses to adopt a new product was so difficult, hospitals would be willing to pay more for a product clinicans were already using than for a totally new product. This dynamic, too, played out differently depending on the product involved and its clinical relevance. But it explains why, for instance, surgical drapes went on contract quickly and robustly while orthopedic implants, much more slowly. Again, this reality was more true of GPOs and medtech products, and played out differently in retail pharmaceuticals. But the common theme is that for a long time, and especially at the beginning of the managed care revolution, medical supply and pharmaceutical companies were largely reluctant and perhaps resistant participants in the transition underway.

62. William Pursche. "Pharmaceuticals—The Consolidation Isn't Over," *The McKinsey Quarterly* (2) (1996): 110–119. According to David Cassak, McKinsey's report also fed the merger frenzy among pharmaceutical companies (and likely consulting engagements for the company).

63. Judith Hellerstein. "The Importance of the Physician in the Generic Versus Trade-Name Prescription Decision," *RAND Journal of Economics* 29(1) (1998): 108–136.

64. Anthony Bower and Gary Burkett. "Family Physicians and Generic Drugs: A Study of Recognition, Information Sources, Prescribing Attitudes, and Practices," *The Journal of Family Practice* 24(6) (1987): 612–616.

65. David Cassak. "Express Scripts' Friendly Data Play," *In Vivo* (May 1997): 39–50.

66. Taylor Christensen. "A Brief History of Pharmacy Benefit Managers (How They Became the 'Shady Middle Men' in the Drug Market)." Available online at: https://theincidentaleconomist.com/wordpress/2021/07/13. Accessed on April 6, 2022.

67. Charles Beever, "Why PBMs Work—And Why They Don't," *In Vivo* (Nov 1994): 8–13.

68. For generic drugs, about three-fourths are reimbursed using limits known as maximum allowable cost (MAC). These limits are established by PBMs, based on the lowest estimated acquisition cost for any of the generic equivalents of a given drug. The MAC tends to be 50 to 60% below AWP. The remaining one-fourth of generics are reportedly reimbursed, like brand-name drugs, at AWP minus 13 to 15%. The dispensing fee for generics tends to be the same as for brand drugs, but sometimes it is 25 or 50 cents higher, to encourage generic substitution by pharmacies.

69. It is worth noting that the PBMs needed a P&T committee by law. The process included the following steps. The P&T committee would medically vet one or a competitive group of drugs. Once the PBM's trade group received the blessing of the P&T committee, they would then go and negotiate with all the P&T-blessed competitors. The one manufacturer that gave them the best economics (volume x rebate) would be "the preferred agent".

70. Congressional Budget Office. *How Increased Competition from Generic Drugs Has Affected Prices and Returns in the Pharmaceutical Industry* (Washington, DC: CBO, July 1998): Fig. 5.

71. Frederick M. Scherer. "How US Antitrust Can Go Astray: The Brand Name Prescription Drug Litigation," *International Journal of the Economics of Business* 4(3) (1997).

72. David Cassak. "Inside Selling—The New Sales/Marketing Mix for Rx Companies," *In Vivo* (January 1990): 12–16.

73. The inclusion of generic drugs on contracts negotiated by chain pharmacies may have served to increase the legitimacy of this mechanism in the eyes of physicians, as well as generate rebate savings. It may have been a natural progression to apply the formularies to branded drugs and seek closer management of these more expensive products.

74. Me-too drugs have been defined as "pharmacologically active compound that is structurally related to a first-in-class compound, regarded as belonging to the same therapeutic class as the original compound, and used for the same therapeutic purposes, but which may differ in some respects, such as specificity of pharmacological action, adverse reactions profile, or drug–drug interactions." Jeffrey Aaronson and A. Richard Green. "Me-Too Pharmaceutical Products: History, Definitions, Examples, and Relevance to Drug Shortages and Essential Medicines Lists," *British Journal of Clinical Pharmacology* 86 (2020): 2114–2122. See also: Congressional Budget Office. *How Increased Competition from Generic Drugs Has Affected Prices and Returns in the Pharmaceutical Industry* (Washington, DC: CBO, July 1998).

75. Marsha Gold, Mark Joffe, Thomas L. Kennedy et al. "Pharmacy Benefits in Health Maintenance Organizations," *Health Affairs* 8(3) (Fall 1989).

76. Jeffrey Harrison, "Comments on Scherer," *International Journal of the Economics of Business* 4(3) (November 1997).

77. No author. "The Drug Industry's Pricing Scare," *In Vivo* (September 1996): 1, 3.

78. Jeffrey Harrison, "Comments on Scherer," *International Journal of the Economics of Business* 4(3) (November 1997).

79. Jeffrey Harrison, "Comments on Scherer," *International Journal of the Economics of Business* 4(3) (November 1997).

80. Congressional Budget Office. *How Increased Competition from Generic Drugs Has Affected Prices and Returns in the Pharmaceutical Industry* (Washington, DC: CBO, July 1998).

81. Marsha Gold, Mark Joffe, and Thomas L. Kennedy. "Pharmacy Benefits in Health Maintenance Organizations," *Health Affairs* (Fall 1989): 182–190.

82. Boston Consulting Group. *The Changing Environment for U.S. Pharmaceuticals: The Role of Pharmaceutical Companies in a Systems Approach to Health Care* (New York: The Boston Consulting Group, Inc., April 1993).

83. Roy Weinstein and John Culbertson. "How US Antitrust Can Be on Target: The Brand Name Prescription Drug Litigation," *International Journal of the Economics of Business* 4(3) (November 1997).

84. Chris Nee. "Uncovering the Mysteries Behind Rebates," *Drug Cost Management Report* (June 2002).

85. Beyond price discounting, there was also a non-discounting strategy that addressed therapeutic substitution—i.e., keeping off the formulary all of the most expensive drugs in a therapeutic category. As noted elsewhere, Merck was the sole drug company that supported Senator David Pryor's legislation: if cost cutting was going to come, Merck wanted it to come in the form of across- the-board discounts, rather than eliminate the most expensive drugs (where most of Merck's drugs fit) and forcing patients to use less expensive products.

86. Stefanie Berman. *A Legislative History of the Medicaid Drug Rebate Law: The Drug Industry and the Crusade of Senator David Pryor*. Harvard Law School, 2004 Third Year Paper.

87. Congressional Budget Office. *How Increased Competition from Generic Drugs Has Affected Prices and Returns in the Pharmaceutical Industry* (Washington, DC: CBO, July 1998).

88. Government Accounting Office. *Medicaid: Changes in Drug Prices Paid by HMOs and Hospitals Since Enactment of Rebate Provisions* (January 1993). HRD-93-43. Government Accounting Office. *Medicaid: Changes in Best Price for Outpatient Drugs Purchased by HMOs and Hospitals* (August 1994). Available online at: https://www.gao.gov/assets/90/89752.pdf.

89. Henry Zaretsky, "Comment on Scherer," *International Journal of the Economics of Business* 4(3) (November 1997).

90. Lynn Etheredge. "Pharmacy Benefit Management: The Right Rx?" Sponsored by the Health Insurance Reform Project of George Washington

University, with funding from the Robert Wood Johnson Foundation (April 1995).

91. Spencer Johnson. *Who Moved My Cheese?* (New York: Putnam's Sons, 1998).

92. Elyse Tanouye. "Big Drug Makers Regaining Control over Their Prices," *Wall Street Journal* (July 12, 1995).

93. David Cassak. Personal communication.

94. Lawrence Van Horn, Lawton R. Burns, and Douglas R. Wholey. "The Impact of Physician Involvement in Managed Care on Efficient Use of Hospital Resources," *Medical Care* 35(9) (1997): 873–889.

95. Kevin Schulman, Elizabeth Rubenstein, Darrell Abernethy et al. "The Effect of Pharmaceutical Benefits Managers: Is it Being Evaluated?" *Annals of Internal Medicine* 124(10) (1996): 906–913.

96. David Cassak. "From Mail Service to Managed Care," *In Vivo* (January 1993): 37–44.

97. No author. "AmHS Takes a Stake in PBM Express Scripts," *In Vivo* (October 1995): 60.

98. No author. "Consolidation in the PBM Industry," *In Vivo* (November 1996): 2.

99. No author. "GPO and PBM: Can They Create a Common Formulary?" *In Vivo* (January 1997): 2.

100. Lawton R. Burns, Ingrid M. Nembhard, and Stephen Shortell. "Integrating Network Theory into the Study of Integrated Healthcare," *Social Science and Medicine* (2022). https://doi.org/10.1016/j.socscimed.2021.114664.

101. Nancy Nichols. "Medicine, Management, and Mergers: An Interview with Merck's Roy Vagelos," *Harvard Business Review* (November–December 1994).

102. David Cassak. "From Mail Service to Managed Care," *In Vivo* (January 1993): 37–44.

103. Roger Longman. "Merck-Medco: Defining a New Pharmaceutical Company," *In Vivo* (September 1993): 29–36.

104. Brian O'Reilly. "Why Merck Married the Enemy," *Fortune* (September 20, 1993).

105. Nancy Nichols. "Medicine, Management, and Mergers: An Interview with Merck's Roy Vagelos," *Harvard Business Review* (November–December 1994).

106. David Cassak. "From Mail Service to Managed Care," *In Vivo* (January 1993): 37–44.

107. Arnon Mishkin, Philippe Chambon, and Eran Broshy. "The Three Strategic Choices for Drug Firms, Part 1," *In Vivo* (May 1994): 7–11.

108. Arnon Mishkin, Philippe Chambon, and Eran Broshy. "The Three Strategic Choices for Drug Firms, Part 1," *In Vivo* (May 1994): 7–11.

109. No author. "The Drug Industry's Pricing Scare," *In Vivo* (October 1996): 1, 3.

110. David Cassak recalls that Roy Vagelos greenlit the Medco deal just a couple of months before he retired (having hit Merck's mandatory retirement age). There were executives within Merck who were furious that he had made this major move without hanging around to see whether it would be successful. Vagelos' replacement was Ray Gilmartin, the CEO of hospital suppler Becton Dickinson. To Cassak, this suggested that Merck's board not only saw Gilmartin as a smart, capable manager but also believed his experience in working with GPOs would be relevant/helpful.

111. David Cassak. "DPS and the Managed Care Revolution," *In Vivo* (May 1991): 17–22.

112. Roger Longman. "The Club of Three," *In Vivo* (July/August 1994): 1–6.

113. Brian O'Reilly. "Why Merck Married the Enemy," *Fortune* (September 20, 1993).

114. *In Vivo* Diarist. "Bridging the Product-Service Divide," *In Vivo* (June 1995): 29.

115. Roger Longman. "SmithKline's Data Challenge," *In Vivo* (January 1995): 41–46.

116. No author. "And Then There Was One," *In Vivo* (March 1999): 77. David Cassak. "Express Scripts—Back to Basics, Only Bigger," *In Vivo* (October 2000): 15–30.

117. No author. "Rite-Aid Buys PCS," *In Vivo* (December 1998): 70.

118. Even the closed-model HMOs had their limitations, based on evidence from California (the home of Kaiser). One study reported that while 77% of California residents got their prescription drug benefits through their health plan, 12% got it through a stand-alone PBM carved out of the insurer, usually by self-insured firms, while another 11% get it through the state's Medicaid program, MediCal. California health plans had more restricted formularies than did the national PBMs, and were less likely to resort to three-tier plans (16% prevalence versus 35% nationally). Nevertheless, more than half of the state's HMOs outsourced major components of their pharmacy benefit services to a carve-out PBM, including: claims processing (#1 outsoured function), mail-order (#2), retail network (#3), formulary and clinical programs (#4). William Mercer, *Prescription Drug Coverage and Formulary Use in California* (May 2001).

119. Scott Hensley. "Prescription Costs," *Modern Healthcare* (August 23, 1999).

120. Peter Fox. "Prescription Drug Benefit: Cost Management Issues for Medicare," *Health Care Financing Review* (Winter 2003–2004).

121. David Cassak. "Express Scripts—Back to Basics, Only Bigger," *In Vivo* (October 2000): 15–30.

122. No author. "In a Hot Political Climate, Drug Prices Continue to Rise," *In Vivo* (July 1999): 2, 4.

123. David Cassak. "Express Scripts—Back to Basics, Only Bigger," *In Vivo* (October 2000): 15–30.

124. David Cassak. "Express Scripts—Back to Basics, Only Bigger," *In Vivo* (October 2000): 15–30.

125. John Hope. "Prescription for Success," *Modern Physician* (April 2000).

126. Eric Adams. "The Other Drug War," *Health Leaders* (November 2001).

127. Russell Gold. "Drug-Benefits Managers Under Fire," *Wall Street Journal* (September 5, 2001).

128. Heather Slowik. "Changes to Medicaid Drug Spending Stirring Manufacturers," *In Vivo* (April 2003): 55–62.

129. Heather Slowik. "Changes to Medicaid Drug Spending Stirring Manufacturers," *In Vivo* (April 2003): 55–62.

130. Amanda Cole, Adrian Towse, Celia Segel et al. *Value, Access, and Incentives for Innovation: Policy Perspectives on Alternative Models for Pharmaceutical Rebates.* Institute for Clinical and Economic Review (March 2019).

131. Congressional Budget Office. *How Increased Competition from Generic Drugs Has Affected Prices and Returns in the Pharmaceutical Industry* (Washington, DC: CBO, July 1998).

132. Anna Cook, Thomas Kornfield, and Marsha Gold. *The Role of PBMs in Managing Drug Costs: Implications for a Medicare Drug Benefit* (Kaiser Family Foundation, January 2000).

133. Kevin Berg and Noah Yosha. *PBM Down Low Vol. II.* Credit Suisse (March 11, 2004).

134. Stephanie Kanwit. Presentation to PCMA (June 6–9, 2004).

135. Thomas Barker, Ross Margulies, Erik Schulwolf. *Antitrust Implications of HHS' Proposed Rule to Limit Manufacturer Rebates.* (Foley Hoag LLP, March 2019).

136. 42 C.F.R. 1001.952(h)(4). See: *Federal Register* 64(223) (November 19, 1999): 63518–63557. In 2003, the OIG-DHHS issued final voluntary guidance for pharmaceutical manufacturers in their dealings and discounted practices with PBMs. See: *Federal Register* 68(86) (May 5, 2003): 23731–23743.

137. Roger Longman opines that this is all true. But two other points about rebates are salient. Plans/employers charge patient copays on the basis of WAC pricing. In simple terms, if a drug's WAC price is $100 and the patient's copay is 20%, the plan gets back $20. If the plan got the drug at a discount—$80—it could only charge the patient $16. That's one reason plans (and their vendors, the PBMs), prefer rebates. And because PBMs bundle all their rebates together, their customers (employers and plans) don't actually know what specific rebates for which specific drugs they're getting. So they don't really have a good handle on what they should be saving and what the PBMs are keeping.

138. Public Advocate for New York City (December 1996). Cited in: "Are PBMs Bad for Your Health?" *In Vivo* (February 1997).

139. Russell Gold. "Drug-Benefits Managers Under Fire," *Wall Street Journal* (September 5, 2001).

140. Chris Nee. "Uncovering the Mysteries Behind Rebates," *Drug Cost Management Report* (June 2002).
141. David Cassak. "Express Scripts' Friendly Data Play," *In Vivo* (May 1997): 39–50.
142. Frederick M. Scherer. "How US Antitrust Can Go Astray: The Brand Name Prescription Drug Litigation," *International Journal of the Economics of Business* 4(3) (1997).

11

PBM Tailwinds in the New Millennium: Specialty Drugs, Specialty Pharmacies, and Insurance Expansion

Lawton Robert Burns and Adam J. Fein

Introduction

PBMs have undergone several significant changes since the start of the new millennium. *First*, PBMs benefitted from long-term underlying trends that fueled demand for pharmaceuticals, including population aging and growing chronic illness. *Second*, PBMs witnessed growth on the supply side with the advent of biotechnology-based innovations in drug discovery that encompass both "orphan drugs" and "specialty medicines." These new types of medications served as additional fuel increasing prescription volumes and revenues. Such drugs grew in salience because of their high individual price tags and their rising, collective share of drug spending. *Third*, PBMs witnessed the consolidation of health plans as well as the emergence of new types of health plan coverage (e.g., high-deductible health plans, or HDHPs). *Fourth*, after a slow start at the beginning of the millennium, PBMs saw their business grow as insurance expansions—particularly the Part D drug benefit in Medicare and the expansion of Medicaid under the Patient Protection and Affordable Care Act (PPACA)—added new fuel to drug utilization and, thus, the flywheel underlying the healthcare quadrilemma. Such insurance expansions have led to enhanced roles of health plans in providing drug coverage. PBMs also saw new pharmacy customers arise due to new cost savings programs for safety net providers like the 340B program. *Fifth*, the PBMs underwent considerable consolidation. This consolidation occasioned

© The Author(s), under exclusive license to Springer Nature Switzerland AG 2022
L. R. Burns, *The Healthcare Value Chain*,
https://doi.org/10.1007/978-3-031-10739-9_11

considerable concern about the potential market power PBMs might wield (see Chapter 12). *Sixth*, the PBMs entered the GPO business (covered in Part II of this volume). These developments have led to a shift in the PBMs' customer mix from enrollees in most private health plans to (increasingly) public enrollees managed by public and private health plans.

This chapter continues the historical chronicle begun in Chapter 10 to bring us into the present day. The chapter reviews each of the major historical developments noted above ("tailwinds") that have shaped the growth and transformation of PBMs—drawing on many of the same forces described at the beginning of the last chapter. These developments include the rise of new classes of expensive drugs and expansions in public insurance.

PBM Tailwind #1: Rising Prescription Volumes & Revenues

PBMs administer drug benefits for nearly all U.S. citizens with third-party insurance coverage through self-insured employers, health insurance plans, labor unions, or government plans. PBMs' services and relationships with payers have grown in tandem with the increasing penetration of drug spending by third-party payers. The PBMs' role waned and then waxed along with spending and utilization trends over the past two decades.

At the start of the millennium, PBMs (and the pharmaceutical industry generally) were faced with slowing organic growth (see Fig. 11.1). Growth in prescription volumes fell from 5% in 2001 to 2% in 2003, due to higher copayments, declining insurance enrollment, and slower rates of product introductions by manufacturers—all in contrast to the more robust 6% prescription compound average growth rate (CAGR) experienced throughout the 1990s. Similarly, mail-order penetration fell and mail-order growth plateaued by 2004–2005. Real per capita spending continued to fall through 2012, in large part due to the 2008 recession and the resulting high level of unemployment.

By contrast, between 2011–2021, revenues grew 67% to more than $200 Billion, with growth accelerating after 2012–2013 (see Fig. 11.2). The growth resulted from a combination of insurance expansions in Medicaid, the end of the recession, and rising employment. More than 80% of that growth was captured by mail pharmacies and chain drugstores: mail pharmacies witnessed 145% revenue growth, even though their prescription volume fell 21%. Other dispensing outlets had slower revenue growth or lost share; retail community pharmacies experienced only 43% revenue growth and

Medicine Spending & Growth 1995–2014

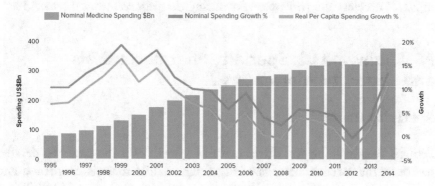

Fig. 11.1 Slowdown in growth (*Source* IMS Health, National Sales Perspectives, December 2014; U.S. Census Bureau of Economic Analysis)

33% prescription volume growth. Revenue growth was also spurred by an increasing number of specialty drugs introduced into the market (covered below) and a plateauing of the generic dispensing rate (due to fewer major brand-name drugs losing exclusivity). The contribution of specialty drugs to the pharmacy industry's revenues grew from 24% in 2013, to 31% in 2016, and then to more than 38% in 2021.

Total prescriptions dispensed at retail, mail, long-term care, and specialty pharmacies have remained fairly stable at 4.1–4.2 billion during the most recent 2017–2021 interval—with a slight downturn during COVID-19. When adjusted for prescription length and standardized on a 30-day basis, the number of prescriptions grew from 5.6 billion to 6.2 Billion, with roughly 2–3% annual growth.[1] Total prescription revenues at retail, mail, long-term

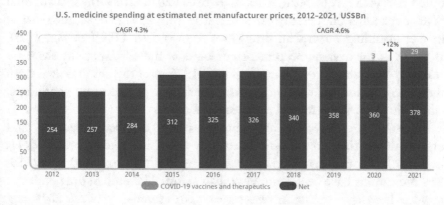

Fig. 11.2 Acceleration in growth (*Source* IQVIA Institute, March 2022. Used by permission)

care, and specialty pharmacies rose from $413 Billion in 2017 to $501 Billion in 2021, accelerating year-over-year during that interval from 0.6 to 7.3%.[2]

PBM Tailwind #2: Specialty Pharmaceuticals and Specialty Pharmacies

Specialty Drugs

Perhaps the single biggest driver of PBM growth over the past two decades has been the ascendance of specialty drugs. While there is no precise and agreed-upon definition, specialty drugs are (a) high cost, e.g., $6,000 annually, (b) often large molecule products which have to be injected, rather than taken orally, (c) initiated and maintained by a specialist, (d) to treat complex diseases requiring careful monitoring of possible, significant side effects, (e) require special handling, storage, and distribution—sometimes referred to as "cold chain," (f) have limited distribution from the manufacturer, and (g) require patient education.[3]

There is considerable overlap (but not identity) between specialty medicines and orphan drugs. Orphan drugs meet with one or more indications approved under the Orphan Drug Act of 1983 to treat rare conditions afflicting less than 200,000 people. According to the U.S. Food and Drug Administration (USFDA), 60% of orphan drugs were specialty medications in 2014. The average annual cost of an orphan drug prescription has been estimated at $18,000, compared to the cost of a specialty drug ($3,000), a branded drug ($182), and a generic drug ($18).[4] In some ways, they are the opposite of blockbuster drugs in that they target small patient populations, oftentimes with rare (orphan) diseases. Between 2010–2019, the share of total invoice spending on specialty medicines rose from 25% to 47%; the share of invoice spending on orphan drugs rose from 6% to 11% (see Fig. 11.3). In terms of the overlap, 36 percentage points of the 47% specialty share are related to specialty non-orphan drugs in 2019. Part of this shift resulted from the genericization of blockbuster drugs that treat primary care conditions, which tilted spending toward the specialty side.

Since 2000, the USFDA has approved a large number of specialty and orphan drugs; they now constitute roughly one-third of all approved drugs (see Fig. 11.4). Between 1983 (passage of the Orphan Drug Act) and 2019, 838 indications have been granted orphan status. The orphan drug approval rate has been accelerating in recent years. For example, between 2014 and 2020, the number of approved orphan drugs rose from 46 to 76. Many of

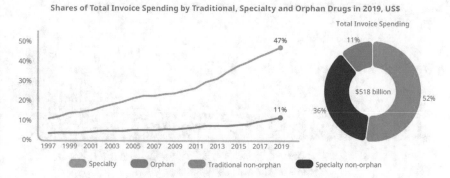

Fig. 11.3 Rise in invoice spending on specialty and orphan drugs (*Source* IQVIA Institute, August 2020; FDA Orphan Drug Designations and Approvals; IQVIA National Sales Perspective, January 2020. Used by permission)

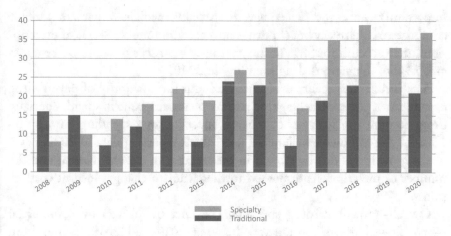

Fig. 11.4 Rise in novel FDA approvals favor specialty medicine

these drugs fall in a discrete set of therapeutic classes, including: multiple sclerosis, HIV, oncology, and inflammatory conditions (e.g., rheumatoid arthritis). Rare cancers have been a focus for manufacturers seeking orphan indications, comprising 42% of approved orphan indications from 2010–2019 (see Fig. 11.5). This is an increase from the 34% of orphan indications approved from 2000–2009.[5]

Specialty Drug Utilization

The number of prescriptions written to treat such conditions has continued to grow, as has their share of total prescriptions, due to the increasing prevalence of such chronic conditions among the (elderly) population. More

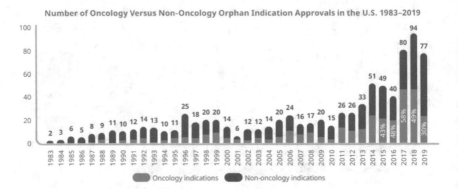

Fig. 11.5 Rise in FDA orphan indication approvals (*Source* IQVIA Institute, August 2020; FDA Orphan Drug Designations and Approvals. Used by permission)

importantly, while the percentage of specialty medicines that are patient-administered pharmacy benefit drugs now account for only 2–3% of prescriptions, they account for 38% of the pharmacy industry's prescription revenues and 52% of the nation's drug spending in 2020.

As a corollary, specialty drugs now account for a majority of payers' drug expenditures. As a percentage of payers' pharmacy benefit spend, specialty drugs account for 50% net of rebates. Specialty drug spending grew by 6–15% for the commercial clients of four PBMs reporting data in 2020. Most of the growth was due to growth in the number of patients treated and the number of prescriptions dispensed to them, not to changes in unit costs or prices.[6]

Overall, growth in drug spending (i.e., net of rebates) by commercial payers slowed down considerably between 2014 and 2019, falling from roughly 13% down to 2.3%. The majority of spending growth was volume-driven, not price-driven. These data highlight an important reality of PBMs for plan sponsors: net plan spending on pharmacy benefit drugs has been growing more slowly than spending on other healthcare services and more slowly than drug list prices (consistent with Fig. 9.9).

Specialty Pharmacies and PBMs

Not surprisingly, PBMs (and other players) began to enter the specialty pharma space due to its growth prospects and their belief that clients wanted a combined solution for both traditional and specialty pharmaceuticals. PBMs (and others) established or acquired specialty pharmacies as new stand-alone PBM businesses to take advantage of the trend. Players in the pharmaceutical supply chain underwent significant re-alignment during the first decade of the new millennium. In 2000, CVS acquired Bergen Brunswig's struggling pharmacy, Stadtlander, which served HIV/AIDS, organ transplant, and cancer patients. That same year, Wellpoint grew its mail-order business by acquiring RxAmerica. In 2003, Express Scripts acquired the specialty pharmacy Cura-Script, while Medco acquired Accredo in 2004. In 2006, CVS Pharmacy acquired Caremark; that same year, Amerisource Bergen acquired the specialty pharmacy igG of America. In 2007, Walgreens acquired Option Care which offered infusion services. That same year, McKesson acquired Oncology Therapeutics Network, which served as a GPO for specialty oncology drugs on behalf of oncology practices.

Specialty drugs do not come to market through retail channels but through specialty pharmacies. Specialty medications are dispensed by pharmacies that self-label themselves as specialty pharmacies; the designation is not regulated or defined by state pharmacy boards. Nevertheless, many PBMs require their specialty pharmacies to be accredited. Such pharmacies not only dispense specialty drugs but also provide patient services such as information, management of side effects, training on how to administer the specialty drugs, etc. Because of these definitional issues, it is hard to chart the rise in the number of specialty pharmacies. According to Drug Channels, the number of pharmacy locations with specialty pharmacy accreditation jumped from 378 in 2015 to 1,570 by 2021. Analysts suggest several drivers of the increase in specialty pharmacies: market entry by smaller PBMs (e.g., Prime Therapeutics), the market entry of private independent specialty pharmacies, multiple accreditation bodies that lower entry barriers, the market entry of hospital systems and integrated delivery networks, the rise of oncology practices dispensing their own oncology drugs, and activity by independent pharmacies to leverage open government payer networks.[7]

PBMs own and operate (internally) the three largest specialty pharmacies, as measured by market share of prescription revenues. The top three include CVS Specialty (28% share); Express Scripts and its two specialty businesses, Accredo and Freedom Fertility (23%); and OptumRx Specialty Pharmacy (14%). Revenue growth at PBMs' pharmacies is driven by the dispensing of more expensive specialty drugs. Specialty pharmacy dispensing revenues grew from $138 Billion to nearly $192 Billion between 2017–2021. Year over year, revenues grew anywhere from 7.3% to 9.1%.[8] By 2026, specialty drugs are forecast to account for 48% of the pharmacy industry's revenues. These specialty drugs drive the revenues of the mail-order pharmacies. As a result, the largest prescription drug dispensers (by revenues) are now central-fill pharmacies, mail pharmacies operated by the PBMs, and the health insurers—displacing the once-central role of retail chains.

Analysts estimate that PBMs now earn more than 50% of their profits from dispensing activities. To maintain and grow this profitability, PBMs increasingly demand that manufacturers pay higher service fees and provide deeper off-invoice discounts. Like any other pharmacy, a PBM's mail and specialty pharmacies earn gross profits from the difference between (1) the reimbursement to the pharmacy minus (2) the pharmacy's net acquisition cost for purchasing the product. This dispensing spread covers the expenses of operating a pharmacy, including pharmacist salaries, inventory holding costs, licensing, and other costs of dispensing. Mail pharmacies typically do not receive dispensing fees, but a PBM's specialty pharmacy could earn service and data fees from a manufacturer. The concentration of specialty and mail dispensing revenues results largely from strategies used by payers and manufacturers to narrow specialty drug channels. In most cases, health plans and plan sponsors require patients to use the mail and specialty pharmacies that the PBM owns and operates.

Cost Containment

Since health plans have fixed budgets, they have sought to limit the utilization of newly launched products. Compared to commercial plans, Medicare Part D plans (covered below) have limited ability to exclude drugs from their formularies. Part D plan formularies are required to include at least two drugs that are not therapeutically equivalent in every category or class. Plans must also include "all or substantially all drugs" in six protected classes: anticonvulsants, antidepressants, antineoplastics, antipsychotics, antiretrovirals, and immunosuppressants.[9] Such restrictions have important implications for drug competition and pricing. Fewer formulary exclusions result in lessened competition among manufacturers to get on the formulary which, in turn, leads to lower rebates.

PBMs have, nevertheless, applied some of the same pharmacy benefit management tools described in Chapter 9 to deal with specialty pharmaceuticals and their high cost. As one illustration, the number of unique products excluded from the formularies of the top three PBMs has risen dramatically between 2019 and 2022 (see Fig. 9.11). These cover not only multi-source drugs but also single-source brand drugs—i.e., those without a generic competitor or a biosimilar alternative. PBMs are now targeting specialty drugs for exclusion, making these therapeutic areas more competitive. From 2014–2020, nearly one-fifth of all formulary exclusions concerned diabetes drugs like insulin; for 2022, PBMs' exclusion lists include many single-source oncology drugs. PBMs have also developed prior authorization, indication-based formularies, step therapy protocols, and other utilization management approaches for other specialty drug classes (e.g., inflammatory conditions). However, compared to commercial plans, Part D plans apply utilization management approaches less frequently (e.g., to only half of the drugs on their formularies).

Thus, the PBMs have migrated (1) from their 1990s' strategy of network management to the 2000s strategy of profiting from the shift to generic drugs to the 2010s' strategy of pharmacy network exclusion, as well as (2) from the 1990s' strategy of three-tier formularies to the 2010s' strategy of formulary exclusions. Some PBMs offer their clients and enrollees a range of options here, much like the older MCOs, spanning from broader network access at higher cost to narrower network access at lower cost. Over time, a growing share of their Medicare Part D enrollees (covered below) have opted for the narrow pharmacy network solution.

Drug and Medical Benefit

The total commercial expenditure on specialty drugs is covered by both the medical benefit (45%) and the pharmacy benefit (55%). Specialty drugs account for 63% of drug spend in the medical benefit, and 51% in the pharmacy benefit. Drugs in the medical benefit are administered by a healthcare professional (e.g., a physician) at a clinic setting, while drugs in the pharmacy benefit are administered by the patient or family member at the home. The former is distributed to the clinics; the latter are distributed via retail, mail-order, or specialty pharmacies.[10]

The overlap in specialty drug spend between the two benefits, combined with the advent of new cancer drug therapies, has brought PBMs into conflict and competition with physicians. In recent years, the treatment of cancer patients has shifted from physician-administered infused or injected chemotherapy (covered under Medicare's Part B medical benefit) to oral oncolytics (covered under Medicare's Part D pharmacy benefit). Medical groups have accused the PBMs and their specialty pharmacies of stifling competition from physician dispensing, without regard to clinical care. Oral chemotherapy has been administered for decades. Now, oral oncolytics are gaining popularity over intravenous chemotherapy for several reasons—particularly patient convenience (self-administer at home versus travel to outpatient center) and clinical precision of the drugs. The oral oncolytics' targeted approach to treatment exhibits a higher degree of safety and effectiveness as compared to traditional chemotherapies. This shift has required dispensing physicians to become increasingly reliant on participation in

Medicare Part D networks, instead of direct billing and fee-for-service payment under Medicare Part B.

It should be noted that Part D drugs carry rebates, while Part B drugs do not; the prices of both sets of drugs continue to rise. Unlike on the commercial payer side, PBMs do not retain rebates on Part D drugs but pass along the vast majority (99% +) to the health plans. Plans utilize these rebates to reduce the monthly premiums they charge to their Medicare enrollees. This enables them to benefit all members and to compete with other Part D plans. Not all enrollees are equally advantaged, however, since beneficiary cost-sharing is tied to the list prices of drugs, not the net prices negotiated by the PBMs and their health plans. Thus, beneficiaries using drugs that carry rebates pay higher out-of-pocket costs.[11] As noted elsewhere in this volume, "tradeoffs are everywhere": all enrollees pay lower premiums, but some enrollees pay higher out-of-pocket costs. Enrollees in some other types of health plans face a similar situation (covered below). Critics allege this set-up provides an incentive for health plans to favor drugs with high rebates, which helps lower their premium costs; they also suggest the possibility that it may also increase federal spending on Part D, but such a determination is difficult.[12]

PBM Tailwind #3: Insurance Changes in the Private Sector

MCO Consolidation

The MCO sector underwent significant consolidation in the new millennium. As shown in Fig. 11.6, the percentage or enrollees across commercial, Medicare, and Medicaid lives increasingly concentrated in a smaller number of health plans. Acquisitions were particularly popular in 2005–2006 (see Fig. 11.7). Such concentration gave the MCOs greater market power relative to providers and product suppliers (such as pharmaceutical companies). MCOs used several cost containment mechanisms and, like GPOs, negotiated lower drug prices from manufacturers in exchange for higher sales and market shares. These mechanisms included formularies and restrictive formularies, number of price tiers, and use of co-pay differentials. It is also possible that the growing concentration of MCOs occasioned two other significant changes in market structure and market power. First, as MCOs consolidated, PBMs may have consolidated to try to achieve an even playing field in terms of winning and negotiating contracts. Second, the larger size of MCOs may have made it more feasible to acquire the concentrating PBMs and add them as an in-house manager of pharmacy benefits to counterbalance the MCOs' growing management of medical benefits.

High Deductible Health Plans

In 2002, the Internal Revenue Service (IRS) clarified that health reimbursement arrangements (HRAs), an employee-specific account established and funded by the employer from which the employee could be reimbursed for medical expenditures, could be excluded from the taxable income of employees. A key limitation of these accounts, however, was that they were tied to a particular employer and often a particular health plan. The Medicare Prescription Drug Improvement and Modernization Act of 2003 (MMA) allowed individuals to establish health savings accounts (HSAs), creating an alternative vehicle for tax-favored spending accounts which addressed the lack of portability of HRAs. The MMA allowed individuals to establish or contribute to an HSA when they are covered by a high-deductible health plan (HDHP). The legislation explicitly defined the minimum deductible and the maximum annual out-of-pocket expenditure for a qualifying plan. This added a new insurance option for employers and their employees, starting in 2006 when MMA went into operation.

Employers can offer their employees a range of health insurance coverage options. These include health maintenance organizations (HMOs), preferred provider organizations (PPOs), point of service (POS), and high-deductible health plans with a savings option (HDHP/SOs). The distribution in the percentage of employees selecting these plans has changed over time (see Fig. 11.8).

The choice among these plans entails a fundamental, well-known tradeoff that workers consciously make: pay a higher premium with lower out-of-pocket costs or a lower premium with higher out-of-pocket costs. According to Fig. 11.9, the HDHP/SO plan option entails the lowest premiums and the lowest worker contributions in exchange for worker responsibility for higher, up-front costs paid out-of-pocket before the insurance coverage begins.

Over the time period from 2007–2019, more employers have chosen to offer the HDHP/SO plan to their workers. Kaiser trend data indicate that workers have increasingly chosen the plan (the HDHP/SO) with a lower annual premium but higher out-of-pocket cost. This is (purportedly) an exercise in consumerism. According to researchers, HDHPs are designed to make the healthcare system more responsive to consumers and make consumers more responsible for the cost of healthcare by exposing them to larger, up-front out-of-pocket expenses. HDHPs entail three types of cost-sharing: the

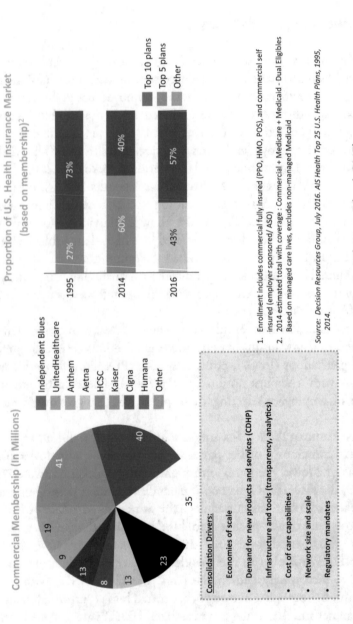

Fig. 11.6 Trends in MCO consolidation (*Source* Brad Fluegel, Presentation to Wharton School, 2017)

M&A in Managed Care Since 2005					
Acquiror	Target	Target Description	Price (mm)	Members (000s)	Announced
WellPoint	Atrium Health Plan	PPO	-	52	May 2005
WellPoint	Lumenos	CDHP	$185	214	May 2005
WellPoint	WellChoice	MCO	$6,600	5,065	September 2005
UnitedHealth Group	Arnett Health Plans	HMO / TPA	-	51	September 2006
UnitedHealth Group	John Deere	HMO	$500	400	December 2005
UnitedHealth Group	PacifiCare	Health plan / Specialty products	$8,100	3,236	July 2005
UnitedHealth Group	Neighborhood Health Partnership	HMO	-	135	July 2005
Cigna	Star HRG	Ltd-benefit medical plans	$175	200	June 2006
Cigna	Managed Care Consulting	(?)	-	100	July 2005
Cigna	Choicelinx	Technology and services; support CDHPs	-	-	August 2005
Cigna	Thai Charoen Insurance Public Co. Ltd.	Supp. Health / Financial Protection (Thailand)	-	-	August 2006
Humana	Corphealth, Inc.	Behavioral health solutions	$54	-	December 2005
Humana	CHA Health	Medical management / claims administration	$54	96	January 2006
Health Net	Universal Care	Public and private healthcare programs (CA)	-	100	January 2006
Aetna	HMS Healthcare	-	$390	-	-
Aetna	Active Health Management	-	$400	-	May 2005
Aveta	PMC Medicare Choice	Medicare advantage (Puerto Rico)	$250	55	May 2006
BCBS IL, TX, NM (H.C. Svcs. Corp.)	BCBS Oklahoma	Private health insurer	-	-	November 2005
Carlyle Group	MultiPlan, Inc.	Healthcare network	$1,000	-	-
Centene	MediPlan	Flexible funding plan	$9	13	January 2006
Centene	OptiCare Health Systems	Managed vision services	$8	-	April 2006
Centene	AirLogix	Respiratory disease management	$35	-	July 2005
Centene	US Script, Inc.	PBM	$40	-	December 2005
Centene	SummaCare	HMO	$31	39	January 2005
Concentra Operating Corp.	Beech Street	National PPO	$165	-	August 2005
Health Insurance Plan of NY	Group Health	Consumer-governed, care and coverage	-	2,600	September 2005
HealthSpring	America's Health Choice Med. Plans	Medical sales and service	$50	13	May 2006
Healthways Inc.	LifeMasters Supported SelfCare	Disease management	$308	600	May 2006
Molina	CAPE Health Plan	Medicaid (MI)	$44	87	January 2006
MultiPlan	Private Healthcare Systems	PPO Network / Independent Care Mgmt.	-	16,000	August 2006
MVP Health Care	Preferred Care	HMO	-	260	July 2005

Fig. 11.7 Health plan acquisitions 2005–2006

Distribution of Health Plan Enrollment for Covered Workers, by Plan Type, 1988-2019

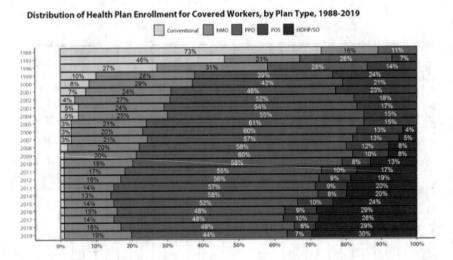

Fig. 11.8 Rise in HDHPs (*Note* Information was not obtained for POS plans in 1988 or for HDHP/SO plans until 2006. A portion of the change in 2005 is likely attributable to incorporating more recent Census Bureau estimates of the number of state and local government workers and removing federal workers from the weights. See the Survey Design and Methods section from the 2005 Kaiser/HRET Survey of Employer Sponsored Health Benefits. *Source* KFF Employer Health Benefits Survey, 2008–2019; Kaiser/HRET Survey of Employer-Sponsored Health Benefits, 1999–2017; KPMG Survey of Employer-Sponsored Health Benefits, 1993 and 1996; The Health Insurance Association of America [HIAA], 1988)

Average Annual Worker and Employer Premium Contributions and Total Premiums for Single and Family Coverage, by Plan Type, 2019

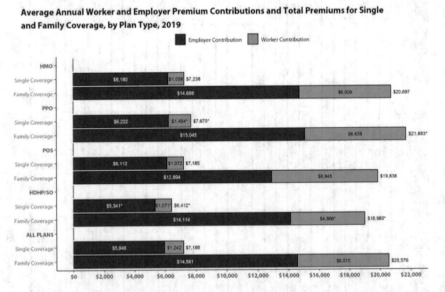

Fig. 11.9 HDHP tradeoff: Premium vs. out of pocket cost (*Note* Estimate is statistically different from all plans estimate within coverage type [$p < 0.05$]. *Source* KFF Employer Health Benefits Survey, 2019)

annual deductible to be paid before coverage begins, the percent of cost-sharing (co-insurance) once the insurance coverage kicks in, and the annual out-of-pocket maximum.

While the Kaiser data do not directly indicate whether the HDHP is an "option" or a "replacement," other data reveal that the vast majority (66%) of enrollees in HDHPs had a choice of plan. Indeed, a higher percentage of HDHP enrollees have greater choice among two or three plans compared to enrollees in national and traditional health plans. The plans from which they choose can include open-network models such as PPOs or more restricted models such as HMOs and POS plans.

It should be noted that HDHP plans have also proved quite popular on the new public health insurance exchanges that came online following the passage of the PPACA. HDHPs were the choice of 85% of enrollees who enrolled in the silver and bronze plans.

Cost-Sharing

Why are these trends relevant? Some background here is helpful. Across all consumers, out-of-pocket spending on drugs (cash-pay, co-payment, coinsurance) as a proportion of outpatient drug expenditures has fallen over time from roughly 90% in 1965 to less than 15% by 2020. On a per capita basis, annual out-of-pocket spending on drugs has remained fairly stable over the last decade, ranging from $141–162. Adjusted for inflation in consumer prices, this spending has fallen 23%.[13] All of these figures suggest that the vast majority of commercially insured enrollees spend less than $200 out-of-pocket annually on drugs; by contrast, a small proportion spend more than $1,000 annually.

Across all employer-sponsored plans, plans with 4+ tiers covered only 3% of workers in 2004 but now cover 51% by 2018. During that same time frame, the average copayments for drugs on the fourth tier rose from $50 to $123. Over time, plans with four or more cost-sharing tiers have also become the most common type of coverage among the HDHP/SOs—rising from 27% of enrollees in 2019 to 44% in 2021. Conversely, the percentage of HDHP enrollees in plans with no cost-sharing fell. Moreover, the HDHP/SO plans are more likely to utilize coinsurance on the lower tiers of such plans. This has likely occasioned the growing dissatisfaction of HDHP/SO enrollees with their out-of-pocket costs for prescription drugs.

It is also important to note that the annual deductibles in most employer plans do not include spending on drugs. This is true for HDHP/HRA plans, but not for HDHP/HSA plans (where workers are required to pay the deductible for all services). This has resulted in a relatively high percentage of workers covered by HDHP/HRA plans (16%) who have no prescription drug coverage prior to meeting their annual deductible compared to those enrolled in HMO plans (5%) and PPO plans (11%).

As a result, the shifts in the benefit designs offered by employers and the plan choices made by workers have exerted huge effects on prescription drug spending and the distribution of the out-of-pocket cost burden. Four shifts in benefit design are important: (1) the shift in benefit designs from fixed copayments to percentage coinsurance amounts, (2) the shift to high deductible plans, (3) the expansion of benefit designs with four or five tiers (where tier five for specialty drugs entails 25% coinsurance), and (4) the absence of any out-of-pocket maximum for drugs on the fourth or fifth tier. Between 2015 and 2021, out-of-pocket spending on drugs based on fixed copayments fell from 66 to 47%; spending based on coinsurance rose from 25 to 39%; and spending during the deductible phase rose from 9 to 15%.[14] Coinsurance amounts incurred during the deductible phase are typically based on a branded drug's list price before any rebates are applied. This generated much attention and litigation against the PBMs (see Chapter 12).

PBM Tailwind #4: Insurance and Service Expansions in the Public Sector

Medicare Modernization Act of 2003

The PBM sector benefitted from several expansions of health insurance coverage in the public sector. First, in 2003, Congress passed the Medicare Modernization Act (MMA), which provided seniors with a retail drug benefit—known as Medicare part D—available from Medicare Prescription Drug Plans (PDPs).[15] The MMA went into operation in 2006.

The legislation also made several changes to the managed care options offered to seniors, primarily the Medicare Advantage (MA) plans. The MA plans were designed to incentivize the elderly to enroll in Medicare HMOs and PPOs by offering them generous coverage. Roughly two-thirds of MA enrollees were enrolled in HMO plans; another 30% were enrolled in PPOs. MA offered several advantages over fee-for-service Medicare, including: avoid cost-sharing in Parts A & B, avoid paying premiums for Medicare supplemental coverage, possibility to enroll in zero-premium MA plans, possible added benefits (vision, dental), and limits on out-of-pocket costs. Not surprisingly, MA plans were quite popular with seniors and witnessed skyrocketing enrollment (see Fig. 11.10).

Medicare enrollees who selected such plans could obtain drug coverage through their MA plan rather than the free-standing PDP plans. By 2021, more than three-quarters of Medicare beneficiaries opted for drug coverage; 43% received it through MA plans while another 40% obtained it through PDP plans. Figure 11.11 shows the trend in enrollment in both types of drug plans since the plans became active in 2006. Between 2005–2006, spending on outpatient drugs as a share of Medicare's total expenditures rose from less than 1% to nearly 10%; it steadily rose after that to approach 14% by 2020. As a percentage of all outpatient drug spending, Medicare's share rose from 2% in 2005 to 17% in 2006 and then to 32% by 2020. This turned Medicare into the second largest payer of outpatient prescription drug spending, just behind employer-sponsored private health insurance (36%). Overall demand for prescription drugs among the elderly was further fueled by the growing percentage of the elderly who are "poly-chronics" (taking five or more prescriptions), which grew from 11% in 1988 to 42% in 2018.

Part D coverage was designed as a federally subsidized program that would mimic commercial market practices. Indeed, it relied on private sector health plans to administer the coverage. Part D plans utilized a retrospective rebate system after the point of sale that preserved the confidentiality of pricing terms between manufacturers and PBMs/plan sponsors. MMA also incentivized the private sector insurers to offer such plans by providing them more generous reimbursement. Part D plans also employ formularies for the

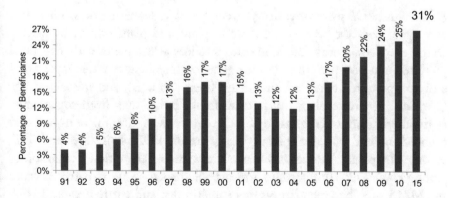

% of Medicare Beneficiaries Enrolled in Medicare Advantage

Fig. 11.10 31% of medicare beneficiaries choose to be in a private medicare advantage (Part C) plan

Medicare Part D Enrollment Has Declined in Stand-alone PDPs While
Increasing Steadily in Medicare Advantage Drug Plans

■ PDP (non-employer) ■ MA-PD (non-employer) ■ Employer-only group PDP   ■ Employer-only group MA-PD

Year	PDP (non-employer)	MA-PD (non-employer)	Employer-only group PDP	Employer-only group MA-PD
2006	15.2M	5.4M		
2007	15.8M	5.9M		
2008	16.1M	6.7M		
2009	16.1M	7.7M		
2010	16.2M	8.5M		
2011	16.7M	9.2M		
2012	17.2M	10.2M		
2013	17.8M	11.2M	4.3M	
2014	18.3M	12.1M	4.6M	
2015	19M	13.3M	4.6M	
2016	19.8M	14.1M	4.5M	
2017	20.3M	15M	4.4M	
2018	20.6M	16M	4.5M	
2019	20.6M	17.4M	4.6M	
2020	20.2M	19.3M	4.6M	
2021	19.5M	21.3M	4.4M	2.8M

Fig. 11.11 Enrollment in PDP and MA-PD plans (*Note* PDP is prescription drug plan. MA-PD is Medicare Advantage drug plan. Analysis includes enrollment in the territories and in employer-only group plans. *Source* KFF analysis of Centers for Medicare & Medicaid Services 2006–2021 Part D plan flies. PNG)

drugs they will cover that include both branded and generic products. Unlike commercial plans, the PDP formularies must allow wider access to drugs in a therapeutic category, thus reducing the power of the formulary to create competition among manufacturers' drugs.

Tiers, Rebates, and PBMs

All MA and PDP plans offer drug coverage with cost-sharing tiers. There was one major contrast between the Part D plans and plans offered by private sector enrollees. Nearly all Medicare enrollees select plans with five tiers: preferred and non-preferred tiers for generic drugs (first two tiers), preferred and non-preferred tiers for brand drugs (next two tiers), and specialty drugs (last tier). Medicare plans utilize coinsurance rather than fixed copayments as the mechanism of cost-sharing on the higher tiers: 40% for non-preferred brand drugs and 25% for specialty drugs among PDP plans, 45% and 33% among MA plans. Another difference is the lower penetration of mail-order among the PDPs compared to the overall market. This is partly because the MMA prohibits mandatory use of mail-order, and partly because MMA requires a level playing field between retail and mail-order.

Medicare Part D plan sponsors have a choice of outsourcing functions to PBMs or performing the activities in-house. Data on 600 sponsors from 2016 revealed that 92% outsourced the adjudication of claims, 81% outsourced drug benefit administration, 78% outsourced pharmacy technical assistance, 76% outsourced pharmacy network development, and 73% outsourced rebate and other price concession negotiations. Conversely, Part D plan sponsors are more likely to insource (provide in-house) functions such as managing the pharmacy and therapeutics (P&T) committee, enrollment processing, and enrollee appeals and grievance process management.[16]

Like their commercial health plan counterparts, Medicare Part D plans engage PBMs to help negotiate rebates with manufacturers. There are no statutorily defined rebates as in Medicaid. PBMs negotiate the rebates with manufacturers based on formulary position and the threat of formulary exclusion. This explains why the tier structures in commercial and Part D benefit plans resemble one another. Drugs in more competitive therapeutic classes have to offer higher rebates to get onto Part D plan formularies. Part D plan sponsors compensate the PBMs for their help by paying them fees, not by allowing them to retain rebates. In 2016, PBMs negotiated roughly two-thirds of total manufacturer rebates, while the plans themselves managed the remainder—consistent with the degree to which Part D plans outsource manufacturer negotiations to the PBMs. The MMA's enactment in 2006 included requirements for transparency and pass-through of manufacturer rebates; as a result, PBMs kept less than 1% of rebates and passed along the remainder to the plans. Such practices may have spilled over to the private plans that PBMs contracted with.

The fact that health plans sponsoring PDP coverage can insource the benefit (rather than outsource it to PBMs) creates competition between the plans and the PBMs for the business of Medicare enrollees. This fosters competition with their MCO customers and increases the number of players in the Part D landscape, making it much less concentrated than drug coverage in the commercial market. Competition is also fostered by the marketing of prescription drug plans (PDPs) in 34 distinct geographic regions, allowing smaller, local players to compete. Moreover, the PBM has traditionally operated as a B2B model, while Part D is a B2C model.

Rebates and other channel discounts paid to PBMs (from manufacturers and pharmacies) constitute "Direct and Indirect Remuneration" (DIR) payments made to Part D Plan Sponsors.[17] These payments were stable from 2010–2012 but began to accelerate beginning in 2013. DIR payments rose from $9.7 Billion in 2012 to $65.6 Billion in 2021, much faster than the Part D program; DIR payments also accounted for a rising share of Part

D drug costs, rising from 11.7% to 30.3% between 2012–2021. Manufacturer rebates constitute the majority of DIR payments ($54.1 Billion out of $65.6 Billion). They also account for 23% of manufacturers' total rebates and discounts for branded drugs. Price concessions made to pharmacies also operate like rebates. The DIR payments do not affect the prices that enrollees pay for their drugs at pharmacies, but they contribute to the gap (disparity) between list and net prices (see Fig. 9.9).

Medicaid Enrollment and Program Expansions

At the start of the millennium, commercial PBMs played a very small role in state Medicaid programs. Of the 30 states that put together either preferred drug lists (similar to a PBM formulary) or operated PBM-like management services, only one state used a commercial PBM in 2003. Instead, states used pharmacy benefit administrators (PBAs) to perform fee-based services.

Medicaid has since become a faster growing source of insurance coverage than Medicare. Enrollment rose from slightly more than 45 million in 2005 to over 75 million by 2020. Enrollment drivers included the 2008–2009 recession, which led to losses in jobs and private insurance coverage and transitions to Medicaid coverage. The COVID-19 pandemic of 2020 exerted a similar effect. Perhaps the biggest driver was passage of the PPACA (2010) which expanded program eligibility to nonelderly adults at or below 138% of the Federal Poverty Line, thereby adding roughly 13 million people. As a consequence, Medicaid now accounts for 10% of all outpatient drug spending.

Most states rely in whole or in part on managed care plans and their carved-in pharmacy benefits to cover enrollees.[18] Given that Medicaid is largely administered at the state level, PBM penetration of the Medicaid managed care market is less concentrated than in the commercial population. While the states can elect to employ PBMs for both their managed care and fee-for-service enrollee populations, the managed care portion of prescriptions and spending has grown to dominate. As in Medicare, PBMs pass along nearly 100% of rebates to the plans.

The 340B Drug Pricing Program

Background[19]

As described in Chapter 10, Congress passed the Medicaid Drug Rebate Program (MDRP) in 1990 to lower the cost of prescription drugs covered by State Medicaid programs. MDRP mandated price rebates on covered outpatient drugs paid by manufacturers based on their best prices. Two years later, Congress passed the Veterans Health Care Act, which established Section 340B of the Public Health Service Act. The Section extended similar price relief for high drug costs to safety net providers. Section 340B required manufacturers to enter pharmaceutical pricing agreements (PPAs) with the Department of Health & Human Services (DHHS) and set price ceilings on their drugs in exchange for having their drugs covered by Medicaid and Medicare Part B. Under the PPA, the manufacturer agreed to provide front-end discounts on covered outpatient drugs purchased by specified providers, called "covered entities," that served the nation's most vulnerable patient populations. Covered entities initially included disproportionate share hospitals, children's hospitals and cancer hospitals exempt from the Medicare prospective payment system, sole community hospitals, rural referral centers, critical access hospitals, and federal grantees such as federally qualified health centers (among others). Hospitals account for 85–90% of all 340B purchases. Manufacturers may not charge more than the 340B ceiling price to covered entities regardless of whether the covered entity purchases pharmaceuticals through a wholesaler or directly from the manufacturer.

The 340B ceiling price is statutorily defined as the average manufacturer price (AMP) reduced by the unit rebate amount (URA). The URA is a minimum rebate percentage of 23.1% for most brand-name prescription drugs, 17.1% for brand-name pediatric drugs and clotting factor, and 13% for generic and over-the-counter drugs. Manufacturers must offer greater discounts on brand-name drugs if the manufacturer's best price for a drug is lower than AMP minus 23.1% for that drug and/or the price of the brand-name drug has increased more quickly than the rate of inflation. The 340B ceiling price is thus equivalent to the Medicaid net price. This mathematical relationship excludes subceiling 340B discounts and supplemental Medicaid rebate agreements.

The 340B program has expanded more rapidly than the overall pharmaceutical market and now exceeds the Medicaid outpatient drug program; some estimate 340B's annual growth at 27%. One main reason is that the eligibility requirements have expanded considerably. First, the PPACA widened the definition of eligible entities to encompass several additional types of hospitals. Second, the list expanded further due to mergers of 340B and non-340B providers. As a consequence, the number of 340B hospitals tripled between 2005–2014 (to 14,000 hospitals and affiliated sites), now encompassing roughly one-third of the hospital industry.[20] Third, the 340B statute did not require these providers to dispense only 340B drugs to needy patients. This allowed providers to buy 340B drugs at big discounts, sell them to non-340B patients, and then retain the difference between the insurance reimbursement rate and the discounted 340B price. Spending on 340B drugs also tripled during that time frame. 340B discounted purchases rose from $30 Billion in 2018 to $38 Billion in 2020 and to an estimated $46 Billion in 2021. The 27% CAGR for 340B purchases from 2014–2020 far outweighed the 4% growth in manufacturers' net drug sales over the same period.[21] Data from 2018 indicate the average discount off list price for 86 branded specialty drugs was 72%. Between 2019 and 2021, 340B discounts have doubled their share of gross-to-net rebates for branded drugs from 10% to 20% (see Fig. 9.14).

Why is this all relevant? Covered entities can purchase and dispense drugs through internal or externally contracted pharmacies. Following upon 2010 changes in DHHS guidance, covered entities have rapidly expanded their use of contract pharmacies; the number of contract pharmacy locations grew from 1,300 in 2010 to nearly 30,000 in 2021; and the proportion of 340B purchases flowing through external pharmacies rose to nearly 30% by 2021. The three largest PBMs operate mail and specialty pharmacy locations that also act as 340B contract pharmacies. Between 2017–2020, 340B sales grew more rapidly than the overall drug market; the fastest growth was observed among mail and specialty pharmacies, which featured 56% growth in the value of 340B purchases. These are the pharmacies where the PBMs have a heavy presence. Analysts estimate that 10% of all specialty prescriptions are dispensed through 340B contract pharmacies.

PBMs may face a loss of business and growing competition from academic medical centers and large hospital systems that (a) have become 340B hospitals, (b) have developed their own specialty pharmacies to serve specific patients in areas such as oncology and home health, and (c) are now partnering with private equity-backed startups in the PBM arena. Such diversification efforts help hospitals to earn substantial revenues and generate positive operating margins that offset their rising compensation expenses resulting from the Great Resignation.

340B Drugs and GPOs

Another aspect of the 340B program that is relevant here concerns the Health Resources and Services Administration (HRSA) that operates within DHHS and oversees the 340B program. The 340B statute initially disallowed certain covered entities (children's hospitals, cancer hospitals, and disproportionate share hospitals) from using GPOs to purchase drugs on the outpatient side; GPO use was legitimate for drugs purchased on the inpatient side. The statute also required HRSA to establish a prime vendor (PV) program to manage the 340B pricing portfolio and to negotiate subceiling prices on 340B drugs for covered entities. While the intent was to have potentially competitive PVs, HRSA's operation of the program and creation of value-added services led to there being just one PV.

This created costly complexity because it would force hospitals to maintain two different pharmacies and two different inventory systems. From 1992–2012, HRSA applied the following solution. It allowed hospitals to operate a two-inventory system whereby hospitals purchased initial drug inventories through their GPOs at a lower rate than WAC. If the drug was used for inpatients, hospitals replenished the drug using drugs acquired via the GPO; if the drug was used for outpatients, the drug was replenished using drugs acquired at the 340B price.

Then, in a Policy Release in early 2013 without notice and comment, HRSA ruled that it did not authorize a GPO replenishment model, and forbade hospitals from making their initial drug acquisitions through a GPO. Instead, HRSA required a three-inventory system where the drugs would be initially acquired based on WAC pricing, creating a financial strain on hospital budgets. As partial relief, HRSA allowed its PV to host a sub-WAC file with a non-GPO, non-340B portfolio of drug prices below WAC, making the PV a monopoly and only source of the sub-WAC portfolio. Creating the sub-WAC contract file entailed group purchasing through the PV, which worked with the drug wholesalers that paid fees to the PV to operate the sub-WAC portfolio. This created a very profitable reality for drug wholesalers and the PV, and reduced the degree of price competition among GPOs for the 340B, sub-WAC business. The GPOs excluded from this new policy sent a letter to the Federal Trade Commission outlining the cost implications:

There is little doubt that Policy Release 2013–1 has driven up the cost of drugs for 340B hospitals. A 2015 survey of 340B hospitals showed that approximately 90 percent of respondents affected by the policy reported increased spending on their non-GPO, non-340B accounts. These hospital drug costs have increased for at least three reasons. First, the prices they must pay by being forced to purchase through non-GPO, non-340B accounts, even with access to the prime vendor's sub-WAC prices, are substantially higher than what they would pay through their GPO accounts. Second, the three-inventory system has created tremendous operating burdens for 340B health systems and has increased labor and software costs. One analysis estimates that the policy has raised costs by $223 Million since its inception. Third, HRSA is enforcing its policy in a draconian fashion which is causing hospitals to err on the side of caution by purchasing through their sub-WAC account when they are clearly entitled to purchase through their GPO account. Our members tell us that, if HRSA discovers that a hospital has used a single GPO drug on a hospital outpatient, even if unintended, HRSA could terminate it from the 340B program or force it to make significant repayments to manufacturers. Hospitals therefore have to invest in rigorous self-auditing programs to prevent inadvertent GPO violations, driving up their operational costs further.[22]

It is worth noting that the 340B prime vendor (PV) is Apexus. Apexus is owned by the GPO Vizient, which itself is owned by its member hospitals. Thus, the federal government has outsourced the operation of the 340B program, which primarily benefits hospitals, to a hospital-owned organization.

PBM Tailwind #5: PBM Mergers

PBMs have been engaged in mergers and acquisitions (M&A) for decades. M&A activity picked up in the new millennium. Figure 11.12 depicts the genealogy of the major PBMs and their M&A history.

Setting the Stage for Consolidation: Slowdown in Growth

As mentioned elsewhere in this volume, PBM consolidation can provide powerful leverage over both manufacturers and pharmacies. Sometimes, mergers and acquisitions (M&A) between PBMs are rationalized as "the pursuit of synergy" but may more simply reflect a growth opportunity— particularly in the presence of a slowing in market growth (see Fig. 11.1). For example, in the early 2000s, analysts at Goldman Sachs commented on the growing saturation of the commercial market and lives covered by existing PBMs, a plateauing of mail-order penetration rates and the slowing growth of mail-order claims (due to lower mail-order utilization, the shrinking spread between retail and mail co-pays, competition from retail pharmacies to offer 90-day refills as well, the low prevalence of mandatory mail-order), as well as the slowing growth in prescription volume beginning in 2000 (due to higher co-pays, declining enrollments in HMOs, a slowdown in new drug product introductions) and the PBMs' historic difficulty in penetrating new market segments such as Medicaid.

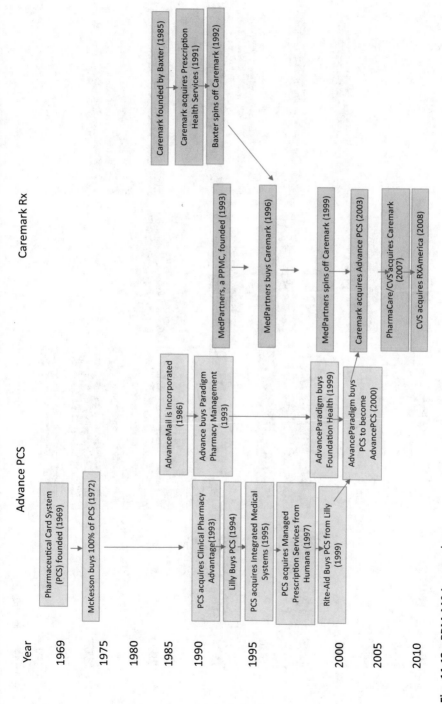

Fig. 11.12 PBM M&A genealogy

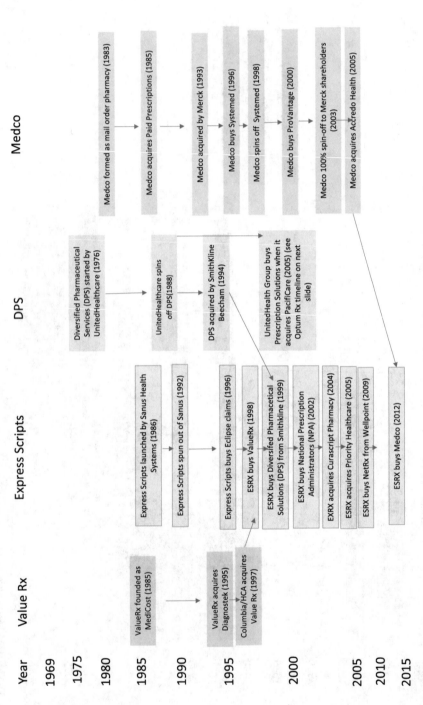

Fig. 11.12 (continued)

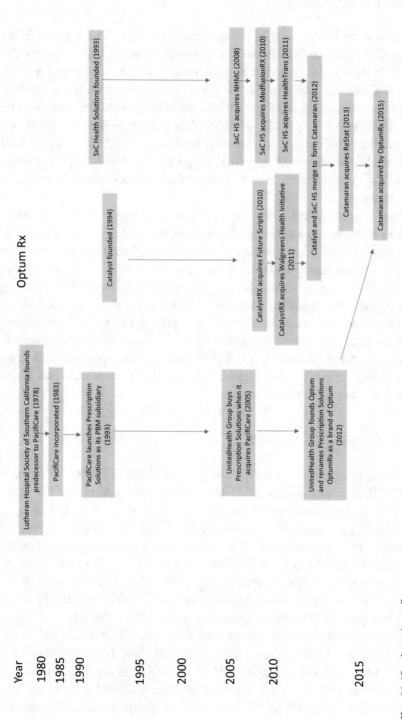

Fig. 11.12 (continued)

Caremark & AdvancePCS

One of the early M&A deals in the new millennium was Caremark's 2003 acquisition of Advance/PCS. According to market analysts, Caremark was the #1 PBM in mail-order but, due to high penetration, faced limited growth prospects. Caremark was also the #1 PBM in specialty pharmacy, offering an integrated package of both oral solids and liquid injectables. For its part, AdvancePCS was the #1 PBM in retail claims processing and offered the largest retail network of 75 million managed lives. However, it had a low share of mail-order claims (9%) which suggested an opportunity to convert AdvancePCS' retail business to mail and penetrate it via Caremark's specialty pharma business.

Analysts suggested that such PBM mergers could exploit scale economies given their fixed-cost structure, significant infrastructure in claims processing, call centers, and mail-order pharmacy. Indeed, both Caremark and Advance PCS operated customer service call centers, mail-order pharmacies, and specialty pharmacies that offered opportunities for combining physical capacity. Operating higher volume over reduced physical capacity are, along with faster speed, the main contributors to economies of scale.[23] Healthcare economists often argue that the main PBM functions of claims adjudication and processing, pharmacy network design and management, and drug formulary design offer clear cost efficiencies associated with scale and focus on prescription drug management.

Express Scripts and Medco

The next big merger was the $29.1 Billion acquisition of Medco by Express Scripts (ESRX) announced in 2011. The merger combined two of the three biggest PBMs that would cover roughly one-third of all prescription drug sales in the U.S., roughly 60% of the mail-order market, and a majority of the specialty pharmacy market. The merger would also more than double the revenue of ESRX from $45 Billion to $110 Billion. One selling point of the deal was the combined purchasing power of ESRX's specialty pharmacy unit (Accredo) with the corresponding unit in Medco, giving it greater leverage to negotiate lower prices on very expensive drugs. For its part, Medco had suffered a recent loss of contracts including CalPERS and FEHBP mail-order (which joined CVS Caremark instead), and United Healthcare (which formed Optum instead). In 2010, CVS Caremark also signed a long-term deal with Aetna and its PBM, blocking Medco's potential acquisition. An additional rationale for ESRX to pursue the deal included ESRX's contract renewal squabble with Walgreens, which generated $5.3 Billion in retail sales and which threatened to withdraw from ESRX's pharmacy network.[24]

Horizontal Mergers: 2013–2015

Following the 2012 merger of Express Scripts and Medco, there were three other notable mergers in three years. First, in 2013, SXC, a regional PBM, agreed to buy Catalyst, another regional PBM, for $4.4 Billion to form a national PBM, known as Catamaran Corp. Second, in 2015, Catamaran was acquired by United, OptumRx's parent company, for $12.8 Billion. The two PBMs integrated operations under one name, OptumRx. Also, in 2015, Rite Aid acquired the PBM EnvisionRx for approximately $2 Billion.

Vertical Mergers: 2018–

Later that decade, several PBMs entered vertical integration arrangements with large health plans. First, CVS Caremark acquired Aetna in 2018; second, Cigna acquired Express Scripts. They joined UnitedHealthcare which had already formed Optum in 2011 (whose PBM operations stemmed from United's 2005 acquisition of the insurer Pacificare and its internal PBM), and Humana which operated its own in-house PBM (Humana Pharmacy Solutions). These and other vertical deals have resulted in a landscape of competing, vertically integrated firms spanning most of the pharmaceutical value chain, and sometimes including providers (see Fig. 11.13). This graphic suggests that a large chunk of U.S. healthcare spending flows through a small number of firms that span value chain players and are reimbursed by public and private payers. The rationales for these deals, and their possible consequences, are discussed in Chapter 13.

PBM Tailwind #6: PBMs Meet GPOs

PBMs serve to aggregate demand across beneficiaries to negotiate discounts and rebates from drug manufacturers. In recent years, the largest PBMs have launched their own group purchasing organizations (GPOs) to aggregate the commercial branded drug purchases of their members, handle rebate negotiations with manufacturers, and provide other services to manufac-turers—just as some GPOs have recently launched PBMs (see Chapter 3). The three largest PBM-owned GPOs are Ascent Health Services (owned by

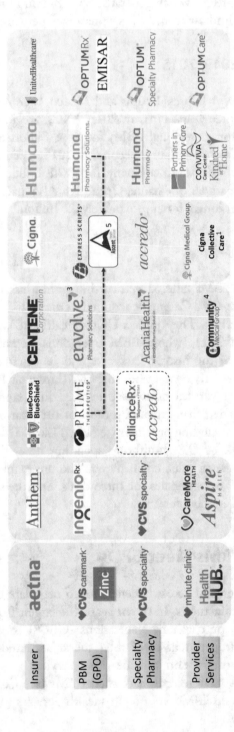

1. Cigna also partners with providers via its Cigna Collaborative Care program.
2. Since January 2021, Prime's Blue Cross and Blue Shield plans have had the option to use Express Scripts or AllianceRx Walgreens Prime for mail and specialty pharmacy services. In December 2021, Walgreens Boots Alliance purchased Prime Therapeutics' 45% ownership in AllianceRx Walgreens Prime.
3. In 2021, Centene has announced its intention to consolidate of all PBM operations onto a single platform and outsource its PBM operations to an external company.
4. In 2021, Centene sold a majority stake in its U.S. Medical Management to a group of private equity firms.
5. Since 2020, Prime has sourced formulary rebates via Ascent Health Services. In 2021, Humana began sourcing formulary rebates via Ascent Health Services for its commercial plans.
Source: Drug Channels Institute research

Fig. 11.13 Recent vertical integration points to a payer-aligned pharmacy supply chain

Cigna, Prime Therapeutics, and Kroger), Emisar Pharma Services (owned by Optum), and Zinc Health Services (formed by CVS Health and Anthem).[25] According to analysts, the PBM-GPOs prefer the term "contracting entity" since (like the GPOs covered in Part II of this volume) they do not actually "purchase" the drugs but rather manage the contracting process and negotiation of discounts; they nevertheless structure their contracts to qualify for the GPO safe harbor.

There are several rationales for PBMs to establish GPOs[26]:

- pool purchases to lower the members' unit costs and reduce their in-house contracting functions, much like the GPOs covered in Part II of this volume;
- expand formulary power by providing contracting and rebate negotiation services for the combined formulary volume of multiple PBMs to try to develop more competitive rebate terms—e.g., combine ESRX's 75 million customers with Prime's 28 million customers;
- equalize the manufacturer rebates and administrative fees among the GPO's owners—e.g., between Cigna and Prime Therapeutics—by raising them for those PBMs with lower initial rebates and fees;
- reduce their pharmacy network costs through increased volume leverage;
- reduce exposure to rebate guarantees offered to clients downstream;
- develop new sources of revenue from manufacturers—GPO administration fees of 1–2%—on top of their PBM administrative service fees (typically 3–5% of WAC list price);
- enable some of the PBM-GPO's owners to be better positioned for the specialty drug market;
- serve as a hedge against future reform of PBM pricing practices by offsetting any reduced rebate income with new GPO admin fees;
- possibly shift manufacturer payments from the rebate pool shared with downstream PBM clients to fees and programs that may be retained at higher levels by the PBM; and
- capture the benefits of international sourcing by setting up the GPOs in other countries and thereby achieve tax efficiencies.

These PBM-GPOs appear to interpose another party between manufacturers and payers. The increased separation appears to be part of a wider trend that reduces direct contracting between manufacturers and payers that include PBM consolidation, PBM sourcing collaborations, and PBM willingness to offer rebate guarantees and price protection for smaller plans. Such separation may complicate efforts by manufacturers to enter value-based

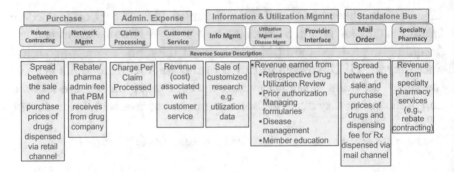

Fig. 11.14 Traditional PBM commercial value chain

contracts with health plans and employers. Analysts are not sure what added value the PBM-GPOs provide to manufacturers. Finally, these PBM-GPOs suggest another challenge to transparency in the retail pharmaceutical supply chain.

Joint Impact of Tailwinds on PBM Value Chain and Revenue Model

The Value Chain of Services

The evolution of PBMs in the twentieth century chronicled in the last chapter resulted in an extended PBM value chain and business model. Figure 11.14 captures this value chain for the PBMs' private sector operations circa 2005.[27]

PBM Business Model and Sources of Revenues (Circa 2005)

PBM consultants provided a window into the sources of PBM earnings at the start of the new millennium. The older administrative functions of claims processing and customer service did not generate revenues but rather incurred losses (−15% earnings before interest, taxes, depreciation, and amortization or EBITDA). Conversely, the newer clinical functions of information, utilization, outcomes research, and disease management developed in the latter 1990s constituted a small percentage (+10%) of EBITDA.[28] A bigger contributor to EBITDA resided in the earlier PBM functions of rebate contracting with manufacturers (+17%: 11% retail, 6% mail-order) and network management on the retail side (+27%).[29] Earnings here were driven by the ability to shift market share which depended on size, formulary control, and geographic penetration (local volume). By far, the biggest contributor to EBITDA were two stand-alone businesses—the earlier mail-order function (+53%: 31% generic, 17% brand) and rebates earned through the emerging sales of specialty drugs in specialty pharmacies (+9%). Earnings here were driven by scale (procurement volume), utilization of generics, and operational efficiency.

Consultants suggested that these functions served to reduce the cost of a retail pharmaceutical by as much as one-third. Assume, for example, that the health plan enrollee begins with an unmanaged, per-member pharmacy cost of $900. Purchase discounts (e.g., moving from AWP +5% to AWP −10%) reduce this cost by $100; negotiated dispensing fees with pharmacies further reduce this by another $30. Generic substitution mechanisms in the drug formulary reduce this amount even further by $80, while utilization management techniques (e.g., drug utilization review, prior authorization) and drug tier co-pays lower it by another $30. Finally, rebates and administrative cost reductions achieve an additional $60 in savings, yielding a total savings of $300.

PBMs can achieve even greater savings with more aggressive cost management approaches. These can include: formularies containing only generics, generic coupons, 4- and 5-tier co-pays, extensive step therapy and prior authorization, exclusion of entire classes of products that become available over-the-counter, exclusion of manufacturers' drugs from formularies, higher consumer cost-sharing by including drugs in health savings accounts with high deductibles and patients bearing full cost after the account is depleted, and mandatory use of mail-order. A 2011 report prepared by Visante for the PBMs' trade association depicted the cost management approaches offered to plan sponsors (see Fig. 11.15).[30]

Revisiting the PBM Business Model and Sources of Revenues (2015–2021)

The same PBM consultants updated their estimates of the sources of PBM earnings starting in 2015. The newer clinical functions of information, utilization, outcomes research, and disease management contributed a higher percentage (+15–20%) of PBM earnings before interest, taxes, depreciation, and amortization (EBITDA), while the older administrative functions of claims processing and customer service continued to incur losses (−5–15% EBITDA). The earlier PBM functions of rebate contracting with manufacturers and network management on the retail side contributed slightly lower

PBM Savings Relative to Unmanaged Drug Expenditures:	20%-30%	30%-40%	40%-50%
Use of PBM Tools	Limited	Average	Best Practice
Plan Sponsor Decisions			
Formulary	Open	Preferred drug list (PDL)	More selective PDL with incentives for generics and preferred brands
Copay Options	Single tier	Two to three tiers with modest copay differentials	Three or more tiers with significant differentials to encourage the use of generics and preferred brands
Utilization Management	None	Pre-approvals for select drugs with safety, efficacy, or cost issues	Pre-approvals plus step therapy to encourage physicians to use first-line treatments
Mail-Service Pharmacy	Minimal copay incentives and usage	Moderate copay incentives and usage	Strong copay and other incentives and high usage
Retail Pharmacy Networks	Open	Network includes vast majority of drugstores in defined geographic areas	Narrower selection of pharmacies able to provide greater discounts
Specialty Pharmacy	None	Specialty pharmacy options available	Use of specialty pharmacy network whenever clinically appropriate

Fig. 11.15 Health plan decisions to drive PBM savings

earnings (+30–40%), as did the mail-order function (+40–50%). The biggest gain in earnings and the biggest contributor were sales of specialty drugs in specialty pharmacies (+20–30%). Across the first two decades of the new millennium, the clinical functions and the new lines of business became larger contributors, while the contributions of rebate contracting and network management somewhat diminished.

A host of other consultants provide a parallel picture of changing PBM revenues using more recent data and a different metric: gross profits (revenues less cost of goods sold). Some of these consultants suggest the two metrics may be closely related, by virtue of their assertion that PBMs can convert ~85% of gross profit into EBITDA. On the other hand, there may be a divergence between gross profits and EBITDA contribution, due to the fact that PBMs have steadily reduced their share of rebates earned from manufacturers and passed a greater share along to plan sponsors. For example, between 2011 and 2019, the share of rebates earned by CVS/Caremark dropped from 27% to 3%, while the value of the rebate per commercial life covered rose from $78 to $282.[31]

Comparisons of changing PBM revenues are further complicated by the use of different reporting periods by different consultants. Consultants studying the 2017–2019 period found that the percentage of gross profits for the top three PBMs derived from retained rebates fell from 17% to 6%. Conversely, administrative fees from manufacturers grew from 15% of gross profits to 20%, while gross profits from mail order and specialty pharmacy operations grew from 35% to 36%; other revenue sources grew from 33% to 38% of gross profits, but could not be distinguished.[32] Rising administrative fees may be due to a host of PBM services, such as conduct of market research, therapeutic substitution, rebate invoicing/administration/collection, access to drug utilization data, etc.

Consultants studying the 2015–2021 period estimated that the top three PBMs earned 35% of their gross profits from the dispensing of specialty drugs in 2021 (up from 17% in 2015). Fees from manufacturers upstream and plan sponsors downstream accounted for another 35% of gross profits (up from 16% in 2015). The remaining sources of gross profits included mail-order pharmacy dispensing (17%, down from 29% in 2015), retained formulary and price protection rebates (9%, down from 31% in 2015), and spreads from network pharmacy dispensing (4%, down from 7% in 2015).[33,34]

In sum, PBM compensation models appear to have evolved as a consequence of higher scrutiny by payers, regulators, and government officials. A crucial part of PBM profits is now specialty pharmacy dispensing and non-rebate fees from manufacturers, while the PBMs' share of gross profits from retained manufacturer rebates and retail network spreads have fallen. Moreover, as noted in Chapter 9, the composition of these rebates has also changed. One consultant reported a decrease during 2017–2021 in the percentage of the gross-to-net price reductions for branded drugs due to commercial rebates (from 27% to 22%) and Medicaid rebates (from 21% to 17%), and a growing percentage of gross-to-net price reductions due to Part D rebates (from 19% to 23%). Between 2019 and 2021, there was also a growing percentage of gross-to-net reductions due to 340B discounts (from 10% to 20%).[35]

An alternate way to display the effect of the PBM tailwinds is to depict the distribution in retail pharmacy prescriptions across payers and network designs. Figure 11.16 highlights the importance of various payer segments to the PBMs, particularly the importance of PDP. The distinctions in network design are important because they show how important narrow pharmacy networks are in Medicare. These figures likely change over time, as does the share of prescriptions accounted for in any given book of business.

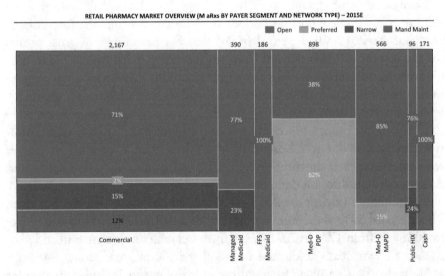

Fig. 11.16 Distribution of retail prescriptions across payers and network design 2015 (*Notes* Includes traditional employer sponsored, off-exchange individual plans and retiree drug; Excludes Mail ~0.5B, ~8% of total market; excludes Rx from "other Public Programs"; ~70 M Rx in FY 2015; all Figs. 90D adjusted. *Source* Bradley Fluegel. Used by permission)

Conclusion

What a difference a couple of decades makes! PBMs have transformed themselves in several ways during the new millennium. They have migrated their strategy away from network management to network pharmacy exclusion and operation of their own in-house pharmacies (particularly for specialty drugs). They have migrated away from three-tier formularies to formulary exclusions. They have migrated away from rebate-based compensation and retail pharmacy spreads to specialty drug fulfillment and administrative fees. Finally, as outlined in the next chapter, they have migrated away from strategies that incurred government investigation and antitrust scrutiny. The end result is that the PBMs of today are not the PBMs of 2000. And, yet, their profit model remains opaque and inscrutable; they are still accused of conflicts of interest such as placing higher-priced drugs on their formularies; and they perhaps still beg for more transparency, although (as pointed out in subsequent chapters) that may not be a good thing.

Notes

1. Drug Channels Institute. *The 2022 Economic Report on U.S. Pharmacies and Pharmacy Benefit Managers*. Exhibit 27.
2. Drug Channels Institute. *The 2022 Economic Report on U.S. Pharmacies and Pharmacy Benefit Managers*. Exhibit 29.
3. Patients may require disease education, frequent dosing adjustments, counseling regarding side effect management, support for medication adherence, monitoring by their physicians, and other services.
4. Libby Meske. "Pharmacy Landscape," Presentation to the Colorado PBM Symposium.
5. IQVIA. *Orphan Drugs in the United States* (Parsippany, NJ: IQVIA Institute, December 2020).
6. Drug Channels Institute. *The 2022 Economic Report on U.S. Pharmacies and Pharmacy Benefit Managers*. Exhibit 76.
7. Drug Channels Institute. *The 2022 Economic Report on U.S. Pharmacies and Pharmacy Benefit Managers*.
8. Drug Channels Institute. *The 2022 Economic Report on U.S. Pharmacies and Pharmacy Benefit Managers*. Exhibit 43.
9. Drug Channels Institute. *The 2022 Economic Report on U.S. Pharmacies and Pharmacy Benefit Managers*. Page 137.
10. Libby Meske. "Pharmacy Landscape," Presentation to the Colorado PBM Symposium.

11. Steven Lieberman, Paul Ginsburg, and Erin Trish. "Sharing Drug Rebates With Medicare Part D Patients: Why and How," *Health Affairs* (September 14, 2020).

12. Steven Lieberman, Paul Ginsburg, and Erin Trish. "Sharing Drug Rebates With Medicare Part D Patients: Why and How," *Health Affairs* (September 14, 2020).

13. Drug Channels Institute. *The 2022 Economic Report on U.S. Pharmacies and Pharmacy Benefit Managers.* Exhibit 124.

14. Drug Channels Institute. *The 2022 Economic Report on U.S. Pharmacies and Pharmacy Benefit Managers.* Exhibit 129.

15. Medicare has four parts. Part A covers hospitalization and hospice care, as well as drugs used in inpatient settings; Part B covers physician and outpatient services (and drugs that cannot be self-administered); Part C was enacted in 1997 as a precursor to Medicare Advantage (MA) plans; Part D covers retail drugs. See Lawton R. Burns, *The U.S. Healthcare Ecosystem* (New York: McGraw-Hill, 2021): Chapter 18.

16. Drug Channels Institute. *The 2022 Economic Report on U.S. Pharmacies and Pharmacy Benefit Managers.* Exhibit 81.

17. While PBMs collect rebates from manufacturers and pharmacies, CMS just finalized a rule that would pass through pharmacy DIR to beneficiaries starting in 2024. See: https://www.federalregister.gov/documents/2022/05/09/2022-09375/medicare-program-contract-year-2023-policy-and-technical-changes-to-the-medicare-advantage-and. Accessed on May 15, 2022.

18. Some large states are moving away from managed care to fee-for-service approaches to pharmacy reimbursement management. See: Drug Channels Institute. *The 2022 Economic Report on U.S. Pharmacies and Pharmacy Benefit Managers.* Section 8.4.

19. For background, one can consult: https://www.hrsa.gov/opa/index.html. Also, consult Chapter 11 in: Drug Channels Institute. *The 2022 Economic Report on U.S. Pharmacies and Pharmacy Benefit Managers.*

20. Joanna Shepherd. "The Prescription for Rising Drug Prices: Competition or Price Controls?" *Health Matrix: The Journal of Law-Medicine* 27(1) (2017): 315–346.

21. Drug Channels Institute. *The 2022 Economic Report on U.S. Pharmacies and Pharmacy Benefit Managers.* Exhibit 195.

22. Letter to the Federal Trade Commission from Three GPOs: HealthTrust, Intalere, and Premier. August 20, 2018. Available from author.

23. Alfred D. Chandler, Jr. *Scale and Scope: The Dynamics of Industrial Capitalism* (Cambridge, MA: Harvard University Press, 1990).

24. "Express Scripts-Medco Deal Showcases New Post-health Reform Reality," *In Vivo* (July 2011).

25. Ascent Health Solutions does not consider itself to be a GPO, since (according to them) they do not purchase medications but only negotiate discounts. However, as noted in Chapter 3, this is true of all GPOs.

26. Eric Percher. *A Closer Look: Cigna/ESI Makes Waves with Ascent Contracting & Econdisc Sourcing GPOs* (Nephron Research, January 23, 2020). Eric Percher. *Optum Launches 'Emisar' Contracting Entity; Navitus Aligns with Ascent via Prime* (Nephron Research, July 26, 2021).

27. The Figure and accompanying earnings data are based on Karl Kellner, Presentation to the Wharton School.

28. This included drug utilization review, co-pay tiers, and generic substitution.

29. This is captured by the reduction in dispensing fees ($2 vs. $4), and the use of lower-cost pharmacy networks.

30. Visante. *Pharmacy Benefit Managers (PBMs): Generating Savings for Plan Sponsors and Consumers.* (2011). Available online at: https://www.pcmanet. org/wp-content/uploads/2016/08/pr-dated-09-19-11-pbms-savings-study-2011-final-2.pdf. Accessed on April 23, 2022.

31. Drug Channels Institute. Prior year. Exhibit 151.

32. Three Axis Advisors. *Understanding the Evolving Business Models and Revenue of Pharmacy Benefit Managers.* PBM Accountability Project 2021. Available online at: https://www.pbmaccountability.org/resources. Accessed on July 12, 2022.

33. Drug Channels Institute. *The 2022 Economic Report on U.S. Pharmacies and Pharmacy Benefit Managers.* Exhibit 188: Top Three PBMs, Sources of Per-Prescription Gross Profit, 2015 vs. 2019. Elsewhere in the report, Adam Fein identifies six types of compensation. These include:

   - Administrative fees: per-claim processing fees paid to the PBM by the plan sponsor.
   - Service revenues: fee-for-service revenues or performance-based payments received from manufacturers for PBM services.
   - Retail network spread: plan sponsors may allow PBMs to retain the spread (difference) between (1) the amount the PBM charges the plan sponsor and (2) the amount the PBM pays to the pharmacy that dispenses the drug.
   - Pharmacy dispensing profit: the difference between (1) what the plan sponsor pays the PBM to reimburse the ingredient cost and (2) the drug acquisition cost to the pharmacy in the PBM's network.
   - Retained rebates: the percentage of manufacturer rebates paid to the PBM that are retained rather than passed along to the plan sponsor.
   - Retained price protection: the percentage of the price protection payment paid by manufacturers to PBMs that is retained by the PBM rather than passed along to the plan sponsor.

34. Another analyst report similarly suggests that, between 2015 and 2021, gross PBM profits shifted away from rebates (down from 27 to 7%) and mail pharmacy (from 28 to 18%) and shifted toward admin fees (up from 15 to 27%) and specialty pharmacy fulfillment (up from 17 to 33%). Flatlining profit sources include spread pricing and price protection (14% in 2015, 15%

in 2021). Eric Percher. *Optum Launches 'Emisar' Contracting Entity; Navitus Aligns with Ascent via Prime* (Nephron Research, July 26, 2021).

35. Drug Channels Institute. *Economic Report on U.S. Pharmacies and Pharmacy Benefit Managers*. Various years.

12

PBM Headwinds in the New Millennium: Court Challenges, Merger Scrutiny, and Congressional Hearings

Introduction

Chapter 11 shows that, as in the prior century, recent PBM growth has been shaped by several environmental changes in technological innovation and insurance coverage. Unlike the past millennium, however, recent PBM growth has been preceded, accompanied, and conditioned by major lawsuits brought by U.S. Attorneys and State Attorneys General. Such lawsuits prompted changes in how the PBMs conducted business. These lawsuits were then followed by federal scrutiny of proposed PBM mergers and then Congressional Hearings on these mergers as well as other PBM business practices.

The historical tailwind developments described in the last chapter led to a shift in the PBMs' customer mix from enrollees in mostly private health plans to (increasingly) public enrollees managed by public and private health plans (see Fig. 11.16). By virtue of the PBMs' increasing presence in government payment programs, these developments may also have occasioned growing regulatory oversight and public hearings on PBM business practices. More-over, such developments are tied to higher spending on expensive drugs, leading some to inquire whether PBMs are somehow responsible.

The growing stature and agency roles played by PBMs (working on behalf of both private and, especially, public payers) have made them a frequent target of criticism for what ails the healthcare ecosystem. Like the GPOs which faced a similar situation in the early 2000s, the PBMs have amended some of their business practices and shifted their revenue models over the

© The Author(s), under exclusive license to Springer
Nature Switzerland AG 2022
L. R. Burns, *The Healthcare Value Chain*,
https://doi.org/10.1007/978-3-031-10739-9_12

past two decades to lessen these concerns. And, yet, the din of criticism has not abated.

Such scrutiny has focused on their historical revenue model of earning manufacturer rebates (which began in the late 1980s and early 1990s), the possible link between these rebates and prescription drug prices, the lack of transparency in the fees obtained from manufacturers and health plan sponsors, and the lack of transparency and disclosure of contract terms (among other issues). These issues have become increasingly popular fodder in the trade and academic literature, as well as subject matter in Congressional hearings and federal agency reports.

The chapter first describes the onset of legal actions taken by the Department of Justice (DOJ) and State Attorneys General to correct PBM business practices. It then briefly sketches the formulation of new rules of PBM behavior that emerged from these legal actions. The chapter then summarizes the antitrust reviews of PBM mergers, the related Congressional Hearings, several contentious issues surrounding PBMs, and any evidence base for these concerns.

New Rules of Behavior for PBMs

Are PBMs Fiduciaries?

Beginning in the early 2000s, PBMs came under scrutiny by the states. In 2003, the State of Maine legislature passed "The Act Against Unfair Prescription Drug Practices." Under this act, PBMs were required to act as "fiduciaries" on behalf of customers, increase financial disclosures, and to pass along manufacturer rebates and fees earned. The PBM's trade association filed suit seeking to reverse the law. This began a sequence of lawsuits alleging that PBMs (not just employers) were fiduciaries under the Employee Retirement and Income Security Act (ERISA).[1]

This Act and the subsequent lawsuit raised an issue that has remained unresolved for nearly two decades. According to the U.S. Department of Labor (USDOL), the primary responsibility of a fiduciary is to run a "plan" solely in the interests of participants and beneficiaries and for the sole purpose of providing benefits and paying plan expenses. Such plans can include retirement plans as well as other benefit plans. In this case (and subsequent lawsuits brought against the PBMs), the State of Maine seemed to stretch the definition to include "health benefit plans," along with their management and assets. The ongoing litigation in this area has been based on allegations that the PBMs have mis-managed the health plan assets.

There have been conflicting court findings over time.[2] In the 2018 Express Scripts/Anthem litigation,[3] the court ruled that the PBM Express Scripts was not a fiduciary because it lacked discretion over pricing. The PBM did not know or control the terms of the contract between the employer health plan and Anthem; the PBM also did not contract directly with the ERISA plan or control the dollar amounts that the insurer charged the plan. Rather, insurers decide what to charge ERISA plans and what these plans pay for prescription drugs.[4]

Appellate courts have generally been unwilling to hold PBMs liable as fiduciaries, especially when the PBM's conduct is subject to the final approval of the party (health plan or employer) contracting with the PBM. Moreover, the courts did not consider the cost-sharing dollars as plan assets and did not agree that PBMs controlled these cost-sharing amounts. According to the Altarum Institute, PBMs rarely have a fiduciary obligation to their plan sponsor clients and prioritize the plan sponsors' best interests.[5]

Legal action to date has turned on whether the PBM satisfies the definition of "fiduciary" under the ERISA statute. Courts have often answered "no," the PBM is not an ERISA fiduciary and hence does not face a fiduciary responsibility to pass the savings they negotiate along to the payers (employers, patients, and health plans). In December 2020, the Second Circuit upheld a district court decision dismissing a class action against insurer Anthem and PBM Express Scripts, alleging that Anthem and Express Scripts were acting as fiduciaries when entering into the 2009 agreement and setting prescription drug prices. The court rejected the plaintiffs' argument that the PBM's ability to set pricing pursuant to its own interpretation of "competitive benchmark pricing" amounted to discretion over pricing, concluding that the PBM was only executing the PBM agreement's pricing scheme. Similarly, the court rejected the plaintiffs' argument that the PBM's ability to maximize the spread between the prices it paid and the amounts it billed to insurance companies and insureds made it a fiduciary, again noting that the PBM agreement contemplated such activity and did not require the PBM to pass on savings to participants.

In September 2014, the ERISA Advisory Council made two recommendations that attempted to increase the accountability of PBMs to plan sponsors. First, The DOL could require PBMs to disclose all direct and indirect compensation to ERISA plans in order for ERISA plans to evaluate whether the compensation to PBMs and downstream to pharmacies—including PBM-owned mail-order pharmacies—and other subcontractors is reasonable.

Second, the DOL could issue guidance to assist plan sponsors to determine whether and how to conduct a PBM audit of direct and indirect compensation. The DOL had not acted on these recommendations (as of early 2018).

Gold Standard of Behavior

As noted at the end of Chapter 10, ominous warnings to the PBMs were sounded by the Eastern District of Pennsylvania in the late 1990s and early 2000s. The U.S. Attorney and Associate Attorney (Pat Meehan and James Sheehan, respectively) conducted two six-year investigations and brought charges against Caremark and Medco Health Solutions. They were joined by lawsuits brought by Attorneys General in 20 states. Caremark served enrollees of FEHBP and Medicare + Choice (forerunner of Medicare Advantage); Medco provided mail-order pharmacy services to enrollees in two federal programs, Federal Employees Health Benefits Program (FEHBP) and TriCare. The complaint against Medco charged the PBM with soliciting kickbacks from pharmaceutical manufacturers to favor their drugs that brought the biggest rebates from manufacturers, not passing all those savings on to its clients (as many of their contracts required), paying kickbacks to health plans to obtain business, and switching or changing patients' prescriptions to different or more expensive or less effective drugs by providing false, misleading, or incomplete information or without the knowledge or consent of the patient or physician or without the approval of the relevant Federal Plan.

The Government's allegations were numerous. Some of the more important ones were:[6]

- Medco failed to provide accurate, complete, timely, and reliable information to patients and physicians concerning: (1) the reasons for, costs relating to, and effect of the drug switches, in order to induce them to approve the switch, or withdraw their objection to the switch; (2) whether and when prescriptions had been received where the prescription had been improperly canceled; and (3) pharmacists' views concerning whether generic drugs sold by Medco were always "just as good as" brand name drugs;
- Medco promoted drugs then likely to remain on patent for long periods of time, and switched patients from drugs which would be subject to generic competition and cost reductions in the near future;

- Medco switched patients from drugs with a generic equivalent to drugs without a generic equivalent;
- Medco promoted a formulary that favored expensive drugs;
- Medco offered or made improper payments in the form of implementation allowances, contract allowances, data fees, credits, up-front payments, cash, and services to certain health plans to induce the plans to select Medco as a pharmacy benefit management subcontractor, or to retain Medco as a pharmacy benefit management subcontractor;
- Medco falsely reported turnaround performance under Federal Plan Contracts, including under the FEHBP contract from 1996 through 2003 on its daily reports, monthly invoice packages reporting turnaround and associated contract penalties, and Annual Statements;
- Medco solicited and received improper payments from pharmaceutical manufacturers to induce or reward Medco for improperly providing favorable consideration to each such pharmaceutical manufacturer's products; to induce Medco to promote the sale of such manufacturers' products; to favor such manufacturers' products over different chemical compounds in the treatment of certain diseases; to favor and advocate such manufacturers' products in formulary placement; and to advocate switches to those favored products by physicians. These payments were allegedly made in the form of rebates, regardless of how characterized, discounts, patient conversion payments, market share movement payments, market share incentives, data fees, commissions, mail service purchase discounts, administrative or management fees, educational grants, outcomes research studies, clinical consulting services, nominally-priced products, disease management program payments, and strategic alliances.

In 2005, Meehan's office reached a $137 Million settlement with Caremark and its AdvancePCS unit (which Caremark acquired in 2004). That investigation also involved kickbacks paid upstream to manufacturers and downstream to customers, and culminated with a corporate integrity agreement and a Consent Decree. This agreement included information disclosure to customers about payments that AdvancePCS receives from pharmaceutical companies, and avoidance of switching patients away from their prescriptions to more expensive medications.

The following year, Medco agreed to pay the U.S. Government $155 Million, on top of the $29 Million it agreed to pay the 20 states (in 2004). Medco also entered into an extensive, five-year corporate integrity agreement (CIA) with the OIG.[7] The contents of the CIA included:

- establish a voluntary compliance program;
- establish a compliance officer and compliance committee;
- develop & disseminate a code of conduct to evaluate the performance of all employees;
- establish written policies and procedures regarding the operation of the compliance program—in particular, adherence to the Anti-Kickback Statute and the False Claims Act;
- regular training of all employees in this code of conduct;
- audit adherence to this code of conduct and policies;
- engage an Independent Review Organization to assist in measuring compliance;
- establish a disclosure program to report any issues concerning Medco's practices;
- submit a written report to the OIG-DHHS regarding the implementation of this CIA, and file an annual report on its compliance activities.

To many industry observers, the Medco CIA represented a milestone in monitoring and disciplining the behavior of the PBMs, a hitherto unregulated sector. The prosecutors stated they expected the code of conduct to become the "gold standard" for the PBM sector.[8] To some, the injunctive relief was more important than the fines levied—particularly as the PBMs were about to enter the Medicare Part D market and compete to administer the billions of dollars in Federal drug spending. Moreover, prosecutors now had a set of standards and rules to apply in all future litigation against suspect PBM practices. They asserted that competitive pressures would drive PBM compliance with these standards. Such standards posed a possible bar that PBMs would have to pass in order to participate in Federal programs such as Medicare Part D and others (chronicled below).

The CIA was remarkable given that, in January 2003, the General Accounting Office published a report lauding the role of PBMs in lowering drug costs for FEHBP employees—the same customer group involved in the Medco investigation.[9] Moreover, in 2003, the OIG issued a report with guidelines regarding sales and marketing programs in the healthcare supply chain, with a focus on PBM rebates.[10] The OIG-DHHS took no issue with the structure of PBM formularies, provided they relied on clinical efficacy and drug appropriateness as judged by the formulary committee. The report further stated that market share rebates are acceptable when disclosed in advance to customers and structured under the GPO safe harbor.

PBM critics argue that the PBMs' disputed practices have continued due to (1) lapses in the agreements noted above, (2) the Federal Trade Commission (FTC) abandonment of active PBM oversight since its opposition to the vertical mergers with pharmaceutical manufacturers in the 1990s, (3) tacit FTC approval of horizontal PBM mergers without challenge (covered below), and (4) the lack of federal regulation. They further argue that PBMs abandoned consumer protection by abridging patients' choice over the types of pharmacies they utilize.[11] According to the critics, these continuing misdeeds are reflected in the number of lawsuits filed against the PBMs since the 2005–2006 cases outlined above. They also frequently mention that, as of 2019, PBMs have paid more than $370 Million in fines and settlements arising from alleged fraudulent and deceptive practices.[12] It should be noted, however, that the majority of these fines stemmed from the early investigations in 2004–2005. Moreover, any fines and judgments against the PBMs since that time (2006–2015) are quite small ($2–60 Million)—perhaps suggesting that PBM infractions on a large scale have diminished.

Indeed, the Medco CIA bears some of the hallmark features of the GPO Code of Conduct developed at roughly the same time (see Chapter 5—Appendix). In both cases, litigation and negative publicity forced both PBMs and GPOs to re-examine their behaviors, change their business practices, be more responsive to external stakeholders, and increase their transparency. The change in business practices, along with new specialty pharmaceuticals and insurance coverage, resulted in changes to the PBMs' revenue model (covered at the end of Chapter 11).

PBM Competition in the Early 2000s

In 2004, the FTC and DOJ issued a joint report on the degree of competition in the healthcare ecosystem, based on hearings conducted the prior year.[13] Section IV of Chapter 7 in the report briefly dealt with PBMs. In summarizing the available evidence, the report relied upon a 2003 GAO report that concluded that PBMs saved money for enrollees in the FEHBP compared to cash-paying customers.[14]

The report also mentioned a subsequent FTC report to be released the following year on savings achieved by PBM-owned mail-order pharmacies compared to retail pharmacies and mail-order pharmacies not owned by the PBMs.[15] An FTC press release summarized the findings of the 240-page document as follows:

- For large PBMs, average total prices in 2002 and 2003 at PBM-owned mail-order pharmacies typically were lower than at mail-order pharmacies not owned by the large PBMs.
- For retailer-owned PBMs, average total prices in 2002 and 2003 were lower for generic and multi-source brand drugs, but not single-source brand drugs, at PBM-owned mail-order pharmacies compared to mail-order pharmacies not owned by PBMs.
- For a common basket of drugs dispensed in December 2003 with the same-size prescriptions, retail prices typically were higher than mail prices at both large PBMs and retailer-owned PBMs. In the 26 PBM-plan sponsor contracts reviewed by the FTC staff, plan sponsors often secured more favorable pharmaceutical pricing for mail dispensing than for retail dispensing.
- There were no significant differences, by therapeutic class, in generic dispensing rates between PBM-owned mail-order pharmacies and mail-order pharmacies not owned by PBMs. However, for large PBMs and retailer-owned PBMs, the generic dispensing rate by therapeutic class was slightly higher at retail pharmacies not owned by PBMs than at mail-order pharmacies owned by PBMs. Formulary status decisions and other aspects of plan designs may explain the differences in these rates.
- Generic substitution rates at PBM-owned mail-order pharmacies were generally equal to those at retail or mail-order pharmacies not owned by PBMs. For large PBMs and small or insurer-owned PBMs, generic drugs were more profitable at their owned mail-order pharmacies than were brand drugs—even when payments to the PBM from pharmaceutical manufacturers for brand drugs were included. Given these profit incentives for the PBM and lower prices to the plan sponsor and member, the PBM-owned mail-order pharmacies' incentives, on average, were consistent with those of their clients in 2002 and 2003.
- PBMs rarely switched patients through a therapeutic interchange from one brand drug to another brand drug or to a chemically distinct generic drug.

Overall, the FTC report suggested that, contrary to suspicions and oft-voiced criticisms, mail-order pharmacies operated by PBMs were not plagued by conflict of interest problems and did not engage in "self-dealing" activities.

PBM Consolidation and Antitrust

Caremark and AdvancePCS (2003)

In addition to business practices, the FTC also scrutinized the growing number of PBM mergers (see Fig. 11.12). In 2004, the FTC investigated the Caremark/AdvancePCS merger and concluded it would not have an anticompetitive impact on either plan sponsors or retail pharmacies. Large and small employers both had alternative PBMs with whom they could contract. As for retail pharmacies, the merger could result in lower dispensing fees, costs, and prices.

Other Uncontested Mergers (2007–2009)

CVS and Caremark combined in 2007, in a merger that was cleared without a Second Request by the FTC. In 2009, Express Scripts acquired NextRX, Wellpoint's PBM, in another merger that was cleared without a Second Request by the FTC. Antitrust attorneys urged the FTC to review these mergers. Their concerns, summarized in white papers issued at the time, were restated by others (see below).[16]

Express Scripts and Medco 2011–2012

The next big merger was the proposed $29.1 Billion acquisition of Medco by Express Scripts. The merger would combine two of the three biggest PBMs that would cover roughly one-third of all prescription drug sales in the U.S., roughly 60% of the mail-order market, and a majority of the specialty pharmacy market.

Congressional Hearings

The merger was the subject of 2011 hearings before the Subcommittee on Intellectual Property, Competition, and the Internet of the U.S. House of Representatives Judiciary Committee. The opening statement by the Subcommittee Chairman evinced little concern, expressing doubts that the merger would engender unlawful and undesirable market power. The Chairman pointed to industry reports regarding the healthcare cost savings delivered by PBMs and the popular agency role that PBMs played for plan sponsors. Committee members also quoted FTC testimony that PBM cost control programs have also "been shown to yield significant savings."

The testimony offered in the Congressional hearing is useful to articulating the "pros and cons" of the merger; the merging parties expressed the pros while industry critics (associations of community pharmacies and other retail outlets) expressed the cons. Here is an itemization of the two sides' arguments:

Pro's

- PBMs have a track record of reducing the prices of medications and increasing the availability of generics. According to a GAO study, PBMs negotiate prices with manufacturers that are 27% below the average cash price at a retail pharmacy for brand drugs, and 53% below the average price for generics.[17] In 2010, Express Scripts whittled down the manufacturer price increase on statins from 9.3% to 6.3% (a 32% reduction).
- The merger will enable the combined parties to extract further price discounts from manufacturers.
- PBMs have a track record of generating savings for employers and their workers.
- PBMs have helped to reduce the annual growth rate in pharmaceutical expenditures from 18% during the late 1990s to 5.3% by 2009 and then to 3.5% in 2010.
- PBMs are projected to save plan sponsors and consumers almost $2 Trillion between 2012–2021, according to a study conducted by Visante for the Pharmaceutical Care Management Association (PCMA), the PBM's trade association.[18] For individual sponsors, such savings range from 20% to 50% depending on the range of PBM tools they draw upon. These tools include: manufacturer rebates, pharmacy discounts, more affordable pharmacy channels (e.g., mail-order, specialty), use of generics, reducing waste, and improving patient adherence. Plan sponsors determine how actively pharmacy benefits are managed, including formularies, copayment tiers, utilization management, and pharmacy channel options.
- PBMs compete for business across a wide array of customer segments: large group employers, small group employers, individual insurance plans, Taft-Hartley union plans, and several public programs (Medicare, Medicaid, Children's Health Insurance Program, TRICARE, state employee benefit plans, and the FEHBP).
- The merger will help the two firms achieve synergies by combining the best of their complementary patient-centered clinical care programs that, in turn, will reduce hospitalizations and gaps in patient care.

- The merger will help federal and state governments decrease the cost of public entitlement programs without the need to reduce enrollee benefits.
- The merger will combine the firms' capabilities to better integrate prescription management, particularly their technology platforms to communicate with both pharmacists and patients, that will improve care management.
- The merger will allow for scale economies in contracting, mail-order pharmacy operations, and designing and operating specialized clinical programs.

Cons?

- Increased PBM leverage upstream over manufacturers, in the form of higher rebates, would capture manufacturers' profits, reduce competition, and reduce drug innovation.
- The rebates negotiated by manufacturers to get on PBM formularies are not always disclosed or passed on to plan sponsors. If the PBM can increase the market share for the manufacturer, the rebates are typically adjusted to incentivize the PBMs to increase the dispensing of the manufacturer's drugs, even if such incentives increase the costs to health plans.
- Plan sponsors are unaware of the "spread" pricing differential earned by PBMs when they bill sponsors for retail pharmacy reimbursement versus what they pay retail pharmacies for drug dispensing.
- PBMs dictate one-sided, unfavorable contract terms to health plans and employers. The PBM consults with employers and health plans regarding what drugs to put on formulary, but without full disclosure of its financial incentives. The PBM thus serves as a "double agent" in negotiations with upstream and downstream stakeholders. PBMs also exert leverage over plan sponsors in the form of higher prices charged to employers and health plans, as well as the reduced choice among PBMs.
- PBMs already dictate one-sided, unfavorable contract terms to pharmacies. Increased PBM leverage downstream over retail pharmacies, in the form of lower reimbursement rates that would reduce their profitability and output, reduces patient access to community pharmacy services, and push more business to the PBMs' own mail-order businesses.
- The increased PBM market concentration following upon the merger would exceed "the tipping point" and adversely impact health plans, employers, and public plans. Increased market concentration in both the mail-order and specialty pharmacy businesses will result in reduced patient access, reduced competition, higher prices, and "self-dealing" (steering patients to the PBMs' own mail-order businesses). Such concentration

will also reduce (1) competition among PBMs along both price and non-price dimensions and (2) the viability of smaller, regional, "captive" (plan-owned), and niche PBMs.

- PBMs are unregulated and operate in an opaque fashion. There are growing allegations of deceptive and fraudulent practices—like those noted in the earlier Caremark and Medco investigations.
- The threat of coordinated action by the merging parties due to the loss of a competitor increases the possibility of collusion, and increases employer and health plan difficulties in determining whether they are receiving the full benefits from their PBM.
- There is no proof that PBMs reduce healthcare costs and pass them along to health plans, employers, and consumers.

FTC Review

The following year, the FTC examined the issue of PBM competition and formally evaluated the proposed Medco-Express Scripts combination. The FTC report is worth reviewing for several reasons. First, federal agencies such as the FTC and the DOJ—as well as state officials such as State Attorney Generals and Insurance Commissioners—usually decide whether or not to challenge corporate mergers, and influence whether they are ultimately blocked or not. It would seem to be important to understand why these decisions are made. Second, these agencies are staffed by economists steeped in antitrust issues and immersed in analyses that are often opaque to the public. Just because a merger results in a bigger, more dominant competitor and/or in a more concentrated market does not necessarily pose harm to the public's welfare. That is, the agencies' decisions are based more on careful empirical analysis rather than rhetoric. Third, the FTC analyses provide an avenue to weigh the pros and cons of evidence offered during the Congressional hearing.

The FTC acknowledged that while the PBM market was moderately concentrated, it nevertheless had at least "ten significant competitors."[19] The FTC staff's analysis suggested that price competition among the PBMs to gain the accounts of plan sponsors (1) was "intense," (2) had driven down prices, and (3) had resulted in declining PBM margins, particularly in the large customer segment. Moreover, the FTC noted that several smaller, standalone PBMs (not the "Big Three") enjoyed recent success in winning employer accounts, including big employers. They competed by differentiating themselves from the Big Three and the payer-owned PBMs by emphasizing a transparent pricing model, providing more individualized account management support, and developing customized PBM offerings.

FTC analysis focused on whether the resulting merger and elimination of a competitor would allow the new firm to unilaterally impose anticompetitive price increases on customers. To assess this issue, FTC staff analyzed data on the price bids that PBMs submitted to health plan sponsors. They found the two parties were not close competitors, and that other PBMs successfully competed for customer contracts. The merger would thus result in a lower "diversion rate" than would be implied by their market shares, and thus exert only small unilateral price effects.

Express Scripts had the most success targeting middle-market plan sponsors and health plans, while Medco had the most success targeting large employers. Indeed, staff interviews found that few customers considered either Express Scripts or Medco to be their first or second choice among the PBMs. This conclusion was further supported by the plan bid data. Express Scripts was just as likely to lose an account to a smaller standalone PBM (e.g., CatalystRx, SXC) or a health plan-based PBM as it would to either Medco or CVS Caremark. Competition from such rivals had become stronger in recent years for both carve-in and carve-out contracts, as customers increasingly included the smaller players in the bidding tournament as part of their request for proposals (RFPs). The FTC also noted that there were dozens of sales opportunities every year among Fortune 500 firms, and even more informal sales opportunities. Another reason for the low diversion rate was the growing competitive threat posed by CVS Caremark. Staff reported the closest competitor to each party was CVS Caremark, not each other. Indeed, CVS Caremark had made great strides in taking business away from Medco. The FTC analysis also concluded that high PBM market shares do not accurately reflect the degree of competition in the market and are not an accurate indicator of merger effects on consumers or competition.

Just as important, the FTC assessed the hypothesized existence of scale economies in the PBM sector in terms of purchasing inputs or operating mail-order pharmacies. The concern is that mergers would confer such economies and thereby advantage larger players relative to smaller players. The FTC reported that the economies were not as significant as hypothesized and, for some inputs, non-existent. This was because the minimum efficient scale (volume) may have already been reached by each of the merging parties. Moreover, many of the PBMs outside of the top three had made significant investments in their operations that reduced, if not eliminated, their historical cost disadvantage. Thus, the size advantage was available to other competing PBMs as well.

Health economists examined four of the cost components in PBM bids to plan sponsors: pharmacy reimbursement rates, manufacturer rebates, mail-order fulfillment costs, and mail-order procurement costs. They reported few scale economies in manufacturer rebates or pharmacy reimbursement; they did find some scale economies in mail-order costs for both procurement and fulfillment.

Another FTC concern was whether a reduced number of competitors would allow the remaining players to engage in collusion. Such collusion requires the parties to reach agreements and then be able to monitor those agreements. However, given the opacity of contracts, the lack of price transparency, and the multiple pricing components submitted in bids to plan sponsors (e.g., separate administrative fees, rebate pass-through, discounts, retail and mail-order pricing for branded and generic drugs, plan design, ancillary services), FTC staff concluded the threat of coordinated pricing was not high. The FTC also did not consider possible coordination by carving up the customer market or deciding not to bid aggressively for another PBM's customers to be a high threat. Indeed, as the FTC opined,

> …The RFP process promotes aggressive competition for employer business and impedes coordinated interaction. Particularly for large employers, the volume of business at stake is substantial, and the incentives to compete aggressively for it are significant. In addition, employers routinely retain expert consultants to identify potential bidders, develop detailed solicitations, and evaluate the proposals before settling on a winner. Because of their repeated interactions with PBMs, industry consultants are particularly well-suited to identify and counteract any attempted coordination by suppliers. RFPs are almost always extended to at least four firms, including the incumbent, typically at least two of the Big Three, one or more smaller PBMs, a carve-in proposal from the customer's health plan provider, and occasionally others on a carve-out basis.

The FTC further found that the merger was unlikely to result in monopsony power, i.e., a competitive advantage in negotiating lower dispensing fees with retail pharmacies downstream. Not only was the proposed merger's resulting share of retail pharmacy sales (29%) too low to exercise such power, but the FTC also found no evidence that PBM size was correlated with pharmacy reimbursement rates. The FTC had previously found that the market for retail dispensing of brand and generic drugs was not susceptible to monopsony power because dispensing fees were negotiated individually between each PBM and each pharmacy. Furthermore, according to the FTC, savings from lower pharmacy reimbursement might be passed along to PBM customers without curtailing pharmacy output or services.

Finally, the FTC did not view the merger as harmful to the distribution of specialty pharmaceuticals from manufacturers, given the low level of market concentration at that time. The proposed merger would give the combined company a market share of only 30%, somewhat below its share of the PBM market. Moreover, there was little evidence of competition between the two firms' specialty pharmacy businesses. Indeed, as the FTC noted, the decision to concentrate specialty drug distribution in limited or exclusive deals with a few players was made by the manufacturers, not the PBMs. Moreover, such decisions are based on the size of the patient population to be served or the drug's specialty safety requirements. Concentration is thus based on ensuring uniform quality, patient safety, and treatment efficacy.

In the end, the FTC did not oppose the merger. However, the FTC did say its decision to close the merger investigation was not an easy one. The agency weighed the concerns over increased market concentration against the other considerations noted above, and decided not to block it. They concluded the merger would not change market dynamics in a competitive sector.

Over time, as critics have correctly observed for several years, the FTC has not weighed in heavily on the PBMs, their consolidation, or efforts to investigate their business practices. As noted before, this likely reflects divisions and diverse opinions within the agency. Indeed, in February 2022, the agency held a vote on whether or not to launch a study of PBM pricing and contractual practices. The 2-2 vote among the four commissioners meant the study would not occur, despite more testimony from independent community pharmacists regarding how their businesses are suffering financially at the hands of the PBMs.[20]

Four months later, after the addition of a fifth commissioner, the FTC voted unanimously to launch an inquiry into specific practices of six, large, vertically-integrated PBMs that might impact patient access and affordability. These practices included:

- fees and clawbacks charged to unaffiliated pharmacies
- methods to steer patients towards pharmacy benefit manager-owned pharmacies
- potentially unfair audits of independent pharmacies
- complicated and opaque methods to determine pharmacy reimbursement
- the prevalence of prior authorizations and other administrative restrictions
- the use of specialty drug lists and surrounding specialty drug policies, and
- the impact of rebates and fees from drug manufacturers on formulary design and the costs of prescription drugs to payers and patients.

It should be noted that the FTC did not make any specific allegations of PBM wrongdoing in these areas.

2015 Hearings in the U.S. House of Representatives

In November 2015, the U.S. House of Representatives' Subcommittee on Regulatory Reform, Commercial and Antitrust Law held another hearing on PBMs and the state of competition among them.[21] Committee members noted that the FTC had not conducted an analysis of the PBM sector since 2005, other than to review the ESRX-Medco merger in 2012 (covered above). The Committee listened to four witnesses, two from the PBM sector, an antitrust attorney who had asked the FTC to conduct Second Reviews of prior mergers (noted above), and a representative of community pharmacies. The antitrust attorney's written comments mirrored many of the "Con" arguments outlined above. They included:

- PBMs are one of the least regulated sectors of the healthcare system. There is no federal regulation and only a modest level of state regulation.
- The PBM market lacks the essential elements for a competitive market: (1) transparency, (2) choice, and (3) a lack of conflicts of interest.
- The FTC has practically abandoned enforcement against PBMs, permitting major PBMs to consolidate without a significant investigation. This consolidation has led to three large PBMs—ExpressScripts, CVS Health (also referred to as "CVS Caremark"), and Optum Rx controlling approximately 80% of the PBM market. Moreover, when states have tried to regulate PBMs, the FTC frequently opposes such efforts at sensible regulation.
- The lack of enforcement, regulation, and competition has created a witches' brew in which PBMs reign free to engage in anticompetitive, deceptive, and fraudulent conduct that harms consumers, employers and unions, and pharmacists. The profits of the major PBMs are increasing at a rapid pace, exceeding $6 Billion annually. As drug prices increase rapidly, PBMs are not adequately fulfilling their function in controlling costs—indeed PBM profits are increasing at the same time drug costs increase because they secure higher rebates from these cost increases. Plan sponsors (employers and unions) cannot attack this problem because PBMs fail to provide adequate transparency on rebates and fail to provide adequate or accurate information on generic drug reimbursement (MAC pricing).
- In addition, PBMs increasingly use restricted pharmacy networks. These restricted networks are especially harmful to vulnerable consumers who

require specialty medications and the elderly and disabled for Part D plans. And these networks drive up costs, reduce patient access to vital healthcare services from their pharmacist of choice, and threaten adequate healthcare.

These same hearings also noted that 24 or more states had passed laws to regulate various PBM business practices; however, such laws did not necessarily cover PBM contracts for self-funded employers.

2018–2019 Hearings

Nearly three years later, the same House Subcommittee held hearings on the proposed vertical merger of CVS Health with Aetna. One expert, an economics professor, highlighted some of the same arguments mentioned above.[22] In particular, he cited research that health plans (insurers like Aetna) that carve-in the pharmacy benefit and coordinate it with the medical benefit in-house have a greater incentive to control total patient costs and therefore provide greater access to drugs that can offset future medical spending. The following year, that same economist stated that, "Confidential rebates are necessary to secure large discounts because when a manufacturer knows all of its customers won't observe a big discount it gives to a particular client, it is more willing to give such a large discount in the first place."[23] Another health economist testified before the Subcommittee that "The PBM's role of seeking out discounts from manufacturers is critical because it is one of the few agents in our commercial pharmaceutical marketplace that creates price competition."[24]

Additional Evidence

Other health economists weighed in two years later and provided a more nuanced picture.[25] They argued *first* that securing a favorable position for a manufacturer's drug on the PBM formulary results from competitive bidding and winning an "all-pay contest" that reduces the cost of the drug for plan enrollees in the form of per-unit rebates off list price. In other words, the position on the formulary reflects an iron triangle access-cost tradeoff: drugs on a more generous tier achieve greater sales due to their lower price, while drugs on less favorable tiers enjoy lower sales due to their higher price. Formularies are far more efficient than the alternative of manufacturers selling their brand drugs at list price. The issue of what PBMs do with the rebates generated in this "near-efficient contest" deals more with the distribution of the surplus rather than market inefficiency. Manufacturers of branded drugs set high list prices to increase the value to consumers of purchasing the drugs on the formulary at a discount. There is a possible inefficiency if (a) some manufacturers set list prices far above monopoly prices and (b) some PBMs include those drugs on their formularies.

In general, PBMs and health plans structure formularies so that, among therapeutically similar drugs, (a) those with lower costs net of rebates are placed on lower, more preferred tiers with lower cost-sharing obligations and/or fewer access restrictions while (b) those with higher costs are placed on higher, less preferred tiers with higher cost-sharing obligations and/or more access restrictions. This structure *incentivizes beneficiaries* to use drugs with lower costs net of rebates and *incentivizes manufacturers* to compete down net prices in order to obtain favorable formulary placement and the corresponding larger share of beneficiaries' prescriptions.[26]

Second, the economists explained that there are further efficiency gains when all health plans delegate the formulary function to particular PBMs. A small number of PBMs that act as the common agent for a large number of plans serve to internalize the externality when payers operate their own formularies and most-favored-nation (MFN) contract provisions. In this manner, they raise the profits of both payers and the PBM and improve market efficiency. In this manner, the PBMs operate as market intermediaries who offer value both upstream (to manufacturers) and downstream (to health plans and consumers). This makes the PBMs' "double agent" role seem less sinister and more beneficial.

Other economists suggested that health plans' concerns with PBMs have less to do with high fees than with the transparency of the PBM revenue flows. Plans may not be clear on what they are being charged, and whether their PBMs are extracting excess profits. Analyses suggest that PBMs earn an operating profit of 4.5% ($11 Billion, excluding mail-order) on their revenues, and are not likely diverting excess profits for themselves.[27] Rather, the profits generated by PBMs are likely shared with their health plan clients, which can translate into lower health plan premiums and more generous formularies for enrollees.

One possible issue is whether health plans evaluate the performance of their PBMs on the level of rebates they generate or on net drug spending. If the former is true, that might provide an incentive for PBMs to negotiate with manufacturers on the basis of higher rebates than lower drug costs.

The Conundrum

At the end of Chapter 10, we noted the conundrum that the PBM market is both concentrated and competitive at the same time. There is an increasing percentage of covered lives in a small number of very large PBMs ("the Big Three") that command 80% market share; simultaneously, there are also many new entrants into the sector (see Figs. 12.1 and 12.2).[28] There were reportedly 66 PBMs in the U.S. in 2019, according to the Pharmacy Benefit Management Institute. The PBMs vary in size, ownership, geographic footprint, customer markets served, service offerings, degree of PBM diversification, expertise, and focus—which serve to increase PBM heterogeneity and, thus, rivalry.

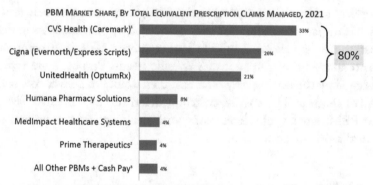

PBM MARKET SHARE, BY TOTAL EQUIVALENT PRESCRIPTION CLAIMS MANAGED, 2021

CVS Health (Caremark)¹	33%
Cigna (Evernorth/Express Scripts)	26%
UnitedHealth (OptumRx)	21%
Humana Pharmacy Solutions	8%
MedImpact Healthcare Systems	4%
Prime Therapeutics²	4%
All Other PBMs + Cash Pay³	4%

(CVS, Cigna, UnitedHealth together: 80%)

1. Includes a full year of Cigna claims, which fully transitioned to Express Scripts by the end of 2020, and the portion of Prime Therapeutics network claims volume for which Express Scripts handles pharmacy network contracting.
2. Excludes Drug Channels Institute estimates of 2021 claims for which Express Scripts handles pharmacy network contracting.
3. Figure includes some patient-paid prescriptions that use a discount card processed by one of the 6 PBMs shown on the chart.
Source: The 2022 Economic Report on U.S. Pharmacies and Pharmacy Benefit Managers, Drug Channels Institute, 2022, Exhibit 87. Total equivalent prescription claims include claims at a PBM's network pharmacies plus prescriptions filled by a PBM's mail and specialty pharmacies. Includes discount card claims. Includes claims for COVID-19 vaccines administered by retail pharmacies. Note that figures may not be comparable with those of previous reports due to changes in publicly reported figures of equivalent prescription claims. Total may not sum due to rounding.
See The Top Pharmacy Benefit Managers of 2021: The Big Get Even Bigger, Drug Channels, April 2022.

Fig. 12.1 PBM market shares

- Abarca Health
- Benecard PBF
- Capital Rx
- Costco Health Solutions
- Elixir (Rite Aid)
- EmpiRx Health
- IPM
- Kroger Prescription Plans
- Magellan Rx
- MaxorPlus

- Navitus Health Solutions
- nirvanaHealth
- PerformRx
- ProCare Rx
- RxBenefits
- Southern Scripts
- Script Care
- WellDyne

- Plus: many small start-ups...

Fig. 12.2 Smaller PBMs

A similar argument was made by an attorney with a prior background at the FTC in testimony before the 2011 Congressional Hearing. She testified that it was a mistake to place too much weight on the market concentration of PBMs for several reasons: e.g., the dynamism of the market based on multiple entries and exits, and the instability of market shares and substantial fluctuations over short time periods in response to changes in the offerings of competitors.[29]

The attorney further testified that the FTC had consistently found the PBM sector to be "vigorously competitive" in competing for contracts with plan sponsors. Indeed, one factor that mitigates concerns over PBM concentration is competition for downstream contracts with plan sponsors (payers). Competition for the PBM's services occurs as part of a bidding process initiated by the plan sponsor. The sponsor issues an RFP that lists the required PBM services and solicits proposals for pricing components to deliver those services. Third-party consultants are often retained by plan sponsors to design and host the RFP process. Multiple PBMs submit bids in a competitive auction to address the plan sponsor's specific needs. Proposals are typically differentiated by the pricing they offer and their ability to deliver cost savings to the plan sponsor. The cost of switching from the incumbent PBM to a different PBM may be considered along with the proposed component costs as part of the pricing comparison.

A Host of Continuing, Contentious Issues

Issue #1: Rebates

Prevalence of Rebates

The issue of manufacturer rebates has never waned in the debate over the PBMs' role. Perhaps a major reason is their prevalence. Rebates are a common feature in the negotiations of PBMs/MCOs with virtually all drug manufacturers. ICER described rebates as "a staple of negotiations between pharmaceutical companies and payer organizations."[30]

According to Milliman researchers, rebates are widely used by a wide array of manufacturers in multiple industrial sectors: automakers, electronics companies, and pharmaceuticals. Rebate contract terms represent "trade secrets," thus explaining the presence of a "black box" in the drug supply chain. Across sectors, rebates average 20%.[31] Moreover, according to Milliman, rebates drive the finances of all supply chain stakeholders. For patients, rebates drive whether the drug is covered and what is the out-of-pocket responsibility. For manufacturers, rebates drive formulary coverage and, thus, sales, revenues, and the growing spread in gross-to-net revenues. For payers, rebates are associated with lower expenditures on prescription drugs and, thus, lower premiums and perhaps more robust benefit packages and lower cost-sharing levels. For wholesalers, rebates drive the demand for specific drugs and thus the volumes of those drugs they carry. And, for PBMs, rebates drive a (declining) share of their earnings.

Large, Growing Amount of Rebate Dollars

Another reason is the sheer amount of money involved. Rebates paid to third-party payers—commercial, Medicare, and Medicaid—now account for the majority of the gross-to-net reductions in drug prices (see Fig. 9.14). In 2016, Altarum estimated that approximately $89 Billion in rebates were paid to payers. Other analysts estimated the total value of manufacturers' off-invoice discounts, rebates, and other price concessions grew from $155 Billion in 2017 to $204 Billion in 2021.[32]

Nevertheless, as noted above, third-party payer rebates as a percentage of gross-to-net reductions have recently fallen over time, from 67% in 2017 to 62% in 2021. Moreover, the composition of those rebates has shifted away from commercial payers to Medicare Part D and 340B programs. Part D rebates accrue to the health plans administering the PDPs, not to the PBMs themselves.

Drivers of Rising Rebates

There are several drivers behind rising rebates flowing through the retail pharmaceutical supply chain—all discussed in Chapters 9 and 11. One powerful driver is the growing DIR payments in Medicare Part D plans. A second driver has been the increase in mandatory Medicaid rebates following the passage of the PPACA and then the Bipartisan Budget Act of 2018 (inflation protection rebate for generic drugs); such rebates now account for 17% of manufacturers' total rebates and discounts. A third driver has been the increasing amount of drug purchases through the 340B program, which now accounts for 20% of manufacturers' total rebates. A fourth driver has been the concentration within the PBM sector, which allows larger PBMs to negotiate larger rebates from manufacturers to attain a position on the formulary and avoid the threat of formulary exclusion. Rebates to commercial payers comprise another 22% of total manufacturer rebates and discounts. On top of these, an additional 12% of manufacturer rebates are captured by PBMs (in the form of administrative fees), wholesalers and pharmacies (in the form of fees and discounts).[33]

Distribution of Rebate Dollars

Overall, Altarum estimated that in 2016 approximately $89 Billion in rebates were paid to payers.[34] The $89 Billion was split among Medicaid ($32 Billion), Medicare Part D plans ($31 Billion), private health plans ($23 Billion), and other payers ($3 Billion), reducing total retail spending by 21%. More recently, analysts have apportioned the destinations of rebates, defined in terms of the gross-to-net reductions for brand-name drugs, as follows: Medicare Part D (23%), Medicaid (17%), commercial payers (22%), 340B program (20%), and PBMs, wholesalers, and pharmacies (12%).

The rebates on branded drugs paid to Medicaid (61%) and Medicare (31%) are much higher than those paid to private plans (16%). It should be obvious that a public payer like Medicaid has extracted higher rebates from manufacturers than have PBMs and private payers extracted from Medicare Part D, and that PBMs have negotiated bigger discounts for public payers than for private payers. This is not to be explained by enrollment size or market power but rather by the fact that (1) Medicaid rebates cover both branded and generic drugs to protect the low-income population, (2) these savings accrue to Medicaid (whereas rebates on generics in Medicare and private plans accrue to pharmacies who select the drugs), and (3) Medicaid uses administered pricing while Medicare relies on contract negotiations. Altarum estimated that Part D plans in Medicare obtain higher rebates (31%) compared to private plans (16%). One explanation is that Medicare Part D plans make more extensive use of utilization management, formulary exclusions, and multi-tiered formularies compared to private plans, thereby giving public payers more leverage in dealing with manufacturers.[35]

Another explanation is the greater price-sensitivity of enrollees in the Medicare program and their willingness to select into restrictive formularies. There is one exception to this pattern, due to the presence of Part D reinsurance for out-of-pocket "catastrophic" spending above $5,000. After meeting this threshold, the financial risk is heavily borne by the government (85%), health plan (10%), and the enrollee (5%). Some analysts believe this gives the Part D plans and their PBMs an incentive to use higher cost, high rebate drugs. This incentive may be particularly strong for expensive specialty drugs.

By contrast, private plans funded by employers are concerned not only with cost containment but also their employees' access to the drugs they prefer. Moreover, drugs are a smaller component of employers' coverage costs (unlike Medicare) and employees are insulated from their insurance premiums (unlike enrollees in Medicare Part D plans); these provide the employer with less bargaining leverage.

The Complexity of Rebates

Rebates are complex. For example, PBMs are paid "stacked" rebates: combined payments related to formulary placement, variously named administrative fees, price increase protection guarantees, and other programs.[36] Moreover, rebate levels change each year as a result of negotiations between manufacturers, PBMs, and insurers. Such changes can affect formulary placement. They take effect at the beginning of a new health insurance contract year, not when manufacturers change their list prices. Rebates also vary by type of drug: a study of Medicare Part D rebates shows they are highest for branded drugs facing brand competition (average 39% of gross cost) and lower for protected class drugs (average 14%). Researchers estimated that rebates are roughly 30% of WAC (list price).[37]

Rebate Benefits

Rebates are thus one important driver through which the government and health plans can reduce overall healthcare spending. Health economists assert that rebates foster price competition among manufacturers, and that PBMs constitute an "institutional innovation that improves the elasticity of demand in buying pharmaceuticals."[38] Plan participants also benefit from rebates through a reduction in premiums and copayments for drugs with more favorable formulary placement, and perhaps also by receipt of enhanced services from their plans.[39]

According to a 2019 report issued by the Government Accountability Office (GAO), PBMs successfully negotiated larger rebates over the period 2014–2016, helping Part D plans hold down their premium levels. Moreover, PBMs passed along 99.6% of these rebates to plan sponsors. Service fees paid to PBMs by manufacturers were only a small percentage (0.4%) of Part D spending; service agreement fees paid by plan sponsors to the PBMs were not tied to the negotiated price of the drugs but to the volume of claims or the size of the enrollee population.[40]

Rebates vs. PBM Profits

PBM profits (excluding mail order) of $11 Billion are quite small in comparison to the $89 Billion in rebates that PBMs generate. Years ago, the FTC argued that rebates promote price competition among manufacturers to get onto PBM formularies and secure more favorable formulary positions; savings from such price competition exist due to the confidential nature of the rebates negotiated.[41]

In 2018, CVS Caremark reported in its Q2 earnings call presentation that it returned roughly 98% of rebates to clients. At the same time, Express Scripts reported that it passed along 95% of rebates, price reductions, and purchase discounts to its health plan clients. The following year, Optum told the Senate Finance Committee that it returned 98% of the value of discounts it collected. The situation is more complex, however, since there are a variety of arrangements for sharing the rebates: e.g., 100% of rebates (with minimum guarantee, no guarantee), percentage share of rebates (with minimum guarantee, no guarantee), flat dollar guaranteed amount, etc. There are also differences between large and small employers in terms of the percentage receiving rebates and the rebate structures utilized.

Overall, rebates have declined both absolutely as well as a share of PBM profits. As one illustration, Medco retained $1.6 Billion in rebates in 2003, more than 50% of the rebates it generated, on $1.5 Billion in gross profits; in 2011, by contrast, it retained only $0.76 Billion in rebates, which accounted for only 12% of total rebates collected on $4.6 Billion in gross profits. Medco's SEC 10-K filing in 2004 and Express Script's Investor Presentation in 2014 explained the transition: an increase in generic drug utilization (particularly in its mail-order business). Generic drug utilization accounted for the majority of earnings growth in the 2000s, while rebates drove earnings during the 1990s. This transition was occasioned by patent expiries and generic drug exploitation of the earlier blockbuster drugs. Between 2004 and 2013, generic drug market share rose from 57% of scripts to 86%.[42] Between 2003 and 2010, the annual sales growth for pharmaceuticals slowed considerably from 11% to 2.6%.[43] Moreover, the rising share of specialty drugs—which often have strong physician and patient preferences, and/or which may have only one competitor in a therapeutic class—made it harder for PBMs to move market share. Another driver may have been the 2004 settlement between Medco and the DOJ and Attorneys General in 20 states over charges that Medco switched patients to higher cost drugs to earn higher rebates—a practice that was now deemed illegal.

The Issue Lingers on

Nevertheless, PBMs have drawn continual fire over rebates on several potential issues: retaining rebates rather than passing them along to plan sponsors, a lack of transparency regarding the amount of rebates and how much is passed along, re-labeling rebates as fees to disguise them, causing manufacturers to raise their list prices to offset the rebates they pay to PBMs, and charging patients list prices for their prescriptions at the point of sale. Another bone of contention is that not all parties have benefitted or benefited equally from these rebate-based savings. One group have been those workers with high drug expenditures but who are enrolled in health plans with high deductibles and high coinsurance; another party has been the independent community pharmacies. Both are discussed below. More generally, PBM critics often historically labeled rebates as suspect "kickbacks", even though they have been protected in a safe harbor since the late 1990s (see Chapter 10).

Indeed, in May 2018, federal policy-makers suggested that the rebate arrangements sanctioned in the late 1990s by the (then) OIG-DHHS encouraged manufacturers, health plans, and PBMs to raise list prices on drugs. The Office of Management and Budget announced it was reviewing a rule proposed by the OIG-DHHS to remove the safe harbor protection of rebates paid to plans or PBMs. The Proposed Rule, issued in February 2019 by OIG-DHHS, argued the current rebate system is a significant cause of high drug prices. In November 2020, the Trump Administration finalized a rule to eliminate the safe harbor shielding rebates paid to Medicare prescription drug plans (PDPs in Medicare Part D) and Medicare Advantage plans (Medicare Part C) from the anti-kickback statute (AKS). The rule also created a new safe harbor to protect point-of-sale ("POS") price reductions paid by manufacturers to Medicare Part D plans, Medicare Advantage plans, and Medicaid managed care organizations ("MCOs"); as well as a new safe harbor to protect fair-market-value service fees paid to PBMs by manufacturers.

The Rebate Rule was to go into effect on January 1, 2022. However, in January 2021, in response to a lawsuit brought by the Pharmaceutical Care Management Association challenging the Rule, the Biden Administration delayed the effective date by two years (January 1, 2023). Later that year, Congress passed the Infrastructure Investment and Jobs Act, signed by President Biden on November 15, 2021. This further delayed implementation of the Rebate Rule to January 2026.[44]

Issue #2: Drug Spending, Drug Prices, and Rebates

Growth in drug expenditures accelerated during the 1990s, peaked at 17% in 2001, and then decelerated through 2012. By 2013–2014, however, drug spending had grown by 13–14%, the largest annual increase observed since 2001. According to the IMS Institute for Healthcare Informatics, the fall in the first decade was due to lower growth in prescription volumes, increased use of generics, and a large number of patent expiries. The subsequent rise was partly due to new product introductions (e.g., specialty and orphan drugs) and fewer drugs losing patent protection; however, the biggest driver in 2014 was the price increase in protected brands.[45]

As outlined more fully above and below, PBM critics have long argued that a big driver of rising drug prices has been PBM consolidation, their growing market power, and the rebates extracted from manufacturers.[46] Thus, the argument goes, the higher rebates negotiated with manufacturers motivate manufacturers to offset them by hiking their list prices. Several studies appear to discount this argument.

First, when IMS decomposed the growth in prices for protected brands, it found that when adjusted for the aggregate level of rebates and discounts, the observed increase in invoice prices of 8.1% fell to only 3.1%. Second, research by Visante has shown no correlation between negotiated rebates and drug price increases.[47] Third, research conducted by MGA shows that the median change in WAC price for rebated and non-rebated drugs between 2018 and 2021 on the formularies of the three largest PBMs were virtually the same (15.6% versus 13.9%).[48] Fourth, the Majority Staff Report on drug pricing issued by the U.S. House of Representatives Committee on Oversight and Reform concluded that:[49]

> Internal data obtained by the Committee reveals that the net prices—the prices manufacturers collect after accounting for rebates, price concessions, and other discounts—of nearly all of the drugs in the investigation increased year over year. Net prices for all of the drugs examined are significantly higher today than at launch. This data, which has never before been shared with the public, undermines industry claims that price increases are primarily due to increasing rebates and discounts paid to pharmacy benefit managers (PBMs).

Instead, the Committee laid the blame for rising drug prices at the feet of pharmaceutical manufacturers and the strategies they followed to allow this pricing behavior. Those strategies included: raising prices at will to meet revenue targets, targeting the U.S. market for their price increases while

Health Plans and PBMs   **Pharma Companies**

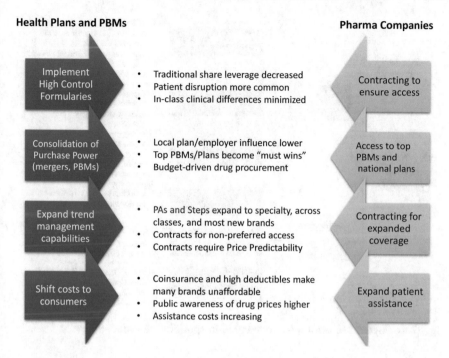

Implement High Control Formularies
- Traditional share leverage decreased
- Patient disruption more common
- In-class clinical differences minimized

Contracting to ensure access

Consolidation of Purchase Power (mergers, PBMs)
- Local plan/employer influence lower
- Top PBMs/Plans become "must wins"
- Budget-driven drug procurement

Access to top PBMs and national plans

Expand trend management capabilities
- PAs and Steps expand to specialty, across classes, and most new brands
- Contracts for non-preferred access
- Contracts require Price Predictability

Contracting for expanded coverage

Shift costs to consumers
- Coinsurance and high deductibles make many brands unaffordable
- Public awareness of drug prices higher
- Assistance costs increasing

Expand patient assistance

Fig. 12.3 Payers using leverage to control costs; pharma working to secure access and growth

maintaining or lowering prices charged in the rest of the world, manipulating the patent system and marketing exclusivities to further extend their monopolies, engaging in anticompetitive behaviors to suppress competition from generic drugs (e.g., loss of exclusivity strategies, evergreening, shadow pricing one another's price hikes), and use of patient assistance programs to increase sales. If anything, PBMs and their health plan trading partners (and, increasingly, parent organizations) stand in opposition to the manufacturers and their efforts to raise prices (see Fig. 12.3). Moreover, PBMs and payers have adopted specific new strategies to contain rising outlays on specialty medicines (see Fig. 12.4). In recent years, payers and PBMs extended their use of formulary exclusions to specialty drugs, making them "less special."[50]

Issue #3: PBMs and Pharmacies

PBMs contract directly with individual pharmacies to reimburse the cost of drugs dispensed to health plan beneficiaries. One controversy deals with "spread pricing," whereby PBMs are reimbursed by health plans and employers at a higher price for generic drugs than what the PBMs actually

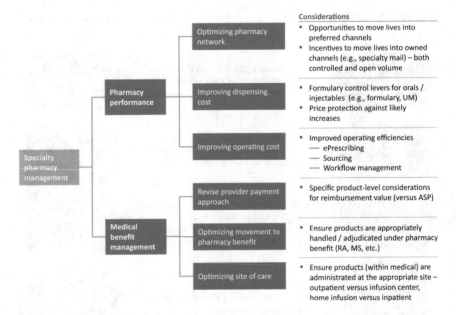

Fig. 12.4 Payer/PBM efforts to drive value in specialty pharmacy

pay pharmacies for these drugs, and then health plans allow the PBMs to keep the difference. This is not an illegal practice; nor is it a signal that PBMs are earning excess profits. However, there may be a lack of transparency regarding the payment schedules PBMs generate for pharmacies that are not disclosed to health plan sponsors. There is also the issue that PBMs may set and control the spread: i.e., they determine how much to bill the insurance plan per prescription and what they will reimburse the pharmacy for dispensing that prescription.

The pharmacy, which has already incurred a cost for stocking and dispensing the medication, has no control over any aspect of the medication's sale. The plan sponsor and PBM determine the patient's copay, and then the PBM determines in advance how much it will reimburse pharmacies for each medication covered under the patient's drug plan. Often the reimbursement rates are below the cost of the drug, putting pharmacies in the position of having to fill a prescription at a loss, which leaves pharmacies unable to predict cash flow, stock inventory, or perhaps meet payroll.[51] PBMs are not required to disclose their formulas for determining cost, which are considered a trade secret. This leaves pharmacies with no choice but to appeal losses they incur in order to fill the prescription. Not surprisingly, pharmacies complain that the PBMs profit off their backs and that they have little recourse to changing PBM practices.

There is the related issue that PBMs compete with the independent pharmacies they are reimbursing. PBMs can own their own pharmacies—both retail stores and mail-order—and make money when patients are incentivized or channeled to use mail-order or only purchase from a PBM-owned pharmacy (e.g., CVS). Critics allege that PBMs reimburse their own pharmacies more than they reimburse non PBM-owned pharmacies, especially small community and independent pharmacies.[52]

The complaints do not stop there. Pharmacies complain that PBMs reclassify generics as brands, paying the pharmacy at the generic rate but reselling it to the client at the brand rate, and keeping the difference. They also suggest PBMs switch a dispensed prescription from its actual NDC (national drug code) to a different NDC of the same drug but at a higher price point (AWP); again, the pharmacy gets paid the lower rate but the PBM gets paid the higher rate, and keeps the difference. Another complaint concerns negative remits, when the member is charged the full copay when the drug costs less; the PBM keeps the difference by paying the pharmacy a negative amount.

A final contentious issue concerns "clawbacks". Clawbacks are controversial not only because they reportedly result in revenues lost by the pharmacy but also in overpayments made by insurance beneficiaries. This happens when the patient's co-pay exceeds the drug's cost: the insurer's PBM instructs the pharmacy to charge the patient an inflated co-pay, and later "claws back" the excess from the pharmacy, keeping it for themselves. More generally, clawbacks may cover several DIR fees under Part D that PBMs charge pharmacies: (1) costs for pharmacies to participate in a PBM's Part D "preferred" network, (2) price reconciliations based on the payer's contractual rates, (3) compliance fees for contract-based performance metrics, wherein performance may offset another fee, and (4) a combination of these fees. Together, these fees allow PBMs to "clawback" millions of dollars based on contracts with pharmacy partners. In some cases, these fees are applied as a flat-rate on prescriptions filled ($2–$7 per claim); in other cases, a percentage is applied, often at three-to-five percent for brand-name drugs. Such instances have led to calls to reform DIR payments made to PBMs and instead include pharmacy DIR in the calculation of Medicare Part D program patient cost sharing at the point of sale to lower the out-of-pocket cost to patients and preserve the financial viability of independent pharmacies.[53]

All of these instances suggest possible abuses of the use of spread pricing. Spread pricing has become highly controversial in Managed Medicaid programs, which account for a majority of Medicaid prescriptions and spending. The Medicaid program in the State of Ohio provides a recent illustration of the issues. The State Auditor issued a report in August 2018 on the

State's contracts with private Medicaid managed care organizations (MCO "plans") that, in turn, contracted with external PBMs to manage the Medicaid pharmacy benefit.[54] According to the Report, the plans reimbursed the PBMs on a pricing model based on publicly available price data (AWP), but the PBMs reimbursed pharmacies using different pricing models based on negotiated contracts. As a result, the amount paid to the pharmacy by the PBM did not correlate with the amount paid by the MCO to the PBM for the same transaction; this was the spread. Moreover, the report found that the $6.14 spread on generic drugs (86% of Medicaid prescriptions) was higher than the spread on branded drugs. The Report also found that (for generics) the PBMs were paid administrative fees that were triple the market rate ($0.95 to $1.90), or an additional $3.81 per prescription, suggesting those fees may have been excessive.

CVS Caremark managed pharmacy benefits for several of the state's Medicaid MCOs; Optum Rx worked on behalf of another MCO. Caremark retained 8.7% of the payments it received, while OptumRx retained 9.4%. An Ohio state official said the state needed more information before it could determine what is a fair share for the PBMs. The state's own report showed the privatization of its Medicaid system saved the state $145 Million compared to the former system where the state insurance program for the poor directly paid fees for services. The report also suggested the state's independent pharmacies were not underpaid but, in fact were paid at equivalent rates to CVS pharmacies for both branded drugs and generics.

The State Attorney General charged the managed care organization Centene and its subsidiary, Buckeye Health Plan, with conspiring to misrepresent the costs of pharmacy services, including the price of prescription drugs. Centene and Buckeye Health Plan administered its pharmacy benefits via sister companies Envolve Health Solutions and Health Net Pharmacy Solutions. The practice of subcontracting with more than one PBM prompted questions about Buckeye Health Plan's business practices and, ultimately, Centene. The AG noted the following breaches by Centene:

- filing reimbursement requests for amounts already paid by third parties,
- failing to accurately disclose the true cost of pharmacy services, including the disclosure of discounts received, and
- artificially inflating dispensing fees.

In June 2021, Centene and its PBM (Envolve Pharmacy Solutions) announced that it settled litigation in both Ohio and Mississippi, agreeing to pay the two states $88 Million and $55 Million, respectively. Centene also announced that it had set aside an additional $1.1 Billion should it decide to settle similar suits in several other states. This possibly marks the largest set of fines imposed since the 2005–2006 litigation against Medco and Caremark. Note that the charges were filed against a Medicaid MCO and its in-house PBM, not one of the three largest PBMs.

In the aftermath of the Ohio investigation, some states have sought to prevent spread pricing by selecting a single PBM to manage Medicaid pharmacy benefits. In February 2021, Ohio moved to a single pharmacy benefit manager system, hiring Gainwell Technologies (previously DXC technologies) to manage all PBM functions; in July 2021, Kentucky awarded its Medicaid pharmacy benefits contract to MedImpact. Other states have elected to run their own internal PBM program and/or drafted legislation to control spread pricing. Finally, as this volume goes to press (June 2022), Republican Senators have just introduced new legislation: the Pharmacy Benefit Manager Transparency Act of 2022. The legislation would (a) make spread pricing illegal, (b) prohibit PBMs from arbitrary or unfair clawbacks, (c) encourage PBMs to pass along 100% of rebates, (d) encourage PBMs to provide full disclosure of drug costs, prices, and reimbursements to pharmacies and health plans, and (e) require PBMs to file annual reports with the FTC on how they charge health plans and pharmacies for prescription drugs.

Issue #4: Safe Harbor Redux

In May 2018, federal policy-makers suggested that the rebate arrangements sanctioned in the late 1990s by the (then) OIG-DHHS encouraged manufacturers, health plans, and PBMs to raise list prices on drugs. The Office of Management and Budget announced it was reviewing a rule proposed by the OIG-DHHS to remove the safe harbor protection of rebates paid to plans or PBMs. The Proposed Rule, issued in February 2019 by OIG-DHHS, argued the current rebate system is a significant cause of high drug prices. The "Rebate Rule" would modify the Safe Harbor for PBM discounts erected during the late 1990s so that it would no longer apply to manufacturer rebates paid to Part D plan sponsors or PBMs. In its place, the new rule would create a new safe harbor that applied only when the discount was applied at the point of sale (the pharmacy), such that the discount was passed along directly to the enrollee and paid to the pharmacy via a chargeback. The rule's intent, ostensibly, was to (a) limit the enrollee's out-of-pocket expenses due to cost-sharing mechanisms (deductibles, copayments, coinsurance), and (b) fit into the growing call for point-of-service (POS) rebates that would be captured by the customer rather than the PBM. The Rule used the threat of liability under the Anti-Kickback Statute (AKS) to eliminate manufacturer payment of retrospective rebates to PBMs and plans, the standard procedure established in the mid-1990s.

CMS evaluated the proposed changes to the safe harbor regulation that would prohibit rebates paid directly to PBMs. It concluded that such a prohibition would lead to a 15% reduction in the discounts paid by manufacturers; the 85% of discounts that would continue to be paid would be split between charge-backs (75%) and lower list prices (25%). There was also considerable concern that payment of rebates at the point of sale would more easily become public information and disclosed to manufacturers, who might more easily discern one another's pricing and engage in price collusion.

In addition to the proposal's impact on net drug prices, the Office of the Actuary (OACT) inside CMS and the Congressional Budget Office explored the estimated impact on health plan premiums. Both projected that premiums for potentially affected plans would rise due to the loss of rebate revenue were the safe harbor removed. OACT forecast that overall drug spending net of rebates and discounts would increase $137 Billion (and perhaps as high as $196 Billion) over ten years, and that a major beneficiary would be the drug manufacturers who would face less price competition. Studies by non-governmental entities also project premium increases. The actuarial and consulting firm Milliman analyzed seven scenarios and concluded the proposed rule would lead to an increase in Medicare Part D premiums by 12–22%;[55] the Wakely Consulting Group estimated an increase of 8 percent.[56] As a result of such pushback, OIG-DHHS withdrew the proposal.

Issue #5: Transparency

One of the most frequent criticisms of PBMs is their lack of transparency. This criticism has been applied to their contracts with manufacturers upstream and their contracts with health plan sponsors downstream. The contract terms struck with manufacturers are never disclosed and are closely kept as trade secrets; disclosure of such terms runs the risk of pricing collusion on the part of manufacturers. Confidentiality may also be necessary to encourage price discounting by the manufacturers and the contracting effort made by the PBMs. The contract terms struck with health plans have variable transparency. Customer satisfaction surveys suggest that plan sponsors view their relationships with smaller PBMs to be more transparent than relationships with larger PBMs. Relationships with smaller PBMs were rated as "completely transparent" by 57% of sponsors and "somewhat transparent" by another 39% of sponsors. By contrast, relationships with larger PBMs were rated as completely transparent by only 24% of plans sponsors, while the majority (63%) rated them as somewhat transparent. Analysts suggest some possible selection effects may characterize these findings, since sponsors may select smaller PBMs which have easier to evaluate business models.

The Congressional Budget Office analyzed the pro and con arguments for price transparency in a 2008 report.[57] It found that increased transparency in healthcare markets characterized by high levels of concentration can result in higher, not lower prices. The FTC evaluated proposed legislation in several states that would mandate disclosure of the contract terms between PBMs and manufacturers. According to the FTC, mandated disclosure is not likely to benefit, and is more likely to harm consumers. This is because there is a lack of evidence that such disclosure of rebates makes PBM markets more competitive. The harms noted above—manufacturer collusion and reduced ability to compel discounts—outweigh the benefits. These conclusions are supported by econometric research that shows that confidentiality lowers prices,[58] while public disclosure of rebate percentages would raise overall costs.[59] Transparency serves to reduce the variation in rebates negotiated, with convergence toward a lower average, thereby raising insurers' costs.[60]

The competitive effects of price transparency resemble the effects of most-favored-nation (MFN) clauses: they both lead to higher prices.[61] Earlier research showed that publication of prices leads to a reduction in the intensity of oligopoly price competition and increased prices.[62]

Nevertheless, federal and state legislators have pushed for greater PBM transparency. Recently, some U.S. Senators introduced the *Pharmacy Benefit Manager Transparency Act of 2022*. The proposed Act empowers the FTC and State Attorneys General to stop unfair and deceptive PBM business (pricing) practices. It would also make illegal spread pricing, clawbacks of reimbursement for drug acquisition costs/dispensing fees, and actions that arbitrarily or unfairly change the fees paid to pharmacies to offset reimbursement changes in federally-funded health plans. The Act would further "encourage" fair and transparent PBM practices, such as 100% pass-through of rebates, provide full disclosure of prices, reimbursements, fees, discounts, markups, as well as require PBMs to file annual reports with the FTC that disclose aggregate spread pricing amounts, total clawback amounts, and why drugs were moved to different tiers.

At the local level, there has been an uptick in proposed and passed PBM-specific legislation in at least 22 states. Efforts here commonly target (1) the transparency of pharmacy prices, (2) pharmacy reimbursement amounts, and (3) specified parameters for contracts between PBMs and plans/pharmacies.

In some states, legislators have required PBMs to have state license and registration.

Other Issues

An earlier section of this chapter discussed the complexity of rebates. Another issue not often considered is the complexity and variety in the pass-through arrangements for rebates. First, rebates can be passed through to health plans as a fixed percentage of the total amount (e.g., 100% of rebate, 90% of rebate, 50% of rebate, etc.). Second, rebates can be passed along as a fixed dollar amount per prescription. Third, rebates can be passed along using a hybrid of the first two approaches. Thus, rebates can be passed along in terms of the greater of two amounts: a fixed dollar amount per prescription or the fixed percentage of the total amount. As a further complexity, some plan sponsors may direct their PBM to retain a portion of the rebates collected as an offset to its "program management fees" (i.e., what it charges the sponsor to process the claim) and its manufacturer administrative fees (i.e., what it charges manufacturers to negotiate the contracts). Moreover, these agreements to offset fees are subject to change annually as PBMs and plan sponsors adjust their contracts. A main point here is that there is a permeable membrane separating rebates from fees in the money flows between PBMs and health plan sponsors—making it difficult to disentangle the two.

A second issue that is often ignored is how health plans utilize the rebates that are passed through. They are used to benefit plan beneficiaries through enhanced plan choice, lower premiums, wider provider networks, lower out-of-pocket costs, and/or better services. Rebates help to keep drug costs lower which, in turn, keeps premiums affordable for enrollees.

A third, related issue is employers' use of rebates. According to PBMI, 68% of employers utilized the rebates to reduce plan spending on drug costs; 11% utilized them to offset member premiums; 15% pursued a combination of plan and member savings; and only 4% used them to reduce member out-of-pocket costs at the point of sale.[63]

Other Possible Headwinds: Employer and Health Plan Purchasing Consortia[64]

The Promise

There are some compelling reasons to think that one key to controlling healthcare prices and costs is the engagement of employers. Employers are the largest provider and purchaser of health insurance in the U.S., covering roughly 150 million workers and their dependents (2018 data), and purchasing one-third of all healthcare. They have leverage approaching that of the federal government. Moreover, they have a stake in controlling these costs, as detailed in Chapter 9.

Prior Employer Strategies and Current Dilemmas

Employers have also been responsible for the growing penetration of HDHP coverage among workers. This has proven to be a two-edged sword, however. On the one hand, HDHPs have helped employers to stabilize healthcare spending as a percentage of workers' compensation (between 8 and 9% from 2010 to 2018). On the other hand, HDHPs have left workers with higher deductibles and out-of-pocket spending, which have resulted in problems in paying for medications (at list price) during the deductible phase. On a related note, the percentage of plans offered on the federal marketplace (health insurance exchange) with separate medical and pharmacy deductibles has risen for the bronze plans from 9% in 2015 to 19% in 2022; however, the percentage has fallen for the three other metal plans (e.g. from 45 to 17% among silver plans).

At a macro level, gains on the cost side have come at the expense of losses on the access and affordability side. This is a thorny topic for employers: rising out-of-pocket costs are increasingly problematic for employees but employers have not found a replacement solution to HDHPs and cost-sharing. They may also be reticent to further increase worker cost-sharing—a reluctance exacerbated by the "Great Resignation" due to Covid and the need to recruit/retain talent.

Prior Employer Consortia in Healthcare

Employer purchasing consortia are not a new phenomenon. Employers formed purchasing consortia in the 1980s and 1990s to contract with providers, such as the Buyers Health Care Action Group (BHCAG) in the Twin Cities and the Pacific Business Group on Health (PBGH) in Northern California. They pool the purchasing power of many employers to try to negotiate more favorable terms from their suppliers/vendors upstream (whether providers or PBMs). Employers form such coalitions because, as individual buyers, they lack the bargaining power in local markets (i.e., not enough covered lives) to compel price concessions. PBGH in the 1990s, for example, had a negotiating alliance with a single request for proposals (RFP) for 25 members representing more than 1 million lives in the San Francisco area. These consortia were led by employed consultants from health benefits firms who served as their chief negotiators.

Limited Success of and Impediments to Employer Consortia

There are any number of reasons why such employer coalition efforts have not generally succeeded. The early BHCAG coalition was thwarted by employer withdrawals (e.g., mergers of employer members that led to a different approach to benefits), sabotage by competitors (e.g., health plans that lowered their prices), and fluctuating employer enthusiasm (e.g., based on rises and declines in the insurance underwriting cycle, lack of enrollment growth, administrative burdens, etc.).

Analysts suggest that special soil and climatic conditions (*terroir*) are required for success. These include competition among the MCO/PBM suppliers from whom the coalitions purchase, aggregated purchasing clout (e.g., sufficient covered lives) on behalf of enough self-insured employers to get their attention, a willingness on the part of human resource managers to confront the tradeoffs in the iron triangle (e.g., cost versus access to drugs) and incorporate them into benefit plan choices, acumen about the health-care ecosystem, and the ability to cooperate with one another.[65] They may also require a willingness among employer members to compromise and settle on a common plan design to simplify negotiations and bidding, rather than insist on customization (i.e., creating multiple plan designs for plans to bid on).

Employers face some barriers here to more effective bargaining.[66] First, borrowing from former Speaker of the House Tip O'Neill, "all healthcare is local." That is, private sector bargaining between suppliers and buyers is conducted at the local level based on relative market power. Providers, insurers, and PBMs are quite concentrated; employers are not. Secondly, employers in diverse industries and sectors, often with their corporate head-quarters scattered across the country, have little experience in collaboration on local market issues. Third, healthcare is a complex ecosystem that few employers understand. Fourth, employer Human Resource departments are risk averse, particularly in managing the tradeoffs in the iron triangle.

Coalitions also face the choice of what healthcare costs to tackle and how to tackle them. One promising avenue is low-value, high-cost care.[67] This can include not only particular treatments rendered by physicians and hospitals, but also particular drugs. Examples of the latter might include: me-too drugs, combination drugs, branded drugs when generic equivalents are available, and prescription drugs when over-the-counter treatments are available. Plan sponsors may contribute to what analysts call "formulary waste" by including these drugs in broad formularies. A study of self-insured employer claims found that 6% of claims (covering 868 drugs in 71 drug groups) were wasteful; the cost difference with higher-value drugs ranged from 25 to 100% per drug; and 42% of wasteful prescriptions involved brand drugs. The savings available here represented 3–24% of the total pharmacy spend administered by the sponsors' PBMs. This suggests that the benefits of coalitions may reside not only in greater bargaining power but also in wiser formulary design and improved oversight of their PBM partners. Employers may also need to confront the tradeoffs they make in PBM contracting between lower administrative fees paid to PBMs and PBM discretion to incorporate drugs on the formulary that carry higher rebates or spreads. Analysts suggest that payment of the higher administrative fees will be more than offset by the reduced spending on expensive/wasteful drugs. Generally, given the rapidly increasing trend in drug spend (roughly two percent higher than the medical trend in 2021), all employers need to find effective strategies to manage their drug costs.

There are, nevertheless, problems with eliminating low-value products and services. First, the movement to improve value (e.g., the Choosing Wisely campaign) has made little progress over the past decade. One problem is defining what is high versus low value. Another problem is that formulary management is a sophisticated competency that (a) PBMs have developed over time and (b) employers have not. A third problem is that failure to understand and tackle the combined pharmacy and medical benefits may hinder efforts to make tradeoffs that increase value. Oftentimes, these benefits are administered separately. Depending on plan design, deductible amounts and out-of-pocket maximums may be combined. For these reasons, many large business coalitions have engaged an expert consultant on pharmacy.

Another approach for employers is to reduce rebates and increase transparency of drug prices. Employer negotiations with PBMs need to focus more on evidence-based cost reduction efforts. One issue here is that transparency of drug prices is not the same as control over drug prices. As pointed out here in this chapter, only the pharmaceutical manufacturers set drug prices; control over this process rests heavily on competition in the drug's therapeutic category, as well as on the timing of patent expiry. Moreover, manufacturers have utilized direct-to-consumer marketing and copayment coupons (that reduce consumer cost-sharing at the point of purchase) to thwart efforts to reduce the utilization of their expensive products.[68] Such efforts increase both drug prices and volumes. Finally, as noted below, transparency of prices brings the risk of collusion and, thus, higher prices (not lower).

Employer Consortia for Drug Purchasing

One employer consortium, Employers Health, was founded in 1983 and began collective purchasing of drugs in 1995. It pools more than $1 Billion in drug purchases for 200 sponsors covering 800,000 lives. In recent years, it contracted with CVS Health and Optum. Employers face an array of contracting options such as direct deal, coalition, or collective. According to PBMI, 21% of survey respondents purchased PBM services using these vehicles in 2017. Since that time, there has been considerable consolidation among the PBMs as well as migration back to PBM ownership by health plans. There are also reports that some health plans have joined together in group purchasing organizations (GPOs) to improve and centralize their expertise in contract negotiations with PBMs (see Chapter 11).

Some employers have enlisted the help of benefits consulting firms such as Aon, Willis Towers Watson, and Mercer to utilize a consortium approach to purchasing PBM services. There may be some hope on the horizon based on several observed shifts. First, executives at one of the three largest PBMs report that more of the RFPs they compete for are run by consultants that intermediate between the PBM and the employer and health plan. Second, these executives report that a growing proportion of their employer contracting business is coming through coalitions rather than direct; this is particularly true for the "middle markets" and smaller groups. Third, these consultants are themselves merging, as illustrated by: Willis Towers Watson, Mercer, Aon, Cambridge Consulting, Health Strategies Group, NFP, etc. As a result, more of the PBM's clients are working through (large and merging) intermediaries to negotiate better terms with the PBM. These terms include greater predictability on the pharmacy network side (e.g., network guarantee price points, rebate guarantee price points, stipulated floors for different types of guarantees in price points), whether for brands or generics. On the manufacturer side, they also want steeper discounts and rebate guarantees (minimums or percentages) on a per-claim basis for branded drugs (e.g., $100 per claim) to be passed through. Finally, clients want increased transparency to help them with their drug cost forecasting, reporting, and auditing activities.

Interestingly, many of the large, influential Fortune 500 companies are members of multiple PBM consortia and negotiating alliances. For example, Boeing belongs to the Mercer Coalition and the new Emsana Rx PBM started by the PBGH of California. This may illustrate the difficulty of maintaining employer loyalty and corresponding negotiation leverage of employee lives.

PBMs have responded to these pressures on their profit margins by resorting to activities they pursued in the mid-1990s when manufacturer discounts were threatened (see Chapter 10). Some have entered value-based contracts (e.g., Express Scripts SafeguardRx portfolio) such that they make payments (per prescription fill) to plans if patients are not adherent after the first, second, or third fill. Others have developed clinical-based contracts where plans pay the PBMs when they achieve improvements in patient outcomes and adherence. The PBM benefits because such efforts to improve adherence not only increase the number of scripts written, but they may also reduce the medical benefit side of spending. Another effort is to move patients to specialty pharmacies that may be better able to drive adherence, supply needed refills in a timely fashion, and provide better reporting and analytics to the client. These pharmacies reportedly have lower costs compared to the hospitals and physicians that deliver such drugs.[69]

Some large PBMs have adopted new approaches to dealing with employers that reduce their financial reliance on rebates. In 2018, Express Scripts announced a novel pharmacy benefit contracting model for members of the National Drug Purchasing Coalition (NDPC), a loose consortium of employers.[70] According to Adam Fein, the deal is structured so that Express Scripts will not profit from the funds flowing from the manufacturer to the plan sponsor. Moreover, the PBM's compensation will be fully delinked from drug list prices. Instead, Express Scripts will earn only fixed management fees plus additional at-risk compensation tied to clinical outcomes. There will be no retail network spreads, no dispensing spreads, and 100% pass-through of all manufacturer formulary rebates and administrative fees. In sum, the new approach would disrupt the traditional PBM revenue model built on rebates. No results have been published on this model.

From the Sublime to the Ridiculous

Particularly during the last six years, PBMs have become bigger targets in litigation involving the high cost of drugs and their inappropriate prescribing. Two cases are noteworthy here. First, the PBMs were accused of causing the rise in the price of Epi-Pens used to treat anaphylactic shock. Second, the PBMs were accused of contributing to the widespread use of opioids. Such litigation overlooked the fact that PBMs did not set drug prices and did not prescribe them to patients. The litigation also overlooked the other, manifold and powerful forces behind these rising costs and utilization. The truth about Epi-Pens is detailed below.

The Brouhaha over Epi-Pens

In litigation brought in U.S. District Court,[71] plaintiffs alleged that the major PBMs leveraged their role in the pharmaceutical supply chain to collude with a pharmaceutical manufacturer (Mylan), jointly conspired to hike list prices on Mylan's Epi-Pen, and earn kickbacks from the higher rebates that derive from the higher list prices. The higher prices hurt employees in employer plans that enrolled in HDHPs, who thus had to cover huge deductibles calculated as a percentage of the list price. These employees served as the plaintiffs. The lengthy complaint (108 pages) leveled several charges at the major PBMs that, when compiled, suggest the flow diagram in Fig. 12.5.

Here is the logic behind this flow model, based on what is stated in the complaint. PBMs leveraged their function as "gatekeepers," managing and administering for health insurance plans their drug benefit, drug formularies, and drug benefits contracts. PBMs got "unprecedented" rebates, fees, discounts, or other financial incentives from Mylan in exchange for inclusion on formulary and/or favorable placement on formulary for the Epi-Pen. The PBMs' main criterion for managing formularies were the "kickbacks." Such kickbacks facilitated favorable placement of the Epi-Pen on PBM formularies, which led to higher Epi-Pen sales and market share for Mylan, as well as hikes in the Epi-Pen list price (see Fig. 12.6).

Chapters 9–12 in this volume deal with most of the components in this flow model. Many of these components are real. The flaw is in the labeling of some components and the causal logic connecting them. First, the astute reader will notice that rebates are characterized here as "kickbacks." This chapter has already established that manufacturer rebates paid to PBMs are protected by the safe harbor and, thus, are not kickbacks. The chapter has also established the value of these rebates. Second, the diagram suggests that

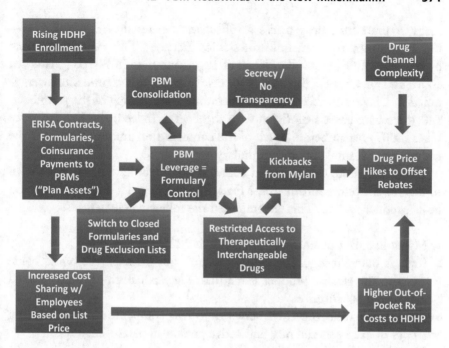

Fig. 12.5 EpiPen litigation claims

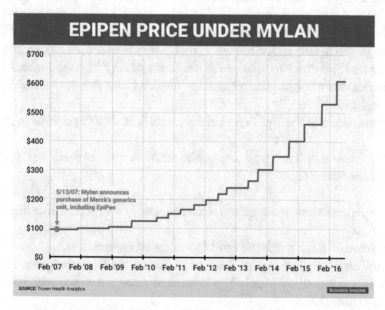

Fig. 12.6 Mylan hiked Epi-Pen price 15 times between 2009 and 2015 by 9–15%, leading to total 400% price surge

manufacturers hike drug prices to offset the rebates they pay to PBMs—i.e., PBMs incentivize manufacturer price increases. This claim was voiced by Mylan's CEO before the House of Representatives in 2016.[72] As noted above and in Chapter 9, there is no evidence for this claim. Moreover, as noted in Chapter 9, there was no correlation in the timing of the price hikes and the rebate levels negotiated with the PBMs. Indeed, the Epi-Pen price hikes (2007) began before much of the consolidation among PBMs and the use of closed formularies and formulary exclusions.

Third, the astute reader should ask what else might have prompted Mylan to hike its list prices for Epi-Pens? First, Mylan enjoyed a dominant position in its product market. This encompassed the following elements:

- Mylan had four patents that ran through 2025.
- Mylan's brand recognition among doctors and patients: the brand name was also the generic product name (like Kleenex). Both of these deterred pharmacist substitution.
- Mylan used anticompetitive activities to halt competitors, entry-delaying tactics to keep generics out, and active pursuit of patent litigation.
- Mylan employed superior marketing practices, including exclusive contracts with schools that was based on favorable federal legislation (*School Access to Emergency Epinephrine Act*). Mylan also successfully lobbied the FDA to change drug labels to include those at risk for reaction in 2010, and added lobbyists in 36 states between 2010 and 2014 to pressure legislatures to require the drug's availability in public schools.
- Epi-Pen was a convergent technology (device and a drug), making it hard to replicate.
- Mylan's share of the Epi-Pen market was 90% in 2007 and 95% in 2015.

Part of this dominant position can be attributed to the weak competition it faced. For example,

- Competitors were weak or non-existent, and never gained much market traction.
- Pharmacies didn't stock the products made by competitors.
- Two PBMs removed one competitor (Adrenaclick) from their formularies.
- Another competitor (Auvi-Q) was yanked from the market in 2015 for faulty operation.
- Such performance and availability issues made physicians skittish to use alternatives.

- Generics showed up only in 2016.

Part of the cause was the presence of third-party insurance coverage, which masked Mylan's price increases. Payers responded to rising Epi-Pen prices by shifting costs to consumers through higher copays. Physicians were not aware of price hikes. Enrollees likewise didn't know about price increases unless and until they lost their insurance coverage or their deductibles jumped or they shifted coverage to HDHPs. Indeed, the lawsuit was brought by HDHP enrollees, and participation in HDHPs sharply increased between 2012 and 2015. In 2017, patients were exposed to list price on only 20% of their prescriptions via coinsurance and deductibles; but that 20% accounted for more than half of patient out-of-pocket expense.[73]

Part of the problem may also have been the executive compensation scheme in place at Mylan. A one-time stock grant allowed executives to be rewarded if Mylan's earnings and stock price met specific goals by the end of 2018. This program started in 2014. Prices start increasing thereafter from 22% annually (2014) to 32% annually (2015)—from $300 to $600 for a two-pack. The CEO's compensation rose from $2 Million to $19 Million.

Following Adam Fein, as the Epi-Pen list prices rose, so did the rebates. Manufacturers ended up paying more and more rebate money into the health insurance system, even when the net amount received by a drug maker was stable or even declining. Employers used these extra payments to offset costs in any area, including hospital and physician payments. Health plans used them to reduce premiums and also offset other healthcare costs. PBMs retained a portion of these rebates as their profits. Wholesalers and pharmacies benefitted, too. Most of the monies went to payers, not the PBMs (who passed back 90%+ of rebates).

In December 2016, the Senate Special Committee on Aging held hearings on the reasons behind the sudden price hikes of off-patent drugs charged by four companies (including Martin Shkreli's Turing Pharmaceuticals).[74] The Committee discovered these companies shared similar business models: acquisition of sole-source drugs that were considered the gold standard of treatment for the targeted condition, small markets served by those drugs that limited entry and competition from other companies, reduced access via closed distribution or specialty pharmacy, and price gouging. The same could be said of Mylan and its pricing of Epi-Pen. These companies raised prices because they could. PBM critics went after the wrong target. The Epi-Pen litigation was thrown out of court by virtue of failing to achieve class certification.

Conclusion

Analysis of the complaints in the Epi-Pen litigation begins to separate fact from fiction in the allegations lodged against the PBMs. Such allegations constitute much of the headwinds considered in this chapter. This analysis suggests that the problem may lie more with the manufacturers upstream than with the players in the retail drug supply chain downstream. The parallel analysis undertaken in Chapter 5—which focused on litigation and Congressional hearings regarding the role of GPOs in the institutional supply chain—concluded that the core problem(s) lay with the small manufacturers making the allegations. This is not meant to demean the manufacturers or fully exonerate the PBMs, but only to highlight the need to carefully examine the specific complaints in each case and whether there are other possible causes.

Notes

1. ERISA is a federal law that sets minimum standards for most voluntarily established pension and health plans in private industry to provide protection for individuals in these plans. ERISA is overseen by the Department of Labor (DOL). ERISA authorizes a participant to sue an entity for breach of its fiduciary duties and to make good on any monetary losses resulting from such fiduciary breach.
2. UnitedHealth Group PBM Litigation (U.S. District Court for the District of Minnesota, 2016). *Negron v. Cigna Health* (U.S. District Court for the District of Connecticut, 2018). Oxford and Optum (U.S. District Court Eastern District of New York, 2019).
3. *Express Scripts/Anthem ERISA Litigation.* Case No. 1:16-cv-03399. United States District Court for the Southern District of New York.
4. Moreover, the health plan Anthem was not a fiduciary because it did not act as a health benefits company setting prices in its role as an insurer. The court also ruled that ERISA plans are neither parties to, nor third-party beneficiaries of, the agreements between health insurers and PBMs.
5. Altarum Institute. *Pharmacy Benefit Managers: Can They Return to Their Client-Centered Origins?* Research Brief No. 23 (January 2018). Available online at: https://www.healthcarevaluehub.org/advocate-resources/public ations/pharmacy-benefit-managers-can-they-return-their-client-centered-ori gins#_edn37. Accessed on April 26, 2022.
6. https://www.sec.gov/Archives/edgar/data/1170650/000119312506217137/dex101.htm. Accessed on April 22, 2022.

7. https://oig.hhs.gov/fraud/cia/agreements/MedcoCIA.pdf. Accessed on April 22, 2022.

8. The Pink Sheet. "Medco Settlement Sets 'Gold Standard' for PBMs Ahead of Medicare Rx" (May 3, 2004).

9. General Accounting Office. *Effects of Using Pharmacy Benefit Managers on Health Plans, Enrollees, Pharmacies.* (Washington, D.C.: GAO, 2003).

10. Office of the Inspector General. *Compliance Program Guidance for Pharmaceutical Manufacturers.* (Washington, D.C.: DHHS, 2003).

11. David A. Balto. "The State of Competition in the Pharmacy Benefits Manager and Pharmacy Marketplaces." Testimony Before the House Judiciary Subcommittee on Regulatory Reform, Commercial and Antitrust Law (November 17, 2015).

12. American Pharmacies. "PBM Issues." Available online at: https://www.aprx.org/-advocacy/pbm-issues. Accessed on April 26, 2022.

13. Department of Justice and Federal Trade Commission. *Improving Health Care: A Dose of Competition* (Washington, D.C.: DOJ & FTC, 2004).

14. U.S. Government Accounting Office. *Federal Employees Health Benefits: Effects of Using Pharmacy Benefit Managers on Health Plans, Enrollees and Pharmacies.* GAO-03-196. (Washington, D.C.: GAO, January 2003).

15. Federal Trade Commission. *Pharmacy Benefit Managers: Ownership of Mail-Order Pharmacies* (August 2005).

16. David Balto and the American Antitrust Institute. *Commentary: The FTC Should Issue a Second Request on Express Scripts' Proposed Acquisition of Wellpoint's PBM Business.* Available online at: https://www.antitrustinstitute.org/wp-content/uploads/2018/08/Express-scripts-white-paper_051220091531.pdf. Accessed on April 15, 2022.

17. U.S. Government Accounting Office. *Federal Employees Health Benefits: Effects of Using Pharmacy Benefit Managers on Health Plans, Enrollees and Pharmacies.* GAO-03-196. (Washington, D.C.: GAO, January 2003).

18. Visante. *Pharmacy Benefit Managers (PBMs): Generating Savings for Plan Sponsors and Consumers* (Pharmaceutical Care Management Association, September 2011).

19. Statement of the Federal Trade Commission Concerning the Proposed Acquisition of Medco Health Solutions by Express Scripts, Inc. FTC File No. 111-0210 April 2, 2012. Available online at https://www.ftc.gov/sites/default/files/documents/public_statements/statement-commission-concerning-proposed-acquisition-medco-health-solutions-express-scripts-inc./120402expressmedcostatement.pdf. Accessed on April 14, 2022.

20. Available online at: https://www.ftc.gov/news-events/events/2022/02/open-commission-meeting-february-17-2022. Accessed on April 27, 2022.

21. State of Competition in the Pharmacy Benefits Manager and Pharmacy Marketplaces. Hearing Before the Subcommittee on Regulatory Reform, Commercial and Antitrust Law of the Committee on the Judiciary. U.S. House of Representatives (November 17, 2015).

22. Craig Garthwaite. Testimony before the House Judiciary Committee Subcommittee on Regulatory Reform, Commercial and Antitrust Law. February 27, 2018.

23. Craig Garthwiate. "Making Markets Work for Pharmaceuticals," *Forbes* (March 12, 2019).

24. Fiona Scott Morton. "Diagnosing the Problem: Exploring the Effects of Consolidation and Anticompetitive Conduct in Health Care Markets" (March 7, 2019). House Judiciary Subcommittee on Regulatory Reform, Commercial and Antitrust Law.

25. Rena Conti, Brigham Frandsen, Michael Powell et al. "Common Agent or Double Agent? Pharmacy Benefit Managers in the Prescription Drug Market," NBER Working Paper No. 28866 (May 2021).

26. Dana Goldman, Geoffrey Joyce, and Yuhui Zheng. "Prescription Drug Cost Sharing: Associations with Medication and Medical Utilization and Spending and Health," *Journal of the American Medical Association* 298(1) (2007): 61–69.

27. Charles Roehrig. *The Impact of Prescription Drug Rebates on Health Plans and Consumers* (Altarum, April 26, 2018).

28. Figures courtesy of Adam Fein, Drug Channels. Taken from presentation by Adam Fein: "PBM Industry Update: Trends, Controversies, and Outlook." (April 22, 2022).

29. Stephanie Kanwit. Prepared Statement. *The Proposed Merger Between Express Scripts and Medco.* Hearing Before the Subcommittee on Intellectual Property, Competition, and the Internet. Committee on the Judiciary. U.S. House of Representatives (September 20, 2011).

30. Amanda Cole, Adrian Towse, Celia Segel et al. *Value, Access, and Incentives for Innovation: Policy Perspectives on Alternative Models for Pharmaceutical Rebates.* Institute for Clinical and Economic Review (March 2019).

31. Gabriela Dieguez, Maggie Alston, and Samantha Tomicki. *A Primer on Prescription Drug Rebates: Insights into Why Rebates are a Target for Reducing Prices* (Seattle, WA: Milliman, 2018).

32. Drug Channels. *The 2022 Economic Report on U.S. Pharmacies and Pharmacy Benefit Managers* (March 2022): Exhibit 168.

33. Drug Channels. *The 2022 Economic Report on U.S. Pharmacies and Pharmacy Benefit Managers* (March 2022): Exhibit 169.

34. Charles Roehrig. *The Impact of Prescription Drug Rebates on Health Plans and Consumers* (Altarum, April 26, 2018).

35. Charles Roehrig. *The Impact of Prescription Drug Rebates on Health Plans and Consumers* (Altarum, April 26, 2018).

36. Amanda Cole, Adrian Towse, Celia Segel et al. *Value, Access, and Incentives for Innovation: Policy Perspectives on Alternative Models for Pharmaceutical Rebates.* Institute for Clinical and Economic Review (March 2019).

37. Cole Werble. "Health Policy Brief: Pharmacy Benefit Managers," *Health Affairs* (September 14, 2017). https://www.healthaffairs.org/content/briefs/pharmacy-benefit-managers.

38. Fiona Scott Morton and Lysle Boller. "Enabling Competition in Pharmaceutical Markets." Center for Health Policy at Brookings. Hutchens Center Working Paper # 30. (May 2017).

39. Gabriela Dieguez, Maggie Alston, and Samantha Tomicki. *A Primer on Prescription Drug Rebates: Insights into Why Rebates are a Target for Reducing Prices* (Seattle, WA: Milliman, 2018).

40. Government Accountability Office. *Medicare Part D: Use of Pharmacy Benefit Managers and Efforts to Manage Drug Expenditures and Utilization.* (Washington, DC: GAO, August 2019).

41. Department of Justice and Federal Trade Commission. *Improving Health Care: A Dose of Competition* (Washington, D.C.: DOJ & FTC, 2004).

42. Patricia Danzon. "Pharmacy Benefit Management: Are Reporting Requirements Pro- or Anticompetitive?" Health Care Management Papers (University of Pennsylvania Scholarly Commons, June 2015).

43. Peter Navarro, Craig Stern, and Rusty Hailey. "Prescription Drug Benefits in Managed Care," In Peter Kongstvedt (Ed.), *Essentials of Managed Health Care* Sixth Edition (Jones & Bartlett, 2013).

44. This chronicle borrows heavily from Ryan Pate. "Future of Discount Safe Harbor for Prescription Drugs Remains Uncertain," ReedSmith Health Industry Washington Watch (December 23, 2021).

45. IMS Institute for Healthcare Informatics. *Medicines Use and Spending Shifts* (Parsippany, NJ: IMS, 2015).

46. Michael Carrier. "A Six-Step Solution to the PBM Problem," *Health Affairs Blog* (August 30, 2018).

47. Visante. *Increasing Prices Set by Drugmakers Not Correlated with Rebates* (June 2017).

48. Alex Brill. *Understanding Drug Rebates and Their Role in Promoting Competition* (MGA, March 2022).

49. Majority Staff Report. *Drug Pricing Investigation.* U.S. House of Representatives Committee on Oversight and Reform (December 2021): p. vi.

50. Drug Channels. "The Big Three PBMs Ramp Up Specialty Drug Exclusions for 2021" (March 22, 2021).

51. Pharmacists Society of the State of New York. "PBM Basics," Available online at: https://www.pssny.org/page/PBMBasics. Accessed on April 26, 2022.

52. Pharmacists Society of the State of New York. "PBM Basics," Available online at: https://www.pssny.org/page/PBMBasics. Accessed on April 26, 2022.

53. T. Joseph Mattingly and Ge Bai. "Reforming Pharmacy Direct and Indirect Remuneration In The Medicare Part D Program," *Health Affairs* (July 19, 2021).

54. Office of the Auditor. *Ohio's Medicaid Managed Care Pharmacy Services - Auditor of State Report* (August 16, 2018). Available online at: https://audits. ohioauditor.gov/Reports/AuditReports/2018/Medicaid_Pharmacy_Services_ 2018_Franklin.pdf. Accessed on April 27, 2022.

55. Jake Klaisner, Katie Holcomb and Troy Filipek. Impact of Potential Changes to the Treatment of Manufacturer Rebates. (Seattle, WA: Milliman. January 31, 2019). Available online at: https://www.regulations.gov/docket? D=HHSIG-2019-0001.

56. Wakely Consulting Group. *Estimate of the Impact on Beneficiaries, CMS, and Drug Manufacturers in CY2020 of Eliminating Rebates for Reduced List Prices at Point-of Sale for the Part D Program* (Aug. 30, 2018).

57. Congressional Budget Office. *Increasing Transparency in the Pricing of Health Care Services and Pharmaceuticals* (Washington, D.C.: CBO, June 2008).

58. David Cutler and Leemore Dafny. "Designing Transparency Systems for Medical Care Prices," *New England Journal of Medicine* 364(2011): 894–895.

59. Amanda Cole, Adrian Towse, Celia Segel et al. *Value, Access, and Incentives for Innovation: Policy Perspectives on Alternative Models for Pharmaceutical Rebates.* Institute for Clinical and Economic Review (March 2019).

60. Peter Orszag, CBO letter to Congress, 2007.

61. David Cutler and Leemore Dafny. "Designing Transparency Systems for Medical Care Prices," *New England Journal of Medicine* 364(2011): 894–895.

62. Svend Albaek, Peter Mollgard, and Per Overgaard. "Government-Assisted Oligopoly Coordination: A Concrete Case," *Journal of Industrial Economics* 45(4) (1997): 429–443.

63. Pharmacy Benefit Management Institute. *Trends in Benefit Design Report* (PBMI, 2017).

64. I wish to thank Mike Taylor, Former Senior Vice-President, Delivery System Transformation at Aon, for his helpful comments on this section of the chapter.

65. Catalyst for Payment Reform. *Aggregated Purchasing of Health Care Services: Lessons Learned and Blueprints for Success.* Available online at: https://www.cat alyze.org/product/aggregated-purchasing-report/. Accessed on May 18, 2022.

66. David Blumenthal, Lovisa Gustafson, and Shawn Bishop. *To Control Health Care Costs, U.S. Employers Should Form Purchasing Alliances.* (New York: Commonwealth Fund, November 2, 2018).

67. Lauren Vela. *Reducing Wasteful Spending in Employers' Pharmacy Benefit Plans* (New York: Commonwealth Fund, August 2019).

68. Leemore Dafny, Kate Ho, and Edward Kong. "How Do Copayment Coupons Affect Branded Drug Prices and Quantities Purchased?" Working paper. (October 21, 2021).

69. AHIP. *Hospital Price Hikes: Markups for Drugs Cost Patients Thousands of Dollars.* (February 2022). Available online at: https://ahiporg-production.s3. amazonaws.com/documents/202202-AHIP_1P_Hospital_Price_Hikes.pdf. Accessed on May 18, 2022.

70. Adam Fein. "PBM Pricing Overhaul: Express Scripts Prepares for a World Without Rebates—But Employers May Not Change," Drug Channels (October 25, 2018).
71. Litigation available online at: https://www.courtlistener.com/docket/629 0515/in-re-epipen-erisa-litigation-klein-v-prime-therapeutics-llc/?filed_ after=&filed_before=&entry_gte=196&entry_lte=196&order_by=asc. Accessed on April 27, 2022.
72. Available online at: https://www.govinfo.gov/content/pkg/CHRG-114hhr g24914/pdf/CHRG-114hhrg24914.pdf. Accessed on April 27, 2022.
73. PhRMA and Amundsen Consulting. *Commercially-Insured Patients Pay Undiscounted List Prices for One in Five Brand Prescriptions, Accounting for Half of Out-of-Pocket Spending on Brand Medicines* (March 2017).
74. United States Senate. *Sudden Price Spikes in Off-Patent Prescription Drugs.* Special Committee on Aging (December 2016).

13

Looking Under the Hood: PBM Contracts

Introduction

The prior chapter discussed the intertwined issues of rebates, administrative fees, and transparency in the relationships between pharmaceutical manufacturers and PBMs. The chapter also discussed the related issue of how these rebates and fees are passed along to health plan clients and how PBMs are compensated for their efforts. These upstream and downstream contracts (and funds flows) lie at the center of the controversy surrounding PBMs.

There are virtually no data on manufacturer-PBM contracts and thus no research evidence. There are also virtually no data on PBM—health plan contracts. This is because, as noted earlier, such contracts and contract terms represent trade secrets. This chapter looks under the hood on these topics using (1) a case example of a real contract struck between one manufacturer and one PBM, as well as the various addenda made to it over time; and (2) another case example of a PBM's downstream contracts with one set of its health plan clients. I do not (and cannot) claim that the contracts or their terms are representative of the universe of such contracts. Other PBMs likely struck different deals with the same upstream manufacturer or downstream health plan. However, such case evidence may help to dispel some of the mystery and misunderstanding about these contractual relationships.

The chapter then examines a series of issues and developments in the contracting relationships between manufacturers, PBMs, and health plans. These include vertical integration between PBMs and health plans, outcomes-based contracts between manufacturers and health plans/PBMs, and analyses

L. R. Burns, *The Healthcare Value Chain*,
https://doi.org/10.1007/978-3-031-10739-9_13

of the value that PBMs provide to payers. Such issues have garnered a lot of attention and warrant a critical appraisal.

Case Example of a Manufacturer-PBM Contract

The Initial Contract

The initial contract was struck as the manufacturer's drug came to market. The contract begins with defining the two parties to the agreement and the terms used therein: client, formulary, national formulary, formulary management services, plan, plan formulary, participating provider, pharmacy & therapeutics committee (P&T), price (WAC), rebate, products, unit, and prior authorization. The next section of the contract covers invoicing for and quarterly payment of rebates and contract administrative fees (CAFs) from the manufacturer to the PBM, as well as the conditions that need to be met for such payment. The next section details the PBM's obligations, which encompass: the approval of the health plans covered under the agreement, provision of copies of the national and plan formularies, inclusion of products in the formulary in accordance with either the PBM's P&T Committee and/or the health plans' P&T Committees, and promise to comply with the provisions of the safe harbor under Social Security [1128B(b) § 42(U.S.C. 1320a—720b(b)]. The following section details the parties' responsibility for records, audit, and confidentiality. The final section covers the contract's term and termination. Exhibits attached to the agreement include: the list of rebated "products" (name, national drug code or NDC, strength), the rebate product schedule with rebate terms and formulas, and a list of the approved health plans to whom these rebates and fees are to be paid.

The agreement was simply called a "rebate and administrative fee agreement," since those were the major contract terms. At that time, there were no competitor products and no prior contracts to compete with. The manufacturer agreed to pay the PBM a rebate of X% off of WAC. The manufacturer also agreed to pay the PBM a CAF of 3%, which would qualify for protection under the safe harbor. The contract stipulated an "agreement period" (certain number of years) and a set of "approved plans" on whose behalf the PBM was negotiating. The contract also specified the products covered under the contract; such products varied in terms of drug dosage and other features. All of the products would receive the same rebate.

Subsequent Amendments

Over the next few years, the manufacturer and PBM entered into a long series of amendments to the initial contract. The first amendment covered the initial contract period and changed the products covered under the contract. Rebates and CAFs remained unchanged.

The second amendment commenced at the termination of the contracting period specified in the first amendment. It, too, would run for the same number of years. However, the contract details now changed to reflect the entrance of competing products. To do so, the contract language now defined a "therapeutic class" of therapeutically-equivalent products.[1] This class included the products made by the manufacturer as well as those made by the new entrants. PBMs value competition. As argued above, they prefer a more crowded therapeutic class that provides more contracting options for health plan clients. If there are limited options and limited new entries to the market, PBMs can consider alternate strategies such as higher rebates and/or "price protection" (i.e., manufacturer price hikes that exceed a percentage threshold require additional rebates to PBM).

The contract specified "tiers" and associated rebates to be paid to the PBM. If the PBM placed the manufacturer's drug on the lowest branded copay tier and if the manufacturer's drug was not disadvantaged relative to other drugs in the same class, the manufacturer would pay the PBM a new, higher rebate of X + 3%. In this case, the manufacturer's drug was considered "equal status." If, however, the PBM placed the manufacturer's drug on the lowest branded copay tier and made it the exclusive brand drug on that tier (and was not disadvantaged), the manufacturer would pay the PBM a rebate of X + 6%. In this case, the manufacturer's drug was labeled the "exclusive brand."

Within a year of signing the second amendment, the two parties inked a third amendment. Instead of two tiers, there were now three—each carrying a different rebate. The base tier designated the manufacturer's drug as "equal status." It lay on the lowest branded copay tier (now labeled 'preferred brand copay tier') and had no restrictions on the drug's use; as before, the rebate was X + 3%. The next tier designated the manufacturer's drug as the "exclusive preferred brand." It again lay on the lowest branded copay tier, but now other competitor drugs lay on the second lowest branded copay tier; the rebate here was X + 9%. Finally, the third tier designated the manufacturer's drug as the "exclusive formulary brand." It lay on the lowest branded copay tier; the drugs of other competitors lay on the second lowest branded copay tier but were either now accompanied by step therapy restrictions or were not covered at all (100% copay). The manufacturer granted an even higher rebate of X +

12% for this tier. One new wrinkle in this amendment was the addition of "price protection," equal to 110% of WAC.[2]

A year later, the two parties entered a fourth amended contract. This contract utilized the same three tiers found in the fourth amendment. One change here was a slight reduction in the price protection clause to 108% of WAC.

Another year later, the parties inked their fifth amended contract with a shorter duration. This contract anticipated possible "generic availability," and stated that the manufacturer's branded drug was still eligible for rebates and administrative fees until a generic competitor is added to the maximum allowable cost (MAC) list used by the patient. In the presence of a generic, the rebates on the manufacturer's products have risen to $X + 6\%$ (equal status), $X + 16\%$ (exclusive preferred brand), and $X + 26\%$ (exclusive formulary brand). Another change was an additional slight reduction in price protection to 107% of WAC.

Within another year and a half, the parties entered their sixth amended contract. There was now a single rebate of $X + 26\%$ for the manufacturer's drug to be on the lowest branded copay tier (the preferred brand). The price protection amount remained stable but the CAF rose to 4% of WAC.

Just months later, the parties entered their seventh amended agreement that broadened the "therapeutic class" members to take account of generic entry. The contract now included two formulary positions (tiers with their own rebate options) for generics and two for branded drugs. Another change was a slight reduction in price protection to 106% of WAC.

Contract Analysis

Formulation of the Formulary

Over time, the contracts shifted from a single tier to multiple tiers that could include: generic, equal status, exclusive preferred brand (lowest copay), and exclusive formulary brand. As noted above, however, health plan clients could construct their own tiers and formularies if they chose to do so. The PBM and its clients followed *several steps* in placing a branded drug on their formulary. They first received the dossier and insert on the drug from the manufacturer. These materials were then reviewed by the PBM's clinical team, who perhaps met with the manufacturer to discuss the clinical trials and results encapsulated and summarized in the product insert.

The PBM's Clinical Committee next met to decide the "clinical threshold levels" (CTLs) for drug inclusion/exclusion from the formulary. These reflected which bucket to place the drug in, based on clinical need and the clients' interests: e.g., must add drug, may add drug, recommend not adding drug. The criteria for deciding whether or not to include the drug on the formulary included net cost, the drug's reception in the marketplace, physician prescribing patterns, and whether the therapeutic class was crowded (allowing more options). After this, the PBM's P&T Committee examined the recommendations of the Clinical Committee and voted on what CTL to place the drug on. This Committee, which included physicians from the outside community, decided on the tiers in the formulary. Health plan clients could also ask the PBM's P&T Committee to develop step edits for specific drugs or drug classes as a utilization management tool (e.g., use the generic drug first, use the preferred branded drug on formulary first before using the non-preferred brand). The P&T Committee's overall goal was to develop a cost-effective formulary that the health plan client could offer to its members. Finally, the pharmacy directors at the health plans decided upon the national formulary as well as customized it for their own formularies.

Variability in Formularies and Tiers

The diversity among the PBM's health plan clients lends itself to immediate variability in their formularies and contract tiers. The plans have different benefit plans, different copays, and different coinsurance structures. There are thus thousands of benefit plans. They also utilize different utilization management tools (e.g., step therapy, prior authorization, quantity limits, formulary exclusion or "NDC block").

Moreover, each health plan may represent employers who are both fully insured and self-insured. As a result, both plans and employers can ask their PBM for more cost-effective formularies, including product exclusions. Moreover, clients did not have to abide by the terms of the negotiated contracts. For example, in the fourth amended contract above, the presence of the middle exclusive tier did not require the PBM's clients to exclude the new competitor from their formularies, although they could resort to utilization management tools. In sum, there is considerable heterogeneity in PBM contracts.

Contract Heterogeneity

As noted above, there is considerable variation in the contracts that PBMs can negotiate with manufacturers upstream and health plan clients downstream. This variation pervades many significant elements and terms of these contracts. These include the following:

- PBM rebate negotiated with the specific manufacturer for the specific drug class;
- PBM contract administrative fee negotiated with the specific manufacturer for the specific drug class;
- PBM retained rebate with the specific health plan client;
- PBM retained contract administrative fee with the specific health plan client;
- PBM reimbursement level paid to a specific network pharmacy;
- Patient cost-sharing by drug placement on the PBM formulary;
- Contract negotiation terms for fully insured versus self-insured employers;
- Contract negotiation terms for insourced versus outsourced PBMs.

There is also variation in the transacted prices between (1) wholesalers and pharmacies, (2) State Medicaid programs and pharmacies, and (3) manufacturers and wholesalers. The net effect of all of this variation is difficulty in drawing firm generalizations and conclusions regarding PBM earnings. It also suggests that the health plan's pharmaceutical spending (and total healthcare spending) is the aggregation of myriad decisions and actions taken by multiple stakeholders, most of whom are unrelated to the health plan sponsors and most of whom have different incentives that may have nothing to do with cost or quality. Apportioning any responsibility for plan cost or quality to their PBM partners may be an impossible task. Thus, observers may not be able to fully lift up the hood on PBMs.

Contract Evolution

It should be noted that while these amended contracts are effective at a given date, they are the result of negotiations that occur throughout the year. New negotiations and thus new amendments constantly occur as new competing drugs come into the market. Moreover, these new amended contracts may not keep pace with the continual price hikes in the manufacturer's drug—which can occur multiple times in a given calendar year.

For example, in preparation for the second amended contract, the PBM and manufacturer each proposed different numbers of tiers with different rebate levels. In general, the PBM would request bids from the manufacturer, who would respond with letters of intent, to which the PBM would respond regarding desired changes in certain tiers or exclusivity provisions. For example, the PBM gave the manufacturer two options: (1) lowest preferred brand with no formulary exclusions and equal access to other brands on that same tier, in exchange for a rebate of X + 5%, *or* (2) lowest preferred brand with all other brands and generics on a higher, more expensive tier with no exclusions, in exchange for a rebate of X + 7%. The manufacturer then counter-proposed three options, which were then modified by the PBM that excluded one of the options. During this back-and-forth negotiation, the PBM exchanged improved formulary placement for a higher level of rebate. The PBM emphasized the cost-effectiveness of the formularies that its health plan clients offered and that the higher rebates were in their clients' interest.

All of these negotiations took place during a time interval where a new competitor was launching its own product. The PBM had a series of parallel negotiations with the competing manufacturer regarding tiers, rebates for each tier, any formulary restrictions, any prior authorization requirements, and price protection terms. The PBM sought price protection to model the product's costs for its health plan clients. The PBM emphasized to the new entrant that the contract must include price protection in order to be added to the formulary. The PBM would then seek to leverage the resulting agreement with the new competitor to extract further contract concessions from the incumbent manufacturer in the form of an "improved offer."

As stated above, these negotiated tiers and formularies are not necessarily what the PBM's clients adopt and utilize. In some PBMs, health plans can structure their own formularies with tiers different from what is depicted above. Health plan clients may also request that the PBM use "step edits" for certain drugs or drug classes as a utilization management tool. Such edits may stipulate (a) try the generic drug first, or (b) use the branded drug on the formulary first before using a non-preferred brand drug. Despite the contract and amendments, the PBM and its health plan clients have discretion in moving drugs around the classifications or removing them entirely from the formulary.

By the time of the fifth agreement, another manufacturer had entered the market, meaning there were now three competitors. The PBM notified the incumbent it had other vendor options who were offering aggressive rebates to get on contract, and that the incumbent should factor this into its negotiations going forward. This likely explains the steep bump in the rebates paid over the fourth and fifth amended contracts. All three manufacturers now offered higher rebates to the PBM to be more competitive.

By the time of the sixth agreement, one of the manufacturer's new competitors had withdrawn their drug from the market (due to reported adverse events). The loss of competition prompted the manufacturer to change the contract terms from three tiers to a single tier (preferred brand rebate). In its view, there was no reason to have anything other than an "on formulary" tier. The PBM was, nevertheless, still able to negotiate an X + 26% rebate for its health plan clients.

Contracting Friction

The case example suggests that the contracts struck between manufacturers and PBMs take place over many months with considerable back-and-forth in proposals and terms. These negotiations become more intense and involved as new competitors enter the market and begin to crowd the therapeutic class. These deliberations are characterized as "arms-length negotiations" between suppliers and buyers, not as collusive relationships. Some executives at the PBM characterized manufacturers as "not easy to work with."

Moreover, these negotiations are further complicated by the unilateral price hikes made by the manufacturers. According to the PBM's executives, decision-making on price hikes remains with the manufacturer, who can engage in "egregious price activity" and "extreme drug pricing." PBMs feel they must respond to, mitigate, and curb these price increases on behalf of their health plan clients. In response to such price hikes, the PBM communicated to the respective manufacturers that it wished "enhancements" to the contract terms, such as higher rebates or price protection levels. The latter explains the fall in the price protection percentage. In this manner, the PBM sought to protect its health plan clients from inflation in drug prices and offer them some cost-sharing to offset such increases. PBM executives also stressed that they were never informed when the manufacturer was going to hike its prices; they also noted that the manufacturer's negotiators also did not know. This poses a huge problem for the PBM who now faces "concerned clients" who want to know what their PBM is going to do about it.

Frequent and unannounced price hikes by manufacturers are not uncommon. As shown in Fig. 13.1, Biogen persistently hiked the price of its multiple sclerosis drug *Avonex* (interferon beta-1a) over a long period of time (2005–2018). The story is similar for other biotechnology drugs which, despite many going off patent, still enjoy strong intellectual property (IP) rights and, thus, continue to earn high revenues. Figure 13.2 lists the number of price hikes and the percentage change in price for several drugs between 2012 and 2017.

These price hikes can be timed to coincide with the manufacturer's revenue goals, the anticipated entry of a new competitor, and/or the exit of a competitor already in the market. PBMs seek price protection particularly when the manufacturer has not taken a price hike recently and one is due. For their part, manufacturers are not crazy about price protection terms and may not offer it if they have "leverage"—e.g., high market share and a near monopoly in the therapeutic class. They may approve such terms only in the face of what they call "a higher level of management" on the part of the PBM: i.e., more exclusivity for their product with the addition of step edits.

U.S. Avonex Price Hikes

Date	% Increase	Approximate Price
May 2005	5%	$15,500
December 2005	9%	$16,900
June 2006	9%	$18,400
February 2007	5%	$19,400
August 2007	6%	$20,500
November 2007	12%	$23,000
June 2008	9%	$25,050
November 2008	9%	$27,300
March 2009	9.5%	$29,900
December 2009	7.5%	$32,100
February 2010	5.5%	$33,900
July 2010	4.5%	$35,400
December 2010	6%	$37,500
May 2011	6%	$39,800
December 2011	6.5%	$42,350
March 2012	8.5%	$45,950
August 2012	6%	$48,600
November 2012	4.5%	$50,900
June 2013	7.5%	$54,700
November 2013	8%	$59,100
September 2014	4%	$62,000
March 2015	5.5%	$65,700
August 2015	6%	$69,600
December 2015	4%	$72,300
May 2016	5%	$75,900
January 2017	8%	$82,000
January 2018	8%	$88,500

Source: PriceRx

Fig. 13.1 Avonex drug price hikes over time (*Source* PriceRx)

Drug	Time Period	# Hikes	% Price Change
Abilify	2012-2017	5	163%
Valcyte	2012-2017	8	187%
Avonex	2012-2017	11	193%
Rebif	2012-2017	12	215%
Byetta	2012-2017	9	229%
Enbrel	2012-2017	12	245%
Humira	2012-2017	12	248%
Percocet	2012-2017	12	298%
Wellbutrin XL	2012-2017	20	596%
Evzio	2014-2017	2	652%

Fig. 13.2 Catch-up race with drug price-hikes

Confidentiality

As noted above, the manufacturer's negotiating team dealing with the PBM can be unaware of future price hikes by their company. Manufacturers do not tell the PBM what their negotiations are with other PBMs; likewise, the PBM does not communicate the content of the negotiations with other PBMs.

PBM View of Rebates

According to the PBM executives involved in these negotiations, the PBM does not rely on the negotiated rebates for its own profit growth. Instead, the PBM pushed for rebates to lower drug costs for its clients who can then offer more cost-effective benefits to their enrollees. In sum the goal is to lower the drug spend and "manage to the lowest net cost for our clients." For this reason, these PBMs return their net cost savings to their health plan clients.

Case Example of a PBM-Health Plan Contract

PBM Services

The PBM served as the health plan clients' exclusive manager (and agent) for the sole purpose of negotiating and obtaining rebates from drug manufacturers. It had a contract term that was similar in length to the manufacturer contract, but without all of the addenda. Pricing terms were renegotiated annually, while other amendments were adopted as needed. Their contract identifies the two parties as "independent contractors."

The PBM contracted to provide a set of basic core services to all clients:

- Rebate management
- Benefit design support
- Electronic processing of pharmacy claims
- Eligibility services
- Client services
- Sales support
- Billing and reconciliation
- Consumer directed health plan tools and
- Web-based tools.

The price for *processing claims* in one contract year was set at roughly $1.20 per claim; the net price for the provision of the core services above amounted to roughly $1.30 per claim. The PBM also offered an additional set of core services, which could vary across health plan clients. These included:

- Formulary management
- Pharmacy network
- Account management
- Clinical management
- Clinical services
- Reporting services and
- Contact center services.

Each of these services had an associated price, ranging from roughly two cents to ten cents per claim, depending on the service. The *clinical management* services included member education, utilization management, drug utilization review, a patient adherence program, and an efficiency program that combined medical and pharmaceutical data to do predictive modeling for patients with significant gaps in their medications. *Utilization management*, in turn, encompassed step therapy, quantity limits, retrospective drug utilization review, and formulary exceptions—all designed to encourage proper drug use to improve outcomes and reduce drug cost.

With regard to *formulary management*, the PBM's P&T Committee helped to establish a national formulary for its health plan clients to use. Representatives from the health plan clients were allowed to attend the P&T Committee meetings and vote on such issues. They also had total discretion on whether or not to use the national formulary or customize it to suit their individual purposes and needs. The contract explicitly stated that the clients determine the formularies used by their plans.

Finally, the PBM offered ancillary services that were priced differently. These included:

- Clinical review
- Contracted medical review
- Paper claims processing
- Network participant (pharmacy) auditing and
- Additional clinical services.

PBM Compensation

The health plan clients utilized several funding mechanisms for the PBM's services. These mechanisms included the rebates collected by the PBM from manufacturers, the CAFs paid to the PBM by manufacturers, transaction fees paid to the PBM by participating network pharmacies, and income from the PBM's mail-order operation. The health plans permitted the PBM to retain a percentage of the rebates it collected. The amount here was formally designated by the plans as one funding mechanism to be used as an offset to the plans' price for core PBM services. This explains the small difference in the PBM's per-claim price for claims processing and its per-claim net price for core services. Similar to the GPOs, the CAFs were capped at 3% of WAC. The contract also stipulated that the PBM was prevented from re-labeling any rebates paid to it by the manufacturer as other types of payment that the PBM might retain for itself.

This compensation approach could change over time. For example, in one contract period, the CAFs might be passed along to the health plan clients; in another period, they may be partially retained by the PBM as an offset to the prices the plans paid to the PBM for its various services. That is, the funding mechanisms could change in a few years' time.

Regardless of the approach, the PBM was required to share with health plan clients all data on rebates and fees collected from manufacturers in quarterly reports. The claims processing fees and other PBM service fees changed considerably from year-to-year. The contract also gave the health plans the right to inspect the PBM's books and records, as well as audit the PBM's contract performance. Government agencies could also audit the PBM.

Pharmacies were paid by the health plans a contracted amount, negotiated roughly every two years. This amount varied according to the particular retail pharmacy chain and its claims volume. The contracted amount represented a combination of ingredient cost and dispensing fee. For drugs in multi-source product categories, ingredient cost was based on maximum allowable cost;

otherwise, ingredient cost was calculated as AWP less a percentage discount. The PBM's agreement with each of its health plan clients involved differences in the amount paid to pharmacies.

The contract with plan sponsors stipulated whether or not the PBM was allowed to engage in spread pricing with network pharmacies. It left it to the discretion of the plans whether or not to use pharmacy spreads as a PBM funding mechanism. Here again, however, this stipulation could change from one year to the next.

Enrollee Out-Of-Pocket Costs

The health plans typically included enrollee out-of-pocket costs for services and drugs utilized. The magnitude and form of these out-of-pocket payments were determined by the plan sponsor, sometimes as a result of explicit negotiations with specific employers or unions. As noted earlier, these drug payments took the form of fixed co-pays, coinsurance payments, and deductibles—what clients refer to as plan design. The fixed co-pays set the amount the enrollee would pay to fill the prescription; they could vary in amount across formulary tiers, but not by drug within a given formulary tier.

Vertical Integration of PBMs With Health Plans

Adversarial Relationships: Anthem—Express Scripts Litigation

Relationships between PBMs and their health plan clients are not always cordial. In 2009, Express Scripts entered a 10-year contract with Anthem to provide exclusive pharmacy benefits. In 2016, Anthem filed a lawsuit arguing that its contract with Express Scripts guaranteed competitive prices for prescription drugs. Anthem or a third-party consultant it retained would conduct a market analysis every three years to determine how competitive the PBM's pricing was; if the pricing was not competitive, then Anthem could renegotiate pricing terms with its PBM. In 2011–2012, Anthem commenced the first round of these renegotiations, which lasted for nearly one year and strained the relationship between the two parties, before they reached an agreement. However, Anthem concluded it was overcharged $3 Billion a year for several years. Anthem began a second round of renegotiations in 2014 by demanding $15 Billion in price concessions from its PBM, and then notified it of a breach of contract. Express Scripts countered that the insurer was responsible to produce a market analysis of drug prices that would serve as the basis of negotiations. It also stated that it earned well below than $3 Billion annually from the PBM agreement and thus could not meet Anthem's demand.

In 2017, Anthem announced it would not renew its contract with Express Scripts. This meant a loss of 20% of the PBM's revenue. In early 2018, a U.S. District Court Judge dismissed Anthem's suit, stating that its contract did not explicitly state that its PBM would ensure competitive pricing; Express Scripts' only obligation was to negotiate based on data the insurer provided.

Downstream Effects of the Litigation

The litigation had several downstream effects—for both insurers and PBMs. First, Anthem had to replace its big-three PBM. In October 2017, Anthem announced its plan to launch its own in-house PBM, IngenioRx, in collaboration with CVS Health; the latter would provide Anthem with claims processing, point-of-sale engagement, and prescription fulfillment services. In 2019, Anthem launched IngenioRx, which reportedly accounted for one-fifth of Anthem's revenue, and served as the insurer's PBM vehicle to target self-insured employers.

Second, Express Scripts faced the loss of its largest health plan client (Anthem) and questions about its future as a stand-alone PBM in an era of consolidation. In April of 2017, Express Scripts reported in its quarterly earnings announcement that it did not expect Anthem to renew its contract; indeed, in January 2019, Anthem terminated the contract a year earlier than scheduled. Express Scripts was soon courted by another insurer, Cigna. Cigna was rebounding from its failed horizontal merger with Anthem: on February 8th of 2017, the District Court for the District of Columbia sided with the Department of Justice in blocking the horizontal merger of Cigna and Anthem. In March of 2018, Cigna announced its plan to acquire Express Scripts for $67 Billion and pursue a vertical merger instead. The deal closed in early December.

The February 2017 District Court ruling also blocked the proposed merger of Aetna and Humana. Within months of the decision, Aetna likewise pursued a vertical merger with CVS Health. CVS Health executives sold the merger to investors as a strategy to develop health hubs for Aetna enrollees at CVS drugstores.

Historical Rationales for Vertical Integration

The combinations of (1) Cigna with Express Scripts and (2) Aetna with CVS Health meant that all three major PBMs now had health plan partners. UnitedHealth had previously formed Optum in 2011 by combining its existing pharmacy benefit and care delivery services within the company. Its PBM operations stemmed from its 2005 acquisition of PacifiCare, a health plan which had a pharmacy benefit manager.

Such combinations are known as "vertical integration." Management researchers often argue that the central decision in corporate strategy concerns "make versus buy": i.e., make it in house or buy it in the marketplace. There are advantages to each approach (see Fig. 13.3), such as: using the company's managerial hierarchy versus market forces to discipline and coordinate the two parties' behaviors, seek the advantages of collaboration versus the benefits of specialization, diversify versus focus, etc. With regard to pharmaceutical benefits, the two approaches are known as "carve-in" versus "carve-out" (see Chapter 9). There is no clearly defined calculus regarding which option to take in the make-vs-buy decision. One has to calculate the costs and benefits of each option—and be satisfied with the tradeoffs.

Taking a long-term perspective, the PBM sector began using a carve-in approach when staff-model HMOs served as their own pharmacy benefit managers working under a capitated budget constraint (see Chapter 10). The objective was to provide comprehensive coverage of both inpatient and outpatient services, including prescription drugs, at an affordable cost ("assurance" rather than insurance). Stand-alone PBMs developed as the staff-model HMOs waxed and then waned in popularity. These PBMs evolved a different set of benefits and services that attracted both employers and health plans as

Market Approach: Outsource	Vertical Integration: Insource
• Invisible hand	• Visible hand
• Specialization	• Coordination
• Scale economies	• Substitution
• Reduce Px drug prices	• Reduce MD, hospital costs
• Focus	• Diversification
• Carve-out	• Carve-in

Fig. 13.3 Vertical integration: insurers and PBMs

clients; while some PBMs could be carved in, many were carved out of the health plan. United's acquisition of Pacificare in 2005 marked the beginning of the current trend to the carve-in approach (back to the roots). United's move was motivated by its desire to acquire Pacificare's health plan operations; the PBM came with the deal. By virtue of acquiring Pacificare's 3.3 million enrollees, United increased its enrollment stature (25.7 million lives) relative to its larger competitor Wellpoint (27.7 million lives), diversified geographically into the West (where Pacificare was located), gained traction in the Medicare risk market, and helped it to prepare for the coming Medicare drug benefit. The deal was also part of the M&A frenzy among health plans in the 2005–2006 era (see Fig. 11.7). Thus, the sector has experimented with both approaches over time, oftentimes based on rationales specific to that point in time that may or may not be based on Fig. 13.3.

Indeed, there have been many rationales for such vertical integration offered over the past decade. These rationales reflect the period's *Zeitgeist* (spirit of the times): care coordination, manage the continuum of care, disease management, chronic disease management, use big data and data analytics to (a) stratify enrollees by their risk level and then (b) identify and intervene for those at high risk. Figure 13.4 illustrates the hypothesized "theory of action."

Vertical integration has also been partly motivated by the growth in spending on specialty drugs. Such spending is split between the pharmacy benefit and the medical benefit. Patients taking specialty medications tend to have more expensive conditions that health plans need to manage. Health plans have argued that spending under both benefits is large and roughly equal in level, thus requiring close management of both. While there is some overlap, specialty drug spend for different disease categories tend to dominate one benefit over the other (e.g., multiple sclerosis on the pharmaceutical benefit side, oncology on the medical benefit side).

The vertical integration strategies were also motivated by the Department of Justice's move to block Aetna's and Cigna's prior horizontal merger efforts (with Humana and Anthem, respectively). The latter observation suggests

Fig. 13.4 Causal model of action in vertical integration of the pharmaceutical and medical benefit

that, at least initially, the underlying rationale for vertical integration was simply growth, not necessarily the specific merger partner.

Current Rationales for Vertical Integration

Adam Fein (at Drug Channels) and Eric Percher (at Nephron Research) have done perhaps the best job of articulating the current vertical integration movement in the pharmaceutical supply chain. Fein suggests that the issue may be control over the drug channel. Vertically integrated payers/PBMs/providers "are poised to restructure U.S. drug channels by exerting greater control over patient access, sites of care/dispensing, and pricing. If they can effectively coordinate their sprawling business operations, they will pose a substantial threat of disruption to the existing commercial strategies of pharma companies."[3] Such control could result from (1) channeling of enrollees to the specialty pharmacies and providers inside these vertical firms, (2) rewarding providers for formulary compliance, and (3) greater management and utilization control over provider-administered drugs and the buy-and-bill practices of in-house physicians.[4]

In his latest 2022 Report,[5] Fein summarizes some additional specific goals of vertical integration that are mentioned by Percher[6]:

- Because healthcare services (e.g., pharmacy) are not subject to the same risk-based capital requirements or profitability regulations as insurers, integration can allow them to retain a greater share of revenues.
- Patients who are on expensive specialty medications have high overall medical spending which can benefit from the combined pharmacy and medical benefit.
- Vertical integration enables insurers to tap into the growing market for specialty pharmaceuticals and perhaps control downstream pharmacy assets.

Challenges to Vertical Integration

In the same report, Fein is also careful to point out the challenges facing the strategy of vertically integrating insurers with PBMs and pharmacies.

- There is no guarantee that an insurer which owns its own PBM and pharmacy operations is assured that prescribing physicians are aware of any pharmacy network restrictions and can direct their drug dispensing.

- Employers may be skeptical about whether the savings from combining the pharmaceutical and medical benefit will accrue to them. This may slow down their adoption of such plans.
- Hospitals have been entering the specialty pharmaceutical business and acquiring oncologist practices. The market for physician-administered drugs is thus shifting from physician offices to hospital outpatient departments. Alternate sites of care such as home infusion account for a portion of the medical benefit spend as well as Medicare Part B spend. Hospitals may enjoy a competitive advantage over integrated insurers in this fragmented market.
- Some prior insurer/PBM/pharmacy joint ventures (e.g., those involving Prime Therapeutics, Centene) and prior insurer-PBM acquisitions (UnitedHealth and DPS) have unwound.

Nevertheless, not all health plans sponsors seem to be beating a path to such integrated plans. According to Drug Channels, 77% of small employers (<1000 workers) contracted with a combined health plan/PBM in 2021. By contrast, only 53% of mid-sized employers (1000–5000 workers) and only 33% of large employers (>5000 workers) did so; the latter two categories were more likely to carve-out the PBM.[7]

Consequences of Vertical Integration

Vertical integration may have important consequences. According to analysts, one outcome of this vertical integration will be more aggressive price competition among health plans and PBMs.[8] This could come about by the merging parties' bundling of medical and pharmacy benefits, which would entail a diminution of carve-out contracts between employers and PBMs for just the pharmacy benefit. This would put pressure on the margins of the free-standing PBMs, because vertically integrated insurers would discount their in-house PBM's services to win the combined business. Any stand-alone PBM contracts would need to lower prices to remain competitive.

Such integration might also reduce heterogeneity in health plans' approaches to strategic alignment with PBMs (which used to vary along an outsourcing-insourcing continuum). Greater homogeneity in strategic alignment across dyads of health plans and PBMs would increase their competitive rivalry.

Such integration also potentially signaled that PBMs would focus increasingly more on the specialty pharmacy business for their profitability and, conversely, focus increasingly less on retained rebates. PBMs have passed along a much greater share of these rebates to health plan sponsors over the past decade, from 75% in 2013 to 90% in 2018. According to some PBM industry presentations, rebates apply to 70% of their branded pharmacy scripts, which in turn account for only 10% of total scripts. Rebates have also diminished in importance due to Medicare's growing share of retail prescription drug spending (from 18% in 2006 to 30% in 2017) and the low amount of rebates retained by PBMs in Part D PDPs.

Finally, growing vertical integration between health plans and PBMs will likely reduce the transparency of freestanding PBMs' financial results. Consider UnitedHealth Group, which had revenues of $226.2 Billion in 2018. For 2018, revenues at its OptumRx subsidiary were $69.5 Billion. Interpreting the OptumRx figure is challenging, because: (1) it includes a combination of prescription revenues from its own mail/specialty pharmacies plus external retail network pharmacies, (2) it is reported net of rebates, (3) it *excludes* the value of members' out-of-pocket payments from revenues from retail network dispensed prescriptions, but *includes* the value of these member payments from prescriptions dispensed by its in-house pharmacies, and (4) it includes revenues of $39.4 Billion (57%) from services provided to other subsidiaries, e.g., UnitedHealthcare.[9]

United's 10-K statement from 2021 includes a depiction of the conglomerate's total revenues. The data indicate huge growth between 2018 and 2021 in the revenues of OptumRx (from $69.5 Billion to $91.3 Billion) and Optum Health (from $24.1 Billion to $54.0 Billion); they appear to be the growth drivers in UnitedHealth's total revenues (from $226.2 Billion to $287.6 Billion). United's biggest revenue source (60%) is the company's Medical and Retirement insurance segment. OptumRx may become increasingly more or less dependent on enrollees outside the parent company. It is difficult to determine the sources of United's profits coming from internal versus external sources given the conglomerate structure and the mix of customers.

Ride into the Danger Zone?

Vertical integration has become a popular strategy in the healthcare ecosystem. Many of these recent vertical integration efforts include providers (e.g., physicians, ambulatory surgery centers or ASCs, retail clinics) as well as insurers, pharmacies, and PBMs. A prominent illustration is United-Health Group which includes the insurer UnitedHealth, its in-house PBM (OptumRx), and its Optum Health division, which employs or contracts with 50,000 physicians and owns a chain of ASCs and urgent care centers.

Another is CVS Health, which encompasses Aetna, CVS pharmacies, and their retail clinics. Such provider markets are typically more fragmented than the core pharmacy and PBM businesses, offer another possible revenue stream, and can involve the key prescriber.

The healthcare sector is in the midst of its second or third iteration of vertical integration involving different providers (e.g., hospitals and physicians) as well as insurers and alternate care sites. The historical evidence has already been published, weighed in the balance, and found wanting.[10] It is not a pretty picture. Most of the vertical combinations that fall into one of three categories—physicians with insurers, hospitals with insurers, physicians with hospitals—suffered from disappointing performance and, sometimes, huge losses. There are an estimated fifty different reasons why combinations of providers with insurers do not work; worse yet, it may only take one of those reasons to sink the deal.

How should one evaluate vertical integration between firms in adjacent stages in the healthcare value chain (see Fig. 2.1)? According to strategy researchers, vertical integration (insourcing) makes more sense than outsourcing when the following *general* conditions hold:

- There are few firms in the adjacent stage
- There is a need to make transaction-specific investments in the upstream/downstream firm
- The integration ensures access to needed inputs
- There is a need for coordination between the firms in the adjacent stages
- The adjacent stages are similar in their optimal scale
- The two stages are strategically similar
- There is high certainty in market demand
- There is low risk in the reliability of the trading partner
- There is low need to continually upgrade capabilities.

Moreover, the following *specific* conditions must also be met **if** the vertical integration is to confer a competitive advantage over rivals:

- The integration achieves coordination and collaboration that other firms cannot accomplish
- The integration improves the joint performance of all value chain activities under one roof
- The integration leverages resources and capabilities across the combined firm
- Ownership is needed to capture all of this value

- Culture clashes between the two firms can be avoided and
- Executives can get the two firms to work together.

The bar is pretty high. Most firms cannot and do not hurdle this bar. What is even worse, most executives do not even consider the general market and specific firm conditions needed to make vertical integration succeed. Vertical integration is a specific type of corporate diversification. The evidence base for the performance of diversified firms is not much better than that for vertically integrated firms. Related diversification outperforms unrelated diversification; but, focus may outperform related diversification. The key question is how big is the overlap between the value chains of the firms that are integrating; the secondary question is whether the overlap occurs in the most important stages of their value chains. This requires a comparison of the health plan's value chain (see Fig. 13.5) and the PBM's value chain (see Fig. 11.14). Another key issue which most strategists fail to consider is this: given the popularity of vertical integration and the large number of firms adopting this strategy, just where is the competitive advantage?

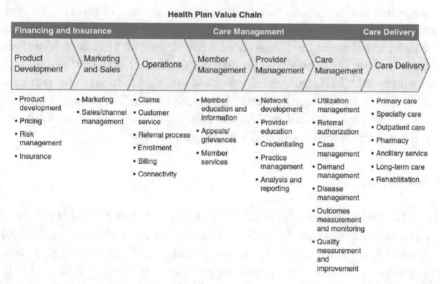

Fig. 13.5 Value chain activities of a health plan (*Source* Brad Fluegel, presentation to Wharton School)

Outcomes-Based Contracting

Rationale

Rather than vertically integrating, PBMs and health plans have entertained a different strategy: jointly engage with pharmaceutical manufacturers upstream in what is variously called value-based contracting (VBC) or outcomes-based contracting (OBC). Such contracts seek to tie drug payments to manufacturers for specific clinical, quality, or utilization outcomes that their drugs help to achieve. This development is somewhat similar to changes in the relationships between PBMs and employer consortia (discussed in Chapter 12), but reflects the general movement from volume to value.

As a recent, visible example, Amgen entered outcomes-based contracts with several payers (e.g., Harvard Pilgrim, Cigna) for its LDL (low-density lipoprotein) cholesterol-lowering drug *Repatha* in 2015–2017. Amgen promised initial discounts with additional rebates if its drug failed to achieve LDL cholesterol reductions similar to those observed in clinical trials; the more recent contract promised a full, money-back guarantee for patients who experienced the rare event of a heart attack or stroke. Amgen entered such agreements because the benefits of its drug relative to statins were unknown at the time; the contract thus constituted a risk-sharing agreement.[11] Moreover, the results from the clinical trial (known as FOURIER) were not "whopping": the reduction in LDL cholesterol led to only modest reductions in such clinical events as cardiovascular death, myocardial infarction, and stroke. Not surprisingly, payers balked at Amgen's initial list price of $14,600/year for the drug. Amgen then countered with its plan for OBC.

Prevalence

In 2021, Avalere released the results of its online survey of 51 health plans and PBMs, covering roughly 59 million lives.[12] Slightly more than half (56%) of payers had such a contract, but the prevalence of contracting was quite concentrated: 12% of these payers reported having 10 + such contracts in place, double the number of payers in 2020. At the same time, there was a decline in the percentage of payers with 5–10 contracts from 19 to 6%. The percentage of payers with 2–5 contracts remained stable at 33%. This suggests the growing use of these contracts among a small subset of health plans; nearly half of health plans surveyed did not utilize such contracts.

Why such a low percentage and low prevalence? Implementation of outcome-based contracts requires significant investments in infrastructure (data collection and analytics capabilities), new partnerships with various stakeholders, and staff training (among others). Therefore, the opposite trend observed between the 5–10 and 10+ categories (noted above) may be an indication that some plans that have had successful experiences with OBCs are reaching efficiency and scalability and are willing to engage in more OBCs. It is also important to note that OBCs are more relevant for some drugs than for others: e.g., high variability in patient response to the drug, a clear link between the drug and the outcomes studied, a reasonably short time period between the drug's administration and the drug's outcome, and the availability and ease of collection of appropriate outcomes data.

Of course, there are likely other reasons for the low prevalence of such contracts that the Avalere report does not mention. Perhaps they don't work. A recent empirical analysis suggests why this might be the case[13]:

- There is general skepticism among health plans that such OBC programs deliver savings.
- Such contracts are limited to commercial payers rather than public payers. Medicaid's stipulation that its program should receive the best price may serve as a price floor that limits manufacturers' ability to offer larger rebates.
- OBC programs face tradeoffs between pursuing rigorous outcome metrics versus using feasible data sources (e.g., in claims databases). Some outcome metrics must be assessed outside of claims data using laboratory test reports, which are expensive and burdensome for health plans to collect.
- Outcome measures are typically set with results from the clinical trials as the hurdle rate. However, patient adherence rates are typically higher in clinical trials than in community practice, making it hard for health plans to hit the adherence thresholds before the rebates kick in.
- Such disparities turn the OBC into a mechanism for the manufacturer to sell more of its drugs and earn a higher market share. Any additional rebates incurred from failing to meet clinical thresholds are more than offset by higher revenues from increased sales and utilization.
- Manufacturers often view OBC and disease management programs as vehicles to (1) ensure coverage of their drugs, (2) sell more of their drugs, and (3) increase their market share in a therapeutic category. Executives from one of the largest pharmaceutical companies met with Wharton School researchers and explained their disease management program this way: there are three classes of patients—those who don't have the condition that our drug addresses, those who do have the condition and do use our drug,

and those that have the condition and do not use our drug; our disease management program targets that last class.

- Another related issue is that OBC may simply represent an alternative mechanism for manufacturers to get (*and keep*) their drug on the PBM formulary, perhaps obtain exclusive or preferential formulary status, and perhaps relegate their competitors' drug to less preferential status.

- OBC benefits manufacturers in the short term but payers in the long term. The manufacturer gets formulary access now; payers have to wait to assemble and analyze data on patient outcomes later on.

- Manufacturers compete on the clinical benefits and quality their drug provides. They are, thus, focused on the numerator of value. By contrast, payers focus on cost and, thus, the denominator of value. The two parties are not focused on the same metrics.

- Outcome metrics may not move the rebate needle that much in comparison to other rebate drivers such as the relative market power of the contracting parties (what some call "the kick-butt ratio")[14] and the degree of competition in the particular therapeutic category. If that is the case, then these contracts will not be a priority among payers since they will not generate sufficient savings, or savings commensurate with the effort and infrastructure (noted above) needed to generate them. Researchers suggest that payer contracts with manufacturers lack the same degree of leverage in their contracts with providers.[15]

- Like pay-for-performance (P4P) and the sustainable growth rate (SGR) discussed below, OBC may be window dressing—i.e., a public relations effort to show that you are trying to do something about the issues of value and rising drug costs—that really serves to do nothing more than postpone the problem and "kick the can down the road".[16] Nevertheless, at the outset of its OBC, Amgen claimed this was not a gimmick but rather part of its commitment to VBC.[17]

- Indeed, early analysis of Amgen's money-back guarantee on *Repatha* indicated a low cost-effectiveness to this approach. The analysis suggested that, in the most optimistic scenario, payers would be refunded the price of the drug for only 2.15% of their patients. More likely, payers would see a reduction in the drug's price from $9,100 to $9,061.[18] Moreover, it would cost $1.6 Million to prevent one myocardial infarction and $5 Million to prevent one stroke.

- OBC may need to consider using "total cost of care" as the appropriate metric and combine data on both pharmaceutical and medical benefit spending to determine the drug's net benefit on downstream utilization of other healthcare services.

Journalists concluded that OBC is not the solution, or even a panacea, to high prices or the rising cost of prescription drugs.[19] Instead, OBC reflects bargaining between manufacturers and payers, who are trading off improved patient access to novel drugs today in exchange for rebate and saving guarantees tomorrow.

Background Issue in OBC: What is Quality?

One should be cautious in drawing any conclusions from this current trend. The use of VBC/OBC has been underway since the late 1990s; the related movement from "volume to value" has been going on for nearly two decades.[20] One major issue is the difficulty in defining "value" that meets the needs and interests of the two contracting parties. Value is simply defined as outcomes (or, alternatively, quality) divided by cost. What quality is, however, is problematic. Quality is actually a vector of **lots** of measures that are loosely linked and weakly correlated with one another. What is quality to one party in a VBC is not likely to be viewed as quality by the other party.[21] Here are just some of the issues with the numerator in value:

- Too many measures
- Most measures focus on "process of care" rather than outcomes
- Numerator is an effort to re-cast clinical practice guidelines (that doctors don't follow)
- These measures do not predict patient outcomes
- These measures do not value what patients value
- These measures are tied to discrete conditions
- These measures do not address multiple chronic conditions and
- These measures track a few outcomes that patients care about (mortality, morbidity).

Moreover, as academic researchers have asked, "if we don't know what value is, then how do we pay for it?".

Questionable Success in Using VBC in PBM Contracts

When applied to contracts between PBMs/health plans and manufacturers, there are some natural issues that require tackling. First, PBMs need to combine the administration of their formulary drugs with particular services that get patients to adhere to the drug therapies over time. That is, they must combine their product with services. Research shows that organizations have difficulty in reaping scale economies from service programs: that is, while product manufacturing may scale, service provision by employees does not. Second, patients' medication adherence has been a thorny problem for decades. PBM executives report that only half of the patients adhere to evidence-based drugs that are prescribed by their physicians. For example, following myocardial infarction, the adherence rate after two years is 40% for statins, 53% for beta-blockers, and 50% for ACEI/ARB (Angiotensin-Converting Enzyme Inhibitor or Angiotensin Receptor Blocker).[22]

The question is, how can the PBM—which lacks a personal relationship with the patient and does not see the patient in an office-based setting—improve on this? One solution adopted by both PBMs and health plans is the use of "big data" and "predictive analytics" to identify which patients to contact and define an intervention strategy for them. A major obstacle here is the growth in the number of poly-chronic patients—those on 5+ medications for chronic conditions, with multiple daily doses—which can decrease adherence rates to as low as 30%. To date, PBMs have relied on service strategies of patient engagement and pharmacy advisors—with mixed success. Other approaches include greater communication between the physician and the pharmacist, as well as the use of direct messaging from the pharmacy and PBM to the patient, and greater physician engagement in pharmaceutical therapy.[23]

One should generally be aware of any promised benefit that relies on the engagement of patients, providers, or both. Research shows that hospitals have sought after provider engagement for decades with little or no success.[24]

Shaky Track Record of VBC in Healthcare Delivery

Another issue is the lack of stellar performance of such contracting strategies. Part of the initial push for VBC began with P4P models. P4P operated by giving providers a small payment bonus if they hit specified quality targets. The P4P strategy served as an escape hatch from the SGR problem in physician payment enacted as part of the 1997 Balanced Budget Act (BBA). The solution postponed the annual SGR cut and ushered in P4P, even though there was little research evidence that paying providers to meet specific performance indicators improved the quality of care. An early P4P program targeted at *hospitals* was the Medicare Premier Hospital Quality Incentive Demonstration (Premier HQID), a six-year P4P demonstration funded by CMS from 2003 to 2009. Premier HQID hospitals could receive a 1–2% bonus or, starting in 2006, penalty adjustments, based on performance on 33 measures.

This demonstration was one of the most widely studied P4P programs. Evidence on its ability to improve quality or reduce costs was tepid, at best.[25]

The program subsequently morphed into the Physician Quality Reporting Initiative (PQRI), and again evolved under the Patient Protection and Affordable Care Act (PPACA) into the Physician Quality Reporting System (PQRS) and a larger P4P initiative called the Medicare Hospital VBP Program (HVBP). Beyond HVBP, CMS launched two additional P4P programs: the Hospital Readmissions Reduction Program (HRRP) and the Hospital-Acquired Conditions (HAC) program. Like HVBP, they were designed to move hospitals away from fee-for-service to value-based payment by withholding some Medicare reimbursements to penalize providers based on their performance on certain quality metrics. HRRP and HAC programs were thus strictly penalty programs. HRRP issued a penalty of up to 3% for hospitals with excessive avoidable readmissions, while HAC issued a 1% penalty for hospitals whose performance was in the bottom quartile for hospital acquired infections. Research suggested that a hospital's performance under VBP was not correlated with its performance under other alternative payment programs, like ACOs. In sum, P4P has been a dud in moving the needle on either quality (the numerator of value) or cost (the denominator of value). Efforts to reduce "low value care" have also not fared well.

PBM Value Proposition for Payers

Health Plans' Return on Investment

An industry-sponsored study suggests that payers earn a healthy return on their investment in services rendered by their PBMs. Visante conducted a study on behalf of the Pharmaceutical Care Management Association.[26] They concluded that:

- PBMs will help reduce prescription drug costs for more than 266 million Americans in 2017. Those served include: 187 million commercial plan enrollees, 41 million Medicare Part D enrollees, and 38 million enrollees in Medicaid managed care plans.
- PBMs save payers and patients 40–50% on their annual prescription drug and related medical costs compared to what they would have spent without PBMs. These savings fall into three buckets: 31–36% savings on negotiated lower unit cost, 11–15% savings on a more affordable drug mix, and up to 2% savings via appropriate utilization.

- PBMs save payers and patients an average of $941 per person per year—a reduction from $2125 annual cost per capita without PBMs to $1184 per capita with PBMs. Of the $1184 in net costs using PBMs, consumers pay only $355, less than one-third of the total.
- For every $1 spent on their services, PBMs reduce costs by $6. For every $100 in drug spending, the PBMs' gross margin is 6–8% ($7) while the costs without PBMs would be $45.
- Annual per capita PBM savings differ across payers: Medicare Part D ($2341), commercial ($747), and Medicaid managed care ($449).
- PBM negotiations with manufacturers reduce the cost of a branded drug from $350 to $268. Of the $268 in net cost, manufacturers capture $235 (88%), while PBMs capture $12 (4%) for their services.
- Over the next 10 years, PBMs will help prevent 1 billion medication errors, primarily in the Medicare population, and largely through the use of drug utilization review.
- Through specialty pharmacy services, PBMs will help extend and improve the quality of life for patients with multiple sclerosis and rheumatoid arthritis by approximately 1 million quality-adjusted life years (QALYs) over 10 years.
- PBMs improve drug therapy and patient adherence in diabetes patients, helping to prevent some 480,000 heart failures; 230,000 incidents of kidney disease; 180,000 strokes; and 8,000 amputations annually.

Employer and Health Plan Satisfaction with PBMs

Part II of this volume presented survey data documenting the continued satisfaction of hospitals with their GPOs. Surveys of health plans and employers suggest growing satisfaction with their PBMs. Data collected by the Pharmacy Benefit Management Institute (PBMI) and then the Pharmaceuticals Strategy Group (PSG)—using a sample of roughly 25% health plans and 50% employers—show that overall satisfaction steadily increased from 7.5 in 2014 to 8.0 in 2018 and then to 8.2 in 2021 (on a 10-point scale).[27] Satisfaction levels were higher for smaller PBMs with 20 million members or less than for larger PBMs with more than 20 million members (8.9 versus 8.1). The satisfaction scores of the different PBMs in each size category varied somewhat, similar to the ratings for the GPOs (see Chapter 8).

Employers rated some aspects of their contracted PBMs higher than others on a variety of service dimensions, as well as on their core and non-core PBM functions (see Chapter 9). With regard to service, PBMs received their highest 2021 rating on "meeting financial guarantees" (8.2) and delivery of promised

Mean Overall Satisfaction Rating, PBMs with >20M Members

Source: Pharmaceutical Strategies Group, 2021 Pharmacy Benefit Manager Customer Satisfaction Report

Fig. 13.6 Employer/plan satisfaction with PBMs (*Source* Pharmaceutical Strategies Group, 2021 Pharmacy Benefit Manager Customer Satisfaction Report)

services (8.2); they received their lowest score on "delivering products that are differentiated in the marketplace" (7.4) and "flexibility" (7.6). With regard to their core functions, PBMs received their highest ratings on "retail network options" (8.7); they received their lowest ratings on "website and mobile apps for members" (8.0). With regard to their non-core functions, PBMs received their highest evaluations on "account team acts as knowledgeable strategic advisor" (8.4) and "formulary management" (8.1); they received their lowest rating on "point of sale rebates for members" (7.4). Satisfaction with their PBM as a proactive partner in managing drug spend was in between (7.8).

The survey also inquired about PBM transparency, a major issue in the PBM debate. Overall satisfaction with PBM transparency was moderate (7.3); there was a slight decrease in the percentage of employers reporting complete or somewhat complete transparency between 2017 and 2021 (91% versus 88%). Dissatisfaction with PBM transparency revolved around contract language, contract complexity, rebate disclosure, and unclear/limited reporting. Among those who were satisfied with financial transparency, the main satisfiers were the ability to audit rebates all the way back to the manufacturer, better and more frequent reporting, and having rebate information available at the drug level.

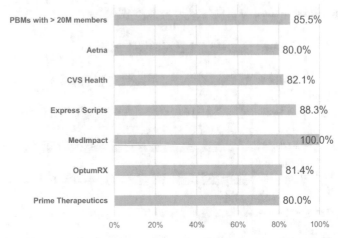

Fig. 13.7 Employer/plan—PBM goal alignment (*Source* Pharmaceutical Strategies Group, 2021 Pharmacy Benefit Manager Customer Satisfaction Report)

Are PBMs Commodities?

One of the more intriguing findings from the 2021 PSG Survey summarized above is the low level of employer/plan satisfaction with their PBM "delivering products that are differentiated in the marketplace." This harkens back to the core issue of Chapter 8: are intermediaries like GPOs differentiated or commoditized? The PSG Survey begins to answer this question for PBMs, albeit using a smaller sample of respondents that lacks statistical power to do more sophisticated analyses.

Figure 13.6 provides the overall satisfaction scores with the large PBMs (greater than 20 million members). The survey data indicate identical, moderate satisfaction ratings by clients of the three largest PBMs (CVS Health, Express Scripts, Optum), lower ratings for two other PBMs (Aetna, Prime Therapeutics), and a higher rating for one other PBM (MedImpact).[28] The pattern of results in Fig. 13.6 is largely repeated in the PBM satisfaction scores on specific dimensions concerning PBM service functions, PBM core functions, and PBM non-core functions. This suggests that, according to their clients downstream, the major PBMs deliver roughly equivalent performance. When these results are compared with the prior survey conducted by PBMI in 2018, one finds that overall satisfaction levels have risen slightly (from 7.8 to 8.1), although there is variability in the trend among the major

PBMs and along the specific dimensions.[29] Similar results have been observed among the GPOs (see Chapter 6).

A slightly different pattern of results is observed for perceived goal alignment reported by PBM clients. Here there is more differentiation (see Fig. 13.7). Two of the three largest PBMs lie below the average for all plans with more than 20 Million members, while the third lies above the average. Overall, the data from the two figures suggests that there is some level of perceived commoditization, but also some indication that clients view the PBMs as their agents.

Notes

1. Medi-Span classifies drugs into therapeutic classes and manages their NDC codes. The therapeutic class can be thought of as a "market basket" of similar, competing drugs. If a drug has no competitor, it is not assigned to a market basket.
2. In order to protect PBM's and their clients from manufacturer increases in the WAC price, which reduce the rebate amount, the PBM can negotiate a price protection rebate. This includes stipulation of a maximum allowable price by which the manufacturer can raise its WAC price. If the drug's WAC price is raised above this maximum amount, the manufacturer must pay a rebate on the same.
3. Adam Fein. "Insurers + PBMs + Specialty Pharmacies + Providers: Will Vertical Consolidation Disrupt Drug Channels in 2020?" Drug Channels (December 12, 2019).
4. Here is what Adam Fein has to say. With regard to *buy-and-bill utilization management:* Ownership of clinics enables much greater control over provider-administered drugs—including opportunities to tighten utilization management, negotiate greater rebates from manufacturers, and drive greater biosimilar adoption. For example, *Optum's MedExpress clinics currently offer infusion therapy in select Florida and Indiana locations for people with UnitedHealthcare or Humana insurance*…commercial health plans try to move infusions to lower-cost sites of care. This is typically achieved with utilization management strategies that guide patients to lower-cost and/or better-performing sites of care. But employed physicians and in-house clinics make site-of-care management much easier. With regard to *buy-and-bill channel management*, a physician office or clinic that is owned by a vertically integrated organization can be required to obtain provider-administered specialty pharmaceuticals from the company's own specialty pharmacy. This practice is called white bagging. It has displaced buy-and-bill for a significant share of provider-administered drugs in commercial health plans. By owning the infusion site, the insurer bypasses the challenge of getting hospitals to accept

white bagging. Adam Fein. "Insurers + PBMs + Specialty Pharmacies + Providers: Will Vertical Consolidation Disrupt Drug Channels in 2020?" Drug Channels (December 12, 2019).

5. Drug Channels Institute. *The 2022 Economic Report on U.S. Pharmacies and Pharmacy Benefit Managers*. Section 12.3.

6. Eric Percher. *Optum Launches 'Emisar' Contracting Entity; Navitus Aligns with Ascent* via *Prime* (Nephron Research, July 26, 2021). Eric Percher. *A Closer Look: Cigna/ESI Makes Waves with Ascent Contracting & Econdisc Sourcing GPOs* (Nephron Research, January 23, 2020).

7. Drug Channels Institute. *The 2022 Economic Report on U.S. Pharmacies and Pharmacy Benefit Managers*. Exhibit 80.

8. Drug Channels Institute. *The 2022 Economic Report on U.S. Pharmacies and Pharmacy Benefit Managers*.

9. Drug Channels Institute. *The 2022 Economic Report on U.S. Pharmacies and Pharmacy Benefit Managers*.

10. David Dranove and Lawton R. Burns. *Big Med: Megaproviders and the High Cost of Healthcare in America*. (Chicago, IL: University of Chicago Press, 2021). Jeff Goldsmith, Lawton R. Burns, Aditi Sen, and Trevor Goldsmith. *Integrated Delivery Networks: In Search of Benefits and Market Effects*. (Washington, D.C.: National Academy of Social Insurance, 2015). Lawton R. Burns, David Asch, and Ralph Muller. "Vertical Integration of Physicians and Hospitals: Three Decades of Futility?" in Mark V. Pauly (Ed.), *Seemed Like a Good Idea: Alchemy versus Evidence-Based Approaches to Healthcare Management Innovation* (Cambridge, UK: Cambridge University Press, 2022). Lawton R. Burns and Darrell P. Thorpe. "Why Provider-Sponsored Health Plans Don't Work." *Healthcare Financial Management: 2001 Resource Guide*: 12–16. 2001.

11. Elizabeth Seeley, Susan Chimonas, and Aaron Kesselheim. "Can Outcomes-Based Pharmaceutical Contracts Reduce Drug Prices in the US? A Mixed Methods Assessment," *Journal of Law, Medicine and Ethics* 46 (2018): 952–963.

12. Kristin McCarthy, Lauren Cricchi, Elizabet Schvets et al. *Avalere Survey: Over Half of Health Plans Use Outcomes-Based Contracts* (Avalere, November 4, 2021).

13. These explanations are drawn from the following sources. Elizabeth Seeley, Susan Chimonas, and Aaron Kesselheim. "Can Outcomes-Based Pharmaceutical Contracts Reduce Drug Prices in the US? A Mixed methods Assessment," *Journal of Law, Medicine and Ethics* 46 (2018): 952–963.

14. The kick-butt ratio (KBR) is defined as the percentage of Firm A's business that comes from its trading partner Firm B divided by the percentage of Firm B's business that comes from Firm A. The higher the value, the more leverage that Firm B has over Firm A: i.e., Firm B is kicking butt.

15. Joseph Kannarkat, Chester Good, and Natasha Parekh. "Value-Based Pharmaceutical Contracts: Value for Whom?" *Value in Health* 23(2) (2020): 154–156.

16. Lawton R. Burns and Mark V. Pauly. "Transformation of the Healthcare Industry: Curb Your Enthusiasm?" *Milbank Quarterly* (March 2018) 96(1): 57–109.

17. John LaMattina. "Outcomes-based Pricing Not a Panacea for High-Priced Drugs," *Forbes* (March 27, 2019).

18. Immaculada Hernandez. "Revisiting Outcomes-Based Pricing Propositions for the PCSK9 Inhibitor Evolocumab," *JAMA Internal Medicine* 177(9) (2017): 1388–1390.

19. John LaMattina. "Outcomes-based Pricing Not a Panacea for High-Priced Drugs," *Forbes* (March 27, 2019).

20. Lawton R. Burns and Mark V. Pauly. "Transformation of the Healthcare Industry: Curb Your Enthusiasm?" *Milbank Quarterly* (March 2018) 96(1): 57–109.

21. Lawton R. Burns. *The U.S. Healthcare Ecosystem* (McGraw-Hill, 2021): Chapters 5, 7.

22. Troyen Brennan. Presentation to the Wharton School (Fall 2015).

23. Troyen Brennan. Presentation to the Wharton School (Fall 2015).

24. Lawton R. Burns, Jeffrey Alexander, and Ronald Andersen. "How Different Governance Models May Impact Physician-Hospital Alignment." *Health Care Management Review* 45(2) (2020, April/June): 173–184.

25. Ash Jha, Karen Joynt, John Orav et al. "The Long-Term Effect of Premier Pay for Performance on Patient Outcomes," *New England Journal of Medicine* 366 (2012): 1606–1615. Gregory Kruse, Daniel Polsky, Elizabeth Stuart et al. "The Impact of Hospital Pay-for-Performance on Hospital and Medicare Costs," *Health Services Research* 47(6) (2012): 2118–2136.

26. Visante. *The Return on Investment (ROI) on PBM Services* (November 2016). Available online at: https://www.pcmanet.org/wp-content/uploads/2016/11/ROI-on-PBM-Services-FINAL.pdf. Accessed on April 28, 2022.

27. Pharmacy Benefit Management Institute. *2018 Pharmacy Benefit Manager Customer Satisfaction Report*. (PBMI, 2018). Pharmaceutical Strategy Group. *Pharmacy Benefit Manager Customer Satisfaction Report* (PSG, 2021).

28. MedImpact is the largest independent PBM and touts itself as being more member-focused, perhaps reflecting its founding by a pharmacist several decades ago. By contrast, Prime Therapeutics is the PBM that serves many Blue Cross/Blue Shield plans.

29. Pharmacy Benefit Management Institute. *2018 Pharmacy Benefit Management Customer Satisfaction Report*. (2018).

Part IV

Summary and Conclusion

14

Conclusion

Revisiting Chapter 1 and the Volume's Purpose

Chapter 1 alerted readers that they were about to enter "dark territory." The allegations leveled against GPOs and/or PBMs included: monopoly power and anticompetitive behavior, collusion with manufacturers, exclusive contracts, market foreclosure of small and innovative firms, impeded patient access to needed technologies, conflicts of interest, excessive fees and outsized profits, kickbacks and secret rebates, lack of transparency and full disclosure, artificially high product prices, reduced provider discretion in decision-making, harms to patient care and quality, and higher consumer costs.

This volume has sought to investigate these claims along several avenues. These have included an understanding of the historical chronicle of both GPOs and PBMs, my own academic research and that of others, industry reports, an understanding of the product sectors in healthcare (e.g., pharmaceuticals, medical devices), analysis of litigation undertaken against GPOs and PBMs in the courts, an understanding of the role such intermediaries play in the wider healthcare ecosystem, and the insights regarding these intermediaries of several seasoned observers (who serve as my co-authors).

Beyond an investigation of these allegations, this volume has also undertaken the following four-fold task:

© The Author(s), under exclusive license to Springer
Nature Switzerland AG 2022
L. R. Burns, *The Healthcare Value Chain*,
https://doi.org/10.1007/978-3-031-10739-9_14

- describe the agency roles of middlemen in U.S. healthcare and the industry context in which they operate
- describe the roles that GPOs/PBMs play in the broader healthcare industry
- chronicle the historical development of GPOs/PBMs and functions they have assumed
- analyze the host of performance issues surrounding the GPOs/PBMs.

I have also tried to answer some basic questions. What "value" do GPOs and PBMs provide, and to whom? Who benefits from the market leverage they exert? Are the agency goals of these two intermediaries consistent with and supportive of the missions of their downstream customers (the principals)? How do such intermediaries solve the dilemmas posed by the "iron triangle" (i.e., balancing the goals of cost, quality, and access)? Does their behavior conform to ethical guidelines developed by government and industry trade groups? The sections below provide some summary answers to these questions.

Lessons of History

Critics of GPOs and PBMs rarely, if ever, bother to confront the historical narrative that led to the formation of these organizations. One likely reason is that, until now, this narrative has never been pulled together from the various archival and eyewitness sources. Doing so requires a lot of work; this volume has devoted at least four chapters to the endeavor. Another, more likely reason is that such a narrative would not support the allegations and conclusions of the critics. The lessons from this narrative are detailed below.

GPOs and PBMs Have Historically Served the Interests of Local Providers

As documented in Chapter 4, GPOs were (a) established by local councils and consortia of hospitals as (b) voluntary associations with the mutual aim to (c) pursue joint purchasing of commonly needed products with the further aim of (d) reducing their input costs. Many of these early organizations were cooperatives organized at the community level as efforts to develop mutual leverage (over suppliers) for their mutual benefit. The overall goal was to reduce cost.

One might argue that community hospitals began the same way as voluntary, community organizations designed to provide community benefits.

Then, years later, these hospitals transformed into "megaproviders" that have acted in ways that reduced competition, increased costs, and possibly reduced quality.[1] There is one major difference, however. GPOs, unlike hospitals, do not make anything, sell anything, or price anything.

As documented in Chapter 10, the early PBMs began the same way as local cooperatives that provided medical and pharmaceutical services to community members on a prepaid, capitated basis through physician group practices. They were not so much healthcare insurance as they were healthcare assurance providers. They were typically organized around health maintenance organizations (HMOs) that took responsibility not only for the medical benefit but also for the pharmacy benefit. They did so for two reasons: to cover the total healthcare needs of their enrollees and manage these needs under an affordable budget constraint. The early PBMs were thus tied to providers; they were also tied to health insurers, just like they are today. Subsequent generations of PBMs operated under a different, convenience-based model to make it easy for consumers to obtain their prescriptions at local pharmacies without having to submit the bills to their insurer. The overall goal was to improve access to needed services. And, like the GPOs, the PBMs do not make anything, sell anything, or price anything.

There is another important point here. GPOs and PBMs served providers of health services, but they did not supply these health services or charge for them. Thus, they are at least one (or more) degrees of separation from where healthcare costs and quality are rendered. Efforts by critics to lay the responsibility for rising healthcare costs or harms to patient quality at their feet are misguided.

GPOs and PBMs Seek Leverage Over Product Suppliers

GPOs (first) and PBMs (later) sought to amass purchasing volume to negotiate better (lower) prices from product manufacturers. GPOs aggregated the purchases of independent hospitals; HMO-PBMs aggregated the prescription orders of scores (and then hundreds) of physicians on their medical staffs. Both routed these orders through a centralized negotiating hub to contract as "one" with manufacturers. The game has always been one of "leverage" over suppliers and exchange of higher volumes from buyers for lower unit price offered by suppliers. Moreover, this game became more important for survival and customer service as input cost pressures (e.g., due to wartime shortages, rising drug costs) and/or reimbursement pressures (e.g., emanating from managed care, public payers) intensified. When squeezed downstream, GPOs and PBMs sought to squeeze manufacturers upstream.

GPOs and PBMs Serve as the Agents of Providers and Health Plans, Respectively

GPOs and PBMs seek to exert leverage over suppliers, not over their hospital or health plan sponsors. Their actions are thus consistent with being agents of these hospitals and health plans. This agency role is confirmed in surveys of hospitals and health plans, which express fairly high satisfaction levels (with GPOs and PBMs, respectively) and indicate a concordance in their goals and interests with those of their agents. It is also confirmed in field research studies funded by the National Science Foundation. It is further confirmed by the facts that (a) suppliers have been historically skeptical of intermediaries like GPOs and PBMs, (b) suppliers have sought to render them ineffective, (c) GPOs and PBMs believe that supplier competition is always in their interest, (d) suppliers do not contract with GPOs and PBMs when they do not have to (due to lack of competition), (e) the relationships between suppliers and these intermediaries are characterized as "adversarial," and (f) suppliers raise prices unilaterally "because they can," which the intermediaries seek to counteract.

GPOs and PBMs Have Been Subject to Considerable Federal Oversight

Both sets of intermediaries have been subjected to considerable scrutiny by the U.S. Congress (House and Senate hearings), the Congressional Budget Office, and various Federal Agencies (e.g., Federal Trade Commission, or FTC; Government Accountability Office, or GAO; Office of the Inspector General, or OIG). Such scrutiny had the beneficial effect of the development of "codes of conduct" for both intermediaries in the 2004–2005 period. None of this scrutiny has since resulted in any subsequent change in legislation or regulatory oversight of either intermediary. This latter point suggests that the codes of conduct may have served their purpose, as some research actually suggests. As a long-time observer of the U.S. healthcare ecosystem, I cannot think of another sector withstanding the barrage of accusations listed at the outset of this chapter.

GPOs and PBMs Have Utilized Many of the Same Contracting Tools for Decades

As noted in earlier chapters, certain business practices of the GPOs and PBMs have come to irritate their critics in the new millennium. For GPOs, these include contract administrative fees (CAFs) paid by manufacturers, sole-source contracts, compliance and committed purchasing contracts, and product bundling. For PBMs, they include drug formularies, CAFs paid by manufacturers, discounts and rebates from manufacturers, narrow pharmacy networks, and spread pricing. What the critics do not recognize is that most of these contracting tools have been in place for decades without causing much of a stink or uproar. That is likely because these tools served the economic interests of their sponsoring organizations downstream (hospitals, health plans), who developed them to deal with competitive and reimbursement pressures. Moreover, none of the GPO and PBM contracts were ever publicly disclosed—just like many contracts between buyers and sellers in the private sector—to encourage price discounting by manufacturers (and inhibit any collusion among them).

What a difference a millennium makes! Since the early 2000s, these contracting tools and business practices have been re-cast as suspect, clandestine, hidden, secretive, pernicious, self-serving, ripe with conflicts of interest, anticompetitive, and, if not illegal, then certainly immoral. The chapters in this volume detail when these contracting tools and business practices surfaced, how they were packaged and by whom, and why they developed. As I and my colleagues have argued, these were local solutions crafted to address local financial problems by local (and, often cooperatively organized) institutions. While these small, grass-roots organizations have grown and consolidated over time to become bigger players, they still serve the needs of their sponsoring members and the broader healthcare ecosystem. Their critics and other aggrieved parties in the healthcare supply chain feel otherwise. It is somewhat ironical that, at least for the GPOs, they may be returning to their roots as local and regional cooperatives.

GPO and PBM Business Models Have Changed Over Time

Finally, the historical narrative presented above (see, in particular, Chapters 3 and 11) demonstrates that the business models and revenue sources of these two intermediaries have changed over time. GPOs are now concentrating on their professional services (advisory/consulting and analytics) business; PBMs are now heavily focused on the dispensing of specialty drugs. These are their main growth areas. Yet, GPO and PBM critics continue to attack these intermediaries for the strategies heavily pursued in the past: contract administration fees (for GPOs) and manufacturer rebates and pharmacy network management (for PBMs). Although still a sizeable portion of their revenues, such strategies appear to be on the wane.

Static vs. Allocative Efficiency: Winners and Losers

GPOs and PBMs have sought to serve the interests of hospitals and HMOs/health plans, respectively; as noted above, they do not serve manufacturers. Thus, by definition, GPOs do not seek to maximize the welfare of small medical device startups—such as those that have taken the GPOs and their trading partners (incumbent manufacturers) to court. The GPOs do have a decided interest in having a competitive playing field among manufacturers (both big and small) but do not see their core mission as preserving or enhancing such competition. Likewise, PBMs do not seek to maximize the welfare of the independent retail pharmacies—such as those that have testified against them before Congress.

The FTC and researchers have implicitly recognized that these intermediaries promote what researchers call market (or static) efficiency. However, these intermediaries do not necessarily promote allocative (or distributive) efficiency whereby goods and services are optimally distributed among buyers. This is because (a) the intermediaries generate efficiencies and surpluses and (b) the surpluses accrue as "rents" to the intermediaries but not necessarily to all buyers downstream. For example, the GPOs collect contract administrative fees (CAFs) from suppliers and pass along the bulk of them to their hospital members. What hospitals do with these rebates has never been analyzed; many industry observers believe they help to prop up low hospital margins (see Chapter 3). Through 2019, the FTC has not undertaken any action against the GPOs in the past two decades regarding these practices, other business practices, or combinations.[2] Indeed, a recent analysis conducted by former senior FTC officials suggests that (1) GPOs and their CAF-based funding save money and are pro-competitive, and (2) eliminating the CAFs would raise costs for providers, taxpayers, and consumers.[3] The FTC did not concern itself with whether small medical device manufacturers thrive or struggle in the presence of GPOs.

Similarly, the FTC has not weighed in on PBM contracting practices, intervened to investigate their combinations, or analyzed their impact on independent pharmacists. PBMs generate savings (net brand price reductions) that benefit health plans and ERISA plan sponsors overall, but not necessarily all of their plan participants. Whether the latter benefit depends on what the health plans and plan sponsors do with rebates passed along by the PBMs—e.g., whether or not they utilize "pass through" pricing and, in particular, point-of-sale rebates. Such a solution rests more with the health plans. PBMs also utilize spread pricing whereby they earn a profit based on the difference between what plans pay them for prescription drugs and what they pay pharmacies for those drugs. Mandatory pass-through pricing can also partly address this issue by leaving PBMs with an administrative fee instead of a spread. Such a solution requires actions by health plans in the private sector and federal/state legislative changes in the public sector (Medicaid). With regard to the latter, in Spring 2020 the Congressional Budget Office (CBO) estimated that a federal proposal to require pass-through pricing would produce federal savings of $929 Million over 10 years—i.e., less than a 1% drop in federal Medicaid prescription drug spending.[4] By contrast, during the prior year, the CBO estimated that President Trump's proposal to end the safe harbor legal protection for PBM drug rebates received from manufacturers under the Part D program would increase Part D premiums and increase federal spending by $177 Billion between 2020 and 2029.[5]

To be sure, some stakeholders in the retail drug supply chain may have been disadvantaged by the PBMs' spread pricing. FTC officials note, however, that such "stakeholders frequently attempt to co-opt the government in their battle against rivals … [which is] wary of having the FTC used as a pawn to boost the profitability of certain sectors or insulate them from competition".[6] This is a polite way of someone else (not me) saying that the rise of these intermediaries has occasioned aggrieved stakeholders who have sought redress in Congress, the courts, and the court of public opinion. These stakeholders are the most vocal and vehement critics of the GPOs and PBMs.

Tradeoffs: The Name of the Game

Just as there are winners and losers in the economic competition between buyers and sellers, there are also (unfortunately) inevitable tradeoffs among desired outcomes. As economists will tell you, economics is all about tradeoffs: making one choice means foregoing some other benefit. Economists refer to this as opportunity costs. Such costs result from issues of scarcity and limited resources.

This volume has repeatedly noted the reality of tradeoffs in many health-care sectors. When one examines the different health plans that employers offer workers (see Chapter 9), one finds that those plans that offer wider choice of providers (more open-network models such as preferred provider organizations, or PPOs) come with higher premiums. That is, PPOs trade off wider access for higher cost. The opposite is the case for health maintenance organizations (HMOs): enrollees pay a lower premium but give up free choice of provider in the form of a closed network. Another illustration of trade-offs can be found in the increasingly popular high-deductible health plans (HDHPs), also covered in Chapter 9. Roughly one-third of U.S. workers have opted into such health plans. Why? Because they offer coverage at the lowest premium. There is a downside, however: they face high deductibles (up to several thousand dollars) that must be paid out-of-pocket before their insurance coverage kicks in. So, the tradeoff here is lower premium cost today for higher out-of-pocket expense tomorrow. The same tradeoff is baked into the "metal plans" on the state insurance exchanges (ObamaCare): compared to the gold and platinum plans, bronze and silver plans have lower premiums but more cost-sharing.

Such tradeoffs factor into the strategies employed by GPOs and PBMs. For example, the 'contentious' GPO practices of rebates, compliance, committed contracts, and sole-source contracts all entail tradeoffs between wider product access versus lower product cost. The GPOs have wisely constructed their contracts and contract tiers to allow hospital members to select the partic-ular tradeoff they prefer. In a similar fashion, PBMs (in partnership with health plans) have developed formulary tiers that allow plan participants to decide how to access the drug(s) they prefer at the cost they can afford to pay. GPOs and PBMs do not dictate the choice to their hospital customers and plan enrollees, respectively. To the extent that plan enrollees face hardships in paying list prices for drugs in their deductible phase (e.g., as in the EpiPen litigation), these hardships are imposed by the HDHPs they selected and the cost-sharing features of their employer's benefit plan.

A third area where such tradeoffs are evident is the pursuit of the three-fold goals of the iron triangle: cost, quality, and access. The historical chronicle suggests that GPOs and PBMs have focused their attention on the cost-access tradeoff in constructing their contracts and formularies. Product quality is, nevertheless, evident in the decisions made by hospitals' product selection committees and health plan pharmacy and therapeutics committees. Such committees are heavily comprised of clinicians (physicians, nurses, pharma-cists) who focus primarily on product quality, not on product cost. In other words, these committee mechanisms represent local-level decisions by clinicians on the types of products and quality levels they want. GPOs and PBMs are not in the business of "telling doctors what they can or cannot order or prescribe." To the extent their product choice set is limited, it likely reflects committee (peer) assessments of what are comparable, therapeutically-equivalent products with no evidence-base to differentiate them. There is, thus, no evidence that GPOs and PBMs are "killing patients"—particularly since they do not engage in patient care.

Another area where strategic tradeoffs are evident is national versus local. The GPOs began as local cooperatives and developed contracts for local membership. The proximity and small membership size made it fairly easy to decide upon products and manufacturers to contract with. As they grew, however, the regional and (then) national GPOs faced increasing difficulty in developing contracts that all of their members wanted. The GPOs therefore embarked on several strategies that allowed members to customize contracts to suit local needs and clinician preferences, including: regional GPO affiliates, assistance with custom contracting, contracting tiers, etc. The goal was to balance the economic leverage of centralized national buying with access to desired products at the local level. PBMs have engaged in similar tradeoffs. They, along with their health plan sponsors, developed national drug formularies than could be tailored or disregarded by health plans at the local level.

Finally, as this volume has repeatedly asserted, the GPOs and PBMs have historically and consistently been engaged in the same strategy with manufacturers: exchanging higher purchase volumes for lower product prices. Buying in bulk is not a contentious practice; it is widespread in most consumer sectors (e.g., go to Costco and buy a LOT of toilet paper for lower cost). This definitely benefits big-box retailers at the expense of smaller retail outlets. The rise of these large retailers has definitely disrupted the business of smaller retailers and smaller manufacturers who have seen their brands and margins diminish—what the economist Joseph Schumpeter long ago labeled as "creative destruction."[7] There are definite tradeoffs here. On the one hand, consumers can access multiple products in a centralized location at lower cost. On the other hand, their community loses local businesses, local suppliers, and perhaps higher-wage jobs—similar to what Schumpeter observed when the manufacture of the first automobile rendered obsolete those tradesmen making horse-drawn carriages. Schumpeter argued that the short-term economic dislocation was more than offset by the long-term productivity and welfare-generating benefits. Thus, you will not be surprised to find "mixed results" of the impact of such big-box retailers on the local economy—some stakeholders benefit, others do not.[8] The same is true for GPOs and PBMs.

Consolidation

GPOs and PBMs have also come under increasing fire for being concentrated sectors. Critics routinely note that a small number of these intermediaries account for the vast bulk of sales in their sector. Such observations are correct. But then critics extrapolate to draw the following conclusion: these huge oligopolies raise costs, harm their own members, and engage in anticompetitive practices that harm the public's welfare. For example, consider the following characterization:

> The modern-day GPOs could not be more different than their early predecessors. Rather than mere servants of their hospital masters, the new GPOs are giant behemoths in a very large industry. The GPO industry is a classic example of a highly concentrated oligopolistic structure, where a handful of companies control more than 80 percent of the hospital supplies purchased through GPOs. This oligopolistic market structure has allowed these, mostly privately owned and controlled entities, to extract excessive rates of return for their own benefit and to the detriment of their member hospitals. In an economic situation that has been characterized by drastic increases in healthcare costs and inefficiency, the GPO oligopoly is a major factor of heretofore unrecognized significance.[9]

This volume presents evidence that refutes all of these charges. First, the GPOs save hospitals money. The hospitals say this, multiple industry reports say this, and former senior FTC officials say this. Second, the GPOs serve their hospital members; indeed, they are often owned by the hospitals on whose behalf they contract. Third, there has been no federal antitrust enforcement activity brought against these parties, and a vastly reduced number of lawsuits filed against them since they adopted codes of conduct in the mid-2000s.

If this was not enough, there are two other problems with the broad and inaccurate characterization quoted above. The entire healthcare ecosystem has undergone consolidation since the 1960s, starting with the investor-owned hospital systems discussed in Chapter 4. Indeed, Fig. 14.1 shows the historical trend and spread of consolidation in healthcare. Second, nearly all of the intermediaries in the supply chain are concentrated: not just GPOs and PBMs but also pharmacies, pharmaceutical wholesalers, and specialty distributors (see Fig. 14.2).[10] Like everyone else, supply chain intermediaries have engaged in mergers and acquisitions (M&A) over time, resulting in an oligopolistic market structure. For some reason, however, critics do not usually complain about the oligopolies in these other sectors. If one wants to start pointing fingers at the biggest culprits in consolidation and rising cost, one does not have to look very far: hospital systems.[11]

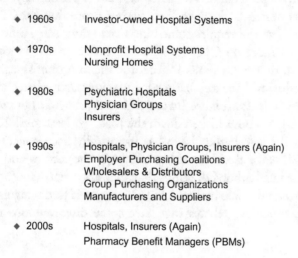

◆ 1960s	Investor-owned Hospital Systems
◆ 1970s	Nonprofit Hospital Systems Nursing Homes
◆ 1980s	Psychiatric Hospitals Physician Groups Insurers
◆ 1990s	Hospitals, Physician Groups, Insurers (Again) Employer Purchasing Coalitions Wholesalers & Distributors Group Purchasing Organizations Manufacturers and Suppliers
◆ 2000s	Hospitals, Insurers (Again) Pharmacy Benefit Managers (PBMs)

Fig. 14.1 Consolidation trend along the healthcare value chain

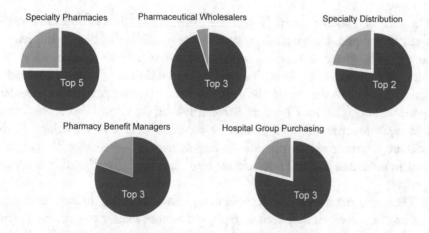

Fig. 14.2 Widespread concentration in the pharmaceutical supply chain (2021) (*Source* Drug Channels Institute research and estimates)

Existential Threats

Safe Harbors

Despite being large firms in an oligopolistic market, both GPOs and PBMs face similar existential threats. There are at least three possible threats—one from the public sector, two from the private sector. The first is revocation of their safe harbor protection. This issue comes up periodically, gets debated, and then gets beaten back down. Safe harbor protection for GPOs is based on statute, so that will require some bipartisan effort; safe harbor protection for PBMs rests more on OIG guidance, so that is perhaps more amenable to change and, thus, vulnerable. Indeed, the Biden Administration has taken steps to whittle down the safe harbor for manufacturer rebates as part of the November 2021 Infrastructure Investment and Jobs Act; however, as noted earlier, "the can has been kicked down the road," at least until 2026.

Moreover, the safe harbor issue has historically been couched as a false dichotomy, either-or decision: either eliminate the rebates and move them outside of the safe harbor OR admit that they are needed and beneficial and keep them inside the safe harbor. One alternative is to distinguish beneficial rebates from predatory rebates that have some discontinuous features (see below).

Disintermediation

The second possible threat is possible disintermediation of the intermediaries. In the past, such a threat rested on the possibility of buyers and sellers engaging in direct contracting which did not require an intermediary. To date, direct contracting in healthcare has been a flop, as witnessed by Medicare's attempts to do this in the 1997 Balanced Budget Act (with "provider sponsored organizations") and more recently with the Global and Professional Direct Contracting (GPDC) Model for accountable care organizations. Both of these efforts relied on providers acting as insurers—basically, diversifying into an unrelated sector. The track record of unrelated diversification is pretty spotty.[12]

There are other possible "supplanters," however, that do not do direct contracting. Instead, they seek to replace the intermediary or gain the upper hand with the intermediary. Certain distributors of medical products in the supply chain offer "wrap around agreements," typically for commodity items. They reportedly entice their hospital customers to increase their aggregate level of spending with them from, say, $10–$40 Million. If hospitals agree to do so, the distributor waives the 2.5% distribution fee, and then delivers a lot of supplies, some good and some not so good, some wanted and some not so much wanted. The hospital may then entertain another offer from a manufacturer or distributor to replace the not so good and not so much wanted items. But if the hospital accepts this second offer, it falls out of compliance with the first agreement, and incurs an immediate penalty on the first dollar spent outside this agreement, which then costs the hospital the entire $2.5 Million as a penalty. The hospital is not free to break up the bundle of products it signed on for the $2.5 Million waiver. In this manner, the distributor is now acting as the hospital's newest GPO and offering to curate the hospital's product formulary. Such wrap-around agreements offer bigger percentage discounts tied to higher percentages of the hospital's medical-surgical spending on the distributor's brand product line.

The existence of such traps in the retail drug supply chain was noted three years ago by a member of the Medicare Payment Advisory Commission (MedPAC). In such traps, manufacturers offer "punitive rebates" on their drugs in order to get them onto the preferred formulary tier of a pharmacy benefit manager. The problem arises when biosimilar drugs come to market, many consumers find themselves with no way to access them. Here is how the scheme works, according to MedPAC testimony:

> …there is an absolute necessity for fees, discounts, and rebates … You have to have that vehicle. But not all fees, discounts, and rebates are created the same. Some are used for legitimate purposes and some are used in very predatory and punitive ways.
>
> And, for example, … if I'm buying $10 Million of something and someone comes to me and says, "Hey, you're a great customer. I want you to have a 25 percent rebate," well … I know I'm getting a proportional 25 percent rebate on those purchases… When I'm buying $10 Million of something and someone says the moment you shift one dollar away from that $10 Million purchase, I'm taking $2.5 Million away from you. These disproportional rebates, these punitive rebates are fundamentally different than legitimate fees, discounts, and rebates that are proportional to the value and volume of products sold.[13]

PBM executives also report their concern with aggregated, aggravated, and activated employers—and, thus, employer purchasing coalitions who seek to impose contract terms on the PBM that are favorable to them. Some of these terms are described in Chapter 12. The employer threat is real in one sense: along with the Federal Government, they are the single largest purchaser of healthcare products and services. They are also in closer proximity to the patient (their employees and their dependents), see them every day, and have a financial incentive to keep them healthy. This trumps the market position and incentives of every other player in the value chain. At the same time, however, the employer threat is fleeting and transitory. Employers become more heavily engaged in healthcare spending during upswings in what were once called the "insurance underwriting cycle": the cycle of rises and falls in the percentage increase in insurance premiums (or healthcare spending). One could count on employer engagement when healthcare premiums were accelerating; one could also count on employers losing interest when healthcare premiums were decelerating.

The Empire (Always) Strikes Back: Supplier Consolidation, Concentration, & Pricing

Perhaps the single greatest existential threat to intermediaries such as GPOs and PBMs is consolidation and/or concentration among the manufacturers upstream with whom they contract. Consolidation has taken place in every sector of the healthcare ecosystem, as noted above. The immediate impact is a reduction in the number of suppliers available for customers to contract with, and the reduction in the competitive rivalry among these suppliers.

In 2009, the top ten medical device firms accounted for 62% of worldwide revenues; by 2017, they accounted for 70% of global revenues.[14] Part of this growing concentration has been driven by mergers and acquisitions (M&A) of smaller companies by larger companies; part of this growing concentration has been driven by product diversification (see Fig. 14.3) whereby large companies acquire other large companies in other product segments. GPOs have noticed that there is a dwindling number for suppliers—sometimes as few as two manufacturers—to contract with in several product areas. The areas of greatest supply concern include: IV solutions, dialysis equipment and fluids, hemodialysis fluids, negative pressure wound therapy, infant formula, pulse oximetry, suction canisters, and contrast media (among others). The GPOs' concerns—which, admittedly, are difficult to empirically document and validate—are manifold: threats to supply and possibilities of supply shortage, higher prices, and lower levels of innovation.

A similar threat of consolidation exists in the pharmaceutical sector. Research suggests that pharmaceutical M&A is sometimes motivated by the desire to limit competition. Researchers have found that a company is 5–7% less likely to complete a drug development project in its acquisition pipeline if those drugs would compete with the acquirer's existing product line (i.e., "killer acquisition").[15] Other research shows that (a) M&A can result in

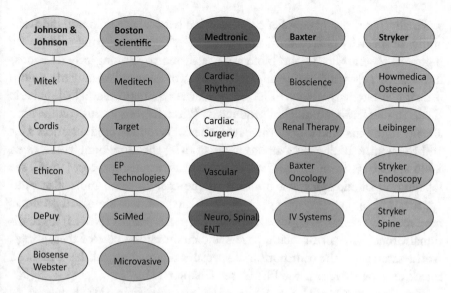

Fig. 14.3 MedTech diversification via M&A

reduced research & development (R&D) spending and patenting for several years,[16] while (b) higher competition spurs R&D spending by firms.[17]

However, the threat is not always due to supplier mergers. M&A activity among large pharmaceutical manufacturers has not resulted in a more concentrated sector. In 2006, the top ten firms accounted for 46% of total sales; ten years later, in 2016, they accounted for only 41% of sales.[18] As noted in Chapter 10, market concentration has historically been more evident at the therapeutic area level than the firm level. Instead, in recent years, the threat has sometimes come from older and/or generic drugs where market demand is too small to support more than one firm and/or all other suppliers have withdrawn for various reasons. The result is a monopoly and egregious pricing behavior. Two prominent examples are (1) Turing Pharmaceuticals and its drug Daraprim, and (2) Mylan Pharmaceuticals and its EpiPen—firms which continually hiked their prices "because they can."

Economists have developed models of drug pricing in the presence of payer formularies that suggest that smaller manufacturers have a greater incentive than larger manufacturers to overcharge for their products.[19] That is because the payer is purchasing a bundle of drugs that include both branded products (with prices reflecting market power) and generic products (which are priced more competitively).[20] Smaller firms are more likely to engage in such behavior because they have smaller drug portfolios and fewer concerns about negative publicity and negative pressure on the prices for its other drugs.

Finally, the threat of supplier concentration particularly resides in the availability of specialty pharmaceuticals—many of which are off-patent. There are higher entry barriers in the biologics space due to (among other reasons) uncertainty regarding the regulatory process for biosimilars and the guidelines for "interchangeability." The result is fewer competitors and little generic threat to these newer biological products.[21] Prior chapters in this volume have already noted the tendency of these manufacturers to hike product prices a lot and frequently. Biologics as a percentage of drug spending doubled between 2006 and 2016, from 13 to 27%. The wholesale acquisition cost (WAC, see Chapter 9) of biologics is a multiple of the cost of small molecules. And approvals of biologic license applications (BLAs) for new biological products have recently overtaken approvals of new molecular entities (NMEs) for traditional drugs. The threat facing payers is containing the cost of these drugs. At the same time, the distribution of specialty pharmaceuticals has become a major revenue driver for the PBMs (see Chapter 11).

The threat of specialty drugs is more nuanced than this, however. As noted earlier, 60%+ of biologics are orphan drugs. Pharmaceutical manufacturers have sought orphan drug status for newly-approved drugs and/or drugs already on the market by identifying the drug's use for an orphan indication. By gaining such status, the drug then gains exclusion from the 340B program described in Chapter 11 and, thus avoids the mandatory price discounts. A drug that gets orphan status for treating one condition gains 340B exclusion for all of its sales.[22]

Moreover, specialty drugs are more buffered from the effects of drug formularies and tiers. Formulary position is driven by competition within the therapeutic area; such competition is greater in some areas than others. Higher competition is observed in areas such as metabolic, cardiovascular, central nervous system, and gastrointestinal; lesser competition is found in areas such as oncology, infectious disease, immunology, and respiratory. In the former areas, there is less clinical differentiation among drug classes and more variation in tiering; in the latter areas, there is more clinical differentiation among drug classes and much less dispersion of formulary drugs across price tiers. This reflects the considerable unmet clinical need and variation in patient response to specialty (e.g., oncologic) drugs, making it harder to restrict and/or channel physician choice among products. Finally, drugs that treat widely prevalent conditions (e.g., diabetes) and thus incur high aggregate spending are more likely to be targeted by formulary tiers than are specialty drugs that incur lower aggregate spending, which are more likely to attract payer strategies such as step therapy.

	GPOS:	PBMS:
Channel Served	Institutional channel: hospitals, nursing homes	Retail channel: community pharmacies, specialty pharmacies, mail-order pharmacies
Contracted Products	Medical-surgical supplies, pharmaceuticals, medical devices and other physician preference items (PPIs), capital equipment, dietary, information technology. Contracted pharmaceuticals are typically used in hospital inpatient or outpatient areas.	Pharmaceuticals (branded and generic), biologics. Most contracted pharmaceuticals are used in retail or mail-order settings.
Customer Served	Healthcare providers downstream: hospitals, physician clinics, nursing homes	Health plans (downstream or in-house), ERISA plan sponsors, labor unions, Federal and State governments
Historical Origin	Local hospital cooperatives, shared services organizations	Prepaid health plan cooperatives, freestanding claims processors
	Control hospital input costs	Control medical group input costs, ensure enrollee access to services
Historical Founding Period	1910-1950	1945-1975
Product Selection Body	Clinical committees, Pharmacy & Therapeutics committees at hospital and GPO level	Pharmacy & Therapeutics committees at health plan and PBM level
Product Listing	Contracted item catalog	Drug formulary
Owner/Sponsor	Hospital shareholders, hospital chains, publicly owned, pharmaceutical wholesalers	Health plans, publicly owned

Fig. 14.4 GPOs vs. PBMs

	GPOS:	PBMS:
Role in the Healthcare Value Chain	GPOs organize the collective purchasing of supplies used by hospitals and other providers into contracts that their members can use. Provider use of the GPO's contracts is voluntary. GPOs negotiate the contracts with product manufacturers (suppliers) but do not do the actual buying, purchasing, or handling.	PBMs administer prescription drug plans on behalf of health insurance plans, employer groups, the Medicare program, and others. PBMs perform administrative functions including plan design and administration, management of drug formularies, enrollment and member services, claims processing & adjudication, utilization review, reporting, etc. PBMs also negotiate drug prices and rebates with pharmaceutical manufacturers. PBMs do not do the actual drug buying, purchasing, or handling.
Business Models	**Purpose:** GPOs pool the buying power of their members to achieve purchasing economies. To do so, they effect a *quid pro quo* with product manufacturers: higher sales volume for the supplier in exchange for lower product price for the member. GPOs can contract with more or fewer manufacturers to drive even lower prices. In this manner, GPOs create price savings for providers. They also create efficiencies in the supply chain processes of members. **Contracting:** Providers join GPOs to gain access to their contracts. GPOs, in turn, contract with manufacturers to get their supplies on the GPO's contract at a negotiated price. The contract may contain one or several "tiers" that allow members to trade off product access for product cost. GPO members then determine which GPO contracts they would like to use to purchase products at the negotiated price and contract tier. **Fees:** The GPO safe harbor protects GPO collection of contract administrative fees (CAFs) from manufacturers upstream up to 3% of the purchase price, with additional transparency requirements for CAFs in excess of 3%. According to the GAO, GPO CAFs average 2%. CAFs are calculated on the net negotiated contract price. In the past, GPOs also collected membership fees from hospitals. **Research:** Independent research has affirmed the GPO business model as an overall cost savings model. The courts and various Federal agencies have also concluded that the GPO business does not violate anti-trust laws.	**Purpose:** PBMs pool the buying power of the health plan enrollees and ERISA plan sponsor employees they represent to achieve purchasing economies. To do so, they effect a *quid pro quo* with a subset of pharmaceutical manufacturers: ensure the presence of the manufacturer's drug on the formulary (and thus patient reimbursement for their drug) in exchange for discounts off the drug's list price. PBMs can accord the manufacturer's drug more favorable placement on the formulary for greater discounts. PBMs also earn markups on expensive specialty drugs. **Contracting:** Health plans, employer groups, and others contract with PBMs to administer their pharmacy benefit and manage their prescription drug plans. PBMs, in turn, contract with manufacturers upstream and develop formulary tiers that patients can access. PBMs also contract with a pharmacy network downstream where patients may access their medications. **Fees:** PBMs collect administrative fees from health plans downstream for processing claims. They also collect contract administrative fees (CAFs) as well as rebates from manufacturers upstream. The CAFs run in the low single digits. The rebates are a negotiated percentage discount off the list price of the manufacturer's drug. The amount of collected rebates that are passed through to a PBM's downstream customer are generally determined contractually; PBMs must pass through 100% of rebates to Medicare Part D plan sponsors. **Research:** There is much less research evaluating the PBM's business model. Studies suggest that PBMs have helped to lower the net price of manufacturers' drugs despite the latter's continual hikes in list price.

Fig. 14.4 (continued)

	GPOS:	PBMS:
Number of Firms	There are 583 GPOs in 2021, according to IBIS World.	There are 39 PBMs in 2021, according to IBIS World. This may be a gross understatement, given the number of purchasing intermediaries in the drug channel (Figure 1.2).
Industry Financials	**Revenue:** The GPO sector has reportedly grown its revenues at 1.3% over the past five years. GPOs earned total revenues of $5 billion in 2021, according to IBIS World. This number is substantially reduced when one includes the financial distributions of CAFs to member providers. This substantially reduces GPO operating revenues by 50% or more. Profit margins reportedly 6.1% (2021).	**Revenue:** The PBM industry has grown its revenues at 2.6% over the last five years to reach a total revenue of $458 billion in 2021. Profit margins reportedly 4.9% (2021).
Operating Guidelines	Safe Harbor: There is both a statutory exception and a regulatory safe harbor under the anti-kickback statute (AKS) for vendor payments to GPOs (42 CFR 1001.952(j)) that specifies transparency requirements. GPOs operate within the scope of the federal GPO Safe Harbor, which requires that: 1. Each provider that uses GPO services has a written contract with the GPO; 2. GPOs disclose their administrative fee arrangements to providers that use GPO services; 3. GPOs report annually to each member the specific administrative fee earned for each contract; and, 4. GPOs provide the above information to the Department of Health and Human Services (DHHS) upon request.	Safe Harbor: There is no statutory safe harbor designed specifically to cover manufacturer payments to PBMs. However, in 1999, the Office of the Inspector General within the Department of Health & Human Services (OIG-DHHS) issued a safe harbor protection to shield drug manufacturers' rebate contracts from the implications of the Anti-Kickback Statute (AKS).
Transparency	Every HSCA member GPO participates in the Healthcare Group Purchasing Initiative (HGPII). Participants maintain a Code of Conduct, established in 2005, and voluntarily participate in the HGPII Ethics and Transparency Initiative. GPO business practices are publicly reported on the HGPII website. Pursuant to the GPO Safe Harbor (see above), GPOs also disclose their administrative fee arrangements to providers that use GPOs and they provide annual reports to each member detailing the specific administrative fee earned for each contract. GPOs also provide the aforementioned information to the Secretary of HHS upon request.	PBMs have operated under "Corporate Integrity Agreements" (CIAs) with the OIG-DHHS since 2005. PBMs providing services to Part D drug plans are required to report and pass on to the plan sponsor the aggregate amount of rebates and discounts received, but there is no public reporting of the specific amount of individual rebates, fees, and other reimbursements.

Fig. 14.4 (continued)

	GPOS:	PBMS:
Rebates Earned	Paid by manufacturers retrospectively, based on purchase volume and/or share	Paid by manufacturers retrospectively, based on purchase volume and/or share
Cost Management Effort	Manage the line-item cost of products on contract	Manage the cost of drugs upstream via formulary placement and rebates Manage the utilization of drugs downstream
Iron Triangle Tradeoff Managed	Product access (on contract) vs. contract price Emphasis on reducing product price, hospital cost	Product access (on formulary, which tier) vs. rebate Product position on formulary tier vs. patient cost-sharing Emphasis on reducing net drug price, health plan cost
Directional Influence in Supply Chain	Leverage product manufacturers upstream	Leverage product manufacturers upstream Leverage independent pharmacies downstream
Aggrieved Parties and Critics	Small medical device start-up firms Medical Device Manufacturers Association (MDMA)	Independent community pharmacies National Community Pharmacists Association (NCPA)

This Figure heavily modifies the following source. Healthcare Supply Chain Association (HSCA) – 2018, "*At a Glance*: Key Differences Between Healthcare Group Purchasing Organizations (GPOs) & Pharmacy Benefit Managers (PBMs)"; Premier Inc., courtesy of Blair Childs, 2022.

Fig. 14.4 (continued)

Summary

This volume argues that GPOs and PBMs occupy parallel roles in the institutional and retail channels of the healthcare value chain. There are multiple similarities in their historical origin, product selection bodies, role in the value chain, roles as agents for downstream buyers, business model, operating guidelines, transparency, rebates earned, cost management efforts, iron triangle tradeoffs managed, and directional influence in the supply chain. These similarities are counter-balanced by their differences in channel served, products contracted for, customers served, founding period, owner/sponsor, number of firms, and industry financials. These comparisons and contrasts are summarized in Fig. 14.4.

Finally, the GPOs and PBMs are intermediaries. They do not buy, sell, or price products conveyed through the institutional and retail supply chains, respectively. They are also not providers of healthcare services. Their impact on the cost and quality of care rendered to patients is thus removed from the parties who play the major roles here. The remarkable finding here is that these intermediaries may nevertheless serve the public's welfare by controlling the rise in healthcare costs.

Notes

1. David Dranove and Lawton R. Burns. *Big Med: Megaproviders and the High Cost of Healthcare in America* (Chicago, IL: University of Chicago Press, 2021).
2. Federal Trade Commission. *Overview of FTC Actions in Health Care Services and Products* (Washington, DC: FTC, June 2019).
3. Dan O'Brien, Jon Leibowitz, and Russell Anello. *Group Purchasing Organizations: How GPOs Reduce Healthcare Costs and Why Changing Their Funding Mechanism Would Raise Costs* (Washington, DC: Healthcare Supply Chain Association, 2017).
4. Available online at: https://www.cbo.gov/system/files/2020-03/PDPRA-SFC.pdf. Accessed on May 11, 2022.
5. Congressional Budget Office. *Incorporating the Effects of the Proposed Rule on Safe Harbors for Pharmaceutical Rebates in CBO's Budget Projections—Supplemental Material for Updated Budget Projections: 2019 to 2029* (Washington, DC: CBO, May 2019).
6. Comments from Christine Wilson. Available online at: https://www.fierce healthcare.com/payers/ftc-deadlocked-whether-study-pbm-contracting-practi ces-such-dir-fees. Accessed on May 11, 2022.

7. Joseph Schumpeter. *Capitalism, Socialism, and Democracy* (New York: Harper & Row, 1942).

8. Emily Freedman, James McConnon, Gary Hunt et al. "An Analysis of the Economic Impacts of Big-Box Stores on a Community's Retail Sector: Evidence from Maine," *The Journal of Regional Analysis and Policy* 46(2) (2016): 138–153. Gian-Claudia Sciara, Kristin Lovejoy, and Susan Handy. "The Impacts of Big Box Retail on Downtown: A Case Study of Target in Davis (CA)," *Journal of the American Planning Association* 84(1) (2018): 45–60. "Big Box Economic Impact Studies." Available online at: https://web.mit.edu/course/4/4.293/!Phoenix/Research/Tenant%20Research/bigboxstudies.pdf. Accessed on May 11, 2022.

9. S. Prakash Sethi. *Group Purchasing Organizations: An Undisclosed Scandal in the U.S. Healthcare Industry* (New York: Palgrave Macmillan, 2009): 17–18.

10. Figure courtesy of Adam Fein of Drug Channels.

11. David Dranove and Lawton R. Burns. *Big Med: Megaproviders and the High Cost of Healthcare in America* (Chicago, IL: University of Chicago Press, 2021).

12. Monika Schommer, Ansgar Richter, and Amit Karna. "Does the Diversification–Firm Performance Relationship Change Over Time? A Meta-Analytical Review," *Journal of Management Studies* 56(1) (2019): 270–298.

13. Testimony of Brian DeBusk. MedPAC Public Meeting. January 18, 2019: pp. 41–42.

14. Kurt Kruger and Max Kruger. "The Medical Device Sector," in Lawton R. Burns (Ed.), *The Business of Healthcare Innovation*, 3rd edition (Cambridge, UK: Cambridge University Press, 2020): Chapter 5.

15. Colleen Cunningham, Florian Ederer, and Song Ma. "Killer Acquisitions," *Journal of Political Economy* 129(3) (2021): 649–702.

16. Government Accountability Office. *Drug Industry: Profits, Research and Development Spending, and Merger and Acquisition Deals.* GAO-18-40 (Washington, DC: GAO, November 2017).

17. Richard Thakor and Andrew Lo. "Competition and R&D Financing: Evidence from the Biopharmaceutical Industry," *Journal of Financial and Quantitative Analysis* (2021). Available online at: https://doi.org/10.1017/S0022109021000284.

18. Lawton R. Burns. *The U.S. Healthcare Ecosystem* (New York: McGraw-Hill, 2021): Chapter 21.

19. David Besanko, David Dranove, and Craig Garthwaite. "Insurance and the High Price of Pharmaceuticals," NBER Working Paper (June 2016).

20. Fiona Scott Morton and Lysle Boller. "Enabling Competition in Pharmaceutical Markets," Hutchens Center Working Paper #30 (May 2017).

21. Lawton R. Burns. *The U.S. Healthcare Ecosystem* (New York: McGraw-Hill, 2021): Chapter 22.

22. Fiona Scott Morton and Lysle Boller. "Enabling Competition in Pharmaceutical Markets," Hutchens Center Working Paper #30 (May 2017).

Index

Printed in the United States
by Baker & Taylor Publisher Services